The Art of Modern Fiction

Alternate Edition

THE ART OF
MODERN FICTION

Alternate Edition

Ray B. West, Jr.
Professor of English · State University of Iowa

Robert Wooster Stallman
Professor of English · University of Connecticut

HOLT, RINEHART AND WINSTON, INC.

NEW YORK • CHICAGO • SAN FRANCISCO • ATLANTA • DALLAS
MONTREAL • TORONTO • LONDON • SYDNEY

COPYRIGHT, 1949, BY RAY B. WEST, JR.

AND ROBERT WOOSTER STALLMAN

Library of Congress Catalog Card Number: 49-10213

ALL RIGHTS RESERVED

SBN: 03-009915-3

PRINTED IN THE UNITED STATES OF AMERICA

90123   68   19181716

❦ A Note to the Reader

Every teacher of fiction is familiar with the student who comes to him and says, "After I have read a story and we have talked about it in class, it is perfectly clear, but when I sit down to read the next assignment I am just as bewildered as ever. How do I know what the author is trying to say? How do I tell whether it is a good story or a bad one?"

The teacher knows that such questions strike at the heart of the problem. He understands, too, that there are no easy answers. Such knowledge as the student demands comes only after time and effort and requires a certain familiarity with general aesthetic principles as well as at least a minimum understanding of the writer's craft. The time allotted a course in modern fiction seldom seems long enough to accomplish all that the teacher hopes to accomplish. Nevertheless, by explaining the basic principles of good fiction and by applying these principles rigorously to outstanding works, a great many teachers do succeed in showing the student how to determine the purpose and value of a work. In other words, a student learns to recognize good craftsmanship through his own reading experience.

In helping the student answer his own questions, which are those that invariably arise in the mind of the reader, the teacher of fiction shows that his final aim is not critical theory but understanding and appreciation—a full appreciation—of the stories themselves. Such is our aim in this book, although we as editors can only set the stage. The real work must be left up to the teacher and his students. We have done what we can by (1) presenting what we consider a collection of the best in modern fiction, (2) so ordering the material that the development of the modern short story may be seen chronologically and so first problems may be considered first.

The short stories in this volume reflect an assumption that the short story as a "modern" literary form began in America with such authors as Hawthorne, Melville, and Crane (although Melville's story is placed out of its order because we classify it as a "short novel"); in Europe with such writers as Maupassant, Tchekhov, Pirandello, and Tolstoi. This fact is of importance only for the teacher who wishes to consider the growth of the short story from the tales and sketches of earlier authors to the more formal products of the nineteenth and twentieth centuries. It does, however, have a special interest for the teacher who wishes to indicate the changes that have taken place in the short fiction forms between the writings of, say, Hawthorne and Hemingway in America, or Maupassant and Sartre in Europe—changes in choice of subject, style, method of character presentation, atmosphere, tone, or point of view. Likewise, similarities may also help in suggesting what has remained relatively unchanged during the same period—what the justification is for calling the present collection examples of *The Art of Modern Fiction*.

Of first importance to the editors themselves is the problem of understanding the individual stories regardless of the date of their composition. The individual teacher will have his own method of achieving such a goal, but it will probably include a preliminary reading to discover what the story is attempting to accomplish; that is, what is the aim—the "intention"—of the story. Each teacher will undoubtedly be concerned then with the various methods used by the author to reveal that aim and to present it in an entertaining and a stimulating manner; the use of a particular style; the creation of atmosphere; the choice of a point of view from which the action is to be displayed or the scene elucidated; details of structure, and so forth. He might ask, for instance, "How does the *atmosphere* of Hawthorne's "Rappaccini's Daughter" differ from that of Crane's "The Open Boat"? What *tone* is set by Pirandello in relating the events of "The Reserved Coffin"? What is the purpose of Joyce's use of a particular *point of view* in his story, "Counterparts"? How does Katherine Mansfield go about making her rather ordinary *characters* interesting to us in "The Daughters of the Late Colonel," and to what purpose in the story have such commonplace characters been selected? What end is served by the various forms of *irony* employed by Henry James in "The Liar"? What is the significance of the final irony at the conclusion of Hemingway's "The Short Happy Life of Francis Macomber"? How does this irony differ from the irony used by James? What is the *structure* of Bunin's "The Gentleman from San Francisco"?

The answer to such questions would demand a close and attentive reading of each story. They reflect the editors' belief that the most effective means of gaining a full understanding of any story is by such close examination, particularly when it is combined with a judicious juxtaposition and comparison of one story with another.

There are, we realize, certain objections by certain teachers and students to close textual analysis. The most common is that it leads to a tendency on the part of a reader to "read into" a story meanings that are no part of the author's intentions. This matter of intentions is difficult, as every teacher well knows. It is, however, extremely important. In our own experience as teachers of fiction, we have found that the student usually does not err in this direction; rather, he tends to miss intentions that are clearly (though often implicitly) stated. He also tends to mistake the explicit statement, which is often intended ironically, for a final statement of the author's meaning. To avoid such underinterpretation it seems desirable to us to examine every possible clue toward a total reading of the story. What Robert Frost has said of poetry we believe to be equally true of fiction: "The poet is entitled to everything the reader can find in his poem." The important thing to remember here is to be sure that what is found *actually is contained* in the work.

Critical reading of fiction has profited by the shift of emphasis in twentieth-century criticism from a concern with the author's life and background to a concern with his work as art. While this recent concern does not mean that the author's life and background cannot often provide valuable information, we have based our own teaching on the assumption that evidence of the writer's artistic excellence is to be found in his work—the stories in his collection were chosen with this in mind.

RAY B. WEST, JR.
ROBERT WOOSTER STALLMAN

Contents

The Short Novel

The Short Story

NATHANIEL HAWTHORNE

Rappaccini's Daughter ℘

From *The Writings of Aubépine*

We do not remember to have seen any translated specimens of the productions of M. de l'Aubépine,—a fact the less to be wondered at, as his very name is unknown to many of his own countrymen as well as to the student of foreign literature. As a writer, he seems to occupy an unfortunate position between the Transcendentalists (who, under one name or another, have their share in all the current literature of the world) and the great body of pen-and-ink men who address the intellect and sympathies of the multitude. If not too refined, at all events too remote, too shadowy and unsubstantial in his modes of development, to suit the taste of the latter class, and yet too popular to satisfy the spiritual or metaphysical requisitions of the former, he must necessarily find himself without an audience, except here and there an individual or possibly an isolated clique. His writings, to do them justice, are not altogether destitute of fancy and originality; they might have won him greater reputation but for an inveterate love of allegory, which is apt to invest his plots and characters with the aspect of scenery and people in the clouds, and to steal away the human warmth out of his conceptions. His fictions are sometimes historical, sometimes of the present day, and sometimes, so far as can be discovered, have little or no reference either to time or space. In any case, he generally contents himself with a very slight embroidery of outward manners,—the faintest possible counterfeit of real life,—and endeavors to create an interest by some less obvious peculiarity of the subject. Occasionally a breath of Nature, a raindrop of pathos and tenderness, or a gleam of humor, will find its way into the midst of his fantastic imagery, and make us feel as if, after all, we were yet within the limits of our native earth. We will only add to this very cursory notice that M. de l'Aubépine's productions, if the reader chance to take them in precisely the proper point of view, may amuse a leisure hour as well as those of a brighter man; if otherwise, they can hardly fail to look excessively like nonsense.

Our author is voluminous; he continues to write and publish with as much praiseworthy and indefatigable prolixity as if his efforts were crowned with the brilliant success that so justly attends those of Eugene Sue. His first appearance was by a collection of stories in a long series of volumes entitled "Contes deux fois racontées." The titles of some of his more recent works (we quote from memory) are as follows: "Le Voyage Céleste à Chemin de Fer," 3 tom., 1838; "Le nouveau Père Adam et la nouvelle Mère Eve," 2 tom., 1839; "Roderic; ou le Serpent à l'estomac," 2 tom., 1840; "Le Culte du Feu," a folio volume of ponderous research into the religion and ritual of the old Persian Ghebers, published in 1841; "La Soirée du Chateau en Espagne," 1 tom., 8vo, 1842; and "L'Artiste du Beau; ou le Papillon Mécanique," 5 tom., 4to, 1843. Our somewhat wearisome perusal of this startling catalogue of volumes has left behind it a certain personal affection and sympathy, though by no means admiration, for M. de l'Aubépine; and we would fain do the little in our power towards introducing him favorably to the American public. The ensuing tale is a translation of his "Beatrice; ou la Belle Empoisonneuse," recently published in *La Revue Anti-Aristocratique*. This journal, edited by the Comte de Bearhaven, has for some years past led the defence of liberal principles and popular rights with a faithfulness and ability worthy of all praise.

A young man, named Giovanni Guasconti, came, very long ago, from the more southern region of Italy, to pursue his studies at the University of Padua. Giovanni, who had but a scanty supply of gold ducats in his pocket, took lodgings in a high and gloomy chamber of an old edifice which looked not unworthy to have been the palace of a Paduan noble, and which, in fact, exhibited over its entrance the armorial bearings of a family long since extinct. The young stranger, who was not unstudied in the great poem of his country, recollected that one of the ancestors of this family, and perhaps an occupant of this very mansion, had been pictured by Dante as a partaker of the immortal agonies of his Inferno. These reminiscences and associations, together with the tendency to heartbreak natural to a young man for the first time out of his native sphere, caused Giovanni to sigh heavily as he looked around the desolate and ill-furnished apartment.

"Holy Virgin, signor!" cried old Dame Lisabetta, who, won by the youth's remarkable beauty of person, was kindly endeavoring to give the chamber a habitable air, "what a sigh was that to come out of a young man's heart! Do you find this old mansion gloomy? For the love of Heaven, then, put your head out of the window, and you will see as bright sunshine as you have left in Naples."

Guasconti mechanically did as the old woman advised, but could not quite agree with her that the Paduan sunshine was as cheerful as that of southern Italy. Such as it was, however, it fell upon a garden beneath the window, and expended its fostering influences on a variety of plants, which seemed to have been cultivated with exceeding care.

"Does this garden belong to the house?" asked Giovanni.

"Heaven forbid, signor, unless it were fruitful of better pot herbs than any that grow there now," answered old Lisabetta. "No; that garden is cultivated by the own hands of Signor Giacomo Rappaccini, the famous doctor, who, I warrant him, has been heard of as far as Naples. It is said that he distills these plants into medicine that are as potent as a charm. Oftentimes you may see the signor doctor at work, and perchance the signora, his daughter, too, gathering the strange flowers that grow in the garden."

The old woman had now done what she could for the aspect of the chamber; and, commending the young man to the protection of the saints, took her departure.

Giovanni still found no better occupation than to look down into the garden beneath his window. From its appearance, he judged it to be one of those botanic gardens which were of earlier date in Padua than elsewhere in Italy, or in the world. Or, not improbably, it might once have been the pleasure-place of an opulent family; for there was the ruin of a marble fountain in the centre, sculptured with rare art, but so wofully shattered that it was impossible to trace the original design from the chaos of remaining fragments. The water, however, continued to gush and sparkle into the sunbeams as cheerfully as ever. A little gurgling sound ascended to the young man's window, and made him feel as if a fountain were an immortal spirit that sung its song unceasingly and without heeding the vicissitudes around it, while one century embodied it in marble and another scattered the perishable garniture on the soil. All about the pool into which the water subsided grew various plants, that seemed to require a plentiful supply of moisture for the nourishment of gigantic leaves, and, in some instances, flowers gorgeously magnificent. There was one shrub in particular, set in a marble vase in the midst of the pool, that bore a profusion of purple blossoms, each of which had the luster and richness of a gem; and the whole together made a show so resplendent that it seemed enough to illuminate the garden, even had there been no sunshine. Every portion of the soil was peopled with plants and herbs, which, if less beautiful, still bore tokens of assiduous care, as if all had their individual virtues, known to the scientific mind that fostered them. Some were placed in urns, rich with old carving, and others in common garden pots; some crept serpent-like along the ground or climbed on high, using whatever means of ascent was offered them. One plant had wreathed itself round a statue of Vertumnus, which was thus quite veiled and shrouded in a drapery of hanging foliage, so happily arranged that it might have served a sculptor for a study.

While Giovanni stood at the window he heard a rustling behind a screen of leaves, and became aware that a person was at work in the garden. His figure soon emerged into view, and showed itself to be that of no common laborer, but a tall, emaciated, sallow, and sickly-looking man dressed in a scholar's garb of black. He was beyond the middle term of life, with gray hair, a thin, gray beard, and a face singularly marked with intellect and cultivation, but which could never, even in his more youthful days, have expressed much warmth of heart.

Nothing could exceed the intentness with which this scientific gardener examined every shrub which grew in his path: it seemed as if he was looking into their inmost nature, making observations in regard to their creative essence, and discovering why one leaf grew in this shape and another in that, and wherefore such and such flowers differed among themselves in hue and perfume. Nevertheless, in spite of this deep intelligence on his part, there was no approach to intimacy between himself and these vegetable existences. On the contrary, he avoided their actual touch or the direct inhaling of their odors with a caution that impressed Giovanni most disagreeably; for the man's demeanor was that of one walking among malignant influences, such as savage beasts, or deadly snakes, or evil spirits, which, should he allow them one moment of license, would wreak upon him some terrible fatality. It was strangely frightful to the young man's imagination to see this air of insecurity in a person cultivating a garden, that most simple and innocent of human toils, and which had been alike the joy and labor of the unfallen parents of the race. Was this garden, then, the Eden of the present world? and this man, with such a perception of harm in what his own hands caused to grow,—was he the Adam?

The distrustful gardener, while plucking away the dead leaves or pruning the too luxuriant growth of the shrubs, defended his hands with a pair of thick gloves. Nor were these his only armor. When, in his walk through the garden, he came to the magnificent plant that hung its purple gems beside the marble fountain, he placed a kind of mask over his mouth and nostrils, as if all this beauty did but conceal a deadlier malice; but, finding his task still too dangerous, he drew back, removed the mask, and called loudly, but in the infirm voice of a person affected with inward disease.

"Beatrice! Beatrice!"

"Here am I, my father. What would you?" cried a rich and youthful voice from the window of the opposite house—a voice as rich as a tropical sunset, and which made Giovanni, though he knew not why, think of deep hues of purple or crimson and of perfumes heavily delectable. "Are you in the garden?"

"Yes, Beatrice," answered the gardener, "and I need your help."

Soon there emerged from under a sculptured portal the figure of a young girl, arrayed with as much richness of taste as the most splendid of the flowers, beautiful as the day, and with a bloom so deep and vivid that one shade more would have been too much. She looked redundant with life, health, and energy; all of which attributes were bound down and compressed as it were, and girdled tensely, in their luxuriance, by her virgin zone. Yet Giovanni's fancy must have grown morbid while he looked down into the garden; for the impression which the fair stranger made upon him was as if here were another flower, the human sister of those vegetable ones, as beautiful as they, more beautiful than the richest of them, but still to be touched only with a glove, nor to be approached without a mask. As Beatrice came down the garden path, it was observable that she handled and inhaled the odor of several of the plants which her father had most sedulously avoided.

"Here, Beatrice," said the latter, "see how many needful offices require to be done to our chief treasure. Yet, shattered as I am, my life might pay the penalty of approaching it so closely as circumstances demand. Henceforth, I fear, this plant must be consigned to your sole charge."

"And gladly will I undertake it," cried again the rich tones of the young lady, as she bent toward the magnificent plant and opened her arms as if to embrace it. "Yes, my sister, my splendor, it shall be Beatrice's task to nurse and serve thee; and thou shalt reward her with thy kisses and perfumed breath, which to her is as the breath of life."

Then, with all the tenderness in her manner that was so strikingly expressed in her words, she busied herself with such attentions as the plant seemed to require; and Giovanni, at his lofty window, rubbed his eyes and almost doubted whether it were a girl tending her favorite flower, or one sister performing the duties of affection to another.

The scene soon terminated. Whether Dr. Rappaccini had finished his labors in the garden or that his watchful eye had caught the stranger's face, he now took his daughter's arm and retired. Night was already closing in; oppressive exhalations seemed to proceed from the plants and steal upward past the open window; and Giovanni, closing the lattice, went to his couch and dreamed of a rich flower and beautiful girl. Flower and maiden were different, and yet the same, and fraught with some strange peril in either shape.

But there is an influence in the light of morning that tends to rectify whatever errors of fancy, or even of judgment, we may have incurred during the sun's decline, or among the shadows of the night, or in the less wholesome glow of moonshine. Giovanni's first movement, on starting from sleep, was to throw open the window and gaze down into the garden which his dreams had made so fertile of mysteries. He was surprised and a little ashamed to find how real and matter-of-fact an affair it proved to be, in the first rays of the sun which gilded the dew-drops that hung upon leaf and blossom, and, while giving a brighter beauty to each rare flower, brought everything within the limits of ordinary experience. The young man rejoiced that, in the heart of the barren city, he had the privilege of overlooking this spot of lovely and luxuriant vegetation. It would serve, he said to himself, as a symbolic language to keep him in communion with Nature. Neither the sickly and thought-worn Dr. Giacomo Rappaccini, it is true, nor his brilliant daughter, were now visible; so that Giovanni could not determine how much of the singularity which he attributed to both was due to their own qualities and how much to his wonder-working fancy; but he was inclined to take a most rational view of the whole matter.

In the course of the day he paid his respects to Signor Pietro Baglioni, professor of medicine in the university, a physician of eminent repute, to whom Giovanni had brought a letter of introduction. The professor was an elderly personage, apparently of genial nature, and habits that might almost be called jovial. He kept the young man to dinner, and made himself very agreeable by the freedom and liveliness of his conversation, especially when warmed by a flask or two of Tuscan wine. Giovanni, conceiving that men of science, inhabitants of the same city, must needs be on familiar terms with one another, took an opportunity to mention the name of Dr. Rappaccini. But the professor did not respond with so much cordiality as he had anticipated.

"Ill would it become a teacher of the divine art of medicine," said Proferror Pietro Baglioni, in answer to a question of Giovanni, "to withhold due and well-considered praise of a physician so eminently skilled as Rappaccini; but, on the other hand, I should answer it but scantily to my conscience were I to permit a worthy youth like yourself, Signor Giovanni, the son of an ancient friend, to imbibe erroneous ideas respecting a man who might hereafter chance to hold your life and death in his hands. The truth is, our worshipful Dr. Rappaccini has as much science as any member of the faculty—with perhaps one single exception—in Padua, or all Italy; but there are certain grave objections to his professional character."

"And what are they?" asked the young man.

"Has my friend Giovanni any disease of body or heart, that he is so inquisitive about physicians?" said the professor, with a smile. "But as for Rappaccini, it is said of him—and I, who know the man well, can answer for its truth—that he cares infinitely more for science than for mankind. His patients are interesting to him only as subjects for some new experiment. He would sacrifice human life, his own among the rest, or whatever else was dearest to him, for the sake of adding so much as a grain of mustard seed to the great heap of his accumulated knowledge."

"Methinks he is an awful man indeed," remarked Guasconti, mentally recalling the cold and purely intellectual aspect of Rappaccini. "And yet, worshipful professor, is it not a noble spirit? Are there many men capable of so spiritual a love of science?"

"God forbid," answered the professor, somewhat testily; "at least, unless they take sounder views of the healing art than those adopted by Rappaccini. It is his theory that all medicinal virtues are comprised within those substances which we term vegetable poisons. These he cultivates with his own hands, and is said even to have produced new varieties of poison, more horribly deleterious than Nature, without the assistance of this learned person, would ever have plagued the world withal. That the signor doctor does less mischief than might be expected with such dangerous substances is undeniable. Now and then, it must be owned, he has effected, or seemed to effect, a marvelous cure; but, to tell you my private mind, Signor Giovanni, he should receive little credit for such instances of success,—they being probably the work of chance,—but should be held strictly accountable for his failures, which may justly be considered his own work."

The youth might have taken Baglioni's opinions with many grains of allowance had he known that there was a professional warfare of long continuance between him and Dr. Rappaccini, in which the latter was generally thought to have gained the advantage. If the reader be inclined to judge for himself, we refer him to certain black-letter tracts on both sides, preserved in the medical department of the University of Padua.

"I know not, most learned professor," returned Giovanni, after musing on what had been said of Rappaccini's exclusive zeal for science,—"I know not how dearly this physician may love his art; but surely there is one object more dear to him. He has a daughter."

"Aha!" cried the professor, with a laugh. "So now our friend Giovanni's secret is out. You have heard of this daughter, whom all the young men in Padua are wild about, though not half a dozen have ever had the good hap to see her face. I know little of the Signora Beatrice save that Rappaccini is said to have instructed her deeply in his science, and that, young and beautiful as fame reports her, she is already qualified to fill a professor's chair. Perchance her father destines her for mine! Other absurd rumors there be, not worth talking about or listening to. So now, Signor Giovanni, drink off your glass of lachryma."

Guasconti returned to his lodgings somewhat heated with the wine he had quaffed, and which caused his brain to swim with strange fantasies in reference to Dr. Rappaccini and the beautiful Beatrice. On his way, happening to pass by a florist's he bought a fresh bouquet of flowers.

Ascending to his chamber, he seated himself near the window, but within the shadow thrown by the depth of the wall, so that he could look down into the garden with little risk of being discovered. All beneath his eye was a solitude. The strange plants were basking in the sunshine, and now and then nodding gently to one another, as if in acknowledgment of sympathy and kindred. In the midst, by the shattered fountain, grew the magnificent shrub, with its purple gems clustering all over it; they glowed in the air, and gleamed back again out of the depths of the pool, which thus seemed to overflow with colored radiance from the rich reflection that was steeped in it. At first, as we have said, the garden was a solitude. Soon, however,—as Giovanni had half hoped, half feared, would be the case,—a figure appeared beneath the antique sculptured portal, and came down between the rows of plants, inhaling their various perfumes as if she were one of those beings of old classic fables that lived upon sweet odors. On again beholding Beatrice the young man was even startled to perceive how much her beauty exceeded his recollection of it; so brilliant, so vivid, was its character, that she glowed amid the sunlight, and, as Giovanni whispered to himself, positively illuminated the more shadowy intervals of the garden path. Her face being now more revealed than on the former occasion, he was struck by its expression of simplicity and sweetness,—qualities that had not entered into his idea of her character, and which made him ask anew what manner of mortal she might be. Nor did he fail again to observe, or imagine, an analogy between the beautiful girl and the gorgeous shrub that hung its gemlike flowers over the fountain,—a resemblance which Beatrice seemed to have indulged a fantastic humor in heightening, both by the arrangement of her dress and the selection of its hues.

Approaching the shrub, she threw open her arms, as with a passionate ardor, and drew its branches into an intimate embrace—so intimate that her features were hidden in its leafy bosom and her glistening ringlets all intermingled with the flowers.

"Give me thy breath, my sister," exclaimed Beatrice; "for I am faint with common air. And give me this flower of thine, which I separate with gentlest fingers from the stem and place it close beside my heart."

With these words the beautiful daughter of Rappaccini plucked one of the richest blossoms of the shrub, and was about to fasten it in her bosom. But now, unless Giovanni's draughts of wine had bewildered his senses, a singular incident occurred. A small orange-colored reptile of the lizard or chameleon species, chanced to be creeping along the path just at the feet of Beatrice. It appeared to Giovanni,—but at the distance from which he gazed, he could scarcely have seen anything so minute,—it appeared to him, however, that a drop or two of moisture from the broken stem of the flower descended upon the lizard's head. For an instant the reptile contorted itself violently, and then lay motionless in the sunshine. Beatrice observed this remarkable phenomenon, and crossed herself, sadly, but without surprise; nor did she therefore hesitate to arrange the fatal flower in her bosom. There it blushed, and almost glimmered with the dazzling effect of a precious stone, adding to her dress and aspect the one appropriate charm which nothing else in the world could have supplied. But Giovanni, out of the shadow of his window, bent forward and shrank back, and murmured and trembled.

"Am I awake? Have I my senses?" said he to himself. "What is this being? Beautiful shall I call her, or inexpressibly terrible?"

Beatrice now strayed carelessly through the garden, approaching closer beneath Giovanni's window, so that he was compelled to thrust his head quite out of its concealment in order to gratify the intense and painful curiosity which she excited. At this moment there came a beautiful insect over the garden wall; it had, perhaps, wandered through the city and found no flowers or verdure among those antique haunts of men until the heavy perfumes of Dr. Rappaccini's shrubs had lured it from afar. Without alighting on the flowers, this winged brightness seemed to be attracted by Beatrice, and lingered in the air and fluttered about her head. Now, here it could not be but that Giovanni Guasconti's eyes deceived him. Be that as it might, he fancied that, while Beatrice was gazing at the insect with childish delight, it grew faint and fell at her feet; its bright wings shivered; it was dead—from no cause that he could discern, unless it were the atmosphere of her breath. Again Beatrice crossed herself and sighed heavily as she bent over the dead insect.

An impulsive movement of Giovanni drew her eyes to the window. There she beheld the beautiful head of the young man—rather a Grecian than an Italian head, with fair, regular features, and a glistening of gold among his ringlets—gazing down upon her like a being that hovered in mid air. Scarcely knowing what he did, Giovanni threw the bouquet which he had hitherto held in his hand.

"Signora," said he, "there are pure and healthful flowers. Wear them for the sake of Giovanni Guasconti."

"Thanks, signor," replied Beatrice, with her rich voice, that came forth as it were like a gush of music, and with a mirthful expression half childish and half woman-like. "I accept your gift, and would fain recompense it with this precious purple flower; but if I toss it into the air it will not reach you. So Signor Guasconti must even content himself with my thanks."

She lifted the bouquet from the ground, and then, as if inwardly ashamed at having stepped aside from her maidenly reserve to respond to a stranger's greeting, passed swiftly homeward through the garden. But few as the moments were, it seemed to Giovanni, when she was on the point of vanishing beneath the sculptured portal, that his beautiful bouquet was already beginning to wither in her grasp. It was an idle thought; there could be no possibility of distinguishing a faded flower from a fresh one at so great a distance.

For many days after this incident the young man avoided the window that looked into Dr. Rappaccini's garden, as if something ugly and monstrous would have blasted his eyesight had he been betrayed into a glance. He felt conscious of having put himself, to a certain extent, within the influence of an unintelligible power by the communication which he had opened with Beatrice. The wisest course would have been, if his heart were in any real danger, to quit his lodgings and Padua itself at once; the next wiser, to have accustomed himself, as far as possible, to the familiar and daylight view of Beatrice,—thus bringing her rigidly and systematically within the limits of ordinary experience. Least of all, while avoiding her sight, ought Giovanni to have remained so near this extraordinary being that the proximity and possibility even of intercourse should give a kind of substance and reality to the wild vagaries which his imagination ran riot continually in producing. Guasconti had not a deep heart—or, at all events, its depths were not sounded now; but he had a quick fancy, and an ardent southern temperament which rose every instant to a higher fever pitch. Whether or no Beatrice possessed those terrible attributes, that fatal breath, the affinity with those so beautiful and deadly flowers which were indicated by what Giovanni had witnessed, she had at least instilled a fierce and subtle poison into his system. It was not love, although her rich beauty was a madness to him; nor horror, even while he fancied her spirit to be imbued with the same baneful essence that seemed to pervade her physical frame; but a wild offspring of both love and horror that had each parent in it, and burned like one and shivered like the other. Giovanni knew not what to dread; still less did he know what to hope; yet hope and dread kept a continual warfare in his breast, alternately vanquishing one another and starting up afresh to renew the contest. Blessed are all simple emotions, be they dark or bright! It is the lurid intermixture of the two that produces the illuminating blaze of the infernal regions.

Sometimes he endeavored to assuage the fever of his spirit by a rapid walk through the streets of Padua or beyond its gates: his footsteps kept time with the throbbings of his brain, so that the walk was apt to accelerate itself to a race. One day he found himself arrested; his arm was seized by a portly personage who had turned back on recognizing the young man and expended much breath in overtaking him.

"Signor Giovanni! Stay, my young friend!" cried he. "Have you forgotten me? That might well be the case if I were as much altered as yourself."

It was Baglioni, whom Giovanni had avoided ever since their first meeting, from a doubt that the professor's sagacity would look too deeply into his secrets. Endeavoring to recover himself, he stared forth wildly from his inner world into the outer one and spoke like a man in a dream.

"Yes; I am Giovanni Guasconti. You are Professor Pietro Baglioni. Now let me pass!"

"Not yet, not yet, Signor Giovanni Guasconti," said the professor, smiling, but at the same time scrutinizing the youth with an earnest glance. "What! Did I grow up side by side with your father? and shall his son pass me like a stranger in these old streets of Padua? Stand still, Signor Giovanni; for we must have a word or two before we part."

"Speedily, then, most worshipful professor, speedily," said Giovanni, with feverish impatience. "Does not your worship see that I am in haste?"

Now, while he was speaking there came a man in black along the street, stooping and moving feebly like a person in inferior health. His face was all overspread with a most sickly and sallow hue, but yet so pervaded with an expression of piercing and active intellect that an observer might easily have overlooked the merely physical attributes and have seen only this wonderful energy. As he passed, this person exchanged a cold and distant salutation with Baglioni, but fixed his eyes upon Giovanni with an intentness that seemed to bring out whatever was within him worthy of notice. Nevertheless, there was a peculiar quietness in the look, as if taking merely a speculative, not a human, interest in the young man.

"It is Dr. Rappaccini!" whispered the professor, when the stranger had passed. "Has he ever seen your face before?"

"Not that I know," answered Giovanni, starting at the name.

"He *has* seen you! he must have seen you!" said Baglioni hastily. "For some purpose or other, this man of science is making a study of you. I know that look of his! It is the same that coldly illuminates his face as he bends over a bird, a mouse, or a butterfly, which, in pursuance of some experiment, he has killed by the perfume of a flower; a look as deep as Nature itself, but without Nature's warmth of love. Signor Giovanni, I will stake my life upon it, you are the subject of one of Rappaccini's experiments."

"Will you make a fool of me?" cried Giovanni passionately. "*That,* signor professor, were an untoward experiment."

"Patience, patience!" replied the imperturbable professor. "I tell thee, my poor Giovanni, that Rappaccini has a scientific interest in thee. Thou hast fallen into fearful hands! And the Signora Beatrice,—what part does she act in this mystery?"

But Guasconti, finding Baglioni's pertinacity intolerable, here broke away, and was gone before the professor could again seize his arm. He looked after the young man intently and shook his head.

"This must not be," said Baglioni to himself. "The youth is the son of my old friend, and shall not come to any harm from which the arcana of medical science can preserve him. Besides, it is too insufferable an impertinence in Rappaccini, thus to snatch the lad out of my own hands, as I may say, and make use of him for his infernal experiments. This daughter of his! It shall be looked to. Perchance, most learned Rappaccini, I may foil you where you little dream of it!"

Meanwhile, Giovanni had pursued a circuitous route, and at length found himself at the door of his lodgings. As he crossed the threshold he was met by old Lisabetta, who smirked and smiled, and was evidently desirous to attract his attention; vainly, however, as the ebullition of his feelings had momentarily subsided into a cold and dull vacuity. He turned his eyes full upon the withered face that was puckering itself into a smile, but seemed to behold it not. The old dame, therefore, laid her grasp upon his cloak.

"Signor! signor!" whispered she, still with a smile over the whole breadth of her visage, so that it looked not unlike a grotesque carving in wood, darkened by centuries. "Listen, signor! There is a private entrance into the garden!"

"What do you say?" exclaimed Giovanni, turning quickly about, as if an inanimate thing should start into feverish life. "A private entrance into Dr. Rappaccini's garden?"

"Hush! hush! Not so loud!" whispered Lisabetta, putting her hand over his mouth. "Yes; into the worshipful doctor's garden, where you may see all this fine shrubbery. Many a young man in Padua would give gold to be admitted among those flowers."

Giovanni put a piece of gold into her hand.

"Show me the way," said he.

A surmise, probably excited by his conversation with Baglioni, crossed his mind, that this interposition of old Lisabetta might perchance be connected with the intrigue, whatever were its nature, in which the professor seemed to suppose that Dr. Rappaccini was involving him. But such a suspicion, though it disturbed Giovanni, was inadequate to restrain him. The instant that he was aware of the possibility of approaching Beatrice, it seemed an absolute necessity of his existence to do so. It mattered not whether she were angel or demon; he was irrevocably within her sphere, and must obey the law that whirled him onward, in ever lessening circles, toward a result which he did not attempt to foreshadow; and yet, strange to say, there came across him a sudden doubt whether this intense interest on his part were not delusory; whether it were really of so deep and positive a nature as to justify him in now thrusting himself into an incalculable position; whether it were not merely the fantasy of a young man's brain, only slightly or not at all connected with his heart.

He paused, hesitated, turned half about, but again went on. His withered guide led him along several obscure passages, and finally undid a door, through which, as it was opened, there came the sight and sound of rustling leaves, with the broken sunshine glimmering among them. Giovanni stepped forth, and, forcing himself through the entanglement of a shrub that wreathed its tendrils over the hidden entrance, stood beneath his own window in the open area of Dr. Rappaccini's garden.

How often is it the case that, when impossibilities have come to pass and dreams have condensed their misty substance into tangible realities, we find ourselves calm, and even coldly self-possessed, amid circumstances which it would have been a delirium of joy or agony to anticipate! Fate delights to thwart us thus. Passion will choose his own time to rush upon the scene, and lingers sluggishly behind when an appropriate adjustment of events would seem to summon his appearance. So was it now with Giovanni. Day after day his pulses had throbbed with feverish blood at the improbable idea of an interview with Beatrice, and of standing with her, face to face, in this very garden, basking in the Oriental sunshine of her beauty, and snatching from her full gaze the mystery which he deemed the riddle of his own existence. But now there was a singular and untimely equanimity within his breast. He threw a glance around the garden to discover if Beatrice or her father were present, and, perceiving that he was alone, began a critical observation of the plants.

The aspect of one and all of them dissatisfied him; their gorgeousness seemed fierce, passionate, and even unnatural. There was hardly an individual shrub which a wanderer, straying by himself through a forest, would not have been startled to find growing wild, as if an unearthly face had glared at him out of the thicket. Several also would have shocked a delicate instinct by an appearance of artificialness indicating that there had been such commixture, and, as it were, adultery, of various vegetable species, that the production was no longer of God's making, but the monstrous offspring of man's depraved fancy, glowing with only an evil mockery of beauty. They were probably the result of experiment, which in one or two cases had succeeded in mingling plants individually lovely into a compound possessing the questionable and ominous character that distinguished the whole growth of the garden. In fine, Giovanni recognized but two or three plants in the collection, and those of a kind that he well knew to be poisonous. While busy with these contemplations he heard the rustling of a silken garment, and, turning, beheld Beatrice emerging from beneath the sculptured portal.

Giovanni had not considered with himself what should be his deportment; whether he should apologize for his intrusion into the garden, or assume that he was there with the privity at least, if not by the desire, of Dr. Rappaccini or his daughter; but Beatrice's manner placed him at his ease, although leaving him still in doubt by what agency he had gained admittance. She came lightly along the path and met him near the broken fountain. There was surprise in her face, but brightened by a simple and kind expression of pleasure.

"You are a connoisseur in flowers, signor," said Beatrice, with a smile, alluding to the bouquet which he had flung her from the window. "It is no marvel, therefore, if the sight of my father's rare collection has tempted you to take a nearer view. If he were here, he could tell you many strange and interesting facts as to the nature and habits of these shrubs; for he has spent a lifetime in such studies, and this garden is his world."

"And yourself, lady," observed Giovanni, "if fame says true,—you likewise are deeply skilled in the virtues indicated by these rich blossoms and these spicy perfumes. Would you deign to be my instructress, I should prove an apter scholar than if taught by Signor Rappaccini himself."

"Are there such idle rumors?" asked Beatrice, with the music of a pleasant laugh. "Do people say that I am skilled in my father's science of plants? What a jest is there! No; though I have grown up among these flowers, I know no more of them than their hues and perfume; and sometimes methinks I would fain rid myself of even that small knowledge. There are many flowers here, and those not the least brilliant, that shock and offend me when they meet my eye. But pray, signor, do not believe these stories about my science. Believe nothing of me save what you see with your own eyes."

"And must I believe all that I have seen with my own eyes?" asked Giovanni, pointedly, while the recollection of former scenes made him shrink. "No, signora; you demand too little of me. Bid me believe nothing save what comes from your own lips."

It would appear that Beatrice understood him. There came a deep flush to her cheek, but she looked full into Giovanni's eyes and responded to his gaze of uneasy suspicion with a queenlike haughtiness.

'I do so bid you, signor," she replied. "Forget whatever you may have fancied in regard to me. If true to the outward senses, still it may be false in its essence; but the words of Beatrice Rappaccini's lips are true from the depths of the heart outward. Those you may believe."

A fervor glowed in her whole aspect and beamed upon Giovanni's consciousness like the light of truth itself; but while she spoke there was a fragrance in the atmosphere around her, rich and delightful, though evanescent, yet which the young man, from an indefinable reluctance, scarcely dared to draw into his lungs. It might be the odor of the flowers. Could it be Beatrice's breath which thus embalmed her words with a strange richness, as if by steeping them in her heart? A faintness passed like a shadow over Giovanni and flitted away; he seemed to gaze through the beautiful girl's eyes into her transparent soul, and felt no more doubt or fear.

The tinge of passion that had colored Beatrice's manner vanished; she became gay, and appeared to derive a pure delight from her communion with the youth not unlike what the maiden of a lonely island might have felt conversing with a voyager from the civilized world. Evidently her experience of life had been confined within the limits of that garden. She talked now about matters as simple as the daylight or summer clouds, and now asked questions in reference to the city, or Giovanni's distant home, his friends, his mother, and his sisters—questions indicating such seclusion, and such lack of familiarity with modes and forms, that Giovanni responded as if to an infant. Her spirit gushed out before him like a fresh rill that was just catching its first glimpse of the sunlight and wondering at the reflections of earth and sky which were flung into its bosom. There came thoughts, too, from a deep source, and fantasies of gemlike brilliancy, as if diamonds and rubies sparkled upward among the bubbles of the fountain. Ever and anon there gleamed across the young man's mind a sense of wonder that he should be walking side by side with the being who had so wrought upon his imagination, whom he had idealized in such hues of terror, in whom he had positively witnessed such manifestations of dreadful attributes,—that he should be conversing with Beatrice like a brother, and should find her so human and so maidenlike. But such reflections were only momentary; the effect of her character was too real not to make itself familiar at once.

In this free intercourse they had strayed through the garden, and now, after many turns among its avenues, were come to the shattered fountain, beside which grew the magnificent shrub with its treasury of glowing blossoms. A fragrance was diffused from it which Giovanni recognized as identical with that which he had attributed to Beatrice's breath, but incomparably more powerful. As her eyes fell upon it, Giovanni beheld her press her hand to her bosom, as if her heart were throbbing suddenly and painfully.

"For the first time in my life," murmured she, addressing the shrub, "I had forgotten thee."

"I remember, signora," said Grovanni, "that you once promised to reward me with one of these living gems for the bouquet which I had the happy boldness to fling to your feet. Permit me now to pluck it as a memorial of this interview."

He made a step toward the shrub with extended hand; but Beatrice darted forward, uttering a shriek that went through his heart like a dagger. She caught his hand and drew it back with the whole force of her slender figure. Giovanni felt her touch thrilling through his fibres.

"Touch it not!" exclaimed she, in a voice of agony. "Not for thy life! It is fatal!"

Then, hiding her face, she fled from him and vanished beneath the sculptured portal. As Giovanni followed her with his eyes, he beheld the emaciated figure and pale intelligence of Dr. Rappaccini, who had been watching the scene, he knew not how long, within the shadow of the entrance.

No sooner was Guasconti alone in his chamber than the image of Beatrice came back to his passionate musings, invested with all the witchery that had been gathering around it ever since his first glimpse of her, and now likewise imbued with a tender warmth of girlish womanhood. She was human; her nature was endowed with all gentle and feminine qualities; she was worthiest to be worshipped; she was capable, surely, on her part, of the height and heroism of love. Those tokens which he had hitherto considered as proofs of a frightful peculiarity in her physical and moral system were now either forgotten, or, by the subtle sophistry of passion transmuted into a golden crown of enchantment, rendering Beatrice the more admirable by so much as she was the more unique. Whatever had looked ugly was now beautiful; or, if incapable of such a change, it stole away and hid itself among those shapeless half ideas which throng the dim region beyond the daylight of our perfect consciousness.

Thus did he spend the night. nor fell asleep until the dawn had begun to awake the slumbering flowers in Dr. Rappaccini's garden, whither Giovanni's dreams doubtless led him. Up rose the sun in his due season, and, flinging his beams upon the young man's eyelids, awoke him to a sense of pain. When thoroughly aroused, he became sensible of a burning and tingling agony in his hand—in his right hand—the very hand which Beatrice had grasped in her own when he was on the point of plucking one of the gemlike flowers. On the back of that hand there was now a purple print like that of four small fingers, and the likeness of a slender thumb upon his wrist.

Oh, how stubbornly does love,—or even that cunning semblance of love which flourishes in the imagination, but strikes no depth of root into the heart,—how stubbornly does it hold its faith until the moment comes when it is doomed to vanish into thin mist! Giovanni wrapped a handkerchief about his hand and wondered what evil thing had stung him, and soon forgot his pain in a reverie of Beatrice.

After the first interview, a second was in the inevitable course of what we call fate. A third; a fourth; and a meeting with Beatrice in the garden was no longer an incident in Giovanni's daily life, but the whole space in which he might be said to live; for the anticipation and memory of that ecstatic hour made up the remainder. Nor was it otherwise with the daughter of Rappaccini. She watched for the youth's appearance, and flew to his side with confidence as unreserved as if they had been playmates from early infancy—as if they were such playmates still. If, by any unwonted chance, he failed to come at the appointed moment, she stood beneath the window and sent up the rich sweetness of her tones to float around him in his chamber and echo and reverberate throughout his heart: "Giovanni! Giovanni! Why tarriest thou? Come down!" and down he hastened into that Eden of poisonous flowers.

But, with all this intimate familiarity, there was still a reserve in Beatrice's demeanor, so rigidly and invariably sustained that the idea of infringing it scarcely occurred to his imagination. By all appreciable signs, they loved; they had looked love with eyes that conveyed the holy secret from the depths of one soul into the depths of the other, as if it were too sacred to be whispered by the way; they had even spoken love in those gushes of passion when their spirits darted forth in articulated breath like tongues of long-hidden flame; and yet there had been no seal of lips, no clasp of hands, nor any slightest caress such as love claims and hallows. He had never touched one of the gleaming ringlets of her hair; her garment—so marked was the physical barrier between them—had never been waved against him by a breeze. On the few occasions when Giovanni had seemed tempted to over-step the limit, Beatrice grew so sad, so stern, and withal wore such a look of desolate separation, shuddering at itself, that not a spoken word was requisite to repel him. At such times he was startled at the horrible suspicions that rose, monster-like, out of the caverns of his heart and stared him in the face; his love grew thin and faint as the morning mist; his doubts alone had substance. But, when Beatrice's face brightened again after the momentary shadow, she was transformed at once from the mysterious, questionable being whom he had watched with so much awe and horror; she was now the beautiful and unsophisticated girl whom he felt that his spirit knew with a certainty beyond all other knowledge.

A considerable time had now passed since Giovanni's last meeting with Baglioni. One morning, however, he was disagreeably surprised by a visit from the professor, whom he had scarcely thought of for whole weeks, and would willingly have forgotten still longer. Given up as he had long been to a pervading excitement, he could tolerate no companions except upon condition of their perfect sympathy with his present state of feeling. Such sympathy was not to be expected from Professor Baglioni.

The visitor chatted carelessly for a few moments about the gossip of the city and the university, and then took up another topic.

"I have been reading an old classic author lately," said he, "and met with a story that strangely interested me. Possibly you may remember it. It is of an Indian prince, who sent a beautiful woman as a present to Alexander the Great. She was as lovely as the dawn and gorgeous as the sunset; but what especially distinguished her was a certain rich perfume in her breath—richer than a garden of Persian roses. Alexander, as was natural to a youthful conqueror, fell in love at first sight with this magnificent stranger; but a certain sage physician, happening to be present, discovered a terrible secret in regard to her."

"And what was that?" asked Giovanni, turning his eyes downward to avoid those of the professor.

"That this lovely woman," continued Baglioni, with emphasis, "had been nourished with poisons from her birth upward, until her whole nature was so imbued with them that she herself had become the deadliest poison in existence. Poison was her element of life. With that rich perfume of her breath she blasted the very air. Her love would have been poison—her embrace death. Is not this a marvelous tale?"

"A childish fable," answered Giovanni, nervously starting from his chair. "I marvel how your worship finds time to read such nonsense among your graver studies."

"By the by," said the professor, looking uneasily about him, "what singular fragrance is this in your apartment? Is it the perfume of your gloves? It is faint, but delicious; and yet, after all, by no means agreeable. Were I to breathe it long, methinks it would make me ill. It is like the breath of a flower; but I see no flowers in the chamber."

"Nor are there any," replied Giovanni, who had turned pale as the professor spoke; "nor, I think, is there any fragrance except in your worship's imagination. Odors being a sort of element combined of the sensual and the spiritual, are apt to deceive us in this manner. The recollection of a perfume, the bare idea of it, may easily be mistaken for a present reality."

"Ay; but my sober imagination does not often play such tricks," said Baglioni; "and, were I to fancy any kind of odor, it would be that of some vile apothecary drug wherewith my fingers are likely enough to be imbued. Our worshipful friend Rappaccini, as I have heard, tinctures his medicaments with odors richer than those of Araby. Doubtless, likewise, the fair and learned Signora Beatrice would minister to her patients with draughts as sweet as a maiden's breath; but woe to him that sips them!"

Giovanni's face evinced many contending emotions. The tone in which the professor alluded to the pure and lovely daughter of Rappaccini was a torture to his soul; and yet the intimation of a view of her character, opposite to his own, gave instantaneous distinctness to a thousand dim suspicions, which now grinned at him like so many demons. But he strove hard to quell them and to respond to Baglioni with a true lover's perfect faith.

"Signor professor," said he, "you were my father's friend; perchance, too, it is your purpose to act a friendly part toward his son. I would fain feel nothing toward you save respect and deference; but I pray you to observe, signor, that there is one subject on which we must not speak. You know not the Signora Beatrice. You cannot, therefore, estimate the wrong—the blasphemy, I may even say—that is offered to her character by a light or injurious word."

"Giovanni! my poor Giovanni!" answered the professor, with a calm expression of pity, "I know this wretched girl far better than yourself. You shall hear the truth in respect to the poisoner Rappaccini and his poisonous daughter; yes, poisonous as she is beautiful. Listen; for, even should you do violence to my gray hairs, it shall not silence me. That old fable of the Indian woman has become a truth by the deep and deadly science of Rappaccini and in the person of the lovely Beatrice."

Giovanni groaned and hid his face.

"Her father," continued Baglioni, "was not restrained by natural affection from offering up his child in this horrible manner as the victim of his insane zeal for science; for, let us do him justice, he is as true a man of science as ever distilled his own heart in an alembic. What, then, will be your fate? Beyond a doubt you are selected as the material of some new experiment. Perhaps the result is to be death; perhaps a fate more awful still. Rappaccini, with what he calls the interest of science before his eyes, will hesitate at nothing."

"It is a dream," muttered Giovanni to himself; "surely it is a dream."

"But," resumed the professor, "be of good cheer, son of my friend. It is not yet too late for the rescue. Possibly we may even succeed in bringing back this miserable child within the limits of ordinary nature, from which her father's madness has estranged her. Behold this little silver vase! It was wrought by the hands of the renowned Benvenuto Cellini, and is well worthy to be a love gift to the fairest dame in Italy. But its contents are invaluable. One little sip of this antidote would have rendered the most virulent poisons of the Borgias innocuous. Doubt not that it will be as efficacious against those of Rappaccini. Bestow the vase, and the precious liquid within it, on your Beatrice, and hopefully await the result."

Baglioni laid a small, exquisitely wrought silver vial on the table and withdrew, leaving what he had said to produce its effect upon the young man's mind.

"We will thwart Rappaccini yet," thought he, chuckling to himself, as he descended the stairs; "but, let us confess the truth of him, he is a wonderful man—a wonderful man indeed; a vile empiric, however, in his practice, and therefore not to be tolerated by those who respect the good old rules of the medical profession."

Throughout Giovanni's whole acquaintance with Beatrice, he had occasionally, as we have said, been haunted by dark surmises as to her character; yet so thoroughly had she made herself felt by him as a simple, natural, most affectionate, and guileless creature, that the image now held up by Professor Baglioni looked as strange and incredible as if it were not in accordance with his own original conception. True, there were ugly recollections connected with his first glimpses of the beautiful girl; he could not quite forget the bouquet that withered in her grasp, and the insect that perished amid the sunny air, by no ostensible agency save the fragrance of her breath. These incidents, however, dissolving in the pure light of her character, had no longer the efficacy of facts, but were acknowledged as mistaken fantasies, by whatever testimony of the senses they might appear to be substantiated. There is something truer and more real than what we can see with the eyes and touch with the finger. On such better evidence had Giovanni founded his confidence in Beatrice, though rather by the necessary force of her high attributes than by any deep and generous faith on his part. But now his spirit was incapable of sustaining itself at the height to which the early enthusiasm of passion had exalted it; he fell down, groveling among earthly doubts, and defiled therewith the pure whiteness of Beatrice's image. Not that he gave her up; he did but distrust. He resolved to institute some decisive test that should satisfy him, once for all, whether there were those dreadful peculiarities in her physical nature which could not be supposed to exist without some corresponding monstrosity of soul. His eyes, gazing down afar, might have deceived him as to the lizard, the insect, and the flowers; but if he could witness, at the distance of a few paces, the sudden blight of one fresh and healthful flower in Beatrice's hand, there would be room for no further question. With this idea he hastened to the florist's and purchased a bouquet that was still gemmed with the morning dew-drops.

It was now the customary hour of his daily interview with Beatrice. Before descending into the garden, Giovanni failed not to look at his figure in the mirror,—a vanity to be expected in a beautiful young man, yet, as displaying itself at that troubled and feverish moment, the token of a certain shallowness of feeling and insincerity of character. He did gaze, however, and said to himself that his features had never before possessed so rich a grace, nor his eyes such vivacity, nor his cheeks so warm a hue of superabundant life.

"At least," thought he, "her poison has not yet insinuated itself into my system. I am no flower to perish in her grasp."

With that thought he turned his eyes on the bouquet, which he had never once laid aside from his hand. A thrill of indefinable horror shot through his frame on perceiving that those dewy flowers were already beginning to droop; they wore the aspect of things that had been fresh and lovely yesterday. Giovanni grew white as marble, and stood motionless before the mirror, staring at his own reflection there as at the likeness of something frightful. He remembered Baglioni's remark about the fragrance that seemed to pervade the chamber. It must have been the poison in his breath! Then he shuddered—shuddered at himself. Recovering from his stupor, he began to watch with curious eye a spider that was busily at work hanging its web from the antique cornice of the apartment, crossing and recrossing the artful system of interwoven lines—as vigorous and active a spider as ever dangled from an old ceiling. Giovanni bent toward the insect, and emitted a deep, long breath. The spider suddenly ceased its toil; the web vibrated with a tremor originating in the body of the small artisan. Again Giovanni sent forth a breath, deeper, longer, and imbued with a venomous feeling out of his heart; he knew not whether he were wicked or only desperate. The spider made a convulsive gripe with his limbs and hung dead across the window.

"Accursed! accursed!" muttered Giovanni, addressing himself. "Hast thou grown so poisonous that this deadly insect perishes by thy breath?"

At that moment a rich, sweet voice came floating up from the garden.

"Giovanni! Giovanni! It is past the hour! Why tarriest thou? Come down!"

"Yes," muttered Giovanni again. "She is the only being whom my breath may not slay! Would that it might!"

He rushed down, and in an instant was standing before the bright and loving eyes of Beatrice. A moment ago his wrath and despair had been so fierce that he could have desired nothing so much as to wither her by a glance; but with her actual presence there came influences which had too real an existence to be at once shaken off: recollections of the delicate and benign power of her feminine nature, which had so often enveloped him in a religious calm; recollections of many a holy and passionate outgush of her heart, when the pure fountain had been unsealed from its depths and made visible in its transparency to his mental eye; recollections which, had Giovanni known how to estimate them, would have assured him that all this ugly mystery was but an earthly illusion, and that, whatever mist of evil might seem to have gathered over her, the real Beatrice was a heavenly angel. Incapable as he was of such high faith, still her presence had not utterly lost its magic. Giovanni's rage was quelled into an aspect of sullen insensibility. Beatrice, with a quick spiritual sense, immediately felt that there was a gulf of blackness between them which neither he nor she could pass. They walked on together, sad and silent, and came thus to the marble fountain and to its pool of water on the ground, in the midst of which grew the shrub that bore gem-like blossoms. Giovanni was affrighted at the eager enjoyment—the appetite, as it were—with which he found himself inhaling the fragrance of the flowers.

"Beatrice," asked he, abruptly, "whence came this shrub?"

"My father created it," answered she, with simplicity.

"Created it! created it!" repeated Giovanni. "What mean you, Beatrice?"

"He is a man fearfully acquainted with the secrets of Nature," replied Beatrice; "and at the hour when I first drew breath this plant sprang from the soil, the offspring of his science, of his intellect, while I was but his earthly child. Approach it not!" continued she, observing with terror that Giovanni was drawing nearer to the shrub. "It has qualities that you little dream of. But I, dearest Giovanni,—I grew up and blossomed with the plant and was nourished with its breath. It was my sister, and I loved it with a human affection; for, alas!—hast thou not suspected it?—there was an awful doom."

Here Giovanni frowned so darkly upon her that Beatrice paused and trembled. But her faith in his tenderness reassured her, and made her blush that she had doubted for an instant.

"There was an awful doom," she continued, "the effect of my father's fatal love of science, which estranged me from all society of my kind. Until Heaven sent thee, dearest Giovanni, oh, how lonely was thy poor Beatrice!"

"Was it a hard doom?" asked Giovanni, fixing his eyes upon her.

"Only of late have I known how hard it was," answered she, tenderly. "Oh, yes; but my heart was torpid, and therefore quiet."

Giovanni's rage broke forth from his sullen gloom like a lightning-flash out of a dark cloud.

"Accursed one!" cried he, with venomous scorn and anger. "And, finding thy solitude wearisome, thou hast severed me likewise from all the warmth of life and enticed me into thy region of unspeakable horror!"

"Giovanni!" exclaimed Beatrice, turning her large bright eyes upon his face. The force of his words had not found its way into her mind; she was merely thunderstruck.

"Yes, poisonous thing!" repeated Giovanni, beside himself with passion. "Thou hast done it! Thou hast blasted me! Thou hast filled my veins with poison! Thou hast made me as hateful, as ugly, as loathsome and deadly a creature as thyself—a world's wonder of hideous monstrosity! Now, if our breath be happily as fatal to ourselves as to all others, let us join our lips in one kiss of unutterable hatred, and so die!"

"What has befallen me?" murmured Beatrice, with a low moan out of her heart. "Holy Virgin, pity me, a poor heart-broken child!"

"Thou,—dost thou pray?" cried Giovanni, still with the same fiendish scorn. "Thy very prayers, as they come from thy lips, taint the atmosphere with death. Yes; let us pray! Let us to church and dip our fingers in the holy water at the portal! They that come after us will perish as by a pestilence! Let us sign crosses in the air! It will be scattering curses abroad in the likeness of holy symbols!"

"Giovanni," said Beatrice calmly, for her grief was beyond passion, "why dost thou join thyself with me thus in those terrible words? I, it is true, am the horrible thing thou namest me. But thou,—what hast thou to do, save with one other shudder at my hideous misery to go forth out of the garden and mingle with thy race, and forget that there ever crawled on earth such a monster as poor Beatrice?"

"Dost thou pretend ignorance?" asked Giovanni, scowling upon her. "Behold! this power have I gained from the pure daughter of Rappaccini."

There was a swarm of summer insects flitting through the air in search of the food promised by the flower odors of the fatal garden. They circled round Giovanni's head, and were evidently attracted toward him by the same influence which had drawn them for an instant within the sphere of several of the shrubs. He sent forth a breath among them, and smiled bitterly at Beatrice as at least a score of the insects fell dead upon the ground.

"I see it! I see it!" shrieked Beatrice. "It is my father's fatal science! No, no, Giovanni; it was not I! Never, never! I dreamed only to love thee and be with thee a little time, and so to let thee pass away, leaving but thine image in mine heart. For, Giovanni, believe it, though my body be nourished with poison, my spirit is God's creature, and craves love as its daily food. But my father,—he has united us in this fearful sympathy. Yes; spurn me, tread upon me, kill me! Oh, what is death after such words as thine? But it was not I. Not for a world of bliss would I have done it."

Giovanni's passion had exhausted itself in its outburst from his lips. There now came across him a sense, mournful, and not without tenderness, of the intimate and peculiar relationship between Beatrice and himself. They stood, as it were, in an utter solitude, which would be made none the less solitary by the densest throng of human life. Ought not, then, the desert of humanity around them to press this insulated pair closely together? If they should be cruel to one another, who was there to be kind to them? Besides, thought Giovanni, might there not still be a hope of his returning within the limits of ordinary nature, and leading Beatrice, the redeemed Beatrice, by the hand? Oh, weak, and selfish, and unworthy spirit, that could dream of an earthly union and earthly happiness as possible after such deep love had been so bitterly wronged as was Beatrice's love by Giovanni's blighting words! No, no; there could be no such hope. She must pass heavily, with that broken heart, across the borders of Time—she must bathe her hurts in some fount of paradise, and forget her grief in the light of immortality, and *there* be well.

But Giovanni did not know it.

"Dear Beatrice," said he, approaching her, while she shrank away as always at his approach, but now with a different impulse, "dearest Beatrice, our fate is not yet so desperate. Behold! there is a medicine, potent, as a wise physician has assured me, and almost divine in its efficacy. It is composed of ingredients the most opposite to those by which thy awful father has brought this calamity upon thee and me. It is distilled of blessed herbs. Shall we not quaff it together, and thus be purified from evil?"

"Give it me!" said Beatrice, extending her hand to receive the little silver vial which Giovanni took from his bosom. She added, with a peculiar emphasis, "I will drink; but do thou await the result."

She put Baglioni's antidote to her lips; and, at the same moment, the figure of Rappaccini emerged from the portal and came slowly toward the marble fountain. As he drew near, the pale man of science seemed to gaze with a triumphant expression at the beautiful youth and maiden, as might an artist who should spend his life in achieving a picture or a group of statuary and finally be satisfied with his success. He paused; his bent form grew erect with conscious power; he spread out his hand over them in the attitude of a father imploring a blessing upon his children; but those were the same hands that had thrown poison into the stream of their lives. Giovanni trembled. Beatrice shuddered nervously, and pressed her hand upon her heart.

"My daughter," said Rappaccini, "thou art no longer lonely in the world. Pluck one of those precious gems from thy sister shrub and bid thy bridegroom wear it in his bosom. It will not harm him now. My science and the sympathy between thee and him have so wrought within his system that he now stands apart from common men, as thou dost, daughter of my pride and triumph, from ordinary women. Pass on, then, through the world, most dear to one another and dreadful to all besides!"

"My father," said Beatrice, feebly,—and still as she spoke she kept her hand upon her heart,—"wherefore didst thou inflict this miserable doom upon thy child?"

"Miserable!" exclaimed Rappaccini. "What mean you, foolish girl? Dost thou deem it misery to be endowed with marvelous gifts against which no power nor strength could avail an enemy—misery, to be able to quell the mightiest with a breath—misery, to be as terrible as thou art beautiful? Wouldst thou, then, have preferred the condition of a weak woman, exposed to all evil and capable of none?"

"I would fain have been loved, not feared," murmured Beatrice, sinking down upon the ground. "But now it matters not. I am going, father, where the evil which thou hast striven to mingle with my being will pass away like a dream—like the fragrance of these poisonous flowers, which will no longer taint my breath among the flowers of Eden. Farewell, Giovanni! Thy words of hatred are like lead within my heart; but they, too, will fall away as I ascend. Oh, was there not, from the first, more poison in thy nature than in mine?"

To Beatrice,—so radically had her earthly part been wrought upon by Rappaccini's skill,—as poison had been life, so the powerful antidote was death; and thus the poor victim of man's ingenuity and of thwarted nature, and of the fatality that attends all such efforts of perverted wisdom, perished there, at the feet of her father and Giovanni.

Just at that moment Professor Pietro Baglioni looked forth from the window, and called loudly, in a tone of triumph mixed with horror, to the thunder-stricken man of science,

"Rappaccini! Rappaccini! And is *this* the upshot of your experiment!"

STEPHEN CRANE

The Open Boat ✌

*A Tale intended to be after the fact. Being the Experience
of Four men from the Sunk Steamer "Commodore"*

I

None of them knew the colour of the sky. Their eyes glanced level,
and were fastened upon the waves that swept toward them. These
waves were of the hue of slate, save for the tops, which were of
foaming white, and all of the men knew the colours of the sea. The horizon
narrowed and widened, and dipped and rose, and at all times its edge was
jagged with waves that seemed thrust up in points like rocks.

Many a man ought to have a bath-tub larger than the boat which here
rode upon the sea. These waves were most wrongfully and barbarously
abrupt and tall, and each froth-top was a problem in small boat navigation.

The cook squatted in the bottom and looked with both eyes at the six
inches of gunwale which separated him from the ocean. His sleeves were
rolled over his fat forearms, and the two flaps of his unbuttoned vest dangled
as he bent to bail out the boat. Often he said: "Gawd! That was a narrow
clip." As he remarked it he invariably gazed eastward over the broken sea.

The oiler, steering with one of the two oars in the boat, sometimes raised
himself suddenly to keep clear of water that swirled in over the stern. It was
a thin little oar and it seemed often ready to snap.

The correspondent, pulling at the other oar, watched the waves and
wondered why he was there.

The injured captain, lying in the bow, was at this time buried in that
profound dejection and indifference which comes, temporarily at least, to
even the bravest and most enduring when, willy nilly, the firm fails, the army
loses, the ship goes down. The mind of the master of a vessel is rooted deep
in the timbers of her, though he command for a day or a decade, and this
captain had on him the stern impression of a scene in the greys of dawn of
seven turned faces, and later a stump of a top-mast with a white ball on it
that slashed to and fro at the waves, went low and lower, and down. Thereafter there was something strange in his voice. Although steady, it was deep
with mourning, and of a quality beyond oration or tears.

"Keep 'er a little more south, Billie," said he.

"A little more south, sir," said the oiler in the stern.

A seat in this boat was not unlike a seat upon a bucking broncho, and, by the same token, a broncho is not much smaller. The craft pranced and reared, and plunged like an animal. As each wave came, and she rose for it, she seemed like a horse making at a fence outrageously high. The manner of her scramble over these walls of water is a mystic thing, and, moreover, at the top of them were ordinarily these problems in white water, the foam racing down from the summit of each wave, requiring a new leap, and a leap from the air. Then, after scornfully bumping a crest, she would slide, and race, and splash down a long incline, and arrive bobbing and nodding in front of the next menace.

A singular disadvantage of the sea lies in the fact that after successfully surmounting one wave you discover that there is another behind it just as important and just as nervously anxious to do something effective in the way of swamping boats. In a ten-foot dingey one can get an idea of the resources of the sea in the line of waves that is not probable to the average experience which is never at sea in a dingey. As each slaty wall of water approached, it shut all else from the view of the men in the boat, and it was not difficult to imagine that this particular wave was the final outburst of the ocean, the last effort of the grim water. There was a terrible grace in the move of the waves, and they came in silence, save for the snarling of the crests.

In the wan light, the faces of the men must have been grey. Their eyes must have glinted in strange ways as they gazed steadily astern. Viewed from a balcony, the whole thing would doubtless have been weirdly picturesque. But the men in the boat had no time to see it, and if they had had leisure there were other things to occupy their minds. The sun swung steadily up the sky, and they knew it was broad day because the colour of the sea changed from slate to emerald-green, streaked with amber lights, and the foam was like tumbling snow. The process of the breaking day was unknown to them. They were aware only of this effect upon the colour of the waves that rolled toward them.

In disjointed sentences the cook and the correspondent argued as to the difference between a life-saving station and a house of refuge. The cook had said: "There's a house of refuge just north of the Mosquito Inlet Light, and as soon as they see us, they'll come off in their boat and pick us up."

"As soon as who see us?" said the correspondent.

"The crew," said the cook.

"Houses of refuge don't have crews," said the correspondent. "As I understand them, they are only places where clothes and grub are stored for the benefit of shipwrecked people. They don't carry crews."

"Oh, yes, they do," said the cook.

"No, they don't," said the correspondent.

"Well, we're not there yet, anyhow," said the oiler, in the stern.

"Well," said the cook, "perhaps it's not a house of refuge that I'm thinking of as being near Mosquito Inlet Light. Perhaps it's a life-saving station."

"We're not there yet," said the oiler, in the stern.

II

As the boat bounced from the top of each wave, the wind tore through the hair of the hatless men, and as the craft plopped her stern down again the spray slashed past them. The crest of each of these waves was a hill, from the top of which the men surveyed, for a moment, a broad tumultuous expanse, shining and wind-driven. It was probably splendid. It was probably glorious, this play of the free sea, wild with lights of emerald and white and amber.

"Bully good thing it's an on-shore wind," said the cook. "If not, where would we be? Wouldn't have a show."

"That's right," said the correspondent.

The busy oiler nodded his assent.

Then the captain, in the bow, chuckled in a way that expressed humour, contempt, tragedy, all in one. "Do you think we've got much of a show now, boys?" said he.

Whereupon the three were silent, save for a trifle of hemming and hawing. To express any particular optimism at this time they felt to be childish and stupid, but they all doubtless possessed this sense of the situation in their mind. A young man thinks doggedly at such times. On the other hand, the ethics of their condition was decidedly against any open suggestion of hopelessness. So they were silent.

"Oh, well," said the captain, soothing his children, "we'll get ashore all right."

But there was that in his tone which made them think, so the oiler quoth: "Yes! If this wind holds!"

The cook was bailing: "Yes! If we don't catch hell in the surf."

Canton flannel gulls flew near and far. Sometimes they sat down on the sea, near patches of brown seaweed that rolled over the waves with a movement like carpets on a line in a gale. The birds sat comfortably in groups, and they were envied by some in the dingey, for the wrath of the sea was no more to them than it was to a covey of prairie chickens a thousand miles inland. Often they came very close and stared at the men with black bead-like eyes. At these times they were uncanny and sinister in their unblinking scrutiny, and the men hooted angrily at them, telling them to be gone. One came, and evidently decided to alight on the top of the captain's head. The bird flew parallel to the boat and did not circle, but made short sidelong jumps in the air in chicken-fashion. His black eyes were wistfully fixed upon the captain's head. "Ugly brute," said the oiler to the bird. "You look as if you were made with a jack-knife." The cook and the correspondent swore darkly at the creature. The captain naturally wished to knock it away with the end of the heavy painter; but he did not dare do it, because anything resembling an emphatic gesture would have capsized this freighted boat and so with his open hand, the captain gently and carefully waved the gull away. After it had been discouraged from the pursuit the captain breathed easier on account of his hair, and others breathed easier because the bird struck their minds at this time as being somehow gruesome and ominous.

In the meantime the oiler and the correspondent rowed. And also they rowed.

They sat together in the same seat, and each rowed an oar. Then the oiler took both oars; then the correspondent took both oars; then the oiler; then the correspondent. They rowed and they rowed. The very ticklish part of the business was when the time came for the reclining one in the stern to take his turn at the oars. By the very last star of truth, it is easier to steal eggs from under a hen than it was to change seats in the dingey. First the man in the stern slid his hand along the thwart and moved with care, as if he were of Sèvres. Then the man in the rowing seat slid his hand along the other thwart. It was all done with the most extraordinary care. As the two sidled past each other, the whole party kept watchful eyes on the coming wave, and the captain cried: "Look out now! Steady there!"

The brown mats of seaweed that appeared from time to time were like islands, bits of earth. They were travelling, apparently, neither one way nor the other. They were, to all intents, stationary. They informed the men in the boat that it was making progress slowly toward the land.

The captain, rearing cautiously in the bow, after the dingey soared on a great swell, said that he had seen the lighthouse at Mosquito Inlet. Presently the cook remarked that he had seen it. The correspondent was at the oars then, and for some reason he too wished to look at the lighthouse, but his back was toward the far shore and the waves were important, and for some time he could not seize an opportunity to turn his head. But at last there came a wave more gentle than the others, and when at the crest of it he swiftly scoured the western horizon.

"See it?" said the captain.

'No," said the correspondent slowly, "I didn't see anything."

"Look again," said the captain. He pointed. "It's exactly in that direction."

At the top of another wave, the correspondent did as he was bid, and this time his eyes chanced an a small still thing on the edge of the swaying horizon. It was precisely like the point of a pin. It took an anxious eye to find a lighthouse so tiny.

"Think we'll make it, captain?"

"If this wind holds and the boat don't swamp, we can't do much else," said the captain.

The little boat, lifted by each towering sea, and splashed viciously by the crests, made progress that in the absence of seaweed was not apparent to those in her. She seemed just a wee thing wallowing, miraculously top up, at the mercy of five oceans. Occasionally, a great spread of water, like white flames, swarmed into her.

"Bail her, cook," said the captain serenely.

"All right, captain," said the cheerful cook.

III

It would be difficult to describe the subtle brotherhood of men that was here established on the seas. No one said that it was so. No one mentioned it. But it dwelt in the boat, and each man felt it warm him. They were a captain, an oiler, a cook, and a correspondent, and they were friends, friends in a more curiously iron-bound degree than may be common. The hurt captain, lying against the water-jar in the bow, spoke always in a low voice and calmly, but he could never command a more ready and swiftly obedient crew than the motley three of the dingey. It was more than a mere recognition of what was best for the common safety. There was surely in it a quality that was personal and heartfelt. And after this devotion to the commander of the boat there was this comradeship that the correspondent, for instance, who had been taught to be cynical of men, knew even at the time was the best experience of his life. But no one said that it was so. No one mentioned it.

"I wish we had a sail," remarked the captain. "We might try my overcoat on the end of an oar and give you two boys a chance to rest." So the cook and the correspondent held the mast and spread wide the overcoat. The oiler steered, and the little boat made good way with her new rig. Sometimes the oiler had to scull sharply to keep a sea from breaking into the boat, but otherwise sailing was a success.

Meanwhile the lighthouse had been growing slowly larger. It had now almost assumed colour, and appeared like a little grey shadow on the sky. The man at the oars could not be prevented from turning his head rather often to try for a glimpse of this little grey shadow.

At last, from the top of each wave the men in the tossing boat could see land. Even as the lighthouse was an upright shadow on the sky, this land seemed but a long black shadow on the sea. It certainly was thinner than paper. "We must be about opposite New Smyrna," said the cook, who had coasted this shore often in schooners. "Captain, by the way, I believe they abandoned that life-saving station there about a year ago."

"Did they?" said the captain.

The wind slowly died away. The cook and the correspondent were not now obliged to slave in order to hold high the oar. But the waves continued their old impetuous swooping at the dingey, and the little craft, no longer under way, struggled woundily over them. The oiler or the correspondent took the oars again.

Shipwrecks are apropos of nothing. If men could only train for them and have them occur when the men had reached pink condition, there would be less drowning at sea. Of the four in the dingey none had slept any time worth mentioning for two days and two nights previous to embarking in the dingey, and in the excitement of clambering about the deck of a foundering ship they had also forgotten to eat heartily.

For these reasons, and for others, neither the oiler nor the correspondent was fond of rowing at this time. The correspondent wondered ingenuously how in the name of all that was sane could there be people who thought it amusing to row a boat. It was not an amusement; it was a diabolical punishment, and even a genius of mental aberrations could never conclude that it was anything but a horror to the muscles and a crime against the back. He mentioned to the boat in general how the amusement of rowing struck him, and the weary-faced oiler smiled in full sympathy. Previously to the foundering, by the way, the oiler had worked double-watch in the engine-room of the ship.

"Take her easy, now, boys," said the captain. "Don't spend yourselves. If we have to run a surf you'll need all your strength, because we'll sure have to swim for it. Take your time."

Slowly the land arose from the sea. From a black line it became a line of black and a line of white, trees and sand. Finally, the captain said that he could make out a house on the shore. "That's the house of refuge, sure," said the cook. "They'll see us before long, and come out after us."

The distant lighthouse reared high. "The keeper ought to be able to make us out now, if he's looking through a glass," said the captain. "He'll notify the life-saving people."

"None of those other boats could have got ashore to give word of the wreck," said the oiler, in a low voice. "Else the lifeboat would be out hunting us."

Slowly and beautifully the land loomed out of the sea. The wind came again. It had veered from the north-east to the south-east. Finally, a new sound struck the ears of the men in the boat. It was the low thunder of the surf on the shore. "We'll never be able to make the lighthouse now," said the captain. "Swing her head a little more north, Billie."

"A little more north, sir," said the oiler.

Whereupon the little boat turned her nose once more down the wind, and all but the oarsman watched the shore grow. Under the influence of this expansion doubt and direful apprehension was leaving the minds of the men. The management of the boat was still most absorbing, but it could not prevent a quiet cheerfulness. In an hour, perhaps, they would be ashore.

Their backbones had become thoroughly used to balancing in the boat, and they now rode this wild colt of a dingey like circus men. The correspondent thought that he had been drenched to the skin, but happening to feel in the top pocket of his coat, he found therein eight cigars. Four of them were soaked with sea-water; four were perfectly scatheless. After a search, somebody produced three dry matches, and thereupon the four waifs rode impudently in their little boat, and with an assurance of an impending rescue shining in their eyes, puffed at the big cigars and judged well and ill of all men. Everybody took a drink of water.

IV

"Cook," remarked the captain, "there don't seem to be any signs of life about your house of refuge."

"No," replied the cook. "Funny they don't see us!"

A broad stretch of lowly coast lay before the eyes of the men. It was of low dunes topped with dark vegetation. The roar of the surf was plain, and sometimes they could see the white lip of a wave as it spun up the beach. A tiny house was blocked out black upon the sky. Southward, the slim lighthouse lifted its little grey length.

Tide, wind, and waves were swinging the dingey northward. "Funny they don't see us," said the men.

The surf's roar was here dulled, but its tone was, nevertheless, thunderous and mighty. As the boat swam over the great rollers, the men sat listening to this roar. "We'll swamp sure," said everybody.

It is fair to say here that there was not a life-saving station within twenty miles in either direction, but the men did not know this fact, and in consequence they made dark and opprobrious remarks concerning the eyesight of the nation's life-savers. Four scowling men sat in the dingey and surpassed records in the invention of epithets.

"Funny they don't see us."

The light-heartedness of a former time had completely faded. To their sharpened minds it was easy to conjure pictures of all kinds of incompetency and blindness and, indeed, cowardice. There was the shore of the populous land, and it was bitter and bitter to them that from it came no sign.

"Well," said the captain, ultimately, "I suppose we'll have to make a try for ourselves. If we stay out here too long, we'll none of us have strength left to swim after the boat swamps."

And so the oiler, who was at the oars, turned the boat straight for the shore. There was a sudden tightening of muscles. There was some thinking.

"If we don't all get ashore—" said the captain. "If we don't all get ashore, I suppose you fellows know where to send news of my finish?"

They then briefly exchanged some addresses and admonitions. As for the reflections of the men, there was a great deal of rage in them. Perchance they might be formulated thus: "If I am going to be drowned—if I am going to be drowned—if I am going to be drowned, why, in the name of the seven mad gods who rule the sea, was I allowed to come thus far and contemplate sand and trees? Was I brought here merely to have my nose dragged away as I was about to nibble the sacred cheese of life? It is preposterous. If this old ninny-woman, Fate, cannot do better than this, she should be deprived of the management of men's fortunes. She is an old hen who knows not her intention. If she has decided to drown me, why did she not do it in the beginning and save me all this trouble? The whole affair is absurd. . . . But no, she cannot mean to drown me. She dare not drown me. She cannot drown me. Not after all this work." Afterward the man might have had an impulse to shake his fist at the clouds: "Just you drown me, now, and then hear what I call you!"

The billows that came at this time were more formidable. They seemed always just about to break and roll over the little boat in a turmoil of foam. There was a preparatory and long growl in the speech of them. No mind unused to the sea would have concluded that the dingey could ascend these sheer heights in time. The shore was still afar. The oiler was a wily surfman. "Boys," he said swiftly, "she won't live three minutes more, and we're too far out to swim. Shall I take her to sea again, captain?"

"Yes! Go ahead!" said the captain.

This oiler, by a series of quick miracles, and fast and steady oarsmanship, turned the boat in the middle of the surf and took her safely to sea again.

There was a considerable silence as the boat bumped over the furrowed sea to deeper water. Then somebody in gloom spoke. "Well, anyhow, they must have seen us from the shore by now."

The gulls went in slanting flight up the wind toward the grey desolate east. A squall, marked by dingy clouds, and clouds brick-red, like smoke from a burning building, appeared from the south-east.

"What do you think of those life-saving people? Ain't they peaches?"

"Funny they haven't seen us."

"Maybe they think we're out here for sport! Maybe they think we're fishin'. Maybe they think we're damned fools."

It was a long afternoon. A changed tide tried to force them southward, but wind and wave said northward. Far ahead, where coastline, sea, and sky formed their mighty angle, there were little dots which seemed to indicate a city on the shore.

"St. Augustine?"

The captain shook his head. "Too near Mosquito Inlet."

And the oiler rowed, and then the correspondent rowed. Then the oiler rowed. It was a weary business. The human back can become the seat of more aches and pains than are registered in books for the composite anatomy of a regiment. It is a limited area, but it can become the theatre of innumerable muscular conflicts, tangles, wrenches, knots, and other comforts.

"Did you ever like to row, Billie?" asked the correspondent.

"No," said the oiler. "Hang it."

When one exchanged the rowing-seat for a place in the bottom of the boat, he suffered a bodily depression that caused him to be careless of everything save an obligation to wiggle one finger. There was cold sea-water swashing to and fro in the boat, and he lay in it. His head, pillowed on a thwart, was within an inch of the swirl of a wave crest, and sometimes a particularly obstreperous sea came in-board and drenched him once more. But these matters did not annoy him. It is almost certain that if the boat had capsized he would have tumbled comfortably out upon the ocean as if he felt sure that it was a great soft mattress.

"Look! There's a man on the shore!"

"Where?"

"There! See 'im? See 'im?"

"Yes, sure! He's walking along."

"Now he's stopped. Look! He's facing us!"

"He's waving at us!"

"So he is! By thunder!"

"Ah, now we're all right! Now we're all right! There'll be a boat out here for us in half an hour."

"He's going on. He's running. He's going up to that house there."

The remote beach seemed lower than the sea, and it required a searching glance to discern the little black figure. The captain saw a floating stick and they rowed to it. A bath-towel was by some weird chance in the boat, and, tying this on the stick, the captain waved it. The oarsman did not dare turn his head, so he was obliged to ask questions.

"What's he doing now?"

"He's standing still again. He's looking, I think. . . . There he goes again. Toward the house. . . . Now he stopped again."

"Is he waving at us?"

"No, not now! he was, though."

"Look! There comes another man!"

"He's running."

"Look at him go, would you."

"Why, he's on a bicycle. Now he's met the other man. They're both waving at us. Look!"

"There comes something up the beach."

"What the devil is that thing?"

"Why, it looks like a boat."

"Why, certainly it's a boat."

"No, it's on wheels."

"Yes, so it is. Well, that must be the life-boat. They drag them along shore on a wagon."

"That's the life-boat, sure."

"No, by God, it's—it's an omnibus."

"I tell you it's a life-boat."

"It is not! It's an omnibus. I can see it plain. See? One of these big hotel omnibuses."

"By thunder, you're right. It's an omnibus, sure as fate. What do you suppose they are doing with an omnibus? Maybe they are going around collecting the life-crew, hey?"

"That's it, likely. Look! There's a fellow waving a little black flag. He's standing on the steps of the omnibus. There come those other two fellows. Now they're all talking together. Look at the fellow with the flag. Maybe he ain't waving it."

"That ain't a flag, is it? That's his coat. Why, certainly, that's his coat."

"So it is. It's his coat. He's taken it off and is waving it around his head. But would you look at him swing it."

"Oh, say, there isn't any life-saving station there. That's just a winter resort hotel omnibus that has brought over some of the boarders to see us drown."

"What's that idiot with the coat mean? What's he signaling, anyhow?"

"It looks as if he were trying to tell us to go north. There must be a life-saving station up there."

"No! He thinks we're fishing. Just giving us a merry hand. See? Ah, there, Willie."

"Well, I wish I could make something out of those signals. What do you suppose he means?"

"He don't mean anything. He's just playing."

"Well, if he'd just signal us to try the surf again, or to go to sea and wait, or go north, or go south, or go to hell—there would be some reason in it. But look at him. He just stands there and keeps his coat revolving like a wheel. The ass!"

"There come more people."

"Now there's quite a mob. Look! Isn't that a boat?"

"Where? Oh, I see where you mean. No, that's no boat."

"That fellow is still waving his coat."

"He must think we like to see him do that. Why don't he quit it? It don't mean anything."

"I don't know. I think he is trying to make us go north. It must be that there's a life-saving station there somewhere."

"Say, he ain't tired yet. Look at 'im wave."

"Wonder how long he can keep that up. He's been revolving his coat ever since he caught sight of us. He's an idiot. Why aren't they getting men to bring a boat out? A fishing boat—one of those big yawls—could come out here all right. Why don't he do something?"

"Oh, it's all right, now."

"They'll have a boat out here for us in less than no time, now that they've seen us."

A faint yellow tone came into the sky over the low land. The shadows on the sea slowly deepened. The wind bore coldness with it, and the men began to shiver.

"Holy smoke!" said one, allowing his voice to express his impious mood, "if we keep on monkeying out here! If we've got to flounder out here all night!"

"Oh, we'll never have to stay here all night! Don't you worry. They've seen us now, and it won't be long before they'll come chasing out after us."

The shore grew dusky. The man waving a coat blended gradually into this gloom, and it swallowed in the same manner the omnibus and the group of people. The spray, when it dashed uproariously over the side, made the voyagers shrink and swear like men who were being branded.

"I'd like to catch the chump who waved that coat. I feel like soaking him one, just for luck."

"Why? What did he do?"

"Oh, nothing, but then he seemed so damned cheerful."

In the meantime the oiler rowed, and then the correspondent rowed, and then the oiler rowed. Grey-faced and bowed forward, they mechanically, turn by turn, plied the leaden oars. The form of the lighthouse had vanished from the southern horizon, but finally a pale star appeared, just lifting from the sea. The streaked saffron in the west passed before the all-merging darkness, and the sea to the east was black. The land had vanished, and was expressed only by the low and drear thunder of the surf.

"If I am going to be drowned—if I am going to be drowned—if I am going to be drowned, why, in the name of the seven mad gods who rule the sea, was I allowed to come thus far and contemplate sand and trees? Was I brought here merely to have my nose dragged away as I was about to nibble the sacred cheese of life?"

The patient captain, drooped over the water-jar, was sometimes obliged to speak to the oarsman.

"Keep her head up! Keep her head up!"

"'Keep her head up,' sir." The voices were weary and low.

This was surely a quiet evening. All save the oarsman lay heavily and listlessly in the boat's bottom. As for him, his eyes were just capable of noting the tall black waves that swept forward in a most sinister silence, save for an occasional subdued growl of a crest.

The cook's head was on a thwart, and he looked without interest at the water under his nose. He was deep in other scenes. Finally he spoke. "Billie," he murmured, dreamfully, "what kind of pie do you like best?"

v

"Pie," said the oiler and the correspondent, agitatedly. "Don't talk about those things, blast you!"

"Well," said the cook, "I was just thinking about ham sandwiches, and—"

A night on the sea in an open boat is a long night. As darkness settled finally, the shine of the light, lifting from the sea in the south, changed to full gold. On the northern horizon a new light appeared, a small bluish gleam on the edge of the waters. These two lights were the furniture of the world. Otherwise there was nothing but waves.

Two men huddled in the stern, and distances were so magnificent in the dingey that the rower was enabled to keep his feet partly warmed by thrusting them under his companions. Their legs indeed extended far under the rowing-seat until they touched the feet of the captain forward. Sometimes, despite the efforts of the tired oarsman, a wave came piling into the boat, an icy wave of the night, and the chilling water soaked them anew. They would twist their bodies for a moment and groan, and sleep the dead sleep once more, while the water in the boat gurgled about them as the craft rocked.

The plan of the oiler and the correspondent was for one to row until he lost the ability, and then arouse the other from his sea-water couch in the bottom of the boat.

The oiler plied the oars until his head drooped forward, and the overpowering sleep blinded him. And he rowed yet afterward. Then he touched a man in the bottom of the boat, and called his name. "Will you spell me for a little while?" he said, meekly.

"Sure, Billie," said the correspondent, awakening and dragging himself to a sitting position. They exchanged places carefully, and the oiler, cuddling down in the sea-water at the cook's side, seemed to go to sleep instantly.

The particular violence of the sea had ceased. The waves came without snarling. The obligation of the man at the oars was to keep the boat headed so that the tilt of the rollers would not capsize her, and to preserve her from filling when the crests rushed past. The black waves were silent and hard to be seen in the darkness. Often one was almost upon the boat before the oarsman was aware.

In a low voice the correspondent addressed the captain. He was not sure that the captain was awake, although this iron man seemed to be always awake. "Captain, shall I keep her making for that light north, sir?"

The same steady voice answered him. "Yes. Keep it about two points off the port bow."

The cook had tied a life-belt around himself in order to get even the warmth which this clumsy cork contrivance could donate, and he seemed almost stove-like when a rower, whose teeth invariably chattered wildly as soon as he ceased his labour, dropped down to sleep.

The correspondent, as he rowed, looked down at the two men sleeping underfoot. The cook's arm was around the oiler's shoulders, and, with their fragmentary clothing and haggard faces, they were the babes of the sea, a grotesque rendering of the old babes in the wood.

Later he must have grown stupid at his work, for suddenly there was a growling of water, and a crest came with a roar and a swash into the boat, and it was a wonder that it did not set the cook afloat in his life-belt. The cook continued to sleep, but the oiler sat up, blinking his eyes and shaking with the new cold.

"Oh, I'm awful sorry, Billie," said the correspondent, contritely.

"That's all right, old boy," said the oiler, and lay down again and was asleep.

Presently it seemed that even the captain dozed, and the correspondent thought that he was the one man afloat on all the oceans. The wind had a voice as it came over the waves, and it was sadder than the end.

There was a long, loud swishing astern of the boat, and a gleaming trail of phosphorescence, like blue flame, was furrowed on the black waters. It might have been made by a monstrous knife.

Then there came a stillness, while the correspondent breathed with the open mouth and looked at the sea.

Suddenly there was another swish and another long flash of bluish light, and this time it was alongside the boat, and might almost have been reached with an oar. The correspondent saw an enormous fin speed like a shadow through the water, hurling the crystalline spray and leaving the long glowing trail.

The correspondent looked over his shoulder at the captain. His face was hidden, and he seemed to be asleep. He looked at the babes of the sea. They certainly were asleep. So, being bereft of sympathy, he leaned a little way to one side and swore softly into the sea.

But the thing did not then leave the vicinity of the boat. Ahead or astern, on one side or the other, at intervals long or short, fled the long sparkling streak, and there was to be heard the whiroo of the dark fin. The speed and power of the thing was greatly to be admired. It cut the water like a gigantic and keen projectile.

The presence of this biding thing did not affect the man with the same horror that it would be if he had been a picnicker. He simply looked at the sea dully and swore in an undertone.

Nevertheless, it is true that he did not wish to be alone with the thing. He wished one of his companions to awaken by chance and keep him company with it. But the captain hung motionless over the water-jar, and the oiler and the cook in the bottom of the boat were plunged in slumber.

VI

"If I am going to be drowned—if I am going to be drowned—if I am going to be drowned, why, in the name of the seven mad gods who rule the sea, was I allowed to come thus far and contemplate sand and trees?"

During this dismal night, it may be remarked that a man would conclude that it was really the intention of the seven mad gods to drown him, despite the abominable injustice of it. For it was certainly an abominable injustice to drown a man who had worked so hard, so hard. The man felt it would be a crime most unnatural. Other people had drowned at sea since galleys swarmed with painted sails, but still—

When it occurs to a man that nature does not regard him as important, and that she feels she would not maim the universe by disposing of him, he at first wishes to throw bricks at the temple, and he hates deeply the fact that there are no bricks and no temples. Any visible expression of nature would surely be pelleted with his jeers.

Then, if there be no tangible thing to hoot he feels, perhaps, the desire to confront a personification and indulge in pleas, bowed to one knee, and with hands supplicant, saying: "Yes, but I love myself."

A high cold star on a winter's night is the word he feels that she says to him. Thereafter he knows the pathos of his situation.

The men in the dingey had not discussed these matters, but each had, no doubt, reflected upon them in silence and according to his mind. There was seldom any expression upon their faces save the general one of complete weariness. Speech was devoted to the business of the boat.

To chime the notes of his emotion, a verse mysteriously entered the correspondent's head. He had even forgotten that he had forgotten this verse, but it suddenly was in his mind.

"A soldier of the Legion lay dying in Algiers,
There was lack of woman's nursing, there was dearth of woman's tears;
But a comrade stood beside him, and he took that comrade's hand,
And he said: 'I shall never see my own, my native land.'"

In his childhood, the correspondent had been made acquainted with the fact that a soldier of the Legion lay dying in Algiers, but he had never regarded the fact as important. Myriads of his school-fellows had informed him of the soldier's plight, but the dinning had naturally ended by making him perfectly indifferent. He had never considered it his affair that a soldier of the Legion lay dying in Algiers, nor had it appeared to him as a matter for sorrow. It was less to him than the breaking of a pencil's point.

Now, however, it quaintly came to him as a human, living thing. It was no longer merely a picture of a few throes in the breast of a poet, meanwhile drinking tea and warming his feet at the grate; it was an actuality—stern, mournful, and fine.

The correspondent plainly saw the soldier. He lay on the sand with his feet out straight and still. While his pale left hand was upon his chest in an attempt to thwart the going of his life, the blood came between his fingers. In the far Algerian distance, a city of low square forms was set against a sky that was faint with the last sunset hues. The correspondent, plying the oars and dreaming of the slow and slower movements of the lips of the soldier, was moved by a profound and perfectly impersonal comprehension. He was sorry for the soldier of the Legion who lay dying in Algiers.

The thing which had followed the boat and waited had evidently grown bored at the delay. There was no longer to be heard the slash of the cut-water, and there was no longer the flame of the long trail. The light in the north still glimmered, but it was apparently no nearer to the boat. Sometimes the boom of the surf rang in the correspondent's ears, and he turned the craft seaward then and rowed harder. Southward, someone had evidently built a watch-fire on the beach. It was too low and too far to be seen, but it made a shimmering, roseate reflection upon the bluff back of it, and this could be discerned from the boat. The wind came stronger, and sometimes a wave suddenly raged out like a mountain-cat, and there was to be seen the sheen and sparkle of a broken crest.

The captain, in the bow, moved on his water-jar and sat erect. "Pretty long night," he observed to the correspondent. He looked at the shore. "Those life-saving people take their time."

"Did you see that shark playing around?"

"Yes, I saw him. He was a big fellow, all right."

"Wish I had known you were awake."

Later the correspondent spoke into the bottom of the boat.

"Billie!" There was a slow and gradual disentanglement. "Billie, will you spell me?"

"Sure," said the oiler.

As soon as the correspondent touched the cold comfortable sea-water in the bottom of the boat, and had huddled close to the cook's life-belt he was deep in sleep, despite the fact that his teeth played all the popular airs. This sleep was so good to him that it was but a moment before he heard a voice call his name in a tone that demonstrated the last stages of exhaustion. "Will you spell me?"

"Sure, Billie."

The light in the north had mysteriously vanished, but the correspondent took his course from the wide-awake captain.

Later in the night they took the boat farther out to sea, and the captain directed the cook to take one oar at the stern and keep the boat facing the seas. He was to call out if he should hear the thunder of the surf. This plan enabled the oiler and the correspondent to get respite together. "We'll give those boys a chance to get into shape again," said the captain. They curled down and, after a few preliminary chatterings and trembles, slept once more the dead sleep. Neither knew they had bequeathed to the cook the company of another shark, or perhaps the same shark.

As the boat caroused on the waves, spray occasionally bumped over the side and gave them a fresh soaking, but this had no power to break their repose. The ominous slash of the wind and the water affected them as it would have affected mummies.

"Boys," said the cook, with the notes of every reluctance in his voice, "she's drifted in pretty close. I guess one of you had better take her to sea again." The correspondent, aroused, heard the crash of the toppled crests.

As he was rowing, the captain gave him some whisky-and-water, and this steadied the chills out of him. "If I ever get ashore and anybody shows me even a photograph of an oar—"

At last there was a short conversation.

"Billie . . . Billie, will you spell me?"

"Sure," said the oiler.

VII

When the correspondent again opened his eyes, the sea and the sky were each of the grey hue of the dawning. Later, carmine and gold was painted upon the waters. The morning appeared finally, in its splendour, with a sky of pure blue, and the sunlight flamed on the tips of the waves.

On the distant dunes were set many little black cottages, and a tall white windmill reared above them. No man, nor dog, nor bicycle appeared on the beach. The cottages might have formed a deserted village.

The voyagers scanned the shore. A conference was held in the boat. "Well," said the captain, "if no help is coming, we might better try a run through the surf right away. If we stay out here much longer we will be too weak to do anything for ourselves at all." The others silently acquiesced in this reasoning. The boat was headed for the beach. The correspondent wondered if none ever ascended the tall wind-tower, and if then they never looked seaward. This tower was a giant, standing with its back to the plight of the ants. It represented in a degree, to the correspondent, the serenity of nature amid the struggles of the individual—nature in the wind, and nature in the vision of men. She did not seem cruel to him then, nor beneficent, nor treacherous, nor wise. But she was indifferent, flatly indifferent. It is, perhaps, plausible that a man in this situation, impressed with the unconcern of the universe, should see the innumerable flaws of his life, and have them taste wickedly in his mind and wish for another chance. A distinction between right and wrong seems absurdly clear to him, then, in this new ignorance of the grave-edge, and he understands that if he were given another opportunity he would mend his conduct and his words, and be better and brighter during an introduction or at a tea.

"Now, boys," said the captain, "she is going to swamp sure. All we can do is to work her in as far as possible, and then when she swamps, pile out and scramble for the beach. Keep cool now, and don't jump until she swamps sure."

The oiler took the oars. Over his shoulders he scanned the surf. "Captain," he said, "I think I'd better bring her about, and keep her head-on to the seas and back her in."

"All right, Billie," said the captain. "Back her in." The oiler swung the boat then and, seated in the stern, the cook and the correspondent were obliged to look over their shoulders to contemplate the lonely and indifferent shore.

The monstrous in-shore rollers heaved the boat high until the men were again enabled to see the white sheets of water scudding up the slanted beach. "We won't get in very close," said the captain. Each time a man could wrest his attention from the rollers, he turned his glance toward the shore, and in the expression of the eyes during this contemplation there was a singular quality. The correspondent, observing the others, knew that they were not afraid, but the full meaning of their glances was shrouded.

As for himself, he was too tired to grapple fundamentally with the fact. He tried to coerce his mind into thinking of it, but the mind was dominated at this time by the muscles, and the muscles said they did not care. It merely occurred to him that if he should drown it would be a shame.

There were no hurried words, no pallor, no plain agitation. The men simply looked at the shore. "Now, remember to get well clear of the boat when you jump," said the captain.

Seaward the crest of a roller suddenly fell with a thunderous crash, and the long white comber came roaring down upon the boat.

"Steady now," said the captain. The men were silent. They turned their eyes from the shore to the comber and waited. The boat slid up the incline, leaped at the furious top, bounced over it, and swung down the long back of the waves. Some water had been shipped and the cook bailed it out.

But the next crest crashed also. The tumbling boiling flood of white water caught the boat and whirled it almost perpendicular. Water swarmed in from all sides. The correspondent had his hands on the gunwale at this time, and when the water entered at that place he swiftly withdrew his fingers, as if he objected to wetting them.

The little boat, drunken with this weight of water, reeled and snuggled deeper into the sea.

"Bail her out, cook! Bail her out," said the captain.

"All right, captain," said the cook.

"Now, boys, the next one will do for us, sure," said the oiler. "Mind to jump clear of the boat."

The third wave moved forward, huge, furious, implacable. It fairly swallowed the dingey, and almost simultaneously the men tumbled into the sea. A piece of life-belt had lain in the bottom of the boat, and as the correspondent went overboard he held this to his chest with his left hand.

The January water was icy, and he reflected immediately that it was colder than he had expected to find it off the coast of Florida. This appeared to his dazed mind as a fact important enough to be noted at the time. The coldness of the water was sad; it was tragic. This fact was somehow so mixed and confused with his opinion of his own situation that it seemed almost a proper reason for tears. The water was cold.

When he came to the surface he was conscious of little but the noisy water. Afterward he saw his companions in the sea. The oiler was ahead in the race. He was swimming strongly and rapidly. Off to the correspondent's left, the cook's great white and corked back bulged out of the water, and in the rear the captain was hanging with his one good hand to the keel of the overturned dingey.

There is a certain immovable quality to a shore, and the correspondent wondered at it amid the confusion of the sea.

It seemed also very attractive, but the correspondent knew that it was a long journey, and he paddled leisurely. The piece of life-preserver lay under him, and sometimes he whirled down the incline of a wave as if he were on a hand-sled.

But finally he arrived at a place in the sea where travel was beset with difficulty. He did not pause swimming to inquire what manner of current had caught him, but there his progress ceased. The shore was set before him like a bit of scenery on a stage, and he looked at it and understood with his eyes each detail of it.

As the cook passed, much farther to the left, the captain was calling to him, "Turn over on your back, cook! Turn over on your back and use the oar."

"All right, sir." The cook turned on his back, and, paddling with an oar, went ahead as if he were a canoe.

Presently the boat also passed to the left of the correspondent with the captain clinging with one hand to the keel. He would have appeared like a man raising himself to look over a board fence, if it were not for the extraordinary gymnastics of the boat. The correspondent marvelled that the captain could still hold to it.

They passed on, nearer to shore—the oiler, the cook, the captain—and following them went the water-jar, bouncing gaily over the seas.

The correspondent remained in the grip of this strange new enemy—a current. The shore, with its white slope of sand and its green bluff, topped with little silent cottages, was spread like a picture before him. It was very near to him then, but he was impressed as one who in a gallery looks at a scene from Brittany or Algiers.

He thought: "I am going to drown? Can it be possible? Can it be possible? Can it be possible?" Perhaps an individual must consider his own death to be the final phenomenon of nature.

But later a wave perhaps whirled him out of this small deadly current, for he found suddenly that he could again make progress toward the shore. Later still, he was aware that the captain, clinging with one hand to the keel of the dingey, had his face turned away from the shore and toward him, and was calling his name. "Come to the boat! Come to the boat!"

In his struggle to reach the captain and the boat, he reflected that when one gets properly wearied, drowning must really be a comfortable arrangement, a cessation of hostilities accompanied by a large degree of relief, and he was glad of it, for the main thing in his mind for some moments had been horror of the temporary agony. He did not wish to be hurt.

Presently he saw a man running along the shore. He was undressing with most remarkable speed. Coat, trousers, shirt, everything flew magically off him.

"Come to the boat," called the captain.

"All right, captain." As the correspondent paddled, he saw the captain let himself down to bottom and leave the boat. Then the correspondent performed his one little marvel of the voyage. A large wave caught him and flung him with ease and supreme speed completely over the boat and far beyond it. It struck him even then as an event in gymnastics, and a true miracle of the sea. An overturned boat in the surf is not a plaything to a swimming man.

The correspondent arrived in water that reached only to his waist, but his condition did not enable him to stand for more than a moment. Each wave knocked him into a heap, and the under-tow pulled at him.

Then he saw the man who had been running and undressing, and undressing and running, come bounding into the water. He dragged ashore the cook, and then waded toward the captain, but the captain waved him away, and sent him to the correspondent. He was naked, naked as a tree in winter, but a halo was about his head, and he shone like a saint. He gave a strong pull, and a long drag, and a bully heave at the correspondent's hand. The correspondent, schooled in the minor formulæ, said: "Thanks, old man."

But suddenly the man cried: "What's that?" He pointed a swift finger. The correspondent said: "Go."

In the shallows, face downward, lay the oiler. His forehead touched sand that was periodically, between each wave, clear of the sea.

The correspondent did not know all that transpired afterward. When he achieved safe ground he fell, striking the sand with each particular part of his body. It was as if he had dropped from a roof, but the thud was grateful to him.

It seems that instantly the beach was populated with men, with blankets, clothes, and flasks, and women with coffee-pots and all the remedies sacred to their minds. The welcome of the land to the men from the sea was warm and generous, but a still and dripping shape was carried slowly up the beach, and the land's welcome for it could only be the different and sinister hospitality of the grave.

When it came night, the white waves paced to and fro in the moonlight, and the wind brought the sound of the great sea's voice to the men on shore, and they felt that they could then be interpreters.

LUIGI PIRANDELLO

The Reserved Coffin 🙖

When the cabriolet was moving along the road below the little
church of San Biagio, Mèndola, coming back from the farm,
thought he had better go up to the cemetery on the hill to see
what truth there was in the complaints lodged with the municipality against
that custodian, Nocio Pàmpina, called *Sacramento*.

City Councillor for about a year, Nino Mèndola, from the very day he had
assumed office, hadn't felt very well. He suffered from attacks of dizziness.
He didn't like to confess it even to himself, but he was afraid he might be
struck with apoplexy any day—an ill of which all his people had died before
their time. Hence he was always in a bad humor; and that sorry old nag of
his that was pulling the cabriolet knew something about it, too.

And all that day, in the country, he had not felt well. Movement and
diversion were futile—and finally, to brave his secret fear, he had made
up his mind then and there to make that long-promised inspection of
the cemetery, promised to himself and to his colleagues of the city
council.

"It isn't only the living," he was thinking as he went up the hill, "even the
dead give you something to think about and to do in this blessed town.
Yes, indeed. The dead know whether they are guarded well or badly.
Perhaps—I don't say they don't: to think that as soon as we are dead we'll
be treated badly, turned over to the tender mercies of Pàmpina, stolid fellow
that he is, and a drunkard to boot, furnishes food for thought—all right;
now I'll see."

Pure slander.

As custodian of the cemetery, Nocio Pàmpina, called *Sacramento*, was
ideal—a ghost, with a voice like a mosquito's—he seemed a corpse just
come out of the grave to do as well as he could the chores about the
house.

What was to be done about it then? All honest folk, up—at length—and
peace.

The leaves, yes. A leaf or two fallen from the hedges encumbered the
paths. A few sprouts had grown up here and there. And the sparrows—the
little scamps—ignorant of the fact that the tombstones needed no punctuation marks, had sown among the magnificent and multitudinous virtues in

This translation, made by Professor J. E. Harry, was published in *The Golden Book*,
January, 1926. It is used with his permission.

which the inscriptions of those monuments abounded, too many commas, perhaps, and too many exclamation points.

Trifles.

Nevertheless, Mèndola, entering the hovel of the keeper at the right of the gate, stopped:

"And what's that—there?"

Nocio Pàmpina, called *Sacramento,* opened his lips to a shade of a smile and whispered:

"A coffin for a dead man, Excellency."

It was, in fact, a very beautiful coffin for a dead man. Polished chestnut, with bosses and gilding. Made really without thinking of the expense. There, almost in the middle of the little room.

"Thanks; I see it," replied Mèndola. "I mean, what's it there for?"

"It's the Cavaliere Piccarone's, Excellency."

"Piccarone? And why? Why, he's not dead!"

"No, no, Excellency! Not at all!" said Pàmpina. "But your Lordship must know that his wife died last month, poor man."

"Well?"

"He accompanied her here, on foot; oldish as he is. Yes, sir. Then he called me, and said: 'Listen, Sacramento. Before another month's gone, you'll have me too.' 'But what is your Lordship saying?' says I. 'Hush!' says he. 'Listen: This coffin, my dear child, cost me more than twenty ounces. Handsome, you see that. I didn't spare expense, you understand. But now that the appearance has been made,' says he, 'of what use will this handsome coffin be to her now, to the blessed spirit under the ground? It's a pity to waste it,' says he. 'I'll tell you what we'll do. Let's lower the sainted spirit,' says he, 'just as it is, in the zinc which is inside; and then put this aside, if you please: it will do for me too. One of these days, toward dusk, I'll send for it.' "

Mèndola didn't linger to hear anything more. He simply couldn't wait till he got to town to spread the news about that coffin which Piccarone had had put aside for himself.

Famous in the town was Gerolamo Piccarone, lawyer, and, at the time of the Bourbons, Cavaliere of San Gennaro, famous for his stinginess and for his knavery. Bad pay was he. Stories were told about his closeness that would make you stand agape. But this—Mèndola was saying to himself—this beats all; and true, ohè, true as truth itself. He had seen it himself, there, the coffin, with his own eyes.

He was enjoying by anticipation the bursts of laughter with which his tale would be received, whispered in the thin voice of Pàmpina; he didn't even notice the cloud of dust raised and the noise that the cabriolet made as his nag rushed furiously along, when lo! "Stop, stop!" he heard somebody yell at the top of his voice from the *Hunters' Tavern,* which a man named Dolcemascolo kept there by the wayside.

Two friends, Bartolo Gaglio and Gaspare Ficarra, ardent hunters, sitting out in front of the tavern under the pergola, had begun to shout in that way because they thought Mèndola's horse was running off with him.

"Running off indeed! I was running——"

"Oh! You were running, were you?" said Gaglio. "Have you got a spare neck at home?"

"If you only knew, *cari miei!*"[1] exclaimed Mèndola joyfully, jumping down, and out of breath; and he told the story of the coffin to those two friends.

They feigned, from time to time, disbelief, but only to manifest their wonder. And then Mèndola swearing—word of honor—that he had seen it, with his own eyes, the coffin, in Sacramento's hovel.

The other two, in turn, began to tell other well-known deeds of prowess of Piccarone. Mèndola was for getting into his cabriolet again at once; but they had already ordered Dolcemascolo to bring a glass for their friend, the Councillor, and would have him drink it.

But Dolcemascolo had been standing there as if stunned.

"Dolcemascolo, ohè!" cried Gaglio.

The tavern-keeper, with his sailor fur cap aslant on his ear, without a jacket, and his shirt sleeves rolled up on his hairy arms, roused himself, and said with a sigh:

"Pardon me," said he, "stupid man that I am, I have been standing here like an idiot listening to this story. Only this morning, Cavaliere Piccarone's dog, Turco, that ugly old brute which comes and goes as he pleases from the Cannatello farm up here to the little villa—say, do you know what he did? Stole more than twenty pieces of sausage that I had hanging out there on the balcony! It's a good thing, I say, that I have two witnesses."

Mèndola, Gaglio, Ficarra burst out laughing. Said Mèndola:

"You like it, *caro mio!*"[2]

Dolcemascolo raised a fist; fire darted from his eyes.

"Ah, *perdio,*[3] no! he'll pay me for those sausages, he will! He'll pay me for them; yes, he'll pay me," he shot back at the incredulous laughs and at the stubborn denials of his three customers. "You gentlemen will see. I've found the way to make him. I know the color of his hair!"

And with a shrewd gesture, habitual with him, he winked one eye as he pulled down the lid of the other with his forefinger.

What way he had found he wouldn't state; but he did say that he was waiting for two farmers who had been present, in the morning, and had

---

[1] My friends (literally, my dears).
[2] My friend (masculine).
[3] My God.

seen the theft of the sausage, and that he was going up to the villa with them before evening.

Mèndola got into his cabriolet again, not even waiting to drain his glass; Gaglio and Ficarra paid their bills; and after advising the tavern-keeper to renounce, for his own good, his famous plan of getting himself paid by Piccarone, they left.

To construct that little one-story villa, on the avenue at the edge of the town, Gerolamo Piccarone, lawyer and cavalier of San Gennaro at the time of King Bomba, had worked for more than twenty years, and rumor had it that it had not cost him a penny.

Evil tongues said that it was made of small stones found on the highway and pushed to the place, one by one, by the feet of the selfsame Piccarone.

He was, besides, a man learned in jurisprudence, and one of deep mind and profound philosophic spirit. One of his books on Gnosticism, and another on Christian Philosophy, they said, had even been translated into German.

But he was *malva di tre cotte,*[4] was Piccarone, that is to say, an enemy of all innovations. He dressed in the style of 1821; wore a necklace beard; was thickset, coarse, baggy at the shoulders. Always frowning, his eyes half-closed, he kept continually rubbing his chin and approving his secret thoughts with frequent grunts:

"Uh—uh—uh—Italy!—they've—made Italy—what a fine thing, uh, Italy —bridges and roads—uh—illumination—army and navy—uh—uh—uh— compulsory education—taxes! and Piccarone pays——"

He paid little or nothing, in reality, for by dint of most subtle quibbles he wore out and exasperated the greatest patience. He always wound up thus:

"What have I got to do with it? Railways? I don't travel. Light? I never go out evenings. I don't ask for anything, thanks; I don't want anything. Only a little air, to breathe. Did you make the air, too? Must I pay also for the air I breathe?"

He had, in fact, withdrawn to that little villa of his and retired from his profession, which had, however, yielded him magnificent returns up to the time of his retirement a few years before. He must have laid by a snug little sum. To whom would he leave it at his death? He had no relatives, near or distant. And banknotes?—could he take them with him in that handsome coffin which he had reserved for himself? And the little villa? And the farm over there at Cannatello?

When Dolcemascolo, accompanied by the two countrymen, came up to the gate, Turco, the old ugly watchdog, as if he understood that the tavern-keeper was coming for him, rushed furiously against the bars. The old servant ran out, but was unable to quiet him or to get him away. Piccarone, who was reading in the kiosk in the middle of the little garden, had to

---

[4] Mallow thrice brewed; hence strong.

whistle for him and then hold him fast by the collar until the servant came
to chain him up.

Dolcemascolo, who knew what was what, had put on his best Sunday
clothes and, clean shaven, between those two poor country clodhoppers who
were coming back dirty and tired from their work, he appeared more than
commonly prosperous and lordly. His face like rose and milk—he was fair
to look upon.

He entered the kiosk exclaiming, with feigned admiration:

"Fine dog! Large animal, noble and handsome! Good watchdog! Worth
his weight in gold!"

Piccarone, frowning and eyes half-closed, grunted several times, nodding
assent to the eulogies of Dolcemascolo; then he said:

"What do you want? Sit down."

And he pointed to the little iron stools arranged all around the kiosk.

Dolcemascolo drew one up near the table, saying to the farmers:

"Sit down there, you. I come to your Lordship, a man of the law, for an
opinion."

Piccarone opened his eyes.

"An opinion? But I haven't practiced law, *caro mio,* for a long time."

"I know it," Dolcemascolo hastened to add. "Your Lordship is, however, a
lawyer of the old school. And my father, blessed be his soul, always used to
say to me: 'Stick to the old, my son!' Now I know how conscientious your
Lordship was in your profession. I have very little faith in the young petti-
foggers of today. I don't want to go to law, understand, with anybody. I'd
be a fool to do that—I've come simply for an opinion, which your Lordship
alone can give me."

Piccarone closed his eyes:

"Speak. I am listening."

"Your Lordship knows," began Dolcemascolo. But Piccarone started and
snorted:

"Uh, what do I know! What do you know? *I know, I know, he knows*—
oh, come to the point, *caro mio!*"

Dolcemascolo was a little taken back, disconcerted; still he smiled and
began again:

"Yes, sir. I meant that your Lordship knows that I have on the highroad,
a restaurant."

"Hunters'? Yes: I've passed it many a time."

"Going to Cannatello, of course. And you must certainly have seen that
on the balcony, under the pergola, I always have some of my wares displayed: bread, fruit, ham."

Piccarone nodded, then added mysteriously: "Seen, and smelled too, sometimes."

"Smelled?"

"Which smelled of sand, *figliuolo*.[5] You understand—dust from the road—No matter. Come to the point."

"Here it is, yes, sir," answered Dolcemascolo, swallowing. "Let us assume that I have displayed on the balcony a few—sausages, for instance. Now, your Lordship—perhaps this—of course!—I was about to repeat—it's a habit of mine—your Lordship perhaps doesn't know it, but these are the days we have quail migrating. Hence, on the road, hunters, dogs, all the time. I'm coming, I'm coming to the point! A dog passes, Signor Cavaliere, jumps up, and seizes the sausages on the balcony."

"A dog?"

"Yes, sir. I run after him, and with me these two poor fellows who had come in to buy some victuals to take to the country with them. Is that so, yes or no? All three of us start to run after the dog; but we can't overtake him. Besides, even if we do, tell me, your Lordship, what could we do with that sausage which the dog had bitten and dragged all along the road—no good, even if we do get it back! But I recognize the dog; I know who he belongs to."

"Uh—a moment," interrupted Piccarone. "Wasn't the owner there?"

"No, sir!" answered Dolcemascolo quickly. "It wasn't one of those hunters. The dog had evidently run away from home. Hunting dogs, you understand, smell the chase, allow themselves to be locked up; then they escape. No matter. Well, as I said, I know who owns the dog; these two friends of mine know it too, and they witnessed the theft. Now, your Lordship, a man of the law, is to tell me simply whether the owner of the dog is bound to pay me damages, *ecco!*"[6]

Piccarone answered without hesitation:

"Of course he is bound to pay, *figliuolo*."

Dolcemascolo leaped for joy, but quickly restrained himself, and, turning to his companions, said:

"Did you hear? The Signor lawyer says that the owner of the dog is bound to pay damages."

"Absolutely bound, absolutely," reaffirmed Piccarone. "Did you hear me say he wasn't?"

"No, sir," replied Dolcemascolo, jumping for joy and clasping his hands. "But your Lordship must pardon me if I, poor ignorant man that I am, have beat around the bush in this feeble way to come to tell you that your Lordship must pay me for the sausages, because the dog that stole it from me was your own, Turco."

Piccarone looked at Dolcemascolo a little while as if he had gone crazy; then, all at once, he lowered his eyes—and began to read in the big book he had before him open on the table.

[5] Little son.
[6] See, behold.

The two rustics looked at each other; Dolcemascolo raised a hand to make a sign to them not to breathe.

Piccarone, pretending all the time to read, rubbed his chin with one hand, grunted, and said:

"So it was Turco?"

"I can swear it, Signor Cavaliere!" exclaimed Dolcemascolo, getting up and crossing his hands over his breast.

"And you have come here," resumed Piccarone, dark and calm, "with two witnesses, eh?"

"No, sir!" said Dolcemascolo quickly. "In case your Lordship did not believe me——"

"Ah, that was the reason?" muttered Piccarone.

"But I believe you, caro mio. Sit down. You are a very honest man. I believe you and I'll pay you. Do I enjoy the reputation of being bad pay, eh?"

"Who says so, Signor Cavaliere?"

"Everybody says so! And you think so too, now, don't you? Two—uh—two witnesses——"

"For the truth, as much for you as for me!"

"Bravo, yes: as much for me as for you; well said. The unjust taxes, caro mio, I refuse to pay; but what is just, yes, I pay that willingly—have always paid that. Turco stole your sausage? Tell me, how much?"

Dolcemascolo, having come anticipating that he would have to fight God knows what kind of battles against the quibbles and snares of this old toad, when he was confronted with such meekness, lost courage, mortified.

"A trifle, Signor Cavaliere. Must have been about twenty pieces, more or less—hardly worth mentioning."

"No, no," replied Piccarone firmly. "Tell me how much I owe you and I want to pay. Tell me quickly, figliuolo! You work; you have suffered a loss; you must be reimbursed. How much?"

Dolcemascolo shrugged his shoulders, smiled, and said:

"Twenty pieces of those big ones—two kilos—at one lira[7] twenty a kilo——"

"You sell them so cheap?" asked Piccarone.

"You must understand," replied Dolcemascolo, all honey, "your Lordship didn't eat them. I charge—I wouldn't—I charge you what they cost me."

"Not at all! If I didn't eat them, my dog did. So let's say—roughly—two kilos. Two lire a kilo all right?"

"As you will."

"Four lire. Good. Now tell me, figliuolo! twenty-five less four make how many? Twenty-one, if I mistake not. Good. You give me twenty-one lire and let's talk no more about it."

[7] A lira at the time was about twenty cents.

Dolcemascolo thought he had not heard aright.

"What's that?"

"Twenty-one lire," repeated Piccarone placidly.

"Here are two witnesses to the truth, as much for me as for you—all right? You come to me for an opinion. Now I, *figliuolo,* charge twenty-five lire for an opinion. Fixed price. I owe you four of them for the sausage; give me twenty-one and don't mention the matter again."

Dolcemascolo looked at Piccarone hard, perplexed, not knowing whether he should laugh or cry, unwilling to believe that Piccarone was serious; yet he did not seem to be jesting.

"I—to—to you?" he stammered.

"It seems clear to me, *figliuolo,*" explained Piccarone. "Your business is keeping an inn; mine giving opinions about the law—feebly though it may be. Now, as I do not deny your right to reimbursement, so you will not deny mine for the information you asked me for, and which I gave you. *Now* you know that if a dog steals your sausage, the owner of the dog is liable for damages and is obliged to indemnify you for the loss you have sustained. You didn't know that before? No! You have to pay for knowledge, *caro mio*. I had to work and spend so much to learn it! Do you think I am jesting?"

"Yes, sir!" confessed Dolcemascolo with tears on his cheeks, lifting and opening wide his arms. "I'll forget about the sausage, Signor Cavaliere; I am a poor ignorant man; pardon me, and let's not talk about it any more, in very truth."

"Ah no, ah no, *caro mio,*" exclaimed Piccarone. "I don't make reductions, *I* don't. Right is right, as much for you as for me. *I* pay, I pay, I want to pay. To pay and be paid. I was here studying, as you see; you have made me lose an hour's time. Twenty-one lire. That's my price. If you are not fully persuaded of it, give ear, *caro mio:* go to any other lawyer and ask him whether this remuneration is due me or not. I give you three days. If at the end of the third day you have not paid me, rest assured, *figliuolo,* I'll sue you."

Piccarone raised his chin, raised his hands: "I'll not listen to any excuses. I'll sue you!"

Dolcemascolo then lost the light of his eyes. Anger seized him by the hair; blinded him. What were the damages? There were no damages. He thought of the bantering he would get, the raillery which he already divined as he gazed into the faces of those two countrymen: he who considered himself so clever, so shrewd, he who had boasted he would display his cunning, and had victory almost within his grasp. Seeing himself caught in his own net, when he least expected it, made him so furious that he suddenly turned into a wild beast.

"Ah, that's the reason, is it?" said he, walking up to Piccarone with his hand raised and his fist clenched, "that's the reason your dog is such a thief? You taught him!"

Piccarone rose to his feet, turbulent, and raised an arm:

"Get out of here! You'll answer also for insults to a man of honor who——"

"Man of honor?" roared Dolcemascolo, grasping the lawyer's arm and shaking it furiously.

The two rustics rushed forward to restrain him but suddenly, before they knew it, Piccarone collapsed, inert, and fell into the violent grasp of Dolcemascolo. And as the latter, amazed, opened his arms to catch him, Piccarone dropped first to the stool, reeled to one side and slumped to the floor in a heap.

Before the terrified countrymen, the features of Dolcemascolo contracted as if by a burst of laughter. Oh—what—? Why, he hadn't even touched him!

They leaned over the man, as he lay on the floor; they moved one of his arms.

"Escape!—escape!——"

Dolcemascolo looked at them both, as if stunned. Escape?

At this point they heard the gate creak, and the coffin, which the old man had reserved for himself, appeared, borne along in triumph on the shoulders of two stalwart, panting bearers, in truth, as if it had been sent for at that very moment for immediate use.

At the apparition of the coffin the three men remained rooted to the spot; they almost fainted.

It did not occur to Dolcemascolo that Nocio Pàmpina, called *Sacramento,* after the visit and inspection of the Councillor, had hastened to put himself in regular standing by forwarding the coffin to its destination; but he recalled in a flash what Mèndola had said that morning down at the restaurant; and suddenly, in that empty coffin which was waiting and which had come unexpectedly, at the very moment it was needed, as if sent for mysteriously, Dolcemascolo saw the hand of fate which had made use of his own hand.

He put his hands to his head and began to shriek:

"There it is! There it is! That was calling him! Bear witness, all of you, that I didn't even touch him! That was calling him! He had put it aside for himself! And lo! here it comes, because he was fated to die!"

And he seized the two bearers by the arms to rouse them from their stupor.

"Isn't it true? Isn't it true? Say!"

But the two bearers were not at all astonished. Since they had brought the coffin, it was the most natural thing in the world to them that they should find the lawyer dead. They shrugged their shoulders, and said:

"Why, yes, here it is."

GUY DE MAUPASSANT

La Mère Sauvage[1] ♉

I had not been at Virelogne for fifteen years. I went back there
in the autumn, to shoot with my friend Serval, who had at last
rebuilt his château, which had been destroyed by the Prussians.

I loved that district very much. It is one of those corners of the world
which have a sensuous charm for the eyes. You love it with a bodily love.
We, whom the country seduces, we keep tender memories for certain springs,
for certain woods, for certain pools, for certain hills, seen very often, and
which have stirred us like joyful events. Sometimes our thoughts turn back
towards a corner in a forest, or the end of a bank, or an orchard powdered
with flowers, seen but a single time, on some gay day; yet remaining in
our hearts like the images of certain women met in the street on a spring
morning, with bright transparent dresses; and leaving in soul and body an
unappeased desire which is not to be forgotten, a feeling that you have just
rubbed elbows with happiness.

At Virelogne I loved the whole countryside, dotted with little woods, and
crossed by brooks which flashed in the sun and looked like veins, carrying
blood to the earth. You fished in them for crawfish, trout, and eels! Divine
happiness! You could bathe in places, and you often found snipe among the
high grass which grew along the borders of these slender watercourses.

I was walking, lightly as a goat, watching my two dogs ranging before
me. Serval, a hundred metres to my right, was beating a field of lucern. I
turned the thicket which forms the boundary of the wood of Sandres, and
I saw a cottage in ruins.

All of a sudden, I remembered it as I had seen it the last time, in 1869,
neat, covered with vines, with chickens before the door. What is sadder
than a dead house, with its skeleton standing upright, bare and sinister?

I also remembered that in it, one very tiring day, the good woman had
given me a glass of wine to drink, and that Serval had then told me the
history of its inhabitants. The father, an old poacher, had been killed by the
gendarmes. The son, whom I had once seen, was a tall, dry fellow who also
passed for a ferocious destroyer of game. People called them "les Sauvage."

Was that a name or a nickname?

I hailed Serval. He came up with his long strides like a crane.

I asked him:

"What's become of those people?"

[1] In English, "The Savage Mother."

And he told me this story:

When war was declared, the son Sauvage, who was then thirty-three years old, enlisted, leaving his mother alone in the house. People did not pity the old woman very much because she had money; they knew it.

But she remained quite alone in that isolated dwelling so far from the village, on the edge of the wood. She was not afraid, however, being of the same strain as her menfolk; a hardy old woman, tall and thin, who laughed seldom, and with whom one never jested. The women of the fields laugh but little in any case; that is men's business, that! But they themselves have sad and narrowed hearts, leading a melancholy, gloomy life. The peasants learn a little boisterous merriment at the tavern, but their helpmates remain grave, with countenances which are always severe. The muscles of their faces have never learned the movements of the laugh.

La Mère Sauvage continued her ordinary existence in her cottage, which was soon covered by the snows. She came to the village once a week, to get bread and a little meat; then she returned into her house. As there was talk of wolves, she went out with a gun upon her back—her son's gun, rusty, and with the butt worn by the rubbing of the hand; and she was strange to see, the tall "Sauvage," a little bent, going with slow strides over the snow, the muzzle of the piece extending beyond the black headdress, which pressed close to her head and imprisoned her white hair, which no one had ever seen.

One day a Prussian force arrived. It was billeted upon the inhabitants, according to the property and resources of each. Four were allotted to the old woman, who was known to be rich.

They were four great boys with blond skin, with blond beards, with blue eyes, who had remained stout notwithstanding the fatigues which they had endured already, and who also, though in a conquered country, had remained kind and gentle. Alone with this aged woman, they showed themselves full of consideration, sparing her, as much as they could, all expenses and fatigue. They would be seen, all four of them, making their toilet round the well, of a morning, in their shirt-sleeves, splashing with great swishes of water, under the crude daylight of the snowy weather, their pink-white Northman's flesh, while La Mère Sauvage went and came, making ready the soup. Then they would be seen cleaning the kitchen, rubbing the tiles, splitting wood, peeling potatoes, doing up all the housework, like four good sons about their mother.

But the old woman thought always of her own, so tall and thin, with his hooked nose and his brown eyes and his heavy mustache which made a roll of black hairs upon his lip. She asked each day of each of the soldiers who were installed beside her hearth:

"Do you know where the French Marching Regiment No. 23 was sent? My boy is in it."

They answered, "No, not know, not know at all."

And, understanding her pain and her uneasiness (they, who had mothers too, there at home), they rendered her a thousand little services. She loved them well, moreover, her four enemies, since the peasantry feels no patriotic hatred; that belongs to the upper class alone. The humble, those who pay the most, because they are poor, and because every new burden crushes them down; those who are killed in masses, who make the true cannon's-meat, because they are so many; those, in fine, who suffer most cruelly the atrocious miseries of war, because they are the feeblest, and offer least resistance—they hardly understand at all those bellicose ardors, that excitable sense of honor, or those pretended political combinations which in six months exhaust two nations, the conqueror with the conquered.

They said on the countryside in speaking of the Germans of La Mère Sauvage:

"There are four who have found a soft place."

Now, one morning, when the old woman was alone in the house, she perceived far off on the plain a man coming towards her dwelling. Soon she recognized him; it was the postman charged to distribute the letters. He gave her a folded paper, and she drew out of her case the spectacles which she used for sewing; then she read:

"MADAME SAUVAGE,—The present letter is to tell you sad news. Your boy Victor was killed yesterday by a shell which near cut him in two. I was just by, seeing that we stood next each other in the company, and he would talk to me about you to let you know on the same day if anything happened to him.

"I took his watch, which was in his pocket, to bring it back to you when the war is done.

"I salute you very friendly.

"CÉSAIRE RIVOT,

"Soldier of the 2d class, March. Reg. No. 23"

The letter was dated three weeks back.

She did not cry at all. She remained motionless, so seized and stupefied that she did not even suffer as yet. She thought: "V'la Victor who is killed now." Then little by little the tears mounted to her eyes, and the sorrow caught her heart. The ideas came to her, one by one, dreadful, torturing. She would never kiss him again, her child, her big boy, never again! The gendarmes had killed the father, the Prussians had killed the son. He had been cut in two by a cannon-ball. She seemed to see the thing, the horrible thing: the head falling, the eyes open, while he chewed the corner of his big mustache as he always did in moments of anger.

What had they done with his body afterwards? If they had only let her have her boy back as they had given her back her husband—with the bullet in the middle of his forehead!

But she heard a noise of voices. It was the Prussians returning from the village. She hid her letter very quickly in her pocket, and she received them quietly, with her ordinary face, having had time to wipe her tears.

They were laughing, all four, delighted, since they brought with them a fine rabbit—stolen, doubtless—and they made signs to the old woman that there was to be something good to eat.

She set herself to work at once to prepare breakfast; but when it came to killing the rabbit, her heart failed her. And yet it was not the first. One of the soldiers struck it down with a blow of his fist behind the ears.

The beast once dead, she separated the red body from the skin; but the sight of the blood which she was touching, and which covered her hands, of the warm blood which she felt cooling and coagulating, made her tremble from head to foot; and she kept seeing her big boy cut in two, and quite red also, like this still-palpitating animal.

She set herself at table with the Prussians, but she could not eat, not even a mouthful. They devoured the rabbit without troubling themselves about her. She looked at them askance, without speaking, ripening a thought, and with a face so impassible that they perceived nothing.

All of a sudden she said: "I don't even know your names, and here's a whole month that we've been together." They understood, not without difficulty, what she wanted, and told their names. That was not sufficient; she had them written for her on a paper, with the addresses of their families, and, resting her spectacles on her great nose, she considered that strange hand writing, then folded the sheet and put it in her pocket, on top of the letter which told her of the death of her son.

When the meal was ended, she said to the men:

"I am going to work for you."

And she began to carry up hay into the loft where they slept.

They were astonished at her taking all this trouble; she explained to them that thus they would not be so cold; and they helped her. They heaped the trusses of hay as high as the straw roof; and in that manner they made a sort of great chamber with four walls of fodder, warm and perfumed, where they should sleep splendidly.

At dinner, one of them was worried to see that La Mère Sauvage still ate nothing. She told him that she had the cramps. Then she kindled a good fire to warm herself up, and the four Germans mounted to their lodging-place by the ladder which served them every night for this purpose.

As soon as they closed the trap, the old woman removed the ladder, then opened the outside door noiselessly, and went back to look for more bundles of straw, with which she filled her kitchen. She went barefoot in the snow, so softly that no sound was heard. From time to time she listened to the sonorous and unequal snorings of the four soldiers who were fast asleep.

When she judged her preparations to be sufficient, she threw one of the bundles into the fireplace, and when it was alight she scattered it all over the others. Then she went outside again and looked.

In a few seconds the whole interior of the cottage was illumined with a violent brightness and became a dreadful brasier, a gigantic fiery furnace, whose brilliance spouted out of the narrow window and threw a glittering beam upon the snow.

Then a great cry issued from the summit of the house; it was a clamor of human shriekings, heartrending calls of anguish and of fear. At last, the trap having fallen in, a whirlwind of fire shot up into the loft, pierced the straw roof, rose to the sky like the immense flame of a torch; and all the cottage flared.

Nothing more was heard therein but the crackling of the fire, the crackling sound of the walls, the falling of the rafters. All of a sudden the roof fell in, and the burning carcass of the dwelling hurled a great plume of sparks into the air, amid a cloud of smoke.

The country, all white, lit up by the fire, shone like a cloth of silver tinted with red.

A bell, far off, began to toll.

The old "Sauvage" remained standing before her ruined dwelling, armed with her gun, her son's gun, for fear lest one of those men might escape.

When she saw that it was ended, she threw her weapon into the brasier. A loud report rang back.

People were coming, the peasants, the Prussians.

They found the woman seated on the trunk of a tree, calm and satisfied.

A German officer, who spoke French like a son of France, demanded of her:

"Where are your soldiers?"

She extended her thin arm towards the red heap of fire which was gradually going out, and she answered with a strong voice:

"There!"

They crowded round her. The Prussian asked:

"How did it take fire?"

She said:

"It was I who set it on fire."

They did not believe her, they thought that the sudden disaster had made her crazy. So, while all pressed round and listened, she told the thing from one end to the other, from the arrival of the letter to the last cry of the men who were burned with her house. She did not forget a detail of all which she had felt, nor of all which she had done.

When she had finished, she drew two pieces of paper from her pocket, and, to distinguish them by the last glimmers of the fire, she again adjusted her spectacles; then she said, showing one: "That, that is the death of Victor." Showing the other, she added, indicating the red ruins with a bend of the head: "That, that is their names, so that you can write home." She calmly held the white sheet out to the officer, who held her by the shoulders, and she continued:

"You must write how it happened, and you must say to their mothers that it was I who did that, Victoire Simon, la Sauvage! Do not forget."

The officer shouted some orders in German. They seized her, they threw her against the walls of her house, still hot. Then twelve men drew quickly up before her, at twenty paces. She did not move. She had understood; she waited.

An order rang out, followed instantly by a long report. A belated shot went off by itself, after the others.

The old woman did not fall. She sank as though they had mowed off her legs.

The Prussian officer approached. She was almost cut in two, and in her withered hand she held her letter bathed with blood.

My friend Serval added:

"It was by way of reprisal that the Germans destroyed the château of the district, which belonged to me."

As for me, I thought of the mothers of those four gentle fellows burned in that house; and of the atrocious heroism of that other mother shot against the wall.

And I picked up a little stone still blackened by the flames.

ANTON TCHEKHOV

La Cigale[1] 🦗

I

To Olga Ivanovna's wedding came all her friends and acquaintances.

"Look at him! Isn't it true there is something in him?" she said to them, nodding towards her husband, as if to justify her marriage to this simple, commonplace, in no way remarkable man.

The bridegroom, Osip Stepanych Dymov, was a doctor, with the rank of Titular Councillor. He worked at two hospitals; in one as supernumerary ordinator; as dissector in the other. At one, from nine in the morning till midday, he received out-patients and worked in the wards; and, finished with this, he took a tram to the second hospital, and dissected bodies. His private practice was small, worth some five hundred rubles a year. That was all. What more could be said of him? On the other hand, Olga Ivanovna, her friends and acquaintances, were by no means ordinary. All were noted for something, and fairly well known; they had names; they were celebrated, or if not celebrated yet, they inspired great hope for the future. A talented actor, clever, modest, a fine gentleman, a master of declamation, who taught Olga Ivanovna to recite; a good-humoured opera-singer who told Olga Ivanovna with a sigh that she was throwing herself away—if she gave up idling and took herself in hand, she would make a famous singer; a few artists, chief of them the genre-ist, animal- and landscape-painter Riabovsky, handsome, fair-haired, twenty-five, successful at exhibitions who sold his last picture for five hundred rubles—he touched up Olga Ivanovna's *études,* and predicted a future for her; a violoncellist, whose instrument wept, who frankly said that of all the women he knew Olga Ivanovna alone could accompany; a man of letters, young, but already known for his short stories, sketches, and plays. Who else? Yes, Vasily Vasilych, country gentleman, dilettante illustrator and vignettist, with his love of the national epos and his passion for old Russian art—on paper, china, and smoked plates he turned out veritable masterpieces. In such society—artistic, free, and spoiled by fate; and (though delicate and modest) oblivious of doctors save when ill; to whom "Dymov" sounded as impersonal as "Tarasov" or "Sidorov"—in such society, the bridegroom seemed out-of-place, needless, and even insignificant, although he was really a very tall and very broad-shouldered man. His

[1] In English, "The Cicada."

evening dress seemed made for someone else. His beard was like a shop-man's. Though it is true that had he been a writer or artist, this beard would have reminded them of Zola.

The artist told Olga Ivanovna that with her flaxen hair and wedding dress she was a graceful cherry-tree covered with tender, white blossoms in spring.

"No, but listen!" replied Olga Ivanovna, seizing his hand. "How suddenly all this happened! Listen, listen! . . . I should tell you that Dymov and my father were at the same hospital. While my poor father was ill, Dymov watched day and night at his bedside. Such self-sacrifice! Listen, Riabovsky! . . . And you, writer, listen—this is very interesting! Come nearer! Such sacri-fice of self, such sincere concern! I myself could not sleep at night, and sat at my father's bedside, and suddenly! . . . I captivated the poor young man! My Dymov was up to his neck in love! In truth, things happened strangely. Well, after my father's death we sometimes met in the street; he paid me occasional visits, and one fine evening suddenly—he proposed to me! . . . I cried all night, and myself fell in love with him. And now, you see, I am married. Don't you think there is something in him? Something strong, mighty, leonine! Just now his face is turned three-quarters from us and the light is bad, but when he turns round just look at his forehead! Riabovsky, what do you think of his forehead? Dymov, we are speaking of you." She turned to her husband. "Come here! Give your honest hand to Riabovsky. . . . That's right. Be friends!"

With a simple, kindly smile, Dymov gave his hand to the artist, and said—

"I'm delighted! There was a Riabovsky at college with me. Was he a relation of yours?"

II

Olga Ivanovna was twenty-two years old, Dymov thirty-one. After the mar-riage they lived well. Olga Ivanovna hung the drawing-room with drawings, her own and her friends', framed and unframed; and about the piano and furniture, arranged in pretty confusion Chinese parasols, easels, many-coloured draperies, poniards, busts, photographs. The dining-room she decked with the bright-coloured oleographs beloved by peasants, bast-shoes and sickles, and these, with the scythe and hay-rake in the corner, made a room in national style. To make her bedroom like a cave, she draped the ceiling and walls with dark cloth, hung a Venetian lantern over the bed, and set near the door a figure with a halberd. And every one agreed that the young couple had a charming flat.

Rising every day at eleven, Olga Ivanovna sat at the piano, or, if the sun shone, painted in oils. At one o'clock she drove to her dressmaker's. As neither she nor Dymov was rich, many ingenious shifts were resorted to to keep her in the new-looking dresses which made such an impression on all.

Pieces of old dyed cloth; worthless patches of tulle, lace, plush, and silk, came back from the dressmaker miracles, not dresses but ravishing dreams. Done with the dressmaker, Olga Ivanovna drove to some actress friend to learn theatrical news and get tickets for first-nights or benefits; thence to an artist's studio or picture gallery, ending up with some other celebrity whom she invited to visit her, or simply gossiped to. And those whom she counted celebrities and great men received her as an equal, and told her in one voice that if she did not throw away her opportunities, her talents, taste, and intellect would yield something really great. She sang, played, painted, modelled, acted in amateur theatricals; and did everything well: if she merely made lanterns for illuminations, or dressed herself up, or tied someone's necktie, the result was invariably graceful, artistic, charming. But none of her talents outshone her skill in meeting and getting on terms of intimacy with men of note. Let a man get the least reputation, or even be talked about, and in a single day she had met him, established friendly relations, and invited him to her home. And each new acquaintance was a festival in himself. She worshipped the well-known, was proud of them, and dreamed of them all night. Her thirst was insatiable. The old celebrities departed and were forgotten, and new celebrities replaced them; and to these last she grew accustomed in time; they lost their charm, so that she sought for more.

She dined at home with her husband at five o'clock. She was in ecstasies over his simplicity, common sense, and good humour. She jumped up from her chair, embraced his head, and covered it with kisses.

"You are clever, a noble man, Dymov!" she exclaimed. "You have only one drawback. You take no interest in art. You deny music and painting."

"I don't understand them," he answered kindly. "All my life I have studied only science and medicine. I have not time for art."

"But that is awful, Dymov!"

"Why awful? Your friends know nothing of science or medicine, yet you don't blame them for that. To each man his own! I don't understand landscapes or operas, but I look at the matter thus: if talented men devote their lives to such things, and clever men pay vast sums for them, that means they are useful. I don't understand them, but not to understand does not mean to deny."

"Give me your hand! Let me press your honest hand!"

After dinner Olga Ivanovna drove away to her friends; after that followed theatres or concerts. She returned after midnight. And so every day.

On Wednesday she gave evening parties. There were no cards and no dancing. Hostess and guests devoted themselves to art. The actor recited, the singer sang, artists sketched in Olga Ivanovna's numberless albums; the hostess painted, modelled, accompanied, and sang. In the pauses between these recreations, they talked of books, the theatre, and art. No women were present, because Olga Ivanovna considered all women, except actresses and dressmakers, tiresome and contemptible. When the hall bell rang the hostess started, and exclaimed triumphantly, "It's he!" meaning thereby some newly met celebrity. Dymov kept out of sight, and few remembered his existence. But at half-past eleven the dining-room door flew open, and Dymov appeared with a kindly smile, rubbing his hands, and said—

"Come, gentlemen, to supper!"

Whereupon all thronged to the dining-room, and each time found awaiting them the same things: a dish of oysters, a joint of ham or veal, sardines, cheese, caviar, mushrooms, vodka, and two decanters of wine.

"My dear *maître d'hôtel!*" cried Olga Ivanovna, waving her hands ecstatically. "You are simply adorable! Gentlemen, look at his forehead! Dymov, show us your profile. Look at him, gentlemen: it is the face of a Bengal tiger with an expression as kind and good as a deer's. My sweetheart!"

And the guests ate steadily and looked at Dymov. But soon they forgot his presence, and returned to theatre, music, and art.

The young couple were happy. Their life, it seemed, flowed as smoothly as oil. But the third week of the honeymoon was crossed by a cloud. Dymov got erysipelas at the hospital, and his fine black hair was cut off. Olga Ivanovna sat with him and cried bitterly, but when he got better she bound a white handkerchief around his head and sketched him as a Bedouin. And both were happy. Three days after he had returned to the hospital a second misfortune occurred.

"I am in bad luck, mama!" he said at dinner. "To-day I had four dissections, and I cut two fingers. I noticed it only just now."

Olga Ivanovna was frightened. But Dymov smiled, dismissed the accident as a trifle, and said that he cut himself often.

"I am carried away by my work, mama, and forget what I'm about."

Olga Ivanovna dreaded blood-poisoning, and at night prayed to God. But no consequences followed, and life, serene and happy, flowed without trouble or alarm. The present was all delight, and behind it came spring—spring already near, beaming and beckoning, with a thousand joys. Pleasures it promised without end. In April, May, and June a villa far from town, with walks, fishing, studies, nightingales. From June till autumn the artists' tour on the Volga, and in this tour, as member of the Artists' Association, Olga Ivanovna would take part. She had already ordered two expensive dresses of gingham, and laid in a stock of colours, brushes, canvas, and a new palette. Almost every day came Riabovsky to watch her progress in painting. When she showed him her work he thrust his hands deep in his pockets, compressed tightly his lips, grunted, and said—

"So! . . . This cloud of yours glares; the light is not right for evening. The foreground is somehow chewed up, and there is something, you understand. . . . And the cabin is somehow crushed . . . you should make that corner a little darker. But on the whole it's not bad. . . . I can praise it."

And the less intelligibly he spoke the better Olga Ivanovna understood.

III

After dinner, on the second day of Trinity week, Dymov bought some *hors d'œuvres* and sweets and took train for his villa in the country. Two whole weeks he had not seen his wife, and he longed to be with her again. During the journey and afterwards, as he searched for the villa in a big wood, he felt hungry and fatigued, and rejoiced at the thought of supping in freedom with his wife and having a sound sleep. So, looking at his parcel of caviar, cheese, and white-fish, he felt happy.

Before he found the villa the sun had begun to set. The old servant said that her mistress was not at home, but that she would soon return. The villa, a very ugly villa, with low ceilings, papered with writing-paper, and uneven, chinky floors, contained only three rooms. In one was a bed, in another canvas, brushes, dirty paper, and men's clothes and hats scattered on chairs and window-sills; and in the third Dymov found three strangers, two dark and bearded, the third—evidently an actor—clean-shaven and stout.

"What do you want?" asked the actor in a bass voice, looking at Dymov shyly. "You wanted Olga Ivanovna? Wait: she'll be back shortly."

Dymov sat down and waited. One of the dark men, looking at him drowsily and lazily, poured tea into his glass and asked—

"Would you like some tea?"

Dymov wanted both to eat and drink, but, fearing to spoil his appetite, he refused the tea. Soon afterwards came footsteps and a familiar laugh; the door flew open, and in came Olga Ivanovna wearing a big hat. On her arm hung a basket, and behind her, with a big parasol and a deck-chair, came merry, rosy-cheeked Riabovsky.

"Dymov!" cried Olga Ivanovna, radiant with joy. "Dymov!" she repeated, laying her head and both hands on his shoulder. "It is you? Why did you not come sooner? Why? Why?"

"I couldn't, mama! I am always busy, and when I end my work there's generally no train."

"How glad I am you've come! I dreamed of you all, all last night. *Akh*, if you knew how I love you—and how opportunely you've come! You are my saviour! To-morrow we have a most original wedding." She laughed and re-tied her husband's tie. "A young telegraphist at the station, a certain Chikeldeyev, is going to be married. A handsome boy, not at all stupid; in his face, you know, there's something strong, bearish. . . . He'd sit admirably as model for a Varangian. We are all interested in him, and promised to come to the wedding. . . . He is a poor man, solitary and shy, and it would be a sin to refuse. Imagine! . . . after church there'll be the wedding, then all go to the bride's house . . . you understand . . . the woods, the birds' songs, sun-spots on the grass, and we ourselves—variegated spots on a bright green background. . . . Most original, quite in the style of the French impressionists! But what am I to wear, Dymov? I have nothing here, literally nothing. . . . No dress, no flowers, no gloves! . . . You must save me. Your arrival means that fate is on my side. Here are the keys, sweetheart! take the train home and bring my rose-coloured dress from the wardrobe. You know it; it's the first you'll see. Then in the chest of drawers—the bottom right-hand drawer—you'll find two boxes. At the top there's only tulle and other rags, but underneath you'll find flowers. Bring all the flowers—carefully! I don't know . . . then I'll choose. . . . And buy me some gloves."

"All right," said Dymov. "I'll get them to-morrow!"

"How to-morrow?" asked Olga Ivanovna, looking at him with surprise. "You can't do it to-morrow. The first train leaves at nine, and the wedding is at eleven. No, dear; go to-night! If you can't get back yourself tomorrow send a messenger. The train is nearly due. Don't miss it, my soul!"

"All right!"

"*Akh,* how sorry I am to have to send you!" she said, and tears came into her eyes. "Why did I promise the telegraph clerk, like a fool!"

Dymov hastily gulped down a glass of tea, and, still smiling kindly, returned to the station. And the caviar, the cheese, and the white-fish were eaten by the actor and the two dark men.

IV

It was a still moonlight night of July. Olga Ivanovna stood on the deck of a Volga steamer and looked now at the river, now at its beautiful banks. Beside her stood Riabovsky, and affirmed that the black shadows on the water were not shadows but a dream; that this magic stream with its fantastic shimmer, this unfathomable sky, these mournful banks—which expressed but the vanity of life, and the existence of something higher, something eternal, something blessed—called to us to forget ourselves, to die, to fade into memories. The past was trivial and tedious, the future insignificant; and this magic night, this one night of life, would soon be past, would have hurried into eternity. Why, then, live?

And Olga Ivanovna listened, first to Riabovsky's voice, then to the midnight silence, and thought that she was immortal, and would never die. The river's turquoise hue, a hue she had never seen before, the sky, the banks, the black shadows, and the irresponsible joy which filled her heart, all whispered to her that she would become a great artist, that somewhere far away, beyond these distances, beyond the moonlight night, somewhere in infinite space there awaited success and glory, and the love of the world. When she looked earnestly into the distance, she saw crowds, lights; she heard solemn music and cries of rapture; she saw herself in a white dress surrounded by flowers cast at her from all sides. And she believed that here beside her, leaning on the bulwark, stood a really great man, a genius, the elected of God. He had already accomplished things beautiful, new, uncommon; what he would do when time had ripened his great talents would be greater immeasurably—that was written legibly in his face, his expressions, his relations to the world around. Of the shadows, the hues of night, the moonlight, he spoke in language all his own, and unconsciously betrayed the power of his magic mastery over Nature. He was handsome and original; and his life, unhampered, free, alien to the trifles of the world, seemed the life of a bird.

"It is getting cold!" said Olga Ivanovna, shuddering.

Riabovsky wrapped her in his cloak and said mournfully—

"I feel myself in your power. I am a slave. Why are you so ravishing to-night?"

He looked at her steadily, and his eyes were so terrible that she feared to look at him.

"I love you madly . . ." he whispered, breathing against her cheek. "Say to me but one word, and I will not live . . . I will abandon my art. . . ." He stammered in his extreme agitation. "Love me, love. . . ."

"Don't speak in that way!" said Olga Ivanovna, closing her eyes. "It is terrible. And Dymov?"

"What is Dymov? Why Dymov? What have I to do with Dymov? The Volga, the moon, beauty, my love, my raptures . . . and no Dymov at all! . . . Akh, I know nothing. . . . I do not want the past; give me but one moment . . . one second!"

Olga Ivanovna's heart beat quickly. She tried to think of her husband; but her whole past, her marriage, Dymov, even the evening parties seemed to her trivial, contemptible, dull, needless, and remote. . . . And, indeed, who was Dymov? Why Dymov? What had she to do with Dymov? Did he exist really in Nature; was he only a dream?

"He has had more happiness than he could expect, a simple and ordinary man," she thought, closing her eyes. "Let them condemn me, let them curse me; but I will take all and perish, take all and perish. . . . We must experience everything in life. . . . Lord, how painful and how good!"

"Well, what? What?" stammered the artist, embracing her. He kissed her hands greedily, while she strove to withdraw them. "You love me? Yes? O what a night! O night divine!"

"Yes, what a night!" she whispered, looking into his eyes which glittered with tears. Then she looked around her, clasped her arms about him, and kissed him firmly on the lips.

"We are near Kineshma," said a voice somewhere across the deck.

Heavy footfalls echoed behind them. A waiter passed from the buffet.

"Waiter!" cried Olga Ivanovna, laughing and crying in her joy. "Bring us some wine."

Pale with excitement, the artist sat on a bench, and stared at Olga Ivanovna with grateful, adoring eyes. But in a moment he shut these eyes, and said with a weary smile—

"I am tired."

And he leaned his head against the bulwark.

v

The second of September was warm and windless but dull. Since early morning a light mist had wandered across the Volga, and at nine o'clock it began to rain. There was no hope of a clear sky. At breakfast Riabovsky told Olga Ivanovna that painting was the most thankless and tedious of arts, that he was no artist, and that only fools thought him talented. Then, for no cause whatever, he seized a knife and cut to pieces his best study. After breakfast, in bad humour, he sat at a window and looked at the river, and found it without life—dull, dead; and cold. All around spoke of frowning autumn's approach. It seemed already that the green carpet on the banks, the diamond flashes from the water, the clear blue distances—all the vanity and parade of Nature had been taken from the Volga and packed in a box until the coming spring; and the ravens flying over the river mocked it and cried, "Naked! Naked!" Riabovsky listened to their cry, and brooded on the exhaustion and loss of his talent: and he thought that all the world was conditional, relative, and stupid, and that he should not have tied himself up with this woman. In one word he was out of spirits and sulked.

On her bed behind the partition, pulling at her pretty hair, sat Olga Ivanovna; and pictured herself at home, first in the drawing-room, then in her bedroom, then in her husband's study; imagination bore her to theatres, to her dressmaker, to her friends. What was Dymov doing now? Did he think of her? The season had already begun; it was time to think of the evening parties. And Dymov? Dear Dymov! How kindly, with what infantile complaints, he begged her in his letters to come home! Every month he sent her seventy-five rubles, and when she wrote that she had borrowed a hundred from the artists he sent her also that hundred. The good, the generous man! Olga Ivanovna was tired of the tour; she suffered from tedium, and wished to escape as soon as possible from the muzhiks, from the river damp, from the feeling of physical uncleanliness caused by living in huts and wandering from village to village. Had Riabovsky not promised his brother artists to stay till the twentieth of September, they might have left at once. And how good it would be to leave!

"My God!" groaned Riabovsky. "Will the sun ever come out? I cannot paint a landscape without the sun!"

"But your study of a cloudy sky?" said Olga Ivanovna, coming from behind the partition. "You remember, the one with the trees in the foreground to the right, and the cows and geese at the left. You could finish that."

"What?" The artist frowned. "Finish it? Do you really think I'm so stupid that I don't know what to do?"

"What I do think is that you've changed to me!" sighed Olga Ivanovna.

"Yes; and that's all right."

Olga Ivanovna's face quivered; she went to the stove and began to cry.

"We only wanted tears to complete the picture! Do stop! I have a thousand reasons for crying, but I don't cry."

"A thousand reasons!" burst out Olga Ivanovna. "The chief reason is that you are tired of me. Yes!" She began to sob. "I will tell you the truth; you are ashamed of your love. You try to hide it, to prevent the others noticing, but that is useless, because they knew about it long ago."

"Olga, I ask only one thing," said the artist imploringly. He put his hand to his ear. "One thing only; do not torture me! I want nothing more from you!"

"Then swear to me that you love me still!"

"This is torture!" hissed Riabovsky through his teeth. He jumped up. "It will end in my throwing myself into the Volga, or going out of my mind. Leave me alone!"

"Then kill me! Kill me!" cried Olga Ivanovna. "Kill me!"

She again sobbed, and retired behind the partition. Raindrops pattered on the cabin roof. Riabovsky with his hands to his head walked from corner to corner; then with a determined face, as if he wanted to prove something, put on his cap, took his gun, and went out of the hut.

When he left, Olga Ivanovna lay on her bed and cried. At first she thought that it would be good to take poison, so that Riabovsky on his return would find her dead. But soon her thoughts bore her back to the drawing-room and to her husband's study; and she fancied herself sitting quietly beside Dymov, enjoying physical rest and cleanliness; and spending the evening listening to *Cavalleria Rusticana*. And a yearning for civilisation, for the sound of cities, for celebrities filled her heart. A peasant woman entered the hut, and lazily prepared the stove for dinner. There was a smell of soot, and the air turned blue from smoke. Then in came several artists in muddy top boots, their faces wet with rain; and they looked at the drawings, and consoled themselves by saying that even in bad weather the Volga had its especial charm. The cheap clock on the wall ticked away; half-frozen flies swarmed in the ikon-corner and buzzed; and cockroaches could be heard under the benches.

Riabovsky returned at sunset. He flung his cap on the table, and, pale, tired, and muddy, dropped on a bench and shut his eyes.

"I am tired," he said, and wrinkled his brows, trying to open his eyes.

To show him kindness, and prove that her anger had passed, Olga Ivanovna came up to him, kissed him silently, and drew a comb through his long, fair hair.

"What are you doing?" he asked, starting as if something cold had touched him. He opened his eyes. "What are you doing? Leave me alone, I beg of you!"

He repulsed her with both hands; and his face seemed to express repugnance and vexation. The peasant woman cautiously brought him a plate, and Olga Ivanovna noticed how she stuck her big fingers in the soup. And the dirty peasant woman with her pendent stomach, the soup which Riabovsky ate greedily, the hut, which she had loved at first for its plainness and artistic disorder, seemed to her unbearable. She felt a deep sense of offence, and said coldly—

"We must part for a time, otherwise we'll only quarrel seriously out of sheer tedium. I am tired of this. I am going to-day."

"Going, how? On the steamer?"

"To-day is Thursday—there is a steamer at half-past nine."

"Eh? Yes! . . . All right, go," said Riabovsky softly, using a towel for a table-napkin. "It's tiresome here for you, and there's nothing to do. Only a great egoist would try to keep you. Go . . . we will meet after the twentieth."

Olga Ivanovna, in good spirits, packed her clothes. Her cheeks burnt with pleasure. "Is it possible?" she asked herself. "Is it possible I shall soon paint in the drawing-room and sleep in a bedroom and dine off a tablecloth?" Her heart grew lighter, and her anger with the artist disappeared.

"I'll leave you the colours and brushes, Riabusha," she said. "You'll bring everything. . . . And, mind, don't idle when I am gone; don't sulk, but work. You are my boy, Riabusha!"

At ten o'clock Riabovsky kissed her good-bye in the hut, to avoid—as she saw—kissing her on the landing-stage in the presence of others. Soon afterwards the steamer arrived and took her away.

Two and a half days later she reached home. Still in her hat and waterproof cloak, panting with excitement, she went through the drawing-room into the dining-room. In his shirt-sleeves, with unbuttoned waistcoat, Dymov sat at the table and sharpened a knife; on a plate before him was a grouse. As Olga Ivanovna entered the house she resolved to hide the truth from her husband, and felt that she was clever and strong enough to succeed. But when she saw his broad, kindly, happy smile and his bright, joyful eyes, she felt that to deceive such a man would be base and impossible, as impossible as to slander, steal, or kill; and she made up her mind in a second to tell him the whole story. When he had kissed and embraced her she fell upon her knees and hid her face.

"What? What is it, mama?" he asked tenderly. "You got tired of it?"

She raised her face, red with shame, and looked at him guiltily and imploringly. But fear and shame forbade her to tell the truth.

"It is nothing," she said. "I only . . ."

"Sit down here!" he said, lifting her and seating her at the table. "There we are! Eat the grouse! You are starving, of course, poor child!"

She breathed in greedily her native air and ate the grouse. And Dymov looked at her with rapture and smiled merrily.

VI

Apparently about the middle of winter Dymov first suspected his wife's unfaithfulness. He behaved as if his own conscience reproached him. He no longer looked her straight in the face; no longer smiled radiantly when she came in sight; and, to avoid being alone with her, often brought home to dinner, his colleague, Korostelev, a little short-haired man, with a crushed face, who showed his confusion in Olga Ivanovna's society by buttoning and unbuttoning his coat and pinching his right moustache. During dinner the doctors said that when the diaphragm rises abnormally high the heart sometimes beats irregularly, that neuritis had greatly increased, and they discussed Dymov's discovery made during dissection that a case of cancer of the pancreas had been wrongly diagnosed as "malignant anæmia." And it was plain that both men spoke only of medicine in order that Olga Ivanovna might be silent and tell no lies. After dinner, Korostelev sat at the piano, and Dymov sighed and said to him—

"*Akh,* brother! Well! Play me something mournful."

Whereupon, raising his shoulders and spreading his hands, Korostelev strummed a few chords and sang in terror, "Show me but one spot where Russia's peasants do not groan!" and Dymov sighed again, rested his head on his hands, and seemed lost in thought.

Of late Olga Ivanovna had behaved recklessly. She awoke each morning in bad spirits, tortured by the thought that Riabovsky no longer loved her, that—thanks to the Lord, all the same!—all was over. But as she drank her coffee she reasoned that Riabovsky had stolen her from her husband, and that now she belonged to neither. Then she remembered a friend's remark that Riabovsky was getting ready for the exhibition a striking picture, a mixture of landscape and *genre,* in the style of Polienov, and that this picture sent everyone into raptures; this, she consoled herself, he had done under her influence. Thanks to her influence, indeed, he had on the whole changed for the better, and deprived of it, he would probably perish. She remembered that when last he visited her he came in a splashed cloth coat and a new tie and asked her languidly, "Am I good-looking?" And, in truth, elegant Riabovsky with his blue eyes and long curls was very good-looking—or, it may be, he merely seemed so and he had treated her with affection.

Having remembered and reasoned much, Olga Ivanovna dressed, and in deep agitation drove to Riabovsky's studio. He was in good humour, delighted with what was indeed a fine picture; he hopped, played the fool, and

answered every serious question with a joke. Olga Ivanovna was jealous
of the picture, and hated it, but for the sake of good manners, she stood
before it five minutes, and, sighing as people sigh before holy things, said
softly—

"Yes, you never painted like that before. Do you know, it almost frightens
me."

And she began to implore him to love her, not to forsake her, to pity her
—poor and unfortunate! She kissed his hand, cried, made him swear his
love, and boasted that without her influence he would go off the track and
perish utterly. Thus having spoilt his good humour, and humiliated herself,
she would drive away to a dressmaker, or to some actress friend to ask for
free tickets.

Once when she found Riabovsky out she left a note swearing that if he did
not visit her at once she would take poison. And he, frightened, came and
stayed to dinner. Ignoring her husband's presence, he spoke to her impudently; and she answered in the same tone. They felt chained to one another;
they were despots and foes; and their anger hid from them their own rude-
ness, which even close-clipped Korostelev remarked. After dinner Riabovsky
said good-bye hastily and went.

"Where are you going?" asked Olga Ivanovna. She stood in the hall, and
looked at him with hatred.

Riabovsky frowned and blinked, and named a woman she knew, and
it was plain that he enjoyed her jealousy, and wished to annoy her. Olga Ivanovna went to her bedroom and lay on her bed; from jealousy, anger, and
a sense of humiliation and shame, she bit her pillow, and sobbed aloud.
Dymov left Korostelev alone, came into the bedroom, and, confused and
abstracted, said softly—

"Don't cry so loudly, mama! . . . What good is it? We must keep silence
about this. . . . People mustn't see. . . . You know yourself that what has
happened is beyond recall."

Unable to appease the painful jealousy which made her temples throb,
thinking, nevertheless, that what had happened was not beyond recall, she
washed and powdered her face, and flew off to the woman friend. Finding
no Riabovsky there she drove to another, then to a third. . . . At first she felt
ashamed of these visits, but she soon reconciled herself; and one evening even
called on every woman she knew and sought Riabovsky; and all of them
understood her.

Of her husband she said to Riabovsky—

"This man tortures me with his magnanimity."

And this sentence so pleased her that, meeting artists who knew of her
affair with Riabovsky, she repeated with an emphatic gesture—

"This man tortures me with his magnanimity."

In general, her life remained unchanged. She resumed her Wednesday-

evening parties. The actor declaimed, the painters sketched, the violoncellist
played, the singers sang; and invariably half an hour before midnight the
dining-room door opened, and Dymov said with a smile—

"Come, gentlemen, supper is ready."

As before, Olga Ivanovna sought celebrities, found them, and, insatiable,
sought for more. As before, she returned home late. But Dymov, no longer
sleeping as of old, sat in his study and worked. He went to bed at three, and
rose at eight.

Once as she stood before the pier-glass dressing for the theatre, Dymov, in
evening dress and a white tie, came into the bedroom. He smiled kindly, with
his old smile, and looked his wife joyfully in the face. His face shone.

"I have just defended my dissertation," he said. He sat down and stroked
his leg.

"Your dissertation?" said Olga Ivanovna.

"Yes," he laughed. He stretched forward so as to see in the mirror the face
of his wife, who continued to stand with her back to him and dress her hair.
"Yes," he repeated. "Do you know what? I expect to be offered a privat-
docentship in general pathology. That is something."

It was plain from his radiant face that had Olga Ivanovna shared his joy
and triumph he would have forgiven and forgotten everything. But "privat-
docentship" and "general pathology" had no meaning for her, and, what's
more, she feared to be late for the theatre. She said nothing.

Dymov sat still for a few minutes, smiled guiltily, and left the room.

VII

This was an evil day.

Dymov's head ached badly; he ate no breakfast, and did not go to the
hospital, but lay on the sofa in his study. At one o'clock Olga Ivanovna went
to Riabovsky's, to show him her *Nature morte,* and ask why he had not come
the day before. The *Nature morte* she herself did not take seriously; she had
painted it only as an excuse to visit the artist.

She went to his apartment unannounced. As she took off her goloshes in
the hall she heard hasty footsteps, and the rustle of a woman's dress; and as
she hurried into the studio a brown skirt flashed for a moment before her
and vanished behind a big picture, which together with its easel was hung
with black calico. There was no doubt that a woman hid there. How often
had Olga Ivanovna herself hidden behind that picture! Riabovsky, in confusion, stretched out both hands as if surprised at her visit, and said with a
constrained smile—

"Ah, I am glad to see you. What is the news?"

Olga Ivanovna's eyes filled with tears. She was ashamed and angered, and
would have given millions to be spared speaking before the strange woman,

the rival, the liar, who hid behind the picture and tittered, no doubt, maliciously.

"I have brought a study . . ." she said in a thin, frightened voice. Her lips trembled. *"Nature morte."*

"What? What? A study?"

The artist took the sketch, looked at it, and walked mechanically into another room. Olga Ivanovna followed submissively.

"Nature morte . . ." he stammered, seeking rhymes. *"Kurort . . . sort . . . porte . . ."*

From the studio came hasty footfalls and the rustle of a skirt. She had gone. Olga Ivanovna felt impelled to scream and strike the artist on the head; but tears blinded her, she was crushed by her shame, and felt as if she were not Olga Ivanovna the artist, but a little beetle.

"I am tired . . ." said Riabovsky languidly. He looked at the study, and shook his head as if to drive away sleep. "This is charming, of course, but . . . it is study to-day, and study to-morrow, and study last year, and study it will be again in a month. . . . How is it you don't get tired? If I were you, I should give up painting, and take up seriously music, or something else. . . . You are not an artist but a musician. You cannot imagine how tired I am. Let me order some tea. Eh?"

He left the room, and Olga Ivanovna heard him giving an order. To avoid good-byes and explanations, still more to prevent herself sobbing, she went quickly into the hall, put on her goloshes, and went out. Once in the street she sighed faintly. She felt that she was for ever rid of Riabovsky and painting, and the heavy shame which had crushed her in the studio. All was over! She drove to her dressmaker, then to Barnay, who had arrived the day before, and from Barnay to a music shop, thinking all the time how she would write Riabovsky a cold, hard letter, full of her own worth; and that the spring and summer she would spend with Dymov in the Crimea, free herself for ever from the past, and begin life anew.

On her return, late as usual, she sat in her street clothes in the drawing-room, and prepared to write. Riabovsky had told her she was no artist; in revenge she would write that he had painted every year one and the same tiresome thing, that he had exhausted himself, and would never again produce original work. She would write also that he owed much to her beneficent influence; and that if he made mistakes it was only because her influence was paralysed by various ambiguous personages who hid behind his pictures.

"Mama!" cried Dymov from his study, without opening the door.

"What it is?"

"Mama, don't come in, but just come to the door. It is this. The day before yesterday I took diphtheria at the hospital, and now . . . I feel bad. Send at once for Korostelev."

Olga Ivanovna called her husband and men-friends by their surnames;

she disliked his name Osip, which reminded her of Gogol's Osip, and the pun *"Osip okrip, a Arkhip osip."* But this time she cried—

"Osip, that is impossible!"

"Send! I am ill," said Dymov from behind the door; and she heard him walking to the sofa and lying down. "Send!" came his hoarse voice.

"What can it be?" thought Olga Ivanovna, chilled with fear. "Why, this is dangerous!"

Without any aim she took a candle, and went into her room, and there, wondering what she should do, she saw herself unexpectedly in the glass. With her pale, terrified face, her high-sleeved jacket with the yellow gathers on the breast, her skirt with its strange stripes, she seemed to herself frightful and repulsive. And suddenly she felt sorry for Dymov, sorry for his infinite love, his young life, the forsaken bed on which he had not slept so long. And remembering his kindly, suppliant smile, she cried bitterly, and wrote Korostelev an imploring letter. It was two o'clock in the morning.

VIII

When at eight next morning Olga Ivanovna, heavy from sleeplessness, untidy, unattractive, and guilty-faced, came out of her bedroom, an unknown, black-bearded man, obviously a doctor, passed her in the hall. There was a smell of drugs. Outside Dymov's study stood Korostelev, twisting his left moustache with his right hand.

"Excuse me, I cannot let you in," he said, looking at her savagely. "You might catch the disease. And in any case, what's the use? He's raving."

"Is it really diphtheria?" whispered Olga Ivanovna.

"People who do foolish things ought to pay for them," muttered Korostelev, ignoring Olga Ivanovna's question. "Do you know how he got this diphtheria? On Tuesday he sucked through a tube the diphtheria laminæ from a boy's throat. And why? Stupid. . . . Like a fool!"

"Is it dangerous? Very?" asked she.

"Yes, it's a very bad form, they say. We must send for Schreck, we must . . ."

First came a little, red-haired, long-nosed man with a Jewish accent; then a tall, stooping, untidy man like a proto-deacon; lastly a young, very stout, red-faced man with spectacles. All these doctors came to attend their sick colleague. Korostelev, having served his turn, remained in the house, wandering about like a shadow. The maid-servant was kept busy serving the doctors with tea, and running to the apothecary's, and no one tidied the rooms. All was still and sad.

Olga Ivanovna sat in her room, and reflected that God was punishing her for deceiving her husband. That silent, uncomplaining, inexplicable man— impersonified, it seemed, by kindness and mildness, weak from excessive goodness—lay on his sofa and suffered alone, uttering no groan. And if he did complain in his delirium, the doctors would guess that the diphtheria was not the only culprit. They would question Korostelev, who knew all, and not without cause looked viciously at his friend's wife as if she were chief and real offender, and disease only her accomplice. She no longer thought of the moonlight Volga night, the love avowal, the romance of life in the peasant's hut; she remembered only that from caprice and selfishness she had smeared herself from head to feet with something vile and sticky which no washing would wash away.

"*Akh,* how I lied to him!" she said, remembering her restless love of Riabovsky. "May it be accursed!"

At four o'clock she dined with Korostelev, who ate nothing, but drank red wine, and frowned. She too ate nothing. But she prayed silently, and vowed to God that if Dymov only recovered, she would love him again and be his faithful wife. Then, forgetting herself for a moment, she looked at Korostelev and thought: "How tiresome it is to be such a simple, undistinguished, obscure man, and to have such bad manners." It seemed to her that God would strike her dead for her cowardice in keeping away from her husband. And altogether she was oppressed by a dead melancholy, and a feeling that her life was ruined, and that nothing now would mend it.

After dinner, darkness. Olga Ivanovna went into the drawing-room, and found Korostelev asleep on a couch, his head resting on a silken cushion embroidered with gold. He snored loudly.

Alone, the doctors, coming on and off duty, ignored the disorder. The strange man sleeping and snoring in the drawing-room, the studies on the walls, the wonderful decorations, the mistress's dishevelled hair and untidy dress—none of these awakened the least interest. One of the doctors laughed; and this laugh had such a timid sound that it was painful to hear.

When next Olga Ivanovna entered the drawing-room Korostelev was awake. He sat up and smoked.

"He has got diphtheria . . . in the nasal cavity," he said quietly. "Yes . . . and his heart is weak. . . . It is a bad business."

"Better send for Schreck," said Olga Ivanovna.

"He's been. It was he noticed that the diphtheria had got into the nose. Yes . . . but what is Schreck? In reality, Schreck is nothing. He is Schreck, I am Korostelev, and nothing more!"

Time stretched into eternity. Olga Ivanovna lay dressed on her unmade bed, and slumbered. She felt that the whole flat from roof to ceiling was filled with a giant block of iron, and that if the iron were only removed, all would be well again. But then she remembered that there was no iron, but only Dymov's illness.

"*Nature morte . . .*" she thought, again losing consciousness. "Sport, *kurort.* . . . And what about Schreck? Schreck, greck, vreck, kreck. Where are my friends now? Do they know of the sorrow that has overtaken us? O Lord, save . . . deliver us! Schreck, greck. . . ."

And again the iron. Time stretched into eternity, and the clock downstairs struck innumerable times. Now and then the bell was rung. Doctors came. . . . In came the servant with an empty glass on a salver, and said—

"Shall I make the bed, ma'am?"

And, receiving no answer, she went out. Again the clock struck—dreams of rain on the Volga—and again someone arrived, this time, it seemed, a stranger. Olga Ivanovna started, and saw Korostelev.

"What time is it?" she asked.

"About three."

"Well, what?"

"Just that I came to say that he's dying."

He sobbed, sat down on her bed, and wiped away his tears with his sleeve. At first Olga Ivanovna understood nothing; then she turned cold, and began to cross herself.

"He is dying," he repeated in a thin voice; and again he sobbed. "He is dying—because he sacrificed himself. What a loss to science!" He spoke bitterly. "This man, compared with the best of us, was a great man, an exceptional man! What gifts! What hopes he awakened in us all!" Korostelev wrung his hands. "Lord, my God, you will not find such a scholar if you search till judgment day! Oska Dymov, Oska Dymov, what have you done? My God!"

In despair he covered his face with his hands and shook his head.

"And what moral fortitude!" he continued, each second increasing in anger. "Good, pure, loving soul—not a man, but a crystal! How he served his science, how he's died for it. Worked—day and night—like an ox, sparing himself never; and he, the young scholar, the coming professor, was forced to seek a practice and spend his nights translating to pay for these . . . these dirty rags!"

Korostelev looked fiendishly at Olga Ivanovna, seized the sheet with both hands, and tore it as angrily as if it, and not she, were guilty.

"And he never spared himself . . . nor did others spare him. And for what purpose . . . why?"

"Yes, a man in a hundred!" came a deep voice from the dining-room.

Olga Ivanovna recalled her life with Dymov, from beginning to end, in all its details; and suddenly she realised that her husband was indeed an exceptional man, a rare—compared with all her other friends—a great man. And remembering how he was looked up to by her late father and by all his colleagues, she understood that there was indeed good reason to predict for him future fame. The walls, the ceiling, the lamp, the carpet winked at her derisively, as if saying, "You have let it slip by, slip by!" With a cry, she rushed out of the room, slipped past some unknown man in the dining-room, and rushed into her husband's study. Covered with a counterpane to the waist, Dymov lay, motionless, on the couch. His face had grown thin, and was a greyish-yellow never seen on the living; his black eyebrows and his kindly smile were all that remained of Dymov. She felt his chest, his forehead, his hands. His chest was still warm, his forehead and hands were icy. And his half-closed eyes looked not at Olga Ivanovna, but down at the counterpane.

"Dymov!" she cried loudly. "Dymov!"

She wished to explain to him that the past was but a mistake; that all was not yet lost; that life might yet be happy and beautiful; that he was a rare, an uncommon, a great man; that she would worship him from this day forth, and pray, and torture herself with holy dread. . . .

"Dymov!" she cried, tapping his shoulder, refusing to believe that he would never awaken. "Dymov! Dymov!"

But in the drawing-room Korostelev spoke to the maid-servant.

"Don't ask silly questions! Go at once to the church watchman, and get the women's addresses. They will wash the body, and lay it out, and do all that's wanted."

IVAN BUNIN

The Gentleman from San Francisco ❧

"Alas, alas, that great city Babylon, that mighty city!"—
—Revelation of St. John.

The Gentleman from San Francisco—neither at Naples nor on Capri could any one recall his name—with his wife and daughter, was on his way to Europe, where he intended to stay for two whole years, solely for the pleasure of it.

He was firmly convinced that he had a full right to a rest, enjoyment, a long comfortable trip, and what not. This conviction had a two-fold reason: first he was rich, and second, despite his fifty-eight years, he was just about to enter the stream of life's pleasures. Until now he had not really lived, but simply existed, to be sure—fairly well, yet putting off his fondest hopes for the future. He toiled unweariedly—the Chinese, whom he imported by thousands for his works, knew full well what it meant,—and finally he saw that he had made much, and that he had nearly come up to the level of those whom he had once taken as a model, and he decided to catch his breath. The class of people to which he belonged was in the habit of beginning its enjoyment of life with a trip to Europe, India, Egypt. He made up his mind to do the same. Of course, it was first of all himself that he desired to reward for the years of toil, but he was also glad for his wife and daughter's sake. His wife was never distinguished by any extraordinary impressionability, but then, all elderly American women are ardent travelers. As for his daughter, a girl of marriageable age, and somewhat sickly,—travel was the very thing she needed. Not to speak of the benefit to her health, do not happy meetings occur during travels? Abroad, one may chance to sit at the same table with a prince, or examine frescoes side by side with a multimillionaire.

The itinerary the Gentleman from San Francisco planned out was an extensive one. In December and January he expected to relish the sun of southern Italy, monuments of antiquity, the tarantella, serenades of wandering minstrels, and that which at his age is felt most keenly—the love, not entirely disinterested though, of young Neapolitan girls. The Carnival days he planned to spend at Nice and Monte-Carlo, which at that time of the year

Reprinted from *The Gentleman from San Francisco and Other Stories* by Ivan Bunin, by permission of Alfred A. Knopf, Inc. Copyright 1923 by Alfred A. Knopf, Inc.

is the meeting-place of the choicest society, the society upon which depend all the blessings of civilization: the cut of dress suits, the stability of thrones, the declaration of wars, the prosperity of hotels. Some of these people passionately give themselves over to automobile and boat races, others to roulette, others, again, busy themselves with what is called flirtation, and others shoot pigeons, which soar so beautifully from the dove-cote, hover a while over the emerald lawn, on the background of the forget-me-not colored sea, and then suddenly hit the ground, like little white lumps. Early March he wanted to devote to Florence, and at Easter, to hear the Miserere in Paris. His plans also included Venice, Paris, bull-baiting at Seville, bathing on the British Islands, also Athens, Constantinople, Palestine, Egypt, and even Japan, of course, on the way back. . . . And at first things went very well indeed.

It was the end of November, and all the way to Gibraltar the ship sailed across seas which were either clad by icy darkness or swept by storms carrying wet snow. But there were no accidents, and the vessel did not even roll. The passengers,—all people of consequence—were numerous, and the steamer, the famous "Atlantis," resembled the most expensive European hotel with all improvements; a night refreshment-bar, Oriental baths, even a newspaper of its own. The manner of living was a most aristocratic one; passengers rose early, awakened by the shrill voice of a bugle, filling the corridors at the gloomy hour when the day broke slowly and sulkily over the grayish-green watery desert, which rolled heavily in the fog. After putting on their flannel pajamas, they took coffee, chocolate, cocoa; they seated themselves in marble baths, went through their exercises, whetting their appetites and increasing their sense of well-being, dressed for the day, and had their breakfast. Till eleven o'clock they were supposed to stroll on the deck, breathing in the chill freshness of the ocean, or they played table-tennis, or other games which arouse the appetite. At eleven o'clock a collation was served consisting of sandwiches and bouillon, after which people read their newspapers, quietly waiting for luncheon, which was more nourishing and varied than the breakfast. The next two hours were given to rest; all the decks were crowded then with steamer chairs, on which the passengers, wrapped in plaids, lay stretched, dozing lazily, or watching the cloudy sky and the foamy-fringed water hillocks flashing beyond the sides of the vessel. At five o'clock, refreshed and gay, they drank strong, fragrant tea; at seven the sound of the bugle announced a dinner of nine courses. . . . Then the Gentleman from San Francisco, rubbing his hands in an onrush of vital energy, hastened to his luxurious state-room to dress.

In the evening, all the decks of the "Atlantis" yawned in the darkness, shone with their innumerable fiery eyes, and a multitude of servants worked with increased feverishness in the kitchens, dish-washing compartments, and wine-cellars. The ocean, which heaved about the sides of the ship, was dreadful, but no one thought of it. All had faith in the controlling power of the captain, a red-headed giant, heavy and very sleepy, who, clad in a uniform with broad golden stripes, looked like a huge idol, and but rarely emerged, for the benefit of the public, from his mysterious retreat. On the forecastle, the siren gloomily roared or screeched in a fit of mad rage, but few of the diners heard the siren: its hellish voice was covered by the sounds of an excellent string orchestra, which played ceaselessly and exquisitely in a vast hall, decorated with marble and spread with velvety carpets. The hall was flooded with torrents of light, radiated by crystal lustres and gilt chandeliers; it was filled with a throng of bejeweled ladies in low-necked dresses, of men in dinner-coats, graceful waiters, and deferential maîtres-d'hôtel. One of these,—who accepted wine orders exclusively—wore a chain on his neck like some lord-mayor. The evening dress, and the ideal linen made the Gentleman from San Francisco look very young. Dry-skinned, of average height, strongly, though irregularly built, glossy with thorough washing and cleaning, and moderately animated, he sat in the golden splendor of this palace. Near him stood a bottle of amber-colored Johannisberg, and goblets of most delicate glass and of varied sizes, surmounted by a frizzled bunch of fresh hyacinths. There was something Mongolian in his yellowish face with its trimmed silvery moustache; his large teeth glimmered with gold fillings, and his strong, bald head had a dull glow, like old ivory. His wife, a big, broad and placid woman, was dressed richly, but in keeping with her age. Complicated, but light, transparent, and innocently immodest was the dress of his daughter, tall and slender, with magnificent hair gracefully combed; her breath was sweet with violet-scented tablets, and she had a number of tiny and most delicate pink dimples near her lips and between her slightly-powdered shoulder blades. . . .

The dinner lasted two whole hours, and was followed by dances in the dancing hall, while the men—the Gentleman from San Francisco among them—made their way to the refreshment-bar, where Negroes in red jackets and with eyeballs like shelled hard-boiled eggs, waited on them. There, with their feet on tables, smoking Havana cigars, and drinking themselves purple in the face, they settled the destinies of nations on the basis of the latest political and stock-exchange news. Outside, the ocean tossed up black mountains with a thud; and the snow-storm hissed furiously in the rigging grown heavy with slush; the ship trembled in every limb, struggling with the storm and ploughing with difficulty the shifting and seething mountainous masses that threw far and high their foaming tails; the siren groaned in agony, choked by storm and fog; the watchmen in their towers froze and almost went out of their minds under the superhuman stress of attention. Like the gloomy and sultry mass of the inferno, like its last, ninth circle, was the submersed womb of the steamer, where monstrous furnaces yawned with red-hot open jaws, and emitted deep, hooting sounds, and where the stokers, stripped to the waist, and purple with reflected flames, bathed in their own dirty, acid sweat. And here, in the refreshment-bar, carefree men, with their feet, encased in dancing shoes, on the table, sipped cognac and liqueurs, swam in waves of spiced smoke, and exchanged subtle remarks, while in the dancing-hall everything sparkled and radiated light, warmth and joy. The couples now turned around in a waltz, now swayed in the tango; and the music, sweetly shameless and sad, persisted in its ceaseless entreaties. . . . There were many persons of note in this magnificent crowd: an ambassador, a dry, modest old man; a great millionaire, shaved, tall, of an indefinite age, who, in his old-fashioned dress-coat, looked like a prelate; also a famous Spanish writer, and an international belle, already slightly faded and of dubious morals. There was also among them a loving pair, exquisite and refined, whom everybody watched with curiosity and who did not conceal their bliss; he danced only with her, sang—with great skill—only to her accompaniment, and they were so charming, so graceful. The captain alone knew that they had been hired by the company at a good salary to play at love, and that they had been sailing now on one, now on another steamer, for quite a long time.

In Gibraltar everybody was gladdened by the sun, and by the weather which was like early Spring. A new passenger appeared aboard the "Atlantis" and aroused everybody's interest. It was the crown-prince of an Asiatic state, who traveled incognito, a small man, very nimble, though looking as if made of wood, broad-faced, narrow-eyed, in gold-rimmed glasses, somewhat disagreeable because of his long moustache, which was sparse like that of a corpse, but otherwise—charming, plain, modest. In the Mediterranean the breath of winter was again felt. The seas were heavy and motley like a peacock's tail and the waves stirred up by the gay gusts of the tramontane, tossed their white crests under a sparkling and perfectly clear sky. Next morning, the sky grew paler and the skyline misty. Land was near. Then Ischia and Capri came in sight, and one could descry, through an opera-glass, Naples, looking like pieces of sugar strewn at the foot of an indistinct dove-colored mass, and above them, a snow-covered chain of distant mountains. The decks were crowded, many ladies and gentlemen put on light fur-coats; Chinese servants, bandy-legged youths—with pitch black braids down to the heels and with girlish, thick eyelashes,—always quiet and speaking in a whisper, were carrying to the foot of the staircases, plaid wraps, canes, and crocodile-leather valises and handbags. The daughter of the Gentleman from San Francisco stood near the prince, who, by a happy chance, had been introduced to her the evening before, and feigned to be looking steadily at something far-off, which he was pointing out to her, while he was, at the same time, explaining something, saying something rapidly and quietly. He was so small that he looked like a boy among other men, and he was not handsome at all. And then there was something strange about him; his glasses, derby and coat were most commonplace, but there was something horse-like in the hair of his sparse moustache, and the thin, tanned skin of his flat face looked as though it were somewhat stretched and varnished. But the girl listened to him, and so great was her excitement that she could hardly grasp the meaning of his words, her heart palpitated with incomprehensible rapture and with pride that he was standing and speaking with her and nobody else. Everything about him was different; his dry hands, his clean skin, under which flowed ancient kingly blood, even his light shoes and his European dress, plain, but singularly tidy—everything hid an inexplicable fascination and engendered thoughts of love. And the Gentleman from San Francisco, himself, in a silk-hat, gray leggings, patent leather shoes, kept eyeing the famous beauty who was standing near him, a tall, stately blonde, with eyes painted according to the latest Parisian fashion, and a tiny, bent peeled-off pet-dog, to whom she addressed herself. And the daughter, in a kind of vague perplexity, tried not to notice him.

Like all wealthy Americans he was very liberal when traveling, and believed in the complete sincerity and good-will of those who so painstakingly fed him, served him day and night, anticipating his slightest desire, protected him from dirt and disturbance, hauled things for him, hailed carriers, and delivered his luggage to hotels. So it was everywhere, and it had to be so at Naples. Meanwhile, Naples grew and came nearer. The musicians, with their shining brass instruments, had already formed a group on the deck, and all of a sudden deafened everybody with the triumphant sounds of a ragtime march. The giant captain, in his full uniform appeared on the bridge and like a gracious Pagan idol, waved his hands to the passengers,—and it seemed to the Gentleman from San Francisco,—as it did to all the rest,—that for him alone thundered the march, so greatly loved by proud America, and that him alone did the captain congratulate on the safe arrival. And when the "Atlantis" had finally entered the port and all its many-decked mass leaned against the quay, and the gang-plank began to rattle heavily,—what a crowd of porters, with their assistants, in caps with golden galloons, what a crowd of various boys and husky ragamuffins with pads of colored postal cards attacked the Gentleman from San Francisco, offering their services! With kindly contempt he grinned at these beggars, and, walking towards the automobile of the hotel where the prince might stop, muttered between his teeth, now in English, now in Italian—"Go away! Via . . ."

Immediately, life at Naples began to follow a set routine. Early in the morning breakfast was served in the gloomy dining-room, swept by a wet draught from the open windows looking upon a stony garden, while outside the sky was cloudy and cheerless, and a crowd of guides swarmed at the door of the vestibule. Then came the first smiles of the warm roseate sun, and from the high suspended balcony, a broad vista unfolded itself: Vesuvius, wrapped to its base in radiant morning vapors; the pearly ripple, touched to silver, of the bay, the delicate outline of Capri in the skyline; tiny asses dragging two-wheeled buggies along the soft, sticky embankment, and detachments of little soldiers marching somewhere to the tune of cheerful and defiant music.

Next on the day's program was a slow automobile ride along crowded, narrow, and damp corridors of streets, between high, many-windowed buildings. It was followed by visits to museums, lifelessly clean and lighted evenly and pleasantly, but as though with the dull light cast by snow;—then to churches, cold, smelling of wax, always alike; a majestic entrance, closed by a ponderous, leather curtain, and inside—a vast void, silence, quiet flames of seven-branched candlesticks, sending forth a red glow from where they stood at the farther end, on the bedecked altar,—a lonely, old woman lost among the dark wooden benches, slippery grave-stones under the feet, and somebody's "Descent from the Cross," infallibility famous. At one o'clock— luncheon, on the mountain of San-Martius, where at noon the choicest people gathered, and where the daughter of the Gentleman from San Francisco once almost fainted with joy, because it seemed to her that she saw the Prince in the hall, although she had learned from the newspapers that he had temporarily left for Rome. At five o'clock it was customary to take tea at the hotel, in a smart *salon,* where it was far too warm because of the carpets and the blazing fireplaces; and then came dinner-time—and again did the mighty, commanding voice of the gong resound throughout the building, again did silk rustle and the mirrors reflect files of ladies in low-necked dresses ascending the staircases, and again the splendid palatial dining hall opened with broad hospitality, and again the musicians' jackets formed red patches on the estrade, and the black figures of the waiters swarmed around the maître-l'hôtel, who, with extraordinary skill, poured a thick pink soup into plates. . . As everywhere, the dinner was the crown of the day. People dressed for it as for a wedding, and so abundant was it in food, wines, mineral waters, sweets and fruits, that about eleven o'clock in the evening chamber-maids would carry to all the rooms hot-water bags.

That year, however, December did not happen to be a very propitious one. The doormen were abashed when people spoke to them about the weather, and shrugged their shoulders guiltily, mumbling that they could not recollect such a year, although, to tell the truth, it was not the first year they mumbled those words, usually adding that "things are terrible everywhere"; that unprecedented showers and storms had broken out on the Riviera, that it was snowing in Athens, that Aetna, too, was all blocked up with snow, and glowed brightly at night, and that tourists were fleeing from Palermo to save themselves from the cold spell. . . .

That winter, the morning sun daily deceived Naples; toward noon the sky would invariably grow gray, and a light rain would begin to fall, growing thicker and duller. Then the palms at the hotel-porch glistened dis-

agreeably like wet tin, the town appeared exceptionally dirty and congested,
the museums too monotonous, the cigars of the drivers in their rubber rain-
coats, which flattened in the wind like wings, intolerably stinking, and the
energetic flapping of their whips over their thin-necked nags—obviously false.
The shoes of the signors, who cleaned the street-car tracks, were in a frightful state, the women who splashed in the mud, with black hair unprotected
from the rain, were ugly and short legged, and the humidity mingled with
the foul smell of rotting fish, that came from the foaming sea, was simply
disheartening. And so, early-morning quarrels began to break out between
the Gentleman from San Francisco and his wife; and their daughter now
grew pale and suffered from headaches, and now became animated, enthusiastic over everything, and at such times was lovely and beautiful. Beautiful
were the tender, complex feelings which her meeting with the ungainly
man aroused in her,—the man in whose veins flowed unusual blood, for
after all, it does not matter what in particular stirs up a maiden's soul: money,
or fame, or nobility of birth. . . . Everybody assured the tourists that it was
quite different at Sorrento and on Capri, that lemon-trees were blossoming
there, that it was warmer and sunnier there, the morals purer, and the wine
less adulterated. And the family from San Francisco decided to set out with
all their luggage for Capri. They planned to settle down at Sorrento, but first
to visit the island, tread the stones where stood Tiberius's palaces, examine
the fabulous wonders of the Blue Grotto, and listen to the bagpipes of
Abruzzi, who roam about the island during the whole month preceding
Christmas and sing the praises of the Madonna.

On the day of departure—a very memorable day for the family from San
Francisco—the sun did not appear even in the morning. A heavy winter fog
covered Vesuvius down to its very base and hung like a gray curtain low over
the leaden surge of the sea, hiding it completely at a distance of half a mile.
Capri was completely out of sight, as though it had never existed on this
earth. And the little steamboat which was making for the island tossed and
pitched so fiercely that the family lay prostrated on the sofas in the miserable cabin of the little steamer, with their feet wrapped in plaids and their
eyes shut because of their nausea. The older lady suffered, as she thought,
most; several times she was overcome with sea-sickness, and it seemed to her
then she was dying, but the chambermaid, who repeatedly brought her the
basin, and who for many years, in heat and in cold, had been tossing on these
waves, ever on the alert, ever kindly to all,—the chambermaid only laughed.
The lady's daughter was frightfully pale and kept a slice of lemon between
her teeth. Not even the hope of an unexpected meeting with the prince at
Sorrento, where he planned to arrive on Christmas, served to cheer her. The
Gentleman from San Francisco, who was lying on his back, dressed in a
large overcoat and a big cap, did not loosen his jaws throughout the voyage.
His face grew dark, his moustache white, and his head ached heavily; for

the last few days, because of the bad weather, he had drunk far too much in the evenings.

And the rain kept on beating against the rattling window panes, and water dripped down from them on the sofas; the howling wind attacked the masts, and sometimes, aided by a heavy sea, it laid the little steamer on its side, and then something below rolled about with a rattle.

While the steamer was anchored at Castellamare and Sorrento, the situation was more cheerful; but even here the ship rolled terribly, and the coast with all its precipices, gardens and pines, with its pink and white hotels and hazy mountains clad in curling verdure, flew up and down as if it were on swings. The rowboats hit against the sides of the steamer, the sailors and the deck passengers shouted at the top of their voices, and somewhere a baby screamed as if it were being crushed to pieces. A wet wind blew through the door, and from a wavering barge flying the flag of the Hotel Royal, an urchin kept on unwearyingly shouting "Kgoyal-al! Hotel Kgoyal-al! . . ." inviting tourists. And the Gentleman from San Francisco felt like the old man that he was,—and it was with weariness and animosity that he thought of all these "Royals," "Splendids," "Excelsiors," and of all those greedy bugs, reeking with garlic, who are called Italians. Once, during a stop, having opened his eyes and half-risen from the sofa, he noticed in the shadow of the rock beach a heap of stone huts, miserable, mildewed through and through, huddled close by the water, near boats, rags, tin-boxes, and brown fishing nets,—and as he remembered that this was the very Italy he had come to enjoy, he felt a great despair. . . . Finally, in twilight, the black mass of the island began to grow nearer, as though burrowed through at the base by red fires, the wind grew softer, warmer, more fragrant; from the dock-lanterns huge golden serpents flowed down the tame waves which undulated like black oil. . . . Then, suddenly, the anchor rumbled and fell with a splash into the water, the fierce yells of the boatman filled the air,—and at once everyone's heart grew easy. The electric lights in the cabin grew more brilliant, and there came a desire to eat, drink, smoke, move. . . . Ten minutes later the family from San Francisco found themselves in a large ferry-boat; fifteen minutes later they trod the stones of the quay, and then seated themselves in a small lighted car, which, with a buzz, started to ascend the slope, while vineyard stakes, half-ruined stone fences, and wet, crooked lemon-trees, in spots shielded by straw sheds, with their glimmering orange-colored fruit and thick glossy foliage, were sliding down past the open car windows. . . . After rain, the earth smells sweetly in Italy, and each of her islands has a fragrance of its own.

The Island of Capri was dark and damp on that evening. But for a while it grew animated and lit up, in spots, as always in the hour of the steamer's arrival. On the top of the hill, at the station of the *funiculaire,* there stood already the crowd of those whose duty it was to receive properly the Gentleman from San Francisco. The rest of the tourists hardly deserved any attention. There were a few Russians, who had settled on Capri, untidy, absent-minded people, absorbed in their bookish thoughts, spectacled, bearded, with the collars of their cloth overcoats raised. There was also a company of long-legged, long-necked, round-headed German youths in Tyrolean costume, and with linen bags on their backs, who need no one's services, are everywhere at home, and are by no means liberal in their expenses. The Gentleman from San Francisco, who kept quietly aloof from both the Russians and the Germans, was noticed at once. He and his ladies were hurriedly helped from the car, a man ran before them to show them the way, and they were again surrounded by boys and those thickset Caprean peasant women, who carry on their heads the trucks and valises of wealthy travelers. Their tiny, wooden, foot-stools rapped against the pavement of the small square, which looked almost like an opera square, and over which an electric lantern swung in the damp wind; the gang of urchins whistled like birds and turned somersaults, and as the Gentleman from San Francisco passed among them, it all looked like a stage scene; he went first under some kind of mediaeval archway, beneath houses huddled close together, and then along a steep echoing lane which led to the hotel entrance, flooded with light. At the left, a palm tree raised its tuft above the flat roofs, and higher up, blue stars burned in the black sky. And again things looked as though it was in honor of the guests from San Francisco that the stony damp little town had awakened on its rocky island in the Mediterranean, that it was they who had made the owner of the hotel so happy and beaming, and that the Chinese gong, which had sounded the call to dinner through all the floors as soon as they entered the lobby, had been waiting only for them.

The owner, an elegant young man, who met the guests with a polite and exquisite bow, for a moment startled the Gentleman from San Francisco. Having caught sight of him, the Gentleman from San Francisco suddenly recollected that on the previous night, among other confused images which disturbed his sleep, he had seen this very man. His vision resembled the hotel keeper to a dot, had the same head, the same hair, shining and scrupulously combed, and wore the same frock-coat with rounded skirts. Amazed, he almost stopped for a while. But as there was not a mustard-seed of what is called mysticism in his heart, his surprise subsided at once; in passing the corridor of the hotel he jestingly told his wife and daughter about this strange coincidence of dream and reality. His daughter alone glanced at him with alarm, longing suddenly compressed her heart, and such a strong feeling of solitude on this strange, dark island seized her that she almost began to cry. But, as usual, she said nothing about her feeling to her father.

A person of high dignity, Rex XVII, who had spent three entire weeks on Capri, had just left the island, and the guests from San Francisco were given the apartments he had occupied. At their disposal was put the most handsome and skillful chambermaid, a Belgian, with a figure rendered slim and firm by her corset, and with a starched cap, shaped like a small, indented crown; and they had the privilege of being served by the most well-appearing and portly footman, a black, fiery-eyed Sicilian, and by the quickest waiter, the small, stout Luigi, who was a fiend at cracking jokes and had changed many places in his life. Then the maître-d'hôtel, a Frenchman, gently rapped at the door of the American gentleman's room. He came to ask whether the gentleman and the ladies would dine, and in case they would, which he did not doubt, to report that there was to be had that day lobsters, roast beef, asparagus, pheasants, etc., etc.

The floor was still rocking under the Gentleman from San Francisco—so sea-sick had the wretched Italian steamer made him—yet, he slowly, though awkwardly, shut the window which had banged when the maître-d'hôtel entered, and which let in the smell of the distant kitchen and wet flowers in the garden, and answered with slow distinctiveness, that they would dine, that their table must be placed farther away from the door, in the depth of the hall, that they would have local wine and champagne, moderately dry and but slightly cooled. The maître-d'hôtel approved the words of the guest in various intonations, which all meant, however, only one thing; there is and can be no doubt that the desires of the Gentleman from San Francisco are right, and that everything would be carried out, in exact conformity with his words. At last he inclined his head and asked delicately:

"Is that all, sir?"

And having received in reply a slow "Yes," he added that to-day they were going to have the tarantella danced in the vestibule by Carmella and Giuseppe, known to all Italy and to "the entire world of tourists."

"I saw her on post-card pictures," said the Gentleman from San Francisco in a tone of voice which expressed nothing. "And this Giuseppe, is he her husband?"

"Her cousin, sir," answered the maître-d'hôtel.

The Gentleman from San Francisco tarried a little, evidently musing on something, but said nothing, then dismissed him with a nod of his head.

Then he started making preparations, as though for a wedding: he turned on all the electric lamps, and filled the mirrors with reflections of light and the sheen of furniture, and opened trunks; he began to shave and to wash himself, and the sound of his bell was heard every minute in the corridor, crossing with other impatient calls which came from the rooms of his wife and daughter. Luigi, in his red apron, with the ease characteristic of stout people, made funny faces at the chambermaids, who were dashing by with tile buckets in their hands, making them laugh until the tears came. He rolled head over heels to the door, and, tapping with his knuckles, asked with feigned timidity and with an obsequiousness which he knew how to render idiotic:

"Ha sonata, Signore?" (Did you ring, sir?)

And from behind the door a slow, grating, insultingly polite voice, answered:

"Yes, come in."

What did the Gentleman from San Francisco think and feel on that evening forever memorable to him? It must be said frankly; absolutely nothing exceptional. The trouble is that everything on this earth appears too simple. Even had he felt anything deep in his heart, a premonition that something was going to happen, he would have imagined that it was not going to happen so soon, at least not at once. Besides, as is usually the case just after sea-sickness is over, he was very hungry, and he anticipated with real delight the first spoonful of soup, and the first gulp of wine; therefore, he was performing the habitual process of dressing, in a state of excitement which left no time for reflection.

Having shaved and washed himself, and dexterously put in place a few false teeth, he then, standing before the mirror, moistened and vigorously plastered what was left of his thick pearly-colored hair, close to his tawny-yellow skull. Then he put on, with some effort, a tight-fitting undershirt of cream-colored silk, fitted tight to his strong, aged body with its waist swelling out because of an abundant diet; and he pulled black silk socks and patent-leather dancing shoes on his dry feet with their fallen arches. Squatting down, he set right his black trousers, drawn high by means of silk suspenders, adjusted his snow-white shirt with its bulging front, put the buttons into the shining cuffs, and began the painful process of hunting up the front button under the hard collar. The floor was still swaying under him, the tips of his fingers hurt terribly, the button at times painfully pinched the flabby skin in the depression under his Adam's apple, but he persevered, and finally, with his eyes shining from the effort, his face blue because of the narrow collar which squeezed his neck, he triumphed over the difficulties—and all exhausted, he sat down before the pier-glass, his reflected image repeating itself in all the mirrors.

"It's terrible!" he muttered, lowering his strong, bald head and making no effort to understand what was terrible; then, with a careful and habitual gesture, he examined his short fingers with gouty callosities in the joints, and their large, convex, almond-colored nails, and repeated with conviction, "It's terrible!"

But here the stentorian voice of the second gong sounded throughout the house, as in a heathen temple. And having risen hurriedly, the Gentleman from San Francisco drew his tie more taut and firm around his collar, and pulled together his abdomen by means of a tight waistcoat, put on a dinner-coat, set to rights the cuffs, and for the last time he examined himself in the mirror. . . . This Carmella, tawny as a mulatto, with fiery eyes, in a dazzling dress in which orange-color predominated, must be an extraordinary dancer,

—it occurred to him. And cheerfully leaving his room, he walked on the carpet, to his wife's chamber, and asked in a loud tone of voice if they would be long.

"In five minutes, papa!" answered cheerfully and gaily a girlish voice. "I am combing my hair."

"Very well," said the Gentleman from San Francisco.

And thinking of her wonderful hair, streaming on her shoulders, he slowly walked down along corridors and staircases, spread with red velvet carpets,—looking for the library. The servants he met hugged the walls, and he walked by as if not noticing them. An old lady, late for dinner, already bowed with years, with milk-white hair, yet bare-necked, in a light-gray silk dress, hurried at top speed, but she walked in a mincing, funny, hen-like manner, and he easily overtook her. At the glass door of the dining hall where the guests had already gathered and started eating, he stopped before the table crowded with boxes of matches and Egyptian cigarettes, took a great Manilla cigar, and threw three liras on the table. On the winter veranda he glanced into the open window; a stream of soft air came to him from the darkness, the top of the old palm loomed up before him afar-off, with its boughs spread among the stars and looking gigantic, and the distant even noise of the sea reached his ear. In the library-room, snug, quiet, a German in round silver-bowed glasses and with crazy, wondering eyes—stood turning the rustling pages of a newspaper. Having coldly eyed him, the Gentleman from San Francisco seated himself in a deep leather arm-chair near a lamp under a green hood, put on his pince-nez and twitching his head because of the collar which choked him, hid himself from view behind a newspaper. He glanced at a few headlines, read a few lines about the interminable Balkan war, and turned over the page with an habitual gesture. Suddenly, the lines blazed up with a glassy sheen, the veins of his neck swelled, his eyes bulged out, the pince-nez fell from his nose. . . . He dashed forward, wanted to swallow air—and made a wild, rattling noise; his lower jaw dropped, dropped on his shoulder and began to shake, the shirt-front bulged out,—and the whole body, writhing, the heels catching in the carpet, slowly fell to the floor in a desperate struggle with an invisible foe. . . .

Had not the German been in the library, this frightful accident would have been quickly and adroitly hushed up. The body of the Gentleman from San Francisco would have been rushed away to some far corner—and none of the guests would have known of the occurrence. But the German dashed out of the library with outcries and spread the alarm all over the house. And many rose from their meal, upsetting chairs, others growing pale, ran along the corridors to the library, and the question, asked in many languages, was heard: "What is it? What has happened?" And no one was able to answer it clearly, no one understood anything, for until this very day men still wonder most at death and most absolutely refuse to believe in it. The owner rushed from one guest to another, trying to keep back those who were running and soothe them with hasty assurances, that this was nothing, a mere trifle, a little fainting-spell by which a Gentleman from San Francisco had been overcome. But no one listened to him, many saw how the footman and waiters tore from the gentleman his tie, collar, waistcoat, the rumpled evening coat, and even—for no visible reason—the dancing shoes from his black silk-covered feet. And he kept on writhing. He obstinately struggled with death, he did not want to yield to the foe that attacked him so unexpectedly and grossly. He shook his head, emitted rattling sounds like one throttled, and turned up his eye-balls like one drunk with wine. When he was hastily brought into Number 43,—the smallest, worst, dampest, and coldest room at the end of the lower corridor,—and stretched on the bed,—his daughter came running, her hair falling over her shoulders, the skirts of her dressing-gown thrown open, with bare breasts raised by the corset. Then came his wife, big, heavy, almost completely dressed for dinner, her mouth round with terror.

In a quarter of an hour all was again in good trim at the hotel. But the evening was irreparably spoiled. Some tourists returned to the dining-hall and finished their dinner, but they kept silent, and it was obvious that they took the accident as a personal insult, while the owner went from one guest to another, shrugging his shoulders in impotent and appropriate irritation, feeling like one innocently victimized, assuring everyone that he understood perfectly well "how disagreeable this is," and giving his word that he would take all "the measures that are within his power" to do away with the trouble. Yet it was found necessary to cancel the tarantella. The unnecessary electric lamps were put out, most of the guests left for the beer-hall, and it grew so quiet in the hotel that one could distinctly hear the tick-tock of the clock in the lobby, where a lonely parrot babbled something in its expressionless manner, stirring in its cage, and trying to fall asleep with its paw clutching the upper perch in a most absurd manner. The Gentleman from San Francisco lay stretched in a cheap iron bed, under coarse woolen blankets, dimly lighted by a single gas-burner fastened in the ceiling. An ice-bag slid down on his wet, cold forehead. His blue, already lifeless face grew gradually cold; the hoarse, rattling noise which came from his mouth, lighted by the glimmer of the golden fillings, gradually weakened. It was not the Gentleman from San Francisco that was emitting those weird sounds; he was no more,—someone else did it. His wife and daughter, the doctor, the servants were standing and watching him apathetically. Suddenly, that which they expected and feared happened. The rattling sound ceased. And slowly, slowly, in everybody's sight a pallor stole over the face of the dead man, and his features began to grow thinner and more luminous, beautiful with the beauty that he had long shunned and that became him well. . . .

The proprietor entered. "Gia é morto," whispered the doctor to him. The proprietor shrugged his shoulders indifferently. The older lady, with tears slowly running down her cheeks, approached him and said timidly that now the deceased must be taken to his room.

"O no, madam," answered the proprietor politely, but without any amiability and not in English, but in French. He was no longer interested in the trifle which the guests from San Francisco could now leave at his cash-office. "This is absolutely impossible," he said, and added in the form of an explanation that he valued this apartment highly, and if he satisfied her desire, this would become known over Capri and the tourists would begin to avoid it.

The girl, who had looked at him strangely, sat down, and with her handkerchief to her mouth, began to cry. Her mother's tears dried up at once, and her face flared up. She raised her tone, began to demand, using her own language and still unable to realize that the respect for her was absolutely gone. The proprietor, with polite dignity, cut her short: "If madam does not like the ways of this hotel, he dare not detain her." And he firmly announced that the corpse must leave the hotel that very day, at dawn, that the police had been informed, that an agent would call immediately and attend to all the necessary formalities. . . . "Is it possible to get on Capri at least a plain coffin?" madam asks. . . . Unfortunately not; by no means, and as for making one, there will be no time. It will be necessary to arrange things some other way. . . . For instance, he gets English soda-water in big, oblong boxes. . . . The partitions could be taken out from such a box. . . .

By night, the whole hotel was asleep. A waiter opened the window in Number 43—it faced a corner of the garden where a consumptive banana-tree grew in the shadow of a high stone wall set with broken glass on the top—turned out the electric light, locked the door, and went away. The deceased remained alone in the darkness. Blue stars looked down at him from the black sky, the cricket in the wall started his melancholy, care-free song. In the dimly lighted corridor two chambermaids were sitting on the window-sill, mending something. Then Luigi came in, in slippered feet, with a heap of clothes on his arm.

"*Pronto?*"—he asked in a stage whisper, as if greatly concerned, directing his eyes toward the terrible door, at the end of the corridor. And waving his free hand in that direction, "*Partenza!*" he cried out in a whisper, as if seeing off a train,—and the chambermaids, choking with noiseless laughter, put their heads on each other's shoulders.

Then, stepping softly, he ran to the door, slightly rapped at it, and inclining his ear, asked most obsequiously in a subdued tone of voice:

"*Ha sonata, Signore?*"

And, squeezing his throat and thrusting his lower jaw forward, he answered himself in a drawling, grating, sad voice, as if from behind the door:

"Yes, come in. . . ."

At dawn, when the window panes in Number 43 grew white, and a damp wind rustled in the leaves of the banana-tree, when the pale-blue morning sky rose and stretched over Capri, and the sun, rising from behind the distant mountains of Italy, touched into gold the pure, clearly outlined summit of Monte Solaro, when the masons, who mended the paths for the tourists on the island, went out to their work,—an oblong box was brought to room Number 43. Soon it grew very heavy and painfully pressed against the knees of the assistant doorman who was conveying it in a one-horse carriage along the white highroad which winded on the slopes, among stone fences and vineyards, all the way down to the seacoast. The driver, a sickly man, with red eyes, in an old short-sleeved coat and in worn-out shoes, had a drunken headache; all night long he had played dice at the eatinghouse—and he kept on flogging his vigorous little horse. According to Sicilian custom, the animal was heavily burdened with decorations: all sorts of bells tinkled on the bridle, which was ornamented with colored woolen fringes; there were bells also on the edge of the high saddle; and a bird's feather, two feet long, stuck in the trimmed crest of the horse, nodded up and down. The driver kept silence: he was depressed by his wrongheadedness and vices, by the fact that last night he had lost in gambling all the copper coins with which his pockets had been full,—neither more nor less than four liras and forty centesimi. But on such a morning, when the air is so fresh, and the sea stretches nearby, and the sky is serene with a morning serenity,—a headache passes rapidly and one becomes carefree again. Besides, the driver was also somewhat cheered by the unexpected earnings which the Gentleman from San Francisco, who bumped his dead head against the walls of the box behind his back, had brought him. The little steamer, shaped like a great bug, which lay far down, on the tender and brilliant blue, filling to the brim the Neapolitan bay, was blowing the signal of departure,—and the sounds swiftly resounded all over Capri. Every bend of the island, every ridge and stone was seen as distinctly as if there were no air between heaven and earth. Near the quay the driver was overtaken by the head doorman who conducted in an auto the wife and daughter of the Gentleman from San Francisco. Their faces were pale and their eyes sunken with tears and a sleepless night. And in ten minutes the little steamer was again stirring up the water and picking its way toward Sorrento and Castellamare, carrying the American family away from Capri forever. . . . Meanwhile, peace and rest were restored on the island.

Two thousand years ago there had lived on that island a man who became utterly entangled in his own brutal and filthy actions. For some unknown reason he usurped the rule over millions of men and found himself bewildered by the absurdity of this power, while the fear that someone might kill him unawares, made him commit deeds inhuman beyond all measure. And mankind has forever retained his memory, and those who, taken together, now rule the world, as incomprehensibly and, essentially, as cruelly as he did,

—come from all the corners of the earth to look at the remnants of the stone house he inhabited, which stands on one of the steepest cliffs of the island. On that wonderful morning the tourists, who had come to Capri for precisely that purpose, were still asleep in the various hotels, but tiny long-eared asses under red saddles were already being led to the hotel entrances. Americans and Germans, men and women, old and young, after having arisen and breakfasted heartily, were to scramble on them, and the old beggar-women of Capri, with sticks in their sinewy hands, were again to run after them along stony, mountainous paths, all the way up to the summit of Monte Tiberia. The dead old man from San Francisco, who had planned to keep the tourists company but who had, instead, only scared them by reminding them of death, was already shipped to Naples, and soothed by this, the travelers slept soundly, and silence reigned over the island. The stores in the little town were still closed, with the exception of the fish and greens market on the tiny square. Among the plain people who filled it, going about their business, stood idly by, as usual, Lorenzo, a tall old boatman, a carefree reveller and once a handsome man, famous all over Italy, who had many times served as a model for painters. He had brought and already sold—for a song —two big sea-crawfish, which he had caught at night and which were rustling in the apron of Don Cataldo, the cook of the hotel where the family from San Francisco had been lodged,—and now Lorenzo could stand calmly until nightfall, wearing princely airs, showing off his rags, his clay pipe with its long reed mouth-piece, and his red woolen cap, tilted on one ear. Meanwhile, among the precipices of Monte Solare, down the ancient Phoenician road, cut in the rocks in the form of a gigantic staircase, two Abruzzi mountaineers were coming from Anacapri. One carried under his leather mantle a bagpipe, a large goat's skin with two pipes; the other, something in the nature of a wooden flute. They walked, and the entire country, joyous, beautiful, sunny, stretched below them; the rocky shoulders of the island, which lay at their feet, the fabulous blue in which it swam, the shining morning vapors over the sea westward, beneath the dazzling sun, and the wavering masses of Italy's mountains, both near and distant, whose beauty human word is powerless to render. . . . Midway they slowed up. Overshadowing the road stood, in a grotto of the rock wall of Monte Solare, the Holy Virgin, all radiant, bathed in the warmth and the splendor of the sun. The rust of her snow-white plaster-of-Paris vestures and queenly crown was touched into gold, and there were meekness and mercy in her eyes raised toward the heavens, toward the eternal and beatific abode of her thrice-blessed Son. They bared their heads, applied the pipes to their lips, and praises flowed on, candid and humbly-joyous, praises to the sun and the morning, to Her, the Immaculate Intercessor for all who suffer in this evil and beautiful world, and to Him who had been born of her womb in the cavern of Bethlehem, in a hut of lowly shepherds in distant Judea.

As for the body of the dead Gentleman from San Francisco, it was on its way home, to the shores of the New World, where a grave awaited it. Having undergone many humiliations and suffered much human neglect, having wandered about a week from one port warehouse to another, it finally got on that same famous ship which had brought the family, such a short while ago and with such a pomp, to the Old World. But now he was concealed from the living: in a tar-coated coffin he was lowered deep into the black hold of the steamer. And again did the ship set out on its far sea journey. At night it sailed by the island of Capri, and, for those who watched it from the island, its lights slowly disappearing in the dark sea, it seemed infinitely sad. But there, on the vast steamer, in its lighted halls shining with brilliance and marble, a noisy dancing party was going on, as usual.

On the second and the third night there was again a ball—this time in mid-ocean, during the furious storm sweeping over the ocean, which roared like a funeral mass and rolled up mountainous seas fringed with mourning silvery foam. The Devil, who from the rocks of Gibraltar, the stony gateway of two worlds, watched the ship vanish into night and storm, could hardly distinguish from behind the snow the innumerable fiery eyes of the ship. The Devil was as huge as a cliff, but the ship was even bigger, a many-storied, many-stacked giant, created by the arrogance of the New Man with the old heart. The blizzard battered the ship's rigging and its broad-necked stacks, whitened with snow, but it remained firm, majestic—and terrible. On its uppermost deck, amidst a snowy whirlwind there loomed up in loneliness the cozy, dimly lighted cabin, where, only half awake, the vessel's ponderous pilot reigned over its entire mass, bearing the semblance of a pagan idol. He heard the wailing moans and the furious screeching of the siren, choked by the storm, but the nearness of that which was behind the wall and which in the last account was incomprehensible to him, removed his fears. He was reassured by the thought of the large, armored cabin, which now and then was filled with mysterious rumbling sounds and with the dry creaking of blue fires, flaring up and exploding around a man with a metallic headpiece, who was eagerly catching the indistinct voices of the vessels that hailed him, hundreds of miles away. At the very bottom, in the under-water womb of the "Atlantis," the huge masses of tanks and various other machines, their steel parts shining dully, wheezed with steam and oozed hot water and oil; here was the gigantic kitchen, heated by hellish furnaces, where the motion of the vessel was being generated; here seethed those forces terrible in their concentration which were transmitted to the keel of the vessel, and into that endless round tunnel, which was lighted by electricity, and looked like a gigantic cannon barrel, where slowly, with a punctuality and certainty that crushes the human soul, a colossal shaft was revolving in its oily nest, like a living monster stretching in its lair. As for the middle part of the "Atlantis," its warm, luxurious cabins, dining-rooms, and halls, they radiated light and joy, were astir with a chattering smartly-dressed crowd, were filled with the fragrance of fresh flowers, and resounded with a string orchestra. And again did the slender supple pair of hired lovers painfully turn and twist and at times clash convulsively amid the splendor of lights, silks, diamonds, and bare feminine shoulders: she—a sinfully modest pretty girl, with lowered eyelashes and an innocent hair-dressing, he—a tall, young man, with black hair, looking as if it were pasted, pale with powder, in most exquisite patent-leather shoes, in a narrow, long-skirted dresscoat,—a beautiful man resembling a leech. And no one knew that this couple had long since been weary of torturing themselves with a feigned beatific torture under the sounds of shamefully-melancholy music; nor did any one know what lay deep, deep, beneath them, on the very bottom of the hold, in the neighborhood of the gloomy and sultry maw of the ship, that heavily struggled with the ocean, the darkness, and the storm. . . .

Translated by A. Yarmolinsky

LEO N. TOLSTOI

Three Arshins of Land

or

How Much Land Does a Man Need? ❦

A woman came from the city, to visit her younger sister in the country. The elder was a city merchant's wife; the younger, a country mujik's. The two sisters drank tea together and talked. The older sister began to boast—to praise up her life in the city; how she lived roomily and elegantly, and went out, and how she dressed her children, and what rich things she had to eat and drink, and how she went to drive, and to walk, and to the theater.

The younger sister felt affronted, and began to deprecate the life of the merchant, and to set forth the advantages of her own,—that of the peasant.

"I wouldn't exchange my life for yours," says she. "Granted that we live coarsely, still we don't know what fear is. You live more elegantly; but you have to sell a great deal, else you find yourselves entirely sold. And the proverb runs, 'Loss is Gain's bigger brother.' It also happens, today you're rich, but tomorrow you're a beggar. But our mujiks' affairs are more reliable; the mujik's life is meager, but long; we may not be rich, but we have enough."

The elder sister began to say:

"Enough,—I should think so! So do pigs and calves! No fine dresses, no good society. How your goodman works! How you live in the dunghill! And so you will die and it will be the same thing with your children."

"Indeed," said the younger, "our affairs are all right. We live well. We truckle to no one, we stand in fear of no one. But you in the city all live in the midst of temptations; today it's all right; but tomorrow up comes some improper person, I fear, to tempt you, and tempts your khozyaïn either to cards, or to wine, or to women. And everything goes to ruin. Isn't it so?"

Pakhom, the "goodman," was listening on the oven, as the women discussed.

"That's true," says he, "the veritable truth. As we peasants from childhood turn up mother earth, so folly stays in our head, and does not depart. Our one trouble is,—so little land. If I only had as much land as I wanted, I shouldn't be afraid of any one—even of the Devil."

From *Popular Legends,* published by Thomas Y. Crowell Company.

The women drank up their tea, talked some more about dresses, put away the dishes, and went to bed.

But the Devil was sitting behind the oven; he heard everything. He was delighted because the peasant woman had induced her husband to boast with her; he had boasted that, if he had land enough, the Devil could not get him!

"All right," he thinks; "you and I'll have to fight it out. I will give you a lot of land. I'll get you through the land."

Pakhom's neighbor was a lady who owned a little estate. She had one hundred and twenty dessyatins.[1] For a long time she had never harmed the peasants in any way, living in peace with them. But lately she had installed a retired soldier as superintendent, and he worried the peasants with fines. No matter how careful Pakhom was, a horse would invade his neighbor's oat-field, or his cow would stray into her garden or the calves into the pasture. There was a fine for everything.

Pakhom paid, growled, beat his family, and in the course of the summer laid up much sin upon his soul because of the superintendent. He found relief only by keeping his cattle in the yard. He begrudged the fodder, but he was thus spared much anxiety.

In the winter the rumor spread that his neighbor meant to dispose of her land and that the superintendent thought of buying it. When the peasants heard this they were greatly troubled.

If the superintendent becomes the master, they judged, there will be no end to the fines.

They importuned the lady to sell the land to the community and not to the superintendent. As they promised to pay her more than the latter, she agreed. The peasants held a meeting, then met again, but came to no understanding. The Devil sowed dissensions. Finally they decided that each should buy land according to his means, and the owner consented again.

When Pakhom heard that a neighboring peasant had bought twenty dessyatins of the land, with time extension to pay one-half of the purchase price, he became envious. "They'll sell the whole land, and I'll go empty-handed." He consulted with his wife. "The peasants are buying land. We must get ten dessyatins," he said. They considered how to arrange the matter.

They had saved a hundred rubles. They sold a foal, one-half of their bee-hives, hired the son out as a laborer, and thus succeeded in scraping one-half of the money together.

Pakhom looked over a tract of land of fifteen dessyatins, with a grove, and negotiated with his neighbor. He contracted for the fifteen dessyatins and paid his earnest money. Then they drove to the city and made out the

[1] A dessyatin is about 2.7 acres.

deed. He paid one-half of the money and agreed to pay the rest in two years. Pakhom now had land.

He borrowed money from his brother-in-law, bought seed and sowed the purchased land. Everything came up beautifully. Inside of a year he was able to pay off his debts to the neighbor and to his brother-in-law. Pakhom was now a landowner in his own right. He cultivated his own ground, and cut his own pasturage. He was overjoyed. The grass had another look; different kinds of flowers seemed to bloom on it. Once upon a time this land had looked to him the same as any other, but now is was a specially blessed piece of God's earth.

Pakhom was enjoying life. Everything would be well now if the peasants only left his fields alone, if they did not let their cattle graze on his meadows. He admonished them in a friendly fashion. But they did not desist from driving their cows on his land, and at night the strangers' horses invaded his grain. Pakhom chased them and for a time did not lay it up against the peasants. Finally, however, he lost patience and made a complaint to the court. He knew very well, tho, that necessity forced the peasants to do this, not love of wrongdoing. Still, he thought, he would have to teach them a lesson, or they would graze his land bare. A good lesson might be useful.

With the help of the court he taught them more than one lesson; more than one peasant was fined. And so it happened that the peasants were in no amiable mood towards him and were eager to play tricks on him. He was soon at loggerheads with all his neighbors. His land had grown, but the confines of the community seemed all too narrow now.

One day, as he was seated at home, a traveling peasant asked for a lodging. Pakhom kept him over night, gave him plenty of meat and drink, inquired where he came from and talked of this and that. The peasant related that he was on the way from the lower Volga region, where he had been working. Many peasants had settled there. They were received into the community and ten dessyatins were allotted to each. Beautiful land! It made the heart feel glad to see it full of sheaves. A peasant had come there naked and poor, with empty hands, and now he had fifty dessyatins under wheat. Last year he sold his one crop of wheat for five thousand rubles.

Pakhom listened with delight. He thought: why plague oneself in this crowded section, if one can live fine elsewhere? I will sell my land and property and from the proceeds I will buy land on the lower Volga and start a farm. Here in this crowded corner there is nothing but quarreling. I will go and look things over for myself.

When summer came he started on his journey. He went by boat to Samara on the Volga, then four hundred versts[2] on foot. When he arrived at his journey's end he found things even as they had been reported to him. Ten

---

[2] A verst is approximately seven-tenths of a mile.

dessyatins were allotted to each person, and the mujiks were glad to receive the stranger into the community. If a man brought money with him he was welcome and could buy as much land as he pleased. Three rubles a dessyatin was the price for the best land.

When Pakhom had investigated everything, he returned home, sold his land at a profit, sold his homestead and cattle, took leave from his community, and, when the spring came around, he journeyed with his family to the new lands.

When he reached his destination with his family, Pakhom settled in a large village and registered in the community. Having treated the elders, he received his papers in good order. He had been taken into the community, and, in addition to the pasturage, land for five souls—fifty dessyatins in all—were allotted to him. He built a homestead and bought cattle. His allotment was twice as large as his former holdings. And what fertile land! He had enough of everything and could keep as many head of cattle as he wished.

In the beginning, while he was building and equipping his homestead, he was well satisfied. But after he had lived there a while he began to feel that the new lands were too narrow. The first year Pakhom sowed wheat on his allotted land. It came up bountifully, and this created a desire to have more land at his disposal. He drove over to the merchant and leased some land for a year. The seed yielded a plentiful harvest. Unfortunately the fields were quite far from the village and the gathered grain had to be carted for a distance of fifteen versts. He saw peasant traders in the neighborhood owning dairies and amassing wealth. How much better were it, thought Pakhom, to buy land instead of leasing it, and to start dairying. That would give me a well-rounded property, all in one hand.

Then he came across a peasant who owned five hundred dessyatins of land, but found himself ruined and was eager to dispose of his property at a low figure. They closed a deal. Pakhom was to pay fifteen hundred rubles, one-half down, one-half later.

About this time a traveling merchant stopped at Pakhom's farm to feed his horses. They drank tea and spoke of this and that. The merchant told him that he was on his way home from the land of the Bashkirs. He had bought land there, about five thousand dessyatins, and had paid one thousand rubles for it. Pakhom made inquiries. The merchant willingly gave information.

"Only one thing is needful," he explained, "and that is to do some favor to their chief. I distributed raiment and rugs among them, which cost me a hundred rubles, and I divided a chest of tea between them, and whoever wanted it had his fill of vodka. I got the dessyatin land for twenty copeks. Here is the deed. The land along the river and even on the steppes is wheat-growing land."

Pakhom made further inquiries.

"You couldn't walk the land through in a year," reported the merchant. "All this is Bashkir-land. The men are as simple as sheep; one could buy from them almost for nothing."

And Pakhom thought: "Why should I buy for my thousand rubles five hundred dessyatins of land and hang a debt around my neck, while for the same amount I can acquire immeasurable property."

Pakhom inquired the way to the land of the Bashkirs. As soon as he had seen the merchant off, he made ready for the journey. He left the land and the homestead in his wife's charge and took only one of his farm-hands along. In a neighboring city they bought a chest of tea, other presents, and some vodka, as the merchant had instructed them.

They rode and rode. They covered five hundred versts and on the seventh day they came into the land of the Bashkirs and found everything just as the merchant had described. On the riverside and in the steppes the Bashkirs live in kibitkas. They do not plow. They eat no bread. Cows and horses graze on the steppes. Foals are tied behind the tents, and mares are taken to them twice daily. They make kumyss out of mare's milk, and the women shake the kumyss to make cheese. The men drink kumyss and tea, eat mutton, and play the flute all day long. They are all fat and merry, and idle the whole summer through. Ignorant folk, they cannot speak Russian, but they were very friendly.

When they caught sight of Pakhom, the Bashkirs left their tents and surrounded him. An interpreter was at hand, whom Pakhom informed that he had come to buy land. The Bashkirs showed their joy and led Pakhom into their good tent. They bade him sit down on a fine rug, propped him up with downy cushions and treated him to tea and kumyss. They also slaughtered a sheep and offered him meat. Pakhom fetched from his tarantass the chest of tea and other presents and distributed them among the Bashkirs. The Bashkirs were overjoyed. They talked and talked among themselves and finally they ordered the interpreter to speak.

"They want me to tell you," said the interpreter, "that they have taken a liking to you. It is our custom to favor the guest in all possible ways and to return gifts for gifts. You have given us presents, now tell us what do you like of what we have so that we may give you presents also."

"Most of all I like land," replied Pakhom. "We're crowded where I am at home and everything is already under the plow. But you have good land and plenty of it. In all my born days I have never seen land like yours."

The Bashkirs were now talking again, and all at once it looked as though they were quarrelling. Pakhom asked why they were quarrelling. The interpreter replied:

"Some of them think that the chief should be consulted, and that no agreement ought to be made without him; but the others say it can be done without the chief just as well."

While the Bashkirs were yet arguing, a man with a hat of fox fur entered the tent. Everybody stopped talking and they all rose.

"This is the chief."

Pakhom immediately produced the best sleeping robe and five pounds of tea. The chief accepted the presents and sat down in the place of honor. The Bashkirs spoke to him. He listened, smiled and addressed Pakhom in Russian.

"Well," he said, "that can be done. Help yourself, wherever it suits you. There is plenty of land."

"How can I do this, tho," thought Pakhom. "Some official confirmation is necessary. Otherwise they say today, help yourself, but afterwards they may take it away again." And he said:

"Thank you for these good words. You have plenty of land, and I need but little. Only I must know what land belongs to me. It must be measured and I need some sort of a confirmation. For God's will rules over life and death. You are good people and you give me the land; but it may happen that your children will take it away again."

The chief laughed. "Surely this can be done," he agreed. "A confirmation so strong that it cannot be made stronger."

Pakhom replied: "I heard that a merchant had been here among you. You sold him land and gave him a deed. I should like to have it the same way."

The chief immediately understood. "This too can be done," he exclaimed. "We have a writer. We will drive to the city and have the seals put on."

"We have but one price: one thousand rubles a day."

Pakhom failed to comprehend what sort of measure a day would be. "How many dessyatins will that make?"

"That we cannot figure out. For one day we sell you as much land as you can walk around in one day. The price of one day is one thousand rubles."

Pakhom looked surprised. "One can walk around a lot of land in one day," he said.

The chief smiled. "Everything will be yours, but on one condition. If in the course of the day you do not return to the place you start from, your money is lost."

"But how can it be noted how far I have gone?"

"We will stay right at the starting point. Our lads will ride behind you. Where you command they will drive in a stake. Then we shall mark furrows from stake to stake. Choose your circle to suit yourself, only before sunset be back at the spot where you started from. All the land that you walk around shall be yours."

Pakhom assented. It was decided to start early in the morning. They conversed for a while, drank kumyss and tea and ate more mutton. When the night set in Pakhom retired to sleep and the Bashkirs dispersed. In the morning they were to meet again in order to journey to the starting point.

Pakhom could not fall asleep. He had his mind on the land. What manner of things he thought of introducing there! "A whole principality I have before me! I can easily make fifty versts in one day. The days are long now. Fifty versts encompass ten thousand dessyatins. I will have to knuckle down to no one. I'll plow as much as may suit me; the rest I'll use for a pasturage."

The whole night through he was unable to close his eyes; only towards morning he dozed restlessly. Hardly had he begun to doze when he saw a vision. He was lying in his kibitka and heard laughter outside. To see who it was that laughed he stepped out of the kibitka and found the chief of the Bashkirs. He was holding his hands to his sides and fairly shaking with laughter. Pakhom approached him in his dream to find out why he was laughing, but now, instead of the Bashkir, he saw the merchant who had come to his farm and told him of this land. Just as he wanted to ask him how long he had been there, he saw that it was no longer the merchant but that mujik who had called on him at his old homestead and told him of the lower Volga region. And now again it was no longer the mujik but the Devil himself, with horns and hoofs, and he laughed and stared at one spot. What is he looking upon? wondered Pakhom; why is he laughing? In his dream he saw a man lying outstretched, barefoot, clad only in a shirt and pair of trousers, with his face turned upward, white as a sheet. As he looked again to see what manner of man it was, he saw clearly that it was he himself.

He awoke with the horror of it. What dreadful things one sees in a dream! He looked about. It was commencing to dawn. The people must be roused. It was time to journey to the starting place.

Pakhom arose, waked his servant, who had been sleeping in the tarantass, harnessed the horses and went to wake the Bashkirs.

"It is time," he said, "to travel to the steppe."

The Bashkirs got up, assembled, and the chief came among them. Again they drank tea and wanted to treat Pakhom, but he urged them to be off.

"If we go, let it be done at once," he remarked. "It is high time."

The Bashkirs made ready, some of them on horseback, others in tarantasses. Pakhom, accompanied by his servant, drove in his own cart. They came to the steppe as the morning sun was beginning to crimson the sky, and driving over to a little hillock they gathered together. The chief came towards Pakhom and pointed with his hand to the steppes.

"All this land that you see," he said, "as far as your eye can reach, is ours. Choose to suit yourself."

Pakhom's eyes shone. In the distance he saw grass land, smooth as the palm of his hand, black as poppy seeds. In the deeper places the grass was growing shoulder high.

The chief took his fur cap and placed it in the middle of the hill.

"This is the landmark. Here place your gold. Your servant will stay here. Go from this point hence and come back again. All the land which you encompass walking is yours."

Pakhom took out the money and laid it on the cap. He took off his coat, keeping the vest on, took a bag of bread, tied a flat water bottle to his belt, pulled up his top boots and made ready to go. He hesitated for a while which direction to take. The view was everywhere enchanting. Finally he said to himself: "I'll go towards the rising of the sun." He faced the East and stretched himself waiting for the sun to appear above the horizon. There was no time to lose. It is better walking in the cool of the morning. The riders took up their positions behind him. As soon as the sun was visible, he set off, followed by the men on horseback.

He walked neither briskly nor slowly. He had walked about a verst without stopping when he ordered a stake to be driven in. Once again in motion, he hastened his steps and soon ordered another stake to be put in. He looked back; the hill was still to be seen with the people on it. Looking up at the sun he figured that he had walked about five versts. It had grown warm, so he doffed his vest. Five versts further the heat began to trouble him. Another glance at the sun showed him it was time for breakfast. "I have already covered a good stretch," he thought. "Of course, there are four of these to be covered today; still it is too early to turn yet; but I'll take my boots off." He sat down, took off his boots and went on. The walking was now easier. "I can go five versts more," he thought, "and then turn to the left." The further he went, the more beautiful the land grew. He walked straight ahead. As he looked again, the hill was hardly to be seen, and the people on it looked like ants.

"Now it's time to turn back," he thought. "How hot I am! I feel like having a drink." He took his bottle with water and drank while walking. Then he made them drive in another stake and turned to the left. He walked and walked; the grass was high, the sun beat down with evergrowing fierceness. Weariness now set in. A glance at the sun showed him that it was midday. "I must rest," he thought. He stopped and ate a little bread. "If I sit down to eat, I'll fall asleep." He stood for a while, caught his breath and walked on. For a time it was easy. The food had refreshed him and given him new strength. But it was too oppressively hot, and sleep threatened to overcome him. He felt exhausted. "Well," he thought, "an hour of pain for an age of joy."

In this second direction he walked nearly ten versts. He meant then to turn to the left, but lo! the section was so fine—a luxuriant dale. Pity to give it up! What a wonderful place for flax! And again he walked straight on, appropriated the dale and marked the place with a stake. Now only he made his second turning. Casting his glance at the starting point he could hardly discern any people on the hill. "Must be about fifteen versts away. I have made the two sides too long and I must shorten the third. Though the property will turn out irregular in this way, what else can be done? I must turn in and walk straight toward the hill. I must hasten and guard against useless turns. I have plenty of land now." And he turned and walked straight toward the hill.

Pakhom's feet ached. He had worked them almost to a standstill. His knees were giving away. He felt like taking a rest, but he dared not. He had no time; he must be back before sunset. The sun does not wait. He ran on as though someone were driving him.

"Did I not make a mistake? Did I not try to grab too much? If I only get back in time! It is so far off, and I am all played out. If only all my trouble and labor be not in vain! I must exert myself to the utmost."

He shivered and ran onward in a trot. His feet were bleeding now. Still he ran. He cast off his vest, the boots, the bottle, the cap. "I was too greedy! I have ruined all! I can't get back by sunset!"

It was getting worse all the time. Fear shortened his breath. He ran on. The shirt and trousers were sticking to his body, his mouth was all dried out, his bosom was heaving like the bellows in a forge, his heart was beating like a hammer, the knees felt as though they were another's and gave under him.

He hardly thought of the land now; he merely thought what to do so as not to die from exertion. Yes, he feared to die, but he could not stop. "I have run so much that if I stop now they will call me a fool."

The Bashkirs, he could hear clearly, were screaming and calling. Their noise added fuel to his burning heart. With the last effort of his strength he ran. The sun was close to the horizon, but the hill was quite near now. The Bashkirs were beckoning, calling. He saw the fur cap, saw his money in it, saw the chief squatting on the ground with his hands at his stomach. He remembered his dream. "Earth there is a-plenty," he thought, "but will God let me live thereon? Ah, I have destroyed myself." And still he kept on running.

He looked at the sun. It was large and crimson, touching the earth and beginning to sink. He reached the foot of the hill. The sun had gone down. A cry of woe escaped from his lips. He thought all was lost. But he remembered that the sun must yet be visible from a higher spot. He rushed up the hill. There was the cap. He stumbled and fell, but reached the cap with his hands. "Good lad!" exclaimed the chief. "You have gained much land."

As Pakhom's servant rushed to his side and tried to lift him, blood was flowing from his mouth. He was dead.

The servant lamented.

The chief was still squatting on the ground, and now he began laughing loudly and holding his sides. Then he rose to his feet, threw a spade to the servant and said, "Here, dig!"

The Bashkirs all clambered to their feet and drove away. The servant remained alone with the corpse.

He dug a grave for Pakhom, the measure of his body from head to foot—three arshins[3] and no more. There he buried Pakhom.

[3] An arshin is about two feet.

KATHERINE MANSFIELD

The Daughters of the Late Colonel ❧

I

The week after was one of the busiest weeks of their lives. Even
when they went to bed it was only their bodies that lay down and
rested; their minds went on, thinking things out, talking things
over, wondering, deciding, trying to remember where . . .

Constantia lay like a statue, her hands by her sides, her feet just overlap-
ping each other, the sheet up to her chin. She stared at the ceiling.

"Do you think that father would mind if we gave his top-hat to the
porter?"

"The porter?" snapped Josephine. "Why ever the porter? What a very
extraordinary idea!"

"Because," said Constantia slowly, "he must often have to go to funerals.
And I noticed at—at the cemetery that he only had a bowler." She paused.
"I thought then how very much he'd appreciate a top-hat. We ought to give
him a present, too. He was always very nice to father."

"But," cried Josephine, flouncing on her pillow and staring across the dark
at Constantia, "father's head!" And suddenly, for one awful moment, she
nearly giggled. Not, of course, that she felt in the least like giggling. It must
have been habit. Years ago, when they had stayed awake at night talking,
their beds had simply heaved. And now the porter's head, disappearing,
popped out, like a candle, under father's hat. . . . The giggle mounted,
mounted; she clenched her hands; she fought it down; she frowned fiercely
at the dark and said, "Remember" terribly sternly.

"We can decide tomorrow," she sighed.

Constantia had noticed nothing; she sighed.

"Do you think we ought to have our dressing-gowns dyed as well?"

"Black?" almost shrieked Josephine.

"Well, what else?" said Constantia. "I was thinking—it doesn't seem quite
sincere, in a way, to wear black out of doors when we're fully dressed, and
then when we're at home—"

"But nobody sees us," said Josephine. She gave the bedclothes such a twitch
that both her feet became uncovered, and she had to creep up the pillows to
get them well under again.

"Kate does," said Constantia. "And the postman very well might."

Josephine thought of her dark-red slippers, which matched her dressing-gown, and of Constantia's favorite indefinite green ones which went with hers. Black! Two black dressing-gowns and two pairs of black woolly slippers, creeping off to the bathroom like black cats.

"I don't think it's absolutely necessary," said she.

Silence. Then Constantia said, "We shall have to post the papers with the notice in them tomorrow to catch the Ceylon mail. . . . How many letters have we had up till now?"

"Twenty-three."

Josephine had replied to them all, and twenty-three times when she came to "We miss our dear father so much," she had broken down and had to use her handkerchief, and on some of them even to soak up a very light-blue tear with an edge of blotting-paper. Strange! She couldn't have put it on—but twenty-three times. Even now, though, when she said over to herself sadly, "We miss our dear father *so* much" she could have cried if she'd wanted to.

"Have you got enough stamps?" came from Constantia.

"Oh, how could I tell?" said Josephine crossly. "What's the good of asking me that now?"

"I was just wondering," said Constantia mildly.

Silence again. There came a little rustle, a scurry, a hop.

"A mouse," said Constantia.

"It can't be a mouse because there aren't any crumbs," said Josephine.

"But it doesn't know there aren't," said Constantia.

A spasm of pity squeezed her heart. Poor little thing! She wished she'd left a tiny piece of biscuit on the dressing-table. It was awful to think of it not finding anything. What would it do?

"I can't think how they manage to live at all," she said slowly.

"Who?" demanded Josephine.

And Constantia said more loudly than she meant to, "Mice."

Josephine was furious. "Oh, what nonsense, Con!" she said. "What have mice got to do with it? You're asleep."

"I don't think I am," said Constantia. She shut her eyes to make sure. She was.

Josephine arched her spine, pulled up her knees, folded her arms so that her fists came under her ears, and pressed her cheek hard against the pillow.

II

Another thing that complicated matters was they had Nurse Andrews staying on with them that week. It was their own fault; they had asked her. It was Josephine's idea. On the morning—well, on the last morning, when the doctor had gone, Josephine had said to Constantia, "Don't you think it would be rather nice if we asked Nurse Andrews to stay on for a week as our guest?"

"Very nice," said Constantia.

"I thought," went on Josephine quickly, "I should just say this afternoon, after we've paid her, 'My sister and I would be very pleased, after all you've done for us, Nurse Andrews, if you would stay on for a week as our guest.' I'd have to put that in about being our guest in case—"

"Oh, but she could hardly expect to be paid!" cried Constantia.

"One never knows," said Josephine sagely.

Nurse Andrews had, of course, jumped at the idea. But it was a bother. It meant they had to have regular sit-down meals at the proper times, whereas if they'd been alone they could have just asked Kate if she wouldn't have minded bringing them a tray wherever they were. And meal-times now that the strain was over were rather a trial.

Nurse Andrews was simply fearful about butter. Really they couldn't help feeling that about butter, at least, she took advantage of their kindness. And she had that maddening habit of asking for just an inch more bread to finish what she had on her plate, and then, at the last mouthful, absentmindedly— of course it wasn't absentmindedly—taking another helping. Josephine got very red when this happened, and she fastened her small, bead-like eyes on the table-cloth as if she saw a minute strange insect creeping through the web of it. But Constantia's long, pale face lengthened and set, and she gazed away—away—far over the desert to where that line of camels unwound like a thread of wool.

"When I was with Lady Tukes," said Nurse Andrews, "she had such a dainty little contrayvance for the buttah. It was a silvah Cupid balanced on the—on the bordah of a glass dish, holding a tayny fork. And when you wanted some buttah you simply pressed his foot and he bent down and speared you a piece. It was quite a gayme."

Josephine could hardly bear that. But "I think those things are very extravagant," was all she said.

"But whey?" asked Nurse Andrews, beaming through her eye-glasses. "No one, surely, would take more buttah than one wanted—would one?"

"Ring, Con," cried Josephine. She couldn't trust herself to reply.

And proud young Kate, the enchanted princess, came in to see what the old tabbies wanted now. She snatched away their plates of mock something or other and slapped down a white, terrified blanc-mange.

"Jam, please, Kate," said Josephine kindly.

Kate knelt and burst open the side-board, lifted the lid of the jam-pot, saw it was empty, put it on the table, and stalked off.

"I'm afraid," said Nurse Andrews a moment later, "there isn't any."

"Oh, what a bother!" said Josephine. She bit her lip. "What had we better do?"

Constantia looked dubious. "We can't disturb Kate again," she said softly.

Nurse Andrews waited, smiling at them both. Her eyes wandered, spying at everything behind her eye-glasses. Constantia in despair went back to her camels. Josephine frowned heavily—concentrated. If it hadn't been for this idiotic woman she and Con would, of course, have eaten their blanc-mange without. Suddenly the idea came.

"I know," she said. "Marmalade. There's some marmalade in the sideboard. Get it, Con."

"I hope," laughed Nurse Andrews, and her laugh was like a spoon tinkling against a medicine-glass—"I hope it's not very bittah marmalayde."

III

But, after all, it was not long now, and then she'd be gone for good. And there was no getting away from the fact that she had been very kind to father. She had nursed him day and night at the end. Indeed, both Constantia and Josephine felt privately that she had rather overdone the not leaving him at the very last. For when they had gone in to say good-bye Nurse Andrews had sat beside his bed the whole time, holding his wrist and pretending to look at her watch. It couldn't have been necessary. It was so tactless, too. Supposing father had wanted to say something—something private to them. Not that he had. Oh, far from it! He lay there, purple, a dark, angry purple in the face, and never even looked at them when they came in. Then, as they were standing there, wondering what to do, he had suddenly opened one eye. Oh, what a difference it would have made, what a difference to their memory of him, how much easier to tell people about it, if he had only opened both! But no—one eye only. It glared at them a moment and then . . . went out.

IV

It had made it very awkward for them when Mr. Farolles, of St. John's, called the same afternoon.

"The end was quite peaceful, I trust?" were the first words he said as he glided towards them through the dark drawing-room.

"Quite," said Josephine faintly. They both hung their heads. Both of them felt certain that eye wasn't at all a peaceful eye.

"Won't you sit down?" said Josephine.

"Thank you, Miss Pinner," said Mr. Farolles gratefully. He folded his coat-tails and began to lower himself into father's armchair, but just as he touched it he almost sprang up and slid into the next chair instead.

He coughed. Josephine clasped her hands; Constantia looked vague.

"I want you to feel, Miss Pinner," said Mr. Farolles, "and you, Miss Constantia, that I'm trying to be helpful. I want to be helpful to you both, if you will let me. These are the times," said Mr. Farolles, very simply and earnestly, "when God means us to be helpful to one another."

"Thank you very much, Mr. Farolles," said Josephine and Constantia.

"Not at all," said Mr. Farolles gently. He drew his kid gloves through his fingers and leaned a little forward. "And if either of you would like a little Communion, either or both of you, here *and* now, you have only to tell me. A little Communion is often very helpful—a great comfort," he added tenderly.

But the idea of a little Communion terrified them. What! In the drawing-room by themselves—with no—no altar or anything! The piano would be much too high, thought Constantia, and Mr. Farolles could not possibly lean over it with the chalice. And Kate would be sure to come bursting in and interrupt them, thought Josephine. And supposing the bell rang in the middle? It might be somebody important—about their mourning. Would they get up reverently and go out, or would they have to wait . . . in torture?

"Perhaps you will send round a note by your good Kate if you would care for it later," said Mr. Farolles.

"Oh, yes, thank you very much!" they both said.

Mr. Farolles got up and took his black straw hat from the round table.

"And about the funeral," he said softly. "I may arrange that—as your dear father's old friend and yours, Miss Pinner—and Miss Constantia?"

Josephine and Constantia got up too.

"I should like it to be quite simple," said Josephine firmly, "and not too expensive. At the same time, I should like—"

"A good one that will last," thought dreamy Constantia, as if Josephine were buying a night-gown. But of course Josephine didn't say that. "One suitable to our father's position." She was very nervous.

"I'll run round to our good friend Mr. Knight," said Mr. Farolles soothingly. "I will ask him to come and see you. I am sure you will find him very helpful indeed."

v

Well, at any rate, all that part of it was over, though neither of them could possibly believe that father was never coming back. Josephine had had a moment of absolute terror at the cemetery, while the coffin was lowered, to think that she and Constantia had done this thing without asking his permission. What would father say when he found out? For he was bound to find out sooner or later. He always did. "Buried. You two girls had me *buried!*" She heard his stick thumping. Oh, what would they say? What possible excuse could they make? It sounded such an appallingly heartless thing to do. Such a wicked advantage to take of a person because he happened to be helpless at the moment. The other people seemed to treat it all as a matter of course. They were strangers; they couldn't be expected to understand that father was the very last person for such a thing to happen to. No, the entire blame for it all would fall on her and Constantia. And the expense, she thought, stepping into the tight-buttoned cab. When she had to show him the bills. What would he say then?

She heard him absolutely roaring, "And do you expect me to pay for this gimcrack excursion of yours?"

"Oh," groaned poor Josephine aloud, "we shouldn't have done it, Con!"

And Constantia, pale as a lemon in all that blackness, said in a frightened whisper, "Done what, Jug?"

"Let them bu-bury father like that," said Josephine, breaking down and crying into her new, queer-smelling mourning handkerchief.

"But what else could we have done?" asked Constantia wonderingly. "We couldn't have kept him, Jug—we couldn't have kept him unburied. At any rate, not in a flat that size."

Josephine blew her nose; the cab was dreadfully stuffy.

"I don't know," she said forlornly. "It is all so dreadful. I feel we ought to have tried to, just for a time at least. To make perfectly sure. One thing's certain"—and her tears sprang out again—"father will never forgive us for this—never!"

VI

Father would never forgive them. That was what they felt more than ever when, two mornings later, they went into his room to go through his things. They had discussed it quite calmly. It was even down on Josephine's list of things to be done. *Go through father's things and settle about them.* But that was a very different matter from saying after breakfast:

"Well, are you ready, Con?"

"Yes, Jug—when you are."

"Then I think we'd better get it over."

It was dark in the hall. It had been a rule for years never to disturb father in the morning, whatever happened. And now they were going to open the door without knocking even. . . . Constantia's eyes were enormous at the idea; Josephine felt weak in the knees.

"You—you go first," she gasped, pushing Constantia.

But Constantia said, as she always had said on those occasions. "No, Jug, that's not fair. You're eldest."

Josephine was going to say—what at other times she wouldn't have owned to for the world—what she kept for her very last weapon, "But you're tallest," when they noticed that the kitchen door was open, and there stood Kate. . . .

"Very stiff," said Josephine, grasping the door-handle and doing her best to turn it. As if anything ever deceived Kate.

It couldn't be helped. That girl was . . . Then the door was shut behind them, but—but they weren't in father's room at all. They might have suddenly walked through the wall by mistake into a different flat altogether. Was the door just behind them? They were too frightened to look. Josephine knew that if it was it was holding itself tight shut; Constantia felt that, like the doors in dreams, it hadn't any handle at all. It was the coldness which made it so awful. Or the whiteness—which? Everything was covered. The blinds were down, a cloth hung over the mirror, a sheet hid the bed; a huge fan of white paper filled the fireplace. Constantia timidly put out her hand; she almost expected a snowflake to fall. Josephine felt a queer tingling in her nose, as if her nose was freezing. Then a cab klop-klopped over the cobbles below, and the quiet seemed to shake into little pieces.

"I had better pull up a blind," said Josephine bravely.

"Yes, it might be a good idea," whispered Constantia.

They only gave the blind a touch, but it flew up and the cord flew after, rolling round the blind-stick, and the little tassel tapped as if trying to get free. That was too much for Constantia.

"Don't you think—don't you think we might put it off for another day?" she whispered.

"Why?" snapped Josephine, feeling, as usual, much better now that she knew for certain that Constantia was terrified. "It's got to be done. But I do wish you wouldn't whisper, Con."

"I didn't know I was whispering," whispered Constantia.

"And why do you keep staring at the bed?" said Josephine, raising her voice almost defiantly. "There's nothing on the bed."

"Oh, Jug, don't say so!" said poor Connie. "At any rate, not so loudly."

Josephine felt herself that she had gone too far. She took a wide swerve over to the chest of drawers, put out her hand, but quickly drew it back again.

"Connie!" she gasped, and she wheeled round and leaned with her back against the chest of drawers.

"Oh, Jug—What?"

Josephine could only glare. She had the most extraordinary feeling that she had just escaped something awful. But how could she explain to Constantia that father was in the chest of drawers? He was in the top drawer with his handkerchiefs and neckties, or in the next with his shirts and pajamas, or in the lowest of all with his suits. He was watching there, hidden away—just behind the door-handle—ready to spring.

She pulled a funny old-fashioned face at Constantia, just as she used to in the old days when she was going to cry.

"I can't open," she nearly wailed.

"No, don't, Jug," whispered Constantia, earnestly. "It's much better not to. Don't let's open anything. At any rate, not for a long time."

"But—but it seems so weak," said Josephine, breaking down.

"But why not be weak for once, Jug?" argued Constantia, whispering quite fiercely. "If it is weak." And her pale stare flew from the locked writing-table—so safe—to the huge glittering wardrobe, and she began to breathe in a queer, panting way. "Why shouldn't we be weak for once in our lives, Jug? It's quite excusable. Let's be weak—be weak, Jug. It's much nicer to be weak than to be strong."

And then she did one of those amazingly bold things that she'd done about twice before in their lives; she marched over to the wardrobe, turned the key, and took it out of the lock. Took it out of the lock and held it up to Josephine, showing Josephine by her extraordinary smile that she knew what she'd done, she'd risked deliberately father being in there among his overcoats.

If the huge wardrobe had lurched forward, had crashed down on Constantia, Josephine wouldn't have been surprised. On the contrary, she would have thought it the only suitable thing to happen. But nothing happened. Only the room seemed quieter than ever, and bigger flakes of cold air fell on Josephine's shoulders and knees. She began to shiver.

"Come, Jug," said Constantia, still with that awful callous smile, and Josephine followed just as she had that last time, when Constantia had pushed Benny into the round pond.

VII

But the strain told on them when they were back in the dining-room. They sat down, very shaky, and looked at each other.

"I don't feel I can settle to anything," said Josephine, "until I've had something. Do you think we could ask Kate for two cups of hot water?"

"I really don't see why we shouldn't," said Constantia carefully. She was quite normal again. "I won't ring. I'll go to the kitchen door and ask her."

"Yes, do," said Josephine, sinking down into a chair. "Tell her, just two cups, Con, nothing else—on a tray."

"She needn't even put the jug on, need she?" said Constantia, as though Kate might very well complain if the jug had been there.

"Oh, no, certainly not! The jug's not at all necessary. She can pour it direct out of the kettle," cried Josephine, feeling that would be a labour-saving indeed.

Their cold lips quivered at the greenish brims. Josephine curved her small red hands round the cup; Constantia sat up and blew on the wavy steam, making it flutter from one side to the other.

"Speaking of Benny," said Josephine.

And though Benny hadn't been mentioned Constantia immediately looked as though he had.

"He'll expect us to send him something of father's, of course. But it's so difficult to know what to send to Ceylon."

"You mean things get unstuck so on the voyage," murmured Constantia.

"No, lost," said Josephine sharply. "You know there's no post. Only runners."

Both paused to watch a black man in white linen drawers running through the pale fields for dear life, with a large brown-paper parcel in his hands. Josephine's black man was tiny; he scurried along glistening like an ant. But there was something blind and tireless about Constantia's tall, thin fellow which made him, she decided, a very unpleasant person indeed . . . On the veranda, dressed all in white and wearing a cork helmet, stood Benny. His right hand shook up and down, as father's did when he was impatient. And behind him, not in the least interested, sat Hilda, the unknown sister-in-law. She swung in a cane rocker and flicked over the leaves of the *Tatler*.

"I think his watch would be the most suitable present," said Josephine.

Constantia looked up; she seemed surprised.

"Oh, would you trust a gold watch to a native?"

"But of course I'd disguise it," said Josephine. "No one would know it was a watch." She liked the idea of having to make a parcel such a curious shape that no one could possibly guess what it was. She even thought for a moment of hiding the watch in a narrow cardboard corset-box that she'd kept by her for a long time, waiting for it to come in for something. It was such a beautiful firm cardboard. But, no, it wouldn't be appropriate for this occasion. It had lettering on it: *Medium Women's 28. Extra Firm Busks.* It would be almost too much of a surprise for Benny to open that and find father's watch inside.

"And of course it isn't as though it would be going—ticking, I mean," said Constantia, who was still thinking of the native love of jewellery. "At least," she added, "it would be very strange if after all that time it was."

VIII

Josephine made no reply. She had flown off on one of her tangents. She had suddenly thought of Cyril. Wasn't it more usual for the only grandson to have the watch? And then dear Cyril was so appreciative, and a gold watch meant so much to a young man. Benny, in all probability, had quite got out of the habit of watches; men so seldom wore waistcoats in those hot climates. Whereas Cyril in London wore them from year's end to year's end. And it would be so nice for her and Constantia, when he came to tea, to know it was there. "I see you've got on grandfather's watch, Cyril." It would be somehow so satisfactory.

Dear boy! What a blow his sweet, sympathetic little note had been. Of course they quite understood; but it was most unfortunate.

"It would have been such a point, having him," said Josephine.

"And he would have enjoyed it so," said Constantia, not thinking what she was saying.

However, as soon as he got back he was coming to tea with his aunties. Cyril to tea was one of their rare treats.

"Now, Cyril, you mustn't be frightened of our cakes. Your Auntie Con and I bought them at Buzzard's this morning. We know what a man's appetite is. So don't be ashamed of making a good tea."

Josephine cut recklessly into the rich dark cake that stood for her winter gloves or the soling and heeling of Constantia's only respectable shoes. But Cyril was most unmanlike in appetite.

"I say, Aunt Josephine, I simply can't. I've only just had lunch, you know."

"Oh, Cyril, that can't be true! It's after four," cried Josephine. Constantia sat with her knife poised over the chocolate-roll.

"It is, all the same," said Cyril, "I had to meet a man at Victoria, and he kept me hanging about till . . . there was only time to get lunch and to come on here. And he gave me—phew"—Cyril put his hand to his forehead—"a terrific blowout," he said.

It was disappointing—today of all days. But still he couldn't be expected to know.

"But you'll have a meringue, won't you, Cyril?" said Aunt Josephine. "These meringues were bought specially for you. Your dear father was so fond of them. We were sure you are, too."

"I *am*, Aunt Josephine," cried Cyril ardently. "Do you mind if I take half to begin with?"

"Not at all, dear boy; but we mustn't let you off with that."

"Is your dear father still so fond of meringues?" asked Auntie Con gently. She winced faintly as she broke through the shell of hers.

"Well, I don't quite know, Auntie Con," said Cyril breezily.

At that they both looked up.

"Don't know?" almost snapped Josephine. "Don't know a thing like that about your own father, Cyril?"

"Surely," said Auntie Con softly.

Cyril tried to laugh it off. "Oh, well," he said, "it's such a long time since—" He faltered. He stopped. Their faces were too much for him.

"Even *so*," said Josephine.

And Auntie Con looked.

Cyril put down his teacup. "Wait a bit," he cried. "Wait a bit, Aunt Josephine. What am I thinking of?"

He looked up. They were beginning to brighten. Cyril slapped his knee.

"Of course," he said, "it was meringues. How could I have forgotten? Yes,

Aunt Josephine, you're perfectly right. Father's most frightfully keen on meringues."

They didn't only beam. Aunt Josephine went scarlet with pleasure; Auntie Con gave a deep, deep sigh.

"And now, Cyril, you must come and see father," said Josephine. "He knows you were coming today."

"Right," said Cyril, very firmly and heartily. He got up from his chair; suddenly he glanced at the clock.

"I say, Auntie Con, isn't your clock a bit slow? I've got to meet a man at —at Paddington just after five. I'm afraid I shan't be able to stay very long with grandfather."

"Oh he won't expect you to stay *very* long!" said Aunt Josephine.

Constantia was still gazing at the clock. She couldn't make up her mind if it was fast or slow. It was one or the other, she felt almost certain of that. At any rate, it had been.

Cyril still lingered. "Aren't you coming along, Auntie Con?"

"Of course," said Josephine, "we shall all go. Come on, Con."

IX

They knocked at the door, and Cyril followed his aunts into grandfather's hot, sweetish room.

"Come on," said Grandfather Pinner. "Don't hang about. What is it? What've you been up to?"

He was sitting in front of a roaring fire, clasping his stick. He had a thick rug over his knees. On his lap there lay a beautiful pale yellow silk handkerchief.

"It's Cyril, father," said Josephine shyly. And she took Cyril's hand and led him forward.

"Good afternoon, grandfather," said Cyril, trying to take his hand out of Aunt Josephine's. Grandfather Pinner shot his eyes at Cyril in the way he was famous for. Where was Auntie Con? She stood on the other side of Aunt Josephine; her long arms hung down in front of her; her hands were clasped. She never took her eyes off grandfather.

"Well," said Grandfather Pinner, beginning to thump, "what have you got to tell me?"

What had he, what had he got to tell him? Cyril felt himself smiling like a perfect imbecile. The room was stifling, too.

But Aunt Josephine came to his rescue. She cried brightly, "Cyril says his father is still very fond of meringues, father dear."

"Eh?" said Grandfather Pinner, curving his hand like a purple meringue-shell over one ear.

Josephine repeated, "Cyril says his father is still very fond of meringues."

"Can't hear," said old Colonel Pinner. And he waved Josephine away with his stick, then pointed to Cyril. "Tell me what she's trying to say," he said.

(My God!) "Must I?" said Cyril, blushing and staring at Aunt Josephine.

"Do, dear," she smiled. "It will please him so much."

"Come on, out with it!" cried Colonel Pinner testily, beginning to thump again.

And Cyril leaned forward and yelled, "Father's still very fond of meringues."

At that Grandfather Pinner jumped as though he had been shot.

"Don't shout!" he cried. "What's the matter with the boy? *Meringues!* What about 'em?"

"Oh, Aunt Josephine, must we go on?" groaned Cyril desperately.

"It's quite all right, dear boy," said Aunt Josephine, as though he and she were at the dentist's together. "He'll understand in a minute." And she whispered to Cyril, "He's getting a bit deaf, you know." Then she leaned forward and really bawled at Grandfather Pinner, "Cyril only wanted to tell you, father dear, that *his* father is still very fond of meringues."

Colonel Pinner heard that time, heard and brooded, looking Cyril up and down.

"What an esstraordinary thing!" said old Grandfather Pinner. "What an esstraordinary thing to come all this way here to tell me!"

And Cyril felt it *was*.

"Yes, I shall send Cyril the watch," said Josephine.

"That would be very nice," said Constantia. "I seem to remember last time he came here there was some little trouble about the time."

x

They were interrupted by Kate bursting through the door in her usual fashion, as though she had discovered some secret panel in the wall.

"Fried or boiled?" asked the bold voice.

Fried or boiled? Josephine and Constantia were quite bewildered for the moment. They could hardly take it in.

"Fried or boiled what, Kate?" asked Josephine, trying to begin to concentrate.

Kate gave a loud sniff. "Fish."

"Well, why didn't you say so immediately?" Josephine reproached her gently. "How could you expect us to understand? There are a great many things in this world, you know, which are fried or boiled." And after such a display of courage, she said quite brightly to Constantia, "Which do you prefer, Con?"

"I think it might be nice to have it fried," said Constantia. "On the other

hand, of course boiled fish is very nice. I think I prefer both equally well.
. . . Unless you . . . In that case—"

"I shall fry it," said Kate, and she bounced back, leaving their door open
and slamming the door of her kitchen.

Josephine gazed at Constantia; she raised her pale eyebrows until they
rippled away into her pale hair. She got up. She said in a very lofty, imposing way, "Do you mind following me into the drawing-room, Constantia?
I've something of great importance to discuss with you."

For it was always to the drawing-room they retired when they wanted to
talk over Kate.

Josephine closed the door meaningly. "Sit down, Constantia," she said, still
very grand. She might have been receiving Constantia for the first time. And
Con looked round vaguely for a chair, as though she felt indeed quite a
stranger.

"Now, the question is," said Josephine, bending forward, "whether we
shall keep her or not."

"That is the question," agreed Constantia.

"And this time," said Josephine firmly, "we must come to a definite
decision."

Constantia looked for a moment as though she might begin going over all
the other times, but she pulled herself together and said, "Yes, Jug."

"You see, Con," explained Josephine, "everything is so changed now."
Constantia looked up quickly. "I mean," went on Josephine, "we're not
dependent on Kate as we were." And she blushed faintly. "There's not father
to cook for."

"That is perfectly true," agreed Constantia. "Father certainly doesn't want
any cooking now, whatever else—"

Josephine broke in sharply, "You're not sleepy, are you, Con?"

"Sleepy, Jug?" Constantia was wide-eyed.

"Well, concentrate more," said Josephine sharply, and she returned to the
subject. "What it comes to is, if we did"—and this she barely breathed, glancing at the door—"give Kate notice"—she raised her voice again—"we could
manage our own food."

"Why not?" cried Constantia. She couldn't help smiling. The idea was
so exciting. She clasped her hands. "What should we live on, Jug?"

"Oh, eggs in various forms!" said Jug, lofty again. "And besides, there
are all the cooked foods."

"But I've always heard," said Constantia, "they are considered so very
expensive."

"Not if one buys them in moderation," said Josephine. But she tore herself
away from the fascinating bypath and dragged Constantia after her.

"What we've got to decide now, however, is whether we really do trust
Kate or not."

Constantia leaned back. Her flat little laugh flew from her lips.

"Isn't it curious, Jug," said she, "that just on this one subject I've never been able to quite make up my mind."

XI

She never had. The whole difficulty was to prove anything. How did one prove things, how could one? Suppose Kate had stood in front of her and deliberately made a face. Mightn't she very well have been in pain? Wasn't it impossible, at any rate, to ask Kate if she was making a face at her? If Kate answered "No"—and of course she would say "No"—what a position! How undignified! Then again Constantia suspected, she was almost certain that Kate went to her chest of drawers when she and Josephine were out, not to take things but to spy. Many times she had come back to find her amethyst cross in the most unlikely places, under her lace ties or on top of her evening Bertha. More than once she had laid a trap for Kate. She had arranged things in a special order and then called Josephine to witness.

"You see, Jug?"

"Quite, Con."

"Now we shall be able to tell."

But, oh, dear, when she did go to look, she was as far off from proof as ever! If anything was displaced, it might so very well have happened as she closed the drawer; a jolt might have done it so easily.

"You come, Jug, and decide. I really can't. It's too difficult."

But after a long pause and a long glare Josephine would sigh, "Now you've put the doubt into my mind, Con, I'm sure I can't tell myself."

"Well, we can't postpone it again," said Josephine. "If we postpone it this time—"

XII

But at that moment in the street below a barrel-organ struck up. Josephine and Constantia sprang to their feet together.

"Run, Con," said Josephine. "Run quickly. There's six-pence on the—"

Then they remembered. It didn't matter. They would never have to stop the organ-grinder again. Never again would she and Constantia be told to make that monkey take his noise somewhere else. Never would sound that loud, strange bellow when father thought they were not hurrying enough. The organ-grinder might play there all day and the stick would not thump.

It never will thump again,
It never will thump again,

played the barrel-organ.

What was Constantia thinking? She had such a strange smile; she looked different. She couldn't be going to cry.

"Jug, Jug," said Constantia softly, pressing her hands together. "Do you know what day it is? It's Saturday. It's a week today, a whole week."

A week since father died,
A week since father died,

cried the barrel-organ. And Josephine, too, forgot to be practical and sensible; she smiled faintly, strangely. On the Indian carpet there fell a square of sunlight, pale red; it came and went and came—and stayed, deepened—until it shone almost golden.

"The sun's out," said Josephine, as though it really mattered.

A perfect fountain of bubbling notes shook from the barrel-organ, round, bright notes, carelessly scattered.

Constantia lifted her big, cold hands as if to catch them, and then her hands fell again. She walked over to the mantel-piece to her favourite Buddha. And the stone and gilt image, whose smile always gave her such a queer feeling, almost a pain and yet a pleasant pain, seemed today to be more than smiling. He knew something; he had a secret. "I know something you don't know," said her Buddha. Oh, what was it, what could it be? And yet she had always felt there was . . . something.

The sunlight pressed through the windows, thieved its way in, flashed its light over the furniture and the photographs. Josephine watched it. When it came to mother's photograph, the enlargement over the piano, it lingered as though puzzled to find so little remained of mother, except the earrings shaped like tiny pagodas and a black feather boa. Why did the photographs of dead people always fade so? wondered Josephine. As soon as a person was dead her photograph died too. But, of course, this one of mother was very old. It was thirty-five years old. Josephine remembered standing on a chair and pointing out that feather boa to Constantia and telling her that it was a snake that had killed their mother in Ceylon. . . . Would everything have been different if mother hadn't died? She didn't see why. Aunt Florence had lived with them until they had left school, and they had moved three times and had their yearly holiday and . . . and there'd been changes of servants, of course.

Some little sparrows, young sparrows they sounded, chirped on the window-ledge. *Yeep-eyeep-yeep*. But Josephine felt they were not sparrows, not on the window-ledge. It was inside her, that queer little crying noise. *Yeep-eyeep-yeep*. Ah, what was it crying, so weak and forlorn?

If mother had lived, might they have married? But there had been nobody for them to marry. There had been father's Anglo-Indian friends before he quarrelled with them. But after that she and Constantia never met a single man except clergymen. How did one meet men? Or even if they'd met them, how could they have got to know men well enough to be more than strangers? One read of people having adventures, being followed, and so on. But nobody had ever followed Constantia and her. Oh, yes, there had been one year at Eastbourne a mysterious man at their boarding-house who had put a note on the jug of hot water outside their bedroom door! But by the time Connie had found it the steam had made the writing too faint to read; they couldn't even make out to which of them it was addressed. And he had left the next day. And that was all. The rest had been looking after father, and at the same time keeping out of father's way. But now? But now? The thieving sun touched Josephine gently. She lifted her face. She was drawn over to the window by gentle beams . . .

Until the barrel-organ stopped playing Constantia stayed before the Buddha, wondering, but not as usual, not vaguely. This time her wonder was like longing. She remembered the times she had come in here, crept out of bed in her nightgown when the moon was full, and lain on the floor with her arms outstretched, as though she was crucified. Why? The big, pale moon had made her do it. The horrible dancing figures on the carved screen had leered at her and she hadn't minded. She remembered too how, whenever they were at the seaside, she had gone off by herself and got as close to the sea as she could, and sung something, something she had made up, while she gazed all over that restless water. There had been this other life, running out, bringing things home in bags, getting things on approval, discussing them with Jug, taking them back to get more things on approval, and arranging father's trays and trying not to annoy father. But it all seemed to have happened in a kind of tunnel. It wasn't real. It was only when she came out of the tunnel into the moonlight or by the sea or into a thunderstorm that she really felt herself. What did it mean? What did it all lead to? Now? Now?

She turned away from the Buddha with one of her vague gestures. She went over to where Josephine was standing. She wanted to say something to Josephine, something frightfully important, about—about the future and what . . .

"Don't you think perhaps—" she began.

But Josephine interrupted her. "I was wondering if now—" she murmured. They stopped; they waited for each other.

"Go on, Con," said Josephine.

"No, no, Jug; after you," said Constantia.

"No, say what you were going to say. You began," said Josephine.

"I . . . I'd rather hear what you were going to say first," said Constantia.

"Don't be absurd, Con."

"Really, Jug."

"Connie!"

"Oh, *Jug!*"

A pause. Then Constantia said faintly, "I can't say what I was going to say, Jug, because I've forgotten what it was . . . that I was going to say."

Josephine was silent for a moment. She stared at a big cloud where the sun had been. Then she replied shortly, "I've forgotten too."

JAMES JOYCE

Counterparts ℣

The bell rang furiously and, when Miss Parker went to the tube, a furious voice called out in a piercing North of Ireland accent: "Send Farrington here!"

Miss Parker returned to her machine, saying to a man who was writing at a desk: "Mr. Alleyne wants you upstairs."

The man muttered *"Blast* him!" under his breath and pushed back his chair to stand up. When he stood up he was tall and of great bulk. He had a hanging face, dark wine-colored, with fair eyebrows and mustache: his eyes bulged forward slightly and the whites of them were dirty. He lifted up the counter and, passing by the clients, went out of the office with a heavy step.

He went heavily upstairs until he came to the second landing, where a door bore a brass plate with the inscription: MR. ALLEYNE. Here he halted, puffing with labor and vexation, and knocked. The shrill voice cried: "Come in!"

The man entered Mr. Alleyne's room. Simultaneously Mr. Alleyne, a little man wearing gold-rimmed glasses on a clean-shaven face, shot his head up over a pile of documents. The head itself was so pink and hairless it seemed like a large egg reposing on the papers. Mr. Alleyne did not lose a moment: "Farrington? What is the meaning of this? Why have I always to complain of you? May I ask you why you haven't made a copy of that contract between Bodley and Kirwan? I told you it must be ready by four o'clock."

"But Mr. Shelley said, sir——"

"Mr. Shelley said, sir . . . Kindly attend to what I say and not to what *Mr. Shelley says, sir.* You have always some excuse or another for shirking work. Let me tell you that if the contract is not copied before this evening I'll lay the matter before Mr. Crosbie. . . . Do you hear me now?"

"Yes, sir."

"Do you hear me now? . . . Ay, and another little matter! I might as well be talking to the wall as talking to you. Understand once for all that you get a half an hour for your lunch and not an hour and a half. How many courses do you want, I'd like to know. . . . Do you mind me now?"

"Yes, sir."

Mr. Alleyne bent his head again upon his pile of papers. The man stared fixedly at the polished skull which directed the affairs of Crosbie & Alleyne, gauging its fragility. A spasm of rage gripped his throat for a few moments and then passed, leaving after it a sharp sensation of thirst. The man recognized the sensation and felt that he must have a good night's drinking. The middle of the month was passed and, if he could get the copy done in time, Mr. Alleyne might give him an order on the cashier. He stood still, gazing fixedly at the head upon the pile of papers. Suddenly Mr. Alleyne began to upset all the papers, searching for something. Then, as if he had been unaware of the man's presence till that moment, he shot up his head again, saying: "Eh? Are you going to stand there all day? Upon my word, Farrington, you take things easy!"

"I was waiting to see——"

"Very good, you needn't wait to see. Go downstairs and do your work."

The man walked heavily toward the door, and as he went out of the room he heard Mr. Alleyne cry after him that if the contract was not copied by evening Mr. Crosbie would hear of the matter.

He returned to his desk in the lower office and counted the sheets which remained to be copied. He took up his pen and dipped it in the ink, but he continued to stare stupidly at the last words he had written: "In no case shall the said Bernard Bodley be" . . . The evening was falling, and in a few minutes they would be lighting the gas: then he could write. He felt that he must slake the thirst in his throat. He stood up from his desk and, lifting the counter as before, passed out of the office. As he was passing out the chief clerk looked at him inquiringly.

"It's all right, Mr. Shelley," said the man, pointing with his finger to indicate the objective of his journey.

The chief clerk glanced at the hatrack, but, seeing the row complete, offered no remark. As soon as he was on the landing the man pulled a shepherd's-plaid cap out of his pocket, put it on his head, and ran quickly down the rickety stairs. From the street door he walked on furtively on the inner side of the path toward the corner and all at once dived into a doorway. He was now safe in the dark snug of O'Neill's shop, and filling up the little window that looked into the bar with his inflamed face, the color of dark wine or dark meat, he called out: "Here, Pat, give us a G.P., like a good fellow."

The curate brought him a glass of plain porter. The man drank it at a gulp and asked for a caraway seed. He put his penny on the counter and, leaving the curate to grope for it in the gloom, retreated out of the snug as furtively as he entered it.

Darkness, accompanied by a thick fog, was gaining upon the dusk of February, and the lamps in Eustace Street had been lit. The man went up by the houses until he reached the door of the office, wondering whether he could finish his copy in time. On the stairs a moist, pungent odor of perfumes aluted his nose: evidently Miss Delacour had come while he was out in O'Neill's. He crammed his cap back again into his pocket and re-entered the office, assuming an air of absent-mindedness.

"Mr. Alleyne has been calling for you," said the chief clerk severely. "Where were you?"

The man glanced at the two clients who were standing at the counter as to intimate that their presence prevented him from answering. As the clients were both male the chief clerk allowed himself a laugh.

"I know that game," he said. "Five times in one day is a little bit. . . . Well, you better look sharp and get a copy of our correspondence in the Delacour case for Mr. Alleyne."

This address in the presence of the public, his run upstairs, and the porter he had gulped down so hastily confused the man, and as he sat down at his desk to get what was required he realized how hopeless was the task of finishing his copy of the contract before half past five. The dark damp night was coming and he longed to spend it in the bars, drinking with his friends amid the glare of gas and the clatter of glasses. He got out the Delacour correspondence and passed out of the office. He hoped Mr. Alleyne would not discover that the last two letters were missing.

The moist, pungent perfume lay all the way up to Mr. Alleyne's room. Miss Delacour was a middle-aged woman of Jewish appearance. Mr. Alleyne was said to be sweet on her or on her money. She came to the office often and stayed a long time when she came. She was sitting beside his desk now in an aroma of perfumes, smoothing the handle of her umbrella and nodding the great black feather in her hat. Mr. Alleyne had swiveled his chair round to face her and thrown his right foot jauntily upon his left knee. The man put the correspondence on the desk and bowed respectfully, but neither Mr. Alleyne nor Miss Delacour took any notice of his bow. Mr. Alleyne tapped a finger on the correspondence and then flicked it toward him as if to say: "That's all right: you can go."

The man returned to the lower office and sat down again at his desk. He stared intently at the incomplete phrase: "In no case shall the said Bernard Bodley be" . . . and thought how strange it was that the last three words began with the same letter. The chief clerk began to hurry Miss Parker, saying she would never have the letters typed in time for post. The man listened to the clicking of the machine for a few minutes and then set to work to finish his copy. But his head was not clear, and his mind wandered away to the glare and rattle of the public house. It was a night for hot punches. He struggled on with his copy, but when the clock struck five he had still fourteen pages to write. Blast it! He couldn't finish it in time. He longed to execrate aloud, to bring his fist down on something violently. He was so enraged that he wrote "Bernard Bernard" instead of "Bernard Bodley" and had to begin again on a clean sheet.

He felt strong enough to clear out the whole office singlehanded. His body ached to do something, to rush out and revel in violence. All the indignities of his life enraged him. . . . Could he ask the cashier privately for an advance? No, the cashier was no good, no damn good: he wouldn't give an advance ... He knew where he would meet the boys: Leonard and O'Halloran and Nosey Flynn. The barometer of his emotional nature was set for a spell of riot.

His imagination had so abstracted him that his name was called twice before he answered. Mr. Alleyne and Miss Delacour were standing outside the counter, and all the clerks had turned round in anticipation of something. The man got up from his desk. Mr. Alleyne began a tirade of abuse, saying that two letters were missing. The man answered that he knew nothing about them, that he had made a faithful copy. The tirade continued: it was so bitter and violent that the man could hardly restrain his fist from descending upon the head of the manikin before him.

"I know nothing about any other two letters," he said stupidly.

"*You—know—nothing.* Of course you know nothing," said Mr. Alleyne. "Tell me," he added, glancing first for approval to the lady beside him, "do you take me for a fool? Do you think me an utter fool?"

The man glanced from the lady's face to the little egg-shaped head and back again, and almost before he was aware of it, his tongue had found a felicitous moment: "I don't think, sir," he said, "that that's a fair question to put to me."

There was a pause in the very breathing of the clerks. Everyone was astounded (the uthor of the witticism no less than his neighbors), and Miss Delacour, who was a stout, amiable person, began to smile broadly. Mr. Alleyne flushed to the hue of a wild rose, and his mouth twitched with a dwarf's passion. He shook his fist in the man's face till it seemed to vibrate like the knob of some electric machine: "You impertinent ruffian! You impertinent ruffian! I'll make short work of you! Wait till you see! You'll apologize to me for your impertinence or you'll quit the office instanter! You'll quit this, I'm telling you, or you'll apologize to me!"

He stood in a doorway opposite the office, watching to see if the cashier would come out alone. All the clerks passed out, and finally the cashier came out with the chief clerk. It was no use trying to say a word to him when he was with the chief clerk. The man felt that his position was bad enough. He had been obliged to offer an abject apology to Mr. Alleyne for his impertinence, but he knew what a hornet's nest the office would be for him. He could remember the way in which Mr. Alleyne had hounded little Peake out of the office in order to make room for his own nephew. He felt savage and thirsty and revengeful, annoyed with himself and with everyone else. Mr. Alleyne would never give him an hour's rest; his life would be a hell o him. He had made a proper fool of himself this time. Could he not keep his tongue in his cheek? But they had never pulled together from the first, he and Mr. Alleyne, ever since the day Mr. Alleyne had overheard him mimicking his North of Ireland accent to amuse Higgins and Miss Parker: that had been the beginning of it. He might have tried Higgins for the money, but sure, Higgins never had anything for himself. A man with two establishments to keep up, of course he couldn't. . . .

He felt his great body again aching for the comfort of the public house. The fog had begun to chill him, and he wondered could he touch Pat in O'Neill's. He could not touch him for more than a bob—and a bob was no use. Yet he must get money somewhere or other: he had spent his last penny for the G.P., and soon it would be too late for getting money anywhere. Suddenly, as he was fingering his watch chain, he thought of Terry Kelly's pawn office in Fleet Street. That was the dart! Why didn't he think of it sooner?

He went through the narrow alley of Temple Bar quickly, muttering to himself that they could all go to hell, because he was going to have a good night of it. The clerk in Terry Kelly's said a crown, but the consignor held out for six shillings; and in the end the six shillings was allowed him literally. He came out of the pawn office joyfully, making a little cylinder of the coins between his thumb and fingers. In Westmoreland Street the footpaths were crowded with young men and women returning from business, and ragged urchins ran here and there yelling out the names of the evening editions. The man passed through the crowd, looking on the spectacle generally with proud satisfaction and staring masterfully at the office girls. His head was full of the noises of tram gongs and swishing trolleys, and his nose already sniffed the curling fumes of punch. As he walked on he reconsidered the terms in which he would narrate the incident to the boys:

"So I just looked at him—coolly, you know, and looked at her. Then I looked back at him again—taking my time, you know. 'I don't think that that's a fair question to put to me,' says I."

Nosey Flynn was sitting up in his usual corner of Davy Byrne's, and when he heard the story he stood Farrington a half one, saying it was as smart a thing as ever he heard. Farrington stood a drink in his turn. After a while O'Halloran and Paddy Leonard came in, and the story was repeated to them. O'Halloran stood tailors of malt, hot, all round, and told the story of the retort he had made to the chief clerk when he was in Callan's of Fownes's Street; but as the retort was after the manner of the liberal shepherds in the eclogues, he had to admit that it was not as clever as Farrington's retort. At this Farrington told the boys to polish off that and have another.

Just as they were naming their poisons who should come in but Higgins! Of course he had to join in with the others. The men asked him to give his version of it, and he did so with great vivacity; for the sight of five small

hot whiskies was very exhilarating. Everyone roared laughing when he
showed the way in which Mr. Alleyne shook his fist in Farrington's face.
Then he imitated Farrington, saying, "And here was my nabs, as cool as
you please," while Farrington looked at the company out of his heavy, dirty
eyes, smiling and at times drawing forth stray drops of liquor from his
mustache with the aid of his lower lip.

When that round was over there was a pause. O'Halloran had money,
but neither of the other two seemed to have any; so the whole party left the
shop somewhat regretfully. At the corner of Duke Street, Higgins and
Nosey Flynn beveled off to the left, while the other three turned back toward
the city. Rain was drizzling down on the cold streets, and when they reached
the Ballast Office, Farrington suggested the Scotch House. The bar was full
of men and loud with the noise of tongues and glasses. The three men pushed
past the whining matchsellers at the door and formed a little party at the
corner of the counter. They began to exchange stories. Leonard introduced
them to a young fellow named Weathers who was performing at the Tivoli
as an acrobat and knockabout *artiste*. Farrington stood a drink all round.
Weathers said he would take a small Irish and Apollinaris. Farrington, who
had definite notions of what was what, asked the boys would they have an
Apollinaris too; but the boys told Tim to make theirs hot. The talk became
theatrical. O'Halloran stood a round, and then Farrington stood another
round, Weathers protesting that the hospitality was too Irish. He promised
to get them in behind the scenes and introduce them to some nice girls.
O'Halloran said that he and Leonard would go but that Farrington wouldn't
go, because he was a married man; and Farrington's heavy, dirty eyes leered
at the company in token that he understood he was being chaffed. Weathers
made them all have just one little tincture at his expense and promised to
meet them later on at Mulligan's in Poolbeg Street.

When the Scotch House closed they went round to Mulligan's. They went
into the parlor at the back, and O'Halloran ordered small hot specials all
round. They were all beginning to feel mellow. Farrington was just standing
another round when Weathers came back. Much to Farrington's relief, he
drank a glass of bitter this time. Funds were getting low, but they had
enough to keep them going. Presently two young women with big hats and
a young man in a check suit came in and sat at a table close by. Weathers
saluted them and told the company that they were out of the Tivoli. Farrington's eyes wandered at every moment in the direction of one of the
young women. There was something striking in her appearance. An immense
scarf of peacockblue muslin was wound round her hat and knotted in a great
bow under her chin, and she wore bright yellow gloves, reaching to the
elbow. Farrington gazed admiringly at the plump arm which she moved
very often and with much grace, and when, after a little time, she answered
his gaze, he admired still more her large dark brown eyes. The oblique, star-

ing expression in them fascinated him. She glanced at him once or twice, and when the party was leaving the room, she brushed against his chair and said, "Oh, pardon!" in a London accent. He watched her leave the room in the hope that she would look back at him, but he was disappointed. He cursed his want of money and cursed all the rounds he had stood, particularly all the whiskies and Apollinaris which he had stood to Weathers. If there was one thing that he hated, it was a sponge. He was so angry that he lost count of the conversation of his friends.

When Paddy Leonard called him, he found that they were talking about feats of strength. Weathers was showing his biceps muscle to the company and boasting so much that the other two had called on Farrington to uphold the national honor. Farrington pulled up his sleeve accordingly and showed his biceps muscle to the company. The two arms were examined and compared, and finally it was agreed to have a trial of strength. The table was cleared, and the two men rested their elbows on it, clasping hands. When Paddy Leonard said "Go!" each was to try to bring down the other's hand on to the table. Farrington looked very serious and determined.

The trial began. After about thirty seconds Weathers brought his opponent's hand slowly down on to the table. Farrington's dark wine-colored face flushed darker still with anger and humiliation at having been defeated by such a stripling.

"You're not to put the weight of your body behind it. Play fair," he said.

"Who's not playing fair?" said the other.

"Come on again. The two best out of three."

The trial began again. The veins stood out on Farrington's forehead, and the pallor of Weathers' complexion changed to peony. Their hands and arms trembled under the stress. After a long struggle Weathers again brought his opponent's hand slowly on to the table. There was a murmur of applause from the spectators. The curate, who was standing beside the table, nodded his red head towards the victor and said with stupid familiarity: "Ah! that's the knack!"

"What the hell do you know about it?" said Farrington fiercely, turning on the man. "What do you put in your gab for?"

"Sh, sh!" said O'Halloran, observing the violent expression of Farrington's face: "Pony up, boys. We'll have just one little smahan more and then we'll be off."

A very sullen-faced man stood at the corner of O'Connell Bridge waiting for the little Sandymount tram to take him home. He was full of smoldering anger and revengefulness. He felt humiliated and discontented; he did not even feel drunk; and he had only two pence in his pocket. He cursed everything. He had done for himself in the office, pawned his watch, spent all his money; and he had not even got drunk. He began to feel thirsty again, and he longed to be back again in the hot, reeking public house. He had lost his reputation as a strong man, having been defeated twice by a mere boy. His heart swelled with fury, and when he thought of the woman in the big hat who had brushed against him and said "Pardon!" his fury nearly choked him.

His tram let him down at Shelbourne Road, and he steered his great body along in the shadow of the wall of the barracks. He loathed returning to his home. When he went in by the side door he found the kitchen empty and the kitchen fire nearly out. He bawled upstairs: "Ada! Ada!"

His wife was a little sharp-faced woman who bullied her husband when he was sober and was bullied by him when he was drunk. They had five children. A little boy came running down the stairs.

"Who is that?" said the man, peering through the darkness.

"Me, Pa."

"Who are you? Charlie?"

"No, Pa. Tom."

"Where's your mother?"

"She's out at the chapel."

"That's right. . . . Did she think of leaving any dinner for me?"

"Yes, Pa. I——"

"Light the lamp. What do you mean by having the place in darkness? Are the other children in bed?"

The man sat down heavily on one of the chairs while the little boy lit the lamp. He began to mimic his son's flat accent, saying half to himself: "'At the chapel.' 'At the chapel,' if you please!" When the lamp was lit he banged his fist on the table and shouted: "What's for my dinner?"

"I'm going to . . . cook it, Pa," said the little boy.

The man jumped up furiously and pointed to the fire. "On that fire! You let the fire out! By God, I'll teach you to do that again!" He took a step to the door and seized the walking stick which was standing behind it. "I'll teach you to let the fire out!" he said, rolling up his sleeves in order to give his arm free play.

The little boy cried, "Oh, Pa!" and ran whimpering round the table, but the man followed him and caught him by the coat. The little boy looked about him wildly but, seeing no way of escape, fell upon his knees.

"Now, you'll let the fire out the next time!" said the man, striking at him vigorously with the stick. "Take that, you little whelp!"

The boy uttered a squeal of pain as the stick cut his thigh. He clasped his hands together in the air, and his voice shook with fright.

"Oh, Pa!" he cried. "Don't beat me, Pa! And I'll . . . I'll say a Hail Mary for you . . . I'll say a Hail Mary for you, Pa, if you don't beat me . . . I'll say a Hail Mary . . ."

HENRY JAMES

The Liar 🜚

I

The train was half an hour late and the drive from the station
longer than he had supposed, so that when he reached the house
its inmates had dispersed to dress for dinner and he was conducted straight to his room. The curtains were drawn in this asylum, the
candles lighted, the fire bright, and when the servant had quickly put out
his clothes the comfortable little place might have been one of the minor
instruments in a big orchestra—seemed to promise a pleasant house, a various
party, talk, acquaintances, affinities, to say nothing of very good cheer.
He was too occupied with his profession often to pay country visits, but he
had heard people who had more time for them speak of establishments
where "they do you very well." He foresaw that the proprietors of Stayes
would do him very well. In his bedroom on such occasions he always looked
first at the books on the shelf and the prints on the walls; these things would
give in a sort the social, the conversational value of his hosts. Though he
had but little time to devote to them on this occasion a cursory inspection
assured him that if the literature, as usual, was mainly American and humorous the art consisted neither of the water-colour studies of the children nor
of "goody" engravings. The walls were adorned with old-fashioned litho-
graphs, mostly portraits of country gentlemen with high collars and riding-
gloves: this suggested—and it was encouraging—that the tradition of por-
traiture was held in esteem. There was the customary novel of Mr. Le Fanu
for the bedside, the ideal reading in a country house for the hours after midnight. Oliver Lyon could scarcely forbear beginning it while he buttoned
his shirt.

Perhaps that is why he not only found every one assembled in the hall
when he went down, but saw from the way the move to dinner was instantly
made that they had been waiting for him. There was no delay to introduce
him to a lady, for he went out unimportant and in a group of unmated men.
The men, straggling behind, sidled and edged as usual at the door of the
dining-room, and the *dénouement* of this little comedy was that he came
to his place last of all. This made him suppose himself in a sufficiently dis-

tinguished company, for if he had been humiliated—which he was not—he couldn't have consoled himself with the reflection that such a fate was natural to an obscure and struggling young artist. He could no longer think of himself as notably young, alas, and if his position wasn't so brilliant as it ought to be he could no longer justify it by calling it a struggle. He was appreciably "known" and was now apparently in a society of the known if not of the knowing. This idea added to the curiosity with which he looked up and down the long table as he settled himself in his place.

It was a numerous party—five-and-twenty people; rather an odd occasion to have proposed to him, as he thought. He wouldn't be surrounded by the quiet that ministers to good work; however, it had never interfered with his work to feel the human scene enclose it as a ring. And though he didn't know this, it was never quiet at Stayes. When he was working well he found himself in that happy state—the happiest of all for an artist—in which things in general interweave with his particular web and make it thicker and stronger and more many-coloured. Moreover there was an exhilaration (he had felt it before) in the rapid change of scene—the jump, in the dusk of the afternoon, from foggy London and his familiar studio to a centre of festivity in the middle of Hertfordshire and a drama half-acted, a drama of pretty women and noted men and wonderful orchids in silver jars. He observed as a not unimportant fact that one of the pretty women was beside him: a gentleman sat on his other hand. But he appraised his neighbours little as yet: he was busy with the question of Sir David, whom he had never seen and about whom he naturally was curious.

Evidently, however, Sir David was not at dinner, a circumstance sufficiently explained by the other circumstance forming our friend's principal knowledge of him—his being ninety years of age. Oliver Lyon had looked forward with pleasure to painting a picked nonagenarian, so that though the old man's absence from table was something of a disappointment—it was an opportunity the less to observe him before going to work—it seemed a sign that he was rather a sacred and perhaps therefore an impressive relic. Lyon looked at his son with the greater interest—wondered if the glazed bloom of such a cheek had been transmitted from Sir David. That would be jolly to paint in the old man—the withered ruddiness of a winter apple, especially if the eye should be still alive and the white hair carry out the frosty look. Arthur Ashmore's hair had a midsummer glow, but Lyon was glad his call had been for the great rather than the small bearer of the name, in spite of his never having seen the one and of the other's being seated there before him now in the very highest relief of impersonal hospitality.

Arthur Ashmore was a fresh-coloured thick-necked English gentleman, but he was just not a subject; he might have been a farmer and he might have been a banker; you could scarcely paint him in character. His wife didn't make up the amount; she was a large bright negative woman who had the same air as her husband of being somehow tremendously new; an appearance as of fresh varnish—Lyon could scarcely tell whether it came from her complexion or from her clothes—so that one felt she ought to sit in a gilt frame and be dealt with by reference to a catalogue or a price-list. It was as if she were already rather a bad though expensive portrait, knocked off by an eminent hand, and Lyon had no wish to copy that work. The pretty woman on his right was engaged with her neighbour, while the gentleman on his other side looked detached and desperate, so that he had time to lose himself in his favourite diversion of watching face after face. This amusement gave him the greatest pleasure he knew, and he often thought it a mercy the human mask did interest him and that it had such a need, frequently even in spite of itself, to testify, since he was to make his living by reproducing it. Even if Arthur Ashmore wouldn't be inspiring to paint (a certain anxiety rose in him lest, should he make a hit with her father-in-law, Mrs. Arthur should take it into her head that he had now proved himself worthy to handle her husband); even if he had looked a little less like a page —fine as to print and margin—without punctuation, he would still be a refreshing iridescent surface. But the gentleman four persons off—what was he? Would he be a subject, or was his face only the legible door-plate of his identity, burnished with punctual washing and shaving—the least thing that was decent you might know him by?

This face arrested Oliver Lyon, striking him at first as very handsome. The gentleman might still be called young, and his features were regular: he had a plentiful fair moustache that curled up at the ends, a brilliant gallant almost adventurous air, together with a big shining breastpin in the middle of his shirt. He appeared a fine satisfied soul, and Lyon perceived that wherever he rested his friendly eye there fell an influence as pleasant as the September sun—as if he could make grapes and pears or even human affection ripen by looking at them. What was odd in him was a certain mixture of the correct and the extravagant: as if he were an adventurer imitating a gentleman with rare perfection, or a gentleman who had taken a fancy to go about with hidden arms. He might have been a dethroned prince or the war-correspondent of a newspaper: he represented both enterprise and tradition, good manners and bad taste. Lyon at length fell into conversation with the lady beside him—they dispensed, as he had had to dispense at dinner-parties before, with an introduction—by asking who this personage might be.

"Oh Colonel Capadose, don't you know?" Lyon didn't know and asked for further information. His neighbour had a sociable manner and evidently was accustomed to quick transitions; she turned from her other interlocutor with the promptness of a good cook who lifts the cover of the next saucepan. "He has been a great deal in India—isn't he rather celebrated?" she put it. Lyon confessed he had never heard of him, and she went on: "Well, perhaps he isn't; but he says he is, and if you think it that's just the same, isn't it?"

"If *you* think it?"

"I mean if he thinks it—that's just as good, I suppose."

"Do you mean if he thinks he has done things he hasn't?"

"Oh dear no; because I never really know the difference between what people say—! He's exceedingly clever and amusing—quite the cleverest person in the house, unless indeed you're more so. But that I can't tell yet, can I? I only know about the people I know; I think that's celebrity enough!"

"Enough for them?"

"Oh I see you're clever. Enough for me! But I've heard of you," the lady went on. "I know your pictures; I admire them. But I don't think you look like them."

"They're mostly portraits," Lyon said; "and what I usually try for is not my own resemblance."

"I see what you mean. But they've much more colour. Don't you suppose Vandyke's things tell a lot about him? And now you're going to do some one here?"

"I've been invited to do Sir David. I'm rather disappointed at not seeing him this evening."

"Oh he goes to bed at some unnatural hour—eight o'clock, after porridge and milk. You know he's rather an old mummy."

"An old mummy?" Oliver Lyon repeated.

"I mean he wears half a dozen waistcoats and sits by the fire. He's always cold."

"I've never seen him and never seen any portrait or photograph of him," Lyon said. "I'm surprised at his never having had anything done—at their waiting all these years."

"Ah that's because he was afraid, you know; it was his pet superstition. He was sure that if anything were done he would die directly afterwards. He has only consented today."

"He's ready to die then?"

"Oh now he's so old he doesn't care."

"Well, I hope I shan't kill him," said Lyon. "It was rather unnatural of his son to send for me."

"Oh they've nothing to gain—everything is theirs already!" his companion rejoined, as if she took this speech quite literally. Her talkativeness was systematic—she fraternized as seriously as she might have played whist. "They do as they like—they fill the house with people—they have *carte blanche*."

"I see—but there's still the 'title.'"

"Yes, but what's the tuppenny title?"

Our artist broke into laughter at this, whereat his companion stared. Before he had recovered himself she was scouring the plain with her other neighbour. The gentleman on his left at last risked an observation as if it had been a move at chess, exciting in Lyon however a comparative wantonness. This personage played his part with difficulty: he uttered a remark as a lady fires a pistol, looking the other way. To catch the ball Lyon had to bend his ear, and this movement led to his observing a handsome creature who was seated on the same side, beyond his interlocutor. Her profile was presented to him and at first he was only struck with its beauty; then it produced an impression still more agreeable—a sense of undimmed remembrance and intimate association. He had not recognised her on the instant only because he had so little expected to see her there; he had not seen her anywhere for so long, and no news of her now ever came to him. She was often in his thoughts, but she had passed out of his life. He thought of her twice a week; that may be called often, even for fidelity, when it has been kept up a dozen years. The moment after he recognised her he felt how true it was that only she could carry that head, the most charming head in the world and of which there could never be a replica. She was leaning forward a little; she remained in profile, slightly turned to some further neighbour. She was listening, but her eyes moved, and after a moment Lyon followed their direction. They rested on the gentleman who had been described to him as Colonel Capadose—rested, he made out, as with an habitual visible complacency. This was not strange, for the Colonel was unmistakably formed to attract the sympathetic gaze of woman; but Lyon felt it as the source of an ache that she could let *him* look at her so long without giving him a glance. There was nothing between them today and he had no rights, but she must have known he was coming—it was of course no such tremendous event, but she couldn't have been staying in the house without some echo of it—and it wasn't natural this should absolutely fail to affect her.

She was looking at Colonel Capadose as if she had been in love with him —an odd business for the proudest, most reserved of women. But doubtless it was all right if her husband was satisfied: he had heard indefinitely, years before, that she was married, and he took for granted—as he had not heard —the presence of the happy man on whom she had conferred what she had refused to a poor art-student at Munich. Colonel Capadose seemed aware of nothing, and this fact, incongruously enough, rather annoyed Lyon than pleased him. Suddenly the lady moved her head, showing her full face to our hero. He was so prepared with a greeting that he instantly smiled, as a shaken jug overflows; but she made no response, turned away again and sank back in her chair. All her face said in that instant was "You see I'm as handsome as ever." To which he mentally subjoined: "Yes, and as much good as ever it does me!" He asked the young man beside him if he knew who that beautiful thing was—the fourth person beyond him. The young man leaned forward, considered and then said: "I think she's Mrs. Capadose."

"Do you mean his wife—that fellow's?" And Lyon indicated the subject of the information given him by his other neighbour.

"Oh is *he* Mr. Capadose?" said the young man, to whom it appeared to

mean little. He admitted his ignorance of these values and explained it by
saying that there were so many people and he had come but the day before.
What was definite to our friend was that Mrs. Capadose was in love with
her husband—so that he wished more than ever he might have married
her.

"She's very fond and true," he found himself saying three minutes later,
with a small ironic ring, to the lady on his right. He added that he meant
Mrs. Capadose.

"Ah you know her then?"

"I knew her once upon a time—when I was living abroad."

"Why then were you asking me about her husband?"

"Precisely for that reason." Lyon was clear. "She married after that—I
didn't even know her present name."

"How then do you know it now?"

"This gentleman has just told me—he appears to know."

"I didn't know he knew anything," said the lady with a crook that took
him in.

"I don't think he knows anything but that."

"Then you've found out for yourself that she's—what do you call it?—
tender and true? What do you mean by that?"

"Ah you mustn't question me—I want to put things to *you*," Lyon said.
"How do you all like her here?"

"You ask too much! I can only speak for myself. I think she's hard."

"That's only because she's honest and straightforward."

"Do you mean I like people in proportion as they deceive?"

"I think we all do, so long as we don't find them out," Lyon said. "And
then there's something in her face—a sort of nobleness of the Roman type,
in spite of her having such English eyes. In fact she's English down to the
ground; but her complexion, her low forehead and that beautiful close little
wave in her dark hair make her look like a transfigured Trasteverina."

"Yes, and she always sticks pins and daggers into her head, to bring out
that effect. I must say I like her husband better: he *gives* so much."

"Well, when I knew her there was no comparison that could injure her,"
Lyon richly sighed. "She was altogether the most delightful thing in
Munich."

"In Munich?"

"Her people lived there; they weren't rich—in pursuit of economy in fact,
and Munich was very cheap. Her father was the younger son of some noble
house; he had married a second time and had a lot of little mouths to feed.
She was the child of the first wife and didn't like her stepmother, but she was
charming to her little brothers and sisters. I once made a sketch of her as
Werther's Charlotte cutting bread and butter while the children clustered
round her. All the artists in the place were in love with her, but she wouldn't

ook at 'the likes' of us. She was too proud—I grant you that, but not stuck
up nor young-ladyish, only perfectly simple and frank about it. She used to
remind me of Thackeray's Ethel Newcome. She told me she must marry
well: it was the one thing she could do for her family. I suppose you'd say
she *has* married well."

"She told *you?*" smiled Lyon's neighbour.

"Oh of course I proposed to her too. But she evidently thinks so herself!"
he added. "I mean that it's no mistake."

When the ladies left the table the host as usual bade the gentlemen draw
together, so that Lyon found himself opposite to Colonel Capadose. The
conversation was mainly about the "run," for it had apparently been a great
day in the hunting-field. Most of the men had a comment or an anecdote,
several had many; but the Colonel's pleasant voice was the most audible in
the chorus. It was a bright and fresh but masculine organ, just such a voice
as, to Lyon's sense, such a "fine man" ought to have had. It appeared from
his allusions that he was a very straight rider, which was also very much what
Lyon would have expected. Not that he swaggered, for his points were all
quietly and casually made; but they had all to do with some dangerous experiment or close shave. Lyon noted after a little that the attention paid by the
company to the Colonel's remarks was not in direct proportion to the interest
they seemed to offer; the result of which was that the speaker, who noticed
that *he* at least was listening, began to treat him as his particular auditor and
to fix his eyes on him as he talked. Lyon had nothing to do but to look
sympathetic and assent—the narrator building on the tribute so rendered. A
neighbouring squire had had an accident; he had come a cropper in an
awkward place—just at the finish—with consequences that looked grave. He
had struck his head; he remained insensible up to the last accounts: there
had evidently been concussion of the brain. There was some exchange of
views as to his recovery, how soon it would take place or whether it would
take place at all; which led the Colonel to confide to our artist across the
table that *he* shouldn't despair of a fellow even if he didn't come round for
weeks—for weeks and weeks and weeks—for months, almost for years. He
leaned forward (Lyon leaned forward to listen) and mentioned that he knew
from personal experience how little limit there really was to the time a fellah
might lie like a stone without being the worse for it. It had happened to him
in Ireland years before; he had been pitched out of a dogcart, had turned a
sheer somersault and landed on his head. They had thought he was dead,
but he wasn't; they had carried him first to the nearest cabin, where he lay
for some days with the pigs, and then to an inn in a neighbouring town—it
was a near thing they hadn't put him underground. He had been completely
insensible—without a ray of recognition of any human thing—for three
whole months; hadn't had a glimmer of consciousness of any blessed thing.
It had been touch and go to that degree that they couldn't come near him,

couldn't feed him, could scarcely look at him. Then one day he had opened his eyes—as fit as a flea!

"I give you my honour it had done me good—it rested my brain." He conveyed, though without excessive emphasis, that with an intelligence so active as his these periods of repose were providential. Lyon was struck by his story, but wanted to ask if he hadn't shammed a little; not in relating it, only in keeping so quiet. He hesitated however, in time, to betray a doubt —he was so impressed with the tone in which Colonel Capadose pronounced it the turn of a hair that they hadn't buried him alive. That had happened to a friend of his in India—a fellow who was supposed to have died of jungle-fever and whom they clapped into a coffin. He was going on to recite the further fate of this unfortunate gentleman when Mr. Ashmore said a word and every one rose for the move to the drawing-room. Lyon noticed that by this time no one was heeding his new friend's prodigies. These two came round on either side of the table and met while their companions hung back for each other.

"And do you mean your comrade was literally buried alive?" asked Lyon in some suspense.

The Colonel looked at him as with the thread of the conversation already lost. Then his face brightened—and when it brightened it was doubly handsome. "Upon my soul he was shoved into the ground!"

"And left there?"

"Left there till I came and hauled him out."

"*You* came?"

"I dreamed about him—it's the most extraordinary story: I heard him calling to me in the night. I took on myself to dig him up. You know there are people in India—a kind of beastly race, the ghouls—who violate graves. I had a sort of presentiment that they would get at him first. I rode straight I can tell you; and, by Jove, a couple of them had just broken ground! Crack —crack from a couple of barrels, and they showed me their heels as you may believe. Would you credit that I took him out myself? The air brought him round and he was none the worse. He has got his pension—he came home the other day. He'd do anything for me," the narrator added.

"He called to you in the night?" said Lyon, much thrilled.

"That's the interesting point. Now *what was it*? It wasn't his ghost because he wasn't dead. It wasn't himself, because he couldn't. It was some confounded brain-wave or other! You see India's a strange country—there's an element of the mysterious: the air's full of things you can't explain."

They passed out of the dining-room, and this master of anecdote, who went among the first, was separated from his newest victim; but a minute later before they reached the drawing-room, he had come back. "Ashmore tells me who you are. Of course I've often heard of you. I'm very glad to make your acquaintance. My wife used to know you."

"I'm glad she remembers me. I recognised her at dinner and was afraid she didn't."

"Ah I dare say she was ashamed," said the Colonel with genial ease.

"Ashamed of me?" Lyon replied in the same key.

"Wasn't there something about a picture? Yes; you painted her portrait."

"Many times," Lyon said; "and she may very well have been ashamed of what I made of her."

"Well, *I* wasn't, my dear sir; it was the sight of that picture, which you were so good as to present to her, that made me first fall in love with her."

Our friend lived over again for a few seconds a lost felicity. "Do you mean one with the children—cutting bread and butter?"

"Bread and butter? Bless me, no—vine-leaves and a leopard-skin. A regular Bacchante."

"Ah yes," said Lyon; "I remember. It was the first decent portrait I painted. I should be curious to see it today."

"Don't ask her to show it to you—she'll feel it awkward," the Colonel went on.

"Awkward?"—our artist wondered.

"We parted with it—in the most disinterested manner," the other laughed. "An old friend of my wife's—her family had known him intimately when they lived in Germany—took the most extraordinary fancy to it: the Grand Duke of Silberstadt-Schreckenstein, don't you know? He came out to Bombay while we were there and he spotted your picture (you know he's one of the greatest collectors in Europe) and made such eyes at it that, upon my word—it happened to be his birthday—she told him he might have it to get rid of him. He was perfectly enchanted—but we miss the picture."

"It's very good of you," Lyon said. "If it's in a great collection—a work of my incompetent youth—I'm infinitely honoured."

"Oh he keeps it in one of his castles; I don't know which—you know he has so many. He sent us, before he left India—to return the compliment—a magnificent old vase."

"That was more than the thing was worth," Lyon modestly urged.

Colonel Capadose gave no heed to this observation; his thoughts now seemed elsewhere. After a moment, however, he said: "If you'll come and see us in town she'll show you the vase." And as they passed into the drawing-room he gave his fellow visitor a friendly propulsion. "Go and speak to her; there she is. She'll be delighted."

Oliver Lyon took but a few steps into the wide saloon; he stood there a moment looking at the bright composition of the lamplit group of fair women, the single figures, the great setting of white and gold, the panels of old damask, in the centre of each of which was a single celebrated picture. There was a subdued lustre in the scene and an air as of the shining trains of dresses tumbled over the carpet. At the furthest end of the room sat Mrs. Capadose, rather isolated; she was on a small sofa with an empty place beside her. Lyon couldn't flatter himself she had been keeping it for him; her failure to take up his shy signal at table contradicted this, but his desire to join her was too strong. Moreover he had her husband's sanction; so he crossed the room, stepping over the tails of gowns, and stood before her with his appeal. "I hope you don't mean to repudiate me."

She looked up at him with frank delight. "I'm so glad to see you. I was charmed when I heard you were coming."

"I tried to get a smile from you at dinner—but I couldn't," Lyon returned.

"I didn't see—I didn't understand. Besides, I hate smirking and telegraphing. Also I'm very shy—you won't have forgotten that. Now we can communicate comfortably." And she made a better place for him on her sofa. He sat down and they had a talk that smote old chords in him; the sense of what he had loved her for came back to him, as well as not a little of the actual effect of that cause. She was still the least spoiled beauty he had ever seen, with an absence of the "wanton" or of any insinuating art that resembled an omitted faculty: she affected him at moments as some fine creature from an asylum—a surprising deaf-mute or one of the operative blind. Her noble pagan head gave her privileges that she neglected, and when people were admiring her brow she was wondering if there were a good fire in her bedroom, or at the very most in theirs. She was simple, kind and good; inexpressive but not inhuman, not stupid. Now and again she dropped something, some small fruit of discrimination, that might have come from a mind, have been an impression at first hand. She had no imagination and only the simpler feelings, but several of these had grown up to full size. Lyon talked of the old days in Munich, reminded her of incidents, pleasures and pains, asked her about her father and the others; and she spoke in return of her being so impressed with his own fame, his brilliant position in the world, that she hadn't felt sure he would notice her or that his mute appeal at table was meant for her. This was plainly a perfectly truthful speech—she was incapable of any other—and he was affected by such humility on the part of a woman whose grand line was unique. Her father was dead; one of her brothers was in the navy and the other on a ranch in America; two of her sisters were married and the youngest just coming out and very pretty. She didn't mention her stepmother. She questioned him on his own story, and he described it mainly as his not having married.

"Oh you ought to," she answered. "It's the best thing."

"I like that—from you!"

"Why not from me? I'm very happy."

"That's just why I can't be," he returned. "It's cruel of you to praise your state. But I've had the pleasure of making the acquaintance of your husband. We had a good bit of talk in the other room."

"You must know him better—you must know him really well," said Mrs. Capadose.

"I'm sure that the further you go the more you find. But he makes a fine show too."

She rested her good grey eyes on this recovered "backer." "Don't you think he's handsome?"

"Handsome and clever and entertaining. You see I'm generous."

"Yes; you must know him well," Mrs. Capadose repeated.

"He has seen a great deal of life," said her companion.

"Ah we've been in so many situations. You must see my little girl. She's nine years old—she's too beautiful."

Lyon rose fully to the occasion. "You must bring her to my studio some day—I should like to paint her."

"Oh don't speak of that," said Mrs. Capadose. "It reminds me of something so distressing."

"I hope you don't mean of when *you* used to sit to me—though that may well have bored you."

"It's not what you did—it's what we've done. It's a confession I must make—it's a weight on my mind! I mean on the subject of the lovely picture you gave me—it used to be so much admired. When you come to see me in London—and I count on your doing that very soon—I shall see you looking all round. I can't tell you I keep it in my own room because I love it so, for the simple reason—" It fairly pulled her up.

"Because you can't tell wicked lies," said Lyon.

"No, I can't. So before you ask for it—"

"Oh I know you parted with it—the blow has already fallen," Lyon interrupted.

"Ah then you've heard? I was sure you would! But do you know what we got for it? Two hundred pounds."

"You might have got much more," the artist smiled.

"That seemed a great deal at the time. We were in want of the money—it was a good while ago, when we first married. Our means were very small then, but fortunately that has changed rather for the better. We had the chance; it really seemed a big sum, and I'm afraid we jumped at it. My husband had expectations which have partly come into effect, so that now we do well enough. But meanwhile the picture went."

"Fortunately the original remained. But do you mean that two hundred was the value of the vase?" Lyon asked.

"Of the vase?"

"The beautiful old Indian vase—the Grand Duke's offering."

"The Grand Duke?"

"What's his name?—Silberstadt-Schreckenstein. Your husband mentioned the transaction."

"Oh my husband!" said Mrs. Capadose; and Lyon now saw her change colour.

Not to add to her embarrassment, but to clear up the ambiguity, which he perceived the next moment he had better have left alone, he went on: "He tells me it's now in his collection."

"In the Grand Duke's? Ah you know its reputation? I believe it contains treasures." She was bewildered, but she recovered herself, and Lyon made the mental reflection that for some reason which would seem good when he knew it the husband and the wife had prepared different versions of the same incident. It was true that he didn't exactly see Everina Brant preparing a version; that wasn't her line of old, and indeed there was no such subterfuge in her eyes today. At any rate they both had the matter too much on their conscience. He changed the subject—said Mrs. Capadose must really bring the little girl. He sat with her some time longer and imagined—perhaps too freely—her equilibrium slightly impaired, as if she were annoyed at their having been even for a moment at cross-purposes. This didn't prevent his saying to her at the last, just as the ladies began to gather themselves for bed: "You seem much impressed, from what you say, with my renown and my prosperity, and you are so good as greatly to exaggerate them. Would you have married me if you had known I was destined to success?"

"I did know it."

"*I* didn't, then!"

"You were too modest."

"You didn't think so when I proposed to you."

"Well, if I had married you I couldn't have married *him*—and he's so awfully nice," Mrs. Capadose said. Lyon knew this was her faith—he had learned that at dinner—but it vexed him a little to hear her proclaim it. The gentleman designated by the pronoun came up, amid the prolonged handshaking for good-night, and Mrs. Capadose remarked to her husband as she turned away, "He wants to paint Amy."

"Ah she's a charming child, a most interesting little creature," the Colonel said to Lyon. "She does the most remarkable things."

Mrs. Capadose stopped in the rustling procession that followed the hostess out of the room. "Don't tell him, please don't," she said.

"Don't tell him what?"

"Why, what she does. Let him find out for himself." And she passed on.

"She thinks I swagger about the child—that I bore people," said the Colonel. "I hope you smoke." He appeared ten minutes later in the smoking-room, brilliantly equipped in a suit of crimson foulard covered with little white spots. He gratified Lyon's eye, made him feel that the modern age has its splendour too and its opportunities for costume. If his wife was an antique he was a fine specimen of the period of colour: he might have passed for a Venetian of the sixteenth century. They were a remarkable couple, Lyon thought, and as he looked at the Colonel standing in bright erectness before the chimney-piece and emitting great smoke-puffs he didn't wonder Everina couldn't regret she hadn't married *him*. All the men collected at Stayes were not smokers and some of them had gone to bed. Colonel Capadose remarked that there probably would be a smallish muster, they had had such a hard day's work. That was the worst of a hunting-house—the men were so sleepy after dinner; it was a great sell for the ladies, even for those who hunted themselves, women being so tough that they never showed it. But most fellows revived under the stimulating influences of the smoking-room, and some of them, in this confidence, would turn up yet. Some of the grounds of their confidence—not all—might have been seen in a cluster of glasses and bottles on a table near the fire, which made the great salver and its contents twinkle sociably. The others lurked as yet in various improper corners of the minds of the most loquacious. Lyon was alone with Colonel Capadose for some moments before their companions, in varied eccentricities of uniform, straggled in, and he felt how little loss of vital tissue this wonderful man had to repair.

They talked about the house, Lyon having noticed an oddity of construction in the smoking-room; and the Colonel explained that it consisted of two distinct parts, one of very great antiquity. They were two complete houses in short, the old and the new, each of great extent and each very fine in its way. The two formed together an enormous structure—Lyon must make a point of going all over it. The modern piece had been erected by the old man when he bought the property; oh yes, he had bought it forty years before—it hadn't been in the family: there hadn't been any particular family for it to be in. He had had the good taste not to spoil the original house—he had not touched it beyond what was just necessary for joining it on. It was very curious indeed —a most irregular rambling mysterious pile, where they now and then discovered a walled-up room or a secret staircase. To his mind it was deadly depressing, however; even the modern additions, splendid as they were, failed to make it cheerful. There was some story of how a skeleton had been found years before, during some repairs, under a stone slab of the floor of one of the passages; but the family were rather shy of its being talked about. The place they were in was of course in the old part, which contained after all some of the best rooms: he had an idea it had been the primitive kitchen, half-modernised at some intermediate period.

"My room is in the old part too then—I'm very glad," Lyon said. "It's very comfortable and contains all the latest conveniences, but I observed the depth of the recess of the door and the evident antiquity of the corridor and staircase—the first short one—after I came out. That panelled corridor is admirable; it looks as if it stretched away, in its brown dimness (the lamps didn't seem to me to make much impression on it) for half a mile."

"Oh don't go to the end of it!" the Colonel warningly smiled.

"Does it lead to the haunted room?" Lyon asked.

His companion looked at him a moment. "Ah you know about that?"

"No, I don't speak from knowledge, only from hope. I've never had any luck—I've never stayed in a spooky house. The places I go to are always as safe as Charing Cross. I want to see—whatever there is, the regular thing. *Is* there a ghost here?"

"Of course there is—a rattling good one."

"And have you seen him?"

"Oh don't ask me what *I've* seen—I should tax your credulity. I don't like to talk of these things. But there are two or three as bad—that is, as good!—rooms as you'll find anywhere."

"Do you mean in my corridor?" Lyon asked.

"I believe the worst is at the far end. But you'd be ill-advised to sleep there."

"Ill-advised?"

"Until you've finished your job. You'll get letters of importance the next morning and take the 10.20."

"Do you mean I shall invent a pretext for running away?"

"Unless you're braver than almost any one has ever been. They don't often put people to sleep there, but sometimes the house is so crowded that they have to. The same thing always happens—ill-concealed agitation at the breakfast-table and letters of the greatest importance. Of course it's a bachelor's room, and my wife and I are at the other end of the house. But I saw the comedy three days ago—the day after we got here. A young fellow had been put there—I forget his name—the house was so full; and the usual consequence followed. Letters at breakfast—an awfully queer face—an urgent call to town—so sorry his visit was cut short. Ashmore and his wife looked at each other and off the poor devil went."

"Ah that wouldn't suit me; I must do my job," said Lyon. "But do they mind your speaking of it? Some people who've a good ghost are very proud of it, you know."

What answer Colonel Capadose was on the point of making to this query our hero was not to learn, for at that moment their host had walked into the room accompanied by three or four of their fellow guests. Lyon was conscious that he was partly answered by the Colonel's not going on with the subject. This on the other hand was rendered natural by the fact that one of the gentlemen appealed to him for an opinion on a point under discussion, something to do with the everlasting history of the day's run. To Lyon himself Mr. Ashmore began to talk, expressing his regret for the delay of this pleasure. The topic that suggested itself was naturally that most closely connected with the motive of the artist's visit. The latter observed that it was a great disadvantage to him not to have had some preliminary acquaintance with Sir David—in most cases he found this so important. But the present sitter was so far advanced in life that there was doubtless no time to lose. "Oh

I can tell you all about him," said Mr. Ashmore; and for half an hour he told him a good deal. It was very interesting as well as a little extravagant, and Lyon felt sure he was a fine old boy to have endeared himself so to a son who was evidently not a gusher. At last he got up—he said he must go to bed if he wished to be fresh for his work in the morning. To which his host replied "Then you must take your candle; the lights are out; past this hour I don't keep my servants up."

In a moment Lyon had his glimmering taper in hand, and as he was leaving the room—he didn't disturb the others with a good-night, they were absorbed in the lemon-squeezer and the soda-water cork—he remembered other occasions on which he had made his way to bed alone through a darkened countryhouse: such occasions had not been rare, for he was almost always the first to leave the smoking-room. If he hadn't stayed at places of markedly evil repute he had, none the less—having too much imagination—sometimes found the great black halls and staircases rather "creepy": there had been often a sinister effect for his nerves in the sound of his tread through the long passages or the way the winter moon peeped into tall windows on landings. It occurred to him that if houses without supernatural pretensions could look so wicked at night the old corridors of Stayes would certainly give him a sensation. He didn't know whether the proprietors were sensitive; very often, as he had said to Colonel Capadose, people enjoyed the impeachment. What determined him to speak despite the risk was a need that had suddenly come to him to measure the Colonel's accuracy. As he had his hand on the door he said to his host: "I hope I shan't meet any ghosts."

"Any ghosts?"

"You ought to have some—in this fine old part."

"We do our best, but they're difficult to raise," said Mr. Ashmore. "I don't think they like the hot-water pipes."

"They remind them too much of their own climate? But haven't you a haunted room—at the end of my passage?"

"Oh there are stories—we try to keep them up."

"I should like very much to sleep there," Lyon said.

"Well, you can move there tomorrow if you like."

"Perhaps I had better wait," Lyon smiled, "till I've done my work." But he was to have presently the slightly humiliated sense of having been "arch" about nothing.

"Very good; but you won't work there, you know. My father will sit to you in his own apartments."

"Oh it isn't that; it's the fear of running away—like that gentleman three days ago."

"Three days ago? What gentleman?" Mr. Ashmore asked.

"The one who got urgent letters at breakfast and fled by the 10.20. Did he stand more than one night?"

"I don't know what you're talking about"—the son of Stayes was sturdy and blank. "There was no such gentleman—three days ago."

"Ah so much the better," said Lyon, nodding good-night and departing. He took his course, as he remembered it, with his wavering candle, and, though he encountered a great many gruesome objects, safely reached the passage out of which his room opened. In the complete darkness it seemed to stretch away still further, but he followed it, for the curiosity of the thing, to the end. He passed several doors with the name of the room painted up, but found nothing else. He was tempted to try the last door, to look into the room his friend had incriminated; but he felt this would be indiscreet, that gentleman's warrant was somehow a document of too many flourishes. There might be apparitions or other uncanny things and there mightn't; but there was surely nothing in the house so odd as Colonel Capadose.

II

Lyon found Sir David Ashmore a beautiful subject as well as the serenest and blandest of sitters. Moreover he was a very informing old man, tremendously puckered but not in the least dim; and he wore exactly the furred dressing-gown his portrayer would have chosen. He was proud of his age but ashamed of his infirmities, which however he greatly exaggerated and which didn't prevent his submitting to the brush as bravely as he might have to the salutary surgical knife. He sat there with the firm eyes and set smile of "Well, do your worst!" He demolished the legend of his having feared the operation would be fatal, giving an explanation which pleased our friend much better. He held that a gentleman should be painted but once in his life—that it was eager and fatuous to be hung up all over the place. That was good for women, who made a pretty wall-pattern; but the male face didn't lend itself to decorative repetition. The proper time for the likeness was at the last, when the whole man was there, when you got the sum of his experience. Lyon couldn't reply, as he would have done in many a case, that this was not a real synthesis—you had to allow so for leakage; since there had been no crack in Sir David's crystallisation. He spoke of his portrait as a plain map of the country, to be consulted by his children in a case of uncertainty. A proper map could be drawn up only when the country had been travelled. He gave Lyon his mornings, till luncheon, and they talked of many things, not neglecting, as a stimulus to gossip, the company at Stayes. Now that he didn't "go out," as he said, he saw much less of the people in his house—processions that came and went, that he knew nothing about and that he liked to hear Lyon describe. The artist sketched with a fine point and didn't caricature, and it usually befell that when Sir David didn't know the sons and daughters he had known the fathers and mothers. He was one of those terrible old persons who keep the book of antecedents. But in the case of the Capadose family, at whom they arrived by an easy stage, his knowledge embraced two, or even three, generations. General Capadose was an old crony, and he remembered his father before him. The General was rather a smart soldier, but in private life of too speculative a turn—always sneaking into the City to put his money into some rotten thing. He had married a girl who brought him something—and with it half a dozen children. He scarcely knew what had become of the rest of them, except that one was in the Church and had found preferment—wasn't he Dean of Rockingham? Clement, the fellow who was at Stayes, had apparently some gift for arms; he had served in the East and married a pretty girl. He had been at Eton with Arthur and used then to come to Stayes in his holidays. Lately, back in England, he had turned up with his wife again; that was before he—the old man—had been put to grass. He was a taking dog but had a monstrous foible.

"A monstrous foible?" Lyon echoed.

"He pulls the long bow—the longest that ever was."

Lyon's brush stopped short, while he repeated, for somehow the words both startled him and brought light: " 'The longest that ever was'?"

"You're very lucky not to have had to catch him."

Lyon debated. "Well, I think I *have* rather caught him. He revels in the miraculous."

"Oh it isn't always the miraculous. He'll lie about the time of day, about the name of his hatter. It's quite disinterested."

"Well, it's very base," Lyon declared, feeling rather sick for what Everina Brant had done with herself.

"Oh it's an extraordinary trouble to take," said the old man, "but this fellow isn't in himself at all base. There's no harm in him and no bad intention; he doesn't steal nor cheat nor gamble nor drink; he's very kind—he sticks to his wife, is fond of his children. He simply can't give you a straight answer."

"Then everything he told me last night, I now see, was tarred with that brush: he delivered himself of a series of the steepest statements. They stuck when I tried to swallow them, yet I never thought of so simple an explanation."

"No doubt he was in the vein," Sir David went on. "It's a natural peculiarity—as you might limp or stutter or be left-handed. I believe it comes and goes with changes of the wind. My son tells me that his friends quite allow for it and don't pin him down—for the sake of his wife, whom every one likes."

"Oh his wife—his wife!" Lyon murmured, painting fast.

"I dare say she's used to it."

"Never in the world, Sir David. How can she be used to it?"

"Why, my dear sir, when a woman's fond—! And don't they mostly rather

handle that instrument themselves? They're connoisseurs in the business,"
Sir David cackled with a harmless old-time cynicism. "They've a sympathy
for a fellow performer."

Lyon wondered; he had no ground for denying that Mrs. Capadose was
attached to her husband. But after a little he rejoined: "Oh not this one! I
knew her years ago—before her marriage; knew her well and admired her.
She was as clear as a bell."

"I like her very much," Sir David said, "but I've seen her back him up."

Lyon considered his host a moment not in the light of a sitter. "Are you
very sure?"

The old man grinned and brought out: "My dear sir, you're in love with
her."

"Very likely. God knows I used to be!"

"She must help him out—she can't expose him."

"She can hold her tongue," Lyon returned.

"Well, before you probably she will."

"That's what I'm curious to see." And he added privately: "Mercy on us,
what he must have made of her!" He kept this reflexion to himself, for he
considered that he had sufficiently betrayed his state of mind with regard
to Mrs. Capadose. None the less it occupied him now immensely, the question of how such a woman would arrange herself in such a position. He
watched her with an interest deeply quickened when he mingled with the
company; he had had his own troubles in life, but had rarely been so anxious
about anything as about this question of what the loyalty of a wife and the
infection of an example would have made of a perfectly candid mind. Oh he
would answer for it that whatever other women might be prone to do she,
of old, had stuck to the truth as a bather who can't swim sticks to shallow
water. Even if she hadn't been too simple for deviations she would have been
too proud, and if she hadn't had too much conscience would have had too
little eagerness. The lie was the last thing she would have endured or con-
doned—the particular thing she wouldn't have forgiven. Did she sit in
torment while her husband gave the rein, or was she now too so perverse
that she thought it a fine thing to be striking at the expense—Lyon would
have been ready to say—of one's decency? It would have taken a wondrous
alchemy—working backwards, as it were—to produce this latter result.
Besides these alternatives—that she suffered misery in silence and that she
was so much in love that her husband's exorbitance seemed to her but an
added richness, a proof of life and talent—there was still the possibility that
she hadn't found him out, that she took his false coinage at his own valuation. A little reflexion rendered this hypothesis untenable; it was too evident
that the account he gave of things must repeatedly have contradicted her
own knowledge. Within an hour or two of his meeting them Lyon had seen
her confronted with that perfectly gratuitous invention about the profit they

had made of his early picture. Even then indeed she had not, so far as he could see, smarted, and—but for the present he could only stare at the mystery!

Even if it hadn't been interfused, through his uneradicated interest in Mrs. Capadose, with an element of suspense, the question would still have been attaching and worrying; since, truly, he hadn't painted portraits so many years without becoming curious of queer cases. His attention was limited for the moment to the opportunity the following three days might yield, as the Colonel and his wife were going on to another house. It fixed itself largely of course upon the Colonel too—the fellow was *so* queer a case. Moreover it had to go on very quickly. Lyon was at once too discreet and too fond of his own intimate inductions to ask other people how they answered his conundrum—too afraid also of exposing the woman he once had loved. It was probable indeed that light would come to him from the talk of their companions; the Colonel's idiosyncrasy, both as it affected his own situation and as it affected his wife, would be a familiar theme in any house in which he was in the habit of staying. Lyon hadn't observed in the circles in which he visited any marked abstention from comment on the singularities of their members. It interfered with his progress that the Colonel hunted all day, while he plied his brushes and chatted with Sir David; but a Sunday intervened and that partly made it up. Mrs. Capadose fortunately didn't hunt and, his work done, was not inaccessible. He took a couple of good walks with her—she was fond of good walks—and beguiled her at tea into a friendly nook in the hall. Regard her as he might he couldn't make out to himself that she was consumed by a hidden shame; the sense of being married to a man whose word had no worth was not, in her spirit, so far as he could guess, the canker within the rose. Her mind appeared to have nothing on it but its own placid frankness, and when he sounded her eyes—with the long plummet he occasionally permitted himself to use—they had no uncomfortable consciousness. He talked to her again and still again of the dear old days—reminded her of things he hadn't had (before this reunion) any sense of himself remembering. Then he spoke to her of her husband, praised his appearance, his talent for conversation, professed to have felt a quick friendship for him and asked, with an amount of "cheek" for which he almost blushed, what manner of man he was. "What manner?" she echoed. "Dear me, how can one describe one's husband? I like him very much."

"Ah you've insisted on that to me already!" Lyon growled to exaggeration.

"Then why do you ask me again?" She added in a moment, as if she were so happy that she could afford to take pity on him: "He's everything that's good and true and kind. He's a soldier and a gentleman and a dear! He hasn't a fault. And he has great, great ability."

"Yes, he strikes one as having great, great ability. But of course I can't think him a dear."

"I don't care what you think him!" Everina laughed, looking still handsomer in the act than he had ever seen her. She was either utterly brazen or of a contrition quite impenetrable, and he had little prospect of extorting from her what he somehow so longed for—some avowal that she had after all better have married a man who was not a by-word for the most contemptible, the least heroic of vices. Hadn't she seen, hadn't she felt, the smile, the cold faded smile of complete depreciation, go round when her husband perjured himself to some particularly characteristic blackness? How could a woman of her quality live with that day after day, year after year, except by her quality's altering? But he would believe in the alteration only when he should have heard *her* lie. He was held by his riddle and yet impatient of it, he asked himself all kinds of questions. Didn't she lie, after all, when she let *his* lies pass without turning a hair? Wasn't her life a perpetual complicity, and didn't she aid and abet him by the simple fact that she wasn't disgusted with him? Then again perhaps she *was* disgusted and it was the mere desperation of her pride that had given her an inscrutable mask. Perhaps she protested in private, passionately; perhaps every night, in their own apartments, after the day's low exhibition, she had things out with him in a manner known only to the pair themselves. But if such scenes were of no avail and he took no more trouble to cure himself, how could she regard him, and after so many years of marriage too, with the perfectly artless complacency that Lyon had surprised in her in the course of the first day's dinner? If our friend hadn't been in love with her he would surely have taken the Colonel's delinquencies less to heart. As the case stood they fairly turned to the tragical for him, even while he was sharply aware of how merely "his funny way" they were to others—and of how funny his, Oliver Lyon's, own way of regarding them would have seemed to every one.

The observation of these three days showed him that if Capadose was an abundant he was not a malignant liar and that his fine faculty exercised itself mainly on subjects of small direct importance. "He's the liar platonic," he said to himself; "he's disinterested, as Sir David said, he doesn't operate with a hope of gain or with a desire to injure. It's art for art—he's prompted by some love of beauty. He has an inner vision of what might have been, of what ought to be, and he helps on the good cause by the simple substitution of a shade. He lays on colour, as it were, and what less do I do myself?" His disorder had a wide range, but a family likeness ran through all its forms, which consisted mainly of their singular futility. It was this that made them an affliction; they encumbered the field of conversation, took up valuable space, turned it into the desert of a perpetual shimmering mirage. For the falsehood uttered under stress a convenient place can usually be found, as for a person who presents himself with an author's order at the first night of a play. But the mere luxurious lie is the gentleman without a voucher or a ticket who accommodates himself with a stool in the passage.

Of one possible charge Lyon acquitted his successful rival; it had puzzled him that, irrepressible as he was, he had never got into a mess in the Service. But it was to be made out that he drew the line at the Service—over that august institution he never flapped his wings. Moreover, for all the personal pretension in his talk it rarely came, oddly enough, to swagger about his military exploits. He had a passion for the chase, he had followed it in far countries, and some of his finest flowers were reminiscences of what he had prodigiously done and miraculously escaped when off by himself. The more by himself he had been of course the bigger the commemorative nosegay bloomed. A new acquaintance always received from him, in honour of their meeting, one of the most striking of these tributes—that generalisation Lyon very promptly made. And the extraordinary man had inconsistencies and unexpected lapses—lapses into the very commonplace of the credible. Lyon recognised what Sir David had told him, that he flourished and drooped by an incalculable law and would sometimes keep the truce of God for a month at a time. The muse of improvisation breathed on him at her pleasure and appeared sometimes quite to avert her face. He would neglect the finest openings and then set sail with everything against him. As a general thing he affirmed the impossible rather than denied the certain, though this too had lively exceptions. Very often, when it was loud enough—for he liked a noise about him—he joined in the reprobation that cast him out, he allowed he was trying it on and that one didn't know what had happened to one till one *had* tried. Still, he never completely retracted nor retreated—he dived and came up in another place. Lyon guessed him capable on occasion of defending his position with violence, though only when it was very bad. Then he might easily be dangerous—then he would hit out and not care whom he touched. Such moments as those would test his wife's philosophy—Lyon would have liked to see her there. In the smoking-room and elsewhere the company, so far as it was composed of his familiars, had an hilarious protest always at hand; but among the men who had known him long his big brush was an old story, so old that they had ceased to talk about it, and Lyon didn't care, as I have said, to bring to a point those impatiences that might have resembled his own.

The oddest thing of all was that neither surprise nor familiarity prevented the Colonel's being liked; his largest appeals even to proved satiety passed for an overflow of life and high spirits—almost of simple good looks. If he was fond of treating his gallantry with a flourish he was none the less unmistakably gallant. He was a first-rate rider and shot, in spite of his fund of anecdote illustrating these accomplishments: in short he was very nearly as clever and brave, and his adventures and observations had been very nearly as numerous and wonderful, as the list he unrolled. His best quality however remained that indiscriminate sociability which took interest and favour for granted and about which he bragged least. It made him cheap, it made him

even in a manner vulgar; but it was so contagious that his listener was more
or less on his side as against the probabilities. It was a private reflexion of
Oliver Lyon's that he not only was mendacious but made any charmed con-
verser feel as much so by the very action of the charm—of a certain guilty
submission of which no intention of ridicule could yet purge you. In the
evening, at dinner and afterwards, our friend, better placed for observation
than the first night, watched his wife's face to see if some faint shade or
spasm never passed over it. But she continued to show nothing, and the
wonder was that when he spoke she almost always listened. That was her
pride: she wished not to be even suspected of not facing the music. Lyon
had none the less an importunate vision of a veiled figure coming the next
day in the dusk to certain places to repair the Colonel's ravages, as the relatives of kleptomaniacs punctually call at the shops that have suffered from
their depredations.

"I must apologise; of course it wasn't true; I hope no harm is done; it's
only his incorrigible—" oh to hear that woman's voice in that deep abase-
ment! Lyon had no harsh design, no conscious wish to practise on her sensi-
bility or her loyalty; but he did say to himself that he should have liked to
bring her round, liked to see her *show* him that a vision of the dignity of not
being married to a mountebank sometimes haunted her dreams. He even
imagined the hour when, with a burning face, she might ask *him* not to
take the question up. Then he should be almost consoled—he would be
magnanimous.

He finished his picture and took his departure, after having worked in a
glow of interest which made him believe in his success, until he found he had
pleased every one, especially Mr. and Mrs. Ashmore, when he began to be
sceptical. The party at any rate changed: Colonel and Mrs. Capadose went
their way. He was able to say to himself however that his parting with
Everina wasn't so much an end as a beginning, and he called on her soon
after his return to town. She had told him the hours she was at home—she
seemed to like him. If she liked him why hadn't she married him, or at any
rate why wasn't she sorry she hadn't? If she was sorry she concealed it too
well. The point he made of some visible contrition in her on this head may
strike the reader as extravagant, but something must be allowed so disappointed a man. He didn't ask much after all; not that she should love him
today or that she should allow him to tell her that he loved her, but only that
she should give him some sign she didn't feel her choice as *all* gain. Instead
of this, for the present, she contented herself with exhibiting her small
daughter to him. The child was beautiful and had the prettiest eyes of
innocence he had ever seen: which didn't prevent his wondering if she told
horrid fibs. This idea much occupied and rather darkly amused him—the
picture of the anxiety with which her mother would watch as she grew older
for symptoms of the paternal strain. That was a pleasant care for such a

woman as Everina Brant! Did she lie to the child herself about her father—was that necessary when she pressed her daughter to her bosom to cover up his tracks? Did he control himself before the little girl—so that she mightn't hear him say things she knew to be other than his account of them? Lyon scarcely thought that probable: his genius would be ever too strong for him, and the only guard for Amy would be in her being too simple for criticism. One couldn't judge yet—she was too young to show. If she should grow up clever she would be sure to tread in his steps—a delightful improvement in her mother's situation! Her little face was not shifty, but neither was her father's big one; so that proved nothing.

Lyon reminded his friends more than once of their promise that Amy should sit to him, and it was now only a question of his own leisure. The desire grew in him to paint the Colonel also—an operation from which he promised himself a rich private satisfaction. He would draw him out, he would set him up in that totality about which he had talked with Sir David, and none but the initiated would know. They, however, would rank the picture high, and it would be indeed six rows deep—a masterpiece of fine characterisation, of legitimate treachery. He had dreamed for years of some work that should show the master of the deeper vision as well as the mere reporter of the items, and here at last was his subject. It was a pity it wasn't better, but that wasn't *his* fault. It was his impression that already no one "drew" the Colonel in the social sense more effectively than he, and he did this not only by instinct but on a plan. There were moments when he almost winced at the success of his plan—the poor gentleman went so terribly far. He would pull up some day, look at his critic between the eyes and guess he was being played upon—which would lead to his wife's guessing it also. Not that Lyon cared much for that however, so long as she failed to suppose —and she couldn't divine it—that *she* was a part of his joke. He formed such a habit now of going to see her of a Sunday afternoon that he was angry when she went out of town. This occurred often, as the couple were great visitors and the Colonel was always looking for sport, which he liked best when it could be had at the expense of others. Lyon would have supposed the general gregarious life, the constant presence of a gaping "gallery," particularly little to her taste, for it was naturally in country-houses that her husband came out strongest. To let him go off without her, not to see him expose himself—that ought properly to have been her relief and her nearest approach to a luxury. She mentioned to her friend in fact that she preferred staying at home, but she didn't say it was because in other people's houses she was on the rack: the reason she gave was that she liked so to be with the child. It wasn't perhaps criminal to deal in such "whoppers," but it was damned vulgar: poor Lyon was delighted when he arrived at that formula. Certainly some day too he would cross the line—he would practise the fraud to which his talked "rot" had the same relation as the experiments of the forger have to the signed cheque. And in the meantime, yes, he was vulgar, in spite of his facility, his impunity, his so remarkably fine person. Twice, by exception, toward the end of the winter, when he left town for a few days' hunting, his wife remained at home. Lyon hadn't yet reached the point of asking himself if the wish not to miss two of his visits might have had something to do with this course. That enquiry would perhaps have been more in place later, when he began to paint her daughter and she made a rule of coming with her. But it wasn't in her to give the wrong name, to affect motives, and Lyon could see she had the maternal passion in spite of the bad blood in the little girl's veins.

She came inveterately, though Lyon multiplied the sittings: Amy was never entrusted to the governess or the maid. He had knocked off poor old Sir David in ten days, but the simple face of the child held him and worried him and gave him endless work. He asked for sitting after sitting, and it might have struck a solicitous spectator that he was wearing the little girl out. He knew better, however, and Mrs. Capadose also knew: they were present together at the long intermissions he gave her, when she left her pose and roamed about the great studio, amusing herself with its curiosities, playing with the old draperies and costumes, having unlimited leave to handle. Then her mother and their so patient friend—much more patient than her piano-mistress—sat and talked; he laid aside his brushes and leaned back in his chair; he always gave her tea. What Mrs. Capadose couldn't suspect was the rate at which, during these weeks, he neglected other orders: women have no faculty of imagination with regard to a man's work beyond a vague idea that it doesn't matter. Lyon in fact put off everything and made high celebrities wait. There were half-hours of silence, when he plied his brushes, during which he was mainly conscious that Everina was sitting there. She easily fell into that if he didn't insist on talking, and she wasn't embarrassed nor bored by any lapse of communication. Sometimes she took up a book— there were plenty of them about; sometimes, a little way off in her chair, she watched his progress—though without in the least advising or correcting— as if she cared for every stroke that was to contribute to his result. These strokes were occasionally a little wild; he was thinking so much more of his heart than of his hand. He wasn't more embarrassed than she, but he was more agitated: it was as if in the sittings (for the child too was admirably quiet) something had beautifully settled itself between them or had already grown—a tacit confidence, an inexpressible secret. He at least felt it that way, but he after all couldn't be sure she did. What he wanted her to do for him was very little; it wasn't even to allow that she was unhappy. She would satisfy him by letting him know even by some quite silent sign that she could imagine her happiness with him—well, more unqualified. Perhaps indeed— his presumption went so far—that was what she did mean by contentedly sitting there.

III

At last he broached the question of painting the Colonel: it was now very late in the season—there would be little time before the common dispersal. He said they must make the most of it; the great thing was to begin; then in the autumn, with the resumption of their London life, they could go forward. Mrs. Capadose objected to this that she really couldn't consent to accept another present of such value. Lyon had sacrificed to her the portrait of herself of old—he knew what they had had the indelicacy to do with it. Now he had offered her this wondrous memorial of the child—wondrous it would evidently be when he should be able to bring it to a finish; a precious possession that, this time, they would cherish for ever. But his generosity and their indiscretion must stop there—they couldn't be so tremendously "beholden" to him. They couldn't order the picture, which of course he would understand without her explaining: it was a luxury beyond their reach, since they knew the great prices he received. Besides, what had they ever done—what above all had *she* ever done, that he should overload them with benefits? No, he was too dreadfully good; it was really impossible that Clement should sit. Lyon listened to her without protest, without interruption, while he bent forward at his work; and at last returned: "Well, if you won't take it why not let him sit just for my own pleasure and profit? Let it be a favour, a service I ask of him. All the generosity and charity will so be on your side. It will do me a lot of good to paint him and the picture will remain in my hands."

"How will it do you a lot of good?" Mrs. Capadose asked.

"Why he's such a rare model—such an interesting subject. He has such an expressive face. It will teach me no end of things."

"Expressive of what?" said Mrs. Capadose.

"Why of his inner man."

"And you want to paint his inner man?"

"Of course I do. That's what a great portrait gives you, and with a splendid comment on it thrown in for the money. I shall make the Colonel's a great one. It will put me up high. So you see my request is eminently interested."

"How can you be higher than you are?"

"Oh I'm an insatiable climber. So don't stand in my way," said Lyon.

"Well, everything in him is very noble," Mrs. Capadose gravely contended.

"Ah trust me to bring everything out!" Lyon returned, feeling a little ashamed of himself.

Mrs. Capadose, before she went, humoured him to the point of saying that her husband would probably comply with his invitation; but she added: "Nothing would induce me to let you pry into *me* that way!"

"Oh you," her friend laughed—"I could do you in the dark!"

The Colonel shortly afterwards placed his leisure at the painter's disposal and by the end of July had paid him several visits. Lyon was disappointed neither in the quality of his sitter nor in the degree to which he himself rose to the occasion; he felt really confident of producing what he had conceived. He was in the spirit of it, charmed with his motive and deeply interested in his problem. The only point that troubled him was the idea that when he should send his picture to the Academy he shouldn't be able to inscribe it in the catalogue under the simple rubric to which all propriety pointed. He couldn't in short send in the title as "The Liar"—more was the pity. However, this little mattered, for he had now determined to stamp that sense on it as legibly—and to the meanest intelligence—as it was stamped for his own vision on the living face. As he saw nothing else in the Colonel today, so he gave himself up to the joy of "rendering" nothing else. How he did it he couldn't have told you, but he felt a miracle of method freshly revealed to him every time he sat down to work. It was in the eyes and it was in the mouth, it was in every line of the face and every fact of the attitude, in the indentation of the chin, in the way the hair was planted, the moustache was twisted, the smile came and went, the breath rose and fell. It was in the way he looked out at a bamboozled world in short—the way he would look out for ever. There were half a dozen portraits in Europe that Lyon rated as supreme; he thought of them always as immortal things, for they were as perfectly preserved as they were consummately painted. It was to this small exemplary group that he aspired to attach the canvas on which he was now engaged. One of the productions that helped to compose it was the magnificent Moroni of the National Gallery—the young tailor in the white jacket at his board with his shears. The Colonel was not a tailor, nor was Moroni's model, unlike many tailors, a liar; the very man, body and soul, should bloom into life under his hand with just that assurance of no loss of a drop of the liquor. The Colonel, as it turned out, liked to sit, and liked to talk while sitting: which was very fortunate, as his talk was half the inspiration of his artist. Lyon applied without mercy his own gift of provocation; he couldn't possibly have been in a better relation to him for the purpose. He encouraged, beguiled, excited him, manifested an unfathomable credulity, and his own sole lapses were when the Colonel failed, as he called it, to "act." He had his intermissions, his hours of sterility, and then Lyon knew that the picture also drooped. The higher his companion soared, the more he circled and sang in the blue, the better he felt himself paint; he only couldn't make the flights and the evolutions last. He lashed his victim on when he flagged; his one difficulty was his fear again that his game might be suspected. The Colonel, however, was easily beguiled; he basked and expanded in the fine steady light of the painter's attention. In this way the picture grew very fast, astonishingly faster, in spite of its so much greater "importance," than the simple-faced little girl's. By the fifth of August it was pretty well finished: that was the date of the last sitting the Colonel was for the present able to give—he was leaving town the next day with his wife. Lyon was amply content—he saw his way so clear: he should be able to do at leisure the little that remained, in respect to which his friend's attendance would be a minor matter. As there was no hurry, in any case, he would let the thing stand over till his own return to London, in November, when he should come back to it with a fresh eye. On the Colonel's asking him if Everina might have a sight of it next day, should she find a minute—this being so greatly her desire —Lyon begged as a special favour that she would wait: what he had yet to do was small in amount, but it would make all the difference. This was the repetition of a proposal Mrs. Capadose had made on the occasion of his last visit to her, and he had then recommended her not coming till he should be himself better pleased. He had really never been, at a corresponding stage, better pleased; and he blushed a little for his subtlety.

By the fifth of August the weather was very warm, and on that day, while the Colonel sat at his usual free practice Lyon opened for the sake of ventilation a little subsidiary door which led directly from his studio into the garden and sometimes served as an entrance and an exit for models and for visitors of the humbler sort, and as a passage for canvases, frames, packing-boxes and other professional gear. The main entrance was through the house and his own apartments, and this approach had the charming effect of admitting you first to a high gallery, from which a winding staircase, happily disposed, dropped to the wide decorated encumbered room. The view of this room beneath them, with all its artistic ingenuities and the objects of value that Lyon had collected, never failed to elicit exclamations of delight from persons stepping into the gallery. The way from the garden was plainer and at once more practicable and more private. Lyon's domain, in Saint John's Wood, was not vast, but when the door stood open of a summer's day it offered a glimpse of flowers and trees, there was a sweetness in the air and you heard the birds. On this particular morning the side-door had been found convenient by an unannounced visitor, a youngish woman who stood in the room before the Colonel was aware of her, but whom he was then the first to see. She was very quiet—she looked from one of the men to the other. "Oh, dear, here's another!" Lyon exclaimed as soon as his eyes rested on her. She belonged in fact to the somewhat importunate class of the model in search of employment, and she explained that she had ventured to come straight in, that way, because very often when she went to call upon gentlemen the servants played her tricks, turned her off and wouldn't take in her name.

"But how did you get into the garden?" Lyon asked.

"The gate was open, sir—the servants' gate. The butcher's cart was there."

"The butcher ought to have closed it," said Lyon.

"Then you don't require me, sir?" the lady continued.

Lyon continued to paint; he had given her a sharp look at first, but now his eyes were only for his work. The Colonel, however, examined her with interest. She was a person of whom you could scarcely say whether being young she looked old or old looked young; she had at any rate clearly rounded several of the corners of life; she had a face that was rosy, yet that failed to suggest freshness. She was nevertheless rather pretty and even looked as if at one time she might have sat for the complexion. She wore a hat with many feathers, a dress with many bugles, long black gloves encircled with silver bracelets, and very bad shoes. There was something about her not exactly of the governess out of place nor completely of the actress seeking an engagement, but that savoured of a precarious profession, perhaps even of a blighted career. She was perceptibly solid and tarnished, and after she had been in the room a few moments the air, or at any rate the nostril, became acquainted with a vague alcoholic waft. She was unpractised in the *h,* and when Lyon at last thanked her and said he didn't want her—he was doing nothing for which she could be useful—she replied in rather a wounded manner: "Well, you know you *'ave* 'ad me!"

"I don't remember you," Lyon protested.

"Well, I dare say the people who saw your pictures do! I haven't much time, but I thought I'd look in."

"I'm much obliged to you."

"If ever you should require me and just send me a postcard—"

"I never send postcards," said Lyon.

"Oh well, I should value a private letter! Anything to Miss Geraldine, Mortimer Terrace Mews, Notting 'ill—"

"Very good; I'll remember," said Lyon.

Miss Geraldine lingered. "I thought I'd just stop on the chance."

"I'm afraid I can't hold out hopes, I'm so busy with portraits," Lyon continued.

"Yes; I see you are. I wish I was in the gentleman's place."

"I'm afraid in that case it wouldn't look like the gentleman," the Colonel sociably laughed.

"Oh of course it couldn't compare—it wouldn't be so 'andsome! But I do hate them portraits!" Miss Geraldine declared. "It's so much bread out of our mouths."

"Well, there are many who can't paint them," Lyon suggested for comfort.

"Oh I've sat to the very first—and only to the first! There's many that couldn't do anything without me."

"I'm glad you're in such demand." Lyon's amusement had turned to impatience and he added that he wouldn't detain her—he would send for her in case of need.

"Very well; remember it's the Mews—more's the pity! You don't sit so well as *us!*" Miss Geraldine pursued, looking at the Colonel. "If *you* should require me, sir—"

"You put him out; you embarrass him," said Lyon.

"Embarrass him, oh gracious!" the visitor cried with a laugh that diffused a fragrance. "Perhaps *you* send postcards, eh?" she went on to the Colonel; but she retreated with a wavering step. She passed out into the garden as she had come.

"How very dreadful—she's drunk!" said Lyon. He was painting hard, but looked up, checking himself: Miss Geraldine, in the open doorway, had thrust in her head again.

"Yes, I do hate it—that sort of thing!" she cried with an explosion of mirth which confirmed Lyon's charge. On which she disappeared.

"What sort of thing—what does she mean?" the Colonel asked.

"Oh my painting you when I might be painting her."

"And have you ever painted her?"

"Never in the world; I've never seen her. She's quite mistaken."

The Colonel just waited; then he remarked: "She was very pretty—ten years ago."

"I dare say, but she's quite ruined. For me the least 'drop too much' spoils them; I shouldn't care for her at all."

"My dear fellow, she's not a model," the Colonel laughed.

"Today, no doubt, she's not worthy of the name; but she has done her time."

"*Jamais de la vie!* That's all a pretext."

"A pretext?" Lyon pricked up his ears—he wondered what now would come.

"She didn't want you—she wanted *me.*"

"I noticed she paid you some attention. What then does she want of you?"

"Oh to do me an ill turn. She hates me—lots of women do. She's watching me—she follows me."

Lyon leaned back in his chair—without a single grain of faith. He was all the more delighted with what he heard and with the Colonel's bright and candid manner. The story had shot up and bloomed, from the dropped seed, on the spot. "My dear Colonel!" he murmured with friendly interest and commiseration.

"I was vexed when she came in—but I wasn't upset," his sitter continued.

"You concealed it very well if you were."

"Ah when one has been through what I have! Today, however, I confess I was half-prepared. I've noticed her hanging about—she knows my movements. She was near my house this morning—she must have followed me."

"But who is she then—with such charming 'cheek'?"

"Yes, she has plenty of cheek," said the Colonel; "but as you observe she was primed. Still, she carried it off as a cool hand. Oh she's a bad 'un! She isn't a model and never was; no doubt she has known some of those women and picked up their form. She had hold of a friend of mine ten years ago—a young jackanapes who might have been left to be plucked but whom I was obliged to take an interest in for family reasons. It's a long story—I had really forgotten all about it. She's thirty-seven if she's a day. I was able to make a diversion and let him get off—after which I sent her about her business. She knew it was me she had to thank. She has never forgiven me—I think she's off her head. Her name isn't Geraldine at all and I doubt very much if that's her address."

"Ah what *is* her name?" Lyon was all participation. He had always noted that when once his friend was launched there was no danger in asking; the more you asked the more abundantly you were served.

"It's Pearson—Harriet Pearson; but she used to call herself Grenadine—wasn't that a rum notion? Grenadine—Geraldine—the jump was easy." Lyon was charmed with this flow of facility, and his interlocutor went on: "I hadn't thought of her for years—I had quite lost sight of her. I don't know what her idea is, but practically she's harmless. As I came in I thought I saw her a little way up the road. She must have found out I come here and have arrived before me. I dare say—or rather I'm sure—she's waiting for me there now."

"Hadn't you better have protection?" Lyon asked with amusement.

"The best protection's five shillings—I'm willing to go that length. Unless indeed she has a bottle of vitriol. But they only throw vitriol on the fellows who have 'undone' them, and I never undid her—I told her the first time I saw her that it wouldn't do. Oh if she's there we'll walk a little way together and talk it over, and, as I say, I'll go as far as five shillings."

"Well," said Lyon, "I'll contribute another five." He felt this little to pay for what he was getting.

That entertainment was interrupted, however, for the time, by the Colonel's departure. Lyon hoped for some sequel to match—a report, by note, of the next scene in the drama as his friend had met it, but this genius apparently didn't operate with the pen. At any rate he left town without writing—they had taken a tryst for three months later. Oliver Lyon always passed the holidays in the same way; during the first weeks he paid a visit to his elder brother, the happy possessor, in the south of England, of a rambling old house with formal gardens, in which he delighted, and then he went abroad—usually to Italy or Spain. This year he carried out his custom after taking a last look at his all but finished work and feeling as nearly pleased with it as decency permitted, the translation of the idea by the hand appearing always to him at the best a pitiful compromise. One yellow afternoon in the country, as he smoked his pipe on one of the old terraces, he was taken with a fancy for another look at what he had lately done, and with that in particular of doing two or three things more to it: he had been much haunted with this unrest while he lounged there. The provocation was not to be resisted, and though he was at any rate so soon to be back in London he was unable to brook delay. Five minutes with his view of the Colonel would be enough—it would clear up questions that hummed in his brain; so that the next morning, to give himself this luxury, he took the train for town. He sent no word in advance; he would lunch at his club and probably return into Sussex by the 5.45.

In Saint John's Wood the tide of human life flows at no time very fast, and in the first days of September Lyon found mere desolation in the straight sunny roads where the little plastered garden-walls, with their incommunicative doors, looked feebly Oriental. There was definite stillness in his own house, to which he admitted himself by his pass-key, it being a matter of conscience with him sometimes to take his servants unawares. The good woman set in authority over them and who cumulated the functions of cook and housekeeper was, however, quickly summoned by his step, and—as he cultivated frankness of intercourse with his domestics—received him without the confusion of surprise. He reassured her as to any other effect of unpreparedness—he had come up but for a few hours and should be busy in the studio. She announced that he was just in time to see a lady and a gentleman who were there at the moment—they had arrived five minutes before. She had told them he was absent but they said it was all right; they only wanted to look at a picture and would be very careful of everything. "I hope it's all right, sir," this informant concluded. "The gentleman says he's a sitter and he gave me his name—rather an odd name; I think it's military. The lady's a very fine lady, sir; at any rate there they are."

"Oh it's all right"—Lyon read the identity of his visitors. The good woman couldn't know, having when he was at home so little to do with the comings and goings; his man, who showed people in and out, had accompanied him to the country. He was a good deal surprised at the advent of Mrs. Capadose, who knew how little he wished her to see the portrait unfinished, but it was a familiar truth to him that she was a woman of a high spirit. Besides, perhaps the lady wasn't Everina; the Colonel might well have brought some inquisitive friend, a person who perhaps wanted a portrait of *her* husband. What were they doing in town, in any case, at that moment? Lyon made his way to the studio with a certain curiosity; he wondered vaguely what his friends were "up to." He laid his hand upon the curtain draping the door of communication, the door opening upon the gallery constructed for relief at the time the studio was added to the house; but with his motion to slide the tapestry on its rings arrested in the act. A singular startling sound reached him from the room beneath; it had the appearance of a passionate wail, or perhaps rather a smothered shriek, accompanied by a violent burst of tears. Oliver Lyon listened intently and then passed in to the balcony, which was covered with an old thick Moorish rug. His step was noiseless without his trying to keep it so, and after that first instant he found himself profiting irresistibly by the accident of his not having attracted the attention of the two persons in the studio, who were some twenty feet below him. They were in truth so deeply and strangely engaged that their unconsciousness of observation was explained. The scene that took place before Lyon's eyes was more extraordinary than any he had ever felt free to overlook. Delicacy and the failure to understand kept him at first from interfering—what he saw was a woman who had thrown herself in a flood of tears on her companion's bosom; after which surprise and discretion gave way to a force that made him step back behind the curtain. This same force, further—the force of a *need* to know—caused him to avail himself for better observation of a crevice formed by his gathering together the two halves of his swinging tapestry. He was perfectly aware of what he was about—he was for the moment an eavesdropper and a spy; but he was also aware that something irregular, as to which his confidence had been trifled with, was on foot, and that he was as much concerned with the reasons of it as he might be little concerned with the taken form. His observation, his reflexions, accomplished themselves in a flash.

His visitors were in the middle of the room; Mrs. Capadose clung to her husband, weeping; she sobbed as if her heart would break. Her distress was horrible to Oliver Lyon, but his astonishment was greater than his horror when he heard the Colonel respond to it by the vehement imprecation "Damn him, damn him, damn him!" What in the world had happened? why was she sobbing and whom was he damning? What had happened, Lyon saw the next instant, was that the Colonel had finally rummaged out the canvas before which he had been sitting—he knew the corner where the artist usually placed it, out of the way and its face to the wall —and had set it up for his wife on an empty easel. She had looked at it a few moments and then—apparently—what she saw in it had produced an explosion of dismay and resentment. She was too overcome, and the Colonel too busy holding her and re-expressing his wrath, to look round or look up. The scene was so unexpected to Lyon that all impulse failed in him on the spot for a proof of the triumph of his hand—of a tremendous hit: he could only wonder what on earth was the matter. The idea of the triumph was yet to come. He could see his projected figure, however, from where he stood; he was startled with its look of life—he hadn't supposed the force of the thing could so prevail. Mrs. Capadose flung herself away from her husband—she dropped into the nearest chair, leaned against a table, buried her face in her arms. The sound of her woe diminished, but she shuddered there as if overwhelmed with anguish and shame. Her husband stood a moment glaring at the picture, then went to her, bent over her, took hold of her again, soothed her. "What is it, darling—what the devil is it?"

Lyon fairly drank in her answer, "It's cruel—oh it's too cruel!"

"Damn him, damn him, damn him!" the Colonel repeated.

"It's all there—it's all there!" Mrs. Capadose went on.

"Hang it, what's all there?"

"Everything there oughtn't to be—everything he has seen. It's too dreadful!"

"Everything he has seen? Why, ain't I a good-looking fellow? I'll be bound to say he has made me handsome."

Mrs. Capadose had sprung up again; she had darted another glance at the painted betrayal. "Handsome? Hideous, hideous! Not that—never, never!"

"Not *what*, in heaven's name?" the Colonel almost shouted. Lyon could see his flushed bewildered face.

"What he has made of you—what you know! *He* knows—he has seen. Every one will, every one know and see. Fancy that thing in the Academy!"

"You're going wild, darling; but if you hate it so it needn't go," the poor branded man declared.

"Ah he'll send it—it's so good! Come away—come away!" Mrs. Capadose wailed, seizing her husband.

"It's so good?" the victim cried.

"Come away—come away," she only repeated, and she turned toward the staircase that ascended to the gallery.

"Not that way—not through the house in the state you're in," Lyon heard her companion object. "This way—we can pass," he added; and he drew his wife to the small door that opened into the garden. It was bolted, but he pushed the bolt and opened the door. She passed out quickly, but he stood there looking back into the room. "Wait for me a moment!" he cried out to her; and with an excited stride he re-entered the studio. He came up to the picture again—again he covered it with his baffled glare. "Damn him—damn him—damn him!" he broke out once more. Yet it wasn't clear to Lyon whether this malediction had for object the guilty original or the guilty painter. The Colonel turned away and moved about as if looking for something; Lyon for the moment wondered at his intentions; saying to himself the next, however, below his breath: "He's going to do it a harm!" His first impulse was to raise a preventive cry, but he paused with the sound of Everina Brant's sobs still in his ears. The Colonel found what he was looking for—found it among some odds and ends on a small table and strode back with it to the easel. At one and the same moment Lyon recognised the object seized as a small Eastern dagger and saw that he had plunged it into the canvas. Animated as with a sudden fury and exercising a rare vigour of hand, he dragged the instrument down—Lyon knew it to have no very fine edge—making a long and abominable gash. Then he plucked it out and dashed it again several times into the face of the likeness, exactly as if he were stabbing a human victim: it had the most portentous effect—that of some act of prefigured or rehearsed suicide. In a few seconds more the Colonel had tossed the dagger away—he looked at it in this motion as for the sight of blood—and hurried out of the place with a bang of the door.

The strangest part of all was—as will doubtless appear—that Oliver Lyon lifted neither voice nor hand to save his picture. The point is that he didn't feel as if he were losing it or didn't care if he were, so much more was he conscious of gaining a certitude. His old friend *was* ashamed of her husband, and he had made her so, and he had scored a great success, even at the sacrifice of his precious labour. The revelation so excited him—as indeed the whole scene did—that when he came down the steps after the Colonel had gone he trembled with his happy agitation; he was dizzy and had to sit down a moment. The portrait had a dozen jagged wounds—the Colonel literally had hacked himself to death. Lyon left it there where it grimaced, never touched it, scarcely looked at it; he only walked up and down his studio with a sense of such achieved success as nothing finished and framed, varnished and delivered and paid for had ever given him. At the end of this time his good woman came to offer him luncheon; there was a passage under the staircase from the offices.

"Ah the lady and gentleman have gone, sir? I didn't hear them."

"Yes; they went by the garden."

But she had stopped, staring at the picture on the easel. "Gracious, how you 'ave served it, sir!"

Lyon imitated the Colonel. "Yes, I cut it up—in a fit of disgust."

"Mercy, after all your trouble! Because they weren't pleased, sir?"

"Yes; they weren't pleased."

"Well, they must be very grand! Blest if I would!"

"Have it chopped up; it will do to light fires," Lyon magnificently said.

He returned to the country by the 3.30 and a few days later passed over to France. There was something he found himself looking for during these two months on the Continent; he had an expectation—he could hardly have said of what; of some characteristic sign or other on the Colonel's part. Wouldn't he write, wouldn't he explain, wouldn't he take for granted Lyon had discovered the way he had indeed been "served" and hold it only decent to show some form of pity for his mystification? Would he plead guilty or would he repudiate suspicion? The latter course would be difficult, would really put his genius to the test, in view of the ready and responsible witness who had admitted the visitors the day of the ravage and would establish the connexion between their presence and that perpetration. Would the Colonel proffer some apology or some amends, or would any word from him be only a further expression of that exasperated wonder which our friend had seen his wife so suddenly and so fatally communicate? He would have either to take oath that he hadn't touched the picture or to admit that he had, and in either case would be at cost for a difficult version. Lyon was impatient for this probably remarkable story, and as no letter came was disappointed at the failure of the exhibition. His impatience however was much greater in respect to Mrs. Capadose's inevitable share in the report, if report there was to be; for certainly that would be the real test, would show how far she would go for her husband on the one side or for himself on the other. He could scarcely wait to see what line she would take—whether she would simply adopt the Colonel's, whatever it might be. It would have met his impatience most to draw her out without waiting, to get an idea in advance. He wrote to her, to this end, from Venice, in the tone of their established friendship, asking for news, telling her of his movements, hoping for their reunion in London and not saying a word about the picture. Day followed day, after the time, and he received no answer; on which he reflected that she couldn't trust herself to write—was still too deeply ruffled, too disconcerted, by his "betrayal." Her husband had espoused her resentment and she had espoused the action he had taken in consequence of it; the rupture was therefore complete and everything at an end. Lyon was frankly rueful over this prospect, at the same time that he thought it deplorable such charming people should have put themselves so grossly in the wrong. He was at last cheered, though little further enlightened, by the arrival of a letter, brief but breathing good humour and hinting neither at a grievance nor at a bad conscience. The most interesting part of it to him was the postscript, which ran as follows: "I have a confession to make to you. We were in town for a couple of days, early in September, and I took the occasion to defy your authority: this was very bad of me but I couldn't help it. I made Clement take me to your studio—I wanted so dreadfully to see what you had done with him, your wishes to the contrary notwithstanding. We made your servants let us in and I took a good look at the picture. It is really wonderful!" "Wonderful" was non-committal, but at least with this letter there was no rupture.

The third day after his return was a Sunday, so that he could go and ask Mrs. Capadose for luncheon. She had given him in the spring a general invitation to do so and he had several times profited by it. These had been the occasions, before his sittings, when he saw the Colonel most familiarly. Directly after the meal his host disappeared (went out, as he said, to call on *his* women) and the second half-hour was the best, even when there were other people. Now, in the first days of December, Lyon had the luck to find the pair alone, without even Amy, who appeared but little in public. They were in the drawing-room waiting for the repast to be announced, and as soon as he came in the Colonel broke out: "My dear fellow, I'm delighted to see you! I'm so keen to begin again."

"Oh do go on; it's so beautiful," Mrs. Capadose said as she gave him her hand.

Lyon looked from one to the other; he didn't know what he had expected, but he hadn't expected this. "Ah then you think I've got something?"

"You've got everything." And Mrs. Capadose smiled from her golden-brown eyes.

"She wrote you of our little crime?" her husband asked. "She dragged me there—I had to go." Lyon wondered for a moment whether he meant by their little crime the assault on the canvas; but his friend's next words made this impossible. "You know I like to sit—you want me animated, and it leaves me so to wag my tongue. And just now I've time."

"You must remember how near I had got to the end," Lyon returned.

"So you had. More's the pity. I should like you to begin again."

"My dear fellow, I shall have to begin again!" laughed the painter with his eyes on Mrs. Capadose. She didn't meet them—she had got up to ring for luncheon. "The picture has been smashed," Lyon continued.

"Smashed? Ah what did you do that for?" cried Everina, standing there before him in all her clear rich beauty. Now that she did look at him she was impenetrable.

"I didn't—I found it so—with a dozen holes punched in it!"

"I say!" cried the Colonel—"what a jolly shame!"

Lyon took him in with a wide smile. "I hope *you* didn't go for it?"

"Is it done for?" the Colonel earnestly asked. He was as brightly true as his wife and he looked simply as if Lyon's question couldn't be serious. "For the love of sitting to you? My dear fellow, if I had thought of it I would!"

"Nor you either?" the painter demanded of Mrs. Capadose.

Before she had time to reply her husband had seized her arm as if a lurid light had come to him. "I say, my dear, that woman—that woman!"

"That woman?" Mrs. Capadose repeated; and Lyon too wondered what woman he meant.

"Don't you remember when we came out, she was at the door—or a little way from it? I spoke to you of her—I told you about her. Geraldine—Grenadine—the one who burst in that day," he explained to Lyon. "We saw her hanging about—I called Everina's attention to her."

"Do you mean she got at my picture?"

"Ah yes, I remember," said Mrs. Capadose with a vague recovery.

"She burst in again—she had learned the way—she was waiting for her chance," the Colonel continued. "Ah the horrid little brute!"

Lyon looked down; he felt himself colouring. This was what he had been waiting for—the day the Colonel should wantonly sacrifice some innocent person. And could his wife be a party to that final atrocity? He had reminded himself repeatedly during the previous weeks that when her husband perpetrated his misdeed she had already quitted the room; but he had argued none the less—it was a virtual certainty—that he had on rejoining her at once mentioned his misdeed. He was in the flush of performance; and even if he hadn't reported what he had done she would have guessed it. Lyon didn't for an instant believe poor Miss Geraldine to have been hovering about his door, nor had the account given by the Colonel the summer before of his relations with this lady affected him as in the least convincing. Lyon had never seen her till the day she planted herself in his studio, but he knew her and classified her as if he had made her. He was acquainted with the London model in all her feminine varieties—in every phase of her development and every step of her decay. When he entered his house that September morning just after the arrival of his two friends there had been no symptoms whatever, up and down the road, of Miss Geraldine's reappearance. That fact had been fixed in his mind by his recollecting the vacancy of the prospect when his cook told him that a lady and a gentleman were in his studio: he had wondered there was neither carriage nor cab at his door. Then he had reflected that they would have come by the underground railway; he was near the Marlborough Road station and he knew the Colonel, repeating his pilgrimage so often, habitually made use of that convenience. "How in the world did she get in?" He addressed the question to his companions indifferently.

"Let us go down to luncheon," said Mrs. Capadose, passing out of the room.

"We went by the garden—without troubling your servant—I wanted to show my wife." Lyon followed his hostess with her husband, and the Colonel stopped him at the top of the stairs. "My dear fellow, I *can't* have been guilty of the folly of not fastening the door?"

"I'm sure I don't know, Colonel," Lyon said as they went down. "It was a very determined hand that did the deed—in the spirit of a perfect wild-cat."

"Well, she *is* a wild-cat—confound her! That's why I wanted to get him away from her."

"But I don't understand her motive."

"Well, she's practically off her head—and she hates me. That was her motive."

"But she doesn't hate me, my dear fellow!" Lyon amusedly urged.

"She hated the picture—don't you remember she said so? The more portraits, the less employment for such as her."

"Yes; but if she's not really the model she pretends to be, how can that hurt her?" Lyon asked.

The question baffled the Colonel an instant—but only an instant. "Ah she's so bad she goes it blind. She doesn't know where she is."

They passed into the dining-room, where Mrs. Capadose was taking her place. "It's too low; it's too horrid!" she said. "You see the fates are against you. Providence won't let you be so disinterested—throwing off masterpieces for nothing."

"Did *you* see the woman?" Lyon put to her with something like a sternness he couldn't mitigate.

She seemed not to feel it, or not to heed it if she did. "There was a person, not far from your door, whom Clement called my attention to. He told me something about her, but we were going the other way."

"And do you think she did it?"

"How can I tell? If she did she was mad, poor wretch."

"I should like very much to get hold of her," said Lyon. This was a false plea for the truth: he had no desire for any further conversation with Miss Geraldine. He had exposed his friends to his own view, but without wish to expose them to others, and least of all to themselves.

"Oh depend upon it she'll never show again. You're all right *now!*" the Colonel guaranteed.

"But I remember her address—Mortimer Terrace Mews, Notting Hill."

"Oh that's pure humbug. There isn't any such place."

"Lord, what a practised deceiver!" said Lyon.

"Is there any one else you suspect?" his host went on.

"Not a creature."

"And what do your servants say?"

"They say it wasn't *them,* and I reply that I never said it was. That's about the substance of our interviews."

"And when did they discover the havoc?"

"They never discovered it at all. I noticed it first—when I came back."

"Well, she could easily have stepped in," said the subject of Miss Geraldine's pursuit. "Don't you remember how she turned up that day like the clown in the ring?"

"Yes, yes; she could have done the job in three seconds, except that the picture wasn't out."

"Ah my dear fellow," the Colonel groaned, "don't utterly curse me!—but of course I dragged it out."

"You didn't put it *back?*" Lyon tragically cried.

"Ah Clement, Clement, didn't I tell you to?" Mrs. Capadose reproachfully wailed.

The Colonel almost howled for compunction; he covered his face with his hands. His wife's words were for Lyon the finishing touch; they made his whole vision crumble—his theory that she had secretly kept herself true. Even to her old lover she wouldn't be so! He was sick; he couldn't eat; he knew how strange he must have looked. He attempted some platitude about spilled milk and the folly of crying over it—he tried to turn the talk to other things. But it was a horrid effort and he wondered how it pressed upon *them.* He wondered all sorts of things: whether they guessed he disbelieved them—that he had seen them of course they would never guess; whether they had arranged their story in advance or it was only an inspiration of the moment; whether she had resisted, protested, when the Colonel proposed it to her, and then had been borne down by him; whether in short she didn't loathe herself as she sat there. The cruelty, the cowardice of fastening their unholy act upon the wretched woman struck him as monstrous—no less monstrous indeed than the levity that could make them run the risk of her giving them, in her righteous indignation, the lie. Of course that risk could only exculpate her and not inculpate them—the probabilities protected them so perfectly; and what the Colonel counted on—what he would have counted upon the day he delivered himself, after first seeing her, at the studio, if he had thought about the matter then at all and not spoken from the pure spontaneity of his genius—was simply that Miss Geraldine must have vanished for ever into her native unknown. Lyon wanted so much to cut loose, in his disgust, that when after a little Mrs. Capadose said to him "But can nothing be done, can't the picture be repaired? You know they do such wonders in that way now," he only made answer: "I don't know, I don't care, it's all over, *n'en parlons plus!*" Her hypocrisy revolted him. And yet by way of plucking off the last veil of her shame he broke out to her again, shortly afterwards: "And you *did* like it, really?" To which she returned, looking him straight in his face, without a blush, a pallor, an evasion: "Oh *cher grand maître,* I loved it!" Truly her husband had trained her well. After that Lyon said no more, and his companions forbore temporarily to insist, like people of tact and sympathy aware that the odious accident had made him sore.

When they quitted the table the Colonel went away without coming upstairs; but Lyon returned to the drawing-room with his hostess, remarking to her however on the way that he could remain but a moment. He spent that moment—it prolonged itself a little—standing with her before the chimney-piece. She neither sat down nor asked him to; her manner betrayed some purpose of going out. Yes, her husband had trained her well; yet Lyon dreamed for a moment that now he was alone with her she would perhaps break down, retract, apologise, confide, say to him: "My dear old friend, forgive this hideous comedy—you understand!" And then how he would have loved her and pitied her, guarded her, helped her always! If she weren't ready to do something of that sort why had she treated him so as a dear old friend; why had she let him for months suppose certain things—or almost; why had she come to his studio day after day to sit near him on the pretext of her child's portrait, as if she liked to think what might have been? Why had she come so near a tacit confession if she wasn't willing to go an inch further? And she wasn't willing—she wasn't; he could see that as he lingered there. She moved about the room a little, rearranging two or three objects on the tables, but she did nothing more. Suddenly he said to her: "Which way was she going when you came out?"

"She—the woman we saw?"

"Yes, your husband's strange friend. It's a clue worth following." He didn't want to scare or to shake her; he only wanted to communicate the impulse that would make her say: "Ah spare me—and spare *him!* There was no such person."

Instead of this Everina replied: "She was going away from us—she crossed the road. We were coming toward the station."

"And did she appear to recognise the Colonel—did she look round?"

"Yes; she looked round, but I didn't notice much. A hansom came along and we got into it. It wasn't till then that Clement told me who she was: I remember he said that she was there for no good. I suppose we ought to have gone back."

"Yes, you'd have saved the picture."

For a moment she said nothing; then she smiled. "For you, *cher maître,* I'm very sorry. But you must remember I possess the original!"

At this he turned away. "Well, I must go," he said; and he left her without any other farewell and made his way out of the house. As he went slowly up the street the sense came back to him of that first glimpse of her he had had at Stayes—of how he had seen her gaze across the table at her husband. He stopped at the corner, looking vaguely up and down. He would never go back—he couldn't. Nor should he ever sound her abyss. He believed in her absolute straightness where she and her affairs alone might be concerned, but she was still in love with the man of her choice, and since she couldn't redeem him she would adopt and protect him. So he had trained her.

D. H. LAWRENCE

The Captain's Doll 🦌

The Countess Hannele sat in a low chair under a reading lamp, a basket of colored silk pieces beside her, and in her hands a doll or mannikin that she was dressing. She was doing something to the knee of the mannikin, so that the poor little gentleman flourished downward with arms wildly tossed out. And it was not at all seemly, because the doll was a Scotch soldier in tight-fitting tartan trews.

She was a fair woman with dark blonde hair and a beautiful fine skin. Her face seemed luminous; a certain quick gleam of life about it as she looked up. But she was restless. She pressed her arms into her lap, as if holding them bent had wearied her. Then she looked at the little clock on the writing table. It was long after dinner-time—why hadn't the Captain come?

She went to the table and looked at his letter-clip with letters in it and at his sealing-wax and his stampbox, touching things and moving them a little, just for the sake of the contrast, not really noticing what she touched. Then she took a pencil, and in stiff gothic characters began to write her name—Johanna zu Rassentlow—time after time her own name—and then once bitterly, curiously, with a curious sharpening of her nose: Alexander Hepburn.

But she threw the pencil down, having no more interest in her own writing. Then she drifted restlessly back to her chair. She had picked up her puppet when she heard him on the stairs. She lifted her face and watched as he entered.

"Hello, you there!" he said quietly, as he closed the door. She glanced at him swiftly, but did not answer.

He took off his overcoat, with quick, quiet movements, and went to hang it up on the pegs. She heard his step, and looked again. He was like the doll, a tall, slender, well-bred man in uniform. When he turned, his dark eyes seemed very wide open. His black hair was growing gray at the temples—the first touch.

She was sewing her doll. Without saying anything, he wheeled round the chair from the writing table, so that he sat with his knees almost touching her. For some moments he watched her, as she sat sewing. The light fell on her soft, delicate hair, that was full of strands of gold and of tarnished gold and shadow. She did not look up.

In silence he held out his small, naked-looking brown hand for the doll.

"Do you want to see it?" she asked, in natural English.

She broke off her thread of cotton and handed him the puppet. He sat with one leg thrown over the other, holding the doll in one hand, and smiling inscrutably with his dark eyes.

"You are very late, aren't you?" she ventured.

"Yes. I am rather late."

"Why are you?"

"Well, as a matter of fact, I was talking with the Colonel."

"About me?"

"Yes. It was about you."

She went pale as she sat looking up into his face. But it was impossible to tell whether there was distress on his dark brow.

"Anything nasty?" she said.

"Well, yes. It was rather nasty. Not about you, I mean. But rather awkward for me."

She watched him. But still he said no more.

"What was it?" she said.

"Oh, well—only what I expected. They seem to know rather too much about you—about you and me, I mean. Not that anybody cares one bit, you know, unofficially. The trouble is, they are apparently going to have to take official notice."

"Why?"

"Oh, well—it appears my wife has been writing letters to the Major-General. He is one of her family acquaintances—known her all his life. And I suppose she's been hearing rumors. In fact, I know she has. She said so in her letter to me."

"And what do you say to her then?"

"Oh, I tell her I'm all right—not to worry."

"You don't expect *that* to stop her worrying, do you?"

"Oh, I don't know. Why should she worry?" he said.

"I think she might have some reason," said Hannele. "You've not seen her for a year—and if she adores you—"

"Oh, I don't think she adores me. I think she quite likes me."

He rose, and began to walk uneasily up and down the room.

He returned to her like a piece of iron returning to a magnet. He sat down again in front of her and put his hands out to her, looking into her face.

"Give me your hands," he said softly, with that strange, mindless soft suggestive tone which left her powerless to disobey. "Give me your hands and let me feel that we are together. Words mean so little. They mean nothing.

And all that one thinks and plans doesn't amount to anything. Let me feel that we are together, and I don't care about the rest."

He spoke in his slow melodious way, and closed her hands in his. She struggled still for voice.

"But you'll have to care about it. You'll *have* to make up your mind. You'll just *have* to," she insisted.

"Yes, I suppose I shall. I suppose I shall. But now that we are together, I won't bother. Let us forget it."

"But when you *can't* forget it any more?"

"Well—then I don't know. But tonight—it seems to me we might just as well forget it."

Countess zu Rassentlow had a studio in one of the main streets. She was really a refugee. And nowadays you can be a Grand Duke and a pauper, if you are a refugee. But Hannele was not a pauper, because she and her friend Mitchka made these dolls, and beautiful cushions of embroidered colored wools, and such like objects of feminine art. The dolls were quite famous, so the two women did not starve.

Hannele did not work much in the studio. She preferred to be alone in her own room, which was another fine attic, not quite so large as the Captain's, under the same roof.

The Alexander doll was never intended for sale. What made Hannele take it to the studio one afternoon will never be known, but she did so, and stood it on a little bureau. It was a wonderful little portrait of an officer and gentleman.

"*Aber nein!* But you won't leave him there?" Mitchka asked.

"Why not?" said Hannele, satirically.

"You love the man. You can't leave his puppet standing there. Only think —he is an English officer."

"He isn't sacrosanct even then."

"When you are not here, I shall put the puppet away in a drawer, I shall show it to nobody, nobody."

It was no good, however, Hannele was obstinate.

So, one sunny afternoon there was a ring at the door; a little lady in white, with a wrinkled face that still had its prettiness.

"Good afternoon!"—in rather lardy-dardy middle-class English. "I wonder if I may see your things in your studio."

"Oh yes!" said Mitchka. "Please to come in."

Entered the little lady in her finery and her crumpled prettiness. She would not be very old; perhaps younger than fifty. And it was odd that her face had gone so crumpled, because her figure was very trim, her eyes were bright, and she had pretty teeth when she laughed. She was very fine in her clothes: a dress of thick knitted white silk, a large ermine scarf with the tails only at the ends, and a black hat over which dipped a trail of green feathers of the osprey sort. She wore rather a lot of jewelry, and two bangles tinkled over her white kid gloves as she put up her fingers to touch her hair, whilst she stood complacently and looked round.

"You've got a *charming* studio—perfectly delightful!"

Mitchka gave a slight bow, and said in her odd, plangent English:

"Oh, yes. We like it very much also."

Hannele, who had dodged behind a screen, now came forth.

"Oh, how do you do!" smiled the elderly lady. "I heard there were two of you. Now which is which, if I may be so bold? This"—and she gave a winsome smile and pointed a white kid finger at Mitchka—"is the—"

"Annamaria von Prielau-Carolath," said Mitchka, bowing.

"Ah, yes!"—and the white kid finger jerked away, "This then is—"

"Johanna zu Rassentlow," said Hannele, smiling.

"Oh! Countess von Rassentlow! And this is Baroness von-von—but I shall never remember even if you tell me, for I am awful at names. Anyhow, I shall call one *Countess* and the other *Baroness*. That will do, won't it, for poor me! Now I should like awfully to see your things, if I may. I want to buy a little present to take back to England with me. I've heard so much about your dolls. I hear they're perfectly exquisite, quite works of art. May I see some, please?"

"Oh yes," came Mitchka's invariable answer, this exclamation being the foundation stone of all her English.

There were never more than three or four dolls in stock. This time there were only two. The famous Captain was hidden in his drawer.

"Perfectly beautiful! Perfectly wonderful," murmured the little lady.

She went over the things very carefully, and thought more than twice. The dolls attracted her, but she thought them expensive, and hung fire.

"I do wish," she said wistfully, "there had been a larger selection of the dolls. I feel, you know, there might have been one which I *just loved*. Of course these are darlings, and worth every *penny,* considering the work there is in them. And the art, of course. But I have a feeling, don't you know how it is, that if there had been just one or two more, I should have found one which I absolutely couldn't live without. Don't you know how it is? One is so foolish, of course."

"Yes," said Hannele, "there is one. But it is ordered. It isn't for sale."

Hannele went quietly to the drawer and took out the Captain. She handed him to the little woman. The latter looked frightened. Her eyes became round, her face went yellowish.

"Not that—isn't *that*—" and she laughed hysterically, then she turned round, as if to escape.

"Do you mind if I sit down," she said, "I think the standing—" and she subsided into a chair. She kept her face averted. But she held the puppet fast, her small white fingers with their heavy jeweled rings clasped round his waist.

"You know," rushed in Mitchka, who was terrified, "you know that is a life picture of an Englishman, of a gentleman we know."

"A portrait," said Hannele brightly.

"Yes," murmured the visitor vaguely. "I'm sure it is. I'm sure it is a very clever portrait indeed."

She fumbled with a chain, and put up a small gold lorgnette before her eyes, as if to screen herself. And from behind the screen of her lorgnette she peered at the image in her hand.

"May I ask the name of the gentleman—if it is not too indiscreet of me?"

"Captain Hepburn," said Hannele.

"Yes, of course it is. I knew him at once. I've known him for many years."

"Oh please," broke in Mitchka. "Oh please do not tell him you have seen it! Please not to tell anyone!"

The visitor looked up with a gray little smile.

"But why not?" she said. "Anyhow, I can't tell him at once, because I hear he is away at present. You don't happen to know when he will be back?"

"I believe tomorrow," said Hannele.

"And please," pleaded Mitchka, "please not to tell anybody that you have seen it."

"Must I promise?" smiled the little lady wanly. "Very well then, I won't tell him I've seen it. And now I think I must be going. Yes, I'll just take the cushion cover, thank you."

That evening Hannele was restless. He had been away for three days. He was returning that night—should have been back in time for dinner. But he had not arrived, and his room was locked and dark.

Yes—there was a sound. Yes, there was his slow step on the stairs, and the slow, straying purr of his voice. She heard the steps echo up the hollows of the stone staircase, slowly, as if wearily, and voices slowly, confusedly mingle. The slow, soft trail of his voice—and then the peculiar quick tones —yes, of a woman. Hannele's quick ears caught the sound of what she was saying: "Yes, I thought the Baroness a perfectly beautiful creature, perfectly lovely. But so extraordinarily like a Spaniard. Do you remember, Alec, at Malaga?

"I thought they fascinated you then, with their mantillas. Perfectly lovely she would look in a mantilla. Only perhaps she is too open-hearted, too impulsive, poor thing. She lacks the Spanish reserve. Baroness, Countess, it sounds just a little ridiculous, when you're buying woolen embroideries from them. But I suppose, poor things, they can't help it. Better drop the titles altogether, I think—"

"Well, they do, if people will let them. Only English and American people find it so much easier to say Baroness or Countess than Fraulein Annamaria von Prielau-Carolath, or whatever it is."

There was a little platform out on the roof, where he used sometimes to stand his telescope and observe the stars or the moon—the moon particularly, when possible.

Hannele heard him quite late in the night, wandering about. She heard him also on the ledge outside. She could not sleep.

She rose, wrapped herself in a dark wrap, and went down the landing to the window at the end. The sky outside was full of moonlight. He was squatted like a great cat peering up at his telescope, sitting on a stool, with his knees wide apart.

She tapped softly on the windowpane. He looked round; then he reached down his hand and pulled the window open.

"Hello," he said quietly. "You're not asleep?"

"Aren't *you* tired?" she replied, rather resentfully.

"No, I was as wide awake as I could be. Isn't the moon fine tonight! What? Perfectly amazing."

At length he turned round to her. "You know I had a visitor?" he said.

"Yes."

"My wife."

She looked up really astonished. She had thought it might be an acquaintance—perhaps his aunt—or even an elder sister.

"But she's years older than you," she said.

"Eight years," he said.

There was a silence.

"Yes," he mused. "She arrived quite suddenly, by surprise, yesterday, and found me away. She's staying in the hotel, in the Vier Jahreszeiten."

There was a very long pause. He remained seated on his stool on the roof, looking with dilated, blank black eyes at nothingness.

"Do you want to go to her at the hotel?" asked Hannele.

"Well, I don't, particularly. But I don't mind, really. We're very good friends. Why we've been friends for eighteen years—we've been married seventeen. Oh, she's a nice little woman. I don't want to hurt her feelings."

"But you—your—yourself!" Hannele's amazement was reaching the point of incredulity. She began to feel that he was making it up. It was all so different from her own point of view.

"I don't consider I count," he said naïvely.

"But do you never count, then?" she asked, and there was a touch of derision, of laughter in her tone. He took no offense.

"Well—very rarely," he said. "I count very rarely. That's how life appears to me. One matters so *very* little."

She felt dizzy with astonishment. "But if you matter so very little, what do you do anything at all for?" she asked.

"Oh, one has to. And then, why not? Why not do things, even if oneself hardly matters."

She gazed at him in such utter amazement that she felt something would really explode in her if she heard another word. Was this man?—or what was it? It was too much for her, that was all.

"Well, good-bye," she said. "I hope you will have a nice time at the Vier Jahreszeiten."

So she left him sitting on the roof.

"I suppose," she said to herself, "that is love *à l'anglaise*. But It's more than I can swallow."

"Won't you come and have tea with me—do! Come right along, now. But perhaps you don't take tea?"

"Oh yes. I got so used to it in England," she said.

"Did you now! Well, were you in England long?"

The two women had met in the Domplatz. Mrs. Hepburn was looking very like one of Hannele's dolls.

"My husband may or may not be in. But that makes no difference to you and me, does it?"

He *was* in, however, standing with his feet apart and his hands in his trouser pockets. He raised his eyebrows the smallest degree, seeing Hannele enter.

"Ah, Countess Hannele—"

"Have you rung for tea, dear?" asked Mrs. Hepburn.

"Er—yes. I said as soon as you came in they were to bring it."

"Yes—well, won't you ring again, dear, and say for *three*—"

"Yes—certainly. Certainly."

He rang, and stood about with his hands in his pockets, waiting for the tea to be brought in.

"Well, now," said Mrs. Hepburn, as she lifted the teapot, and her bangles tinkled, and her huge rings of brilliants twinkled, and her big earrings of clustered seed-pearls bobbed against her rather withered cheek, "isn't it charming of Countess zu—"

"Rassentlow," said he. "I believe most people say Countess Hannele. I know we always do among ourselves. We say Countess Hannele's shop—"

"Countess Hannele's shop! Now isn't that perfectly delightful; such a romance in the very sound of it. You take cream?"

"Thank you," said Hannele.

The tea passed in a cloud of chatter.

"Alec dear," said Mrs. Hepburn. "You won't forget to leave that message for me at Mrs. Rackham's. I'm so afraid it will be forgotten."

"No dear, I won't forget. Er—I may as well go now."

And he went. Mrs. Hepburn detained her guest.

"He *is* so charming to me," said the little woman. "He's really wonderful. And he always has been the same—invariably. So that if he *did* make a little slip—I don't have to take it so seriously."

"No," said Hannele, feeling as if her ears were stretching with astonishment.

"It's the war. It's had a terrible deteriorating effect on the men. Really, there's hardly one man left the same as he was before the war. Terribly degenerated.

"Still I'm thankful my husband isn't that sort." The little laugh tinkled. "Oh he's been perfect to me, perfect. Hardly a cross word. Why, on our wedding night, he kneeled down in front of me and promised, with God's help to make my life happy. And I must say, as far as possible he's kept his word.

"Well, perhaps one can feel too safe. Perhaps one needs a tiny pinch of the salt of jealousy. I believe one does. And I have not had one jealous moment for seventeen years. So that, really when I heard a whisper of something going on here, I felt almost pleased. I felt exonerated for my own little peccadilloes, for one thing.

"I had just a hint that she was a German—a refugee aristocrat—and that he used to call at the studio—" The little lady eyed Hannele sharply, and gave a breathless little laugh, clasping her hands nervously.

"Of course," resumed Mrs. Hepburn, "that was enough. That was quite a sufficient clue. I'm afraid my intentions when I called at the studio were not as pure as they might have been. I'm afraid I wanted to see something more than the dolls. But when you showed me *his* doll, then I knew. Of course there wasn't a shadow of doubt about that. And I saw at once that she loved him, poor thing. She was *so* agitated. And I must say she's very lovely—she's very, very lovely. I think she's much too dangerous for my husband to see much of her."

"Oh, but really," stammered Hannele. "There's nothing in it, really."

"Well," said the little lady, cocking her head shrewdly aside, "I shouldn't like there to be any *more* in it."

"Well, now," she said, breaking again suddenly into life. "What are we to do? I mean what is to be done? You are the Baroness's nearest friend. And I wish her no harm, none whatever—"

"What can we do?" said Hannele.

"I have been urging my husband for some time to get his discharge from the army," said the little woman. "I know he could have it in three months' time. But like so many men, he has no income of his own, and he doesn't want to feel dependent. Perfect nonsense! So he says he wants to stay on in the army. I have never known him before to go against my real wishes—"

Hannele went her way pondering. A man never is quite such an abject specimen as his wife makes him look, talking about "my husband." Therefore, if any woman wishes to rescue her husband from the clutches of another female, let her only invite this female to tea and talk quite sincerely about "my husband, you know." The picture of Alec at his wife's feet on his wedding night, vowing to devote himself to her lifelong happiness—this picture strayed across Hannele's mind time after time, whenever she thought of her dear captain.

And then a dreadful thing happened: really a very dreadful thing. Hannele read of it in the evening newspaper of the town.

Mrs. Hepburn had fallen out of her bedroom window, from the third floor of the hotel, down onto the pavement below, and was killed. She was dressing for dinner. And apparently she had in the morning washed a certain little camisole, and put it on the window sill to dry.

Her husband who had been in the dressing room, heard a queer little noise, a sort of choking cry, and came into her room to see what it was. And she wasn't there. When he looked out of the window down into the street, he fainted.

The very next day the Captain came back to his attic. Hannele did not know, until quite late at night when he tapped softly on her door.

"Won't you come over for a chat?" he said.

"Yes, in a minute," she said, closing her door in his face.

She found him sitting quite still, not even smoking, in his quiet attic. He did not rise, but just glanced round with a faint smile. And she thought his face seemed different, more flexible. But in the half-light she could not tell. She sat down at some little distance from him.

"I suppose you've heard," he said.

"Yes."

After a long pause, he resumed: "Yes. It seems an impossible thing to have happened. Yet it has happened."

Hannele's ears were sharp. But strain them as she might she could not catch the meaning of his voice.

"It must have been terrible for you, too," she said.

"Ah yes," he said in his slow voice. "At the time it was awful. Awful. I felt the smash right inside me. But now I feel very strangely happy about it. I feel she has got out of some great tension. I feel she's free now for the first time in her life. She was a gentle soul, and an original soul, but she was like a fairy who is condemned to live in houses and sit on furniture and all that."

There was a long pause.

"And perhaps I was to blame. For my life, I didn't know what to do, except try to make her happy. . . . I always had astronomy. It's been an

immense relief to me, watching the moon. Instead of looking into the
cage, at her—I looked right out—into freedom."

"The moon, you mean?"

"Yes, the moon."

"And that's your freedom?"

"That's where I've found the greatest sense of freedom," he said.

In a little while, she bade him good night and left him.

The chief thing that the Captain knew, at this juncture, was that a
hatchet had gone through the ligatures and veins that connected him with
the people of his affection, and that he was left with the bleeding ends
of all his vital human relationships. So he went to England, to settle his
affairs, and out of duty to see his children. He wished his children all the
well in the world—everything except any emotional connection with himself.

The Captain decided also to leave the army as soon as he could be free.
And he thought he would wander about for a time, till he came upon
something he wanted. And during all the time he never wrote once to
Hannele.

Nevertheless, a man hasn't finished his life at forty. And Alexander
Hepburn was not the man to live alone. At last he wrote to Hannele: and
got no answer. So he wrote to Mitchka and still got no answer. So he wrote
for information—and there was none, except that they had gone to Munich.

For the time being, he left it at that. To him, Hannele did not exactly
represent rosy love. Rather a hard destiny. He did not feel one bit of adoration for her. As a matter of fact, not all the beauties and virtues of women
put together with all the gold in the Indies would have tempted him into
the business of adoration any more.

But in the end he suddenly took the train to Munich. And when he
got there he found the town beastly uncomfortable, the Bavarians rude and
disagreeable, and no sign of the missing females, not even in the Café
Stephanie. He wandered round and round.

And then one day, Oh, heaven, he saw his doll in a shop-window; a
little art shop. He stood and stared quite spellbound. "Well, if that isn't
the devil," he said. "Seeing yourself in a shop-window!"

He was so disgusted that he would not go into the shop.

Then, every day for a week he walked down that little street and took
a look at himself in the shop-window. Yes, there he stood, with one hand
in his pocket. And the figure had one hand in its pocket. There he stood, his
head rather forward, gazing with fixed dark eyes. Himself in little, that
wretched figure, stood there with its head rather forward, staring with
fixed dark eyes. It was such a real little *man,* that it fairly staggered him.
The oftener he saw it, the more it staggered him. And the more he hated it.
Yet it fascinated him, and he came again to look.

It was always there. A lonely little individual lounging there with one hand in its pocket, and nothing to do, among the bric-à-brac and the bibelots. Poor devil, stuck so incongruously in the world. And yet losing none of his masculinity.

A male little devil, for all his forlornness. But such an air of isolation, of not belonging. Yet taut and male, in his tartan trews. And what a situation to be in. Poor little devil: It was like a deliberate satire.

And then one day it was gone. There was the cabinet and the tiresome inkstand tray and the little gentleman wasn't there. The Captain at once walked into the shop.

"Have you sold that doll?—that unknown soldier?" he added, without knowing quite what he was saying.

The doll was sold.

"Do you know who bought it?"

The girl looked at him very coldly, and did not know.

"I once knew the lady who made it. In fact, the doll was *me*," he said.

The girl now looked at him with sudden interest.

"Don't you think it was like me?" he said.

"Perhaps—" she began to smile.

"It was me. And the lady who made it was a friend of mine. Do you know her name?"

"Yes."

"Gräfin zu Rassentlow," he cried, his eyes shining.

"Oh yes. But her dolls are famous."

"Do you know where she is? Is she in Munich?"

"That I don't know. I can ask."

"Or the Baroness von Prielau-Carolath?"

"The Baroness is dead. She was shot in a riot in Salzburg. They say a lover—"

"How do you know?"

"From the newspapers."

There was a pause.

"Well," he said, "if you would inquire about the address—I'll call again." Then he turned back from the door.

"By the way, do you mind telling me how much you sold the doll for?"

The girl hesitated. She was by no means anxious to give away any of her trade details. But at length she answered reluctantly: "Five hundred marks."

"So cheap," he said. "Good day. Then I will call again."

Then again he got a trace in the Chit-Chat column of the *Muenchener Neue Zeitung* under Studio-Comments. "Theodor Worpswede's latest picture is a still-life, containing an entertaining group of a doll, two sunflowers in a glass jar, and a poached egg on toast. The contrast between the three subjects is highly diverting and instructive, and this is perhaps one of the most interesting of Worpswede's works. The doll, by the way, is one of the creations of our fertile Countess Hannele. It is the figure of an English, or rather a Scottish officer, in the famous tartan trousers. The doll itself is a masterpiece, and has begotten another masterpiece in Theodor Worpswede's still-life. We have heard, by the way, a rumor of Countess zu Rassentlow's engagement. Apparently the Herr Regierungsrat von Poldi, of that most beautiful of summer-resorts, Kaprun, in the Tyrol, is the fortunate man—"

The Captain bought the still-life. This new version of himself along with the poached egg and the sunflowers was rather frightening. So he packed up for Austria, for Kaprun, with his picture, and had a fight to get the beastly thing out of Germany, and then another fight to get it into Austria. Fatigued and furious he arrived in Salzburg, seeing no beauty in anything. Next day he was in Kaprun.

The Herr Regierungsrat was not at first sight prepossessing. He was approaching fifty, and had gone stout and rather loose.

Hannele was attracted to him by his talk. The summer night was still and warm: the lake lay deep and full, and the old town twinkled away across.

And on and on talked Herr Regierungsrat, with all the witty volubility of the more versatile Austrian. That subtle stoicism, that unsentimental epicureanism, that kind of reckless hopelessness fascinated the women. And particularly Hannele.

She became engaged. But something made her hesitate before marriage. Being in Austria was like being on a wrecked ship that *must* sink after a certain short length of time.

It was August when Alexander met Hannele. She was walking under a chintz parasol, wearing a dress of blue cotton with little red roses, and a red silk apron. She had no hat. Herr Regierungsrat was at her side, large, nimble, and laughing with a new witticism. Alexander saw her coming along from the Amtsgericht, and with the Herr Regierungsrat at her side, across the space of sunshine. She was laughing, and did not notice him.

"How do you do, Countess! I hoped I should meet you."

She heard his slow, sad-clanging, straying voice again, and she pressed her hand with the umbrella stick against her breast.

She presented him to the Herr Regierungsrat, who was stiff and cold. She asked where the Captain was staying. Then, not knowing what else to say, she said: "Won't you come to tea?"

She was staying in a villa across the lake. And yes, he would come to tea.

Hepburn and Hannele made a small excursion to the glacier which stood there always in sight, coldly grinning in the sky. He and Hannele were not in good company together. There was a sort of silent hostility between them. She hated the effort of climbing; but the high air, the cold in the air, the savage cat-howling sound of the water, these awful flanks of livid rock, all this thrilled and excited her to another sort of savageness.

"Wonderful! Wonderful!" she cried, taking great breaths in her splendid chest.

"Yes. And horrible. Detestable, very detestable. I want to live near the sea-level. I am no mountain-topper."

"Evidently not," she said.

They ate venison and spinach in the hotel, then set off down again. Both felt happier.

But a fume of cloud was blowing up thick from behind the glacier. Hannele was uneasy. She wanted to get down. So they did not stay to rest, but dropped easily down the steep dark valley toward the motorcar terminus. There they had tea, rather tired but comfortably so. The big hotel restaurant was hideous, and seemed sordid. So in the gloom of a gray, early twilight they went out again and sat on a seat, watching the tourists.

"Do you think," said Alexander, "you will marry the Herr Regierungsrat?"

She looked round, making wide eyes.

"It looks like it, doesn't it?" she said.

"Quite," he said.

"What makes you ask such a question?" she said.

"Well," he said, "if you were not going to marry the Herr Regierungsrat, I should suggest that you marry me."

She stared away at the auto garage, a very faint little look of amusement, or pleasure, or ridicule on her face: or all three.

"Why should you suggest that I should marry you?"

"Why?" he replied, in his lingering tones. "Why?—well, for what purpose does a man ask a woman to marry him?"

"For what purpose!" she repeated, rather haughtily.

"For what reason, then!" he corrected.

"There is usually only one reason," she replied, in a rather small voice.

"Yes," he replied curiously. "What would you say that was?"

She hesitated. Then rather stiffly: "Because he really loved her, I suppose. That seems to me the only excuse for a man asking a woman to marry him."

She did not attempt to break the silence that followed.

"Leaving aside the question of whether you love me or I love you—" he began.

"I certainly won't leave it aside," she interrupted swiftly.

"And I certainly won't consider it," he said, just as obstinately.

She turned now and looked full at him with amazement, ridicule and anger in her face. "I really think you must be mad."

"I doubt if you do think that," he replied. "It is only a method of retaliation, that is. I think you see my point very clearly."

"I assure you I do *not* see your point. I don't see any point at all. I see only impertinence."

"Very good," he replied. "The point is whether we marry on a basis of love."

"Indeed! Marry! We, marry! I don't think that is by any means the point."

"When," he said, "we were supposed to be in love with one another, you made that doll of me, didn't you?"

"I never for one moment was deluded that you really loved me," she said bitterly.

"Take the other point, whether you loved me, or not," said he.

"How could I love you, when I couldn't believe in your love for me?" she cried.

"All this about love," he said, "is very confusing and very complicated."

"Very! In your case. Love to me is simple enough," she said.

"Is it? Is it? And was it simple love when you made that doll of me?"

"Why shouldn't I make a doll of you? Does it do you any harm? And weren't you a doll? Good heavens! You were nothing *but* a doll, so what hurt does it do?"

"Yes, it does. It does me the greatest possible damage," he replied. "When I think of it—then I know that there's no love between you and me."

"Then why are you talking to me in this shameful way?" she flashed at him, tears of anger and mortification rising to her eyes. "You want your little revenge on me, I suppose, because I made that doll of you."

"That may be so in a small measure."

"That is *all*. That is all and everything," she cried. "And that is all you came back to me for—for this petty revenge. Well, you've had it now. But please don't speak to me any more. I shall go home."

The tourists who had arrived in the big bus now began to collect. And soon the huge drab vehicle itself rolled up, and stood big as a house before the hotel door. Hannele took her seat and Hepburn got in beside her. The driver snapped up the tickets and climbed in past them. With a vindictive screech the car glided away down the ravine.

"I think," said Hepburn, "I may as well finish what I had to say."

"What?" cried Hannele, fluttering in the wind of the rushing car.

"I may as well finish what I had to say," he shouted, his breath blown away.

"Finish then," she screamed, the ends of her scarf flickering behind her.

"When my wife died," he said loudly, "I knew I couldn't love any more."

"Oh-h!" she screamed ironically.

"In fact," he shouted, "I realized that, as far as I was concerned, love was a mistake."

"What was a mistake?" she screamed.

"Love," he bawled.

"Love!" she screamed. "A mistake?" Her tone was derisive.

"For me personally," he said shouting.

"Oh, only for you personally," she cried, with a pouf of laughter.

"That is why I came back to you," he continued. "I don't want to love you. I don't want marriage based on love."

"On a basis of what, then?"

"It isn't very easy to put into words," he said. "But I tried marriage once on a basis of love and I must say, it was a ghastly affair in the long run. And I believe it would be so, for me, whatever woman I had."

"There must be something wrong with you, then," said she.

"As far as love goes. And yet I want marriage. I want marriage. I want a woman to honor me and obey me—"

They were silent now until the car stopped at the station. There they descended and walked on under the trees by the lake.

"Honor and obedience, and the proper physical feelings," he said. "To me that is marriage. Nothing else."

"But what are the proper physical feelings, but love?" asked Hannele.

"No," he said. "A woman wants you to adore her, and be in love with her—and I shan't. I will not do it again, if I live a monk for the rest of my days. I will neither adore you nor be in love with you."

"You won't get a chance, thank you. And what do you call the proper physical feelings, if not love?"

"If a woman honors me—absolutely from the bottom of her nature honors me—and obeys me because of that, I take it, my desire for her goes very much deeper than if I was in love with her, or if I adored her."

"It's the same thing. If you love, then everything is there—all the lot—your honor and obedience and all."

"That isn't true," he replied. "A woman may love you, she may adore you, but she'll neither honor you nor obey you. The most loving and adoring woman today could any minute start and make a doll of her husband—as you made of me."

"Oh, that eternal doll! What makes it stick so in your mind?"

"I don't know. But there it is. It wasn't malicious. It was flattering, if you like. But it just sticks in me like a thorn, and you can say what you like, but *any* woman today, no matter how much she loves her man—she could start any minute and make a doll of him. And the doll would be her hero —and her hero would be no more than her doll. And when she's got her doll, that's all she wants. And that's what love means. It is an insult. I won't be loved. And I won't love. I'll be honored and obeyed, or nothing."

"And you?" she cried. "You! I suppose all you've got to do is to sit there like a sultan and sup it up."

"Oh, no, I have many things to do. I'm going to East Africa to join a man who's breaking his neck to get his three thousand acres of land under control."

"And the woman?—supposing you got the poor thing."

"Well," he said slowly, "she'll be my wife, and I shall treat her as such. If the marriage service says love and cherish—well, in that sense I shall—"

"To be loved and cherished just because you're his wife! All I can admire is the conceit and impudence of it."

"Very well then," he said, rising.

As they were rowing in silence over the lake, he said: "I shall leave tomorrow."

She made no answer. She sat and watched the lights of the villa draw near, and then she said:

"I'll come to Africa with you. But I won't promise to honor and obey you."

"I don't want you otherwise," he said, very quietly.

The boat was drifting to the little landing stage. Hannele's friends were hallooing to her from the balcony.

"You'll come in?"

"No, I'll row straight back."

"But you won't have me even if I love you?" she asked him.

"You must promise the other," he said, "it comes in the marriage service."

"Don't be a solemn ass. Do come in."

"No," he said, "I don't want to come in."

"Do you want to go away tomorrow? Go, if you do. But anyway I won't say it before the marriage service. I needn't, need I?"

She stepped from the boat.

"And come to me tomorrow, will you?" she said.

"Yes, in the morning."

He pulled back quietly into the dark.

ERNEST HEMINGWAY

The Short Happy Life of Francis Macomber ❦

It was now lunch time and they were all sitting under the double green fly of the dining tent pretending that nothing had happened.

"Will you have lime juice or lemon squash?" Macomber asked.

"I'll have a gimlet," Robert Wilson told him.

"I'll have a gimlet too. I need something," Macomber's wife said.

"I suppose it's the thing to do," Macomber agreed. "Tell him to make three gimlets."

The mess boy had started them already, lifting the bottles out of the canvas cooling bags that sweated wet in the wind that blew through the trees that shaded the tents.

"What had I ought to give them?" Macomber asked.

"A quid would be plenty," Wilson told him. "You don't want to spoil them."

"Will the headman distribute it?"

"Absolutely."

Francis Macomber had, half an hour before, been carried to his tent from the edge of the camp in triumph on the arms and shoulders of the cook, the personal boys, the skinner and the porters. The gun-bearers had taken no part in the demonstration. When the native boys put him down at the door of his tent, he had shaken all their hands, received their congratulations, and then gone into the tent and sat on the bed until his wife came in. She did not speak to him when she came in and he left the tent at once to wash his face and hands in the portable wash basin outside and go over to the dining tent to sit in a comfortable canvas chair in the breeze and the shade.

"You've got your lion," Robert Wilson said to him, "and a damned fine one too."

Mrs. Macomber looked at Wilson quickly. She was an extremely handsome and well-kept woman of the beauty and social position which had, five years before, commanded five thousand dollars as the price of endorsing, with photographs, a beauty product which she had never used. She had been married to Francis Macomber for eleven years.

"He is a good lion, isn't he?" Macomber said. His wife looked at him now. She looked at both these men as though she had never seen them before.

One, Wilson, the white hunter, she knew she had never truly seen before. He was about middle height with sandy hair, a stubby mustache, a very red face and extremely cold blue eyes with faint white wrinkles at the corners that grooved merrily when he smiled. He smiled at her now and she looked away from his face at the way his shoulders sloped in the loose tunic he wore with the four big cartridges held in loops where the left breast pocket should have been, at his big brown hands, his old slacks, his very dirty boots and back to his red face again. She noticed where the baked red of his face stopped in a white line that marked the circle left by his Stetson hat that hung now from one of the pegs of the tent pole.

"Well, here's to the lion," Robert Wilson said. He smiled at her again and, not smiling, she looked curiously at her husband.

Francis Macomber was very tall, very well built if you did not mind that length of bone, dark, his hair cropped like an oarsman, rather thin-lipped, and was considered handsome. He was dressed in the same sort of safari clothes that Wilson wore except that his were new, he was thirty-five years old, kept himself very fit, was good at court games, had a number of big-game fishing records, and had just shown himself, very publicly, to be a coward.

"Here's to the lion," he said. "I can't ever thank you for what you did."

Margaret, his wife, looked away from him and back to Wilson.

"Let's not talk about the lion," she said.

Wilson looked over at her without smiling and now she smiled at him.

"It's been a very strange day," she said. "Hadn't you ought to put your hat on even under the canvas at noon? You told me that, you know."

"Might put it on," said Wilson.

"You know you have a very red face, Mr. Wilson," she told him and smiled again.

"Drink," said Wilson.

"I don't think so," she said. "Francis drinks a great deal, but his face is never red."

"It's red today," Macomber tried a joke.

"No," said Margaret. "It's mine that's red today. But Mr. Wilson's is always red."

"Must be racial," said Wilson. "I say, you wouldn't like to drop my beauty as a topic, would you?"

"I've just started on it."

"Let's chuck it," said Wilson.

"Conversation is going to be so difficult," Margaret said.

"Don't be silly, Margot," her husband said.

"No difficulty," Wilson said. "Got a damn fine lion."

Margot looked at them both and they both saw that she was going to cry. Wilson had seen it coming for a long time and he dreaded it. Macomber was past dreading it.

"I wish it hadn't happened. Oh, I wish it hadn't happened," she said and started for her tent. She made no noise of crying but they could see that her shoulders were shaking under the rose-colored, sun-proofed shirt she wore.

"Women upset," said Wilson to the tall man. "Amounts to nothing. Strain on the nerves and one thing'n another."

"No," said Macomber. "I suppose that I rate that for the rest of my life now."

"Nonsense. Let's have a spot of the giant killer," said Wilson. "Forget the whole thing. Nothing to it anyway."

"We might try," said Macomber. "I won't forget what you did for me though."

"Nothing," said Wilson. "All nonsense."

So they sat there in the shade where the camp was pitched under some wide-topped acacia trees with a boulder-strewn cliff behind them, and a stretch of grass that ran to the bank of a boulder-filled stream in front with forest beyond it, and drank their just-cool lime drinks and avoided one another's eyes while the boys set the table for lunch. Wilson could tell that the boys all knew about it now and when he saw Macomber's personal boy looking curiously at his master while he was putting dishes on the table he snapped at him in Swahili. The boy turned away with his face blank.

"What were you telling him?" Macomber asked.

"Nothing. Told him to look alive or I'd see he got about fifteen of the best."

"What's that? Lashes?"

"It's quite illegal," Wilson said. "You're supposed to fine them."

"Do you still have them whipped?"

"Oh, yes. They could raise a row if they chose to complain. But they don't. They prefer it to the fines."

"How strange!" said Macomber.

"Not strange, really," Wilson said. "Which would you rather do? Take a good birching or lose your pay?"

Then he felt embarrassed at asking it and before Macomber could answer he went on, "We all take a beating every day, you know, one way or another."

This was no better. Good God, he thought. I'm a diplomat, aren't I?

"Yes, we take a beating," said Macomber, still not looking at him. "I'm awfully sorry about that lion business. It doesn't have to go any further, does it? I mean no one will hear about it, will they?"

"You mean will I tell it at the Mathaiga Club?" Wilson looked at him now coldly. He had not expected this. So he's a bloody four-letter man as well as a bloody coward, he thought. I rather liked him too until today. But how is one to know about an American?

"No," said Wilson. "I'm a professional hunter. We never talk about our clients. You can be quite easy on that. It's supposed to be bad form to ask us not to talk though."

He had decided now that to break would be much easier. He would eat, then, by himself and could read a book with his meals. They would eat by themselves. He would see them through the safari on a very formal basis—what was it the French called it? Distinguished consideration—and it would be a damn sight easier than having to go through this emotional trash. He'd insult him and make a good clean break. Then he could read a book with his meals and he'd still be drinking their whisky. That was the phrase for it when a safari went bad. You ran into another white hunter and you asked, "How is everything going?" and he answered, "Oh, I'm still drinking their whisky," and you knew everything had gone to pot.

"I'm sorry," Macomber said and looked at him with his American face that would stay adolescent until it became middle-aged, and Wilson noted his crew-cropped hair, fine eyes only faintly shifty, good nose, thin lips and handsome jaw. "I'm sorry I didn't realize that. There are lots of things I don't know."

So what could he do, Wilson thought. He was all ready to break it off quickly and neatly and here the beggar was apologizing after he had just insulted him. He made one more attempt. "Don't worry about me talking," he said. "I have a living to make. You know in Africa no woman ever misses her lion and no white man ever bolts."

"I bolted like a rabbit," Macomber said.

Now what in hell were you going to do about a man who talked like that, Wilson wondered.

Wilson looked at Macomber with his flat, blue, machine-gunner's eyes and the other smiled back at him. He had a pleasant smile if you did not notice how his eyes showed when he was hurt.

"Maybe I can fix it up on buffalo," he said. "We're after them next, aren't we?"

"In the morning if you like," Wilson told him. Perhaps he had been wrong. This was certainly the way to take it. You most certainly could not tell a damned thing about an American. He was all for Macomber again. If you could forget the morning. But, of course, you couldn't. The morning had been about as bad as they come.

"Here comes the Memsahib," he said. She was walking over from her tent looking refreshed and cheerful and quite lovely. She had a very perfect oval face, so perfect that you expected her to be stupid. But she wasn't stupid, Wilson thought, no, not stupid.

"How is the beautiful red-faced Mr. Wilson? Are you feeling better, Francis, my pearl?"

"Oh, much," said Macomber.

"I've dropped the whole thing," she said, sitting down at the table. "What importance is there to whether Francis is any good at killing lions? That's not his trade. That's Mr. Wilson's trade. Mr. Wilson is really very impressive killing anything. You do kill anything, don't you?"

"Oh, anything," said Wilson. "Simply anything." They are, he thought, the hardest in the world; the hardest, the cruelest, the most predatory and the most attractive and their men have softened or gone to pieces nervously as they have hardened. Or is it that they pick men they can handle? They can't know that much at the age they marry, he thought. He was grateful that he had gone through his education on American women before now because this was a very attractive one.

"We're going after buff in the morning," he told her.

"I'm coming," she said.

"No, you're not."

"Oh, yes, I am. Mayn't I, Francis?"

"Why not stay in camp?"

"Not for anything," she said. "I wouldn't miss something like today for anything."

When she left, Wilson was thinking, when she went off to cry, she seemed a hell of a fine woman. She seemed to understand, to realize, to be hurt for him and for herself and to know how things really stood. She is away for twenty minutes and now she is back, simply enamelled in that American female cruelty. They are the damnedest women. Really the damnedest.

"We'll put on another show for you tomorrow," Francis Macomber said.

"You're not coming," Wilson said.

"You're very mistaken," she told him. "And I want *so* to see you perform again. You were lovely this morning. That is if blowing things' heads off is lovely."

"Here's the lunch," said Wilson. "You're very merry, aren't you?"

"Why not? I didn't come out here to be dull."

"Well, it hasn't been dull," Wilson said. He could see the boulders in the river and the high bank beyond with the trees and he remembered the morning.

"Oh, no," she said. "It's been charming. And tomorrow. You don't know how I look forward to tomorrow."

"That's eland he's offering you," Wilson said.

"They're the big cowy things that jump like hares, aren't they?"

"I suppose that describes them," Wilson said.

"It's very good meat," Macomber said.

"Did you shoot it, Francis?" she asked.

"Yes."

"They're not dangerous, are they?"

"Only if they fall on you," Wilson told her.

"I'm so glad."

"Why not let up on the bitchery just a little, Margot," Macomber said, cutting the eland steak and putting some mashed potato, gravy and carrot on the down-turned fork that tined through the piece of meat.

"I suppose I could," she said, "since you put it so prettily."

"Tonight we'll have champagne for the lion," Wilson said. "It's a bit too hot at noon."

"Oh, the lion," Margot said. "I'd forgotten the lion!"

So, Robert Wilson thought to himself, she *is* giving him a ride, isn't she. Or do you suppose that's her idea of putting up a good show? How should a woman act when she discovers her husband is a bloody coward? She's damn cruel but they're all cruel. They govern, of course, and to govern one has to be cruel sometimes. Still, I've seen enough of their damn terrorism.

"Have some more eland," he said to her politely.

That afternoon, late, Wilson and Macomber went out in the motor car with the native driver and the two gun-bearers. Mrs. Macomber stayed in the camp. It was too hot to go out, she said, and she was going with them in the early morning. As they drove off Wilson saw her standing under the big tree, looking pretty rather than beautiful in her faintly rosy khaki, her dark hair drawn back off her forehead and gathered in a knot low on her neck, her face as fresh, he thought, as though she were in England. She waved to them as the car went off through the swale of high grass and curved around through the trees into the small hills of orchard bush.

In the orchard bush they found a herd of impala, and leaving the car they stalked one old ram with long, wide-spread horns and Macomber killed it with a very creditable shot that knocked the buck down at a good two hundred yards and sent the herd off bounding wildly and leaping over one another's backs in long, leg-drawn-up leaps as unbelievable and as floating as those one makes sometimes in dreams.

"That was a good shot," Wilson said. "They're a small target."

"Is it a worth-while head?" Macomber asked.

"It's excellent," Wilson told him. "You shoot like that and you'll have no trouble."

"Do you think we'll find buffalo tomorrow?"

"There's a good chance of it. They feed out early in the morning and with luck we may catch them in the open."

"I'd like to clear away that lion business," Macomber said. "It's not very pleasant to have your wife see you do something like that."

I should think it would be even more unpleasant to do it, Wilson thought, wife or no wife, or to talk about it having done it. But he said, "I wouldn't think about that any more. Any one could be upset by his first lion. That's all over."

But that night after dinner and a whisky and soda by the fire before going to bed, as Francis Macomber lay on his cot with the mosquito bar over him and listened to the night noises it was not all over. It was neither all over nor was it beginning. It was there exactly as it happened with some parts of it indelibly emphasized and he was miserably ashamed at it. But more than shame he felt cold, hollow fear in him. The fear was still there like a cold slimy hollow in all the emptiness where once his confidence had been and it made him feel sick. It was still there with him now.

It had started the night before when he had wakened and heard the lion roaring somewhere up along the river. It was a deep sound and at the end there were sort of coughing grunts that made him seem just outside the tent, and when Francis Macomber woke in the night to hear it he was afraid. He could hear his wife breathing quietly, asleep. There was no one to tell he was afraid, nor to be afraid with him, and, lying alone, he did not know the Somali proverb that says a brave man is always frightened three times by a lion; when he first sees his track, when he first hears him roar and when he first confronts him. Then while they were eating breakfast by lantern light out in the dining tent, before the sun was up, the lion roared again and Francis thought he was just at the edge of camp.

"Sounds like an old-timer," Robert Wilson said, looking up from his kippers and coffee. "Listen to him cough."

"Is he very close?"

"A mile or so up the stream."

"Will we see him?"

"We'll have a look."

"Does his roaring carry that far? It sounds as though he were right in camp."

"Carries a hell of a long way," said Robert Wilson. "It's strange the way it carries. Hope he's a shootable cat. The boys said there was a very big one about here."

"If I get a shot, where should I hit him," Macomber asked, "to stop him?"

"In the shoulders," Wilson said. "In the neck if you can make it. Shoot for bone. Break him down."

"I hope I can place it properly," Macomber said.

"You shoot very well," Wilson told him. "Take your time. Make sure of him. The first one in is the one that counts."

"What range will it be?"

"Can't tell. Lion has something to say about that. Don't shoot unless it's close enough so you can make sure."

"At under a hundred yards?" Macomber asked.

Wilson looked at him quickly.

"Hundred's about right. Might have to take him a bit under. Shouldn't chance a shot at much over that. A hundred's a decent range. You can hit him wherever you want at that. Here comes the Memsahib."

"Good morning," she said. "Are we going after that lion?"

"As soon as you deal with your breakfast," Wilson said. "How are you feeling?"

"Marvellous," she said. "I'm very excited."

"I'll just go and see that everything is ready." Wilson went off. As he left the lion roared again.

"Noisy beggar," Wilson said. "We'll put a stop to that."

"What's the matter, Francis?" his wife asked him.

"Nothing," Macomber said.

"Yes, there is," she said. "What are you upset about?"

"Nothing," he said.

"Tell me," she looked at him. "Don't you feel well?"

"It's that damned roaring," he said. "It's been going on all night, you know."

"Why didn't you wake me," she said. "I'd love to have heard it."

"I've got to kill the damned thing," Macomber said, miserably.

"Well, that's what you're out here for, isn't it?"

"Yes. But I'm nervous. Hearing the thing roar gets on my nerves."

"Well then, as Wilson said, kill him and stop his roaring."

"Yes, darling," said Francis Macomber. "It sounds easy, doesn't it?"

"You're not afraid, are you?"

"Of course not. But I'm nervous from hearing him roar all night."

"You'll kill him marvellously," she said. "I know you will. I'm awfully anxious to see it."

"Finish your breakfast and we'll be starting."

"It's not light yet," she said. "This is a ridiculous hour."

Just then the lion roared in a deep-chested moaning, suddenly guttural, ascending vibration that seemed to shake the air and ended in a sigh and a heavy, deep-chested grunt.

"He sounds almost here," Macomber's wife said.

"My God," said Macomber. "I hate that damned noise."

"It's very impressive."

"Impressive. It's frightful."

Robert Wilson came up then carrying his short, ugly, shockingly big-bored .505 Gibbs and grinning.

"Come on," he said. "Your gun-bearer has your Springfield and the big gun. Everything's in the car. Have you solids?"

"Yes."

"I'm ready," Mrs. Macomber said.

"Must make him stop that racket," Wilson said. "You get in front. The Memsahib can sit back here with me."

They climbed into the motor car and, in the gray first daylight, moved off up the river through the trees. Macomber opened the breech of his rifle and saw he had metal-cased bullets, shut the bolt and put the rifle on safety. He saw his hand was trembling. He felt in his pocket for more cartridges and moved his fingers over the cartridges in the loops of his tunic front. He turned back to where Wilson sat in the rear seat of the doorless, box-bodied motor car beside his wife, them both grinning with excitement, and Wilson leaned forward and whispered,

"See the birds dropping. Means the old boy has left his kill."

On the far bank of the stream Macomber could see, above the trees, vultures circling and plummeting down.

"Chances are he'll come to drink along here," Wilson whispered. "Before he goes to lay up. Keep an eye out."

They were driving slowly along the high bank of the stream which here cut deeply to its boulder-filled bed, and they wound in and out through big trees as they drove. Macomber was watching the opposite bank when he felt Wilson take hold of his arm. The car stopped.

"There he is," he heard the whisper. "Ahead and to the right. Get out and take him. He's a marvellous lion."

Macomber saw the lion now. He was standing almost broadside, his great head up and turned toward them. The early morning breeze that blew toward them was just stirring his dark mane, and the lion looked huge, silhouetted on the rise of bank in the gray morning light, his shoulders heavy, his barrel of a body bulking smoothly.

"How far is he?" asked Macomber, raising his rifle.

"About seventy-five. Get out and take him."

"Why not shoot from where I am?"

"You don't shoot them from cars," he heard Wilson saying in his ear. "Get out. He's not going to stay there all day."

Macomber stepped out of the curved opening at the side of the front seat, onto the step and down onto the ground. The lion still stood looking majestically and coolly toward this object that his eyes only showed in silhouette, bulking like some super-rhino. There was no man smell carried toward him and he watched the object, moving his great head a little from side to side. Then watching the object, not afraid, but hesitating before going down the bank to drink with such a thing opposite him, he saw a man figure detach itself from it and he turned his heavy head and swung away toward the cover of the trees as he heard a cracking crash and felt the slam of a .30-06 220-grain solid bullet that bit his flank and ripped in sudden hot scalding nausea through his stomach. He trotted, heavy, big-footed, swinging wounded full-bellied, through the trees toward the tall grass and cover, and the crash came again to go past him ripping the air apart. Then it crashed again and he felt the blow as it hit his lower ribs and ripped on through, blood sudden hot and frothy in his mouth, and he galloped toward the high grass where he could crouch and not be seen and make them bring the crashing thing close enough so he could make a rush and get the man that held it.

Macomber had not thought how the lion felt as he got out of the car. He only knew his hands were shaking and as he walked away from the car it was almost impossible for him to make his legs move. They were stiff in the thighs, but he could feel the muscles fluttering. He raised the rifle, sighted on the junction of the lion's head and shoulders and pulled the trigger. Nothing happened though he pulled until he thought his finger would break. Then he knew he had the safety on and as he lowered the rifle to move the safety over he moved another frozen pace forward, and the lion seeing his silhouette now clear of the silhouette of the car, turned and started off at a trot, and, as Macomber fired, he heard a whunk that meant that the bullet was home; but the lion kept on going. Macomber shot again and every one saw the bullet throw a spout of dirt beyond the trotting lion. He shot again, remembering to lower his aim, and they all heard the bullet hit, and the lion went into a gallop and was in the tall grass before he had the bolt pushed forward.

Macomber stood there feeling sick at his stomach, his hands that held the Springfield still cocked, shaking, and his wife and Robert Wilson were standing by him. Beside him too were the two gun-bearers chattering in Wakamba.

"I hit him," Macomber said. "I hit him twice."

"You gut-shot him and you hit him somewhere forward," Wilson said without enthusiasm. The gun-bearers looked very grave. They were silent now.

"You may have killed him," Wilson went on. "We'll have to wait a while before we go in to find out."

"What do you mean?"

"Let him get sick before we follow him up."

"Oh," said Macomber.

"He's a hell of a fine lion," Wilson said cheerfully. "He's gotten into a bad place though."

"Why is it bad?"

"Can't see him until you're on him."

"Oh," said Macomber.

"Come on," said Wilson. "The Memsahib can stay here in the car. We'll go to have a look at the blood spoor."

"Stay here, Margot," Macomber said to his wife. His mouth was very dry and it was hard for him to talk.

"Why?" she asked.

"Wilson says to."

"We're going to have a look," Wilson said. "You stay here. You can see even better from here."

"All right."

Wilson spoke in Swahili to the driver. He nodded and said, "Yes, Bwana."

Then they went down the steep bank and across the stream, climbing over and around the boulders and up the other bank, pulling up by some projecting roots, and along it until they found where the lion had been trotting when Macomber first shot. There was dark blood on the short grass that the gun-bearers pointed out with grass stems, and that ran away behind the river bank trees.

"What do we do?" asked Macomber.

"Not much choice," said Wilson. "We can't bring the car over. Bank's too steep. We'll let him stiffen up a bit and then you and I'll go in and have a look for him."

"Can't we set the grass on fire?" Macomber asked.

"Too green."

"Can't we send beaters?"

Wilson looked at him appraisingly. "Of course we can," he said. "But it's just a touch murderous. You see we know the lion's wounded. You can drive an unwounded lion—he'll move on ahead of a noise—but a wounded lion's going to charge. You can't see him until you're right on him. He'll make himself perfectly flat in cover you wouldn't think would hide a hare. You can't very well send boys in there to that sort of a show. Somebody is bound to get mauled."

"What about the gun-bearers?"

"Oh, they'll go with us. It's their *shauri*. You see, they signed on for it. They don't look too happy though, do they?"

"I don't want to go in there," said Macomber. It was out before he knew he'd said it.

"Neither do I," said Wilson very cheerily. "Really no choice though." Then, as an afterthought, he glanced at Macomber and saw suddenly how he was trembling and the pitiful look on his face.

"You don't have to go in, of course," he said. "That's what I'm hired for, you know. That's why I'm so expensive."

"You mean you'd go in by yourself? Why not leave him there?"

Robert Wilson, whose entire occupation had been with the lion and the problem he presented, and who had not been thinking about Macomber except to note that he was rather windy, suddenly felt as though he had opened the wrong door in a hotel and seen something shameful.

"What do you mean?"

"Why not just leave him?"

"You mean pretend to ourselves he hasn't been hit?"

"No. Just drop it."

"It isn't done."

"Why not?"

"For one thing, he's certain to be suffering. For another, some one else might run onto him."

"I see."

"But you don't have to have anything to do with it."

"I'd like to," Macomber said. "I'm just scared, you know."

"I'll go ahead when we go in," Wilson said, "with Kongoni tracking. You keep behind me and a little to one side. Chances are we'll hear him growl. If we see him we'll both shoot. Don't worry about anything. I'll keep you backed up. As a matter of fact, you know, perhaps you'd better not go. It might be much better. Why don't you go over and join the Mensahib while I just get it over with?"

"No, I want to go."

"All right," said Wilson. "But don't go in if you don't want to. This is my *shauri* now, you know."

"I want to go," said Macomber.

They sat under a tree and smoked.

"Want to go back and speak to the Memsahib while we're waiting?" Wilson asked.

"No."

"I'll just step back and tell her to be patient."

"Good," said Macomber. He sat there, sweating under his arms, his mouth dry, his stomach hollow feeling, wanting to find courage to tell Wilson to go on and finish off the lion without him. He could not know that Wilson was furious because he had not noticed the state he was in earlier and sent him back to his wife. While he sat there Wilson came up. "I have your big gun," he said. "Take it. We've given him time, I think. Come on."

Macomber took the big gun and Wilson said:

"Keep behind me and about five yards to the right and do exactly as I tell you." Then he spoke in Swahili to the two gun-bearers who looked the picture of gloom.

"Let's go," he said.

"Could I have a drink of water?" Macomber asked. Wilson spoke to the older gun-bearer, who wore a canteen on his belt, and the man unbuckled it, unscrewed the top and handed it to Macomber, who took it noticing how heavy it seemed and how hairy and shoddy the felt covering was in his hand. He raised it to drink and looked ahead at the high grass with the flat-topped trees behind it. A breeze was blowing toward them and the grass rippled gently in the wind. He looked at the gun-bearer and he could see the gun-bearer was suffering too with fear.

Thirty-five yards into the grass the big lion lay flattened out along the ground. His ears were back and his only movement was a slight twitching up and down of his long, black-tufted tail. He had turned at bay as soon as he had reached this cover and he was sick with the wound through his full belly, and weakening with the wound through his lungs that brought a thin foamy red to his mouth each time he breathed. His flanks were wet and hot and flies were on the little openings the solid bullets had made in his tawny hide, and his big yellow eyes, narrowed with hate, looked straight ahead, only blinking when the pain came as he breathed, and his claws dug in the soft baked earth. All of him, pain, sickness, hatred and all of his remaining strength, was tightening into an absolute concentration for a rush. He could hear the men talking and he waited, gathering all of himself into this preparation for a charge as soon as the men would come into the grass. As he heard their voices his tail stiffened to twitch up and down, and, as they came into the edge of the grass, he made a coughing grunt and charged.

Kongoni, the old gun-bearer, in the lead watching the blood spoor, Wilson watching the grass for any movement, his big gun ready, the second gun-bearer looking ahead and listening, Macomber close to Wilson, his rifle cocked, they had just moved into the grass when Macomber heard the blood-choked coughing grunt, and saw the swishing rush in the grass. The next thing he knew he was running; running wildly, in panic in the open, running toward the stream.

He heard the *ca-ra-wong!* of Wilson's big rifle, and again in a second crashing *carawong!* and turning saw the lion, horrible-looking now, with half his head seeming to be gone, crawling toward Wilson in the edge of the tall grass while the red-faced man worked the bolt on the short ugly rifle and aimed carefully as another blasting *carawong!* came from the muzzle, and the crawling, heavy, yellow bulk of the lion stiffened and the huge, mutilated head slid forward and Macomber, standing by himself in the clearing where he had run, holding a loaded rifle, while two black men and a white man looked back at him in contempt, knew the lion was dead. He came toward Wilson, his tallness all seeming a naked reproach, and Wilson looked at him and said:

"Want to take pictures?"

"No," he said.

That was all any one had said until they reached the motor car. Then Wilson had said:

"Hell of a fine lion. Boys will skin him out. We might as well stay here in the shade."

Macomber's wife had not looked at him nor he at her and he had sat by her in the back seat with Wilson sitting in the front seat. Once he had reached over and taken his wife's hand without looking at her and she had removed her hand from his. Looking across the stream to where the gun-bearers were skinning out the lion he could see that she had been able to see the whole thing. While they sat there his wife had reached forward and put her hand on Wilson's shoulder. He turned and she had leaned forward over the low seat and kissed him on the mouth.

"Oh, I say," said Wilson, going redder than his natural baked color.

"Mr. Robert Wilson," she said. "The beautiful red-faced Mr. Robert Wilson."

Then she sat down beside Macomber again and looked away across the stream to where the lion lay, with uplifted, white-muscled, tendon-marked naked forearms, and white bloating belly, as the black men fleshed away the skin. Finally the gun-bearers brought the skin over, wet and heavy, and climbed in behind with it, rolling it up before they got in, and the motor car started. No one had said anything more until they were back in camp.

That was the story of the lion. Macomber did not know how the lion had felt before he started his rush, nor during it when the unbelievable smash of the .505 with a muzzle velocity of two tons had hit him in the mouth, nor what kept him coming after that, when the second ripping crash had smashed his hind quarters and he had come crawling on toward the crashing, blasting thing that had destroyed him. Wilson knew something about it and only expressed it by saying, "Damned fine lion," but Macomber did not know how Wilson felt about things either. He did not know how his wife felt except that she was through with him.

His wife had been through with him before but it never lasted. He was very wealthy, and would be much wealthier, and he knew she would not leave him ever now. That was one of the few things that he really knew. He knew about that, about motor cycles—that was earliest—about motor cars, about duck-shooting, about fishing, trout, salmon and big-sea, about sex in books, many books, too many books, about all court games, about dogs, not much about horses, about hanging on to his money, about most of the other things his world dealt in, and about his wife not leaving him. His wife had been a great beauty and she was still a great beauty in Africa, but she was not a great enough beauty any more at home to be able to leave him and better herself and she knew it and he knew it. She had missed the chance to leave him and he knew it. If he had been better with women she would probably have started to worry about him getting another new, beautiful wife; but she knew too much about him to worry about him either. Also, he had always had a great tolerance which seemed the nicest thing about him if it were not the most sinister.

All in all they were known as a comparatively happily married couple, one of those whose disruption is often rumored but never occurs, and as the society columnist put it, they were adding more than a spice of *adventure* to their much envied and ever-enduring *Romance* by a *Safari* in what was known as *Darkest Africa* until the Martin Johnsons lighted it on so many silver screens where they were pursuing *Old Simba* the lion, the buffalo, *Tembo* the elephant and as well collecting specimens for the Museum of Natural History. This same columnist had reported them *on the verge* at least three times in the past and they had been. But they always made it up. They had a sound basis of union. Margot was too beautiful for Macomber to divorce her and Macomber had too much money for Margot ever to leave him.

It was now about three o'clock in the morning and Francis Macomber, who had been asleep a little while after he had stopped thinking about the lion, wakened and then slept again, woke suddenly, frightened in a dream of the bloody-headed lion standing over him, and listening while his heart pounded, he realized that his wife was not in the other cot in the tent. He lay awake with that knowledge for two hours.

At the end of that time his wife came into the tent, lifted her mosquito bar and crawled cozily into bed.

"Where have you been?" Macomber asked in the darkness.

"Hello," she said. "Are you awake?"

"Where have you been?"

"I just went out to get a breath of air."

"You did, like hell."

"What do you want me to say, darling?"

"Where have you been?"

"Out to get a breath of air."

"That's a new name for it. You *are* a bitch."

"Well, you're a coward."

"All right," he said. "What of it?"

"Nothing as far as I'm concerned. But please let's not talk, darling, because I'm very sleepy."

"You think that I'll take anything."

"I know you will, sweet."

"Well, I won't."

"Please, darling, let's not talk. I'm so very sleepy."

"There wasn't going to be any of that. You promised there wouldn't be."

"Well, there is now," she said sweetly.

"You said if we made this trip that there would be none of that. You promised."

"Yes, darling. That's the way I meant it to be. But the trip was spoiled yesterday. We don't have to talk about it, do we?"

"You don't wait long when you have an advantage, do you?"

"Please let's not talk. I'm so sleepy, darling."

"I'm going to talk."

"Don't mind me then, because I'm going to sleep." And she did.

At breakfast they were all three at the table before daylight and Francis

Macomber found that, of all the many men that he had hated, he hated Robert Wilson the most.

"Sleep well?" Wilson asked in his throaty voice, filling a pipe.

"Did you?"

"Topping," the white hunter told him.

You bastard, thought Macomber, you insolent bastard.

So she woke him when she came in, Wilson thought, looking at them both with his flat, cold eyes. Well, why doesn't he keep his wife where she belongs? What does he think I am, a bloody plaster saint? Let him keep her where she belongs. It's his own fault.

"Do you think we'll find buffalo?" Margot asked, pushing away a dish of apricots.

"Chance of it," Wilson said and smiled at her. "Why don't you stay in camp?"

"Not for anything," she told him.

"Why not order her to stay in camp?" Wilson said to Macomber.

"You order her," said Macomber coldly.

"Let's not have any ordering, nor," turning to Macomber, "any silliness, Francis," Margot said quite pleasantly.

"Are you ready to start?" Macomber asked.

"Any time," Wilson told him. "Do you want the Memsahib to go?"

"Does it make any difference whether I do or not?"

The hell with it, thought Robert Wilson. The utter complete hell with it. So this is what it's going to be like. Well, this is what it's going to be like, then.

"Makes no difference," he said.

"You're sure you wouldn't like to stay in camp with her yourself and let me go out and hunt the buffalo?" Macomber asked.

"Can't do that," said Wilson. "Wouldn't talk rot if I were you."

"I'm not talking rot. I'm disgusted."

"Bad word, disgusted."

"Francis, will you please try to speak sensibly?" his wife said.

"I speak too damned sensibly," Macomber said. "Did you ever eat such filthy food?"

"Something wrong with the food?" asked Wilson quietly.

"No more than with everything else."

"I'd pull yourself together, laddybuck," Wilson said very quietly. "There's a boy waits at table that understands a little English."

"The hell with him."

Wilson stood up and puffing on his pipe strolled away, speaking a few words in Swahili to one of the gun-bearers who was standing waiting for him. Macomber and his wife sat on at the table. He was staring at his coffee cup.

"If you make a scene I'll leave you, darling," Margot said quietly.

"No, you won't."

"You can try it and see."

"You won't leave me."

"No," she said. "I won't leave you and you'll behave yourself."

"Behave myself? That's a way to talk. Behave myself."

"Yes. Behave yourself."

"Why don't *you* try behaving?"

"I've tried it so long. So very long."

"I hate that red-faced swine," Macomber said. "I loathe the sight of him."

"He's really *very* nice."

"Oh, *shut up,*" Macomber almost shouted. Just then the car came up and stopped in front of the dining tent and the driver and the two gun-bearers got out. Wilson walked over and looked at the husband and wife sitting there at the table.

"Going shooting?" he asked.

"Yes," said Macomber, standing up. "Yes."

"Better bring a woolly. It will be cool in the car," Wilson said.

"I'll get my leather jacket," Margot said.

"The boy has it," Wilson told her. He climbed into the front with the driver and Francis Macomber and his wife sat, not speaking, in the back seat.

Hope the silly beggar doesn't take a notion to blow the back of my head off, Wilson thought to himself. Women *are* a nuisance on safari.

The car was grinding down to cross the river at a pebbly ford in the gray daylight and then climbed, angling up the steep bank, where Wilson had ordered a way shovelled out the day before so they could reach the parklike wooded rolling country on the far side.

It was a good morning, Wilson thought. There was a heavy dew and as the wheels went through the grass and low bushes he could smell the odor of the crushed fronds. It was an odor like verbena and he liked this early morning smell of the dew, the crushed bracken and the look of the tree trunks showing black through the early morning mist, as the car made its way through the untracked, parklike country. He had put the two in the back seat out of his mind now and was thinking about buffalo. The buffalo that he was after stayed in the daytime in a thick swamp where it was impossible to get a shot, but in the night they fed out into an open stretch of country and if he could come between them and their swamp with the car, Macomber would have a good chance at them in the open. He did not want to hunt buff with Macomber in thick cover. He did not want to hunt buff or anything else with Macomber at all, but he was a professional hunter and he had hunted with some rare ones in his time. If they got buff today there would only be rhino to come and the poor man would have gone through his dangerous game and things might pick up. He'd have nothing more to do with the woman and Macomber would get over that too. He must have gone through plenty of that before by the look of things. Poor beggar. He must have a way of getting over it. Well, it was the poor sod's own bloody fault.

He, Robert Wilson, carried a double size cot on safari to accommodate any windfalls he might receive. He had hunted for a certain clientele, the international, fast, sporting set, where the women did not feel they were getting their money's worth unless they had shared that cot with the white hunter. He despised them when he was away from them although he liked some of them well enough at the time, but he made his living by them; and their standards were his standards as long as they were hiring him.

They were his standards in all except the shooting. He had his own standards about the killing and they could live up to them or get some one else to hunt them. He knew, too, that they all respected him for this. This Macomber was an odd one though. Damned if he wasn't. Now the wife. Well, the wife. Yes, the wife. Hm, the wife. Well he'd dropped all that. He looked around at them. Macomber sat grim and furious. Margot smiled at him. She looked younger today, more innocent and fresher and not so professionally beautiful. What's in her heart God knows, Wilson thought. She hadn't talked much last night. At that it was a pleasure to see her.

The motor car climbed up a slight rise and went on through the trees and then out into a grassy prairie-like opening and kept in the shelter of the trees along the edge, the driver going slowly and Wilson looking carefully out across the prairie and all along its far side. He stopped the car and studied the opening with his field glasses. Then he motioned to the driver to go on and the car moved slowly along, the driver avoiding wart-hog holes and driving around the mud castles ants had built. Then, looking across the opening, Wilson suddenly turned and said,

"By God, there they are!"

And looking where he pointed, while the car jumped forward and Wilson spoke in rapid Swahili to the driver, Macomber saw three huge, black animals looking almost cylindrical in their long heaviness, like big black tank cars, moving at a gallop across the far edge of the open prairie. They moved at a stiff-necked, stiff bodied gallop and he could see the upswept wide black horns on their heads as they galloped heads out; the heads not moving.

"They're three old bulls," Wilson said. "We'll cut them off before they get to the swamp."

The car was going a wild forty-five miles an hour across the open and as Macomber watched, the buffalo got bigger and bigger until he could see the gray, hairless, scabby look of one huge bull and how his neck was a part of his shoulders and the shiny black of his horns as he galloped a little behind the others that were strung out in that steady plunging gait; and then, the car swaying as though it had just jumped a road, they drew up close and he could see the plunging hugeness of the bull, and the dust in his sparsely haired hide, the wide boss of horn and his outstretched, wide-nostrilled muzzle, and he was raising his rifle when Wilson shouted, "Not from the car, you fool!" and he had no fear, only hatred of Wilson, while the brakes clamped on and the car skidded, plowing sideways to an almost stop and Wilson was out on one side and he on the other, stumbling as his feet hit the still speeding-by of the earth, and then he was shooting at the bull as he moved away, hearing the bullets whunk into him, emptying his rifle at him as he moved steadily away, finally remembering to get his shots forward into the shoulder, and as he fumbled to re-load, he saw the bull was down. Down on his knees, his big head tossing, and seeing the other two still galloping he shot at the leader and hit him. He shot again and missed and he heard the *carawonging* roar as Wilson shot and saw the leading bull slide forward onto his nose.

"Get that other," Wilson said. "Now you're shooting!"

But the other bull was moving steadily at the same gallop and he missed, throwing a spout of dirt, and Wilson missed and the dust rose in a cloud and Wilson shouted, "Come on. He's too far!" and grabbed his arm and they were in the car again, Macomber and Wilson hanging on the sides and rocketing swayingly over the uneven ground, drawing up on the steady, plunging, heavy-necked, straight-moving gallop of the bull.

They were behind him and Macomber was filling his rifle, dropping shells onto the ground, jamming it, clearing the jam, then they were almost up with the bull when Wilson yelled "Stop," and the car skidded so that it almost swung over and Macomber fell forward onto his feet, slammed his bolt forward and fired as far forward as he could aim into the galloping, rounded black back, aimed and shot again, then again, then again, and the bullets, all of them hitting, had no effect on the buffalo that he could see. Then Wilson shot, the roar deafening him, and he could see the bull stagger. Macomber shot again, aiming carefully, and down he came, onto his knees.

"All right," Wilson said. "Nice work. That's the three."

Macomber felt a drunken elation.

"How many times did you shoot?" he asked.

"Just three," Wilson said. "You killed the first bull. The biggest one. I helped you finish the other two. Afraid they might have got into cover. You had them killed. I was just mopping up a little. You shot damn well."

"Let's go to the car," said Macomber. "I want a drink."

"Got to finish off that buff first," Wilson told him. The buffalo was on his knees and he jerked his head furiously and bellowed in pig-eyed, roaring rage as they came toward him.

"Watch he doesn't get up," Wilson said. Then, "Get a little broadside and take him in the neck just behind the ear."

Macomber aimed carefully at the center of the huge, jerking, rage-driven neck and shot. At the shot the head dropped forward.

"That does it," said Wilson. "Got the spine. They're a hell of a looking thing, aren't they?"

"Let's get the drink," said Macomber. In his life he had never felt so good.

In the car Macomber's wife sat very white faced. "You were marvellous, darling," she said to Macomber. "What a ride."

"Was it rough?" Wilson asked.

"It was frightful. I've never been more frightened in my life."

"Let's all have a drink," Macomber said.

"By all means," said Wilson. "Give it to the Memsahib." She drank the neat whisky from the flask and shuddered a little when she swallowed. She handed the flask to Macomber who handed it to Wilson.

"It was frightfully exciting," she said. "It's given me a dreadful headache. I didn't know you were allowed to shoot them from cars though."

"No one shot from cars," said Wilson coldly.

"I mean chase them from cars."

"Wouldn't ordinarily," Wilson said. "Seemed sporting enough to me though while we were doing it. Taking more chance driving that way across the plain full of holes and one thing and another than hunting on foot. Buffalo could have charged us each time we shot if he liked. Gave him every chance. Wouldn't mention it to any one though. It's illegal if that's what you mean."

"It seemed very unfair to me," Margot said, "chasing those big helpless things in a motor car."

"Did it?" said Wilson.

"What would happen if they heard about it in Nairobi?"

"I'd lose my license for one thing. Other unpleasantnesses," Wilson said, taking a drink from the flask. "I'd be out of business."

"Really?"

"Yes, really."

"Well," said Macomber, and he smiled for the first time all day. "Now she has something on you."

"You have such a pretty way of putting things, Francis," Margot Macomber said. Wilson looked at them both. If a four-letter man marries a five-letter woman, he was thinking, what number of letters would their children be? What he said was, "We lost a gun-bearer. Did you notice it?"

"My God, no," Macomber said.

"Here he comes," Wilson said. "He's all right. He must have fallen off when we left the first bull."

Approaching them was the middle-aged gun-bearer, limping along in his knitted cap, khaki tunic, shorts and rubber sandals, gloomy-faced and disgusted looking. As he came up he called out to Wilson in Swahili and they all saw the change in the white hunter's face.

"What does he say?" asked Margot.

"He says the first bull got up and went into the bush," Wilson said with no expression in his voice.

"Oh," said Macomber blankly.

"Then it's going to be just like the lion," said Margot, full of anticipation.

"It's not going to be a damned bit like the lion," Wilson told her. "Did you want another drink, Macomber?"

"Thanks, yes," Macomber said. He expected the feeling he had had about the lion to come back but it did not. For the first time in his life he really felt wholly without fear. Instead of fear he had a feeling of definite elation.

"We'll go and have a look at the second bull," Wilson said. "I'll tell the driver to put the car in the shade."

"What are you going to do?" asked Margaret Macomber.

"Take a look at the buff," Wilson said.

"I'll come."

"Come along."

The three of them walked over to where the second buffalo bulked blackly in the open, head forward on the grass, the massive horns swung wide.

"He's a very good head," Wilson said. "That's close to a fifty-inch spread."

Macomber was looking at him with delight.

"He's hateful looking," said Margot. "Can't we go into the shade?"

"Of course," Wilson said. "Look," he said to Macomber, and pointed. "See that patch of bush?"

"Yes."

"That's where the first bull went in. The gun-bearer said when he fell off the bull was down. He was watching us helling along and the other two buff galloping. When he looked up there was the bull up and looking at him. Gun-bearer ran like hell and the bull went off slowly into that bush."

"Can we go in after him now?" asked Macomber eagerly.

Wilson looked at him appraisingly. Damned if this isn't a strange one, he thought. Yesterday he's scared sick and today he's a ruddy fire eater.

"No, we'll give him a while."

"Let's please go into the shade," Margot said. Her face was white and she looked ill.

They made their way to the car where it stood under a single, wide-spreading tree and all climbed in.

"Chances are he's dead in there," Wilson remarked. "After a little we'll have a look."

Macomber felt a wild unreasonable happiness that he had never known before.

"By God, that was a chase," he said. "I've never felt any such feeling. Wasn't it marvellous, Margot?"

"I hated it."

"Why?"

"I hated it," she said bitterly. "I loathed it."

"You know I don't think I'd ever be afraid of anything again," Macomber said to Wilson. "Something happened in me after we first saw the buff and started after him. Like a dam bursting. It was pure excitement."

"Cleans out your liver," said Wilson. "Damn funny things happen to people."

Macomber's face was shining. "You know something did happen to me," he said. "I feel absolutely different."

His wife said nothing and eyed him strangely. She was sitting far back in the seat and Macomber was sitting forward talking to Wilson who turned sideways talking over the back of the front seat.

"You know, I'd like to try another lion," Macomber said. "I'm really not afraid of them now. After all, what can they do to you?"

"That's it," said Wilson. "Worst one can do is kill you. How does it go? Shakespeare. Damned good. See if I can remember. Oh, damned good. Used to quote it to myself at one time. Let's see. 'By my troth, I care not; a man can die but once; we owe God a death and let it go which way it will, he that dies this year is quit for the next.' Damned fine, eh?"

He was very embarrassed, having brought out this thing he had lived by, but he had seen men come of age before and it always moved him. It was not a matter of their twenty-first birthday.

It had taken a strange chance of hunting, a sudden precipitation into action without opportunity for worrying beforehand, to bring this about with Macomber, but regardless of how it had happened it had most certainly happened. Look at the beggar now, Wilson thought. It's that some of them stay little boys so long, Wilson thought. Sometimes all their lives. Their figures stay boyish when they're fifty. The great American boy-men. Damned strange people. But he liked this Macomber now. Damned strange fellow. Probably meant the end of cuckoldry too. Well, that would be a damned good thing. Damned good thing. Beggar had probably been afraid all his life. Don't know what started it. But over now. Hadn't had time to be afraid with the buff. That and being angry too. Motor car too. Motor cars made it familiar. Be a damn fire eater now. He'd seen it in the war work the same way. More of a change than any loss of virginity. Fear gone like an operation. Something else grew in its place. Main thing a man had. Made him into a man. Women knew it too. No bloody fear.

From the far corner of the seat Margaret Macomber looked at the two of them. There was no change in Wilson. She saw Wilson as she had seen him the day before when she had first realized what his great talent was. But she saw the change in Francis Macomber now.

"Do you have that feeling of happiness about what's going to happen?" Macomber asked, still exploring his new wealth.

"You're not supposed to mention it," Wilson said, looking in the other's face. "Much more fashionable to say you're scared. Mind you, you'll be scared too, plenty of times."

"But you *have* a feeling of happiness about action to come?"

"Yes," said Wilson. "There's that. Doesn't do to talk too much about all this. Talk the whole thing away. No pleasure in anything if you mouth it up too much."

"You're both talking rot," said Margot. "Just because you've chased some helpless animals in a motor car you talk like heroes."

"Sorry," said Wilson. "I have been gassing too much." She's worried about it already, he thought.

"If you don't know what we're talking about why not keep out of it?" Macomber asked his wife.

"You've gotten awfully brave, awfully suddenly," his wife said contemptuously, but her contempt was not secure. She was very afraid of something.

Macomber laughed, a very natural hearty laugh. "You know I *have*," he said. "I really have."

"Isn't it sort of late?" Margot said bitterly. Because she had done the best she could for many years back and the way they were together now was no one person's fault.

"Not for me," said Macomber.

Margot said nothing but sat back in the corner of the seat.

"Do you think we've given him time enough?" Macomber asked Wilson cheerfully.

"We might have a look," Wilson said. "Have you any solids left?"

"The gun-bearer has some."

Wilson called in Swahili and the older gun-bearer, who was skinning out one of the heads, straightened up, pulled a box of solids out of his pocket and brought them over to Macomber, who filled his magazine and put the remaining shells in his pocket.

"You might as well shoot the Springfield," Wilson said. "You're used to it. We'll leave the Mannlicher in the car with the Memsahib. Your gun-bearer can carry your heavy gun. I've this damned cannon. Now let me tell you about them." He had saved this until the last because he did not want to worry Macomber. "When a buff comes he comes with his head high and thrust straight out. The boss of the horns covers any sort of a brain shot. The only shot is straight into the nose. The only other shot is into his chest or, if you're to one side, into the neck or the shoulders. After they've been hit once they take a hell of a lot of killing. Don't try anything fancy. Take the easiest shot there is. They've finished skinning out that head now. Should we get started?"

He called to the gun-bearers, who came up wiping their hands, and the older one got into the back.

"I'll only take Kongoni," Wilson said. "The other can watch to keep the birds away."

As the car moved slowly across the open space toward the island of brushy trees that ran in a tongue of foliage along a dry water course that cut the open swale, Macomber felt his heart pounding and his mouth was dry again, but it was excitement, not fear.

"Here's where he went in," Wilson said. Then to the gun-bearer in Swahili, "Take the blood spoor."

The car was parallel to the patch of bush. Macomber, Wilson and the gun-bearer got down. Macomber, looking back, saw his wife, with the rifle by her side, looking at him. He waved to her and she did not wave back.

The brush was very thick ahead and the ground was dry. The middle-aged gun-bearer was sweating heavily and Wilson had his hat down over his eyes and his red neck showed just ahead of Macomber. Suddenly the gun-bearer said something in Swahili to Wilson and ran forward.

"He's dead in there," Wilson said. "Good work," and he turned to grip Macomber's hand and as they shook hands, grinning at each other, the gun-bearer shouted wildly and they saw him coming out of the bush sideways, fast as a crab, and the bull coming, nose out, mouth tight closed, blood dripping, massive head straight out, coming in a charge, his little pig eyes bloodshot as he looked at them. Wilson, who was ahead, was kneeling shooting, and Macomber, as he fired, unhearing his shot in the roaring of Wilson's gun, saw fragments like slate burst from the huge boss of the horns, and the head jerked, he shot again at the wide nostrils and saw the horns jolt again and fragments fly, and he did not see Wilson now and, aiming carefully, shot again with the buffalo's huge bulk almost on him and his rifle almost level with the on-coming head, nose out, and he could see the little wicked eyes and the head started to lower and he felt a sudden white-hot, blinding flash explode inside his head and that was all he ever felt.

Wilson had ducked to one side to get in a shoulder shot. Macomber had stood solid and shot for the nose, shooting a touch high each time and hitting the heavy horns, splintering and chipping them like hitting a slate roof, and Mrs. Macomber, in the car, had shot at the buffalo with the 6.5 Mannlicher as it seemed about to gore Macomber and had hit her husband about two inches up and a little to one side of the base of his skull.

Francis Macomber lay now, face down, not two yards from where the buffalo lay on his side and his wife knelt over him with Wilson beside her.

"I wouldn't turn him over," Wilson said.

The woman was crying hysterically.

"I'd get back in the car," Wilson said. "Where's the rifle?"

She shook her head, her face contorted. The gun-bearer picked up the rifle.

"Leave it as it is," said Wilson. Then, "Go get Abdulla so that he may witness the manner of the accident."

He knelt down, took a handkerchief from his pocket, and spread it over Francis Macomber's crew-cropped head where it lay. The blood sank into the dry, loose earth.

Wilson stood up and saw the buffalo on his side, his legs out, his thinly-haired belly crawling with ticks. "Hell of a good bull," his brain registered automatically. "A good fifty inches, or better. Better." He called to the driver and told him to spread a blanket over the body and stay by it. Then he walked over to the motor car where the woman sat crying in the corner.

"That was a pretty thing to do," he said in a toneless voice. "He *would* have left you too."

"Stop it," she said.

"Of course it's an accident," he said. "I know that."

"Stop it," she said.

"Don't worry," he said. "There will be a certain amount of unpleasantness but I will have some photographs taken that will be very useful at the inquest. There's the testimony of the gun-bearers and the driver too. You're perfectly all right."

"Stop it," she said.

"There's a hell of a lot to be done," he said. "And I'll have to send a truck off to the lake to wireless for a plane to take the three of us into Nairobi. Why didn't you poison him? That's what they do in England."

"Stop it. Stop it. Stop it," the woman cried.

Wilson looked at her with his flat blue eyes.

"I'm through now," he said. "I was a little angry. I'd begun to like your husband."

"Oh, please stop it," she said. "Please, please stop it."

"That's better," Wilson said. "Please is much better. Now I'll stop."

WILLIAM FAULKNER

A Rose for Emily 🐛

When Miss Emily Grierson died, our whole town went to her
funeral: the men through a sort of respectful affection for a fallen
monument, the women mostly out of curiosity to see the inside of
her house, which no one save an old manservant—a combined gardener and
cook—had seen in at least ten years.

It was a big, squarish frame house that had once been white, decorated
with cupolas and spires and scrolled balconies in the heavily lightsome style
of the seventies, set on what had once been our most select street. But garages
and cotton gins had encroached and obliterated even the august names of
that neighborhood; only Miss Emily's house was left, lifting its stubborn
and coquettish decay above the cotton wagons and the gasoline pumps—an
eyesore among eyesores. And now Miss Emily had gone to join the repre-
sentatives of those august names where they lay in the cedar-bemused cemetery among the ranked and anonymous graves of Union and Confederate
soldiers who fell at the battle of Jefferson.

Alive, Miss Emily had been a tradition, a duty, and a care; a sort of heredi-
tary obligation upon the town, dating from that day in 1894 when Colonel
Sartoris, the mayor—he who fathered the edict that no Negro woman should
appear on the streets without an apron—remitted her taxes, the dispensation
dating from the death of her father on into perpetuity. Not that Miss Emily
would have accepted charity. Colonel Sartoris invented an involved tale to
the effect that Miss Emily's father had loaned money to the town, which the
town, as a matter of business, preferred this way of repaying. Only a man of
Colonel Sartoris' generation and thought could have invented it, and only
a woman could have believed it.

When the next generation, with its more modern ideas, became mayors
and aldermen, this arrangement created some little dissatisfaction. On the
first of the year they mailed her a tax notice. February came, and there was
no reply. They wrote her a formal letter, asking her to call at the sheriff's
office at her convenience. A week later the mayor wrote her himself, offering
to call or to send his car for her, and received in reply a note on paper of an

Copyright 1931 by William Faulkner. Reprinted by permission of Random House,
Inc.

archaic shape, in a thin, flowing calligraphy in faded ink, to the effect that she no longer went out at all. The tax notice was also enclosed, without comment.

They called a special meeting of the Board of Aldermen. A deputation waited upon her, knocked at the door through which no visitor had passed since she ceased giving china-painting lessons eight or ten years earlier. They were admitted by the old Negro into a dim hall from which a stairway mounted into still more shadow. It smelled of dust and disuse—a close, dank smell. The Negro led them into the parlor. It was furnished in heavy, leather-covered furniture. When the Negro opened the blinds of one window, they could see that the leather was cracked; and when they sat down, a faint dust rose sluggishly about their thighs, spinning with slow motes in the single sun-ray. On a tarnished gilt easel before the fireplace stood a crayon portrait of Miss Emily's father.

They rose when she entered—a small, fat woman in black, with a thin gold chain descending to her waist and vanishing into her belt, leaning on an ebony cane with a tarnished gold head. Her skeleton was small and spare; perhaps that was why what would have been merely plumpness in another was obesity in her. She looked bloated, like a body long submerged in motionless water, and of that pallid hue. Her eyes, lost in the fatty ridges of her face, looked like two small pieces of coal pressed into a lump of dough as they moved from one face to another while the visitors stated their errand.

She did not ask them to sit. She just stood in the door and listened quietly until the spokesman came to a stumbling halt. Then they could hear the invisible watch ticking at the end of the gold chain.

Her voice was dry and cold. "I have no taxes in Jefferson. Colonel Sartoris explained it to me. Perhaps one of you can gain access to the city records and satisfy yourselves."

"But we have. We are the city authorities, Miss Emily. Didn't you get a notice from the sheriff, signed by him?"

"I received a paper, yes," Miss Emily said. "Perhaps he considers himself the sheriff. . . . I have no taxes in Jefferson."

"But there is nothing on the books to show that, you see. We must go by the—"

"See Colonel Sartoris. I have no taxes in Jefferson."

"But, Miss Emily—"

"See Colonel Sartoris." (Colonel Sartoris had been dead almost ten years.) "I have no taxes in Jefferson. Tobe!" The Negro appeared. "Show these gentlemen out."

II

So she vanquished them, horse and foot, just as she had vanquished their fathers thirty years before about the smell. That was two years after her father's death and a short time after her sweetheart—the one we believed would marry her—had deserted her. After her father's death she went out very little; after her sweetheart went away, people hardly saw her at all. A few of the ladies had the temerity to call, but were not received, and the only sign of life about the place was the Negro man—a young man then—going in and out with a market basket.

"Just as if a man—any man—could keep a kitchen properly," the ladies said; so they were not surprised when the smell developed. It was another link between the gross, teeming world and the high and mighty Griersons.

A neighbor, a woman, complained to the mayor, Judge Stevens, eighty years old.

"But what will you have me do about it, madam?" he said.

"Why, send her word to stop it," the woman said. "Isn't there a law?"

"I'm sure that won't be necessary," Judge Stevens said. "It's probably just a snake or a rat that nigger of hers killed in the yard. I'll speak to him about it."

The next day he received two more complaints, one from a man who came in diffident deprecation. "We really must do something about it, Judge. I'd be the last one in the world to bother Miss Emily, but we've got to do something." That night the Board of Aldermen met—three graybeards and one younger man, a member of the rising generation.

"It's simple enough," he said. "Send her word to have her place cleaned up. Give her a certain time to do it in, and if she don't . . ."

"Dammit, sir," Judge Stevens said, "will you accuse a lady to her face of smelling bad?"

So the next night, after midnight, four men crossed Miss Emily's lawn and slunk about the house like burglars, sniffing along the base of the brickwork and at the cellar openings while one of them performed a regular sowing motion with his hand out of a sack slung from his shoulder. They broke open the cellar door and sprinkled lime there, and in all the outbuildings. As they recrossed the lawn, a window that had been dark was lighted and Miss Emily sat in it, the light behind her, and her upright torso motionless as that of an idol. They crept quietly across the lawn and into the shadow of the locusts that lined the street. After a week or two the smell went away.

That was when people had begun to feel really sorry for her. People in our town, remembering how old lady Wyatt, her great-aunt, had gone completely crazy at last, believed that the Greirsons held themselves a little too high for what they really were. None of the young men were quite good enough for Miss Emily and such. We had long thought of them as a tableau: Miss Emily a slender figure in white in the background, her father a spraddled silhouette in the foreground, his back to her and clutching a horsewhip, the two of them framed by the back-flung front door. So when she got to be thirty and was still single, we were not pleased exactly, but vindicated; even with insanity in the family she wouldn't have turned down all of her chances if they had really materialized.

When her father died, it got about that the house was all that was left to her; and in a way, people were glad. At last they could pity Miss Emily. Being left alone, and a pauper, she had become humanized. Now she too would know the old thrill and the old despair of a penny more or less.

The day after his death all the ladies prepared to call at the house and offer condolence and aid, as is our custom. Miss Emily met them at the door, dressed as usual and with no trace of grief on her face. She told them that her father was not dead. She did that for three days, with the ministers calling on her, and the doctors, trying to persuade her to let them dispose of the body. Just as they were about to resort to law and force, she broke down, and they buried her father quickly.

We did not say she was crazy then. We believed she had to do that. We remembered all the young men her father had driven away, and we knew that with nothing left, she would have to cling to that which had robbed her, as people will.

III

She was sick for a long time. When we saw her again, her hair was cut short, making her look like a girl, with a vague resemblance to those angels in colored church windows—sort of tragic and serene.

The town had just let the contracts for paving the sidewalks, and in the summer after her father's death they began the work. The construction company came with niggers and mules and machinery, and a foreman named Homer Barron, a Yankee—a big, dark, ready man, with a big voice and eyes lighter than his face. The little boys would follow in groups to hear him cuss the niggers, and the niggers singing in time to the rise and fall of picks. Pretty soon he knew everybody in town. Whenever you heard a lot of laughing anywhere about the square, Homer Barron would be in the center of the group. Presently we began to see him and Miss Emily on Sunday afternoons driving in the yellow-wheeled buggy and the matched team of bays from the livery stable.

At first we were glad that Miss Emily would have an interest, because the ladies all said, "Of course a Grierson would not think seriously of a Northerner, a day laborer." But there were still others, older people, who said that even grief could not cause a real lady to forget *noblesse oblige*— without calling it *noblesse oblige*. They just said, "Poor Emily. Her kinsfolk should come to her." She had some kin in Alabama; but years ago her father had fallen out with them over the estate of old lady Wyatt, the crazy woman, and there was no communication between the two families. They had not even been represented at the funeral.

And as soon as the old people said, "Poor Emily," the whispering began. "Do you suppose it's really so?" they said to one another. "Of course it is. What else could . . ." This behind their hands; rustling of craned silk and satin behind jalousies closed upon the sun of Sunday afternoon as the thin, swift clop-clop-clop of the matched team passed: "Poor Emily."

She carried her head high enough—even when we believed that she was fallen. It was as if she demanded more than ever the recognition of her dignity as the last Grierson; as if it had wanted that touch of earthiness to reaffirm her imperviousness. Like when she bought the rat poison, the arsenic. That was over a year after they had begun to say "Poor Emily," and while the two female cousins were visiting her.

"I want some poison," she said to the druggist. She was over thirty then, still a slight woman, though thinner than usual, with cold, haughty black eyes in a face the flesh of which was strained across the temples and about the eyesockets as you imagine a lighthouse-keeper's face ought to look. "I want some poison," she said.

"Yes, Miss Emily. What kind? For rats and such? I'd recom—"

"I want the best you have. I don't care what kind."

The druggist named several. "They'll kill anything up to an elephant. But what you want is—"

"Arsenic," Miss Emily said. "Is that a good one?"

"Is . . . arsenic? Yes, ma'am. But what you want—"

"I want arsenic."

The druggist looked down at her. She looked back at him, erect, her face like a strained flag. "Why, of course," the druggist said. "If that's what you want. But the law requires you to tell what you are going to use it for."

Miss Emily just stared at him, her head tilted back in order to look him eye for eye, until he looked away and went and got the arsenic and wrapped it up. The Negro delivery boy brought her the package; the druggist didn't come back. When she opened the package at home there was written on the box, under the skull and bones: "For rats."

IV

So the next day we all said, "She will kill herself"; and we said it would be the best thing. When she had first begun to be seen with Homer Barron, we had said, "She will marry him." Then we said, "She will persuade him yet," because Homer himself had remarked—he liked men, and it was known that he drank with the younger men in the Elks' Club—that he was not a marrying man. Later we said, "Poor Emily," behind the jalousies as they passed on Sunday afternoon in the glittering buggy, Miss Emily with her head high and Homer Barron with his hat cocked and a cigar in his teeth, reins and whip in a yellow glove.

Then some of the ladies began to say that it was a disgrace to the town and a bad example to the young people. The men did not want to interfere, but at last the ladies forced the Baptist minister—Miss Emily's people were Episcopal—to call upon her. He would never divulge what happened during that interview, but he refused to go back again. The next Sunday they again drove about the streets, and the following day the minister's wife wrote to Miss Emily's relations in Alabama.

So she had blood-kin under her roof again and we sat back to watch developments. At first nothing happened. Then we were sure that they were to be married. We learned that Miss Emily had been to the jeweler's and ordered a man's toilet set in silver, with the letters H.B. on each piece. Two days later we learned that she had bought a complete outfit of men's clothing, including a nightshirt, and we said, "They are married." We were really glad. We were glad because the two female cousins were even more Grierson than Miss Emily had ever been.

So we were not surprised when Homer Barron—the streets had been finished some time since—was gone. We were a little disappointed that there was not a public blowing-off, but we believed that he had gone on to prepare for Miss Emily's coming, or to give her a chance to get rid of the cousins. (By that time it was a cabal, and we were all Miss Emily's allies to help circumvent the cousins.) Sure enough, after another week they departed. And, as we had expected all along, within three days Homer Barron was back in town. A neighbor saw the Negro man admit him at the kitchen door at dusk one evening.

And that was the last we saw of Homer Barron. And of Miss Emily for some time. The Negro man went in and out with the market basket, but the front door remained closed. Now and then we would see her at a window for a moment, as the men did that night when they sprinkled the lime, but for almost six months she did not appear on the streets. Then we knew that this was to be expected too; as if that quality of her father which had thwarted her woman's life so many times had been too virulent and too furious to die.

When we next saw Miss Emily, she had grown fat and her hair was turning gray. During the next few years it grew grayer and grayer until it attained an even pepper-and-salt iron-gray, when it ceased turning. Up to the day of her death at seventy-four it was still that vigorous iron-gray, like the hair of an active man.

From that time on her front door remained closed, save for a period of six or seven years, when she was about forty, during which she gave lessons in china-painting. She fitted up a studio in one of the downstairs rooms, where the daughters and granddaughters of Colonel Sartoris' contemporaries were sent to her with the same regularity and in the same spirit that they were sent on Sundays with a twenty-five cent piece for the collection plate. Meanwhile her taxes had been remitted.

Then the newer generation became the backbone and the spirit of the town, and the painting pupils grew up and fell away and did not send their children to her with boxes of color and tedious brushes and pictures cut from the ladies' magazines. The front door closed upon the last one and remained closed for good. When the town got free postal delivery Miss Emily alone refused to let them fasten the metal numbers above her door and attach a mailbox to it. She would not listen to them.

Daily, monthly, yearly we watched the Negro grow grayer and more stooped, going in and out with the market basket. Each December we sent her a tax notice, which would be returned by the post office a week later, unclaimed. Now and then we would see her in one of the downstairs windows—she had evidently shut up the top floor of the house—like the carven torso of an idol in a niche, looking or not looking at us, we could never tell which. Thus she passed from generation to generation—dear, inescapable, impervious, tranquil, and perverse.

And so she died. Fell ill in the house filled with dust and shadows, with only a doddering Negro man to wait on her. We did not even know she was sick; we had long since given up trying to get any information from the Negro. He talked to no one, probably not even to her, for his voice had grown harsh and rusty, as if from disuse.

She died in one of the downstairs rooms, in a heavy walnut bed with a curtain, her gray head propped on a pillow yellow and moldy with age and lack of sunlight.

v

The Negro met the first of the ladies at the front door and let them in, with their hushed, sibilant voices and their quick, curious glances, and then he disappeared. He walked right through the house and out the back and was not seen again.

The two female cousins came at once. They held the funeral on the second day, with the town coming to look at Miss Emily beneath a mass of bought flowers, with the crayon face of her father musing profoundly above the bier and the ladies sibilant and macabre; and the very old men—some in their brushed Confederate uniforms—on the porch and the lawn, talking of Miss Emily as if she had been a contemporary of theirs, believing that they had danced with her and courted her perhaps, confusing time with its mathematical progression, as the old do, to whom all the past is not a diminishing road, but, instead, a huge meadow which no winter ever quite touches, divided from them now by the narrow bottleneck of the most recent decade of years.

Already we knew that there was one room in that region above stairs which no one had seen in forty years, and which would have to be forced. They waited until Miss Emily was decently in the ground before they opened it.

The violence of breaking down the door seemed to fill this room with pervading dust. A thin, acrid pall as of the tomb seemed to lie everywhere upon this room decked and furnished as for a bridal: upon the valance curtains of faded rose color, upon the rose-shaded lights, upon the dressing table, upon the delicate array of crystal and the man's toilet things backed with tarnished silver, silver so tarnished that the monogram was obscured. Among them lay a collar and tie, as if they had just been removed, which, lifted, left upon the surface a pale crescent in the dust. Upon a chair hung the suit, carefully folded; beneath it the two mute shoes and the discarded socks.

The man himself lay in the bed.

For a long while we just stood there, looking down at the profound and fleshless grin. The body had apparently once lain in the attitude of an embrace, but now the long sleep that outlasts love, that conquers even the grimace of love, had cuckolded him. What was left of him, rotted beneath what was left of the nightshirt, had become inextricable from the bed in which he lay; and upon him and upon the pillow beside him lay that even coating of the patient and biding dust.

Then we noticed that in the second pillow was the indentation of a head. One of us lifted something from it, and leaning forward, that faint and invisible dust dry and acrid in the nostrils, we saw a long strand of iron-gray hair.

KATHERINE ANNE PORTER

Flowering Judas ❦

Braggioni sits heaped upon the edge of a straight-backed chair much too small for him, and sings to Laura in a furry, mournful voice. Laura has begun to find reasons for avoiding her own house until the latest possible moment, for Braggioni is there almost every night. No matter how late she is, he will be sitting there with a surly, waiting expression, pulling at his kinky yellow hair, thumbing the strings of his guitar, snarling a tune under his breath. Lupe the Indian maid meets Laura at the door, and says with a flicker of a glance towards the upper room, "He waits."

Laura wishes to lie down, she is tired of her hairpins and the feel of her long tight sleeves, but she says to him, "Have you a new song for me this evening?" If he says yes, she asks him to sing it. If he says no, she remembers his favorite one, and asks him to sing it again. Lupe brings her a cup of chocolate and a plate of rice, and Laura eats at the small table under the lamp, first inviting Braggioni, whose answer is always the same: "I have eaten, and besides, chocolate thickens the voice."

Laura says, "Sing, then," and Braggioni heaves himself into song. He scratches the guitar familiarly as though it were a pet animal, and sings passionately off key, taking the high notes in a prolonged painful squeal. Laura, who haunts the markets listening to the ballad singers, and stops every day to hear the blind boy playing his reed-flute in Sixteenth of September Street, listens to Braggioni with pitiless courtesy, because she dares not smile at his miserable performance. Nobody dares to smile at him. Braggioni is cruel to everyone, with a kind of specialized insolence, but he is so vain of his talents, and so sensitive to slights, it would require a cruelty and vanity greater than his own to lay a finger on the vast cureless wound of his self-esteem. It would require courage, too, for it is dangerous to offend him, and nobody has this courage.

Braggioni loves himself with such tenderness and amplitude and eternal charity that his followers—for he is a leader of men, a skilled revolutionist, and his skin has been punctured in honorable warfare—warm themselves in the reflected glow, and say to each other: "He has a real nobility, a love of humanity raised above mere personal affections." The excess of this self-love has flowed out, inconveniently for her, over Laura, who, with so many others, owes her comfortable situation and her salary to him. When he is in a very good humor, he tells her, "I am tempted to forgive you for being a *gringa, gringita!*" and Laura, burning, imagines herself leaning forward suddenly, and with a sound back-handed slap wiping the suety smile from his face. If he notices her eyes at these moments he gives no sign.

She knows what Braggioni would offer her, and she must resist tenaciously without appearing to resist, and if she could avoid it she would not admit even to herself the slow drift of his intention. During these long evenings which have spoiled a long month for her, she sits in her deep chair with an open book on her knees, resting her eyes on the consoling rigidity of the printed page when the sight and sound of Braggioni singing threaten to identify themselves with all her remembered afflictions and to add their weight to her uneasy premonitions of the future. The gluttonous bulk of Braggioni has become a symbol of her many disillusions, for a revolutionist should be lean, animated by heroic faith, a vessel of abstract virtues. This is nonsense, she knows it now and is ashamed of it. Revolution must have leaders, and leadership is a career for energetic men. She is, her comrades tell her, full of romantic error, for what she defines as cynicism in them is merely "a developed sense of reality." She is almost too willing to say, "I am wrong, I suppose I don't really understand the principles," and afterward she makes a secret truce with herself, determined not to surrender her will to such expedient logic. But she cannot help feeling that she has been betrayed irreparably by the disunion between her way of living and her feeling of what life should be, and at times she is almost contented to rest in this sense of grievance as a private store of consolation. Sometimes she wishes to run away, but she stays. Now she longs to fly out of this room, down the narrow stairs, and into the street where the houses lean together like conspirators under a single mottled lamp, and leave Braggioni singing to himself.

Instead she looks at Braggioni, frankly and clearly, like a good child who understands the rules of behavior. Her knees cling together under sound blue serge, and her round white collar is not purposely nun-like. She wears the uniform of an idea, and has renounced vanities. She was born Roman Catholic, and in spite of her fear of being seen by someone who might make a scandal of it, she slips now and again into some crumbling little church, kneels on the chilly stone, and says a Hail Mary on the gold rosary she bought in Tehuantepec. It is no good and she ends by examining the altar with its tinsel flowers and ragged brocades, and feels tender about the battered doll-shape of some male saint whose white, lace-trimmed drawers hang limply around his ankles below the hieratic dignity of his velvet robe. She has encased herself in a set of principles derived from her early training, leaving no detail of gesture or of personal taste untouched, and for this reason she will not wear lace made on machines. This is her private heresy, for in her special group the machine is sacred, and will be the salvation of the workers. She loves fine lace, and there is a tiny edge of fluted cobweb on this collar, which is one of twenty precisely alike, folded in blue tissue paper in the upper drawer of her clothes chest.

Braggioni catches her glance solidly as if he had been waiting for it, leans forward, balancing his paunch between his spread knees, and sings with tremendous emphasis, weighing his words. He has, the song relates, no father and no mother, nor even a friend to console him; lonely as a wave of the sea he comes and goes, lonely as a wave. His mouth opens round and yearns sideways, his balloon cheeks grow oily with the labor of song. He bulges marvelously in his expensive garments. Over his lavender collar, crushed upon a purple necktie, held by a diamond hoop: over his ammunition belt of tooled leather worked in silver, buckled cruelly around his gasping middle: over the tops of his glossy yellow shoes Braggioni swells with ominous ripeness, his mauve silk hose stretched taut, his ankles bound with the stout leather thongs of his shoes.

When he stretches his eyelids at Laura she notes again that his eyes are the true tawny yellow cat's eyes. He is rich, not in money, he tells her, but in power, and this power brings with it the blameless ownership of things, and the right to indulge his love of small luxuries. "I have a taste for the elegant refinements," he said once, flourishing a yellow silk handkerchief before her nose. "Smell that? It is Jockey Club, imported from New York." Nonetheless he is wounded by life. He will say so presently. "It is true everything turns to dust in the hand, to gall on the tongue." He sighs and his leather belt creaks like a saddle girth. "I am disappointed in everything as it comes. Everything." He shakes his head. "You, poor thing, you will be disappointed too. You are born for it. We are more alike than you realize in some things. Wait and see. Some day you will remember what I have told you, you will know that Braggioni was your friend."

Laura feels a slow chill, a purely physical sense of danger, a warning in her blood that violence, mutilation, a shocking death, wait for her with lessening patience. She has translated this fear into something homely, immediate, and sometimes hesitates before crossing the street. "My personal fate is nothing, except as the testimony of a mental attitude," she reminds herself, quoting from some forgotten philosophic primer, and is sensible enough to add, "Anyhow, I shall not be killed by an automobile if I can help it."

"It may be true I am as corrupt, in another way, as Braggioni," she thinks in spite of herself, "as callous, as incomplete," and if this is so, any kind of death seems preferable. Still she sits quietly, she does not run. Where could she go? Uninvited she has promised herself to this place; she can no longer imagine herself as living in another country, and there is no pleasure in remembering her life before she came here.

Precisely what is the nature of this devotion, its true motives, and what are its obligations? Laura cannot say. She spends part of her days in Xochimilco, near by, teaching Indian children to say in English, "The cat is on the mat." When she appears in the classroom they crowd about her with smiles on their wise, innocent, clay-colored faces, crying, "Good morning, my titcher!" in immaculate voices, and they make of her desk a fresh garden of flowers every day.

During her leisure she goes to union meetings and listens to busy important voices quarreling over tactics, methods, internal politics. She visits the prisoners of her own political faith in their cells, where they entertain themselves with counting cockroaches, repenting of their indiscretions, composing their memoirs, writing out manifestoes and plans for their comrades who are still walking about free, hands in pockets, sniffing fresh air. Laura brings them food and cigarettes and a little money, and she brings messages disguised in equivocal phrases from the men outside who dare not set foot in the prison for fear of disappearing into the cells kept empty for them. If the prisoners confuse night and day, and complain, "Dear little Laura, time doesn't pass in this infernal hole, and I won't know when it is time to sleep unless I have a reminder," she brings them their favorite narcotics, and says in a tone that does not wound them with pity, "Tonight will really be night for you," and though her Spanish amuses them they find her comforting, useful. If they lose patience and all faith, and curse the slowness of their friends in coming to their rescue with money and influence, they trust her not to repeat everything, and if she inquires, "Where do you think we can find money, or influence?" they are certain to answer, "Well, there is Braggioni, why doesn't he do something?"

She smuggles letters from headquarters to men hiding from firing squads in back streets in mildewed houses, where they sit in tumbled beds and talk bitterly as if all Mexico were at their heels, when Laura knows positively they might appear at the band concert in the Alameda on Sunday morning, and no one would notice them. But Braggioni says, "Let them sweat a little. The next time they may be careful. It is very restful to have them out of the way for a while." She is not afraid to knock on any door in any street after midnight, and enter in the darkness, and say to one of these men who is really in danger: "They will be looking for you—seriously—tomorrow morning after six. Here is some money from Vicente. Go to Vera Cruz and wait."

She borrows money from the Roumanian agitator to give to his bitter enemy the Polish agitator. The favor of Braggioni is their disputed territory, and Braggioni holds the balance nicely, for he can use them both. The Polish agitator talks love to her over café tables, hoping to exploit what he believes is her secret sentimental preference for him, and he gives her misinformation which he begs her to repeat as the solemn truth to certain persons. The Roumanian is more adroit. He is generous with his money in all good causes, and lies to her with an air of ingenuous candor, as if he were her good friend and confidant. She never repeats anything they may say. Braggioni never asks questions. He has other ways to discover all that he wishes to know about them.

Nobody touches her, but all praise her gray eyes, and the soft, round under lip which promises gayety, yet is always grave, nearly always firmly closed: and they cannot understand why she is in Mexico. She walks back and forth on her errands, with puzzled eyebrows, carrying her little folder of drawings and music and school papers. No dancer dances more beautifully than Laura walks, and she inspires some amusing, unexpected ardors, which cause little gossip, because nothing comes of them. A young captain who had been a soldier in Zapata's army attempted, during a horseback ride near Cuernavaca, to express his desire for her with the noble simplicity befitting a rude folk-hero: but gently, because he was gentle. This gentleness was his defeat, for when he alighted, and removed her foot from the stirrup, and essayed to draw her down into his arms, her horse, ordinarily a tame one, shied fiercely, reared and plunged away. The young hero's horse careened blindly after his stable-mate, and the hero did not return to the hotel until rather late that evening. At breakfast he came to her table in full charro dress, gray buckskin jacket and trousers with strings of silver buttons down the leg, and he was in a humorous, careless mood. "May I sit with you?" and "You are a wonderful rider. I was terrified that you might be thrown and dragged. I should never have forgiven myself. But I cannot admire you enough for your riding."

"I learned to ride in Arizona," said Laura.

"If you will ride with me again this morning, I promise you a horse that will not shy with you," he said. But Laura remembered that she must return to Mexico City at noon.

Next morning the children made a celebration and spent their playtime writing on the blackboard, "We lov ar titcher," and with tinted chalks they drew wreaths of flowers around the words. The young hero wrote her a letter: "I am a very foolish, wasteful, impulsive man. I should have first said I love you, and then you would not have run away. But you shall see me again." Laura thought, "I must send him a box of colored crayons," but she was trying to forgive herself for having spurred her horse at the wrong moment.

A brown shock-haired youth came and stood in her patio one night and sang like a lost soul for two hours, but Laura could think of nothing to do about it. The moonlight spread a wash of gauzy silver over the clear spaces of the garden, and the shadows were cobalt blue. The scarlet blossoms of the Judas tree were dull purple, and the names of the colors repeated themselves automatically in her mind, while she watched not the boy, but his shadow, fallen like a dark garment across the fountain rim, trailing in the water. Lupe came silently and whispered expert counsel in her ear: "If you will throw him one little flower, he will sing another song or two and go away." Laura threw the flower, and he sang a last song and went away with the flower tucked in the band of his hat. Lupe said, "He is one of the organizers of the Typographers Union, and before that he sold corridos in the Merced market, and before that, he came from Guanajuato, where I was born. I would not trust any man, but I trust least those from Guanajuato."

She did not tell Laura that he would be back again the next day, and the next, nor that he would follow her at a certain fixed distance around the Merced market, through the Zocolo, up Francesco I. Madero Avenue, and so along the Paseo de la Reforma to Chapultepec Park, and into the Philosopher's Footpath, still with that flower withering in his hat, and an indivisible attention in his eyes.

Now Laura is accustomed to him, it means nothing except that he is nineteen years old and is observing a convention with all propriety, as though it were founded on a law of nature, which in the end it might very well prove to be. He is beginning to write poems which he prints on a wooden press, and he leaves them stuck like handbills in her door. She is pleasantly disturbed by the abstract, unhurried watchfulness of his black eyes which will in time turn easily towards another object. She tells herself that throwing the flower was a mistake, for she is twenty-two years old and knows better; but she refuses to regret it, and persuades herself that her negation of all external events as they occur is a sign that she is gradually perfecting herself in the stoicism she strives to cultivate against that disaster she fears, though she cannot name it.

She is not at home in the world. Every day she teaches children who remain strangers to her, though she loves their tender round hands and their charming opportunistic savagery. She knocks at unfamiliar doors not knowing whether a friend or a stranger shall answer, and even if a known face emerges from the sour gloom of that unknown interior, still it is the face of a stranger. No matter what this stranger says to her, nor what her message to him, the very cells of her flesh reject knowledge and kinship in one monotonous word. No. No. No. She draws her strength from this one holy talismanic word which does not suffer her to be led into evil. Denying everything, she may walk anywhere in safety, she looks at everything without amazement.

No, repeats this firm unchanging voice of her blood; and she looks at Braggioni without amazement. He is a great man, he wishes to impress this simple girl who covers her great round breasts with thick dark cloth, and who hides long, invaluably beautiful legs under a heavy skirt. She is almost thin except for the incomprehensible fullness of her breasts, like a nursing mother's, and Braggioni, who considers himself a judge of women, speculates again on the puzzle of her notorious virginity, and takes the liberty of speech which she permits without a sign of modesty, indeed, without any sort of sign, which is disconcerting.

"You think you are so cold, *gringita!* Wait and see. You will surprise yourself someday! May I be there to advise you!" He stretches his eyelids at her, and his ill-humored cat's eyes waver in a separate glance for the two points of light marking the opposite ends of a smoothly drawn path between the swollen curve of her breasts. He is not put off by that blue serge, nor by her resolutely fixed gaze. There is all the time in the world. His cheeks are bellying with the wind of song. "O girl with the dark eyes," he sings, and reconsiders. "But yours are not dark. I can change all that. O girl with the green eyes, you have stolen my heart away." Then his mind wanders to the song, and Laura feels the weight of his attention being shifted elsewhere. Singing thus, he seems harmless, he is quite harmless, there is nothing to do but sit patiently and say "No," when the moment comes. She draws a full breath, and her mind wanders also, but not far. She dares not wander too far.

Not for nothing has Braggioni taken pains to be a good revolutionist and a professional lover of humanity. He will never die of it. He has the malice, the cleverness, the wickedness, the sharpness of wit, the hardness of heart, stipulated for loving the world profitably. He *will never die of it.* He will live to see himself kicked out from his feeding trough by other hungry world-saviours. Traditionally he must sing in spite of his life which drives him to bloodshed, he tells Laura, for his father was a Tuscany peasant who drifted to Yucatan and married a Maya woman: a woman of race, an aristocrat. They gave him the love and knowledge of music, thus: and under the rip of his thumbnail, the strings of the instrument complain like exposed nerves.

Once he was called Delgadito by all the girls and married women who ran after him; he was so scrawny all his bones showed under his thin cotton clothing, and he could squeeze his emptiness to the very backbone with his two hands. He was a poet and the revolution was only a dream then; too many women loved him and sapped away his youth, and he could never find enough to eat anywhere, anywhere! Now he is a leader of men, crafty men who whisper in his ear, hungry men who wait for hours outside his office for a word with him, emaciated men with wild faces who waylay him at the street gate with a timid, "Comrade, let me tell you . . ." and they blow the foul breath from their empty stomachs in his face.

He is always sympathetic. He gives them handfuls of small coins from his own pockets, he promises them work, there will be demonstrations, they must join the unions and attend the meetings, above all they must be on the watch for spies. They are closer to him than his own brothers, without them he can do nothing—until tomorrow, comrade!

Until tomorrow. "They are stupid, they are lazy, they are treacherous, they would cut my throat for nothing," he says to Laura. He has good food and abundant drink, he hires an automobile and drives in the Paseo on Sunday morning, and enjoys plenty of sleep in a soft bed beside a wife who dares not disturb him; and he sits pampering his bones in easy billows of fat, singing to Laura, who knows and thinks these things about him. When he was fifteen, he tried to drown himself because he loved a girl, his first love, and she laughed at him. "A thousand women have paid for that," and his tight little mouth turns down at the corners. Now he perfumes his hair with Jockey Club, and confides to Laura: "One woman is really as good as another for me in the dark. I prefer them all."

His wife organizes unions among the girls in the cigarette factories, and walks in picket lines, and even speaks at meetings in the evening. But she cannot be brought to acknowledge the benefits of true liberty. "I tell her I must have my freedom, net. She does not understand my point of view." Laura has heard this many times. Braggioni scratches the guitar and meditates. "She is an instinctively virtuous woman, pure gold, no doubt of that. If she were not, I should lock her up, and she knows it."

His wife, who works so hard for the good of the factory girls, employs part of her leisure lying on the floor weeping because there are so many women in the world, and only one husband for her, and she never knows where nor when to look for him. He told her: "Unless you can learn to cry when I am not here, I must go away for good." That day he went away and took a room at the Hotel Madrid.

It is this month of separation for the sake of higher principles that has been spoiled not only for Mrs. Braggioni, whose sense of reality is beyond criticism, but for Laura, who feels herself bogged in a nightmare. Tonight Laura envies Mrs. Braggioni, who is alone, and free to weep as much as she pleases about a concrete wrong. Laura has just come from a visit to the prison, and she is waiting for tomorrow with a bitter anxiety as if tomorrow may not come, but time may be caught immovably in this hour, with herself transfixed, Braggioni singing on forever, and Eugenio's body not yet discovered by the guard.

Braggioni says: "Are you going to sleep?" Almost before she can shake her head, he begins telling her about the May-day disturbances coming on in Morelia, for the Catholics hold a festival in honor of the Blessed Virgin, and the Socialists celebrate their martyrs on that day. "There will be two independent processions, starting from either end of town, and they will march until they meet, and the rest depends . . ." He asks her to oil and load his pistols. Standing up, he unbuckles his ammunition belt, and spreads it laden across her knees. Laura sits with the shells slipping through the cleaning cloth dipped in oil, and he says again he cannot understand why she works so hard for the revolutionary idea unless she loves some man who is in it. "Are you not in love with someone?" "No," says Laura. "And no one is in love with you?" "No." "Then it is your own fault. No woman need go begging. Why, what is the matter with you? The legless beggar woman in the Alameda has a perfectly faithful lover. Did you know that?"

Laura peers down the pistol barrel and says nothing, but a long, slow faintness rises and subsides in her; Braggioni curves his swollen fingers around the throat of the guitar and softly smothers the music out of it, and when she hears him again he seems to have forgotten her, and is speaking in the hypnotic voice he uses when talking in small rooms to a listening, close-gathered crowd. Some day this world, now seemingly so composed and eternal, to the edges of every sea shall be merely a tangle of gaping trenches, of crashing walls and broken bodies. Everything must be torn from its accustomed place where it has rotted for centuries, hurled skyward and distributed, cast down again clean as rain, without separate identity. Nothing shall survive that the stiffened hands of poverty have created for the rich and no one shall be left alive except the elect spirits destined to procreate a new world cleansed of cruelty and injustice, ruled by benevolent anarchy: "Pistols are good, I love them, cannon are even better, but in the end I pin my faith to good dynamite," he concludes, and strokes the pistol lying in her hands. "Once I dreamed of destroying this city, in case it offered resistance to General Ortiz, but it fell into his hands like an overripe pear."

He is made restless by his own words, rises and stands waiting. Laura holds up the belt to him: "Put that on, and go kill somebody in Morella, and you will be happier," she says softly. The presence of death in the room makes her bold. "Today, I found Eugenio going into a stupor. He refused to allow me to call the prison doctor. He had taken all the tablets I brought him yesterday. He said he took them because he was bored."

"He is a fool, and his death is his own business," says Braggioni, fastening his belt carefully.

"I told him if he had waited only a little while longer, you would have got him set free," says Laura. "He said he did not want to wait."

"He is a fool and we are well rid of him," says Braggioni, reaching for his hat.

He goes away. Laura knows his mood has changed, she will not see him any more for a while. He will send word when he needs her to go on errands into strange streets, to speak to the strange faces that will appear, like clay masks with the power of human speech, to mutter their thanks to Braggioni for his help. Now she is free, and she thinks, I must run while there is time. But she does not go.

Braggioni enters his own house where for a month his wife has spent many hours every night weeping and tangling her hair upon her pillow. She is weeping now, and she weeps more at the sight of him, the cause of all her sorrows. He looks about the room. Nothing is changed, the smells are good and familiar, he is well acquainted with the woman who comes toward him with no reproach except grief on her face. He says to her tenderly: "You are so good, please don't cry any more, you dear good creature." She says, "Are you tired, my angel? Sit here and I will wash your feet." She brings a bowl of water, and kneeling, unlaces his shoes, and when from her knees she raises her sad eyes under her blackened lids, he is sorry for everything, and bursts into tears. "Ah, yes, I am hungry, I am tired, let us eat something together," he says, between sobs. His wife leans her head on his arm and says, "Forgive me!" and this time he is refreshed by the solemn, endless rain of her tears.

Laura takes off her serge dress and puts on a white linen nightgown and goes to bed. She turns her head a little to one side, and lying still, reminds herself that it is time to sleep. Numbers tick in her brain like little clocks, soundless doors close of themselves around her. If you would sleep, you must not remember anything, the children will say tomorrow, good morning, my teacher, the poor prisoners who come every day bringing flowers to their jailor. 1-2-3-4-5—it is monstrous to confuse love with revolution, night with day, life with death—ah Eugenio!

The tolling of the midnight bell is a signal, but what does it mean? Get up, Laura, and follow me: come out of your sleep, out of your bed, out of this strange house. What are you doing in this house? Without a word, without fear she rose and reached for Eugenio's hand, but he eluded her with a sharp, sly smile and drifted away. This is not all, you shall see— Murderer, he said, follow me, I will show you a new country, but it is far away and we must hurry. No, said Laura, not unless you take my hand, no; and she clung first to the stair rail, and then to the topmost branch of the Judas tree that bent down slowly and set her upon the earth, and then to the rocky ledge of a cliff, and then to the jagged wave of a sea that was not water but a desert of crumbling stone. Where are you taking me? she asked in wonder but without fear. To death, and it is a long way off, and we must hurry, said Eugenio. No, said Laura, not unless you take my hand. Then eat these flowers, poor prisoner, said Eugenio in a voice of pity, take and eat: and from the Judas tree he stripped the warm bleeding flowers, and held them to her lips. She saw that his hand was fleshless, a cluster of small white petrified branches, and his eye sockets were without light, but she ate the flowers greedily for they satisfied both hunger and thirst. Murderer! said Eugenio, and Cannibal! This is my body and my blood. Laura cried No! and at the sound of her own voice, she awoke trembling, and was afraid to sleep again.

KAY BOYLE

His Idea of a Mother 🐿

The road wound straight on, with a small branch to the left, and
there seemed no reason at all to turn and cross the stream that slid
along on the other side. A queer thought it would be indeed to
follow the cattle path up over the hill.

But the little boy was on his way home from school one day when he
stopped at Drury's Crossing and looked up at the signpost that was insisting
that the branch to the left led to Shopton and the road before him to something else again. It came into his head that the path and the way it was going
had been left unmentioned. He sat down there to have a good look at the
hill that was stretching away beyond.

Across the stream there seemed to be a great amount of soft, sweet turf and
of greenness spread out all over. Higher, there were trees springing up, as
lyrical as dancing women, though all he could see in them was the way they
moved in the wind. Beside the stream there was a willow or two drying out
its hair.

The path did not quite make the grade to the castle of trees that was
bowing this way and that at the top. Just a minute before it got there, it
threw up its two small white arms in despair and was lost forever in the
blowing weeds. The little boy sat looking at what lay before him and calling
upon the courage that would take him over the fence and the stream and
up the hill.

The whole of the hill itself was spotted with islands of dung, and if he
had summoned any courage at all, it perished at the sight of a cow making
her way down. He thought she must be on her way down to drink, but
when she spied him, she stood quite still and looked at him with her soft dim
eyes. He sat hard and small against the fence, wondering if she had any
young ones behind her and watching her full sagging throat and the gentle
shifting of her jaw. Presently, another great angular cow followed the first
one, and then another, and before the little boy could get to his feet and move
away, at least eight of the beasts were stumbling down the stony path.

He stood for a while in the road, watching them lower their muzzles to
drink at the water, and the bright beads from the stream that gathered on
their sparse beards, and the long ribbons of slobber that hung from the ends
of their mouths. Every time they flung wide their rosy nostrils to drink, he

could see the clear ripples which their breath tossed across the surface of the water. He had no great feeling of pride for himself as he stood on the other side of the fence from them, for if men and their courage were strangers to him, at least he knew that the delicate thing which the sight of big animals set shaking between his ribs was fragile enough to be the ornament of any little girl. His father had been dead eight years, and what he was like he had no idea at all.

His idea of a mother was something else again. How long she had been dead, he did not know. He was thinking of her as he walked backward up the road. His dragging feet were startling up fine clouds of dust in the roadway, and in the soles of them was more than languor, as if he did not care whether he ever found his way back to her or not. "Aunt Petoo, skee-doo," he thought. He looked at the cows and watched their tails moving venomously across their bony rumps. "Aunt Petoo, skee-doo."

He found her squatting down in the garden before the house. She had a trowel in her hand, and she was prodding at her flowers. She looked up at him and pushed her straw bonnet off her brow with the back of her hand.

"Did ye ever take a walk up the path over the hill at Drury's Crossing?" he said to her as he swung on the gate.

She shook her head absently. "Will you get me some water in the can, there you are," was what she said. The little boy set down his books. "Don't set your books down there," she said. "Why do you have to swing on the gate every time you come in like that?"

"Did ye ever take a walk on that path over the hill at Drury's Crossing?" asked the little boy.

"Will you get me some water in the can?" said Aunt Petoo.

The little boy walked off with the can in his hand. He was looking around about him, and up, and over, and looking at the house in its vines, and the trees wavering and the birds flying, over his shoulder; and in this way he tripped on a croquet wicket and fell down.

"Get up," said Reynolds.

The little boy sat rubbing his shins and looking sourly at the toes of Reynolds' boots. Reynolds was the only man he had ever known intimately. His vest was black and yellow, and it was his place to ride behind Aunt Petoo's horses and to mow the grass. He could drown kittens, dispose of rabbits with one whack of the hand, and he could swim. In the summer, he could swim the river with the muscles of his breasts swelling and gathering like snowballs in the water. As he stood above the little boy on the croquet lawn, he was red with anger. In one hand he held a carriage whip, and in the other an urchin.

"Look here at this urchin!" he said in contempt to Aunt Petoo. "He was come across stealing cherries!"

There in the sun shone the flushed and dripping face, the contorted mouth, and the terror of the urchin boy. The little boy himself began to whimper at the sight. When he lifted his hand to wipe off his own tears with the back of it, he could see it was shaking as if in the very teeth of cowardice.

"What are you going to do with the urchin?" said the little boy. He whispered it in terror across the grass.

"Thrash him," said Reynolds. "It's what his own father ought to be giving him, not me!" Reynolds swung about to the old lady. "I'm going to thrash him proper, Miss Petoo," he said. He held the urchin up in the sun.

"Not here," said Aunt Petoo. "The wretches squawk so." With the greatest precision she pinched off the leaves that sprang up along the stalk of a begonia. Her mouth did not relent. "Take him around by the stable," she said. "The slugs got into the very best strawberries last night. Not a sizable one for tea, Reynolds!"

"Aunt Petoo," said the little boy, "don't let him thrash the urchin." Aunt Petoo looked up from the flowers. The little boy was standing beside her. "Don't, don't, ah, please don't, Aunt Petoo!" He spoke very quietly, and the "ah" seemed a strange sound for such a small boy to be making. It was a church, a poetry sound, and to hear him using it for a moment put her out.

"But a thief," she said. "A thief who steals . . ."

The little boy's face was shaking like a small fist in her face. "Aunt Petoo, Aunt Petoo," he said. "Please, please, ah, please, please, don't let him do it!"

The garden was as soft and melting as an all-day sucker between the teeth. Aunt Petoo cracked off a great bite of it. "Oh, skee-doo," she said. "Get along with you! Let Reynolds go his own way, and you get about yours! I've been after you for water in the can . . ."

The little boy flung himself against her knees. "Ah, Aunt Petoo, Aunt Petoo," he cried. "No, no, no, no, Aunt Petoo! Let the urchin go once this time, ah, ah, ah, ah, ah, Aunt Petoo!"

A terrible look of venom crossed Aunt Petoo's face. He had made the garden go sick on her very tongue. Reynolds had walked off with the urchin under his arm, and the little boy lay on the ground at her feet, biting fiercely at the turf. "Now listen here," she said. She shook at his shoulder. "Your Uncle Dan is coming home. What do you think of a soldier hearing all this crying and this screaming?" Her voice would never give in. "It's a shame for a boy, and no soldier would bear it."

The little boy lay still.

"Who is my Uncle Dan?" he said, without lifting his head.

"Your father's brother," said Aunt Petoo. "With long whiskers and a sword."

The day had begun to fade away when the little boy started off down the road. That his father's brother was coming back was the thought that remained in his mind. He thought of this until every tree he passed became a menace to him, and his shoelace, untied and tapping at his ankle, made him skid with terror in the gloom.

When he came to Drury's Crossing, he slipped with the greatest glibness beneath the bars of the fence and leaped across the stream. His blood was singing like a harp, and he was not afraid at all. As he ran, he startled a little group of cottontails across the path. He stopped and watched them scampering off through the impenetrable grass. The water was shining like a mirror far below him, and the willows looked as soft and airy as feathers blowing along the stream.

Milkweed pods were tapping at the cups of his knees, and now and again the wing of a moth caressed his cheek. The sight of a moth in the room with him made his spine crawl, but here in the dark it was natural and left him with no fear at all. When he seated himself in the deep grass, he felt as if he were crouching on the hearth close before the fire. Even the wind that rose was as warm as a scarf around his neck.

Whether he fell asleep then or whether his eyes were open all the time he did not know. But however it was, he had not been sitting there long when he saw the cows beginning to loom out of the darkness and make their way down toward the stream. They were going slowly down, with their heads hanging like heavy copper bells between their forelegs, their jaws endlessly and softly crunching, and when they stopped at all, it was to lift their heads and call softly out through the falling night.

The deep mellow sound of the cows calling to one another was so beautiful that the little boy tried the sound of it in his own throat. He lifted his head to catch the soft shape of the cows' mouths and the turn of their velvet tongues in their jaws. His nostrils were stretched wide open, imitating the cows' rosy nostrils, which were spread full as harvest moons.

The great dark beasts seemed in no great haste to descend the hill, and they loitered here and there in the rich night. Had they been horses, thought the little boy, the least sound of him stirring would have sent them off in alarm, but here were the cows cropping at the grass and munching it almost at his feet, as though the smell of him there meant nothing to them. Any movement he made seemed natural to them, and when he put out his hand and stroked the foreleg of one cow that stood near by, she lifted her head in no dismay whatever and snuffed deeply at his neck. Such a blast of sweet meadowy odor passed across his face that he shuddered with delight.

It was then that the beast he had stroked bent her knees under her and lay down in the grass. He could not perceive her in the darkness, but from the sound and breath of her and the soft swing and crunch of her jaws, he knew that she had folded her gray, horny hoofs under her heart and was chewing gently there beside him in the grass. When he moved closer, she made no sign. Even the touch of his hand on her strong shoulder did not cause her to stir. When he stroked the stiff, sleek curve of her ear in his open hand, she flicked it solemnly back and forth.

The little boy shifted himself against her and pressed his small lean back into her strong covered bones. The endless rhythm of her cud swung easily through all her rich shoulder and bosom. Great tough ribbons of movement ran strongly through her flesh. The little boy had laid his face against her neck, and there was his ear stroked and soothed with it. He could hear the soft humming of her belly as it greeted and returned the food from her fruitful jaws. On the ground he could feel the feast of white violets and clover heads that had been spread there before her. As he lay against her he thought of the great full sack of milk that was hanging between her legs.

He was thinking what a comfort it was to have the great warm body of the cow against him in the field, and while he was drowsing, suddenly she whipped her head about so violently that she gave him a fierce blow in the ribs with the side of her horn. When he had found his senses again, he thought it must have been a fly that had disturbed her, or else she would never have struck him with such force. This was the thought that was in his head when she turned again toward him and rubbed her great bony face against his arm. Such blasts did she thrust from her nose on him, like a mother cat smelling out her young, that he thought he would be blown down the black field. But presently, when she had snuffed in enough of him, her tongue began to move rudely across his hand, lifting his fingers up and turning them over as if they were so many stalks of clover. When she had done with his hands, she licked her way up the coarse stuff of his jacket, and there was his neck and his ear and all the hairs on his head getting such a scrubbing and such a loving as would have taken his hide off had it been anyone else that was doing it to him.

It was when the half-moon was coming up from behind the trees that the mother cow, without any kind of warning at all, suddenly straightened out her legs and stood up in the grass. A terrible feeling of despair pierced the little boy's heart. But she went ambling quietly off, with her tail swinging, and the little boy himself started reluctantly down the hill. The whole world was returning again under the illumination of the moon. The trees were uncurling out of the darkness, and the grass was moving like a sea. When the little boy reached the water, he stopped for a moment. In the middle of the stream lay a little broken moon, rippling back and forth. He knelt down and put his two hands about its moving edges and tried to lift it up. In a moment the little moon was rippling back and forth again and his hands were wet and cold.

The little boy crossed the fence and started up the dusty road. The old landmarks were familiar to him in the strange light. When he came to the gate of the garden, some kind of human fear possessed him. It was a surprise to himself when he pushed the gate open and walked up the path. A man with a pipe in his mouth was turning up and down the terrace. The little boy stood still for a while and watched this sight. When the man turned again he looked down the garden, and he too stopped in his walk.

"Hullo," he remarked. He had no whiskers.

"Are you Uncle Dan?" said the little boy.

"Right you are," said the man.

"Are you going to thrash me?" said the little boy.

"Is that customary in greeting a nephew?" asked Uncle Dan.

"I ran away," explained the little boy. "If my father was here, he'd thrash me—"

"Hold on, sir," said Uncle Dan. The little boy stood staring at him in silence. Uncle Dan glanced over his shoulder. "I say," he remarked in a lower tone, "shall we walk down the road a bit so we shan't be disturbed?"

THOMAS MANN

Little Herr Friedemann 🥨

It was the nurse's fault. When they first suspected, Frau Consul
Friedemann had spoken to her very gravely about the need of
controlling her weakness. But what good did that do? Or the
glass of red wine which she got daily besides the beer which was needed for
the milk? For they suddenly discovered that she even sank so low as to
drink the methylated spirit which was kept for the spirit lamp. Before they
could send her away and get someone to take her place, the mischief was
done. One day the mother and sisters came home to find that little Johannes,
then about a month old, had fallen from the couch and lay on the floor,
uttering an appallingly faint little cry, while the nurse stood beside him quite
stupefied.

The doctor came and with firm, gentle hands tested the little creature's
contracted and twitching limbs. He made a very serious face. The three girls
stood sobbing in a corner and the Frau Consul in the anguish of her heart
prayed aloud.

The poor mother, just before the child's birth, had already suffered a
crushing blow: her husband, the Dutch Consul, had been snatched away
from her by sudden and violent illness, and now she was too broken to cherish any hope that little Johannes would be spared to her. But by the second
day the doctor had given her hand an encouraging squeeze and told her that
all immediate danger was over. There was no longer any sign that the brain
was affected. The facial expression was altered, it had lost the fixed and
staring look. . . . Of course, they must see how things went on—and hope for
the best, hope for the best.

The grey gabled house in which Johannes Friedemann grew up stood by
the north gate of the little old commercial city. The front door led into a
large flag-paved entry, out of which a stair with a white wooden balustrade
led up into the second storey. The faded wall-paper in the living-room had
a landscape pattern, and straight-backed chairs and sofas in dark-red plush
stood round the heavy mahogany table.

Often in his childhood—Johannes sat here at the window, which always
had a fine showing of flowers, on a small footstool at his mother's feet, listen-

Reprinted from *Stories of Three Decades* by Thomas Mann, by permission of Alfred
A. Knopf, Inc. Copyright 1936 by Alfred A. Knopf, Inc.

ing to some fairy-tale she told him, gazing at her smooth grey head, her mild and gentle face, and breathing in the faint scent she exhaled. She showed him the picture of his father, a kindly man with grey side-whiskers—he was now in heaven, she said, and awaiting them there.

Behind the house was a small garden where in summer they spent much of their time, despite the smell of burnt sugar which came over from the refinery close by. There was a gnarled old walnut tree in whose shade little Johannes would sit, on a low wooden stool, cracking walnuts, while Frau Friedemann and her three daughters, now grown women, took refuge from the sun under a grey canvas tent. The mother's gaze often strayed from her embroidery to look with sad and loving eyes at her child.

He was not beautiful, little Johannes, as he crouched on his stool industriously cracking his nuts. In fact, he was a strange sight, with his pigeon breast, humped back, and disproportionately long arms. But his hands and feet were delicately formed, he had soft red-brown eyes like a doe's, a sensitive mouth, and fine, light-brown hair. His head, had it not sat so deep between his shoulders, might almost have been called pretty.

When he was seven he went to school, where time passed swiftly and uniformly. He walked every day, with the strut deformed people often have, past the quaint gabled houses and shops to the old schoolhouse with the vaulted arcades. When he had done his preparation he would read in his books with the lovely title-page illustrations in colour, or else work in the garden, while his sisters kept house for their invalid mother. They went out too, for they belonged to the best society of the town; but unfortunately they had not married, for they had not much money nor any looks to recommend them.

Johannes too was now and then invited out by his schoolmates, but it is not likely that he enjoyed it. He could not take part in their games, and they were always embarrassed in his company, so there was no feeling of good fellowship.

There came a time when he began to hear certain matters talked about, in the courtyard at school. He listened wide-eyed and large-eared, quite silent, to his companions' raving over this or that little girl. Such things, though they entirely engrossed the attention of these others, were not, he felt, for him; they belonged in the same category as the ball games and gymnastics. At times he felt a little sad. But at length he had become quite used to standing on one side and not taking part.

But after all it came about—when he was sixteen—that he felt suddenly drawn to a girl of his own age. She was the sister of a classmate of his, a blonde, hilarious hoyden, and he met her when calling at her brother's house. He felt strangely embarrassed in her neighbourhood; she too was embarrassed and treated him with such artificial cordiality that it made him sad.

One summer afternoon as he was walking by himself on the wall outside the town, he heard a whispering behind a jasmine bush and peeped cautiously through the branches. There she sat on a bench beside a long-legged, red-haired youth of his acquaintance. They had their arms about each other and he was imprinting on her lips a kiss, which she returned amid giggles. Johannes looked, turned round, and went softly away.

His head was sunk deeper than ever between his shoulders, his hands trembled, and a sharp pain shot upwards from his chest to his throat. But he choked it down, straightening himself as well as he could. "Good," said he to himself. "That is over. Never again will I let myself in for any of it. To the others it brings joy and happiness, for me it can only mean sadness and pain. I am done with it. For me that is all over. Never again."

The resolution did him good. He had renounced, renounced forever. He went home, took up a book, or else played on his violin, which despite his deformed chest he had learned to do.

At seventeen Johannes left school to go into business, like everybody else he knew. He was apprenticed to the big lumber firm of Herr Schlievogt down on the river-bank. They were kind and considerate, he on his side was responsive and friendly, time passed with peaceful regularity. But in his twenty-first year his mother died, after a lingering illness.

This was a sore blow for Johannes Friedemann, and the pain of it endured. He cherished this grief, he gave himself up to it as one gives oneself to a great joy, he fed it with a thousand childhood memories; it was the first important event in his life and he made the most of it.

Is not life in and for itself a good, regardless of whether we may call its content "happiness"? Johannes Friedemann felt that it was so, and he loved life. He, who had renounced the greatest joy it can bring us, taught himself with infinite, incredible care to take pleasure in what it had still to offer. A walk in the springtime in the parks surrounding the town; the fragrance of a flower; the song of a bird—might not one feel grateful for such things as these?

And that we need to be taught how to enjoy, yes, that our education is always and only equal to our capacity for enjoyment—he knew that too, and he trained himself. Music he loved, and attended all the concerts that were given in the town. He came to play the violin not so badly himself, no matter what a figure of fun he made when he did it; and took delight in every beautiful soft tone he succeeded in producing. Also, by much reading he came in time to possess a literary taste the like of which did not exist in the place. He kept up with the new books, even the foreign ones; he knew how to savour the seductive rhythm of a lyric or the ultimate flavour of a subtly told tale—yes, one might almost call him a connoisseur.

He learned to understand that to everything belongs its own enjoyment and that it is absurd to distinguish between an experience which is "happy" and one which is not. With a right good will he accepted each emotion as it came, each mood, whether sad or gay. Even he cherished the unfulfilled desires, the longings. He loved them for their own sakes and told himself that with fulfilment the best of them would be past. The vague, sweet, painful yearning and hope of quiet spring evenings—are they not richer in joy than all the fruition the summer can bring? Yes, he was a connoisseur, our little Herr Friedemann.

But of course they did not know that, the people whom he met on the street, who bowed to him with the kindly, compassionate air he knew so well. They could not know that this unhappy cripple, strutting comically along in his light overcoat and shiny top hat—strange to say, he was a little vain—they could not know how tenderly he loved the mild flow of his life, charged with no great emotions, it is true, but full of a quiet and tranquil happiness which was his own creation.

But Herr Friedemann's great preference, his real passion, was for the theatre. He possessed a dramatic sense which was unusually strong; at a telling theatrical effect or the catastrophe of a tragedy his whole small frame would shake with emotion. He had his regular seat in the first row of boxes at the opera-house; was an assiduous frequenter and often took his sisters with him. Since their mother's death they kept house for their brother in the old home which they all owned together.

It was a pity they were unmarried still; but with the decline of hope had come resignation—Friederike, the eldest, was seventeen years further on than Herr Friedemann. She and her sister Henriette were over-tall and thin, whereas Pfiffi, the youngest, was too short and stout. She had a funny way, too, of shaking herself as she talked, and water came in the corners of her mouth.

Little Herr Friedemann did not trouble himself overmuch about his three sisters. But they stuck together loyally and were always of one mind. Whenever an engagement was announced in their circle they with one voice said how very gratifying that was.

Their brother continued to live with them even after he became independent, as he did by leaving Herr Schlievogt's firm and going into business for himself, in an agency of sorts, which was no great tax on his time. His offices were in a couple of rooms on the ground floor of the house so that at mealtimes he had but the pair of stairs to mount—for he suffered now and then from asthma.

His thirtieth birthday fell on a fine warm June day, and after dinner he sat out in the grey canvas tent, with a new head-rest embroidered by Henriette. He had a good cigar in his mouth and a good book in his hand. But sometimes he would put the latter down to listen to the sparrows chirping

blithely in the old nut tree and look at the clean gravel path leading up to
the house between lawns bright with summer flowers.

Little Herr Friedemann wore no beard, and his face had scarcely changed
at all, save that the features were slightly sharper. He wore his fine light-
brown hair parted on one side.

Once, as he let the book fall on his knee and looked up into the sunny blue
sky, he said to himself: "Well, so that is thirty years. Perhaps there may be
ten or even twenty more, God knows. They will mount up without a sound
or a stir and pass by like those that are gone; and I look forward to them
with peace in my heart."

Now, it happened in July of the same year that a new appointment to the
office of District Commandant had set the whole town talking. The stout
and jolly gentleman who had for many years occupied the post had been
very popular in social circles and they saw him go with great regret. It
was in compliance with goodness knows what regulations that Herr von
Rinnlingen and no other was sent hither from the capital.

In any case the exchange was not such a bad one. The new Commandant
was married but childless. He rented a spacious villa in the southern suburbs
of the city and seemed to intend to set up an establishment. There was a
report that he was very rich—which received confirmation in the fact that
he brought with him four servants, five riding and carriage horses, a landau
and a light hunting-cart.

Soon after their arrival the husband and wife left cards on all the best
society, and their names were on every tongue. But it was not Herr von
Rinnlingen, it was his wife who was the centre of interest. All the men were
dazed, for the moment too dazed to pass judgment; but their wives were
quite prompt and definite in the view that Gerda von Rinnlingen was not
their sort.

"Of course, she comes from the metropolis, her ways would naturally be
different," Frau Hagenström, the lawyer's wife, said, in conversation with
Henriette Friedemann. "She smokes, and she rides. That is of course. But
it is her manners—they are not only free, they are postively brusque, or even
worse. You see, no one could call her ugly, one might even say she is pretty;
but she has not a trace of feminine charm in her looks or gestures or her
laugh—they completely lack everything that makes a man fall in love with
a woman. She is not a flirt—and goodness knows I would be the last to dis-
parage her for that. But it is strange to see so young a woman—she is only
twenty-four—so entirely wanting in natural charm. I am not expressing
myself very well, my dear, but I know what I mean. All the men are simply
bewildered. In a few weeks, you will see, they will be disgusted."

"Well," Fräulein Friedemann said, "she certainly has everything she
wants."

"Yes," cried Frau Hagenström, "look at her husband! And how does she treat him? You ought to see it—you will see it! I would be the first to approve of a married woman behaving with a certain reserve towards the other sex. But how does she behave to her own husband? She has a way of fixing him with an ice-cold stare and saying 'My dear friend!' with a pitying expression that drives me mad. For when you look at him—upright, correct, gallant, a brilliant officer and a splendidly preserved man of forty! They have been married four years, my dear."

Herr Friedemann was first vouchsafed a glimpse of Frau von Rinnlingen in the main street of the town, among all the rows of shops, at midday, when he was coming from the Bourse, where he had done a little bidding.

He was strolling along beside Herr Stephens, looking tiny and important, as usual. Herr Stephens was in the wholesale trade, a huge stocky man with round side-whiskers and bushy eyebrows. Both of them wore top hats; their overcoats were unbuttoned on account of the heat. They tapped their canes along the pavement and talked of the political situation; but half-way down the street Stephens suddenly said:

"Deuce take it if there isn't the Rinnlingen driving along."

"Good," answered Herr Friedemann in his high, rather sharp voice, looking expectantly ahead. "Because I have never yet set eyes on her. And here we have the yellow cart we hear so much about."

It was in fact the hunting-cart which Frau von Rinnlingen was herself driving today with a pair of thoroughbreds; a groom sat behind her, with folded arms. She wore a loose beige coat and skirt and a small round straw hat with a brown leather band, beneath which her well-waved red-blond hair, a good, thick crop, was drawn into a knot at the nape of her neck. Her face was oval, with a dead-white skin and faint bluish shadows lurking under the close-set eyes. Her nose was short but well-shaped, with a becoming little saddle of freckles; whether her mouth was as good or no could not be told, for she kept it in continual motion, sucking the lower and biting the upper lip.

Herr Stephens, as the cart came abreast of them, greeted her with a great show of deference; little Herr Friedemann lifted his hat too and looked at her with wide-eyed attention. She lowered her whip, nodded slightly, and drove slowly past, looking at the houses and shop-windows.

After a few paces Herr Stephens said:

"She has been taking a drive and was on her way home."

Little Herr Friedemann made no answer, but stared before him at the pavement. Presently he started, looked at his companion, and asked: "What did you say?"

And Herr Stephens repeated his acute remark.

Three days after that Johannes Friedemann came home at midday from his usual walk. Dinner was at half past twelve, and he would spend the interval in his office at the right of the entrance door. But the maid came across the entry and told him that there were visitors.

"In my office?" he asked.

"No, upstairs with the mistresses."

"Who are they?"

"Herr and Frau Colonel von Rinnlingen."

"Ah," said Johannes Friedemann. "Then I will—"

And he mounted the stairs. He crossed the lobby and laid his hand on the knob of the high white door leading into the "landscape room." And then he drew back, turned round, and slowly returned as he had come. And spoke to himself, for there was no one else there, and said: "No, better not."

He went into his office, sat down at his desk, and took up the paper. But after a little he dropped it again and sat looking to one side out of the window. Thus he sat until the maid came to say that luncheon was ready; then he went up into the dining-room where his sisters were already waiting, and sat down in his chair, in which there were three music-books.

As she ladled the soup Henriette said:

"Johannes, do you know who were here?"

"Well?" he asked.

"The new Commandant and his wife."

"Indeed? That was friendly of them."

"Yes," said Pfiffi, a little water coming in the corners of her mouth. "I found them both very agreeable."

"And we must lose no time in returning the call," said Friederike. "I suggest that we go next Sunday, the day after tomorrow."

"Sunday," Henriette and Pfiffi said.

"You will go with us, Johannes?" asked Friederike.

"Of course he will," said Pfiffi, and gave herself a little shake. Herr Friedemann had not heard her at all; he was eating his soup, with a hushed and troubled air. It was as though he were listening to some strange noise he heard.

Next evening *Lohengrin* was being given at the opera, and everybody in society was present. The small auditorium was crowded, humming with voices and smelling of gas and perfumery. And every eye-glass in the stalls was directed towards box thirteen, next to the stage; for this was the first appearance of Herr and Frau von Rinnlingen and one could give them a good looking-over.

When little Herr Friedemann, in flawless dress clothes and glistening white pigeon-breasted shirt-front, entered his box, which was number thirteen, he started back at the door, making a gesture with his hand towards his brow. His nostrils dilated feverishly. Then he took his seat, which was next to Frau von Rinnlingen's.

She contemplated him for a little while, with her under lip stuck out; then she turned to exchange a few words with her husband, a tall, broad-shouldered gentleman with a brown, good-natured face and turned-up moustaches.

When the overture began and Frau von Rinnlingen leaned over the balustrade, Herr Friedemann gave her a quick, searching side glance. She wore a light-coloured evening frock, the only one in the theatre which was slightly low in the neck. Her sleeves were full and her white gloves came up to her elbows. Her figure was statelier than it had looked under the loose coat; her full bosom slowly rose and fell and the knot of red-blond hair hung low and heavy at the nape of her neck.

Herr Friedemann was pale, much paler than usual, and little beads of perspiration stood on his brow beneath the smoothly parted brown hair. He could see Frau von Rinnlingen's left arm, which lay upon the balustrade. She had taken off her glove and the rounded, dead-white arm and ringless hand, both of them shot with pale blue veins, were directly under his eye—he could not help seeing them.

The fiddles sang, the trombones crashed, Telramund was slain, general jubilation reigned in the orchestra, and little Herr Friedemann sat there motionless and pallid, his head drawn in between his shoulders, his forefinger to his lips and one hand thrust into the opening of his waistcoat.

As the curtain fell, Frau von Rinnlingen got up to leave the box with her husband. Johannes Friedemann saw her without looking, wiped his handkerchief across his brow, then rose suddenly and went as far as the door into the foyer, where he turned, came back to his chair, and sat down in the same posture as before.

When the bell rang and his neighbours re-entered the box he felt Frau von Rinnlingen's eyes upon him, so that finally against his will he raised his head. As their eyes met, hers did not swerve aside; she continued to gaze without embarrassment until he himself, deeply humiliated, was forced to look away. He turned a shade paler and felt a strange, sweet pang of anger and scorn. The music began again.

Towards the end of the act Frau von Rinnlingen chanced to drop her fan; it fell at Herr Friedemann's feet. They both stooped at the same time, but she reached it first and gave a little mocking smile as she said: "Thank you."

Their heads were quite close together and just for a second he got the warm scent of her breast. His face was drawn, his whole body twitched, and his heart thumped so horribly that he lost his breath. He sat without moving for half a minute, then he pushed back his chair, got up quietly, and went out.

He crossed the lobby, pursued by the music; got his top hat from the cloak-room, his light overcoat and his stick, went down the stairs and out of doors.

It was a warm, still evening. In the gas-lit street the gabled houses towered towards a sky where stars were softly beaming. The pavement echoed the steps of a few passers-by. Someone spoke to him, but he heard and saw nothing; his head was bowed and his deformed chest shook with the violence of his breathing. Now and then he murmured to himself:

"My God, my God!"

He was gazing horror-struck within himself, beholding the havoc which had been wrought with his tenderly cherished, scrupulously managed feelings. Suddenly he was quite overpowered by the strength of his tortured longing. Giddy and drunken he leaned against a lamp-post and his quivering lips uttered the one word: "Gerda!"

The stillness was complete. Far and wide not a soul was to be seen. Little Herr Friedemann pulled himself together and went on, up the street in which the opera-house stood and which ran steeply down to the river, then along the main street northwards to his home.

How she had looked at him! She had forced him, actually, to cast down his eyes! She had humiliated him with her glance. But was she not a woman and he a man? And those strange brown eyes of hers—had they not positively glittered with unholy joy?

Again he felt the same surge of sensual, impotent hatred mount up in him; then he relived the moment when her head had touched his, when he had breathed in the fragrance of her body—and for the second time he halted, bent his deformed torso backwards, drew in the air through clenched teeth, and murmured helplessly, desperately, uncontrollably:

"My God, my God!"

Then went on again, slowly, mechanically, through the heavy evening air, through the empty echoing streets until he stood before his own house. He paused a minute in the entry, breathing the cool, dank inside air; then he went into his office.

He sat down at his desk by the open window and stared straight ahead of him at a large yellow rose which somebody had set there in a glass of water. He took it up and smelt it with his eyes closed, then put it down with a gesture of weary sadness. No, no. That was all over. What was even that fragrance to him now? What any of all those things that up to now had been the well-springs of his joy?

He turned away and gazed into the quiet street. At intervals steps passed and the sound died away. The stars stood still and glittered. He felt so weak, so utterly tired to death. His head was quite vacant, and suddenly his despair began to melt into a gentle, pervading melancholy. A few lines of a poem flickered through his head, he heard the *Lohengrin* music in his ears, he saw

Frau von Rinnlingen's face and her round white arm on the red velvet—
then he fell into a heavy fever-burdened sleep.

Often he was near waking, but feared to do so and managed to sink back
into forgetfulness again. But when it had grown quite light, he opened his
eyes and looked round him with a wide and painful gaze. He remembered
everything, it was as though the anguish had never been intermitted by sleep.

His head was heavy and his eyes burned. But when he had washed up and
bathed his head with cologne he felt better and sat down in his place by the
still open window. It was early, perhaps only five o'clock. Now and then a
baker's boy passed; otherwise there was no one to be seen. In the opposite
house the blinds were down. But birds were twittering and the sky was
luminously blue. A wonderfully beautiful Sunday morning.

A feeling of comfort and confidence came over little Herr Friedemann.
Why had he been distressing himself? Was not everything just as it had
been? The attack of yesterday had been a bad one. Granted. But it should
be the last. It was not too late, he could still escape destruction. He must
avoid every occasion of a fresh seizure; he felt sure he could do this. He felt
the strength to conquer and suppress his weakness.

It struck half past seven and Friederike came in with the coffee, setting it
on the round table in front of the leather sofa against the rear wall.

"Good morning, Johannes," said she; "here is your breakfast."

"Thanks," said little Herr Friedemann. And then: "Dear Friederike, I am
sorry, but you will have to pay your call without me, I do not feel well
enough to go. I have slept badly and have a headache—in short, I must
ask you—"

"What a pity!" answered Friederike. "You must go another time. But you
do look ill. Shall I lend you my menthol pencil?"

"Thanks," said Herr Friedemann. "It will pass." And Friederike went
out.

Standing at the table he slowly drank his coffee and ate a croissant. He
felt satisfied with himself and proud of his firmness. When he had finished
he sat down again by the open window, with a cigar. The food had done
him good and he felt happy and hopeful. He took a book and sat reading
and smoking and blinking into the sunlight.

Morning had fully come, wagons rattled past, there were many voices and
the sound of the bells on passing trams. With and among it all was woven
the twittering and chirping; there was a radiant blue sky, a soft mild air.

At ten o'clock he heard his sisters cross the entry; the front door creaked,
and he idly noticed that they passed his window. An hour went by. He felt
more and more happy.

A sort of hubris mounted in him. What a heavenly air—and how the birds
were singing! He felt like taking a little walk. Then suddenly, without any

transition, yet accompanied by a terror namelessly sweet came the thought: "Suppose I were to go to her!" And suppressing, as though by actual muscular effort, every warning voice within him, he added with blissful resolution: "I will go to her!"

He changed into his Sunday clothes, took his top hat and his stick, and hurried with quickened breath through the town and into the southern suburbs. Without looking at a soul he kept raising and dropping his head with each eager step, completely rapt in his exalted state until he arrived at the avenue of chestnut trees and the red brick villa with the name of Commandant von Rinnlingen on the gate-post.

But here he was seized by a tremor, his heart throbbed and pounded in his breast. He went across the vestibule and rang at the inside door. The die was cast, there was no retreating now. "Come what come may," thought he, and felt the stillness of death within him.

The door suddenly opened and the maid came towards him across the vestibule; she took his card and hurried away up the red-carpeted stair. Herr Friedemann gazed fixedly at the bright colour until she came back and said that her mistress would like him to come up.

He put down his stick beside the door leading into the salon and stole a look at himself in the glass. His face was pale, the eyes red, his hair was sticking to his brow, the hand that held his top hat kept on shaking.

The maid opened the door and he went in. He found himself in a rather large, half-darkened room, with drawn curtains. At his right was a piano, and about the round table in the centre stood several arm-chairs covered in brown silk. The sofa stood along the left-hand wall, with a landscape painting in a heavy gilt frame hanging above it. The wall-paper too was dark in tone. There was an alcove filled with potted palms.

A minute passed, then Frau von Rinnlingen opened the portières on the right and approached him noiselessly over the thick brown carpet. She wore a simply cut frock of red and black plaid. A ray of light, with motes dancing in it, streamed from the alcove and fell upon her heavy red hair so that it shone like gold. She kept her strange eyes fixed upon him with a searching gaze and as usual stuck out her under lip.

"Good morning, Frau Commandant," began little Herr Friedemann, and looked up at her, for he came only as high as her chest. "I wished to pay you my respects too. When my sisters did so I was unfortunately out . . . I regretted sincerely . . ."

He had no idea at all what else he should say; and there she stood and gazed ruthlessly at him as though she would force him to go on. The blood rushed to his head. "She sees through me," he thought, "she will torture and despise me. Her eyes keep flickering. . . ."

But at last she said, in a very high, clear voice:

"It is kind of you to have come. I have also been sorry not to see you before. Will you please sit down?"

She took her seat close beside him, leaned back, and put her arm along the arm of the chair. He sat bent over, holding his hat between his knees. She went on:

"Did you know that your sisters were here a quarter of an hour ago? They told me you were ill."

"Yes," he answered, "I did not feel well enough to go out, I thought I should not be able to. That is why I am late."

"You do not look very well even now," said she tranquilly, not shifting her gaze. "You are pale and your eyes are inflamed. You are not very strong, perhaps?"

"Oh," said Herr Friedemann, stammering, "I've not much to complain of, as a rule."

"I am ailing a good deal too," she went on, still not turning her eyes from him, "but nobody notices it. I am nervous, and sometimes I have the strangest feelings."

She paused, lowered her chin to her breast, and looked up expectantly at him. He made no reply, simply sat with his dreamy gaze directed upon her. How strangely she spoke, and how her clear and thrilling voice affected him! His heart beat more quietly and he felt as though he were in a dream. She began again:

"I am not wrong in thinking that you left the opera last night before it was over?"

"Yes, madam."

"I was sorry to see that. You listened like a music-lover—though the performance was only tolerable. You are fond of music, I am sure. Do you play the piano?"

"I play the violin, a little," said Herr Friedemann. "That is, really not very much—"

"You play the violin?" she asked, and looked past him consideringly. "But we might play together," she suddenly said. "I can accompany a little. It would be a pleasure to find somebody here—would you come?"

"I am quite at your service—with pleasure," he said stiffly. He was still as though in a dream. A pause ensued. Then suddenly her expression changed. He saw it alter for one of cruel, though hardly perceptible mockery, and again she fixed him with that same searching, uncannily flickering gaze. His face burned, he knew not where to turn; drawing his head down between his shoulders he stared confusedly at the carpet, while there shot through him once more that strangely sweet and torturing sense of impotent rage.

He made a desperate effort and raised his eyes. She was looking over his head at the door. With the utmost difficulty he fetched out a few words:

"And you are so far not too dissatisfied with your stay in our city?"

"Oh, no," said Frau Rinnlingen indifferently. "No, certainly not; why should I not be satisfied? To be sure, I feel a little hampered, as though everybody's eyes were upon me, but—oh, before I forget it," she went on quickly, "we are entertaining a few people next week, a small, informal company. A little music, perhaps, and conversation. . . . There is a charming garden at the back, it runs down to the river. You and your sisters will be receiving an invitation in due course, but perhaps I may ask you now to give us the pleasure of your company?"

Herr Friedemann was just expressing his gratitude for the invitation when the door-knob was seized energetically from without and the Commandant entered. They both rose and Frau von Rinnlingen introduced the two men to each other. Her husband bowed to them both with equal courtesy. His bronze face glistened with the heat.

He drew off his gloves, addressing Herr Friedemann in a powerful, rather sharp-edged voice. The latter looked up at him with large vacant eyes and had the feeling that he would presently be clapped benevolently on the shoulder. Heels together, inclining from the waist, the Commandant turned to his wife and asked, in a much gentler tone:

"Have you asked Herr Friedemann if he will give us the pleasure of his company at our little party, my love? If you are willing I should like to fix the date for next week and I hope that the weather will remain fine so that we can enjoy ourselves in the garden."

"Just as you say," answered Frau von Rinnlingen, and gazed past him.

Two minutes later Herr Friedemann got up to go. At the door he turned and bowed to her once more, meeting her expressionless gaze still fixed upon him.

He went away, but he did not go back to the town; unconsciously he struck into a path that led away from the avenue towards the old ruined fort by the river, among well-kept lawns and shady avenues with benches.

He walked quickly and absently, with bent head. He felt intolerably hot, as though aware of flames leaping and sinking within him, and his head throbbed with fatigue.

It was as though her gaze still rested on him—not vacantly as it had at the end, but with that flickering cruelty which went with the strange still way she spoke. Did it give her pleasure to put him beside himself, to see him helpless? Looking through and through him like that, could she not feel a little pity?

He had gone along the river-bank under the moss-grown wall; he sat down on a bench within a half-circle of blossoming jasmine. The sweet, heavy scent was all about him, the sun brooded upon the dimpling water.

He was weary, he was worn out; and yet within him all was tumult and anguish. Were it not better to take one last look and then to go down into that quiet water; after a brief struggle to be free and safe and at peace? Ah, peace, peace—that was what he wanted! Not peace in an empty and sound-less void, but a gentle, sunlit peace, full of good, of tranquil thoughts.

All his tender love of life thrilled through him in that moment, all his profound yearning for his vanished "happiness." But then he looked about him into the silent, endlessly indifferent peace of nature, saw how the river went its own way in the sun, how the grasses quivered and the flowers stood up where they blossomed, only to fade and be blown away; saw how all that was bent submissively to the will of life; and there came over him all at once that sense of acquaintance and understanding with the inevitable which can make those who know it superior to the blows of fate.

He remembered the afternoon of his thirtieth birthday and the peaceful happiness with which he, untroubled by fears or hopes, had looked forward to what was left of his life. He had seen no light and no shadow there, only a mild twilight radiance gently declining into the dark. With what a calm and superior smile had he contemplated the years still to come—how long ago was that?

Then this woman had come, she had to come, it was his fate that she should, for she herself was his fate and she alone. He had known it from the first moment. She had come—and though he had tried his best to defend his peace, her coming had roused in him all those forces which from his youth up he had sought to suppress, feeling, as he did, that they spelled torture and destruction. They had seized upon him with frightful, irresistible power and flung him to the earth.

They were his destruction, well he knew it. But why struggle, then, and why torture himself? Let everything take its course. He would go his appointed way, closing his eyes before the yawning void, bowing to his fate, bowing to the overwhelming, anguishingly sweet, irresistible power.

The water glittered, the jasmine gave out its strong, pungent scent, the birds chattered in the tree-tops that gave glimpses among them of a heavy, velvety-blue sky. Little hump-backed Herr Friedemann sat long upon his bench; he sat bent over, holding his head in his hands.

Everybody agreed that the Rinnlingens entertained very well. Some thirty guests sat in the spacious dining-room, at the long, prettily decorated table, and the butler and two hired waiters were already handing round the ices. Dishes clattered, glasses rang, there was a warm aroma of food and perfumes. Here were comfortable merchants with their wives and daughters; most of the officers of the garrison; a few professional men, lawyers and the popular old family doctor—in short, all the best society.

A nephew of the Commandant, on a visit, a student of mathematics, sat deep in conversation with Fräulein Hagenström, whose place was directly

opposite Herr Friedemann's, at the lower end of the table. Johannes Friedemann sat there on a rich velvet cushion, beside the unbeautiful wife of the
Colonial Director and not far off Frau von Rinnlingen, who had been
escorted to table by Consul Stephens. It was astonishing, the change which
had taken place in little Herr Friedemann in these few days. Perhaps the
incandescent lighting in the room was partly to blame; but his cheeks looked
sunken, he made a more crippled impression even than usual, and his
inflamed eyes, with their dark rings, glowed with an inexpressibly tragic
light. He drank a great deal of wine and now and then addressed a remark
to his neighbour.

Frau von Rinnlingen had not so far spoken to him at all; but now she
leaned over and called out:

"I have been expecting you in vain these days, you and your fiddle."

He looked vacantly at her for a while before he replied. She wore a light-
coloured frock with a low neck that left the white throat bare; a Maréchal
Niel rose in full bloom was fastened in her shining hair. Her cheeks were a
little flushed, but the same bluish shadows lurked in the corners of her eyes.

Herr Friedemann looked at his plate and forced himself to make some
sort of reply; after which the school superintendent's wife asked him if he
did not love Beethoven and he had to answer that too. But at this point the
Commandant, sitting at the head of the table, caught his wife's eye, tapped
on his glass and said:

"Ladies and gentlemen, I suggest that we drink our coffee in the next
room. It must be fairly decent out in the garden too, and whoever wants a
little fresh air, I am for him."

Lieutenant von Deidesheim made a tactful little joke to cover the ensuing
pause, and the table rose in the midst of laughter. Herr Friedemann and his
partner were among the last to quit the room; he escorted her through the
"old German" smoking-room to the dim and pleasant living-room, where
he took his leave.

He was dressed with great care: his evening clothes were irreproachable,
his shirt was dazzlingly white, his slender, well-shaped feet were encased in
patent-leather pumps, which now and then betrayed the fact that he wore
red silk stockings.

He looked out into the corridor and saw a good many people descending
the steps into the garden. But he took up a position at the door of the
smoking-room, with his cigar and coffee, where he could see into the living-
room.

Some of the men stood talking in this room, and at the right of the door
a little knot had formed round a small table, the centre of which was the
mathematics student, who was eagerly talking. He had made the assertion
that one could draw through a given point more than one parallel to a

straight line; Frau Hagenström had cried that this was impossible, and he had gone on to prove it so conclusively that his hearers were constrained to to behave as though they understood.

At the rear of the room, on the sofa beside the red-shaded lamp, Gerda von Rinnlingen sat in conversation with young Fräulein Stephens. She leaned back among the yellow silk cushions with one knee slung over the other, slowly smoking a cigarette, breathing out the smoke through her nose and sticking out her lower lip. Fräulein Stephens sat stiff as a graven image beside her, answering her questions with an assiduous smile.

Nobody was looking at little Herr Friedemann, so nobody saw that his large eyes were constantly directed upon Frau von Rinnlingen. He sat rather droopingly and looked at her. There was no passion in his gaze nor scarcely any pain. But there was something dull and heavy there, a dead weight of impotent, involuntary adoration.

Some ten minutes went by. Then as though she had been secretly watching him the whole time, Frau von Rinnlingen approached and paused in front of him. He got up as he heard her say:

"Would you care to go into the garden with me, Herr Friedemann?"

He answered:

"With pleasure, madam."

"You have never seen our garden?" she asked him as they went down the steps. "It is fairly large. I hope that there are not too many people in it; I should like to get a breath of fresh air. I got a headache during supper; perhaps the red wine was too strong for me. Let us go this way." They passed through a glass door, the vestibule, and a cool little courtyard, whence they gained the open air by descending a couple more steps.

The scent of all the flower-beds rose into the wonderful, warm, starry night. The garden lay in full moonlight and the guests were strolling up and down the white gravel paths, smoking and talking as they went. A group had gathered round the old fountain, where the much-loved old doctor was making them laugh by sailing paper boats.

With a little nod Frau von Rinnlingen passed them by, and pointed ahead of her, where the fragrant and well-cared-for garden blended into the darker park.

"Shall we go down this middle path?" asked she. At the beginning of it stood two low, squat obelisks.

In the vista at the end of the chestnut alley they could see the river shining green and bright in the moonlight. All about them was darkness and coolness. Here and there side paths branched off, all of them probably curving down to the river. For a long time there was not a sound.

"Down by the water," she said, "there is a pretty spot where I often sit. We could stop and talk a little. See the stars glittering here and there through the trees."

He did not answer, gazing, as they approached it, at the river's shimmering green surface. You could see the other bank and the park along the city wall. They left the alley and came out on the grassy slope down to the river, and she said:

"Here is our place, a little to the right, and there is no one there."

The bench stood facing the water, some six paces away, with its back to the trees. It was warmer here in the open. Crickets chirped among the grass, which at the river's edge gave way to sparse reeds. The moonlit water gave off a soft light.

For a while they both looked in silence. Then he heard her voice; it thrilled him to recognize the same low, gentle, pensive tone of a week ago, which now as then moved him so strangely:

"How long have you had your infirmity, Herr Friedemann? Were you born so?"

He swallowed before he replied, for his throat felt as though he were choking. Then he said, politely and gently:

"No, *gnädige Frau*. It comes from their having let me fall, when I was an infant."

"And how old are you now?" she asked again.

"Thirty years old."

"Thirty years old," she repeated. "And these thirty years were not happy ones?"

Little Herr Friedemann shook his head, his lips quivered.

"No," he said, "that was all lies and my imagination."

"Then you have thought that you were happy?" she asked.

"I have tried to be," he replied, and she responded:

"That was brave of you."

A minute passed. The crickets chirped and behind them the boughs rustled lightly.

"I understand a good deal about unhappiness," she told him. "These summer nights by the water are the best thing for it."

He made no direct answer, but gestured feebly across the water, at the opposite bank, lying peaceful in the darkness.

"I was sitting over there not long ago," he said.

"When you came from me?" she asked. He only nodded.

Then suddenly he started up from his seat, trembling all over; he sobbed and gave vent to a sound, a wail which yet seemed like a release from strain, and sank slowly to the ground before her. He had touched her hand with his as it lay beside him on the bench, and clung to it now, seizing the other as he knelt before her, this little cripple, trembling and shuddering; he

buried his face in her lap and stammered between his gasps in a voice which
was scarcely human:

"You know, you understand . . . let me . . . I can no longer . . . my God,
oh, my God!"

She did not repulse him, neither did she bend her face towards him. She
sat erect, leaning a little away, and her close-set eyes, wherein the liquid
shimmer of the water seemed to be mirrored, stared beyond him into space.

Then she gave him an abrupt push and uttered a short, scornful laugh.
She tore her hands from his burning fingers, clutched his arm, and flung
him sidewise upon the ground. Then she sprang up and vanished down the
wooded avenue.

He lay there with his face in the grass, stunned, unmanned, shudders
coursing swiftly through his frame. He pulled himself together, got up
somehow, took two steps, and fell again, close to the water. What were his
sensations at this moment? Perhaps he was feeling that same luxury of hate
which he had felt before when she had humiliated him with her glance,
degenerated now, when he lay before her on the ground and she had treated
him like a dog, into an insane rage which must at all costs find expression
even against himself—a disgust, perhaps of himself, which filled him with a
thirst to destroy himself, to tear himself to pieces, to blot himself utterly out.

On his belly he dragged his body a little further, lifted its upper part,
and let it fall into the water. He did not raise his head nor move his legs,
which still lay on the bank.

The crickets stopped chirping a moment at the noise of the little splash.
Then they went on as before, the boughs lightly rustled, and down the long
alley came the faint sound of laughter.

JEAN-PAUL SARTRE

The Wall ℰ

They pushed us into a large white room and my eyes began to
blink because the light hurt them. Then I saw a table and four
fellows seated at the table, civilians, looking at some papers. The
other prisoners were herded together at one end and we were obliged to
cross the entire room to join them. There were several I knew, and others
who must have been foreigners. The two in front of me were blond with
round heads. They looked alike. I imagine they were French. The smaller
one kept pulling at his trousers, out of nervousness.

This lasted about three hours. I was dog-tired and my head was empty.
But the room was well-heated, which struck me as rather agreeable; we
had not stopped shivering for twenty-four hours. The guards led the prisoners in one after the other in front of the table. Then the four fellows asked
them their names and what they did. Most of the time that was all—or
perhaps from time to time they would ask such questions as: "Did you help
sabotage the munitions?" or, "Where were you on the morning of the ninth
and what were you doing?" They didn't even listen to the replies, or at least
they didn't seem to. They just remained silent for a moment and looked
straight ahead, then they began to write. They asked Tom if it was true he
had served in the International Brigade. Tom couldn't say he hadn't because
of the papers they had found in his jacket. They didn't ask Juan anything,
but after he told them his name, they wrote for a long while.

"It's my brother José who's the anarchist," Juan said. "You know perfectly
well he's not here now. I don't belong to any party. I never did take part in
politics." They didn't answer.

Then Juan said, "I didn't do anything. And I'm not going to pay for
what the others did."

His lips were trembling. A guard told him to stop talking and led him
away. It was my turn.

"Your name is Pablo Ibbieta?"

I said yes.

The fellow looked at his papers and said, "Where is Ramon Gris?"

"I don't know."

"You hid him in your house from the sixth to the nineteenth."

"I did not."

They continued to write for a moment and the guards led me away. In the hall, Tom and Juan were waiting between two guards. We started walking. Tom asked one of the guards, "What's the idea?" "How do you mean?" the guard asked. "Was that just the preliminary questioning, or was that the trial?" "That was the trial," the guard said. "So now what? What are they going to do with us?" The guard answered drily, "The verdict will be told you in your cell."

In reality, our cell was one of the cellars of the hospital. It was terribly cold there because it was very drafty. We had been shivering all night long and it had hardly been any better during the day. I had spent the preceding five days in a cellar in the archbishop's palace, a sort of dungeon that must have dated back to the Middle Ages. There were lots of prisoners and not much room, so they housed them just anywhere. But I was not homesick for my dungeon. I hadn't been cold there, but I had been alone, and that gets to be irritating. In the cellar I had company. Juan didn't say a word; he was afraid, and besides, he was too young to have anything to say. But Tom was a good talker and knew Spanish well.

In the cellar there were a bench and four straw mattresses. When they led us back we sat down and waited in silence. After a while Tom said, "Our goose is cooked."

"I think so too," I said. "But I don't believe they'll do anything to the kid."

Tom said, "They haven't got anything on him. He's the brother of a fellow who's fighting, and that's all."

I looked at Juan. He didn't seem to have heard.

Tom continued, "You know what they do in Saragossa? They lay the guys across the road and then they drive over them with trucks. It was a Moroccan deserter who told us that. They say it's just to save ammunition."

I said, "Well, it doesn't save gasoline."

I was irritated with Tom; he shouldn't have said that.

He went on, "There are officers walking up and down the roads with their hands in their pockets, smoking, and they see that it's done right. Do you think they'd put 'em out of their misery? Like hell they do. They just let 'em holler. Sometimes as long as an hour. The Moroccan said the first time he almost puked."

"I don't believe they do that here," I said, "unless they really are short of ammunition."

The daylight came in through four air vents and a round opening that had been cut in the ceiling, to the left, and which opened directly onto the sky. It was through this hole, which was ordinarily closed by means of a trapdoor, that they unloaded coal into the cellar. Directly under the hole, there was a big pile of coal dust; it had been intended for heating the hospital, but at the beginning of the war they had evacuated the patients and the coal had stayed there unused; it even got rained on from time to time, when they forgot to close the trapdoor.

Tom started to shiver. "God damn it," he said, "I'm shivering. There, it is starting again."

He rose and began to do gymnastic exercises. At each movement, his shirt opened and showed his white, hairy chest. He lay down on his back, lifted his legs in the air and began to do the scissors movement. I watched his big buttocks tremble. Tom was tough, but he had too much fat on him. I kept thinking that soon bullets and bayonet points would sink into that mass of tender flesh as though it were a pat of butter.

I wasn't exactly cold, but I couldn't feel my shoulders or my arms. From time to time, I had the impression that something was missing and I began to look around for my jacket. Then I would suddenly remember they hadn't given me a jacket. It was rather awkward. They had taken our clothes to give them to their own soldiers and had left us only our shirts and these cotton trousers the hospital patients wore in mid-summer. After a moment, Tom got up and sat down beside me, breathless.

"Did you get warmed up?"

"Damn it, no. But I'm all out of breath."

Around eight o'clock in the evening, a Major came in with two falangists.

"What are the names of those three over there?" he asked the guard.

"Steinbock, Ibbieta and Mirbal," said the guard.

The Major put on his glasses and examined his list.

"Steinbock—Steinbock . . . Here it is. You are condemned to death. You'll be shot tomorrow morning."

He looked at his list again.

"The other two, also," he said.

"That's not possible," said Juan. "Not me."

The Major looked at him with surprise. "What's your name?"

"Juan Mirbal."

"Well, your name is here," said the Major, "and you're condemned to death."

"I didn't do anything," said Juan.

The Major shrugged his shoulders and turned toward Tom and me.

"You are both Basque?"

"No, nobody's Basque."

He appeared exasperated.

"I was told there were three Basques. I'm not going to waste my time running after them. I suppose you don't want a priest?"

We didn't even answer.

Then he said, "A Belgian doctor will be around in a little while. He has permission to stay with you all night."

He gave a military salute and left.

"What did I tell you?" Tom said. "We're in for something swell."

"Yes," I said. "It's a damned shame for the kid."

I said that to be fair, but I really didn't like the kid. His face was too refined and it was disfigured by fear and suffering, which had twisted all his features. Three days ago, he was just a kid with a kind of affected manner some people like. But now he looked like an aging fairy, and I thought to myself he would never be young again, even if they let him go. It wouldn't have been a bad thing to show him a little pity, but pity makes me sick, and besides, I couldn't stand him. He hadn't said anything more, but he had turned gray. His face and hands were gray. He sat down again and stared, round-eyed, at the ground. Tom was goodhearted and tried to take him by the arm, but the kid drew himself away violently and made an ugly face. "Leave him alone," I said quietly. "Can't you see he's going to start to bawl?" Tom obeyed regretfully. He would have liked to console the kid; that would have kept him occupied and he wouldn't have been tempted to think about himself. But it got on my nerves. I had never thought about death, for the reason that the question had never come up. But now it had come up, and there was nothing else to do but think about it.

Tom started talking. "Say, did you ever bump anybody off?" he asked me. I didn't answer. He started to explain to me that he had bumped off six fellows since August. He hadn't yet realized what we were in for, and I saw clearly he didn't *want* to realize it. I myself hadn't quite taken it in. I wondered if it hurt very much. I thought about the bullets; I imagined their fiery hail going through my body. All that was beside the real question; but I was calm, we had all night in which to realize it. After a while Tom stopped talking and I looked at him out of the corner of my eye. I saw that he, too, had turned gray and that he looked pretty miserable. I said to myself, "It's starting." It was almost dark, a dull light filtered through the air vents across the coal pile and made a big spot under the sky. Through the hole in the ceiling I could already see a star. The night was going to be clear and cold.

The door opened and two guards entered. They were followed by a blond man in a tan uniform. He greeted us.

"I'm the doctor," he said. "I've been authorized to give you any assistance you may require in these painful circumstances."

He had an agreeable, cultivated voice.

I said to him, "What are you going to do here?"

"Whatever you want me to do. I shall do everything in my power to lighten these few hours."

"Why did you come to us? There are lots of others: the hospital's full of them."

"I was sent here," he answered vaguely. "You'd probably like to smoke, wouldn't you?" he added suddenly. "I've got some cigarettes and even some cigars."

He passed around some English cigarettes and some *puros,* but we refused them. I looked him straight in the eye and he appeared uncomfortable.

"You didn't come here out of compassion," I said to him. "In fact, I know who you are. I saw you with some fascists in the barracks yard the day I was arrested."

I was about to continue, when all at once something happened to me which surprised me: the presence of this doctor had suddenly ceased to interest me. Usually, when I've got hold of a man I don't let go. But somehow the desire to speak had left me. I shrugged my shoulders and turned away. A little later, I looked up and saw he was watching me with an air of curiosity. The guards had sat down on one of the mattresses. Pedro, the tall thin one, was twiddling his thumbs, while the other one shook his head occasionally to keep from falling asleep.

"Do you want some light?" Pedro suddenly asked the doctor. The other fellow nodded, "Yes." I think he was not over-intelligent, but doubtless he was not malicious. As I looked at his big, cold, blue eyes, it seemed to me the worst thing about him was his lack of imagination. Pedro went out and came back with an oil lamp which he set on the corner of the bench. It gave a poor light, but it was better than nothing; the night before we had been left in the dark. For a long while I stared at the circle of light the lamp threw on the ceiling. I was fascinated. Then, suddenly, I came to, the light circle paled, and I felt as if I were being crushed under an enormous weight. It wasn't the thought of death, and it wasn't fear; it was something anonymous. My cheeks were burning hot and my head ached.

I roused myself and looked at my two companions. Tom had his head in his hands and only the fat, white nape of his neck was visible. Juan was by far the worst off; his mouth was wide open and his nostrils were trembling. The doctor came over to him and touched him on the shoulder, as though to comfort him; but his eyes remained cold. Then I saw the Belgian slide his hand furtively down Juan's arm to his wrist. Indifferent, Juan let himself be handled. Then, as though absent-mindedly, the Belgian laid three fingers over his wrist; at the same time, he drew away somewhat and managed to turn his back to me. But I leaned over backward and saw him take out his watch and look at it a moment before relinquishing the boy's wrist. After a moment, he let the inert hand fall and went and leaned against the wall. Then, as if he had suddenly remembered something very important that had to be noted down immediately, he took a notebook from his pocket and wrote a few lines in it. "The son-of-a-bitch," I thought angrily. "He better not come and feel my pulse; I'll give him a punch in his dirty jaw."

He didn't come near me, but I felt he was looking at me. I raised my head and looked back at him. In an impersonal voice, he said, "Don't you think it's frightfully cold here?"

He looked purple with cold.

"I'm not cold," I answered him.

He kept looking at me with a hard expression. Suddenly I understood, and I lifted my hands to my face. I was covered with sweat. Here, in this cellar, in mid-winter, right in a draft, I was sweating. I ran my fingers through my hair, which was stiff with sweat; at the same time, I realized my shirt was damp and sticking to my skin. I had been streaming with perspiration for an hour, at least, and had felt nothing. But this fact hadn't escaped that Belgian swine. He had seen the drops rolling down my face and had said to himself that it showed an almost pathological terror; and he himself had felt normal and proud of it because he was cold. I wanted to get up and go punch his face in, but I had hardly started to make a move before my shame and anger had disappeared. I dropped back onto the bench with indifference.

I was content to rub my neck with my handkerchief because now I felt the sweat dripping from my hair onto the nape of my neck and that was disagreeable. I soon gave up rubbing myself, however, for it didn't do any good; my handkerchief was already wringing wet and I was still sweating. My buttocks, too, were sweating, and my damp trousers stuck to the bench.

Suddenly, Juan said, "You're a doctor, aren't you?"

"Yes," said the Belgian.

"Do people suffer—very long?"

"Oh! When . . . ? No, no," said the Belgian, in a paternal voice, "it's quickly over."

His manner was as reassuring as if he had been answering a paying patient.

"But I . . . Somebody told me—they often have to fire two volleys."

"Sometimes," said the Belgian, raising his head, "it just happens that the first volley doesn't hit any of the vital organs."

"So then they have to reload their guns and aim all over again?" Juan thought for a moment, then added hoarsely, "But that takes time!"

He was terribly afraid of suffering. He couldn't think about anything else, but that went with his age. As for me, I hardly thought about it any more and it certainly was not fear of suffering that made me perspire.

I rose and walked toward the pile of coal dust. Tom gave a start and looked at me with a look of hate. I irritated him because my shoes squeaked. I wondered if my face was as putty-colored as his. Then I noticed that he, too, was sweating. The sky was magnificent; no light at all came into our dark corner and I had only to lift my head to see the Big Bear. But it didn't look the way it had looked before. Two days ago, from my cell in the archbishop's palace, I could see a big patch of sky and each time of day brought back a different memory. In the morning, when the sky was a deep blue, and light, I thought of beaches along the Atlantic; at noon, I could see the sun, and I remembered a bar in Seville where I used to drink manzanilla and eat anchovies and olives; in the afternoon, I was in the shade, and I thought of the deep shadow which covers half of the arena while the other half gleams in the sunlight: it really gave me a pang to see the whole earth reflected in the sky like that. Now, however, no matter how much I looked up in the air, the sky no longer recalled anything. I liked it better that way. I came back and sat down next to Tom. There was a long silence.

Then Tom began to talk in a low voice. He had to keep talking, otherwise he lost his way in his own thoughts. I believe he was talking to me, but he didn't look at me. No doubt he was afraid to look at me, because I was gray and sweating. We were both alike and worse than mirrors for each other. He looked at the Belgian, the only one who was alive.

"Say, do you understand? I don't."

Then I, too, began to talk in a low voice. I was watching the Belgian.

"Understand what? What's the matter?"

"Something's going to happen to us that I don't understand."

There was a strange odor about Tom. It seemed to me that I was more sensitive to odors than ordinarily. With a sneer, I said, "You'll understand, later."

"That's not so sure," he said stubbornly. "I'm willing to be courageous, but at least I ought to know . . . Listen, they're going to take us out into the courtyard. All right. The fellows will be standing in line in front of us. How many of them will there be?"

"Oh, I don't know. Five, or eight. Not more."

"That's enough. Let's say there'll be eight of them. Somebody will shout 'Shoulder arms!' and I'll see all eight rifles aimed at me. I'm sure I'm going to feel like going through the wall. I'll push against the wall as hard as I can with my back, and the wall won't give in. The way it is in a nightmare. . . . I can imagine all that. Ah, if you only knew how well I can imagine it!"

"Skip it!" I said. "I can imagine it too."

"It must hurt like the devil. You know they aim at your eyes and mouth so as to disfigure you," he added maliciously. "I can feel the wounds already. For the last hour I've been having pains in my head and neck. Not real pains —it's worse still. They're the pains I'll feel tomorrow morning. And after that, then what?"

I understood perfectly well what he meant, but I didn't want to seem to understand. As for the pains, I, too, felt them all through my body, like a lot of little gashes. I couldn't get used to them, but I was like him, I didn't think they were very important.

"After that," I said roughly, "you'll be eating daisies."

He started talking to himself, not taking his eyes off the Belgian, who didn't seem to be listening to him. I knew what he had come for, and that what we were thinking didn't interest him. He had come to look at our bodies, our bodies which were dying alive.

"It's like in a nightmare," said Tom. "You want to think of something, you keep having the impression you've got it, that you're going to understand, and then it slips away from you, it eludes you and it's gone again. I say to myself, afterwards, there won't be anything. But I don't really understand what that means. There are moments when I almost do—and then it's gone again. I start to think of the pains, the bullets, the noise of the shooting. I am a materialist, I swear it; and I'm not going crazy, either. But there's something wrong. I see my own corpse. That's not hard, but it's *I* who see it, with *my* eyes. I'll have to get to the point where I think—where I think I won't see anything more. I won't hear anything more, and the world will go on for the others. We're not made to think that way, Pablo. Believe me, I've already stayed awake all night waiting for something. But this is not the same thing. This will grab us from behind, Pablo, and we won't be ready for it."

"Shut up," I said. "Do you want me to call a father confessor?"

He didn't answer. I had already noticed that he had a tendency to prophesy and call me "Pablo" in a kind of pale voice. I didn't like that very much, but it seems all the Irish are like that. I had a vague impression that he smelled of urine. Actually, I didn't like Tom very much, and I didn't see why, just because we were going to die together, I should like him any better. There are certain fellows with whom it would be different—with Ramon Gris, for instance. But between Tom and Juan, I felt alone. In fact, I liked it better that way. With Ramon I might have grown soft. But I felt terribly hard at that moment, and I wanted to stay hard.

Tom kept on muttering, in a kind of absent-minded way. He was certainly talking to keep from thinking. Naturally, I agreed with him, and I could have said everything he was saying. It's not *natural* to die. And since I was going to die, nothing seemed natural any more: neither the coal pile, nor the bench, nor Pedro's dirty old face. Only it was disagreeable for me to think the same things Tom thought. And I knew perfectly well that all night long, within five minutes of each other, we would keep on thinking things at the same time, sweating or shivering at the same time. I looked at him sideways and, for the first time, he seemed strange to me. He had death written on his face. My pride was wounded. For twenty-four hours I had lived side by side with Tom, I had listened to him, I had talked to him, and I knew we had nothing in common. And now we were as alike as twin brothers, simply because we were going to die together. Tom took my hand without looking at me.

"Pablo, I wonder . . . I wonder if it's true that we just cease to exist."

I drew my hand away.

"Look between your feet, you dirty dog."

There was a puddle between his feet and water was dripping from his trousers.

"What's the matter?" he said, frightened.

"You're wetting your pants," I said to him.

"It's not true," he said furiously. "I can't be . . . I don't feel anything."

The Belgian had come closer to him. With an air of false concern, he asked, "Aren't you feeling well?"

Tom didn't answer. The Belgian looked at the puddle without comment. "I don't know what that is," Tom said savagely, "but I'm not afraid. I swear to you, I'm not afraid."

The Belgian made no answer. Tom rose and went to the corner. He came back, buttoning his fly, and sat down, without a word. The Belgian was taking notes.

We were watching the doctor. Juan was watching him too. All three of us were watching him because he was alive. He had the gestures of a living person, the interests of a living person; he was shivering in this cellar the way living people shiver; he had an obedient, well-fed body. We, on the other hand, didn't feel our bodies any more—not the same way, in any case. I felt like touching my trousers, but I didn't dare to. I looked at the Belgian, well-planted on his two legs, master of his muscles—and able to plan for tomorrow. We were like three shadows deprived of blood; we were watching him and sucking his life like vampires.

Finally he came over to Juan. Was he going to lay his hand on the nape of Juan's neck for some professional reason, or had he obeyed a charitable impulse? If he had acted out of charity, it was the one and only time during the whole night. He fondled Juan's head and the nape of his neck. The kid let him do it, without taking his eyes off him. Then, suddenly, he took hold of the doctor's hand and looked at it in a funny way. He held the Belgian's hand between his own two hands and there was nothing pleasing about them, those two gray paws squeezing that fat red hand. I sensed what was going to happen and Tom must have sensed it, too. But all the Belgian saw was emotion, and he smiled paternally. After a moment, the kid lifted the big red paw to his mouth and started to bite it. The Belgian drew back quickly and stumbled toward the wall. For a second, he looked at us with horror. He must have suddenly understood that we were not men like himself. I began to laugh, and one of the guards started up. The other had fallen asleep with his eyes wide open, showing only the whites.

I felt tired and over-excited at the same time. I didn't want to think any more about what was going to happen at dawn—about death. It didn't make sense, and I never got beyond just words, or emptiness. But whenever I tried to think about something else I saw the barrels of rifles aimed at me.

I must have lived through my execution twenty times in succession; one time I thought it was the real thing; I must have dozed off for a moment. They were dragging me toward the wall and I was resisting; I was imploring their pardon. I woke with a start and looked at the Belgian. I was afraid I had cried out in my sleep. But he was smoothing his mustache; he hadn't noticed anything. If I had wanted to, I believe I could have slept for a while. I had been awake for the last forty-eight hours, and I was worn out. But I didn't want to lose two hours of life. They would have had to come and wake me at dawn. I would have followed them, drunk with sleep, and I would have gone off without so much as "Gosh!" I didn't want it that way, I didn't want to die like an animal. I wanted to understand. Besides, I was afraid of having nightmares. I got up and began to walk up and down and, so as to think about something else, I began to think about my past life. Memories crowded in on me, helter-skelter. Some were good and some were bad—at least that was how I had thought of them *before*. There were faces and happenings. I saw the face of a little *novilero* who had gotten himself horned during the *Feria,* in Valencia. I saw the face of one of my uncles, of Ramon Gris. I remembered all kinds of things that had happened: how I had been on strike for three months in 1926, and had almost died of hunger. I recalled a night I had spent on a bench in Granada; I hadn't eaten for three days, I was nearly wild, I didn't want to give up the sponge. I had to smile. With what eagerness I had run after happiness, and women, and liberty! And to what end? I had wanted to liberate Spain, I admired Py Margall, I had belonged to the anarchist movement, I had spoken at public meetings. I took everything as seriously as if I had been immortal.

At that time I had the impression that I had my whole life before me, and I thought to myself, "It's all a god-damned lie." Now it wasn't worth anything because it was finished. I wondered how I had ever been able to go out and have a good time with girls. I wouldn't have lifted my little finger if I had ever imagined that I would die like this. I saw my life before me, finished, closed, like a bag, and yet what was inside was not finished. For a moment I tried to appraise it. I would have liked to say to myself, "It's been a good life." But it couldn't be appraised, it was only an outline. I had spent my time writing checks on eternity, and had understood nothing. Now, I didn't miss anything. There were a lot of things I might have missed: the taste of manzanilla, for instance, or the swims I used to take in summer in a little creek near Cadiz. But death had taken the charm out of everything.

Suddenly the Belgian had a wonderful idea.

"My friends," he said to us, "if you want me to—and providing the military authorities give their consent—I could undertake to deliver a word or some token from you to your loved ones. . . ."

Tom growled, "I haven't got anybody."

I didn't answer. Tom waited for a moment, then he looked at me with curiosity. "Aren't you going to send any message to Concha?"

"No."

I hated that sort of sentimental conspiracy. Of course, it was my fault, since I had mentioned Concha the night before, and I should have kept my mouth shut. I had been with her for a year. Even as late as last night, I would have cut my arm off with a hatchet just to see her again for five minutes. That was why I had mentioned her. I couldn't help it. Now I didn't care any more about seeing her. I hadn't anything more to say to her. I didn't even want to hold her in my arms. I loathed my body because it had turned gray and was sweating—and I wasn't even sure that I didn't loathe hers too. Concha would cry when she heard about my death; for months she would have no more interest in life. But still it was I who was going to die. I thought of her beautiful, loving eyes. When she looked at me something went from her to me. But I thought to myself that it was all over; if she looked at me *now* her gaze would not leave her eyes, it would not reach out to me. I was alone.

Tom too, was alone, but not the same way. He was seated astride his chair and had begun to look at the bench with a sort of smile, with surprise, even. He reached out his hand and touched the wood cautiously, as though he were afraid of breaking something, then he drew his hand back hurriedly, and shivered. I wouldn't have amused myself touching that bench, if I had been Tom, that was just some more Irish play-acting. But somehow it seemed to me too that the different objects had something funny about them. They seemed to have grown paler, less massive than before. I had only to look at the bench, the lamp or the pile of coal dust to feel I was going to die. Naturally, I couldn't think clearly about my death, but I saw it everywhere, even on the different objects, the way they had withdrawn and kept their distance, tactfully, like people talking at the bedside of a dying person. It was *his own death* Tom had just touched on the bench.

In the state I was in, if they had come and told me I could go home quietly, that my life would be saved, it would have left me cold. A few hours, or a few years of waiting are all the same, when you've lost the illusion of being eternal. Nothing mattered to me any more. In a way, I was calm. But it was a horrible kind of calm—because of my body. My body—I saw with its eyes and I heard with its ears, but it was no longer I. It sweat and trembled independently, and I didn't recognize it any longer. I was obliged to touch it and look at it to know what was happening to it, just as if it had been someone else's body. At times I still felt it, I felt a slipping, a sort of headlong plunging, as in a falling airplane, or else I heard my heart beating. But this didn't give me confidence. In fact, everything that came from my body had something damned dubious about it. Most of the time it was silent, it stayed put and I didn't feel anything other than a sort of heaviness, a loathsome presence against me. I had the impression of being bound to an enormous vermin.

The Belgian took out his watch and looked at it.

"It's half-past three," he said.

The son-of-a-bitch! He must have done it on purpose. Tom jumped up. We hadn't yet realized the time was passing. The night surrounded us like a formless, dark mass; I didn't even remember it had started.

Juan started to shout. Wringing his hands, he implored, "I don't want to die! I don't want to die!"

He ran the whole length of the cellar with his arms in the air, then he dropped down onto one of the·mattresses, sobbing. Tom looked at him with dismal eyes and didn't even try to console him any more. The fact was, it was no use; the kid made more noise than we did, but he was less affected, really. He was like a sick person who defends himself against his malady with a high fever. When there's not even any fever left, it's much more serious.

He was crying. I could tell he felt sorry for himself; he was thinking about death. For one second, one single second, I too felt like crying, crying out of pity for myself. But just the contrary happened. I took one look at the kid, saw his thin, sobbing shoulders, and I felt I was inhuman. I couldn't feel pity either for these others or for myself. I said to myself, "I want to die decently."

Tom had gotten up and was standing just under the round opening looking out for the first signs of daylight. I was determined, I wanted to die decently, and I only thought about that. But underneath, ever since the doctor had told us the time, I felt time slipping, flowing by, one drop at a time.

It was still dark when I heard Tom's voice.

"Do you hear them?"

"Yes."

People were walking in the courtyard.

"What the hell are they doing? After all, they can't shoot in the dark."

After a moment, we didn't hear anything more. I said to Tom, "There's the daylight."

Pedro got up yawning, and came and blew out the lamp. He turned to the man beside him. "It's hellish cold."

The cellar had grown gray. We could hear shots at a distance.

"It's about to start," I said to Tom. "That must be in the back courtyard."

Tom asked the doctor to give him a cigarette. I didn't want any; I didn't want either cigarettes or alcohol. From that moment on, the shooting didn't stop.

"Can you take it in?" Tom said.

He started to add something, then he stopped and began to watch the door.

The door opened and a lieutenant came in with four soldiers. Tom dropped his cigarette.

"Steinbock?"

Tom didn't answer. Pedro pointed him out.

"Juan Mirbal?"

"He's the one on the mattress."

"Stànd up," said the Lieutenant.

Juan didn't move. Two soldiers took hold of him by the armpits and stood him up on his feet. But as soon as they let go of him he fell down.

The soldiers hesitated a moment.

"He's not the first one to get sick," said the Lieutenant. "You'll have to carry him, the two of you. We'll arrange things when we get there." He turned to Tom. "All right, come along."

Tom left between two soldiers. Two other soldiers followed, carrying the kid by his arms and legs. He was not unconscious; his eyes were wide open and tears were rolling down his cheeks. When I started to go out, the Lieutenant stopped me.

"Are you Ibbieta?"

"Yes."

"You wait here. They'll come and get you later on."

They left. The Belgian and the two jailers left too, and I was alone. I didn't understand what had happened to me, but I would have liked it better if they had ended it all right away. I heard the volleys at almost regular intervals; at each one, I shuddered. I felt like howling and tearing my hair. But instead, I gritted my teeth and pushed my hands deep into my pockets, because I wanted to stay decent.

An hour later, they came to fetch me and took me up to the first floor in a little room which smelt of cigar smoke and was so hot it seemed to me suffocating. Here there were two officers sitting in comfortable chairs, smoking, with papers spread out on their knees.

"Your name is Ibbieta?"

"Yes."

"Where is Ramon Gris?"

"I don't know."

The man who questioned me was small and stocky. He had hard eyes behind his glasses.

"Come nearer," he said to me.

I went nearer. He rose and took me by the arms, looking at me in a way calculated to make me go through the floor. At the same time he pinched my arms with all his might. He didn't mean to hurt me; it was quite a game; he wanted to dominate me. He also seemed to think it was necessary to blow his fetid breath right into my face. We stood like that for a moment, only I felt more like laughing than anything else. It takes a lot more than that to intimidate a man who's about to die: it didn't work. He pushed me away violently and sat down again.

"It's your life or his," he said. "You'll be allowed to go free if you tell us where he is."

After all, these two bedizened fellows with their riding crops and boots were just men who were going to die one day. A little later than I, perhaps, but not a great deal. And there they were, looking for names among their papers, running after other men in order to put them in prison or do away with them entirely. They had their opinions on the future of Spain and on other subjects. Their petty activities seemed to me to be offensive and ludicrous. I could no longer put myself in their place. I had the impression they were crazy.

The little fat fellow kept looking at me, tapping his boots with his riding crop. All his gestures were calculated to make him appear like a spirited, ferocious animal.

"Well? Do you understand?"

"I don't know where Gris is," I said. "I thought he was in Madrid."

The other officer lifted his pale hand indolently. This indolence was also calculated. I saw through all their little tricks, and I was dumbfounded that men should still exist who took pleasure in that kind of thing.

"You have fifteen minutes to think it over," he said slowly. "Take him to the linen-room, and bring him back here in fifteen minutes. If he continues to refuse, he'll be executed at once."

They knew what they were doing. I had spent the night waiting. After that, they had made me wait another hour in the cellar, while they shot Tom and Juan, and now they locked me in the linen-room. They must have arranged the whole thing the night before. They figured that sooner or later people's nerves wear out and they hoped to get me that way.

They made a big mistake. In the linen-room I sat down on a ladder because I felt very weak, and I began to think things over. Not their proposition, however. Naturally I knew where Gris was. He was hiding in his cousins' house, about two miles outside of the city. I knew, too, that I would not reveal his hiding place, unless they tortured me (but they didn't seem to be considering that). All that was definitely settled and didn't interest me in the least. Only I would have liked to understand the reasons for my own conduct. I would rather die than betray Gris. Why? I no longer liked Ramon Gris. My friendship for him had died shortly before dawn along with my love for Concha, along with my own desire to live. Of course I still admired him—he was hard. But it was not for that reason that I was willing to die in his place; his life was no more valuable than mine. No life was of any value. A man was going to be stood up against a wall and fired at till he dropped dead. It didn't make any difference whether it was I or Gris or somebody else. I knew perfectly well he was more useful to the

Spanish cause than I was, but I didn't give a God damn about Spain or anarchy, either; nothing had any importance now. And yet, there I was. I could save my skin by betraying Gris and I refused to do it. It seemed more ludicrous to me than anything else; it was stubbornness.

I thought to myself, "Am I hard-headed!" And I was seized with a strange sort of cheerfulness.

They came to fetch me and took me back to the two officers. A rat darted out under our feet and that amused me. I turned to one of the falangists and said to him, "Did you see that rat?"

He made no reply. He was gloomy, and took himself very seriously. As for me, I felt like laughing, but I restrained myself because I was afraid that if I started, I wouldn't be able to stop. The falangist wore mustaches. I kept after him, "You ought to cut off those mustaches, you fool."

I was amused by the fact that he let hair grow all over his face while he was still alive. He gave me a kind of half-hearted kick, and I shut up.

"Well," said the fat officer, "have you thought things over?"

I looked at them with curiosity, like insects of a very rare species.

"I know where he is," I said. "He's hiding in the cemetery. Either in one of the vaults, or in the gravediggers' shack."

I said that just to make fools of them. I wanted to see them get up and fasten their belts and bustle about giving orders.

They jumped to their feet.

"Fine. Moles, go ask Lieutenant Lopez for fifteen men. And as for you," the little fat fellow said to me, "if you've told the truth, I don't go back on my word. But you'll pay for this, if you're pulling our leg."

They left noisily and I waited in peace, still guarded by the falangists. From time to time I smiled at the thought of the face they were going to make. I felt dull and malicious. I could see them lifting up the gravestones, or opening the doors of the vaults one by one. I saw the whole situation as though I were another person: the prisoner determined to play the hero, the solemn falangists with their mustaches and the men in uniform running around among the graves. It was irresistibly funny.

After half an hour, the little fat fellow came back alone. I thought he had come to give the order to execute me. The others must have stayed in the cemetery.

The officer looked at me. He didn't look at all foolish.

"Take him out in the big courtyard with the others," he said. "When military operations are over, a regular tribunal will decide his case."

I thought I must have misunderstood.

"So they're not—they're not going to shoot me?" I asked.

"Not now, in any case. Afterwards, that doesn't concern me."

I still didn't understand.

"But why?" I said to him.

He shrugged his shoulders without replying, and the soldiers led me away. In the big courtyard there were a hundred or so prisoners, women, children and a few old men. I started to walk around the grass plot in the middle. I felt absolutely idiotic. At noon we were fed in the dining hall. Two or three fellows spoke to me. I must have known them, but I didn't answer. I didn't even know where I was.

Toward evening, about ten new prisoners were pushed into the courtyard. I recognized Garcia, the baker.

He said to me, "Lucky dog! I didn't expect to find you alive."

"They condemned me to death," I said, "and then they changed their minds. I don't know why."

"I was arrested at two o'clock," Garcia said.

"What for?"

Garcia took no part in politics.

"I don't know," he said. "They arrest everybody who doesn't think the way they do."

He lowered his voice.

"They got Gris."

I began to tremble.

"When?"

"This morning. He acted like a damned fool. He left his cousins' house Tuesday because of a disagreement. There were any number of fellows who would have hidden him, but he didn't want to be indebted to anybody any more. He said, 'I would have hidden at Ibbieta's, but since they've got him, I'll go hide in the cemetery.'"

"In the cemetery?"

"Yes. It was the god-damnedest thing. Naturally they passed by there this morning; that had to happen. They found him in the gravediggers' shack. They opened fire at him and they finished him off."

"In the cemetery!"

Everything went around in circles, and when I came to I was sitting on the ground. I laughed so hard the tears came to my eyes.

SHERWOOD ANDERSON

Seeds 🐣

He was a small man with a beard and was very nervous. I remember how the cords of his neck were drawn taut.

For years he had been trying to cure people of illness by the method called psychoanalysis. The idea was the passion of his life. "I came here because I am tired," he said dejectedly. "My body is not tired but something inside me is old and worn-out. I want joy. For a few days or weeks I would like to forget men and women and the influences that make them the sick things they are."

There is a note that comes into the human voice by which you may know real weariness. It comes when one has been trying with all his heart and soul to think his way along some difficult road of thought. Of a sudden he finds himself unable to go on. Something within him stops. A tiny explosion takes place. He bursts into words and talks, perhaps foolishly. Little side currents of his nature he didn't know were there run out and get themselves expressed. It is at such times that a man boasts, uses big words, makes a fool of himself in general.

And so it was the doctor became shrill. He jumped up from the steps where we had been sitting, talking and walked about. "You come from the West. You have kept away from people. You have preserved yourself—damn you! I haven't——" His voice had indeed become shrill. "I have entered into lives. I have gone beneath the surface of the lives of men and women. Women especially I have studied—our own women, here in America."

"You have loved them?" I suggested.

"Yes," he said. "Yes—you are right there. I have done that. It is the only way I can get at things. I have to try to love. You see how that is? It's the only way. Love must be the beginning of things with me."

I began to sense the depths of his weariness. "We will go swim in the lake," I urged.

"I don't want to swim or do any damn plodding thing. I want to run and shout," he declared. "For a while, for a few hours, I want to be like a dead leaf blown by the winds over these hills. I have one desire and one only—to free myself."

We walked in a dusty country road. I wanted him to know that I thought I understood, so I put the case in my own way.

When he stopped and stared at me I talked. "You are no more and no better than myself," I declared. "You are a dog that has rolled in offal, and because you are not quite a dog you do not like the smell of your own hide."

In turn my voice became shrill. "You blind fool," I cried impatiently. "Men like you are fools. You cannot go along that road. It is given to no man to venture far along the road of lives."

I became passionately in earnest. "The illness you pretend to cure is the universal illness," I said. "The thing you want to do cannot be done. Fool— do you expect love to be understood?"

We stood in the road and looked at each other. The suggestion of a sneer played about the corners of his mouth. He put a hand on my shoulder and shook me. "How smart we are—how aptly we put things!"

He spat the words out and then turned and walked a little away. "You think you understand, but you don't understand," he cried. "What you say can't be done can be done. You're a liar. You cannot be so definite without missing something vague and fine. You miss the whole point. The lives of people are like young trees in a forest. They are being choked by climbing vines. The vines are old thoughts and beliefs planted by dead men. I am myself covered by crawling creeping vines that choke me."

He laughed bitterly. "And that's why I want to run and play," he said. "I want to be a leaf blown by the wind over hills. I want to die and be born again, and I am only a tree covered with vines and slowly dying. I am, you see, weary and want to be made clean. I am an amateur venturing timidly into lives," he concluded. "I am weary and want to be made clean. I am covered by creeping crawling things."

A woman from Iowa came here to Chicago and took a room in a house on the west-side. She was about twenty-seven years old and ostensibly she came to the city to study advanced methods for teaching music.

A certain young man also lived in the west-side house. His room faced a long hall on the second floor of the house and the one taken by the woman was across the hall facing his room.

In regard to the young man—there is something very sweet in his nature. He is a painter but I have often wished he would decide to become a writer. He tells things with understanding and he does not paint brilliantly.

And so the woman from Iowa lived in the west-side house and came home from the city in the evening. She looked like a thousand other women one sees in the streets every day. The only thing that at all made her stand out among the women in the crowds was that she was a little lame. Her right foot was slightly deformed and she walked with a limp. For three months she lived in the house—where she was the only woman except the landlady—and then a feeling in regard to her began to grow up among the men of the house.

The men all said the same thing concerning her. When they met in the hallway at the front of the house they stopped, laughed and whispered. "She wants a lover," they said and winked. "She may not know it but a lover is what she needs." One knowing Chicago and Chicago men would think that an easy want to be satisfied. I laughed when my friend—whose name is LeRoy—told me the story, but he did not laugh. He shook his head. "It wasn't so easy," he said. "There would be no story were the matter that simple."

LeRoy tried to explain. "Whenever a man approached her she became alarmed," he said. Men kept smiling and speaking to her. They invited her to dinner and to the theatre, but nothing would induce her to walk in the streets with a man. She never went into the streets at night. When a man stopped and tried to talk with her in the hallway she turned her eyes to the floor and then ran into her room. Once a young drygoods clerk who lived there induced her to sit with him on the steps before the house.

He was a sentimental fellow and took hold of her hand. When she began to cry he was alarmed and arose. He put a hand on her shoulder and tried to explain, but under the touch of his fingers her whole body shook with terror. "Don't touch me," she cried, "don't let your hands touch me!" She began to scream and people passing in the street stopped to listen. The drygoods clerk was alarmed and ran upstairs to his own room. He bolted the door and stood listening. "It is a trick," he declared in a trembling voice. "She is trying to make trouble. I did nothing to her. It was an accident and anyway what's the matter? I only touched her arm with my fingers."

Perhaps a dozen times LeRoy has spoken to me of the experience of the Iowa woman in the west-side house. The men there began to hate her. Although she would have nothing to do with them she would not let them alone. In a hundred ways she continually invited approaches that when made she repelled. When she stood naked in the bathroom facing the hallway where the men passed up and down she left the door slightly ajar. There was a couch in the living room downstairs, and when men were present she would sometimes enter and without saying a word throw herself down before them. On the couch she lay with lips drawn slightly apart. Her eyes stared at the ceiling. Her whole physical being seemed to be waiting for something. The sense of her filled the room. The men standing about pretended not to see. They talked loudly. Embarrassment took possession of them and one by one they crept quietly away.

One evening the woman was ordered to leave the house. Someone, perhaps the drygoods clerk, had talked to the landlady and she acted at once. "If you leave tonight I shall like it that much better," LeRoy heard the elder woman's voice saying. She stood in the hallway before the Iowa woman's room. The landlady's voice rang through the house.

LeRoy the painter is tall and lean and his life has been spent in devotion to ideas. The passions of his brain have consumed the passions of his body. His income is small and he has not married. Perhaps he has never had a sweetheart. He is not without physical desire but he is not primarily concerned with desire.

On the evening when the Iowa woman was ordered to leave the west-side house, she waited until she thought the landlady had gone downstairs, and then went into LeRoy's room. It was about eight o'clock and he sat by a window reading a book. The woman did not knock but opened the door. She said nothing but ran across the floor and knelt at his feet. LeRoy said that her twisted foot made her run like a wounded bird, that her eyes were burning and that her breath came in little gasps. "Take me," she said, putting her face down upon his knees and trembling violently. "Take me quickly. There must be a beginning to things. I can't stand the waiting. You must take me at once."

You may be quite sure LeRoy was perplexed by all this. From what he has said I gathered that until that evening he had hardly noticed the woman. I suppose that of all the men in the house he had been the most indifferent to her. In the room something happened. The landlady followed the woman when she ran to LeRoy, and the two women confronted him. The woman from Iowa knelt trembling and frightened at his feet. The landlady was indignant. LeRoy acted on impulse. An inspiration came to him. Putting his hand on the kneeling woman's shoulder he shook her violently. "Now behave yourself," he said quickly. "I will keep my promise." He turned to the landlady and smiled. "We have been engaged to be married," he said. "We have quarreled. She came here to be near me. She has been unwell and excited. I will take her away. Please don't let yourself be annoyed. I will take her away."

When the woman and LeRoy got out of the house she stopped weeping and put her hand into his. Her fears had all gone away. He found a room for her in another house and then went with her into a park and sat on a bench.

Everything LeRoy has told me concerning this woman strengthens my belief in what I said to the man that day in the mountains. You cannot venture along the road of lives. On the bench he and the woman talked until midnight and he saw and talked with her many times later. Nothing came of it. She went back, I suppose, to her place in the West.

In the place from which she had come the woman had been a teacher of music. She was one of four sisters, all engaged in the same sort of work and, LeRoy says, all quiet capable women. Their father had died when the eldest girl was not yet ten, and five years later the mother died also. The girls had a house and a garden.

In the nature of things I cannot know what the lives of the women were like but of this one may be quite certain—they talked only of women's affairs, thought only of women's affairs. No one of them ever had a lover. For years no man came near the house.

Of them all only the youngest, the one who came to Chicago, was visibly affected by the utterly feminine quality of their lives. It did something to her. All day and every day she taught music to young girls and then went home to the women. When she was twenty-five she began to think and to dream of men. During the day and through the evening she talked with women of women's affairs, and all the time she wanted desperately to be loved by a man. She went to Chicago with that hope in mind. LeRoy explained her attitude in the matter and her strange behavior in the west-side house by saying she had thought too much and acted too little. "The life force within her became decentralized," he declared. "What she wanted she could not achieve. The living force within could not find expression. When it could not get expressed in one way it took another. Sex spread itself out over her body. It permeated the very fibre of her being. At the last she was sex personified, sex become condensed and impersonal. Certain words, the touch of a man's hand, sometimes even the sight of a man passing in the street did something to her."

Yesterday I saw LeRoy and he talked to me again of the woman and her strange and terrible fate.

We walked in the park by the lake. As we went along the figure of the woman kept coming into my mind. An idea came to me.

"You might have been her lover," I said. "That was possible. She was not afraid of you."

LeRoy stopped. Like the doctor who was so sure of his ability to walk into lives he grew angry and scolded. For a moment he stared at me and then a rather odd thing happened. Words said by the other man in the dusty road in the hills came to LeRoy's lips and were said over again. The suggestion of a sneer played about the corners of his mouth. "How smart we are. How aptly we put things," he said.

The voice of the young man who walked with me in the park by the lake in the city became shrill. I sensed the weariness in him. Then he laughed and said quietly and softly, "It isn't so simple. By being sure of yourself you are in danger of losing all of the romance of life. You miss the whole point. Nothing in life can be settled so definitely. The woman—you see—was like a young tree choked by a climbing vine. The thing that wrapped her about had shut out the light. She was a grotesque as many trees in the forest are grotesques. Her problem was such a difficult one that thinking of it has changed the whole current of my life. At first I was like you. I was quite sure. I thought I would be her lover and settle the matter."

LeRoy turned and walked a little away. Then he came back and took hold of my arm. A passionate earnestness took possession of him. His voice trembled. "She needed a lover, yes, the men in the house were quite right about that," he said. "She needed a lover and at the same time a lover was not what she needed. The need of a lover was, after all, a quite secondary thing. She needed to be loved, to be long and quietly and patiently loved. To be sure she is grotesque, but then all the people in the world are grotesque. We all need to be loved. What would cure her would cure the rest of us also. The disease she had is, you see, universal. We all want to be loved and the world has no plan for creating our lovers."

LeRoy's voice dropped and he walked beside me in silence. We turned away from the lake and walked under trees. I looked closely at him. The cords of his neck were drawn taut. "I have seen under the shell of life and I am afraid," he mused. "I am myself like the woman. I am covered with creeping crawling vine-like things. I cannot be a lover. I am not subtle or patient enough. I am paying old debts. Old thoughts and beliefs—seeds planted by dead men—spring up in my soul and choke me."

For a long time we walked and LeRoy talked, voicing the thoughts that came into his mind. I listened in silence. His mind struck upon the refrain voiced by the man in the mountains. "I would like to be a dead dry thing," he muttered looking at the leaves scattered over the grass. "I would like to be a leaf blown away by the wind." He looked up and his eyes turned to where among the trees we could see the lake in the distance. "I am weary and want to be made clean. I am a man covered by creeping crawling things. I would like to be dead and blown by the wind over limitless waters," he said. "I want more than anything else in the world to be clean."

STEFAN ZWEIG

The Invisible Collection 🦌

An Episode from the Period of the German Inflation

Translated by M. L. Nielsen*

At the first station past Dresden, an elderly gentleman entered our
compartment and, after giving a friendly greeting, looked up and
nodded in my direction with special emphasis as if to an old
friend. I was at a loss to know who he might be. But then he smiled and
mentioned his name. Of course I knew him! He was one of the most
respected art-dealers in Berlin, in whose shop I had often examined and
bought rare books and autographs before the war. After we had chatted for
a time about trivialities, he suddenly said:

"I must tell you the object of the journey I'm returning from, because I've
had an experience which is about the most unusual thing that has ever
happened to me in the thirty-seven years of my activity as an art peddler.
No doubt you know what things are like in the art trade these days, since
money values have become as insubstantial as vapor: the newly-rich have
suddenly discovered a passion for Gothic madonnas and incunabula and
old prints and pictures. You just can't conjure up enough to satisfy them;
in fact you have to be on your guard to prevent them from stripping your
very house and room. They'd like to buy the cuff-links off your shirts and
the lamp from your writing-table. And it's getting more and more difficult
to obtain new merchandise. I see that you're shocked to hear me refer to
these things which we've always looked upon with reverence as merchandise.
But this wretched tribe has accustomed even me to looking upon a wonderful Venetian incunabulum as nothing more than security for so and so
many dollars, and a drawing of Guercino as the incarnation of a few
hundred-franc notes.

"There's no defense against the intrusive insistence of these people with
their sudden mania for buying, and so the other day I found that once more
I had been completely cleaned out over night and was of a mind to close up
the shop altogether. But then I began to feel ashamed to see the store which
my father took over from my grandfather cluttered up with trashy merchandise which not so long ago no second-hand dealer in the north-end
would have bothered to pile onto his cart. In this dilemma I hit upon the

* Used by permission of the translator.

idea of looking through our old account books to ferret out some former customers from whom I might pilfer back a few decent items.

"Such an old list of customers is always a kind of morgue, especially in times like these, and it didn't tell me much. Most of those who had bought from us in earlier days had long since been forced to dispose of their holdings at auction, or had died, and from the few who were still about there was little to hope for. But then I happened to stumble onto a whole bundle of letters from a man who was probably our oldest customer and who had slipped from my memory for the simple reason that, since the start of the World War, since 1914, he had never once sent us any kind of inquiry nor any order. The correspondence went back—and this is truly no exaggeration —almost sixty years; he had bought from my father and even my grandfather, though I couldn't recall that he had ever entered our shop in the thirty-seven years of my own activity.

"Everything pointed to the conclusion that this man must have been a peculiar, old-fashioned, abusive type of person, one of those vanished Menzel or Spitzweg Germans who have survived as unique specimens here and there in provincial towns right up to our own day. His letters were neatly-written calligraphics, with amounts underlined with a ruler or in red ink, and figures invariably written twice in order to allow no chance for error. This, plus the fact that he always wrote on cheap block paper and sent his letters in a motley assortment of cheap envelopes, indicated the pettiness and fanatical miserliness of a hopeless provincial. In addition to his name, these unusual documents invariably bore the ceremonious title: Forestry-and-Agricultural-Commissioner, Retired; Lieutenant, Retired; Holder of the Iron Cross, First Class. As a veteran of 'seventy he must be carrying, if still alive, at least a good eighty years on his back. But this crabbed, ridiculous old miser showed extraordinary shrewdness, excellent knowledge and the finest kind of taste as a collector of old prints. As I gradually put together his orders over a period of nearly sixty years, the first of which ran to no more than a few cents, it became clear that, in the days when one could still buy a whole heap of the most beautiful German woodcuts for a few marks, this little provincial must have quietly brought together a collection of copper-plate prints which could certainly stand honorable comparison with any of the noisily-publicized collections of the newly-rich. Because even what he had bought from us in the course of a half-century for a few marks or a few cents represented today an astonishing value, and it was reasonable to expect that he had struck as good a bargain at auctions and with other dealers. Although no further order had come from him since 1914, I was so familiar with every happening in the art trade that the auction or closed sale of such a stock could not have escaped me. And so this unusual man must still be alive, or the collection must be in the hands of his heirs.

"I became interested in the matter, and the very next day, last evening, I started out on a trip to one of the most outlandish provincial cities of Saxony; and as I sauntered from the railway station through the main street, I could scarcely conceive of the possibility that here, amidst all these banal and shoddy houses with their middle-class rubbish, in one of these rooms, there should live a person possessing the most beautiful pictures of Rembrandt along with prints of Dürer and Mantegnas in perfect condition. When I inquired at the post office whether a forestry or agricultural commissioner of a certain name lived in the city, I was astonished to learn that the old gentleman was still living, and before it was yet noon I set out on the way to his house—not, I must confess, without a certain feeling of excitement.

"I had no trouble finding where he lived. It was in the second story of one of those scanty, small-town houses which was probably hastily thrown together by some speculating building-contractor back in the 'sixties. A worthy master-tailor lived on the first floor; upstairs on the left gleamed the doorplate of a postmaster, and on the right finally a porcelain plate bearing the name of the forestry-and-agricultural-commissioner. In answer to my hesitant ringing the door was opened at once by a very old, white-haired lady wearing a neat little black hood. I handed her my card and asked whether I might speak with the forestry commissioner. Surprised and with a certain air of mistrust, she looked first at me and then at the card. Apparently a visit from the outside world was something of an event in this isolated little town, in this old-fashioned house. I heard her whispering softly, and then suddenly a loud, booming male voice: 'Ah, Herr R. . . . from Berlin, from the big art shop . . . show him in, show him in . . . It's a pleasure!' And now the little old grandmother came tripping back and invited me into the friendly room.

"I took off coat and hat and entered. In the middle of the modest room, standing very erect, was an old but still vigorous-looking man with bushy mustache who wore a belted lounging-robe of semi-military cut. He was holding both hands heartily out toward me, and yet the unmistakably happy and spontaneous welcome indicated by this gesture was contradicted by a strange stiffness in the way the man stood there. He didn't advance a single step toward me, and I was compelled—somewhat taken aback—to go right up to him in order to grasp his hand. As I was about to do so, however, it became clear from the fixed and immoveable way in which these hands were held that they were waiting for mine rather than seeking them. And in the next instant I understood everything: this man was blind.

"From the time of my childhood I have always been uncomfortable in the presence of a blind person. I have never been able to escape a certain feeling of shame and embarrassment stemming from the knowledge that the person before me is so completely alive and yet is incapable of having the same feeling with regard to me. Now too I had to fight to overcome an incipient fright as I looked into the dead eyes, directed fixedly into empty space, under the bristling, bushy white eyebrows. But the blind man didn't leave me much time for such discomfort, for as soon as my hand touched his he began to shake it vigorously and to renew his greeting with hearty and noisy joviality.

" 'A strange visit,' he said, laughing full in my direction, 'really a miracle that one of the fine gentlemen from Berlin should ever wander into our little hamlet . . . But that's the time to be on your guard, when one of the gentlemen dealers gets on a train . . . We have a saying in these parts: Lock your doors and your pocketbooks when the gypsies come around . . . Yes, I have an idea why you've hunted me out . . . Business is bad now in our poor, downtrodden Germany, there are no longer any buyers, and so the fine gentlemen turn their thoughts to their old customers once more and are out looking after their old flocks . . . But I'm afraid you won't have much luck with me; we poor old pensioners are happy to have a piece of bread on the table. We can't compete with the insane prices you're setting these days . . . My type is out of the running forever.'

"I assured him at once that he had misunderstood me, that I hadn't come to sell him something. I told him I just happened to be in the vicinity and hadn't wanted to miss the opportunity of paying my compliments to a person who was a customer of our house of long years' standing and one of the greatest collectors in Germany. Scarcely had I spoken the words 'one of the greatest collectors in Germany' when a striking transformation took place in the old gentleman's face. He still stood straight and stiff in the middle of the room, but now there came into his bearing a sudden expression of brightness and inner pride. He turned in the direction where he judged his wife to be, as if to say 'Do you hear?' and without a trace of that gruff military tone which he had been affecting, but with a happy voice that was actually soft and tender, he said: 'That is really very, very nice of you . . . And you won't have come in vain . . . You'll see something you don't get to see every day, not even in your snobbish Berlin . . . a few items that are as fine as anything you will find in the *Albertina* or in that accursed Paris . . . Yes, when one collects for sixty years, he manages to get together a lot of things that you won't find just lying about in the streets. Luise, hand me the key to the cabinet.'

"But now an unexpected thing happened. The little old grandmother, who had been standing at his side and silently following our conversation with a polite, smiling friendliness, suddenly raised both hands toward me in a gesture of entreaty, and at the same time shook her head vigorously, a sign which at first I didn't understand. Then she went up to her husband and gently placed both hands on his shoulder: 'But Hermann,' she admonished, 'you didn't ask the gentleman whether he had time now to examine the collection. It's nearly noon, and after lunch you must rest for an hour as the doctor has ordered. Wouldn't it be better to show the gentleman all the things after lunch, and then we can drink coffee together. Then Annemarie will be here too; she understands everything so much better and can help you.'

"And once again, as soon as she had finished speaking, she repeated the same insistent gesture of entreaty, looking past the unsuspecting man. Now I understood. I knew that she wished me to decline an immediate inspection, and I quickly made up the excuse that I had an invitation to lunch. It would be a pleasure and an honor to examine his collection, I said, but it would scarcely be possible before three o'clock. At that time I would be happy to return.

"As vexed as a child from whom one has taken its favorite toy, the old man turned around. 'Of course,' he growled, 'the gentlemen from Berlin never have time for anything. But this is once when you'll have to take time, because this is not just three or four pieces. There are twenty-seven portfolios, each one for a different artist, and not one that isn't more than half full. At three o'clock then. But be punctual, otherwise we won't get through.'

"Again he stretched out his hand to me into empty space. 'But mind me now, it may delight you—or it may annoy you. And the more it annoys you, the happier I'll be. After all, that's the way we collectors are: everything for ourselves and nothing for the other fellow!' Once more he heartily shook my hand.

"The little old lady accompanied me to the door. Through it all I had noticed in her an expression of embarrassed, nervous anxiety. And now, right in the doorway, she began to stutter in a suppressed voice: 'Could . . . could . . . my daughter Annemarie call for you, before you come back? . . . It would be better for . . . for several reasons . . . No doubt you will eat at the hotel?'

" 'Certainly, I would be happy, it will be a pleasure,' I said.

"And so it turned out. An hour later, just as I had finished my lunch in the small dining room of the hotel on the *Marktplatz,* a rather spinsterish-looking girl, simply dressed, entered the room and looked about searchingly. I went up to her, introduced myself, and said that I was ready to leave at once to look over the collection. But she reddened suddenly, and with the same nervous embarrassment that her mother had displayed she begged to be permitted to speak a few words with me first. And I could see at a glance that it was very difficult for her. Each time she took hold of herself and tried to speak, this fleeting, agitated redness spread itself all the way up to her forehead, and her hand twined itself in her dress. Finally she began, her speech sticking in her throat and faltering time and again.

" 'My mother sent me to you . . . She told me everything, and . . . we have a great favor to ask of you . . . You see, we want to inform you before you go to father . . . Naturally father will want to show you his collection, and the collection . . . the collection . . . is no longer quite complete . . . A number of items are missing . . . quite a lot, unfortunately . . .' She had to get her breath again, then she suddenly looked full at me and said in a hurried voice:

" 'I must speak frankly to you . . .You know what the times are like, you'll understand everything . . . Father became totally blind after the war broke out. His vision was often impaired even before that, but at that time the excitement robbed him of the light completely. You see, he wanted to join up and march against France in spite of his seventy-six years, and when the army failed to move right along as it had done in 1870, he was terribly disturbed by it all, and his vision began to fail with alarming speed. Otherwise he is still perfectly robust; until a short time ago he was still able to walk for hours and even go hunting, of which he was very fond. But now it's all over with his walks, and the only pleasure that was left to him was his collection. He looks at it every day . . . that is, he doesn't look at it, of course, he can't see anything any more, but every afternoon he takes all the portfolios out, so that he can at least touch the pieces, one after the other, always in the same order, which he has known by memory for decades . . . That's all he's interested in now, and I always have to read to him from the newspaper about the auctions, and the higher the prices he hears about, the happier it makes him . . . because . . . and this is what is so terrible . . . father doesn't understand anything about the prices and about the conditions today . . . He doesn't know that we have lost everything and that we couldn't live two days out of the month on his pension . . . and on top of that my sister's husband was killed in the war and he left her with four small children . . . But father knows nothing of all our material difficulties.

" 'In the beginning we cut expenses, cut them even more than before, but that didn't help. Then we began to sell. Of course we did not touch the beloved collection. We sold the little bit of finery we had, but, Lord in heaven, what did that amount to? For sixty years, after all, father had spent every extra cent for his prints. And one day there wasn't anything left . . . we didn't know which way to turn . . . and then . . . then . . . mother and I sold one of the prints. Father would never have allowed it. He just doesn't know how bad things are, he has no idea how hard it is to scare up a little bit of food undercover somewhere. He doesn't even know that we have lost the war and that Alsace and Lorraine have been lost. We no longer read him all these things from the papers, so that he won't excite himself.

" 'It was a very valuable item that we sold, a Rembrandt etching. The dealer offered us many, many thousands of marks for it, and we hoped it would take care of us for years. But you know how the money melts away . . . We had put all the balance in the bank, and in two months it was all gone. And so we had to sell another piece, and another, and the dealer was always so slow in sending the money that it had already lost its value. Then we tried the auctions, but there too they swindled us in spite of prices that ran into the millions. By the time the millions reached us, they were always worthless paper. In this way the best part of his collection down to a few remaining good items has gradually slipped away, and only to eke out the barest, scantiest kind of existence. And father suspects nothing.

" 'And that's why mother was so worried when you came today . . . because if he opens the portfolios for you everything will be lost. You see, we put cheap copies or sheets of the same size in his old mats, each of which he recognizes when he feels it, so that he doesn't notice anything when he runs his fingers over them. And if only he can touch them and go through them item by item (he knows the exact order by heart), he gets the same pleasure from them that he used to when he could see them. And there is no one else in this small town whom father would consider worthy of seeing his treasures . . . and he loves every single sheet with such a fanatical love that I think his heart would break if he suspected that the whole lot of it has long since slipped away from under his very hands. You are the first one in all these years, since the former director of the Dresden gallery of etchings died, to whom he has wanted to show his collection. And so I beg of you . . .'

"And suddenly the aging girl raised her hands toward me, and there was a sparkle of tears in her eyes. '. . . We beg of you . . . don't make him unhappy . . . all of us unhappy . . . don't destroy this last illusion for him. Help us make him believe that all these prints which he is going to describe to you are still there. He wouldn't live through it if he had the faintest suspicion. Maybe we did wrong him, but there was nothing else we could do. We had to live . . . and human lives, the lives of four fatherless children like my sister's, are surely more important than printed sheets. After all we haven't yet robbed him of a single bit of pleasure; he is happy to be able to leaf through his portfolios every afternoon for three hours, talking with each sheet as if it were a living thing. And today . . . perhaps today would have been his happiest day, for he has been waiting for years for the opportunity to show his favorites to a connoisseur. Please . . . I beg of you with outstretched hand, don't rob him of this happiness!'

"All this was said in a manner more moving than my narrative can possibly convey. Good Lord, as a dealer I had seen many of these people who had been basely swindled by the inflation, people who had been cheated of costly, centuries-old family possessions for a mere piece of buttered bread. But fate had here played an odd trick which I found strangely moving. Of course I promised to keep silent and to do my best.

"So we started out together. On the way I learned with bitterness with what trifling sums these poor, unknowing women had been cheated. But that only strengthened my determination to help them to the limit. We climbed the stairs, and the moment we opened the door we heard from within the room the happy, blustering voice of the old man: 'Come in!

Come in!' With the sensitive ears of the blind he must have heard our footsteps while we were still on the stairway.

" 'Hermann has been so impatient to show you his treasures that he couldn't even sleep today,' said the little old lady with a smile. A single glance from her daughter had reassured her that I had agreed to their request. The piles of portfolios were spread out on the table awaiting us, and as soon as the blind man felt my hand he grasped my arm, and without further greeting pushed me into a chair.

" 'So, and now we can begin—there is a lot to see, and the gentlemen from Berlin never have any time. This first portfolio here is master Dürer, and, as you will soon discover, fairly complete, though of course some of the prints are finer than others. Well, you can judge for yourself. Just look at that!'—he opened to the first page of the portfolio—'the *Great Horse.*'

"And now, with the tender care which one usually employs when handling something fragile, he took from the portfolio with gentle, cautious fingertips a mat which framed a blank, yellowed piece of paper, and enraptured he held the worthless scrap before him. Without really seeing it, he looked at it for minutes on end, holding the empty sheet ecstatically at eye-level, with arm extended. His whole countenance magically expressed the intent look of the beholder, and in his staring eyes with their dead pupils there suddenly appeared—was it a reflection from the paper or a brilliance that came from within?—a mirror-like brightness, a knowing light.

" 'Well,' he said proudly, 'have you ever seen a finer impression? How sharply, how clearly every detail stands out. I've compared the Dresden print with this one and it seems completely dull and lifeless. And on top of that the pedigree! There'—and turning the sheet over he pointed with such exactitude to particular spots that involuntarily I looked to see whether there were not some marks on the back after all—'there you have the stamp of the Nagler collection, and here those of Remy and Esdaile; they didn't dream, these illustrious owners of an earlier day, that their sheet would someday find its way into this little room.'

"I felt a cold chill in my spine as I heard this unsuspecting man praise an empty sheet with such enthusiasm. It was uncanny to see how he pointed with his fingernail with millimeter accuracy to all the invisible collectors' marks which still existed only in his phantasy. My throat was constricted with something very like horror; I could think of nothing to say; but as I looked up in confusion at the two women, I saw again the hand of the trembling and excited old lady raised in supplication. And so I took hold of myself and began to speak my part.

" 'Amazing,' I finally managed to stammer. 'A wonderful specimen.' At once his whole face lit up with pride. 'But that's nothing yet,' he said triumphantly, 'wait until you see the *Melancholia,* or the *Passion* here, an illuminated copy such as you will scarcely find in like quality anywhere. Just look'

—and again his fingers brushed gently across an imaginary picture—'just look at this fresh, warm, pithy tone. With all its fine dealers and museum doctors, Berlin would stand on its head at sight of that.'

"And so it went on, this tumultuous, triumphant commentary, for two whole hours. No, I can't possibly describe to you how ghostly it was to look with him at those hundred or two-hundred empty scraps of paper or shabby reproductions, and to see that in the memory of this tragically deceived man they were so incredibly real that he was able to praise and describe every single one in faultless order and minute detail. The invisible collection which must long since have been scattered to the four winds was still there for this blind man. For him it was unimpaired, and his vision of it was so intense and overpowering that even I almost found myself beginning to believe in it.

"Only once did the awful danger of an awakening break into the dream-like certainty of his visionary rapture. As he came to Rembrandt's *Antiope* (a test impression which must really have had an incalculable value) he had again praised the sharpness of the print, and, as he did so, had run his nervously clairvoyant finger affectionately over the lines of the imprint. But his refined sense of touch was unable to distinguish the expected depressions in the strange sheet, and something like a shadow abruptly passed across his forehead. His voice faltered. 'But that is . . . surely that is the *Antiope?*' he murmured, somewhat embarrassed, whereupon I immediately primed myself, hastily took the framed sheet from his hands and gave a glowing description of the etching in all possible detail, for I knew it very well too. The face of the blind man, which had taken on a confused look, now relaxed once more, and the more I praised, the greater grew the jovial heartiness and ingenuous gaiety of the gnarled, weather-beaten old man.

" 'Here at last is a man who knows what is good,' he cried out in triumph, turning to his family. 'Finally, finally someone from whom you too can hear how much my pictures are worth. You've always been suspicious and scolded me because I put all my money into my collection. It's true. For sixty years no beer, no wine, no tobacco, no trips, no visits to the theater, no books. All that time I have just saved and saved for these pictures. But you'll see some-day, when I am gone—then you will be rich, richer than anyone in town, and as rich as the richest in Dresden. Then at last you will be glad that I was so foolish. But as long as I live not a single picture leaves this house—first they've got to carry me out, and then my collection can go.'

"And with these words he ran his hand tenderly, as if over some living thing, across the long-since empty portfolios. It was frightening and at the same time touching, because in all the years of war I had not seen so complete and pure an expression of happiness in a German countenance. At his side stood the women, uncannily like those female figures in the German

master's etching who, having come to visit the grave of their saviour, stand
before the broken, empty tomb in an attitude expressive at once of fearful
alarm and devout, joyful wonderment. Just as in that picture the disciples
are illumined by a divine presentiment of the saviour, so were these two
aging, worn and simple women illumined by the child-like bliss of this old
man. They stood there half-laughing, half-weeping, a sight more moving
than any I have ever experienced. But the old man couldn't get his fill of
my praise; again and again he piled up the sheets and turned through them,
thirstily drinking in every word. And so it was a relief for me when at last
the deceitful portfolios were put aside and he was reluctantly forced to clear
the table for the coffee.

"But what was my feeling of guilt compared with the soaring spirits of
this man who seemed to have grown thirty years younger! He related a
thousand anecdotes about his purchases and his prize catches, and again
and again, refusing all offers of aid, he got up and felt his way to the portfolios to fetch another picture. He was filled with a gay intoxication as if
from wine. And when I finally said that I must take my leave, he acted as
surly as a self-willed child and sulkily stamped his foot, saying that it was
out of the question, since I had seen scarcely half of the collection. The
women had all they could do to make him understand, in his stubborn ill-
humor, that he mustn't detain me longer or I would miss my train.

"When, after long and desperate resistance, he finally gave in, and it came
time to say farewell, his voice grew very gentle. He took both my hands,
and his fingers felt their way caressingly along them up to my wrists with
that expressiveness peculiar to blind people, as if they wanted to know more
of me and to convey more love than words can possibly do.

"'Your visit has made me so very, very happy,' he began, with an out-
pouring of emotion which I can never forget. 'It has been a real blessing to
be able at last, at long last, to look through my beloved pictures with a
connoisseur. But you shall see that you didn't come to visit this old blind
man in vain. I promise you here in front of my wife as a witness that I
shall put a clause in my will giving your old and tried firm the right to
conduct the auction of my collection. You shall have the honor of admin-
istering this unknown treasure'—and he placed his hand lovingly on the
plundered portfolios—'until the day when it is scattered into the world. Just
promise me that you will prepare a fine catalogue. That shall be my tomb-
stone; I need none better.'

"I looked at the wife and daughter. They held close to one another, and
from time to time a tremor ran from one to the other, as if they were a
single body quivering there in a unity of feeling. As for me, I was filled
with a feeling of solemnity on hearing this pathetically unsuspecting man
hand over into my keeping like a treasure his invisible collection which had
long since been scattered abroad like so much dust. Deeply moved, I

promised him what I could never fulfill. Again a gleam of light came into
the dead pupils of his eyes, and I sensed in him an inner longing which was
trying to grasp me bodily. I sensed it from the tender, loving pressure of the
fingers which were holding mine and sealing a solemn compact.

"The women accompanied me to the door. They did not dare to speak,
because his sensitive ears would have caught every word, but how warm
with tears, how filled with gratitude, were the glances which shone upon
me! I felt my way down the steps in a veritable stupor. Actually I felt
ashamed. I had come like an angel in a fairy-tale into a poor man's humble
dwelling, I had caused a blind man to see for an hour by abetting a pious
fraud and lying without shame, I who had come in truth as a shabby trades-
man to practice my cunning and relieve someone of a few valuable items.
Yet what I took away with me was worth much more: once more I had
been privileged to experience, in a period of insensibility and joylessness,
pure rapture incarnate, a sort of spiritually-illumined ecstasy directed solely
at art. And that is something which our people appear long since to have
forgotten. I was filled with—I do not know how else to say it—with reverence, yet at the same time I was ashamed without knowing exactly why.

"As I reached the street, I heard the rattling of a window from above and
heard a voice calling my name. Yes, it was he. The old man had insisted
on looking out with unseeing eyes in the direction where he judged me
to be. He was leaning out so far that the two women had to take the pre-
caution of holding him. He waved his handkerchief, and with the carefree,
blithe voice of a boy he called out: 'A good journey to you!' It was a sight
I shall not forget: the happy face of the gray-headed old man up there in
the window, hovering far above all the morose, harassed, officious people of
the streets, held gently aloft out of our unpleasant world of reality by the
white cloud of kindly illusion. And I couldn't help thinking again of those
wise, old words—I believe they are Goethe's—: 'Collectors are happy people.'"

FRANZ KAFKA

A Hunger-Artist 𝕐

Translated by M. L. Nielsen

In recent decades there has been a distinct falling-off in the interest
shown in hunger-artists. Whereas in earlier times one could stage
such exhibitions at one's own expense and be quite sure of success,
today such a thing is utterly impossible. Those were other times. In those
days the entire city occupied itself with the hunger-artist; the interest in him
grew from fast day to fast day; every one wanted to see the hunger-artist at
least once a day, and in the latter stages there were regular subscribers who
sat before the small latticed cage for days on end. On sunny days the cage
was carried out into the open, and on these occasions it was especially the
children to whom the hunger-artist was exhibited. But whereas for the adults
he was often no more than a source of amusement, of which they partook
only because it was the stylish thing to do, the children would gaze upon
him open-mouthed, holding one another by the hand for safety's sake, as
he sat there on his straw, scorning even so much as a chair, deathly pale,
dressed in black tights, his ribs protruding powerfully, sometimes nodding
politely and answering questions with a forced smile, even thrusting his arm
through the bars to let them feel his emaciation, then lapsing once more into
complete self-absorption and paying attention to no one, ignoring even the
striking of the clock which was the cage's sole decoration, looking straight
before him with eyes almost closed, and sipping occasionally from a tiny
glass of water to wet his lips.

Besides the spectators who merely came and went, there were also regular
guards chosen by the public—usually butchers, for some remarkable reason,
and always by threes—to whom was assigned the task of watching the
hunger-artist day and night, lest he might succeed after all in surreptitiously
partaking of nourishment. But that was no more than a formality, introduced to satisfy the masses, because the initiated were well aware that the
hunger-artist would never under any circumstances, not even under com-
pulsion, partake of any nourishment during the period of fasting. His honor
as an artist forbade such a thing. Of course not every guard could comprehend this. Sometimes there were groups of watchers who were very lax in
their guard duty, who would purposely sit down together in a distant corner

and absorb themselves in a game of cards with the obvious intention of allowing the hunger-artist a little refreshment which they seemed to believe he could produce from some secret supply. To the hunger-artist nothing was more painful than such guards; they filled him with unspeakable sadness; they made fasting terribly difficult for him. Sometimes he would overcome his weakness and sing during such a watch as this, sing as long as his strength held out, just to show the people how unjust were their suspicions. But it availed him little; in such cases they would simply marvel at the cleverness which enabled him to eat even while singing. Much more to his liking were the guards who sat down close to the cage, and not satisfied with the gloomy illumination of the hall, turned upon him the pocket torches with which they had been provided by the impresario. The bright light bothered him not at all. Sleep was impossible in any case, and he could always drowse a little, under any illumination and at any hour, even when the hall was noisy and overcrowded. He was only too willing to pass the night with such watchers entirely without sleep; he would put himself out to joke with them, to tell them tales of his wanderings or on the other hand to listen to their stories: anything to stay awake, to be able to show them again and again that he had nothing edible in his cage and that he was fasting as none of them could possibly do. But his happiest moment was when morning came and a sumptuous breakfast was brought to them at his expense, and he saw them fall upon it with the appetite of healthy men who had spent a tiresome night in wakeful watching. To be sure there were people who pretended to see in this breakfast an unseemly attempt to influence the guards, but that was going too far, and when they were asked whether they would be willing to take upon themselves the task of watching through the night for the sake of the thing itself and without the breakfast, they made a wry face, though they continued to harbor their suspicions just the same.

After all, this was simply one of the suspicions unavoidably connected with fasting. Obviously no one was in a position to spend every day and night as a watchman at the side of the hunger-artist, and no one could be sure from his own observation that the fasting was really uninterrupted and complete; only the hunger-artist himself could know that, and so only he who was the faster could be at the same time a completely satisfied spectator of his fasting. And yet for another reason he never was satisfied. Perhaps it wasn't fasting at all which made him so emaciated that some people to their great regret had to stay away because they couldn't bear the sight of him; perhaps his emaciation came solely from his dissatisfaction with himself. For the fact was that only he and no one else, not even the initiated, knew how easy a thing it was to fast. It was the easiest thing in the world. He didn't keep it a secret either, but no one would believe him. At best people said he was modest, but usually he was accused of being a publicity hound or even an out-and-out fraud for whom fasting was easy because he knew how to make it easy, and who had the cheek on top of that practically to admit as much. All this he was forced to accept, he had become accustomed to it in the course of years, but inside him was the constant gnawing of dissatisfaction.

And yet never, never once at the end of any hunger period—this all were forced to admit—had he left his cage willingly. The impresario had set forty days as the maximum period for fasting, beyond that he would never let the fasting go, not even in the great world centers—and for a very good reason. Experience had shown that for about forty days, through the use of gradually intensified publicity, the interest of a city could be brought to an ever higher pitch, but that at the end of that time public enthusiasm began to wane and a marked decrease in patronage became apparent. There were of course minor differences in this respect from city to city and country to country, but the rule was that forty days was the maximum time. And so on the fortieth day the door of the flower-bedecked cage was opened, an enthusiastic audience filled the amphitheater, a military band played, two doctors entered the cage to carry out the necessary measurements on the body of the hunger-artist, the results were announced to the hall through a megaphone, and finally there came two young ladies, happy in the knowledge that they and no one else had been chosen for the task, whose duty it was to lead the hunger-artist from his cage and down a few steps at the bottom of which stood a tiny table set with a carefully-chosen invalid's repast. And at this moment the hunger-artist invariably rebelled. He was willing enough to place his bony arms into the helping hands which the young ladies extended as they bent over him, but he didn't want to stand up. Why stop just now, at the end of forty days? He could have borne it much longer, immeasurably longer; why stop just now, at the point when his fasting was at its best—no, not even yet at its best. Why did they want to rob him of the honor of fasting on, of becoming not only the greatest hunger-artist of all time, which he probably was already, but of surpassing himself beyond measure, for he sensed that there was no limit to his capacity for fasting. Why did this throng, which pretended to marvel so at his feat, have so little patience with him? If he could bear to go on fasting, why could they not bear with him? Besides he was weary, his seat in the straw was comfortable, and now they wanted him to rouse himself, stand up, and go to the meal, the very thought of which induced in him a nausea which he was barely able to suppress out of respect for the women. And he looked into the eyes of the women who appeared so friendly but were in reality so cruel and wearily shook the head which was so much too heavy for the fragile neck. But now there happened the thing which always happened at this point. The impresario would come, and silently—for the music rendered speech impossible—he would raise his arms over the hunger-artist as if inviting heaven to look down upon its work here upon the straw, this pitiful martyr—and martyr the hunger-artist was, to be sure, though in an entirely different sense. Then he would grasp the hunger-artist about his frail waist, trying as he did to make it obvious by his exaggerated caution with what a fragile object he was dealing, and, after surreptitiously shaking him a little and causing his legs to wobble and his body to sway uncontrollably, would turn him over to the ladies, who had meanwhile turned as pale as death. Now the hunger-artist offered no further resistance. His head lay on his chest, as if it had rolled there and somehow inexplicably stuck fast; his torso was cavernous; his legs, impelled by the urge to self-preservation, were pressed tightly together at the knees, and yet his feet scraped the earth as if it were not real, as if they were seeking the real one. And the entire weight of his body, light though it was, rested upon one of the ladies, who, breathless and looking about imploringly for help (she had not pictured this post of honor thus), first tried to avoid contact with the hunger-artist by stretching her neck as far as possible, and then—since this availed her nothing and her more fortunate companion did nothing to help her, but simply contented herself with carrying the hand of the hunger-artist, a mere bundle of bones, in her own trembling hand— she broke into tears to the accompaniment of delighted laughter from the audience, and had to be relieved at her post by an attendant who had long been held in readiness. Then came the meal, a little of which the impresario managed to force down the half-unconscious hunger-artist, the while he chattered amiably to divert attention from his condition; then a toast was spoken to the public, which the impresario pretended had been whispered to him by the hunger-artist; the orchestra provided a mighty climax with a flourish of trumpets; the crowd broke up, and no one had the right to be dissatisfied with what he had seen, no one but the hunger-artist, always only he.

And so it went on for many years, with only brief intervals of recuperation. He lived in apparent glory, honored by the world, but for the most part filled with a gloomy melancholy which was deepened by the fact that no one understood it. And indeed what comfort could one offer him? What else could he wish for? And when sometimes a good-natured person appeared who felt sorry for him and tried to explain to him that his sadness was caused by the lack of food, it was quite likely—especially if the fasting period was far advanced—that the hunger-artist would answer by flying into a rage and terrifying all those around him by shaking the bars of his cage like a wild animal. But for such outbreaks the impresario had a method of punishment which he was very fond of employing. He would apologize to the assembled public on behalf of the hunger-artist and admit that his conduct could be pardoned only by understanding the irritability caused by fasting, an irritability which would be less easy to understand in a well-fed person; then he would lead logically to the equally understandable claim of the hunger-artist that he could fast much longer, and would praise the lofty endeavor, worthy determination and great self-denial which were evidenced by this claim. But then he would attempt to refute this claim simply by passing around photographs—which at the same time were offered for sale—in which one could see the hunger-artist on the fortieth day of fasting, lying in bed and so weak that he was on the point of expiring. This perversion of the truth, so well known to the hunger-artist, and yet so unnerving when applied, was more than he could bear. That which was the effect of the premature ending of the fasting was here being set forth as its cause! Against this lack of understanding, this universal lack of understanding, it was impossible to fight. Each time he would stand at the bars and listen eagerly to what the impresario was saying, but always when the photographs were brought forth he would relax his hold on the bars and sink back onto the straw, and once more the reassured public could come near and view him undisturbed.

When the witnesses of such scenes thought back on them a few years later, they found it hard to understand themselves. For meanwhile the aforementioned transformation had taken place. Perhaps there were deep-lying reasons for it; but who was interested in seeking them out? At any rate, the pampered hunger-artist one day found himself abandoned by the pleasure-seeking multitude, which preferred to flock to other spectacles. Once again the impresario raced through half of Europe with him to see whether the old interest would not here and there manifest itself. But in vain; as if by some secret agreement a genuine dislike for fasting exhibitions had everywhere developed. In reality of course it couldn't have come as suddenly as all that, and now one tardily remembered certain warning signs which at the time, in the intoxication of success, had not been sufficiently heeded or sufficiently combatted—but it was too late now to do anything about it. To be sure it was certain that one day the time for fasting would come again, but for the living that was no comfort. What was the hunger-artist to do now?—He whom thousands had acclaimed couldn't put himself on display in the exhibition booths at small annual fairs, and for going into some other profession he was not only too old but above all too fanatically devoted to fasting. And so he dismissed the impresario, the companion of a brilliant carrier, and hired himself out to a great circus. In order to spare his feelings, he did not even examine the terms of his contract.

A great circus with its huge throng of contrasting yet complementary men and animals and its masses of equipment can always find a place for another attraction, even a hunger-artist—that is, if his claims are modest enough. But in this case it was not only the hunger-artist who was engaged, but also his old and well-known name itself. Indeed it wasn't even possible to say, in view of the peculiar nature of this art which showed no flagging with increasing age, that a superannuated artist no longer at the height of his powers had taken refuge in a quiet position with a circus. On the contrary:

the hunger-artist gave assurance that he could fast as well as he ever could —a thoroughly credible claim—indeed, he even maintained that, if allowed to go his own way (a privilege immediately granted to him), he would only now for the first time set the world in justifiable astonishment, a claim which, in view of the temper of times, forgotten by the hunger-artist in his zeal, evinced no more than a smile from those who were in the know.

Actually, however, even the hunger-artist did not lose sight of the true state of affairs, and he was not at all surprised when he saw that his cage was stationed not in the middle of the circus as a feature attraction but out in the vicinity of the stables, a place which in its own way certainly was accessible enough. Large, gaily-colored signs surrounded the cage and proclaimed what was to be seen there. During the intermissions in the performances, when the crowds thronged to the stables to see the animals, it was almost unavoidable that they should pass by the hunger-artist and pause there for a little. Perhaps they would have stayed there longer had it not been for the fact that the people who were pushing impatiently from the rear in the narrow alley way, not understanding the reason for the delay on the way to the eagerly-awaited barns, made a longer and more leisurely view impossible. This explained too why the hunger-artist, though longing impatiently for these visits, which he naturally saw as his reason for existence, couldn't help feeling at the same time a certain apprehension. At first he could scarcely wait for the intermissions; he would note the approach of the throng with charmed anticipation; but only too soon he became convinced of the fact that again and again, without exception, they were on their way to the stables, and his experience in this matter overcame even the most stubborn, almost conscious self-deception. And this view of the throng from a distance continued to be the most agreeable one. For once they had reached his cage, he was immediately submerged in a sea of shouting, cursing people who formed ever-changing groups, one made up of those who wanted to view him at their leisure—not because they had any understanding for him, but simply impelled by a whim or out of sheer willfulness (and these soon became for the hunger-artist the more unpleasant)—and the other consisting of those who were bent on getting immediately to the stalls. Once the great crowd had passed by, there would come the stragglers, and these of course, for whom there was no obstacle to stopping had they only felt the desire, strode by with hurried steps in order not to be late at the barns. And it was no more than a fortunate but infrequent stroke of luck when the father of a family would come by with his children, point to the hunger-artist, and explain in detail what it was all about; and he would tell about earlier times when he had been present at similar but incomparably finer exhibitions. But naturally the children, on account of inadequate preparation in the schools and in life, always remained without any understanding. What did fasting mean to them? And yet in the sparkling of their penetrating eyes they gave a hint of new and more merciful days to come. Perhaps, the hunger-artist would say to himself on such occasions, everything would be better if his station were not quite so close to the barns. It made the choice too easy for the people, to say nothing of the fact that the evil odors from the stalls, the restlessness of the animals at night, the sight of pieces of raw meat for the beasts of prey being carried by, and the screams of the animals at feeding time offended him and kept him in a constant state of depression. But he didn't venture to complain to the management; after all he owed to the animals the fact that he had so many visitors, among whom there might be now and then one destined for him. And who knew to what spot they might banish him if he reminded them of his existence, and of the fact that, when seen aright, he served only as a hindrance on the way to the barns.

A minor hindrance, to be sure, and one that was constantly growing smaller. People came to take for granted the novelty of having anyone demand attention for a hunger-artist in modern times, and this taking-for-granted spelled his doom. Let him fast with all the skill of which he was capable—and he did—but nothing could save him now, people simply passed him by. Just try to explain the art of fasting to some one! He who has no feeling for it simply cannot comprehend it. The beautiful signs grew dirty and illegible; they were torn down, and it occurred to no one to replace them. The little board showing the number of days of fasting achieved, which at first had been conscientiously changed, had remained the same for weeks on end, for the attendants had grown weary even of this little task. And so the hunger-artist fasted on without hindrance, as he had once dreamed of doing, and was able to do it without difficulty, just as he had once predicted, but no one counted the days; no one, not even the hunger-artist himself, knew how great his achievement actually was, and his heart grew heavy. And if on occasion some idler stopped, ridiculed the old numbers on the board, and spoke of fraud, it was the most stupid lie which indifference and inborn malice could possibly invent, because it was not the hunger-artist who was cheating, he was doing his duty honorably, but the world was cheating him of his reward.

And yet more days passed, but that too had its end. Once one of the managers happened to notice the cage, and he asked the attendants why such a good serviceable cage with its putrid straw should be left standing unused. No one could say, until one of them, with the help of the numbered board, remembered the hunger-artist. The straw was probed with poles, and inside they found the hunger-artist. "You're still fasting?" asked the manager. "When in heaven's name will you be done?" "Forgive me, all of you," whispered the hunger-artist. "Certainly," said the manager, and he pointed to his head with his finger to indicate the hunger-artist's condition to the attendants, "we forgive you." "I always wanted you to admire my fasting," said the hunger-artist. "And we do admire it," replied the manager obligingly. "But you shouldn't admire it," said the hunger-artist. "Well, then, we don't admire it," said the manager, "and why shouldn't we admire it?" "Because I have to fast, I can't help myself," said the hunger-artist. "Just listen to that," said the manager, "and why can't you help yourself?" "Because," said the hunger-artist, and he lifted his dainty head a little, and, thrusting his lips forward as if for a kiss, spoke directly into the manager's ear so that no word would be lost, "because I could find no food to my liking. If I had found it, believe me, I should have caused no stir, I should have eaten my fill just as you do, and all others." Those were his last words, but in his glazed eyes there remained the firm, though no longer proud, conviction that he was still fasting.

"Well, now clean things up!" said the manager, and they buried the hunger-artist together with the straw. And into the cage they put a young panther. It was perceptibly refreshing even to the dullest temperament to see this wild animal hurl itself about in this cage which so long had been desolate. He lacked for nothing. Without any delay the keepers brought him just the kind of food he craved. And he appeared not even to miss his freedom. This noble body, healthy to the point of bursting, seemed in fact to carry its own freedom around with it (a freedom which appeared to reside somewhere in the region of its teeth); and its joy in living issued forth from its throat with such fierceness that it wasn't easy for those who watched it to stand firm. But they overcame their hesitation, crowded about the cage, and just couldn't tear themselves away.

LIONEL TRILLING

The Other Margaret ❧

Mark Jennings stood the picture up on the wide counter and he
and Stephen Elwin stepped back and looked at it. It was one of
Rouault's kings. A person looking at it for the first time might
find it repellent, even brutal or cruel. It was full of rude blacks that might
seem barbarically untidy.

But the two men knew the picture well. They looked at it in silence.
The admiration they were sharing made a community between them which
at their age was rare, for they had both passed forty. Jennings waited for
Elwin to speak first—they were friends but Elwin was the customer. Besides,
the frame had been designed by Jennings and in buying a reproduced picture
the frame is of great importance, accounting for more than half the cost.
Elwin had bought the picture some weeks before but he was seeing it
framed for the first time.

Elwin said, "The frame is very good, Mark. It's perfect." He was a
rather tall man with an attractive, competent face. He touched the frame
curiously with the tip of his forefinger.

Jennings replied in a judicious tone, as if it were not his own good taste
but that of a very gifted apprentice of his. "*I* think so," he said. And he too
touched the frame, but intimately, rubbing briskly up and down one mould-
ing with an artisan's possessive thumb, putting an unneeded last touch. He
explained what considerations of color and proportion made the frame right
for the picture. He spoke as if these were simple rules anyone might find
in a book.

The king, blackbearded and crowned, faced in profile to the left. He had
a fierce quality that had modulated, but not softened, to authority. One
could feel of him—it was the reason why Elwin had bought the picture—that
he had passed beyond ordinary matters of personality and was worthy of the
crown he was wearing. Yet he was human and tragic. He was not unlike the
sculptured kings of Chartres. In his right hand he held a spray of flowers.

"Is he a favorite of yours?" Elwin said. He did not know whether he
meant the king or the king's painter. Indeed, as he asked the question, it
seemed to him that he had assumed that the painter was this archaic personage himself. He had never imagined the painter painting the canvas with
a brush. It was the beginning of a new thought about the picture.

Jennings answered with a modified version of the Latin gesture of esteem, a single decisive shake of his lifted hand, thumb and forefinger touching in a circle.

Elwin acknowledged the answer with a nod but said nothing. He did not want Jennings' admiration, even though he had asked for it. Jennings would naturally give as much admiration to most of the fine pictures in fine reproduction with which his shop was filled. At that moment, Elwin was not interested in admiration or in art. But he liked what Jennings said next.

"It will give you a lot of satisfaction," Jennings said. It was exactly as if he had just sold Elwin a suit or a pair of shoes.

Elwin said, "Yes," a little hesitatingly, only politely agreeing, not committing himself in the matter of his money's worth until it should be proved.

From behind the partition that made Jennings' little office they had been hearing a man talking on the telephone. Now the conversation ended and a young soldier, a second lieutenant, came out into the shop. Jennings said to him, "Did the call get through?" and the young man said, "Oh yes, after some difficulty. It was eighty-five cents. Let me pay you for it." "Oh nonsense," said Jennings, and took him by the arm and quickly introduced him to Elwin as a cousin of his wife's. The young man offered Elwin the hand that had been reaching into his pocket and said, "I'm glad to meet you, sir."

He said it very nicely, with the niceness that new young officers are likely to have. Pleased with themselves, they are certain that everyone will be nice to them. This young man's gold bar did a good deal for him, did perhaps more than rank ought to have to do for a man. He was not really much of a person. Yet Elwin, meeting him, felt the familiar emotion in which he could not distinguish guilt from envy. He knew it well, knew how to control it and it did not diminish, not much, the sense of holiday he was having. The holiday was made by his leaving his office a little early. He published scientific books in a small but successful way and the war had made a great pressure of work for him, but he had left his office early when Jennings phoned that the picture was back from the framer's.

The young lieutenant was looking at the picture. He so clearly did not like it that Jennings said quickly, "Mr. Elwin's just bought it."

The lieutenant regarded the picture thoughtfully. "Very nice," he said, with an enthusiastic and insincere shake of his head. He did not want to spoil things for Jennings by undermining the confidence of the customer. Elwin looked from the king to the lieutenant and back to the king. It was perfectly polite, only as if he had looked at the young man to hear his opinion more clearly and then had examined again the thing they were talking about

But Jennings understood the movement of Elwin's glance, for when the lieutenant had shaken hands and left the shop, Jennings said stoutly, "He's a good kid."

"Yes he is," Elwin said serenely.

"It's funny seeing him an officer. He used to be against anything like that. But he was glad to go—he said he did not want to miss sharing the experience of his generation."

"A lot of them say that." Elwin had heard it often from the young men, the clever ones. Someone had started it and all the young men with the semi-political views said it. Their reasons for saying it were various. Elwin liked some of the reasons and disliked others, but whether he liked the reasons or not, he never heard the phrase without a twinge of envy. Now it comforted him to think that this man with the black beard and the flower had done his fighting without any remarks about experience and generations.

The idea of age and death did not present itself to Elwin in any horrifying way. It had first come to him in the form of a sentence from one of Hazlitt's essays. The sentence was, "No young man believes he shall ever die," and the words had come to him suddenly from the past, part of an elaborate recollection of a scene at high-school. When he looked up the quotation, he found that he had remembered it with perfect accuracy, down to that very *shall* which struck his modern ear as odd and even ungrammatical. The memory had begun with the winter sunlight coming through the dirty windows of the classroom. Then there was the color, texture and smell of varnished wood. But these details were only pointing to the teacher himself, and what he was saying. He was a Mr. Baxter, a heron-like man, esteemed as brilliant and eccentric, what some students called "a real person." Suddenly Mr. Baxter in a loud voice had uttered that sentence of Hazlitt's. He held the book in his hand but did not read from it. "No young man believes he shall ever die," he said, just as if he had thought of it himself.

It had been very startling to hear him say that, and this effect was of course just what the teacher wanted. It was the opening sentence of an essay called "On the Feeling of Immortality in Youth," and to Baxter it was important that the class should see what a bold and captivating way it was to begin an essay, how it was exactly as if someone had suddenly said the words, not written them after thought.

The chalky familiar classroom had been glorified by this moment of Mr. Baxter. So many things had been said in the room, but here was one thing that had been said which was true. It was true in two ways. For Mr. Baxter it was true that no *young* man believes he shall ever die, but Mr. Baxter was not exactly a young man. For Stephen Elwin it was true that he would never die—he was scarcely even a young man yet, still only a boy. Between the student and the teacher the great difference was that the student would never die. Stephen Elwin had pitied Mr. Baxter and had been proud of himself. And mixed with the boy's feeling of immortality was a boy's pleasure at being involved with ideas which were not only solemn but complicated, for Mr. Baxter's mortality should have denied, but actually did not deny, the immortality that Stephen felt.

The Hazlitt sentence, once it had been remembered, had not left Elwin.

Every now and then, sometimes just as he was falling asleep, sometimes just as he was waking up, sometimes right in the middle of anything at all, the sentence and the full awareness of what it meant would come to him. It felt like an internal explosion. It was not, however, an explosion of force but rather an explosion of light. It was not without pain but it was not wholly painful.

With the picture neatly wrapped in heavy brown paper, Elwin walked down Madison Avenue. It was still early. On a sudden impulse he walked west at 6oth Street. Usually he came home by taxi, but this evening he thought of the Fifth Avenue bus, for some reason remembering that it was officially called a "coach" and that his father had spoken of it so, and had sometimes even referred to it as a "stage." The "coach" that he signaled was of the old kind, open wooden deck, platform at the rear, stairs connecting platform and deck with a big architectural.curve. He saw it with surprise and affection. He had supposed that this model of bus had long been out of service and as he hailed it his mind sought for and found a word long unused. "DeDion," he said, pleased at having found it. "DeDion Bouton."

He pronounced it *Deedeeon,* the way he and his friends had said it in 1917 when they had discussed the fine and powerful motors from Europe that were then being used for the buses. Some of them had been Fiats, but the most powerful of all were said to be the DeDions from France. No one knew the authority for this superlative judgment, but boys finding a pleasure in firm opinions did not care. Elwin remembered the special note in his friends' voices as they spoke of the DeDions. They talked about the great Mediterranean motors with a respect that was not only technical but historical. There had never been more than a few of the DeDions in America. Even in 1917 they were no longer being imported and the boys thought of them as old and rare.

Elwin took his seat inside the bus, at the rear. As suddenly as the name DeDion, it came to him how the open deck had once been a deck indeed—how, as sometimes the only passenger braving the weather up there, he had been the captain of the adventure, facing into the cold wind, even into the snow or rain, stoic, assailed but unmoved by the elements, inhaling health, fortitude and growth, for he had a boy's certainty that the more he endured, the stronger he would become. And when he had learned to board the bus and alight from it while it was still moving—"board" and "alight" were words the company used in its notices—how far advanced in life he had felt. So many landmarks of Elwin's boyhood in the city had vanished but this shabby bus had endured since the days when it had taken him daily to school.

At 82nd Street the bus stopped for a red light. A boy stood at the curb near the iron stanchion that bore the bus-stop sign. He clutched something in his hand. It must have been a coin, for he said to the conductor, "Mister, how much does it cost to ride on this bus?"

Elwin could not be sure of the boy's age, but he was perhaps twelve, Elwin's own age when he had been touched by his friends' elegiac discussions of the DeDions. The boy was not alone, he had a friend with him, and to see this friend, clearly a follower, was to understand the quality of the chief. The subaltern was a boy like any other, but the face of his leader was alight with the power of mind and a great urgency. Perhaps he was only late and in a hurry, but in any case the urgency illuminated his remarkable face.

The conductor did not answer the question.

"Mister," the boy said again, "how much does it cost to ride on this bus?"

His friend stood by, sharing passively in the question but saying nothing. They did not dare "board" until they knew whether or not their resources were sufficient.

The boy was dressed sturdily enough, perhaps for a boy of his age he was even well dressed. But he had been on the town or in the park most of the afternoon, or perhaps he had been one of those boys who, half in awe, half in rowdy levity, troop incessantly through the Egyptian rooms of the Museum, repeatedly entering and emerging from and entering again the narrow slits of the grave vaults. His knickerbockers were sliding at the knees and his effort to control a drop at his nose further compromised but by no means destroyed his dignity. He had the clear cheeks and well-shaped head of a carefully reared child, but he seemed too far from home at this hour quite to be the child of very careful parents. There was an air about him which suggested that he had learned to expect at least a little resistance from the world and that he was ready to meet it.

The conductor did not reply to the second question. He had taken a large black wallet of imitation leather from some cranny of the rear platform and was making marks with a pencil on the cardboard trip-sheet it contained. He was an old man.

"Mister," said the boy again, and his voice, though tense, was reasonable. It was the very spirit of reasonableness. "Mister, how much does it cost to ride on this bus? A nickel or a dime?"

The conductor elaborately lifted his eyes from his record. He looked at the boy not hostilely nor yet quite facetiously, but with a certain quiet air of settled satisfaction. "What do you want to know for?" he said.

Elwin wanted to lower the window to tell the boy it was a dime. But he had waited too long. The conductor put his hand on the bell-button and gave the driver the signal. The light changed and the bus began to move.

"Mister!" the boy shouted. He may have been late to his supper but it was not this urgency that made his voice go up so loud and high. "For God's sake, mister!"

He of course did not bring in God by way of appeal. There was no longer any hope of his getting an answer. It was rather an expostulation with the unreasonable, the most passionate thing imaginable. Elwin looked back and saw the boy's hatred still following the conductor and, naturally, not only the conductor but the whole bus.

The conductor had now the modest look of a person who has just delivered a rebuke which was not only deserved but witty.

Well, Elwin thought, he is an old man and his pride is somewhere involved. Perhaps it was only that he could not at the moment bring himself to answer a question.

But he believed that in the past it could not have happened. When he was a boy the conductor might have said, "What do you want to know for?"—boys must always be teased a little by men. But the teasing would have stopped in time for him to board the bus. The bus was peculiarly safe. The people who rode in it and paid a dime after they had taken their seats were known to be nicer than the people who rode in the subway for a nickel which they paid before admission. It was the first public conveyance to which "nervous" parents entrusted their children—the conductors were known for their almost paternal kindness. For example, if you found on your trip to school that you had forgotten your money, the conductor would not fail to quiet the fear of authority that clutched your guilty heart. But this old man had outlived his fatherhood, which had once extended to all the bus-world of children. His own sons and daughters by now would have grown and gone and given him the usual causes for bitterness.

The old man's foolish triumph was something that must be understood. Elwin tried to know the weariness and sense of final loss that moved the old conductor to stand on that small dignity of his. He at once brought into consideration the conditions of life of the old man, especially the lack of all the advantages that he himself had had—the gentle rearing and the good education that made a man like Stephen Elwin answerable for all his actions. It had long been the habit of Elwin's mind to raise considerations of just this sort whenever he had reason to be annoyed with anyone who was not more powerful than himself.

But now, strangely, although the habit was in force, it did not check his anger. It was bewildering that he should feel anger at a poor ignorant man, a working man. It was the first time in his life that he had ever felt so. It shamed him. And he was the more bewildered and ashamed when he understood, as he did, that he was just as angry at the boy as at the old man. He was seeing the boy full grown and the self-pity and hatred taking root beside the urgency and power. The conductor and the boy were links in the great chain of the world's rage.

Clearly it was an unreasoning thing to feel. It was not what a wise man would feel. At this time in his life Stephen Elwin had the wish to be wise. He had never known a wise man. The very word sounded like something in a tale read to children. But the occasion for courage had passed. By courage Elwin meant something very simple, an unbending resistance of spirit under extreme physical difficulties. It was a boy's notion, but it had stayed with Elwin through most of his life, through his business and his pleasure, and nothing that he had ever done had given him the proof that he wanted. And now that the chance for that was gone—he was forty-one years old—it seemed to him that perhaps to be wise was almost as manly a thing as to be brave.

Two wars had passed Elwin by. For one he was too young, for the other too old, though by no means, of course, old. Had it not been for the war, and the consideration of age it so ruthlessly raised, the recollection of the sentence from Hazlitt would no doubt have been delayed by several years, and so too would the impulse to which it had given rise, the desire to have "wisdom." More and more in the last few months, Elwin had been able to experience the sensation of being wise, for it was indeed a sensation, a feeling of stamina, poise and illumination.

He was puzzled and unhappy as he "alighted" from the bus at 92nd Street. It seemed to him a great failure that his knowledge of death and his having reached the years of wisdom—they were the same thing—had not prevented him from feeling anger at an old man and a boy. It then occurred to him to think that perhaps he had felt his anger not in despite of wisdom but because of it. It was a disturbing, even a horrifying, fancy. Yet as he walked the two blocks to his home, he could not help recurring to it, with what was, as he had to see, a certain gratification.

In his pleasant living-room, in his comfortable chair, Stephen Elwin watched his daughter as she mixed the drink he usually had before dinner. She was thirteen. About a month ago she had made this her job, almost her duty, and she performed it with an unspeakable seriousness. She measured out the whiskey and poured it into the tumbler. With the ice-tongs she reached the ice gently into the bottom of the glass so that there would not be the least splash of whiskey. She opened the bottle of soda. Holding up the glass for her father's inspection, she poured the soda slowly, ready to stop at her father's word. Elwin cried "Whoa!" and at the word he thought that his daughter had reached the stage of her growth where she did indeed look like a well-bred pony.

Now Margaret was searching for the stirring-spoon. But she had forgotten to put it on the tray with all the other paraphernalia and she gave a little cry of vexation and went to fetch it. Elwin did not tell her not to bother, that it did not matter if the drink was not stirred. He understood that this business had to proceed with a ceremonial completeness.

Margaret returned with the stirring-spoon. She stirred the highball and the soda foamed up. She waited until it subsided, meanwhile shaking the spoon dry over the glass with three precise little shakes. She handed her father the drink and put a coaster on the table by his chair. She watched while he took his first sip. He had taken the whole responsibility for the proportion of soda to whiskey. Still, she wanted to be told that she had made the drink just right. Elwin said, "Fine. Just right," and Margaret tried not to show the absurd pleasure she felt.

For this ritual of Margaret there were, as Elwin guessed, several motives. The honor of her home required that her father not make his own highball in the pantry and bring it out to drink in his chair, not after she had begun to take notice that in the homes of some of her schoolmates, every evening and not only at dinner-parties, a servant brought in, quite as a matter of course, a large tray of drinking equipment. But Margaret had other reasons than snobbishness—Elwin thought that she needed to establish a "custom," not only for now but for the future, against the time when she could say to her children, "And every night before dinner it was the *custom* in our family for me to make my father a drink." He supposed that this ritual of the drink was Margaret's first traffic with the future. It seemed to him that to know a thing like this about his daughter was one of the products of what could be called wisdom and he thought with irony but also with pleasure of his becoming a dim but necessary figure in Margaret's story of the past.

"I bought a picture today," Elwin said.

Margaret cocked an eye at him, as if to say, "Are you on the loose again?" She said, "What is it? Did you bring it home?"

"Oh, just a reproduction, a Rouault."

"Rouault?" she said. She shook her head decisively. "Don't know him." It quite settled Rouault for the moment.

"Don't know him?"

"Never heard of him."

"Well, take a look at it—it's over there."

She untied the string and took off the paper and sat there on the big hassock, her feet far out in front of her, holding the great king at arm's length. It was to Elwin strange and funny, this confrontation of the black, calm, tragic king and this blonde child in her sweater and skirt, in her moccasin shoes. She became abstracted and withdrawn in her scrutiny of the picture. Then Elwin, seeing the breadth and brightness of her brow, the steady intelligence of her gaze, understood that there was really no comic disproportion. What was funny was the equality. The young lieutenant had been quite neutralized by the picture. Even Mark Jennings had been a little diminished by it. But Margaret, with her grave, luminous brow, was able to meet it head on. And not in agreement either.

"You don't like it?" Elwin said.

She looked from the picture to him and said, "I don't think so."

She said it softly but it was pretty positive. She herself painted and she was in a very simple relation to pictures. She rose and placed the picture on the sofa as if to give it another chance in a different position and a better light. She stood at a distance and looked at it and Elwin stood behind her to get the same view of it that she had. He put his hand on her shoulder. After a moment she looked up at him and smiled. "I don't really *like* it," she said. The modulation of her voice was not apology, but simply a gesture of making room for another opinion. She did not think it was important whether she liked or disliked the picture. It said something to her that was not in her experience or that she did not want in her experience. Liking the picture would have given her pleasure. She got no pleasure from not liking it. It seemed to Elwin that in the little shake of her head, in her tone and smile, there was a quality, really monumental, by which he could explain his anger at the old conductor and the boy and forgive himself for having had it.

When Lucy Elwin came in, her face was flushed from the stove and she had a look of triumphant anticipation. She shamelessly communicated this to her family. "It's going to be ve-ry good," she said, not as if she were promising them a fine dinner, rather as if she were threatening them with a grim fate. She meant that her dinner was going to be so very good that if they did not extravagantly admire it, if they merely took it for granted, they would be made to feel sorry. "It will be ready in about ten minutes," she said. "Are you very hungry?"

"Just enough," Elwin said. "Are you tired?" For his wife had stretched out in the armchair and put back her head. She slouched with her long legs at full length, her skirt a little disordered, one ankle laid on the other. Her eyes being closed made her complicated face look simple and she seemed young and self-indulgent, like a girl who escapes from the embarrassment of herself into a broody trance. It was an attitude that had lately become frequent with Margaret.

Lucy Elwin said, "Yes, a little tired. But really, you know, I'd almost rather do the work myself than have that Margaret around."

She spoke with her eyes still closed, and so she did not see her daughter stiffen. But Elwin did. He knew that it was not because Margaret thought that her mother meant her but because of the feelings she had for the other Margaret, the maid. The other Margaret, as so often, had not come to work that day.

Margaret had mixed a drink for her mother and now she was standing beside Lucy's chair, waiting with exaggerated patience for Lucy to open her eyes. She said, "Here's your drink, mother!"

She said it as if she had waited quite long enough, using the lumpish, martyred, unsuccessful irony of thirteen, her eyebrows very weary, the expression of her mouth very dry. Lucy opened her eyes and sat up straight in her chair. She took the drink from Margaret and smiled. "Thank you, dear," she said. For the moment it was as if Margaret were the mother, full of rectitude and manners, and Lucy the careless daughter.

That Lucy was being careless even her husband felt. No one could say of their Negro maid, the other Margaret, that she was a pleasant person. Even Elwin would have to admit to a sense of strain in her presence. But surely Lucy took too passionate a notice of her. Elwin felt that this was not in keeping with his wife's nature. But no, that was really not so. It was often disquieting to Elwin, the willingness that Lucy had to get angry even with simple people when she thought they were not behaving well. And lately she had been full of stories about the nasty and insulted temper that was being shown by the people one daily dealt with. Only yesterday, for example, there had been her story of the soda-fountain man who made a point of mopping and puttering and changing the position of pieces of pie and only after he had shown his indifference and independence would take your order. Elwin had to balance against the notice his wife took of such things the deep, literal, almost childish way she spoke of them, the innocence of her passion. But this particular story of the soda-fountain clerk had really distressed him, actually embarrassing him for Lucy, and he had pointed out to her how frequent such stories had become. She had simply stared at him, the fact was so very clear. "Why, it's the war," she said. "People are just much meaner since the war." And when his rebuke had moved on to the matter of the maid Margaret, Lucy had said in the most matter-of-fact way, "Why, she just hates us." And she had shocked Elwin by giving, just like any middle-class housewife, a list of all the precious things Margaret had broken. "And observe," Lucy had said, "that never once has she broken anything cheap or ordinary, only the things I've pointed out to her that needed care."

Elwin had to admit that the list made a case. Still, even if the number of the green Wedgwood coffee cups had been much diminished, cups for which Elwin himself had a special fondness, and even if the Persian bowl had been dropped and the glass urn they had brought from Sweden had been cracked in the sink, they must surely not talk of such things. The very costliness of the objects which proved Margaret's animosity, the very affection which the Elwins felt for them, made the whole situation impossible to consider.

Lucy must indeed have been unaware of how deeply her husband resisted her carelessness in these matters and of what her daughter was now feeling. Otherwise she would not have begun her story, her eyes narrowing in anger at the recollection, "Oh, such a rotten thing happened on the way home on the bus."

It was Elwin who had had the thing happen on the bus, not quite "rotten" but sufficiently disturbing, and he was startled, as if his wife's consciousness had in some way become mixed up with his own in a clairvoyant experience. And this feeling was not diminished as Lucy told her story about a young woman who had asked the conductor a question. It was a simple, ordinary question, Lucy said, about what street one transferred at. The conductor at first had not answered, and then, when he came around again and the question was as'₍d again, he had looked at the young woman—"looked her straight in the face," Lucy said—and had replied in a loud voice, "Vot deed you shay?"

"*Mother!*" cried Margaret. Her voice was all absolute childish horror.

Elwin at once saw what was happening, but Lucy, absorbed in what she had experienced, only said mildly, "What's the matter, dear?"

"Mother!" Margaret grieved, "you mustn't do that." Her face was quite aghast and she was standing stiff with actual fright.

"Why, do what, Margaret?" said Lucy. She was troubled for her daughter but entirely bewildered.

"Make fun of—fun of—" But Margaret could not say it.

"Of Jews?" said Elwin in a loud, firm, downright voice.

Margaret nodded miserably. Elwin said with enough sharpness, "Margaret, whatever makes you think that Lucy is making fun of Jews? She is simply repeating——"

"Oh," Margaret cried, her face a silly little moon of gratitude and relief. "Oh," she said happily, "what the woman said to the conductor!"

"No, Margaret. How absurd!" Lucy cried. "*Not* what the woman said to the conductor. What the conductor said to the woman."

Margaret just sat there glowering with silence and anger.

Elwin said to Margaret with a pedagogic clearness and patience, "The conductor was making fun of the woman for being Jewish."

"Not at all," Lucy said, beginning to be a little tried by so much misunderstanding. "Not at all, she wasn't Jewish at all. He was insulting her by pretending that she was Jewish."

Margaret had only one question to ask. "The *conductor?*" she cried with desperate emphasis.

And when Lucy said that it was indeed the conductor, Margaret said nothing, but shrugged her shoulders in an elaborate way and made with her hands a large grimace of despairing incomprehension. She was dismissing the grownups by this pantomime, appealing beyond all their sad nonsense to her own world of sure right reason. In that world one knew where one was, one knew that to say things about Jews was bad and that working men were good. And *therefore.*

Elwin, whose awareness was all aroused, wondered in tender amusement what his daughter would have felt if she had known that her gesture, which she had drawn from the large available stock of the folk-culture of children, had originally been a satiric mimicry of a puzzled shrugging Jew. The Margaret who stood there in sullenness was so very different from the Margaret who, only a few minutes before, had looked at the picture with him and had seemed, almost, to be teaching him something. Now he had to teach her. "That isn't a very pretty gesture," he said. "And what, please, is so difficult about Lucy's story? Don't you believe it?"

A mistake, as he saw at once. Margaret was standing there trapped—no, she did not believe it, but she did not dare say so. Elwin corrected himself and gave her her chance. "Do you think Lucy didn't hear right?"

Margaret nodded eagerly, humbly glad to take the way out that was being offered her.

"We studied the transit system," she said by way of explanation. "We made a study of it." She stopped. Elwin knew how her argument ran, but she herself was not entirely sure of it. She said tentatively, by way of a beginning, "They are underpaid."

Lucy was being really irresponsible, Elwin thought, for she said in an abstracted tone, as if she were musing on the early clues of an interesting scientific generalization, "They hate *women*—it's women they're always rude to. Never the men." Margaret's face flushed, and her eyes darkened at this new expression of her mother's moral obtuseness, and Elwin felt a quick impatience with his daughter's sensitivity—it seemed suddenly to have taken on a pedantic air. But he was annoyed with Lucy too, who ought surely be more aware of what her daughter was feeling. No doubt he was the more annoyed because his own incident of the bus was untold and would remain untold. But it was Lucy who saved the situation she had created. She suddenly remembered the kitchen. She hurried out, then came back, caught Margaret by the arm in a bustle of haste and said, "Come and hurl the salad." This was a famous new joke in the family. Elwin had made it, Margaret loved it. It had reference to a "tossed green salad" on a pretentious restaurant menu. Of the salad, when it was served to them in all its wiltedness, Elwin had said that apparently it needed to be more than tossed, it needed to be hurled.

And so all at once the family was restored, a family with a family joke. Margaret stood there grinning in the embarrassment of the voluptuous pleasure she felt at happiness returned. But she must have been very angry with her mother, for she came back and pulled Elwin's head down and whispered into his ear where he would be able to find and inspect the presents she had for Lucy's birthday next week.

He was to look for two things. In the top left-hand drawer of Margaret's desk he would find the "bought present" and on the shelf in the clothes closet he would find the "made present." The bought present was a wallet, a beautiful green wallet, so clearly expensive that Elwin understood why his daughter had had to tease him for money to supplement her savings, and so adult in its expensiveness that he had to understand how inexorably she was growing up.

The made present was also green, a green lamb, large enough to have to be held in two hands, with black feet and wide black eyes. The eyes stared out with a great charming question to the world, expressing the comic grace of the lamb's awkwardness. Elwin wondered if Margaret had been at all aware of how much the lamb was a self-portrait. When Elwin, some two years before, had listened to his daughter playing her first full piece on the recorder, he had thought that nothing could be more wonderful than the impervious gravity of her face as her eyes focussed on the bell of the instrument and on the music-book while she blew her tune in a daze of concentration; yet only a few months later, when she had progressed so far as to be up to airs from Mozart, she had been able, in the very midst of a roulade, with her fingers moving fast, to glance up at him with a twinkling, sidelong look, her mouth puckering in a smile as she kept her lips pursed, amused by the music, amused by the frank excess of its ornamentation and by her own virtuosity. For Elwin the smile was the expression of gay and conscious life, of life innocently aware of itself and fond of itself, and, although there was something painful in having to make the admission, it was even more endearing than Margaret's earlier gravity. Life aware of itself seemed so much more life.

His daughter's room was full of life. His own old microscope stood on Margaret's desk and around it was a litter of slides and of the various objects from which she had been cutting sections, a prune and a dried apricot, a sliver of wood, a piece of cheese and what seemed to be a cockroach. There were tools for carving wood and for cutting linoleum blocks. The books were beginning to be too many for the small bookshelf, starting with *The Little Family* and going on to his own soiled copy of *The Light That Failed* that Margaret had unearthed. There was her easel and on one wall was a print of Picasso's trapeze people in flight, like fierce flames, and on another wall one of Benton's righteous stylizations, both at home, knowing nothing of their antagonism to each other. The dolls were no longer so much to the fore as they once were, but they were still about, and so was the elaborate doll's house which contained in precise miniature, accumulated over years, almost every object of daily living, tiny skillets, lamps, cups, kettles, packaged groceries. Surrounded by all that his daughter made and did and read, Elwin could not understand how she found the time. And then, on the thought of what time could be to a child, there came to him with more painful illumination than usual, the recurrent sentence. "No young man believes he shall ever die." And he stood contemplating the room with a kind of desolation of love for it.

Margaret burst in suddenly as if she were running away from something

—as indeed she was, for her eyes blazed with the anger she was fleeing. She flung herself on the bed, ignoring her father's presence.

"Margaret, what's the matter?" Elwin said.

But she did not answer.

"Margaret!" There was the note of discipline in his voice. "Tell me what the matter is."

She was not crying, but her face, when she lifted it from the pillow, was red and swollen. "It's mother," she said. "The way she talked to Margaret."

"To Margaret? Has Margaret come?"

"Yes, she came." The tone implied: through flood and fire. "And mother —oh!" She broke off and shook her head in a rather histrionic expression of how impossible it was to tell what her mother had done.

"What did she say that was so terrible?"

"She said—she said, 'Look here——' " But Margaret could not go on.

Lucy strode into the room with quite as much impulse as Margaret had and with eyes blazing quite as fiercely as her daughter's. "Look here, Margaret," she said. "I've quite enough trouble with that Margaret without your nonsense. Nobody is being exploited in this house and nobody is being bullied and I'm not going to have you making situations about nothing. I'm sure your Miss Hoxie is very sweet and nice, but you seem to have got your ideas from her all mixed up. You weren't that way about Millie when she was with us. As a matter of fact," Lucy said with remorseless irony, "you were often not at all nice to her."

Margaret had not heard the end of Lucy's speech. At the mention of Miss Hoxie in the tone that Lucy has used—"your Miss Hoxie"—at the sacred name of her teacher blasphemously uttered, she looked at her mother with the horror of seeing her now in her true terrible colors. The last bond between them had snapped at this attack upon her heart's best loyalty.

But Lucy was taking no account of finer feelings. She closed the door and said firmly, "Now look here, the simple fact is that that Margaret is a thoroughly disagreeable person, a nasty, mean person."

"Oh, she is not," Margaret wailed. And then, despite all her passion, the simple fact broke in upon her irresistibly. Elwin's heart quite melted as he saw her confront the fact and struggle with it. For the fact was as Lucy had stated it, and he himself at that moment had to realize it. And it was wonderful to see that Margaret's mind, whatever the inclination of her will, was unable to resist a fact. But the mind that had momentarily deserted her will, came quickly again to its help. "She's not responsible," she said desperately. "It's not her fault. She couldn't help it. Society——" But at that big word she halted, unable to handle it. "We can't blame her," she said defiantly but a little lamely.

At that moment Lucy saw the green clay lamb that Elwin was still holding. She rushed to it and took it and cried, "Margaret, is this yours? I've never seen it, why didn't you show it to me?"

It was, of course, a decided point for Margaret that her birthday surprise was spoiled. She sat there looking dry and indifferent amid the ruins of family custom. Elwin said, "It's a birthday present for you, Lucy. You weren't supposed to see it," and their glances met briefly. He had been a little treacherous, for he could have managed to put the lamb out of sight, but some craftiness, not entirely conscious, had suggested its usefulness for peace.

"It's so *lovely,*" Lucy said. "Is it really for me?"

Margaret had to acknowledge that it was, but with an elaborate ungraciousness from her bruised and empty heart. Her mother might have the gift, meaningless as it now was. But Lucy was in a flood of thanks and praise impossible to withstand—it was lovely, she said, to have a gift in advance of her birthday, it was something she had always wanted as a child and had never been able to induce her parents to allow, that she should have one, just one, of her presents before the others, and the lamb itself was simply beautiful, quite the nicest thing Margaret had ever made. "Oh, I love it," she said, stroking its face and then its rump. "Why darling!" she cried, "it looks exactly like you!" And Margaret had to submit to the child's pain at seeing the eminence of grief and grievance swept away. But at last, carried beyond the vacant moment when the forgiving and forgiven feeling had not yet come, she sat there in an embarrassed glow, beaming shyly as her mother kissed her and said quietly and finally, "Thank you."

When they were in the dining-room, all three of them feeling chastened and purged, Lucy said, "I must have it here by my place." And she put the lamb by her at the table, touching its cheek affectionately.

The dinner that Lucy had cooked was served by the other Margaret. She was a tall, rather light colored girl, with a genteel manner and eyebrows that were now kept very high. As she presented the casserole to Lucy, she looked far off into a distance and stood a little too far away for convenience. Lucy sat there with the serving spoon and fork in her hand and then said, "Come a little closer, Margaret." Margaret Elwin sat rigid, watching. Margaret the maid edged a little closer and continued her gaze. She moved to serve Elwin but Lucy said, "It's Margaret you serve next." Her tone was a little dry. Margaret Elwin flushed and looked mortified. It had been a matter of some satisfaction that she was now of an age to be served at table just after her mother, but she hated to have a point made of it if Margaret objected, and Margaret did seem to object and would not accept the reassuring smile that was being offered her over the casserole.

In the interval between the serving of the casserole and the serving of the salad that had once that evening made the family peace, Margaret held her parents with a stern and desperate eye. But she was unable to suppress a glance her mother sent to her father, a glance that had in it a touch of mild triumph. And her father did not this time fortify himself against it. The odds were terribly against her and she looked from one to the other and said in an intense whisper, "It's not her fault. She's not responsible."

"Why not?" Elwin asked.

It was his voice that made the question baffling to Margaret. She did not answer, or try to. It was not merely that the question was, for the moment, beyond her powers. Nor was it that she was puzzled because her father had seemed to change sides. But she was touched by the sense, so little formulated, so fleeting as scarcely to establish itself in her memory, that something other than the question, or the problem itself, was involved here. She barely perceived, yet she did perceive, her mother's quick glance at her father under lowered lids. It was something more than a glance of surprise. Neither Margaret nor Lucy, of course, knew anything about the sentence from Hazlitt. But this was one of the moments when the sentence had occurred to Elwin and with it the explosion of light. And his wife and daughter had heard the event in his voice. For Elwin an illumination, but a dark illumination, was thrown around the matter that concerned them. It seemed to him —not suddenly, for it had been advancing in his mind for some hours now— that in the aspect of his knowledge of death, all men were equal in their responsibility. The two bus conductors, Lucy's and his own, the boy with his face contorted in rational rage against the injustice he suffered, Margaret the maid with her genteel malice—all of them, quite as much as he himself, bore their own blame. Exemption was not given by age or youth, or sex, or color, or condition of life. It was the sense of this that made his voice so strange at his own dinner-table, as if it came not merely from another place but another time.

"Why not?" he said again. "Why not, Margaret?"

Margaret looked at her father's face and tried to answer. She seriously marshalled her thoughts and, as always, the sight of his daughter actually thinking touched Elwin profoundly. "It's because—because society didn't give her a chance," she said slowly. "She has a handicap. Because she's colored. She has to struggle so hard—against prejudice. It's so *hard* for her."

"It's true," Elwin said. "It's very hard for her. But it's hard for Millie too." Millie had been with the Elwins for nearly seven years. Some months ago she had left them to nurse a dying sister in the South.

Margaret of course knew what her father meant, that Millie, despite "society," was warm and good and capable. Her answer was quick, too quick. "Oh, Millie has a slave-psychology," she said loftily.

Really, Elwin thought, Miss Hoxie went too far. He felt a kind of disgust that a child should have been given such a phrase to use. It was a good school, he approved of its theory; but it must not give Margaret such things to say. He wondered if Margaret had submitted the question of Millie to

Miss Hoxie. If she had, and if this was the answer she had been given, his daughter had been, yes, corrupted. He said, "You should not say such things about Millie. She is a good loyal person and you haven't any right to say she is not."

"Loyal!" said Margaret in triumph. "Loyal!"

"Why yes. To her sister in Alabama, Margaret, just as much as to us. Is it what you call slave-psychology to be loyal to your own sister?"

But Margaret was not to be put down. She kept in mind the main point, which was not Millie but the other Margaret.

"I notice," she said defiantly, "that when Millie sends you parts of the money you lent her, you take it all right."

Poor child, she had fumbled, and Elwin laid his hand on hers on the table. "But Margaret! Of course I do," he said. "If I didn't, wouldn't that be slave-psychology? Millie would feel very lowered if I didn't take it."

"But she can't afford it," Margaret insisted.

"No, she can't afford it."

"Well then!" and she confronted the oppressor in her father.

"But she can't afford not to. She needs it for her pride. She needs to think of herself as a person who pays her debts, as a responsible person."

"I wonder," Lucy said, "I wonder how Millie is. Poor thing!" She was not being irrelevant. She was successful in bringing her husband up short. Yes, all that his "wisdom" had done was to lead him to defeat his daughter in argument. And defeat made Margaret stupid and obstinate. She said, "Well, anyway, it's not Margaret's fault," and sat sulking.

Had he been truly the wise man he wanted to be, he would have been able to explain, to Margaret and himself, the nature of the double truth. As much as Margaret, he believed that "society is responsible." He believed the other truth too. He felt rather tired, as if the little debate with Margaret had been more momentous than he understood. Yet wisdom, a small measure of it, did seem to come. It came suddenly, as no doubt was the way of moments of wisdom, and he perceived what stupidly he had not understood earlier, that it was not the other Margaret but herself that his Margaret was grieving for, that in her foolish and passionate argument, with the foolish phrases derived from the admired Miss Hoxie, she was defending herself from her own impending responsibility. Poor thing, she saw it moving toward her through the air at a great rate, and she did not want it. Naturally enough, she did not want it. And he, for what reason he did not know, was forcing it upon her.

He understood why Lucy, when they had risen from the table, made haste to put her arm around Margaret's shoulders as they went into the living-room.

They were sitting in the living-room, a rather silent family for the moment, when the other Margaret stood in the doorway. "You may as well know," she said, "that I'm through here." And she added, "I've had enough."

There was a little cry, as of horror, from Margaret. She looked at her parents with a bitter and tragic triumph. Lucy said shortly, "Very well, Margaret. Just finish up and I'll pay you." The quick acceptance took the maid aback. Angrier than before, she turned abruptly back into the dining-room.

For the third time that evening, Margaret Elwin sat in wretched isolation. Her father did not watch her, but he knew what she felt. She had been told *she* might go, never to return. She saw the great and frightening world before her. It was after all possible so to offend her parents that this expulsion would follow. Elwin rose to get a cigarette from the table near the sofa on which Margaret sat and he passed his hand over her bright hair. The picture of the king with the flower in his hand was in the other corner of the sofa.

It was as Elwin's hand was on his daughter's head that they heard the crash, and Elwin felt under his hand how Margaret's body experienced a kind of convulsion. He turned and saw Lucy already at the door of the dining-room, while there on the floor, in many pieces, as if it had fallen with force, lay the smashed green lamb, more white clay showing than green glaze. Lucy stooped down to the fragments, examining them, delicately turning them over one by one, as if already estimating the possibility of mending.

The maid Margaret stood there, a napkin in her hand clutched to her breast. All the genteel contempt had left her face. She looked only frightened, as if something was now, at last, going to be done to her. For her, almost more than for his own Margaret, Elwin felt sad. He said, "It's all right, Margaret. Don't worry, it's all right." It was a foolish and weak thing to say. It was not all right, and Lucy was still crouching, heartbroken, over the pieces. But he had had to say it, weak and foolish as it was.

"Ah, darling, don't feel too bad," Lucy said to her daughter as she came back into the living-room, tenderly holding the smashed thing in her hand.

But Margaret did not answer or even hear. She was staring into the dining-room with wide, fixed eyes. "She meant to do it," she said. "She *meant* to do it."

"Oh, no," Lucy said in her most matter-of-fact voice. "Oh, no, dear. It was just an accident."

"She meant to do it, she meant to do it." And then Margaret said, "I *saw* her." She alone had been facing into the dining-room and could have seen. "I saw her—with the napkin. She made a movement," and Margaret made a movement, "like this . . ."

Over her head her parents' eyes met. They knew that they could only offer the feeble lying of parents to a child. But they were determined to continue. "Oh, no," Elwin said, "it just happened." And he wondered if the king, within his line of vision as he stood there trying to comfort his daughter, would ever return to the old, fine, tragic power, for at the moment he seemed only quaint, extravagant and beside the point.

"She meant to. She didn't like me. She hated me," and the great sobs began to come. But Elwin knew that it was not because the other Margaret hated her that his Margaret wept, but because she had with her own eyes seen the actual possibility of what she herself might do, the insupportable fact of her own moral life. She was weeping bitterly now, her whole body shaking with the deepest of sobs, and she found refuge in a corner of the sofa, hiding her head from her parents. She had drawn up her knees, making herself as tight and inaccessible as she could, and Elwin, to comfort her, sat on what little space she allowed him on the sofa beside her, stroking her burrowing head and her heaving back, quite unable, whatever he might have hoped and wanted, to give her any better help than that.

EDWARD DONAHOE

Head by Scopas 🐾

We walked for a long time up the steep path which was supposed
to lead to the quiet place Alan knew. We had started from Leysin
at seven in order to have a full day in the place skiing. Alan
expected to do a water color of the Pic Chaussy. Even the dullest English-
men seem to be able to paint fairly decent water colors. Alan had taught
himself to draw during the three years he had been in a clinic at Leysin. His
delicate little pictures reminded me of the water colors Jane Austen's sister
Cassandra made for *Love and Friendship*. Alan had no business to be
painting Alps.

I said I had brought a bottle of Chambertin. "I can't drink much wine
because of my face,". he said. He had lupus, a tuberculous infection of the
skin. The left side of his face was scarred and discolored. The right one was
like one of the beautiful heads by Scopas in the Boston Museum. It was
always a shock to people in a railway carriage or a restaurant when his left
profile was revealed after they had admired his right.

The surface of the snow was broken up into innumerable hard little
crystal flakes like rhinestones. We had to put on dark glasses because of the
unbearable brightness of the sunlight on the snow. The path was getting
steeper and we were very tired under the weight of our skis and rucksacks
when we reached the little café. There was no one there. It was too early in
the morning for customers. Mme. Veillard had probably gone down to
Leysin village to buy provisions and to gossip. I was outdone with her
because I had planned to have a warming grog there.

"Well, we can at least stop to put on our skis now," Alan said. "It's level,
more or less, from here on." We strapped them on, readjusted our rucksacks,
and glided across a long meadow like sailboats. The tips of our skis scattered
the hard crystals of snow like sea foam. Our breaths blew white. The left
side of Alan's face was bright purple. I tried not to look at it.

"There's the place," he said, pointing to a deep basin of shining snow
fringed at the top on all sides by dark fir trees. A deserted chalet was at the
bottom, its rotten boards stained black. We went inside and undressed. It
is not unusual to ski without clothes at Leysin. The sun is very warm on
one's skin. One must be careful, though, not to fall down into the snow.
Alan wore a gee-string, but I wanted to be brown all over and said so.
Alan climbed to the top of the basin and dropped off into space like a bird.
We made figures and faces in the snow and drew intricate patterns with

our skis, occasionally falling down like collapsing kites, laughing and shouting in our icy graves.

"We've had enough," Alan said, when it was almost noon. "Let's have
some lunch." I poured the wine into aluminum cups. Alan hesitated and
took some. "It will warm me up," he said. The black bread and strong
cheese were delicious. We ate and drank eagerly and noisily. "If you want
a good light you had better begin your water color," I said, after we had sat
smoking for an hour or so. We had finished the bottle of Chambertin.

He began to sketch a little more boldly than usual the outline of the
mountain far to the north of us above the fir trees. As he mixed his colors
I watched him idly, thinking his life unenviable enough. Since childhood
he had had the ugly infection on his face. In London, where he lived, he had
spent many years trying to be cured. Surgeons there had grafted fresh skin
on diseased skin. He had been burned time and again by X rays. The scars
from the burning he would never lose. The infection had ceased spreading
when he came to Switzerland. His left ear was scarcely touched and his left
eye was safe. I refrained from asking him cruel questions: if women ever
kissed him, if people minded his sitting down across from them in restau-
rants, if there was danger of his infecting someone else. It is hard to resist
such natural cruelty. Children do not try. He had told me that he had been
called Nasty-Face by the boys at his school. After that and worse persecu-
tion he had begged to be tutored at home. He was deeply ignorant. He also
knew strange, unusual things. At twenty he was virginal. He would be, I
supposed, repellent to most women only on account of his infection.

"Do you know my girl?" he asked suddenly. I was startled and confused.
It was as if he had guessed what I had been thinking about.

"No, I'm afraid not," I said. "Who is she?"

"Oh she's a jolly girl, pretty as the devil. She's Swiss. You've never seen
her around Leysin, I suppose." He laughed aloud to himself. Clearly he
wanted the pleasure of talking about her.

"Do you like her very much?" I asked. Immediately I regretted the silly
question. I was not interested in knowing whether he liked his girl or not.

"Like her? I say, I *love* her!" He jabbed his brush violently into a mound
of Indian Lake. I was silent. He looked up at me surprised and almost displeased that I did not say something.

"That's very nice," I said weakly. "She must be charming."

"She damn well is. She wants to marry me, too. I wrote mother about it.
Her father is a patient at L'Aiglon. His family are here to be near him, so
she has a dull time. They're from Geneva."

"I've never met anyone from Geneva."

"Would you like to meet Hedwige?"

"Is that her name? Of course. The two of you might have dinner with
me tomorrow night." I was suddenly caught with his own enthusiasm.

"She can't go out unchaperoned." He looked at me, waiting.

"Well, I don't want her mother, thank you," I said. "You've got those clouds a little too heavy. They seem solider than your mountain."

"You know," he said, ignoring my criticism of his picture, "I wish I could have an affair with a girl before I marry Hedwige. I'd be more experienced and sure of myself."

"What about Hedwige herself?" I laughed at my daring. Alan was with the Victorians about women. They were only good or bad.

"Oh, she wouldn't."

Some crows were pecking at the crumbs we had scattered. They were very hungry and not at all frightened.

"Have you ever said anything to her about it?" I ventured.

"No, but she wouldn't. She's going to be my wife, you know. She loves me like anything." He laughed aloud to himself again.

"How can you tell? Does she show she loves you in some particular way? I mean, does she kiss you?"

"Oh yes," he said eagerly. "She doesn't seem to mind my face a bit—and that's something, you know. She writes me wonderful letters every day, too. She was going to the university when her father became ill. She writes frightfully well. I have one of her letters in my 'breeks' in the chalet. Shall I read it to you?"

"If you like."

He was unused to wine. The Chambertin had released him from his usual restraint. He stepped away from the easel and ran over to the chalet to get the letter. He came out reading it to himself. Then he smiled and shook his head. "I think this one's too personal, after all. She wouldn't like to let anyone see it."

I was unable to put aside my sudden curiosity. "Please let me read it. I won't tell anybody. Please let me," I pleaded.

He folded the letter and put it into the envelope. I leaped toward him, caught him round the waist, and we tumbled into the snow, laughing. I got the letter away from him and ran into the chalet, bolting the door on the inside. He pounded his fists against it.

The letter was in French. "My dear Alan," I hastily translated, "you did not come to see me last night, and I had to go to bed without seeing your beautiful face. That made me very restless and sad. I must see your face every day. So I lay awake for hours thinking of it, very lovely like a marble head by some Greek sculptor, which had been dug up by the careless assistant of an archaeologist, who scraped the left cheek with his spade and broke away the warm, luminous surface, spoiling the patina forever. I am in love with you, Alan, because you are English and not Swiss. But, more than that, I am in love with you because of your beautiful Greek fragment of a face . . ."

I unbolted the door. He had walked away and would not turn around when I called.

EUDORA WELTY

Powerhouse 🎺

Powerhouse is playing!

He's here on tour from the city—"Powerhouse and His Keyboard"—"Powerhouse and His Tasmanians"—think of the things
he calls himself! There's no one in the world like him. You can't tell what
he is. "Nigger man"?—he looks more Asiatic, monkey, Jewish, Babylonian,
Peruvian, fanatic, devil. He has pale gray eyes, heavy lids, maybe horny like
a lizard's, but big glowing eyes when they're open. He has African feet of
the greatest size, stomping, both together, on each side of the pedals. He's
not coal black—beverage colored—looks like a preacher when his mouth is
shut, but then it opens—vast and obscene. And his mouth is going every
minute: like a monkey's when it looks for something. Improvising, coming
on a light and childish melody—*smooch*—he loves it with his mouth.

Is it possible that he could be this! When you have him there performing
for you, that's what you feel. You know people on a stage—and people of a
darker race—so likely to be marvelous, frightening.

This is a white dance. Powerhouse is not a show-off like the Harlem boys,
not drunk, not crazy—he's in a trance; he's a person of joy, a fanatic. He
listens as much as he performs, a look of hideous, powerful rapture on his
face. Big arched eyebrows that never stop traveling, like a Jew's—wandering-
Jew eyebrows. When he plays he beats down piano and seat and wears them
away. He is in motion every moment—what could be more obscene? There
he is with his great head, fat stomach, and little round piston legs, and long
yellow-sectioned strong big fingers, at rest about the size of bananas. Of
course you know how he sounds—you've heard him on records—but still you
need to see him. He's going all the time, like skating around the skating
rink or rowing a boat. It makes everybody crowd around, here in this
shadowless steel-trussed hall with the rose-like posters of Nelson Eddy and
the testimonial for the mind-reading horse in handwriting magnified five
hundred times. Then all quietly he lays his finger on a key with the promise
and serenity of a sibyl touching the book.

Powerhouse is so monstrous he sends everybody into oblivion. When any
group, any performers, come to town, don't people always come out and
hover near, leaning inward about them, to learn what it is? What is it?
Listen. Remember how it was with the acrobats. Watch them carefully, hear

the least word, especially what they say to one another, in another language —don't let them escape you; it's the only time for hallucination, the last time. They can't stay. They'll be somewhere else this time tomorrow.

Powerhouse has as much as possible done by signals. Everybody, laughing as if to hide a weakness, will sooner or later hand him up a written request. Powerhouse reads each one, studying with a secret face: that is the face which looks like a mask—anybody's; there is a moment when he makes a decision. Then a light slides under his eyelids, and he says, "92!" or some combination of figures—never a name. Before a number the band is all frantic, misbehaving, pushing, like children in a school-room, and he is the teacher getting silence. His hands over the keys, he says sternly, "You-all ready? You-all ready to do some serious walking?"—waits—then, STAMP. Quiet. STAMP, for the second time. This is absolute. Then a set of rhythmic kicks against the floor to communicate the tempo. Then, O Lord! say the distended eyes from beyond the boundary of the trumpets, Hello and good-by, and they are all down the first note like a waterfall.

This note marks the end of any known discipline. Powerhouse seems to abandon them all—he himself seems lost—down in the song, yelling up like somebody in a whirlpool—not guiding them—hailing them only. But he knows, really. He cries out, but he must know exactly. "Mercy! . . . What I say! . . . Yeah!" And then drifting, listening—"Where that skin beater?"— wanting drums, and starting up and pouring it out in the greatest delight and brutality. On the sweet pieces such a leer for everybody! He looks down so benevolently upon all our faces and whispers the lyrics to us. And if you could hear him at this moment on "Marie, the Dawn is Breaking"! He's going up the keyboard with a few fingers in some very derogatory triplet-routine, he gets higher and higher, and then he looks over the end of the piano, as if over a cliff. But not in a show-off way—the song makes him do it.

He loves the way they all play, too—all those next to him. The far section of the band is all studious, wearing glasses, every one—they don't count. Only those playing around Powerhouse are the real ones. He has a bass fiddler from Vicksburg, black as pitch, named Valentine, who plays with his eyes shut and talking to himself, very young: Powerhouse has to keep encouraging him. "Go on, go on, give it up, bring it on out there!" When you heard him like that on records, did you know he was really pleading?

He calls Valentine out to take a solo.

"What you going to play?" Powerhouse looks out kindly from behind the piano; he opens his mouth and shows his tongue, listening.

Valentine looks down, drawing against his instrument, and says without a lip movement, "'Honeysuckle Rose.'"

He has a clarinet player named Little Brother, and loves to listen to anything he does. He'll smile and say, "Beautiful!" Little Brother takes a step forward when he plays and stands at the very front, with the whites of his eyes like fishes swimming. Once when he played a low note, Powerhouse muttered in dirty praise, "He went clear downstairs to get that one!"

After a long time, he holds up the number of fingers to tell the band how many choruses still to go—usually five. He keeps his directions down to signals.

It's a bad night outside. It's a white dance, and nobody dances, except a few straggling jitterbugs and two elderly couples. Everybody just stands around the band and watches Powerhouse. Sometimes they steal glances at one another, as if to say, Of course, you know how it is with *them*—Negroes—band leaders—they would play the same way, giving all they've got, for an audience of one. . . . When somebody, no matter who, gives everything, it makes people feel ashamed for him.

Late at night they play the one waltz they will ever consent to play—by request, "Pagan Love Song." Powerhouse's head rolls and sinks like a weight between his waving shoulders. He groans, and his fingers drag into the keys heavily, holding on to the notes, retrieving. It is a sad song.

"You know what happened to me?" says Powerhouse.

Valentine hums a response, dreaming at the bass.

"I got a telegram my wife is dead," says Powerhouse, with wandering fingers.

"Uh-huh?"

His mouth gathers and forms a barbarous O while his fingers walk up straight, unwillingly, three octaves.

"Gypsy? Why how come her to die, didn't you just phone her up in the night last night long distance?"

"Telegram say—here the words: Your wife is dead." He puts 4/4 over the 3/4.

"Not but four words?" This is the drummer, an unpopular boy named Scoot, a disbelieving maniac.

Powerhouse is shaking his vast cheeks. "What the hell was she trying to do? What was she up to?"

"What name has it got signed, if you got a telegram?" Scoot is spitting away with those wire brushes.

Little Brother, the clarinet player, who cannot now speak, glares and tilts back.

"Uranus Knockwood is the name signed." Powerhouse lifts his eyes open. "Ever heard of him?" A bubble shoots out on his lip like a plate on a counter.

Valentine is beating slowly on with his palm and scratching the strings with his long blue nails. He is fond of a waltz, Powerhouse interrupts him.

"I don't know him. Don't know who he is." Valentine shakes his head with the closed eyes.

"Say it agin."

"Uranus Knockwood."

"That ain't Lenox Avenue."

"It ain't Broadway."

"Ain't ever seen it wrote out in any print, even for horse racing."

"Hell, that's on a star, boy, ain't it?" Crash of the cymbals.

"What the hell was she up to?" Powerhouse shudders. "Tell me, tell me, tell me." He makes triplets, and begins a new chorus. He holds three fingers up.

"You say you got a telegram." This is Valentine, patient and sleepy, beginning again.

Powerhouse is elaborate. "Yas, the time I go out, go way downstairs along a long cor-ri-dor to where they puts us: coming back along the cor-ri-dor: steps out and hands me a telegram: Your wife is dead."

"Gypsy?" The drummer like a spider over his drums.

"Aaaaaaaa!" shouts Powerhouse, flinging out both powerful arms for three whole beats to flex his muscles, then kneading a dough of bass notes. His eyes glitter. He plays the piano like a drum sometimes—why not?

"Gypsy? Such a dancer?"

"Why you don't hear it straight from your agent? Why it ain't come from headquarters? What you been doing, getting telegrams in the corridor, signed nobody?"

They all laugh. End of that chorus.

"What time is it?" Powerhouse calls. "What the hell place is this? Where is my watch and chain?"

"I hang it on you," whimpers Valentine. "It still there."

There it rides on Powerhouse's great stomach, down where he can never see it.

"Sure did hear some clock striking twelve while ago. Must be midnight."

"It going to be intermission," Powerhouse declares, lifting up his finger with the signet ring.

He draws the chorus to an end. He pulls a big Northern hotel towel out of the deep pocket in his vast, special-cut tux pants and pushes his forehead into it.

"If she went and killed herself!" he says with a hidden face. "If she up and jumped out that window!" He gets to his feet, turning vaguely, wearing the towel on his head.

"Ha, ha!"

"Sheik, sheik!"

"She wouldn't do that." Little Brother sets down his clarinet like a precious vase, and speaks. He still looks like an East Indian queen, implacable, divine, and full of snakes. "You ain't going to expect people doing what they says over long distance."

"Come on!" roars Powerhouse. He is already at the back door, he has pulled it wide open, and with a wild, gathered-up face is smelling the terrible night.

Powerhouse, Valentine, Scoot and Little Brother step outside into the drenching rain.

"Well, they emptying buckets," says Powerhouse in a mollified voice. On the street he holds his hands out and turns up the blanched palms like sieves.

A hundred dark, ragged, silent, delighted Negroes have come around from under the eaves of the hall, and follow wherever they go.

"Watch out, Little Brother, don't shrink," says Powerhouse. "You just the right size now, clarinet don't suck you in. You got a dry throat, Little Brother, you in the desert?" He reaches into the pocket and pulls out a paper of mints. "Now hold 'em in your mouth—don't chew 'em. I don't carry around nothing without limit."

"Go in that joint and have beer," says Scoot, who walks ahead.

"Beer? Beer? You know what beer is? What do they say is beer? What's beer? Where I been?"

"Down yonder where it say World Café—that do?" They are in Negro-town now.

Valentine patters over and holds open a screen door warped like a sea shell, bitter in the wet, and they walk in, stained darker with the rain and leaving footprints. Inside, sheltered dry smells stand like screens around a table covered with a red-checkered cloth, in the center of which flies hang onto an obelisk-shaped ketchup bottle. The midnight walls are checkered again with admonishing "Not Responsible" signs and black-figured, smoky calendars. It is a waiting, silent, limp room. There is a burned-out-looking nickelodeon and right beside it a long-necked wall instrument labeled "Business Phone, Don't Keep Talking." Circled phone numbers are written up everywhere. There is a worn-out peacock feather hanging by a thread to an old, thin, pink, exposed light bulb, where it slowly turns around and around, whoever breathes.

A waitress watches.

"Come here, living statue, and get all this big order of beer we fixing to give."

"Never seen you before anywhere." The waitress moves and comes forward and slowly shows little gold leaves and tendrils over her teeth. She shoves up her shoulders and breasts. "How I going to know who you might be? Robbers? Coming in out of the black of night at midnight, setting down so big at my table?"

"Boogers," says Powerhouse, his eyes opening lazily as in a cave.

The girl screams delicately with pleasure. O Lord, she likes talk and scares.
"Where you going to find enough beer to put out on this here table?"
She runs to the kitchen with bent elbows and sliding steps.

"Here's a million nickels," says Powerhouse, pulling his hand out of his
pockets and sprinkling coins out, all but the last one, which he makes vanish
like a magician.

Valentine and Scoot take the money over to the nickelodeon, which looks
as battered as a slot machine, and read all the names of the records out loud.

"Whose 'Tuxedo Junction'?" asks Powerhouse.

"You know whose."

"Nickelodeon, I request you please to play 'Empty Bed Blues' and let Bessie
Smith sing."

Silence: they hold it like a measure.

"Bring me all those nickels on back here," says Powerhouse. "Look at that!
What you tell me the name of this place?"

"White dance, week night, raining, Alligator, Mississippi, long ways from
home."

"Uh-huh."

"Sent for You Yesterday and Here You Come Today" plays.

The waitress, setting the tray of beer down on a back table, comes up taut
and apprehensive as a hen. "Says in the kitchen, back there putting their
eyes to little hole peeping out, that you is Mr. Powerhouse. . . . They knows
from a picture they seen."

"They seeing right tonight, that is him," says Little Brother.

"You him?"

"That is him in the flesh," says Scoot.

"Does you wish to touch him?" asks Valentine. "Because he don't bite."

"You passing through?"

"Now you got everything right."

She waits like a drop, hands languishing together in front.

"Little-Bit, ain't you going to bring the beer?"

She brings it, and goes behind the cash register and smiles, turning different ways. The little fillet of gold in her mouth is gleaming.

"The Mississippi River's here," she says once.

Now all the watching Negroes press in gently and bright-eyed through the
door, as many as can get in. One is a little boy in a straw sombrero which has
been coated with aluminum paint all over.

Powerhouse, Valentine, Scoot and Little Brother drink beer, and their
eyelids come together like curtains. The wall and the rain and the humble
beautiful waitress waiting on them and the other Negroes watching enclose
them.

"Listen!" whispers Powerhouse, looking into the ketchup bottle and
slowly spreading his performer's hands over the damp, wrinkling cloth with

the red squares. "Listen how it is. My wife gets missing me. Gypsy. She goes to the window. She looks out and sees you know what. Street. Sign saying Hotel. People walking. Somebody looks up. Old man. She looks down, out the window. Well? . . . *Sssst! Plooey!* What she do! Jump out and bust her brains all over the world."

He opens his eyes.

"That's it," agrees Valentine. "You gets a telegram."

"Sure she misses you," Little Brother adds.

"No, it's night time." How softly he tells them! "Sure. It's the night time. She say, What do I hear? Footsteps walking up the hall? That him? Footsteps go on off. It's not me. I'm in Alligator, Mississippi, she's crazy. Shaking all over. Listens till her ears and all grow out like old music-box horns but still she can't hear a thing. She says, All right! I'll jump out the window then. Got on her nightgown. I know that nightgown, and her thinking there. Says, Ho hum, all right, and jumps out the window. Is she mad at me! Is she crazy! She don't leave *nothing* behind her!"

"Ya! Ha!"

"Brains and insides everywhere, Lord, Lord."

All the watching Negroes stir in their delight, and to their higher delight he says affectionately, "Listen! Rats in here."

"That must be the way, boss."

"Only, naw, Powerhouse, that ain't true. That sound too *bad*."

"Does? I even know who finds her," cried Powerhouse. "That no-good pussyfooted crooning creeper, that creeper that follow around after me, coming up like weeds behind me, following around after me everything I do and messing around on the trail I leave. Bets my numbers, sings my songs, gets close to my agent like a Betsy-bug; when I going out he just coming in. I got him now! I got my eye on him."

"Know who he is?"

"Why it's that old Uranus Knockwood!"

"Ya! Ha!"

"Yeah, and he coming now, he going to find Gypsy. There he is, coming around that corner, and Gypsy kadoodling down, oh-oh, watch out! *Sssst! Plooey!* See, there she is in her little old nightgown, and her insides and brains all scattered round."

A sigh fills the room.

"Hush about her brains. Hush about her insides."

"Ya! Ha! You talking about her brains and insides—old Uranus Knockwood," says Powerhouse, "look down and say Jesus! He say, Look here what I'm walking round in!"

They all burst into halloos of laughter. Powerhouse's face looks like a big hot iron stove.

"Why, he picks her up and carries her off!" he says.

"Ya! Ha!"

"Carries her *back* around the corner. . . ."

"Oh, Powerhouse!"

"You know him."

"Uranus Knockwood!"

"Yeahhh!"

"He takes our wives when we gone!"

"He come in when we goes out!"

"Uh-huh!"

"He go out when we comes in!"

"Yeahhh!"

"He standing behind the door!"

"Old Uranus Knockwood."

"You know him."

"Middle-size man."

"Wears a hat."

"That's him."

Everybody in the room moans with pleasure. The little boy in the fine silver hat opens a paper and divides out a jelly roll among his followers.

And out of the breathless ring somebody moves forward like a slave, leading a great logy Negro with bursting eyes, and says, "This here is Sugar-Stick Thompson, that dove down to the bottom of July Creek and pulled up all those drownded white people fall out of a boat. Last summer, pulled up fourteen."

"Hello," says Powerhouse, turning and looking around at them all with his great daring face until they nearly suffocate.

Sugar-Stick, their instrument, cannot speak; he can only look back at the others.

"Can't even swim. Done it by holding his breath," says the fellow with the hero.

Powerhouse looks at him seekingly.

"I his half brother," the fellow puts in.

They step back.

"Gypsy say," Powerhouse rumbles gently again, looking at *them,* " 'What is the use? I'm gonna jump out so far—so far. . . .' *Sssst—!*"

"Don't, boss, don't do it again," says Little Brother.

"It's awful," says the waitress. "I hates that Mr. Knockwoods. All that the truth?"

"Want to see the telegram I got from him?" Powerhouse's hand goes to the vast pocket.

"Now wait, now wait, boss." They all watch him.

"It must be the real truth," says the waitress, sucking in her lower lip, her luminous eyes turning sadly, seeking the windows.

"No, babe, it ain't the truth." His eyebrows fly up and he begins to whisper to her out of his vast oven mouth. His hand stays in his pocket. "Truth is something worse, I ain't said what, yet. It's something hasn't come to me, but I ain't saying it won't. And when it does, then want me to tell you?" He sniffs all at once, his eyes come open and turn up, almost too far. He is dreamily smiling.

"Don't, boss, don't, Powerhouse!"

"Oh!" the waitress screams.

"Go on git out of here!" bellows Powerhouse, taking his hand out of his pocket and clapping after her red dress.

The ring of watchers breaks and falls away.

"*Look* at that! Intermission is up," says Powerhouse.

He folds money under a glass, and after they go out, Valentine leans back in and drops a nickel in the nickelodeon behind them, and it lights up and begins to play "The Goona Goo." The feather dangles still.

"Take a telegram!" Powerhouse shouts suddenly up into the rain over the street. "Take a answer. Now what was that name?"

They get a little tired.

"Uranus Knockwood."

"You ought to know."

"Yas? Spell it to me."

They spell it all the ways it could be spelled. It puts them in a wonderful humor.

"Here's the answer. I got it right here. 'What in the hell you talking about? Don't make any difference: I gotcha.' Name signed: Powerhouse."

"That going to reach him, Powerhouse?" Valentine speaks in a maternal voice.

"Yas, yas."

All hushing, following him up the dark street at a distance, like old rained-on black ghosts, the Negroes are afraid they will die laughing.

Powerhouse throws back his vast head into the steaming rain, and a look of hopeful desire seems to blow somehow like a vapor from his own dilated nostrils over his face and bring a mist to his eyes.

"Reach him and come out the other side."

"That's it, Powerhouse, that's it. You got him now."

Powerhouse lets out a long sigh.

"But ain't you going back there to call up Gypsy long distance, the way you did last night in that other place? I seen a telephone. . . . Just to see if she there at home?"

There is a measure of silence. That is one crazy drummer that's going to get his neck broken some day.

"No," growls Powerhouse. "No! How many thousand times tonight I got to say No?"

He holds up his arm in the rain.

"You sure-enough unroll your voice some night, it about reach up yonder to her," says Little Brother, dismayed.

They go on up the street, shaking the rain off and on them like birds.

Back in the dance hall, they play "San" (99). The jitterbugs start up like windmills stationed over the floor, and in their orbits—one circle, another, a long stretch and a zigzag—dance the elderly couples with old smoothness, undisturbed and stately.

When Powerhouse first came back from intermission, no doubt full of beer, they said, he got the band tuned up again in his own way. He didn't strike the piano keys for pitch—he simply opened his mouth and gave falsetto howls—in A, D and so on—they tuned by him. Then he took hold of the piano, as if he saw it for the first time in his life, and tested it for strength, hit it down in the bass, played an octave with his elbow, lifted the top, looked inside, and leaned against it with all his might. He sat down and played it for a few minutes with outrageous force and got it under his power —a bass deep and coarse as a sea net—then produced something glimmering and fragile, and smiled. And who could ever remember any of the things he says? They are just inspired remarks that roll out of his mouth like smoke.

They've requested "Somebody Loves Me," and he's already done twelve or fourteen choruses, piling them up nobody knows how, and it will be a wonder if he ever gets through. Now and then he calls and shouts, " 'Somebody loves me! Somebody loves me, I wonder who!' " His mouth gets to be nothing but a volcano. "I wonder who!"

"Maybe . . ." He uses all his right hand on a trill.

"Maybe . . ." He pulls back his spread fingers, and looks out upon the place where he is. A vast, impersonal and yet furious grimace transfigures his wet face.

". . . Maybe it's you!"

CAROLINE GORDON

Her Quaint Honour 🐞

The first year I was at Taylor's Grove I raised ten thousand pounds
of tobacco. Five thousands pounds of lugs and seconds and five
thousand pounds of prime leaf. And, boy, was it prime! I ought to
have got thirty cents for that leaf, the way it was selling that year. But I
didn't get but fifteen. That yellow wife of Tom Doty's was the cause of that.

I was raised at the Grove but I had a fuss with my folks one fall and went
off to Louisville and worked in a garage. I got to be a pretty good mechanic
but they kept me at it eighteen hours a day. I figured there was no percentage
in that so I saved up some money and started me a combined garage and
filling station. I made money on the service end, or would have if it hadn't
been for my friends. They came from all over town and were all slow pay.
Then the depression hit us. I started lying awake nights worrying about the
pay roll. One night I got to thinking about all that land at the Grove. It
don't belong to me or to any of us—yet. It belongs to my grandmother. She
is seventy-five years old and hell on wheels. Always has been, they tell me.
Still, I knew that if I could stand the old lady I was welcome to go there
and farm.

I got up the next morning and went to see a man I know. By afternoon
I'd sold the shop, including some high-priced accessories, and was heading
for South Todd.

But I didn't go straight to the old place. I went by to see a nigger I know.
Tom Doty was the house boy at the Grove when I was a kid. Then later
he got to be a hand and finally foreman and he stayed there till he had some
trouble with my grandmother and had to leave. I reckon I'd better stop now
and tell you about my grandmother. She is the only woman in South Todd
old enough to have owned slaves—her parents died when she was little—and
she has never got over it. The niggers say can't anybody get along with her
and don't any of them try it. The poor white people don't know her as well
as the niggers do, and two or three families move on the place every year.
But they never make more than one crop there. As the old lady says, "They
don't suit the place."

But this Tom Doty I was telling you about always could get along with
her when he wanted to. And, besides that, he is the smartest nigger and the
fastest worker I ever knew. I always said that if I ever went to farming I'd

try to get hold of Tom, so I stopped at Price's Station and found he was cropping at a Mr. Bannerman's and went right on over there.

It was just before Christmas but it was a warm day. Tom was sitting on the doorstep, sunning. I thought he must be doing right well at Mr. Bannerman's, for everything he had on was new—leather coat and tan shoes and a pair of those purple corduroy pants the niggers like so much. He looked good in 'em too. Tom is a tall, handsome nigger, with a very black face and a big, real nigger mouth. My grandmother always said he had Coromantee blood in him.

I drove up to the door. "Hello, Tom," I said. "Have you traded for next year?"

He jumped right up. "God help me! If it ain't Mister Jim!"

"It ain't anybody else," I told him. "Have you traded yet?"

"I ain't named it to Mr. Bannerman," he said, "but I reckon he'll let me stay here long as I want to."

"How'd you like to make a crop with me?"

Tom kind of grins. "Whereabouts?"

"Well," I said, "there's a lot of land over at the old place ain't in use."

Tom grins again. "Hi yi! You reckon Miss Jinny'd let us stay on the place long enough to make a crop?"

"I was thinking about trying it."

He stood there looking at me a minute. He scratched his head. He sat down. Then he stood up. "Mister Jim, I got a wife in there I believe can git along with Miss Jinny."

"You *got* something then," I said. "Let me see her."

He called, "Frankie!" A girl came to the door. I didn't like her looks much. For one thing she had on lipstick and rouge. She was almost as tall as Tom and plump. And she had gray eyes and a bright skin. I never did like to see gray eyes in a nigger's head, and a light-skin nigger always looks sassy to me. Still, she had a good-natured smile and good nature was what I was after.

"Howdy, Frankie," I said. "Whose girl are you?"

"I'm Old Man Gus Byars' daughter."

I was glad to hear that. Those Byars niggers are as respectable niggers as we've got in our county. Old Gus is the grandson of a white man, Mister Jim Parlow, who died right after the Civil War. He had four hundred acres of land and in his will he divided it up among his four mulatto sons, said, "They may be niggers but they're damn fine boys." The rest of them had lost their land long ago but old Gus still had fifty acres of his.

"Frankie," I said, "you know Miss Jinny Taylor?"

"Naw, suh, but Papa say he been knowin' her all his life."

"Can your papa get along with her?"

"Naw, suh, he say cain't nobody git along with her, black or white."

"Well, Frankie, Tom here says you can get along with her."

She laughed and ducked her head. "Folks generally likes me," she said.

Tom had sat down and was whittling on a stick. He'd been eyeing Frankie like he'd never seen her before and was trying to make up his mind about her. "Mister Jim, I believe she kin do it," he says finally in that soft voice of his.

"Well, what about it, Frankie?"

She was looking at Tom. I could tell from that look that they were a mighty loving pair, "Whatever Tom says," she told me.

"All right," I said, "we've done traded. Tom, you got a wagon?"

"Yes, sir."

"Well, you be ready to move your stuff around New Year's."

"How you know Miss Jinny got an empty cabin?"

"I'll empty one."

He laughed. "Miss Jinny gwine have something to say to that."

I drove on over to Taylor's Grove. Got there about four o'clock. The front door was locked. I knocked on it a long while. Nobody came but I could hear a radio going full tilt inside. Finally I shouted: "Mama! Mama!" (My mother died when I was little so I always call my grandmother "Mama.") There was a lull in the music. The old lady came to the door. She is a small old lady with white hair and real pretty blue eyes. She wears gray gingham dresses and if it's cold a little shawl. She stuck her face up against the screen. "Who is it? What do you want?"

"It's Jim," I told her. "Looks like you'd let me in after I drove all the way from Louisville to see you."

She opened the door mighty quick then. That old lady likes her own flesh and blood. She just can't stand to have them around long at a time.

"Jim!" she said. "Jim, I'm glad to see you."

"Why'n't you let me in, then?" I asked, kidding her like I always did.

She said: "I heard somebody calling 'Mama' but I thought it was the music. So many of these new songs have 'Mama' in them."

We went in and sat down and she told me all the news, mostly about a polecat had got in the henhouse and how the tenants were drying up her cows. After a while she asked me if I didn't want supper the way people do when they expect you to say "No." I told her I could eat a house. She looked kind of worried and then she said she wasn't figuring on eating any supper and had let the fire go out but she could scramble me some eggs.

I kindled a fire in the stove and she fixed the eggs. But it took her a long time. I could see that she had broken a lot since the last time I was here. I thought it was time some of her own folks came to live with her.

After supper we went and sat in her room some more and listened to the radio. She is hell on politics and likes to know what is going on in Soviet

Russia and China. I sat there looking at her and thinking how she'd kept us all in a stew for twenty or thirty years and would keep it up too till she died.

The way I figure it she isn't mean. She just has more curiosity than most folks. When she has anybody around her she just has to take 'em to pieces to see what makes 'em tick. And when she finds the weak spot she can't help probing it. I decided that if I was going to make a crop there I'd try to stay away from the house as much as possible. I wasn't thinking much about the future in those days. Just to make one crop was all I figured on.

It was ten o'clock. She got up and said it was time to go to bed. I knew it was time to strike.

"Mama," I said, "how'd you like to have me come here and make a crop?"

She blinked. Her face worked like she was going to cry. But that old lady is game from the word "go." "Well," she says, offhand, "I'll have to see what Phil says about it."

Uncle Phil is her brother, lives on the next farm. He is seventy years old and weighs two hundred pounds. He manages her business like he manages his own by sitting on the front porch and hollering at the hands.

"That's right," I told her, "we'll have to see what Uncle Phil says," and I went on upstairs to my old room and went to bed.

In the morning the old lady called Uncle Phil up and had a long talk with him. When she got through she said that Uncle Phil thought it was a good idea but I'd have to talk over the details of the trade with him. I told her that was all right. I'd go over to Uncle Phil that morning. Then I asked her if there was an empty cabin on the place and when she said there was I told her I thought I'd try to get Tom Doty for a cropper. She said that was fine. She always liked Tom.

I thought it was about time to hit the big road so I said I'd go on over and have my talk with Uncle Phil. I stopped at a country store and telephoned him. He must have heard I was there. "What's the matter?" he sings out. "City got you down?"

I said that that was the size of it and told him I'd decided to make a crop at the Grove if he was agreeable.

He didn't say anything for a minute. Finally he said: "What you want to make a crop for? Why'n't you just go there and stay as long as you want to?"

"Listen," I told him, "I've been working eighteen hours a day in that garage but I'm not ready for a nursemaid's job yet. And if I was I wouldn't start on Mama because she is hell on wheels and always has been."

"She don't mellow much," he said and then he gave a sigh. "I reckon you got to get experience. . . . Come on over in a few days and let me know how you make out."

I told him I would, and then I drove over to Bannerman's. Tom was sitting there on the doorstep. "Well, Tom," I said, "you can move in any time you want to."

Tom looked at me kind of funny. "How Miss Jinny gettin' along?" he asked in that polite voice of his.

"Tom," I said, "I ain't goin' to try to fool you. She's just like she always was. But you said Frankie could handle her."

Tom laughed. "That's right," he says.

They moved in three days later. Right then I came near making a big mistake. I went on down to the cabin that first morning and told Tom I reckoned Frankie'd better go up and see about working for Miss Jinny.

Tom looked upset like he always does when he has to go against white folks. Finally he says, "Mister Jim, it ain't *time* for Frankie to go to the house yit."

I told him all right. I was pretty busy for the next week or so and I didn't have time to think about those niggers. All this time the old lady and I'd been having snacks off the kitchen table because it was too much trouble to light a fire in the dining room. Then one night when I rolled in for my scrambled eggs there was a fire going in the dining room and the table was all set. Frankie was in the kitchen standing over the stove and the old lady was ambling around telling her to do this and that. I beat it across the hall and waited till they rang the bell.

There was fried chicken and mashed potatoes and mustard greens. The chicken was fine and the greens were cooked down like I like them but I was waiting for the biscuits. Those old-fashioned housekeepers judge a cook by her bread. I picked one up looking kind of sour as if I expected the worst. It was light as a feather. I ate seven and I could have eaten more but I was afraid the old lady would think I was dissatisfied with her cooking. We had some kind of pudding after that and I had a cup of good coffee. The old lady just picked at a chicken wing and she wouldn't drink any coffee for fear it would keep her awake. I went on across the hall and after the old lady had shown Frankie where to put things and bossed her about the dish washing she came too. The old lady can't read much at night on account of her eyes so she usually keeps the radio going till ten or eleven o'clock. She turned it on tonight same as usual. It was a talk on Soviet Russia but it didn't seem to hold her. She turned it off and came over to the fire.

"That wife of Tom's came up today," she says, "and wanted to know if I wouldn't give her some milk. I told her I'd give her a gallon if she'd churn every day."

I put my paper down. "A gallon of milk! You know what that would cost you in town?"

"I ain't in town," the old lady says, "and ain't going to be if I keep my reason. The milk don't cost me anything and I'm glad for 'em to have it.

I'm going to have Frankie get supper every night too. Of course I'll pay her extra for that."

"You don't really need her, do you?" I asked.

"No, I don't need her," the old lady says, "but when I find one that's willing to work I like to encourage 'em. So many of 'em won't do a hand's turn these days."

"Tom's a good man," I says, "but that Frankie don't look like much of a worker to me."

"She ain't overly strong," the old lady says, "but she's a good cook. All those Byars girls are good cooks."

Well, it went on like that. The way I figured it Frankie got paid for everything she did but every day she'd do a little something extra that she hadn't been paid for and that kept the old lady feeling good. It was like they were running a race, with Frankie lagging on the turns so the old lady'd always keep in the lead. I got to worrying for fear they'd get all the chores done some day and Frankie'd have to pass the old lady.

There was one other thing worried me. Frankie was well named. She and Tom were just like the niggers in the song. They were willing to work but loving came first. Every day after dinner Frankie would leave the dishes there on the table and she and Tom would head for the cabin. I was afraid the old lady'd notice and one day I took the bull by the horns. "Don't Frankie do any work in the afternoons?" I asked. "I came through the kitchen at one o'clock the other day and she'd left all her dinner dishes."

The old lady bridled up. "She goes to the cabin to rest a few minutes right after dinner. Good cooks are all like that. They get nervous, cooking. They have to cool off before they can eat anything."

I thought that as long as the old lady thought Frankie went to the cabin to cool off it was all right. I was pretty busy about that time. I don't know whether you ever raised any dark tobacco. A man ought not to go into it unless he wants to keep on the move. There's something to do every month in the year. We start burning our plant beds in February. In April it's time to take the canvas off and let the plants toughen up. Then from the middle of April on through May and sometimes up to the first of June you're on pins and needles waiting for a good season to set your tobacco. In our country we have some of the worst droughts in the spring. It's a hard proposition, setting tobacco when the ground isn't wet. You have to water every plant by hand and at that you're lucky if you get a stand.

We had some good rains in May, though, that year. I got my whole crop set on two rains. It was a fine stand and grew off pretty. By July my tobacco was waist-high, good, broad, spreading leaves too. She was ready to cut by the first of August. And I got the whole crop—ten thousand pounds of tobacco—cut and into the barn by August fifteenth. I felt pretty good about that but I knew the hardest job was still ahead. It's the curing that tells the tale. You've got to put the smoke to her just right.

I'd been around tobacco barns a lot when I was a kid. I knew it was the devil of a job to get the right color and finish on a leaf but I wasn't worrying. Uncle Phil, for all he is so lazy, knows a lot about farming. I thought I only had to ask him when the time came.

I let my tobacco yellow for about a week before I started the fires: good chunks of hickory going in all four corners of the barn. I fired off and on, according to the season, for two weeks and then I called the old man up and asked him how much longer I ought to let the fires go.

"Hell," he says, "how do I know?"

"You been raising dark tobacco for fifty years," I told him. "You ought to know something about it."

"I know one thing," he says, "you'll house-burn it, sure as God made little apples, if you're let alone."

"Why'n't you come on over and show me how to fire it then?" I asked, knowing he wouldn't stir out of his house if half the barns in the country were burning down.

"I haven't cured a crop of tobacco in thirty years," he says.

"What do you do when firing time comes?"

"I get somebody that knows more about it than I do. Go on over and get Bud Asbury. He's a genius at it."

I drove over to the Asbury place. The first thing I saw was Old Man Asbury coming around the corner of the barn. He hadn't changed since I was a child: little old dried up pea of a man rattling around in his overalls. I had to go in and howdy with old Mrs. Asbury before I could tell him what I wanted. He said Bud wasn't home right now but he knew he'd be glad to help me. "All right, then," I said, "tell him to drop around tomorrow morning."

The old man looked kind of worried. He began all over again, saying Bud would be proud to help me—if he was home when the time came.

"Has he got a job somewhere?" I asked.

The old man said no, he didn't have any job.

"Well, don't he come home to sleep?"

The old man said the fact was he hadn't seen Bud for three, four days. "You know he always was a rambling sort of a boy," he said.

"Well, I hope he'll ramble in here tomorrow morning," I told him, "or I'll have to get somebody else to cure that tobacco."

I went on home. Fifteen minutes after I got there Uncle Phil called up. "Have you read today's *Tobacco-Leaf?*" he asked.

I told him I'd been too busy to even take the paper out of the box.

"It's a good thing for you I read the paper," he said. "You better go on into town and get Bud Asbury out of jail."

"What's he in jail for?"

"For taking a man's car."

"Maybe he'd better stay in jail," I said.

The old man laughed. "Bud wouldn't steal a pin. You go on in there and tell the judge to turn Bud loose, that you need him to fire your tobacco. No, tell him I said I needed him to fire *my* tobacco. You better take some money. There's a drunk and disorderly charge too."

I went on in. The judge is a mighty pleasant old man. We howdied about the healths of both our families and then I told him what Uncle Phil said. "Well, now," he said, "I'm glad Phil can use him. That charge they've laid against Bud is just a piece of Bill Cain's foolishness."

Bill Cain is our prosecuting attorney. "Has he got it in for Bud?" I asked.

The judge explained that Bill Cain and Chief Patterson didn't exactly have it in for Bud. They were just worn out with him. It seems that Bud is a spree drinker, goes on a bat regularly every two or three months. He's also one of these blind drunks that never lose the use of their legs. This time he'd come out of a speakeasy and got in somebody else's car and drove off. The man who lost the car figured that Bud had it because Bud's car was still sitting there in the square next morning. But he goes ahead just the same and swears out a warrant for Bud's arrest.

"And Bill Cain," the judge said testily, "was fool enough to serve it."

I told the judge I thought Uncle Phil would go on Bud's bond and in the meantime I'd take him home and sober him up with a little work. Tom said he'd drive Bud's car over to the Asburys'. I went by police court and paid his fine and then went on over to the county jail.

Mr. Cleaver, the sheriff, and Bud and two niggers were sitting in the hall playing checkers. I told Mr. Cleaver what I wanted and he said all right but he'd be obliged if I'd wait a few minutes: he and Bud were having a tournament with the niggers. "This boy, Billy," he says, pointing over his shoulder, "is the champion of Dunham's warehouse but Bud and me are going to beat him if you'll give us time to finish this game."

I said all right and came in and watched them. Bud looked like he was still drunk or else he had a whale of a hangover. He sat up there stiff as a dead man, pushing those checkers around. He's a tall, lean fellow, about forty years old, one of the handsomest men I ever saw in my life but with a kind of shattered look to him. It wasn't his features or the fact that he'd slept in his clothes. It was his eyes: he had that cold-looking blue eye you see sometimes in steady drinkers or sometimes in men that just don't give a damn. I decided I'd as soon not meet him when he was on one of his sprees.

They finished their game—the niggers beat 'em four out of six. The sheriff went in his office and telephoned Uncle Phil, then came back and told Bud good-bye. "Don't stay away so long next time, Bud," he says, winking at me.

"They ain't goin' to be no next time, Mister Cleaver," Bud tells him.

As we drove home he gave me quite a lecture on drinking. The trouble, he said, was the liquor they sold you nowadays. It had got so that he was almost a teetotaler, never knowing how the liquor would take him. Once he wanted me to stop the car. He was a mind to go back and beat up Lonny Cross who'd sold him the liquor. You'd think, he said, that you could go in a man's bar and have a drink, friendly like, without him poisoning you. I told him he'd better leave Lonny Cross alone. He wasn't out of the woods yet on that larceny charge. He didn't seem worried about that. His idea was that the prosecutor must have been drunk when he let the man swear out the warrant. "Must have been. Mister Cain knows I wouldn't steal anybody's car. Why, a man needs his car to get around in."

We drove into the Grove about five o'clock. Tom had just got back from the Asburys'. I stopped by the barn a minute and then I took Bud on up to the house. I went in the back way like I always do when I've got mud on my boots. Frankie was frying some fish one of the boys had caught in Grinstead's pond. She said the old lady hadn't been feeling so well and was lying down.

The kitchen smelled mighty good with fish frying and coffee making. There was a table in the corner that Frankie always kept covered with a fresh cloth. I thought that as long as the old lady wasn't coming in Bud and I might as well eat at that table so I told Frankie not to bother making a fire in the dining room and then I went on in to see the old lady.

She was lying down, listening to the radio. I stayed with her awhile and then I left her with the radio turned low and went back to the kitchen.

Tom had come in from the barn and was sitting on his bench back of the stove. Frankie had put a chair up to the table for Bud and he was sitting there, smoking. I thought he must be needing a drink bad by this time so I stepped into the dining room and found a pint bottle that was three quarters full of whiskey. I divided it between the four of us, giving Bud a little the best of the deal.

He turned his glass up and downed her at one smack. "You ain't got any more of that?" he says.

I told him that as far as I knew it was the last in the house. "Miss Jinny and Frankie are teetotalers," I said.

Tom lets out a laugh. That was a joke we had. The old lady doesn't believe in using liquor except for medicine and cooking. "I just take it to ease the pain," she says, but one way or another she and Frankie get through with about a quart a week.

Frankie laughs too. "You can leave it around here all you want, Mister Jim. I ain't gwine tech it."

"I'll drink your share, Frankie," Bud says.

He was looking different from what he had when he came in. Those funny blue eyes were shining and he had color in his cheeks. If I hadn't known there wasn't any liquor in the house I'd have thought he was starting on another drunk.

Frankie was taking her fish off the stove. We drew up our chairs. Her coffee was good that night and we had a dozen of those little pond perch fried a golden brown. And every time we turned around Frankie was there with more batter bread. I told her I believed it was the best she'd ever made.

She had just handed me a piece and was going on to Bud. He looked up at her. "Yeah," he said, "and them's mighty pretty little yellow hands that made it."

Nobody said anything for a minute. Before I knew it I'd looked over at Tom. He was sitting on a bench by the stove and he slewed around as sudden as if he'd been pulled by a string. His eyes popped open and fastened on Bud's face. Then he realized that I was looking at him and he ducked his head and began eating again, real slow.

I looked back at Bud. He looked back as unconcerned as you please. I kept on looking at him. I made my voice real hard. "Eat up, Bud," I said; "it's time we were getting to the barn."

"That tobacco ain't goin' to walk off," he says and laughs and looks up at Frankie, who was still standing there by the table.

I pushed my chair back. "I'm ready now," I said. "I'll be obliged if you'd come with me."

He put one last piece of corn bread in his mouth and reached for his hat. We went out the back way and started down to the barn. We hadn't gone far before Bud said he'd have to stop a minute. I thought he had to see a man about a dog and walked on. I hadn't been in the barn more than ten minutes before he came in. And in a little while Tom came too.

We set to work building up the fires. You can't have flames going any length of time. You've got to have red-hot embers and keeping a hickory log at that stage takes doing. But Tom was good at it, as Bud remarked.

Bud seemed to be feeling better and better. He went over the barn, pinching a leaf here and there. He said the tobacco was in exactly the right order. Seems it's all a matter of draft. If you have too much draft the lighter edges of the leaf'll dry out too quick and set in whatever colour they happen to have at the time, instead of making the nice brown everybody wants.

He talked a lot about houseburning. Said there wasn't any use of anybody houseburning their tobacco if they kept their minds on it. Said it comes from letting your fires die out too sudden. That vapor'll stop right in the middle of the barn and condense into sweat. She's gone then, he said, and can't anything bring her back. But the nearer you can bring her to houseburning without burning her the prettier she'll be.

About twelve o'clock we got up to go up to the house for more coffee.

Tom got up too. I'd intended to leave him there to watch the fires but something about the way he looked made me change my mind.

The three of us started back to the house but Bud dropped off as we were crossing the yard. Seemed to me he was having a lot of sudden calls that night and I so remarked to Tom.

Tom laughed, kind of surly. "He done gone to git him some more of that wine. Whilst you in talking to Old Miss he went in the dining room and got him a whole jug of blackberry wine."

"Why'n't you stop him, Tom?"

Tom laughed again. "Mister Jim, you know I couldn't head Mister Bud Asbury off when he wants to do anything."

"Is he mean?" I asked. "Has he got the reputation of being mean?"

"He's hard to head," Tom said. "The jedge or anybody that has the handlin' of him'll tell you that."

Bud was already sitting up to the table when we came in. "Come on," he called, like it was his house and not mine. "Come on and git some of these good sandwiches Frankie made us."

I could see he'd taken on another load of the old lady's wine. He kept laughing most of the time and once when Frankie was passing something he made a swipe low with his hand and caught hold of her ankle.

Frankie was quick. She flopped over against the table, spilling half the sandwiches. " 'Scuse me, Mister Bud," she says, "I mighty nigh fell on you."

"It don't make a bit of difference," Bud says genially. "You fall all over me if you want to."

I was stumped. I've been around a good bit. I know plenty of men that think nothing of sleeping with nigger women but I never saw one in the act of going after a nigger woman before. It gave me a funny feeling. And I was worried about Tom. Tom is a boy that thinks a lot of his raising. I don't reckon he'd ever spoken an out-of-the-way word to a white person in his life—until that night.

Bud finished eating and got up and went out on the porch, to get a drink of water, he said. He was out there a few minutes and then he came to the door. "Frankie," he called, "step here a minute."

Frankie jumped up quick like she always does when there's any waiting on to do and then she must have realized what he wanted, for she stopped short and just stood there, staring at him.

Tom was getting up from his bench behind the stove. He kept on coming till he was right in the middle of the floor and then he stopped. "Mister Bud," he said, "that's my woman."

I saw his hand go up, slow, over his jumper. He wears one of these old-fashioned cutting razors slung around his neck on a piece of string.

I stepped out between them. I looked him straight in the eye. "Tom!" I said, "Tom! You sit down there behind that stove."

That nigger looked at me like he'd never seen me before. Then his eyes changed. "Yas, sir," he said, kind of dazed. "Yas, sir, that's what I was going to do."

I looked at Frankie. I was mad through by that time and it seemed to me that more'n half of it was her fault. Those high yellows just can't help bridling if a man looks at 'em. "Frankie," I said, "do you want to go out on that porch with Mister Asbury?"

She was crying. "Naw, suh, I don't want to go out there with no white man."

"Well, go on over there and sit down by Tom and try behaving yourself for a change."

She went off sniffling and I walked over and stood in front of Tom. "Tom," I told him, "I'm going out there to see Mister Asbury and I don't want any niggers mixing in. You understand?"

"Yas, sir," he said, keeping his eyes on the floor.

I stepped outside. Bud was walking around in the yard. It was dark out there when you stood away from the window. The fool thought I was Frankie. He made a dive at me. "Come on, honey," he says, "let's you and me take a walk."

I caught him by the arm. "You're going to take a walk," I says, "but you ain't going with Frankie. Now, Bud, when you get through that gate you hit the big road and you keep going till you strike your old man's house."

We were passing the window. I could see the surprised look on his face. "Now, Jim," he says, "what have I done to get you down on me like that?"

"You been making passes at Frankie right in my kitchen," I told him. "I ain't going to have it."

"All right," he says sadly, "if that's the way you feel," and he goes off across the yard. He hadn't gone but a few steps before he stopped. "I ain't goin'," he says, sullen like a child. "I ain't ever started curing a crop of tobacco that I didn't finish it. I'm goin' right back to the barn."

I saw there was nothing else for it so I tackled him. I caught him around the knees and we both went down together in the mud. He tried to get up but I shifted my hold and got him around the chest. He broke my hold without half trying and the next thing I knew he had me flat on my back in the mud. "I hate to do this," he says, "but you don't seem to have no sense tonight."

I didn't say anything and after a minute he let me go and got up. I jumped to my feet and went at him again. This time I knocked him over backwards, but he turned, quick as a cat, and had me with a leg hold.

We clinched two or three times after that. I never could break his hold but he'd let me go just so I could come at him again. His blood was up now and he was enjoying himself. As for me I was beginning to think that if anybody hit the big road that night it'd be me.

The last time he threw me plumb over his head. I landed so hard I thought my neck was snapped in two. I lay there a second trying to get my breath. Then I realized that my left hand was hurting like blazes. I moved it. Something rattled. I'd landed against a pile of tobacco sticks. I took another good breath and got up with one of those oak sticks in my hand.

The kitchen door opened, real soft. Tom came out. "Mister Jim," he called, "you want me to come out there and help you tie up Mister Bud?"

"You come out here," I said, "and you'll get the worst beating you ever got in your life."

I walked over and let Bud have that solid oak, whang, on the side of his head. He rocked a little like cattle do when you fell them and then he started towards me. But my legs were still good. I jumped to the side, quick. "Bud," I said, "I'm going to raise knots on the other side of your head if you don't hit the big road."

I don't believe he knew what had hit him till that minute. He stopped and fingered his head and then came at me. I let him have it again, a harder lick this time. It knocked him down but not out. That boy's head was hard as bow-dock. After a bit he got on his feet. He stood there, staggering, then he says, real polite, "All right, if that's the way you feel," and starts for the gate.

I went on in the house. "Come on, Tom," I said, "we better get back to the barn."

We took turns the rest of the night, sleeping and firing. But we had let the fires go plumb out while we were having the ruckus and the barn had got cold. We got the fires going good again and kept a steady fire the rest of the night and the wind had changed so it was making the draft just the way you want it. But before I left the barn, towards daybreak, I pulled down a leaf and felt it. It wasn't what you'd call dry but it had lost that kid-glove feeling. Tobacco has a skin just like a woman. Once that stretchiness is gone out of a leaf it's gone and there ain't anything can bring it back.

Daylight was coming in through the open doors. I looked at the tiers of tobacco hanging all the way up to the roof. Ten thousand pounds and if it had been cured right we'd have got thirty cents for every pound of the prime leaf but now we'd do well to get fifteen.

Tom was just getting up from a pile of sacks, feeling his leg that had gone to sleep. "Tom," I said, "take a look up there."

"What is it," he says, "old possum or something on the rafters?"

"It ain't any possum," I said, "but last night we had nineteen hundred and sixty dollars hanging up over us and now we ain't got but nine hundred and thirty."

Tom looked at the tobacco and then he looked at me. He poked his lip out. "That Mister Bud Asbury," he said, "I don't care how good he can cure tobacco. He better stay away from my woman."

I didn't say anything. A man has to fight if somebody tries to take his woman. But I couldn't stand by and watch that nigger carve Bud up. It struck me as a funny business. Always has.

WALTER VAN TILBURG CLARK

The Portable Phonograph ℘

The red sunset, with narrow, black cloud strips like threats across
it, lay on the curved horizon of the prairie. The air was still and
cold, and in it settled the mute darkness and greater cold of night.
High in the air there was wind, for through the veil of the dusk the clouds
could be seen gliding rapidly south and changing shapes. A queer sensation
of torment, of two-sided, unpredictable nature, arose from the stillness of
the earth air beneath the violence of the upper air. Out of the sunset, through
the dead, matted grass and isolated weed stalks of the prairie, crept the
narrow and deeply rutted remains of a road. In the road, in places, there
were crusts of shallow, brittle ice. There were little islands of an old oiled
pavement in the road too, but most of it was mud, now frozen rigid. The
frozen mud still bore the toothed impress of great tanks, and a wanderer
on the neighboring undulations might have stumbled, in this light, into
large, partially filled-in and weed-grown cavities, their banks channelled
and beginning to spread into badlands. These pits were such as might have
been made by falling meteors, but they were not. They were the scars of
gigantic bombs, their rawness already made a little natural by rain, seed,
and time. Along the road, there were rakish remnants of fence. There was
also, just visible, one portion of tangled and multiple barbed wire still erect,
behind which was a shelving ditch with small caves, now very quiet and
empty, at intervals in its back wall. Otherwise there was no structure or
remnant of a structure visible over the dome of the darkling earth, but only,
in sheltered hollows, the darker shadows of young trees trying again.

Under the wuthering arch of the high wind a V of wild geese fled south.
The rush of their pinions sounded briefly, and the faint, plaintive notes of
their expeditionary talk. Then they left a still greater vacancy. There was the
smell and expectation of snow, as there is likely to be when the wild geese fly
south. From the remote distance, towards the red sky, came faintly the pro-
tracted howl and quick yap-yap of a prairie wolf.

North of the road, perhaps a hundred yards, lay the parallel and deeply
intrenched course of a small creek, lined with leafless alders and willows. The
creek was already silent under ice. Into the bank above it was dug a sort of
cell, with a single opening, like the mouth of a mine tunnel. Within the cell
there was a little red of fire, which showed dully through the opening, like a

reflection or a deception of the imagination. The light came from the chary burning of four blocks of poorly aged peat, which gave off a petty warmth and much acrid smoke. But the precious remnants of wood, old fence posts and timbers from the long-deserted dugouts, had to be saved for the real cold, for the time when a man's breath blew white, the moisture in his nostrils stiffened at once when he stepped out, and the expansive blizzards paraded for days over the vast open, swirling and settling and thickening, till the dawn of the cleared day when the sky was thin blue-green and the terrible cold, in which a man could not live for three hours unwarmed, lay over the uniformly drifted swell of the plain.

Around the smoldering peat, four men were seated cross-legged. Behind them, traversed by their shadows, was the earth bench, with two old and dirty army blankets, where the owner of the cell slept. In a niche in the opposite wall were a few tin utensils which caught the glint of the coals. The host was rewrapping in a piece of daubed burlap four fine, leather-bound books. He worked slowly and very carefully, and at last tied the bundle securely with a piece of grass-woven cord. The other three looked intently upon the process, as if a great significance lay in it. As the host tied the cord, he spoke. He was an old man, his long, matted beard and hair gray to nearly white. The shadows made his brows and cheekbones appear gnarled, his eyes and cheeks deeply sunken. His big hands, rough with frost and swollen by rheumatism, were awkward but gentle at their task. He was like a prehistoric priest performing a fateful ceremonial rite. Also his voice had in it a suitable quality of deep, reverent despair, yet perhaps at the moment, a sharpness of selfish satisfaction.

"When I perceived what was happening," he said, "I told myself, 'It is the end. I cannot take much; I will take these.'

"Perhaps I was impractical," he continued. "But for myself, I do not regret, and what do we know of those who will come after us? We are the doddering remnant of a race of mechanical fools. I have saved what I love; the soul of what was good in us is here; perhaps the new ones will make a strong enough beginning not to fall behind when they become clever."

He rose with slow pain and placed the wrapped volumes in the niche with his utensils. The others watched him with the same ritualistic gaze.

"Shakespeare, the Bible, *Moby Dick*, the *Divine Comedy*," one of them said softly. "You might have done worse, much worse."

"You will have a little soul left until you die," said another harshly. "That is more than is true of us. My brain becomes thick, like my hands." He held the big, battered hands, with their black nails, in the glow to be seen.

"I want paper to write on," he said. "And there is none."

The fourth man said nothing. He sat in the shadow farthest from the fire, and sometimes his body jerked in its rags from the cold. Although he was still young, he was sick and coughed often. Writing implied a greater future than he now felt able to consider.

The old man seated himself laboriously, and reached out, groaning at the movement, to put another block of peat on the fire. With bowed heads and averted eyes, his three guests acknowledged his magnanimity.

"We thank you, Doctor Jenkins, for the reading," said the man who had named the books.

They seemed then to be waiting for something. Doctor Jenkins understood, but was loath to comply. In an ordinary moment he would have said nothing. But the words of *The Tempest,* which he had been reading, and the religious attention of the three made this an unusual occasion.

"You wish to hear the phonograph," he said grudgingly.

The two middle-aged men stared into the fire, unable to formulate and expose the enormity of their desire.

The young man, however, said anxiously, between suppressed coughs, "Oh, please," like an excited child.

The old man rose again in his difficult way, and went to the back of the cell. He returned and placed tenderly upon the packed floor, where the fire-light might fall upon it, an old portable phonograph in a black case. He smoothed the top with his hand, and then opened it. The lovely green-felt-covered disk became visible.

"I have been using thorns as needles," he said. "But tonight, because we have a musician among us"—he bent his head to the young man, almost invisible in the shadow—"I will use a steel needle. There are only three left."

The two middle-aged men stared at him in speechless adoration. The one with the big hands, who wanted to write, moved his lips, but the whisper was not audible.

"Oh, don't!" cried the young man, as if he were hurt. "The thorns will do beautifully."

"No," the old man said. "I have become accustomed to the thorns, but they are not really good. For you, my young friend, we will have good music tonight."

"After all," he added generously, and beginning to wind the phonograph, which creaked, "they can't last forever."

"No, nor we," the man who needed to write said harshly. "The needle, by all means."

"Oh, thanks," said the young man. "Thanks," he said again in a low, excited voice, and then stifled his coughing with a bowed head.

"The records, though," said the old man when he had finished winding, "are a different matter. Already they are very worn. I do not play them more than once a week. One, once a week, that is what I allow myself.

"More than a week I cannot stand it; not to hear them," he apologized.

"No, how could you?" cried the young man. "And with them here like this."

"A man can stand anything," said the man who wanted to write, in his harsh, antagonistic voice.

"Please, the music," said the young man.

"Only the one," said the old man. "In the long run, we will remember more that way."

He had a dozen records with luxuriant gold and red seals. Even in that light the others could see that the threads of the records were becoming worn. Slowly he read out the titles and the tremendous, dead names of the composers and the artists and the orchestras. The three worked upon the names in their minds, carefully. It was difficult to select from such a wealth what they would at once most like to remember. Finally, the man who wanted to write named Gershwin's "New York."

"Oh, no," cried the sick young man, and then could say nothing more because he had to cough. The others understood him, and the harsh man withdrew his selection and waited for the musician to choose.

The musician begged Doctor Jenkins to read the titles again, very slowly, so that he could remember the sounds. While they were read, he lay back against the wall, his eyes closed, his thin, horny hand pulling at his light beard, and listened to the voices and the orchestras and the single instruments in his mind.

When the reading was done he spoke despairingly. "I have forgotten," he complained; "I cannot hear them clearly.

"There are things missing," he explained.

"I know," said Doctor Jenkins. "I thought that I knew all of Shelley by heart. I should have brought Shelley."

"That's more soul than we can use," said the harsh man. "*Moby Dick* is better.

"By God, we can understand that," he emphasized.

The Doctor nodded.

"Still," said the man who had admired the books, "we need the absolute if we are to keep a grasp on anything.

"Anything but these sticks and peat clods and rabbit snares," he said bitterly.

"Shelley desired an ultimate absolute," said the harsh man. "It's too much," he said. "It's no good; no earthly good."

The musician selected a Debussy nocturne. The others considered and approved. They rose to their knees to watch the Doctor prepare for the playing, so that they appeared to be actually in an attitude of worship. The peat glow showed the thinness of their bearded faces, and the deep lines in them, and revealed the condition of their garments. The other two continued to kneel as the old man carefully lowered the needle onto the spinning disk, but the musician suddenly drew back against the wall again, with his knees up, and buried his face in his hands.

At the first notes of the piano the listeners were startled. They stared at each other. Even the musician lifted his head in amazement, but then quickly bowed it again, strainingly, as if he were suffering from a pain he might not be able to endure. They were all listening deeply, without movement. The wet, blue-green notes tinkled forth from the old machine, and were individual, delectable presences in the cell. The individual, delectable presences swept into a sudden tide of unbearably beautiful dissonance, and then continued fully the swelling and ebbing of that tide, the dissonant inpourings, and the resolutions, and the diminishments, and the little, quiet wavelets of interlude lapping between. Every sound was piercing and singularly sweet. In all the men except the musician, there occurred rapid sequences of tragically heightened recollection. He heard nothing but what was there. At the final, whispering disappearance, but moving quietly so that the others would not hear him and look at him, he let his head fall back in agony, as if it were drawn there by the hair, and clenched the fingers of one hand over his teeth. He sat that way while the others were silent, and until they began to breathe again normally. His drawn-up legs were trembling violently.

Quickly Doctor Jenkins lifted the needle off, to save it and not to spoil the recollection with scraping. When he had stopped the whirling of the sacred disk, he courteously left the phonograph open and by the fire, in sight.

The others, however, understood. The musician rose last, but then abruptly, and went quickly out at the door without saying anything. The others stopped at the door and gave their thanks in low voices. The Doctor nodded magnificently.

"Come again," he invited, "in a week. We will have the 'New York.'"

When the two had gone together, out towards the rimed road, he stood in the entrance, peering and listening. At first, there was only the resonant boom of the wind overhead, and then far over the dome of the dead, dark plain, the wolf cry lamenting. In the rifts of clouds the Doctor saw four stars flying. It impressed the Doctor that one of them had just been obscured by the beginning of a flying cloud at the very moment he heard what he had been listening for, a sound of suppressed coughing. It was not near-by, however. He believed that down against the pale alders he could see the moving shadow.

With nervous hands he lowered the piece of canvas which served as his door, and pegged it at the bottom. Then quickly and quietly, looking at the piece of canvas frequently, he slipped the records into the case, snapped the lid shut, and carried the phonograph to his couch. There, pausing often to stare at the canvas and listen, he dug earth from the wall and disclosed a piece of board. Behind this there was a deep hole in the wall, into which he put the phonograph. After a moment's consideration, he went over and reached down his bundle of books and inserted it also. Then, guardedly, he once more sealed up the hole with the board and the earth. He also changed his blankets, and the grass-stuffed sack which served as a pillow, so that he could lie facing the entrance. After carefully placing two more blocks of peat upon the fire, he stood for a long time watching the stretched canvas, but it seemed to billow naturally with the first gusts of a lowering wind. At last he prayed, and got in under his blankets, and closed his smoke-smarting eyes. On the inside of the bed, next the wall, he could feel with his hand the comfortable piece of lead pipe.

WALLACE STEGNER

Butcher Bird 🐦

That summer the boy was alone on the farm except for his parents. His brother was working at Orullian's Grocery in town, and there was no one to run the trap line with or swim with in the dark, weed-smelling reservoir where garter snakes made straight rapid lines in the water and the skaters rowed close to shore. So every excursion was an adventure, even if it was only a trip across the three miles of prairie to Larsen's to get mail or groceries. He was excited at the visit to Garfield's as he was excited by everything unusual. The hot midsummer afternoon was still and breathless, the air harder to breathe than usual. He knew there was a change in weather coming because the gingersnaps in their tall cardboard box were soft and bendable when he snitched two to stick in his pocket. He could tell too by his father's grumpiness accumulated through two weeks of drought, his habit of looking off into the southwest, from which either rain or hot winds might come, that something was brewing. If it was rain everything would be fine, his father would hum under his breath getting breakfast, maybe let him drive the stoneboat or ride the mare down to Larsen's for mail. If it was hot wind they'd have to walk soft and speak softer, and it wouldn't be any fun.

They didn't know the Garfields, who had moved in only the fall before, but people said they had a good big house and a bigger barn and that Mr. Garfield was an Englishman and a little funny talking about scientific farming and making the desert blossom like the rose. The boy's father hadn't wanted to go, but his mother thought it was unneighborly not to call at least once in a whole year when people lived only four miles away. She was, the boy knew, as anxious for a change, as eager to get out of that atmosphere of waiting to see what the weather would do—that tense and teeth-gritting expectancy—as he was.

He found more than he looked for at Garfield's. Mr. Garfield was tall and bald with a big nose, and talked very softly and politely. The boy's father was determined not to like him right from the start.

When Mr. Garfield said, "Dear, I think we might have a glass of lemonade, don't you?", the boy saw his parents look at each other, saw the beginning of a contemptuous smile on his father's face, saw his mother purse her lips and shake her head ever so little. And when Mrs. Garfield, prim and spectacled, with a habit of tucking her head back and to one side while she listened to anyone talk, brought in the lemonade, the boy saw his father taste his and make a little face behind the glass. He hated any summer drink without ice in it, and had spent two whole weeks digging a dugout icehouse just so that he could have ice water and cold beer when the hot weather came.

But Mr. and Mrs. Garfield were nice people. They sat down in their new parlor and showed the boy's mother the rug and the gramophone. When the boy came up curiously to inspect the little box with the petunia-shaped horn and the little china dog with "His Master's Voice" on it, and the Garfields found that he had never seen or heard a gramophone, they put on a cylinder like a big spool of tightly wound black thread and lowered a needle on it, and out came a man's voice singing in Scotch brogue, and his mother smiled and nodded and said, "My land, Harry Lauder! I heard him once a long time ago. Isn't it wonderful, Sonny?"

It was wonderful all right. He inspected it, reached out his fingers to touch things, wiggled the big horn to see if it was loose or screwed in. His father warned him sharply to keep his hands off, but then Mr. Garfield smiled and said, "Oh, he can't hurt it. Let's play something else," and found a record about the saucy little bird on Nelly's hat that had them all laughing. They let him wind the machine and play the record over again, all by himself, and he was very careful. It was a fine machine. He wished he had one.

About the time he had finished playing his sixth or seventh record, and George M. Cohan was singing "She's a grand old flag, she's a high-flying flag, and forever in peace may she wave," he glanced at his father and discovered that he was grouchy about something. He wasn't taking any part in the conversation but was sitting with his chin in his hand staring out of the window. Mr. Garfield was looking at him a little helplessly. His eyes met the boy's and he motioned him over.

"What do you find to do all summer? Only child, are you?"

"No, sir. My brother's in Whitemud. He's twelve. He's got a job."

"So you come out on the farm to help," said Mr. Garfield. He had his hand on the boy's shoulder and his voice was so kind that the boy lost his shyness and felt no embarrassment at all in being out there in the middle of the parlor with all of them watching.

"I don't help much," he said. "I'm too little to do anything but drive the stoneboat, Pa says. When I'm twelve he's going to get me a gun and then I can go hunting."

"Hunting?" Mr. Garfield said. "What do you hunt?"

"Oh, gophers and weasels. I got a pet weasel. His name's Lucifer."

"Well," said Mr. Garfield. "You seem to be a pretty manly little chap. What do you feed your weasel?"

"Gophers." The boy thought it best not to say that the gophers were live ones he threw into the weasel's cage. He thought probably Mr. Garfield would be a little shocked at that.

Mr. Garfield straightened up and looked round at the grown folks. "Isn't it a shame," he said," "that there are so many predatory animals and pests in this country that we have to spend our time destroying them? I hate killing things."

"I hate weasels," the boy said. "I'm just saving this one till he turns into an ermine, and then I'm going to skin him. Once I speared a weasel with the pitchfork in the chicken coop and he dropped right off the tine and ran up my leg and bit me after he was speared clean through."

He finished breathlessly, and his mother smiled at him, motioning him not to talk so much. But Mr. Garfield was still looking at him kindly. "So you want to make war on the cruel things, the weasels and hawks," he said.

"Yes, sir," the boy said. He looked at his mother and it was all right. He hadn't spoiled anything by telling about the weasels.

"Now that reminds me," Mr. Garfield said, rising. "Maybe I've got something you'd find useful."

He went into another room and came back with a .22 in his hand. "Could you use this?"

"I . . . yes, *sir!*" the boy said. He had almost, in his excitement, said "I hope to whisk in your piskers," because that was what his father always said when he meant anything real hard.

"If your parents want you to have it," Mr. Garfield said and raised his eyebrows at the boy's mother. He didn't look at the father, but the boy did.

"Can I, Pa?"

"I guess so," his father said. "Sure."

"Thank Mr. Garfield nicely," said his mother.

"Gee," the boy breathed. "Thanks, Mr. Garfield, ever so much."

"There's a promise goes with it," Mr. Garfield said. "I'd like you to promise never to shoot anything with it but the bloodthirsty animals—the cruel ones like weasels and hawks. Never anything like birds or prairie dogs."

"How about butcher birds?"

"Butcher birds?" Mr. Garfield said.

"Shrikes," said the boy's mother. "We've got some over by our place. They kill all sorts of things, snakes and gophers and other birds. They're worse than the hawks because they just kill for the fun of it."

"By all means," said Mr. Garfield. "Shoot all the shrikes you see. A thing that kills for the fun of it . . ." He shook his head and his voice got solemn, almost like the voice of Mr. McGregor, the Sunday School Superintendent in town, when he was asking the benediction. "There's something about the way the war drags on, or maybe just this country," he said, "that makes me hate killing. I just can't bear to shoot anything any more, even a weasel."

The boy's father turned cold eyes away from Mr. Garfield and looked out of the window. One big brown hand, a little dirty from the wheel of the car, rubbed against the day-old bristles on his jaws. Then he stood up and stretched. "Well, we got to be going," he said.

"Oh, stay a little while," Mr. Garfield said. "You just came. I wanted to show you my trees."

The boy's mother stared at him. "Trees?"

He smiled. "Sounds a bit odd out here, doesn't it? But I think trees will grow. I've made some plantings down below."

"I'd love to see them," she said. "Sometimes I'd give almost anything to get into a good deep shady woods. Just to smell it, and feel how cool . . ."

"There's a little story connected with these," Mr. Garfield said. He spoke to the mother alone, warmly. "When we first decided to come out here I said to Martha that if trees wouldn't grow we shouldn't stick it. That's just what I said, 'If trees won't grow we shan't stick it.' Trees are almost the breath of life to me."

The boy's father was shaken by a sudden spell of coughing, and the mother shot a quick look at him and looked back at Mr. Garfield with a light flush on her cheekbones. "I'd love to see them," she said. "I was raised in Minnesota, and I never will get used to a place as barren as this."

"When I think of the beeches back home in England," Mr. Garfield said, and shook his head with a puckering smile round his eyes.

The father lifted himself heavily out of his chair and followed the rest of them out to the coulee edge. Below them willows grew profusely along the almost-dry creek, and farther back from the water there was a grove of perhaps twenty trees about a dozen feet high.

"I'm trying cottonwoods first because they can stand dry weather," Mr. Garfield said.

The mother was looking down with all her longings suddenly plain and naked in her eyes. "It's wonderful," she said. "I'd give almost anything to have some on our place."

"I found the willows close by here," said Mr. Garfield. "Just at the south end of the hills they call Old-Man-on-His-Back, where the stream comes down."

"Stream?" the boy's father said. "You mean that trickle?"

"It's not much of a stream," Mr. Garfield said apologetically. "But . . ."

"Are there any more there?" the mother said.

"Oh, yes. You could get some. Cut them diagonally and push them into any damp ground. They'll grow."

"They'll grow about six feet high," the father said.

"Yes," said Mr. Garfield. "They're not, properly speaking, trees. Still . . ."

"It's getting pretty smothery," the father said rather loudly. "We better be getting on."

This time Mr. Garfield didn't object, and they went back to the car exchanging promises of visits. The father jerked the crank and climbed into the Ford, where the boy was sighting along his gun. "Put that down," his father said. "Don't you know any better than to point a gun around people?"

"It isn't loaded."

"They never are," his father said. "Put it down now."

The Garfields were standing with their arms round each other's waists, waiting to wave good-by. Mr. Garfield reached over and picked something from his wife's dress.

"What was it, Alfred?" she said peering.

"Nothing. Just a bit of fluff."

The boy's father coughed violently and the car started with a jerk. With his head down almost to the wheel, still coughing, he waved, and the mother and the boy waved as they went down along the badly set cedar posts of the pasture fence. They were almost a quarter of a mile away before the boy, with a last wave of the gun, turned around again and saw that his father was purple with laughter. He rocked the car with his joy, and when his wife said, "Oh, Harry, you big fool," he pointed helplessly to his shoulder. "Would you mind," he said. "Would you mind brushing that bit o' fluff off me showldah?" He roared again, pounding the wheel. "I shawn't stick it," he said. "I bloody well shawn't stick it, you knaow!"

"It isn't fair to laugh at him," she said. "He can't help being English."

"He can't help being a sanctimonious old mudhen either, braying about his luv-ly luv-ly trees. They'll freeze out the first winter."

"How do you know? Maybe it's like he says—if they get a start they'll grow here as well as anywhere."

"Maybe there's a gold mine in our back yard too, but I'm not gonna dig to see. I couldn't stick it."

"Oh, you're just being stubborn," she said. "Just because you didn't like Mr. Garfield . . ."

He turned on her in heavy amazement. "Well, my God! Did you?"

"I thought he was very nice," she said, and sat straighter in the back seat, speaking loudly above the creak of the springs and cough of the motor. "They're trying to make a home, not just a wheat crop. I liked them."

"Uh, huh." He was not laughing any more now. Sitting beside him, the boy could see that his face had hardened and the cold look had come into his eye again. "So I should start talking like I had a mouthful of bran, and planting trees around the house that'll look like clothesline poles in two months."

"I didn't say that."

"You thought it though." He looked irritably at the sky, misted with the same delusive film of cloud that had fooled him for three days, and spat at the roadside. "You thought it all the time we were there. 'Why aren't you more like Mr. Garfield, he's such a nice man.'" With mincing savagery he swung round and mocked her. "Shall I make it a walnut grove? Or a big maple sugar bush? Or maybe you'd like an orange orchard."

The boy was looking down at his gun, trying not to hear them quarrel, but he knew what his mother's face would be like—hurt and a little flushed, her chin trembling into stubbornness. "I don't suppose you could bear to have a rug on the floor, or a gramophone?" she said.

He smacked the wheel hard. "Of course I could bear it if we could afford it. But I sure as hell would rather do without than be like that old sandhill crane."

"I don't suppose you'd like to take me over to the Old-Man-on-His-Back some day to get some willow slips either."

"What for?"

"To plant down in the coulee, by the dam."

"That dam dries up every August. Your willows wouldn't live till snow flies."

"Well, would it do any harm to try?"

"Oh, shut up!" he said. "Just thinking about that guy and his fluff and his trees give me the pleefer."

The topless Ford lurched, one wheel at a time, through the deep burnout by their pasture corner, and the boy clambered out with his gun in his hand to slip the loop from the three-strand gate. It was then that he saw the snake, a striped limp ribbon, dangling on the fence, and a moment later the sparrow, neatly butchered and hung by the throat from the barbed wire. He pointed the gun at them. "Lookit!" he said. "Lookit what the butcher bird's been doing."

His father's violent hand waved at him from the seat. "Come on! Get the wire out of the way!"

The boy dragged the gate through the dust, and the Ford went through and up behind the house, perched on the bare edge of the coulee in the midst of its baked yard and framed by the dark fireguard overgrown with Russian thistle. Walking across that yard a few minutes later, the boy felt its hard heat under his sneakers. There was hardly a spear of grass within the fireguard. It was one of his father's prides that the dooryard should be like cement. "Pour your wash water out long enough," he said, "and you'll have a surface so hard it won't even make mud." Religiously he threw his water out three times a day, carrying it sometimes a dozen steps to dump it on a dusty or grassy spot.

The mother had objected at first, asking why they had to live in the middle of an alkali flat, and why they couldn't let grass grow up to the door. But he snorted her down. Everything round the house ought to be bare as a bone. Get a good prairie fire going and it'd jump that guard like nothing, and if they had grass to the door where'd they be? She said why not plow a wider fireguard then, one a fire couldn't jump, but he said he had other things to do besides plowing fifty-foot fireguards.

They were arguing inside when the boy came up on the step to sit down and aim his empty .22 at a fencepost. Apparently his mother had been persistent, and persistence when he was not in a mood for it angered the father worse than anything else. Their talk came vaguely through his concentration, but he shut his ears on it. If that spot on the fencepost was a coyote now, and he held the sight steady, right on it, and pulled the trigger, that old coyote would jump about eighty feet in the air and come down dead as a mackerel, and he could tack his hide on the barn the way Mr. Larsen had one, only the dogs had jumped' and torn the tail and hind legs off Mr. Larsen's pelt, and he wouldn't get more than the three-dollar bounty out of it. But then Mr. Larsen had shot his with a shotgun anyway, and the hide wasn't worth much even before the dogs tore it. . . .

"I can't for the life of me see why not," his mother said inside. "We could do it now. We're not doing anything else."

"I tell you they wouldn't grow!" said his father with emphasis on every word. "Why should we run our tongues out doing everything that mealy-mouthed fool does?"

"I don't want anything but the willows. They're easy."

He made his special sound of contempt, his half-snort, half-grunt. After a silence she tried again. "They might even have pussies on them in the spring. Mr. Garfield thinks they'd grow, and he used to work in a greenhouse, his wife told me."

"This isn't a greenhouse, for Chrissake."

"Oh, let it go," she said. "I've stood it this long without any green things around. I guess I can stand it some more."

The boy, aiming now toward the gate where the butcher bird, coming back to his prey, would in just a minute fly right into Deadeye's unerring bullet, heard his father stand up suddenly.

"Abused, aren't you?" he said.

The mother's voice rose. "No, I'm not abused! Only I can't see why it would be so awful to get some willows. Just because Mr. Garfield gave me the idea, and you didn't like him . . ."

"You're right I didn't like Mr. Garfield," the father said. "He gave me a pain right under the crupper."

"Because," the mother's voice said bitterly, "he calls his wife 'dear' and puts his arm around her and likes trees. It wouldn't occur to you to put your arm around your wife, would it?"

The boy aimed and held his breath. His mother ought to keep still, because if she didn't she'd get him real mad and then they'd both have to tiptoe around the rest of the day. He heard his father's breath whistle through his teeth, and his voice, mincing, nasty. "Would you like me to kiss you now, *dear?*"

"I wouldn't let you touch me with a ten-foot pole," his mother said. She sounded just as mad as he did, and it wasn't often she let herself get that way. The boy squirmed over when he heard the quick hard steps come up behind him and pause. Then his father's big hand, brown and meaty and felted with fine black hair, reached down over his shoulder and took the .22.

"Let's see this cannon old Scissor-bill gave you," he said.

It was a single-shot, bolt-action Savage, a little rusty on the barrel, the bolt sticky with hardened grease when the father removed it. Sighting up through the barrel, he grunted. "Takes care of a gun like he takes care of his farm. Probably used it to cultivate his luv-ly trees."

He went out into the sleeping porch, and after a minute came back with a rag and a can of machine oil. Hunching the boy over on the step, he sat down and began rubbing the bolt with the oil-soaked rag.

"I just can't bear to shoot anything any more," he said, and laughed suddenly. "I just cawn't stick it, little man." He leered at the boy, who grinned back uncertainly. Squinting through the barrel again, the father breathed through his nose and clamped his lips together, shaking his head.

The sun lay heavy on the baked yard. Out over the corner of the pasture a soaring hawk caught wind and sun at the same time, so that his light breast feathers flashed as he banked and rose. Just wait, the boy thought. Wait till I get my gun working and I'll fix you, you hen-robber. He thought of the three chicks a hawk had struck earlier in the summer, the three balls of yellow with the barred mature plumage just coming through. Two of them dead when he got there and chased the hawk away, the other gasping with its crop slashed wide open and the wheat spilling from it on the ground. His mother had sewed up the crop, and the chicken had lived, but it always looked droopy, like a plant in drought time, and sometimes it would stand and work its bill as if it were choking.

By golly, he thought, I'll shoot every hawk and butcher bird in twenty miles. I'll . . .

"Rustle around and find me a piece of baling wire," his father said. "This barrel looks like a henroost."

Behind the house he found a piece of rusty wire, brought it back and watched his father straighten it, wind a bit of rag round the end, ram it up and down through the barrel, and peer through again. "He's leaded her so you can hardly see the grooves," he said. "But maybe she'll shoot. We'll fill her with vinegar and cork her up to-night."

The mother was behind them, leaning against the jamb and watching. She reached down and rumpled the father's black hair. "The minute you get a gun in your hand you start feeling better," she said. "It's just a shame you weren't born fifty years sooner."

"A gun's a good tool," he said. "It hadn't ought to be misused. Gun like this is enough to make a guy cry."

"Well, you've got to admit it was nice of Mr. Garfield to give it to Sonny," she said. It was the wrong thing to say. The boy had a feeling somehow that she knew it was the wrong thing to say, that she said it just to have one tiny triumph over him. He knew it would make him boiling mad again, even before he heard his father's answer.

"Oh, sure, Mr. Garfield's a fine man. He can preach a better sermon than any homesteader in Saskatchewan. God Almighty! everything he does is better than what I do. All right. All right, *all right!* Why the hell don't you move over there if you like it so well?"

"If you weren't so blind . . ."

He rose with the .22 in his hand and pushed past her into the house. "I'm not so blind," he said heavily in passing. "You've been throwing that bastard up to me for two hours. It don't take very good eyes to see what that means."

His mother started to say, "All because I want a few little . . ." but the boy cut in on her, anxious to help the situation somehow. "Will it shoot now?" he said.

His father said nothing. His mother looked down at him, shrugged, sighed, smiled bleakly with a tight mouth. She moved aside when the father came back with a box of cartridges in his hand. He ignored his wife, speaking to the boy alone in the particular half-jocular tone he always used with him or the dog when he wasn't mad or exasperated.

"Thought I had these around," he said. "Now we'll see what this smoke-pole will do."

He slipped a cartridge in and locked the bolt, looking round for something to shoot at. Behind him the mother's feet moved on the floor, and her voice came purposefully. "I can't see why you have to act this way," she said. "I'm going over and get some slips myself."

There was a long silence. The angled shade lay sharp as a knife across the baked front yard. The father's cheek was pressed against the stock of the gun, his arms and hands as steady as stone.

"How'll you get there?" he said, whispering down the barrel.

"I'll walk."

"Five miles and back."

"Yes, five miles and back. Or fifty miles and back. If there was any earthly reason why you should mind . . ."

"I don't mind," he said, and his voice was soft as silk. "Go ahead."

Close to his mother's long skirts in the doorway, the boy felt her stiffen as if she had been slapped. He squirmed anxiously, but his desperation could find only the question he had asked before. His voice squeaked on it: "Will it shoot now?"

"See that sparrow out there?" his father said, still whispering. "Right out by that cactus?"

"Harry!" the mother said. "If you shoot that harmless little bird!"

Fascinated, the boy watched his father's dark face against the rifle stock, the locked, immovable left arm, the thick finger crooked inside the trigger guard almost too small to hold it. He saw the sparrow, gray, white-breasted, hopping obliviously in search of bugs, fifty feet out on the gray earth. "I just . . . can't . . . bear . . . to . . . shoot . . . anything," the father said, his face like dark stone, his lips hardly moving. "I just . . . can't . . . stick it!"

"Harry!" his wife screamed.

The boy's mouth opened, a dark wash of terror shadowed his vision of the baked yard cut by its sharp angle of shade.

"Don't, pa!"

The rocklike figure of his father never moved. The thick finger squeezed slowly down on the trigger, there was a thin, sharp report, and the sparrow jerked and collapsed into a shapeless wad on the ground. It was as if, in the instant of the shot, all its clean outlines vanished. Head, feet, the white breast, the perceptible outlines of the folded wings, disappeared all at once, were crumpled together and lost, and the boy sat beside his father on the step with the echo of the shot still in his ears.

He did not look at either of his parents. He looked only at the crumpled sparrow. Step by step, unable to keep away, he went to it, stooped, and picked it up. Blood stained his fingers, and he held the bird by the tail while he wiped the smeared hand on his overalls. He heard the click as the bolt was shot and the empty cartridge ejected, and he saw his mother come swiftly out of the house past his father, who sat still on the step. Her hands were clenched, and she walked with her head down, as if fighting tears.

"Ma!" the boy said dully. "Ma, what'll I do with it?"

She stopped and turned, and for a moment they faced each other. He saw the dead pallor of her face, the burning eyes, the not-quite-controllable quiver of her lips. But her words, when they came, were flat and level, almost casual.

"Leave it right there," she said. "After a while your father will want to hang it on the barbed wire."

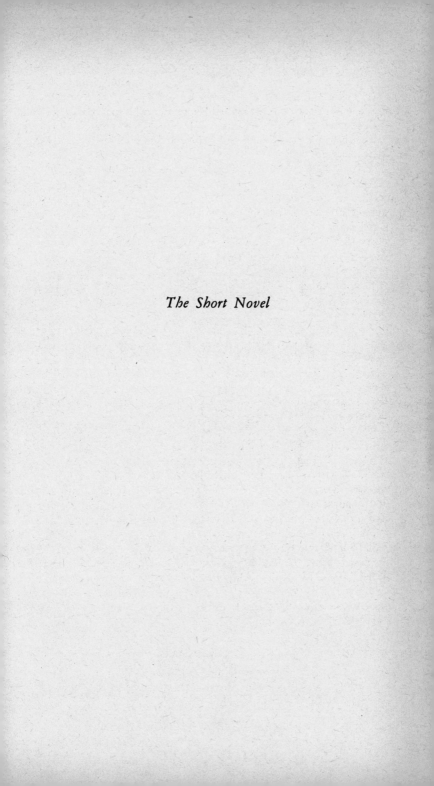

The Short Novel

HERMAN MELVILLE

Benito Cereno 🐌

In the year 1799, Captain Amasa Delano, of Duxbury, in Massachusetts, commanding a large sealer and general trader, lay at anchor, with a valuable cargo, in the harbour of St. Maria—a small, desert, uninhabited island towards the southern extremity of the long coast of Chili. There he had touched for water.

On the second day, not long after dawn, while lying in his berth, his mate came below, informing him that a strange sail was coming into the bay. Ships were then not so plenty in those waters as now. He rose, dressed, and went on deck.

The morning was one peculiar to that coast. Everything was mute and calm; everything grey. The sea, though undulated into long roods of swells, seemed fixed, and was sleeked at the surface like waved lead that has cooled and set in the smelters' mould. The sky seemed a grey mantle. Flights of troubled grey fowl, kith and kin with flights of troubled grey vapours among which they were mixed, skimmed low and fitfully over the waters, as swallows over meadows before storms. Shadows present, foreshadowing deeper shadows to come.

To Captain Delano's surprise, the stranger, viewed through the glass, showed no colours; though to do so upon entering a haven, however uninhabited in its shores, where but a single other ship might be lying, was the custom among peaceful seamen of all nations. Considering the lawlessness and loneliness of the spot, and the sort of stories, at that day, associated with those seas, Captain Delano's surprise might have deepened into some uneasiness had he not been a person of a singularly undistrustful good nature, not liable, except on extraordinary and repeated excitement, and hardly then, to indulge in personal alarms, any way involving the imputation of malign evil in man. Whether, in view of what humanity is capable, such a trait implies, along with a benevolent heart, more than ordinary quickness and accuracy of intellectual perception, may be left to the wise to determine.

But whatever misgivings might have obtruded on first seeing the stranger, would almost, in any seaman's mind, have been dissipated by observing that the ship, in navigating into the harbour, was drawing too near the land, for her own safety's sake, owing to a sunken reef making out off her bow. This seemed to prove her a stranger, indeed, not only to the sealer, but the island; consequently, she could be no wonted freebooter on that ocean. With no small interest, Captain Delano continued to watch her—a proceeding not much facilitated by the vapours partly mantling the hull, through which the far matin light from her cabin streamed equivocally enough; much like the sun—by this time crescented on the rim of the horizon, and apparently, in company with the strange ship, entering the harbour—which, wimpled by the same low, creeping clouds, showed not unlike a Lima intriguante's one sinister eye peering across the Plaza from the Indian loop-hole of her dusk *saya-y-manta*.

It might have been but a deception of the vapours, but, the longer the stranger was watched, the more singular appeared her manœuvres. Ere long it seemed hard to decide whether she meant to come in or no—what she wanted, or what she was about. The wind, which had breezed up a little during the night, was now extremely light and baffling, which the more increased the apparent uncertainty of her movements.

Surmising, at last, that it might be a ship in distress, Captain Delano ordered his whale-boat to be dropped, and, much to the wary opposition of his mate, prepared to board her, and, at the least, pilot her in. On the night previous, a fishing-party of the seamen had gone a long distance to some detached rocks out of sight from the sealer, and, an hour or two before day-break, had returned, having met with no small success. Presuming that the stranger might have been long off soundings, the good captain put several baskets of the fish, for presents, into his boat, and so pulled away. From her continuing too near the sunken reef, deeming her in danger, calling to his men, he made all haste to apprise those on board of their situation. But, some time ere the boat came up, the wind, light though it was, having shifted, had headed the vessel off, as well as partly broken the vapours from about her.

Upon gaining a less remote view, the ship, when made signally visible on the verge of the leaden-hued swells, with the shreds of fog here and there raggedly furring her, appeared like a white-washed monastery after a thunder-storm, seen perched upon some dun cliff among the Pyrenees. But it was no purely fanciful resemblance which now, for a moment, almost led Captain Delano to think that nothing less than a ship-load of monks was before him. Peering over the bulwarks were what really seemed, in the hazy distance, throngs of dark cowls; while fitfully revealed through the open port-holes, other dark moving figures were dimly descried, as of Black Friars pacing the cloisters.

Upon a still nigher approach, this appearance was modified, and the true character of the vessel was plain—a Spanish merchantman of the first class; carrying negro slaves, amongst other valuable freight, from one colonial port to another. A very large, and, in its time, a very fine vessel, such as in those days were at intervals encountered along that main; sometimes superseded Acapulco treasure-ships, or retired frigates of the Spanish king's navy, which, like superannuated Italian palaces, still, under a decline of masters, preserved signs of former state.

As the whale-boat drew more and more nigh, the cause of the peculiar pipe-clayed aspect of the stranger was seen in the slovenly neglect pervading her. The spars, ropes, and great part of the bulwarks, looked woolly, from long unacquaintance with the scraper, tar, and the brush. Her keel seemed laid, her ribs put together, and she launched, from Ezekiel's Valley of Dry Bones.

In the present business in which she was engaged, the ship's general model and rig appeared to have undergone no material change from their original warlike and Froissart pattern. However, no guns were seen.

The tops were large, and were railed about with what had once been octagonal net-work, all now in sad disrepair. These tops hung overhead like three ruinous aviaries, in one of which was seen perched, on a ratlin, a white noddy, a strange fowl, so called from its lethargic somnambulistic character, being frequently caught by hand at sea. Battered and mouldy, the castellated forecastle seemed some ancient turret, long ago taken by assault, and then left to decay. Towards the stern, two high-raised quarter galleries—the balustrades here and there covered with dry, tindery sea-moss —opening out from the unoccupied state-cabin, whose dead lights, for all the mild weather, were hermetically closed and caulked—these tenantless balconies hung over the sea as if it were the grand Venetian canal. But the principal relic of faded grandeur was the ample oval of the shield-like stern-piece, intricately carved with the arms of Castile and Leon, medallioned about by groups of mythological or symbolical devices; uppermost and central of which was a dark satyr in a mask, holding his foot on the prostrate neck of a writhing figure, likewise masked.

Whether the ship had a figure-head, or only a plain beak, was not quite certain, owing to canvas wrapped about that part, either to protect it while undergoing a refurbishing, or else decently to hide its decay. Rudely painted or chalked, as in a sailor freak, along the forward side of a sort of pedestal below the canvas, was the sentence, *"Seguid vuestro jefe,"* (follow your leader); while upon the tarnished headboards, near by, appeared, in stately capitals, once gilt, the ship's name, "SAN DOMINICK," each letter streakingly corroded with tricklings of copper-spike rust; while, like mourning weeds, dark festoons of seagrass slimily swept to and fro over the name, with every hearse-like roll of the hull.

As at last the boat was hooked from the bow along toward the gangway amidship, its keel, while yet some inches separated from the hull, harshly grated as on a sunken coral reef. It proved a huge bunch of conglobated barnacles adhering below the water to the side like a wen; a token of baffling airs and long calms passed somewhere in those seas.

Climbing the side, the visitor was at once surrounded by a clamorous throng of whites and blacks, but the latter outnumbering the former more than could have been expected, negro transportation-ship as the stranger in port was. But, in one language, and as with one voice, all poured out a common tale of suffering; in which the negresses, of whom there were not a few, exceeded the others in their dolorous vehemence. The scurvy, together with a fever, had swept off a great part of their number, more especially the Spaniards. Off Cape Horn, they had narrowly escaped shipwreck; then, for days together, they had lain tranced without wind; their provisions were low; their water next to none; their lips that moment were baked.

While Captain Delano was thus made the mark of all eager tongues, his one eager glance took in all the faces, with every other object about him.

Always upon first boarding a large and populous ship at sea, especially a foreign one, with a nondescript crew such as Lascars or Manila men, the impression varies in a peculiar way from that produced by first entering a strange house with strange inmates in a strange land. Both house and ship, the one by its walls and blinds, the other by its high bulwarks like ramparts, hoard from view their interiors till the last moment; but in the case of the ship there is this addition: that the living spectacle it contains, upon its sudden and complete disclosure, has, in contrast with the blank ocean which zones it, something of the effect of enchantment. The ship seems unreal; these strange costumes, gestures, and faces, but a shadowy tableau just emerged from the deep, which directly must receive back what it gave.

Perhaps it was some such influence as above is attempted to be described which, in Captain Delano's mind, heightened whatever, upon a staid scrutiny, might have seemed unusual; especially the conspicuous figures of four elderly grizzled negroes, their heads like black, doddered willow tops, who, in venerable contrast to the tumult below them, were couched sphynx-like, one on the starboard cathead, another on the larboard, and the remaining pair face to face on the opposite bulwarks above the main-chains. They each had bits of unstranded old junk in their hands, and, with a sort of stoical self-content, were picking the junk into oakum, a small heap of which lay by their sides. They accompanied the task with a continuous, low, monotonous chant; droning and drooling away like so many grey-headed bag-pipers playing a funeral march.

The quarter-deck rose into an ample elevated poop, upon the forward verge of which, lifted, like the oakum-pickers, some eight feet above the general throng, sat along in a row, separated by regular spaces, the cross-legged figures of six other blacks; each with a rusty hatchet in his hand, which, with a bit of brick and a rag, he was engaged like a scullion in scouring; while between each two was a small stack of hatchets, their rusted edges turned forward awaiting a like operation. Though occasionally the four oakum-pickers would briefly address some person or persons in the crowd below, yet the six hatchet-polishers neither spoke to others, nor breathed a whisper among themselves, but sat intent upon their task, except at intervals, when, with the peculiar love in negroes of uniting industry with pastime, two-and-two they sideways clashed their hatchets together, like cymbals, with a barbarous din. All six, unlike the generality, had the raw aspect of unsophisticated Africans.

But that first comprehensive glance which took in those ten figures, with scores less conspicuous, rested but an instant upon them, as, impatient of the hubbub of voices, the visitor turned in quest of whomsoever it might be that commanded the ship.

But as if not unwilling to let nature make known her own case among his suffering charge, or else in despair of restraining it for the time, the Spanish captain, a gentlemanly, reserved-looking, and rather young man to a stranger's eye, dressed with singular richness, but bearing plain traces of recent sleepless cares and disquietudes, stood passively by, leaning against the main-mast, at one moment casting a dreary, spiritless look upon his excited people, at the next an unhappy glance toward his visitor. By his side stood a black of small stature, in whose rude face, as occasionally, like a shepherd's dog, he mutely turned it up into the Spaniard's, sorrow and affection were equally blended.

Struggling through the throng, the American advanced to the Spaniard, assuring him of his sympathies, and offering to render whatever assistance might be in his power. To which the Spaniard returned, for the present, but grave and ceremonious acknowledgments, his national formality dusked by the saturnine mood of ill-health.

But losing no time in mere compliments, Captain Delano, returning to the gangway, had his baskets of fish brought up; and as the wind still continued light, so that some hours at least must elapse ere the ship could be brought to the anchorage, he bade his men return to the sealer, and fetch back as much water as the whaleboat could carry, with whatever soft bread the steward might have, all the remaining pumpkins on board, with a box of sugar, and a dozen of his private bottles of cider.

Not many minutes after the boat's pushing off, to the vexation of all, the wind entirely died away, and the tide turning, began drifting back the ship helplessly seaward. But trusting this would not long last, Captain Delano sought with good hopes to cheer up the strangers, feeling no small satisfaction that, with persons in their condition he could—thanks to his frequent voyages along the Spanish main—converse with some freedom in their native tongue.

While left alone with them, he was not long in observing some things tending to heighten his first impressions; but surprise was lost in pity, both for the Spaniards and blacks, alike evidently reduced from scarcity of water and provisions; while long-continued suffering seemed to have brought out the less good-natured qualities of the negroes, besides, at the same time, impairing the Spaniard's authority over them. But, under the circumstances, precisely this condition of things was to have been anticipated. In armies, navies, cities, or families—in nature herself—nothing more relaxes good order than misery. Still, Captain Delano was not without the idea, that had Benito Cereno been a man of greater energy, misrule would hardly have come to the present pass. But the debility, constitutional or induced by the hardships, bodily and mental, of the Spanish captain, was too obvious to be overlooked. A prey to settled dejection, as if long mocked with hope he would not now indulge it, even when it had ceased to be a mock, the prospect of that day or evening at furthest, lying at anchor, with plenty of water for his people, and a brother captain to counsel and befriend, seemed in no perceptible degree to encourage him. His mind appeared unstrung, if not still more seriously affected. Shut up in these oaken walls, chained to one dull round of command, whose unconditionality cloyed him, like some hypochondriac abbot he moved slowly about at times suddenly pausing, starting, or staring, biting his lip, biting his fingernails, flushing, paling, twitching his beard, with other symptoms of an absent or moody mind. This distempered spirit was lodged, as before hinted, in as distempered a frame. He was rather tall, but seemed never to have been robust, and now with nervous suffering was almost worn to a skeleton. A tendency to some pulmonary complaint appeared to have been lately confirmed. His voice was like that of one with lungs half gone, hoarsely suppressed, a husky whisper. No wonder that, as in this state he tottered about, his private servant apprehensively followed him. Sometimes the negro gave his master his arm, or took his handkerchief out of his pocket for him; performing these and similar offices with that affectionate zeal which transmutes into something filial or fraternal acts in themselves but menial; and which has gained for the negro the repute of making the most pleasing body servant in the world; one, too, whom a master need be on no stiffly superior terms with, but may treat with familiar trust; less a servant than a devoted companion.

Marking the noisy indocility of the blacks in general, as well as what seemed the sullen inefficiency of the whites, it was not without humane satisfaction that Captain Delano witnessed the steady good conduct of Babo.

But the good conduct of Babo, hardly more than the ill-behavior of others, seemed to withdraw the half-lunatic Don Benito from his cloudy languor. Not that such precisely was the impression made by the Spaniard on the mind of his visitor. The Spaniard's individual unrest was, for the present, but noted as a conspicuous feature in the ship's general affliction. Still, Captain Delano was not a little concerned at what he could not help taking for the time to be Don Benito's unfriendly indifference toward himself. The Spaniard's manner, too, conveyed a sort of sour and gloomy disdain, which he seemed at no pains to disguise. But this the American in charity ascribed to the harassing effects of sickness, since, in former instances, he had noted that there are peculiar natures on whom prolonged physical suffering seems to cancel every social instinct of kindness; as if forced to black bread themselves, they deemed it but equity that each person coming nigh them should, indirectly, by some slight or affront, be made to partake of their fare.

But ere long Captain Delano bethought him that, indulgent as he was at the first, in judging the Spaniard, he might not, after all, have exercised charity enough. At bottom it was Don Benito's reserve which displeased him; but the same reserve was shown toward all but his personal attendant. Even the formal reports which, according to sea-usage, were at stated times made to him by some petty underling (either a white, mulatto or black), he hardly had patience enough to listen to, without betraying contemptuous aversion. His manner upon such occasions was, in its degree, not unlike that which might be supposed to have been his imperial countryman's, Charles V., just previous to the anchoritish retirement of that monarch from the throne.

This splenetic disrelish of his place was evinced in almost every function pertaining to it. Proud as he was moody, he condescended to no personal mandate. Whatever special orders were necessary, their delivery was delegated to his body-servant, who in turn transferred them to their ultimate destination, through runners, alert Spanish boys or slave boys, like pages or pilot-fish within easy call continually hovering round Don Benito. So that to have beheld this undemonstrative invalid gliding about, apathetic and mute, no landsman could have dreamed that in him was lodged a dictatorship beyond which, while at sea, there was no earthly appeal.

Thus, the Spaniard, regarded in his reserve, seemed as the involuntary victim of mental disorder. But, in fact, his reserve might, in some degree, have proceeded from design. If so, then in Don Benito was evinced the unhealthy climax of that icy though conscientious policy, more or less adopted by all commanders of large ships, which, except in signal emergencies, obliterates alike the manifestation of sway with every trace of sociality; transforming the man into a block, or rather into a loaded cannon, which, until there is call for thunder, has nothing to say.

Viewing him in this light, it seemed but a natural token of the perverse habit induced by a long course of such hard self-restraint, that, notwithstanding the present condition of his ship, the Spaniard should still persist in a demeanour, which, however harmless—or it may be, appropriate—in a well-appointed vessel, such as the *San Dominick* might have been at the outset of the voyage, was anything but judicious now. But the Spaniard perhaps thought that it was with captains as with gods: reserve, under all events, must still be their cue. But more probably this appearance of slumbering dominion might have been but an attempted disguise to conscious imbecility —not deep policy, but shallow device. But be all this as it might, whether Don Benito's manner was designed or not, the more Captain Delano noted its pervading reserve, the less he felt uneasiness at any particular manifestation of that reserve toward himself.

Neither were his thoughts taken up by the captain alone. Wonted to the quiet orderliness of the sealer's comfortable family of a crew, the noisy confusion of the *San Dominick's* suffering host repeatedly challenged his eye. Some prominent breaches not only of discipline but of decency were observed. These Captain Delano could not but ascribe, in the main, to the absence of those subordinate deck-officers to whom, along with higher duties, is entrusted what may be styled the police department of a populous ship. True, the old oakum-pickers appeared at times to act the part of monitorial constables to their countrymen, the blacks; but though occasionally succeeding in allaying trifling outbreaks now and then between man and man, they could do little or nothing toward establishing general quiet. The *San Dominick* was in the condition of a transatlantic emigrant ship, among whose multitude of living freight are some individuals, doubtless, as little troublesome as crates and bales; but the friendly remonstrances of such with their ruder companions are of not so much avail as the unfriendly arm of the mate. What the *San Dominick* wanted was, what the emigrant ship has, sterner superior officers. But on these decks not so much as a fourth mate was to be seen.

The visitor's curiosity was roused to learn the particulars of those mishaps which had brought about such absenteeism, with its consequences; because, though deriving some inkling of the voyage from the wails which at the first moment had greeted him, yet of the details no clear understanding had been had. The best account would, doubtless, be given by the captain. Yet at first the visitor was loath to ask it, unwilling to provoke some distant rebuff. But plucking up courage, he at last accosted Don Benito, renewing the expression of his benevolent interest, adding, that did he (Captain Delano) but know the particulars of the ship's misfortunes, he would, perhaps, be better able in the end to relieve them. Would Don Benito favour him with the whole story?

Don Benito faltered; then, like some somnambulist suddenly interfered with, vacantly stared at his visitor, and ended by looking down on the deck. He maintained this posture so long, that Captain Delano, almost equally disconcerted, and involuntarily almost as rude, turned suddenly from him, walking forward to accost one of the Spanish seamen for the desired information. But he had hardly gone five paces, when with a sort of eagerness Don Benito invited him back, regretting his momentary absence of mind, and professing readiness to gratify him.

While most part of the story was being given, the two captains stood on the after part of the main-deck, a privileged spot, no one being near but the servant.

"It is now a hundred and ninety days," began the Spaniard, in his husky whisper, "that this ship, well officered and well manned, with several cabin passengers—some fifty Spaniards in all—sailed from Buenos Ayres bound to Lima, with a general cargo, Paraguay tea and the like—and," pointing forward, "that parcel of negroes, now not more than a hundred and fifty, as you see, but then numbering over three hundred souls. Off Cape Horn we had heavy gales. In one moment, by night, three of my best officers, with fifteen sailors, were lost, with the main-yard; the spar snapping under them in the slings, as they sought, with heavers, to beat down the icy sail. To lighten the hull, the heavier sacks of mata were thrown into the sea, with most of the water-pipes lashed on deck at the time. And this last necessity it was, combined with the prolonged detentions afterwards experienced, which eventually brought about our chief causes of suffering. When—"

Here there was a sudden fainting attack of his cough, brought on, no doubt, by his mental distress. His servant sustained him, and drawing a cordial from his pocket placed it to his lips. He a little revived. But unwilling to leave him unsupported while yet imperfectly restored, the black with one arm still encircled his master, at the same time keeping his eye fixed on his face, as if to watch for the first sign of complete restoration, or relapse, as the event might prove.

The Spaniard proceeded, but brokenly and obscurely, as one in a dream.

—"Oh, my God! rather than pass through what I have, with joy I would have hailed the most terrible gales; but—"

His cough returned and with increased violence; this subsiding, with reddened lips and closed eyes he fell heavily against his supporter.

"His mind wanders. He was thinking of the plague that followed the gales," plaintively sighed the servant; "my poor, poor master!" wringing one hand, and with the other wiping the mouth. "But be patient, Señor," again turning to Captain Delano, "these fits do not last long; master will soon be himself."

Don Benito reviving, went on; but as this portion of the story was very brokenly delivered, the substance only will here be set down.

It appeared that after the ship had been many days tossed in storms off the Cape, the scurvy broke out, carrying off numbers of the whites and blacks. When at last they had worked round into the Pacific, their spars and sails were so damaged, and so inadequately handled by the surviving mariners, most of whom were become invalids, that, unable to lay her northerly course by the wind, which was powerful, the unmanageable ship for successive days and nights was blown northwestward, where the breeze suddenly deserted her, in unknown waters, to sultry calms. The absence of the water-pipes now proved as fatal to life as before their presence had menaced it. Induced, or at least aggravated, by the more than scanty allowance of water, a malignant fever followed the scurvy; with the excessive heat of the lengthened calm, making such short work of it as to sweep away, as by billows, whole families of the Africans, and a yet larger number, proportionably, of the Spaniards, including, by a luckless fatality, every officer on board. Consequently, in the smart west winds eventually following the calm, the already rent sails having to be simply dropped, not furled, at need, had been gradually reduced to the beggar's rags they were now. To procure substitutes for his lost sailors, as well as supplies of water and sails, the captain at the earliest opportunity had made for Baldivia, the southernmost civilized port of Chili and South America; but upon nearing the coast the thick weather had prevented him from so much as sighting that harbour. Since which period, almost without a crew, and almost without canvas and almost without water, and at intervals giving its added dead to the sea, the *San Dominick* had been battle-dored about by contrary winds, inveigled by currents, or grown weedy in calms. Like a man lost in woods, more than once she had doubled upon her own track.

"But throughout these calamities," huskily continued Don Benito, painfully turning in the half embrace of his servant, "I have to thank those negroes you see, who, though to your inexperienced eyes appearing unruly, have indeed conducted themselves with less of restlessness than even their owner could have thought possible under such circumstances."

Here he again fell faintly back. Again his mind wandered: but he rallied, and less obscurely proceeded.

"Yes, their owner was quite right in assuring me that no fetters would be needed with his blacks; so that while, as is wont in this transportation, those negroes have always remained upon deck—not thrust below, as in the Guineamen—they have, also from the beginning, been freely permitted to range within given bounds at their pleasure."

Once more the faintness returned—his mind roved—but, recovering, he resumed:

"But it is Babo here to whom, under God, I owe not only my own preservation, but likewise to him, chiefly, the merit is due, of pacifying his more ignorant brethren, when at intervals tempted to murmurings."

"Ah, master," sighed the black, bowing his face, "don't speak of me; Babo is nothing; what Babo has done was but duty."

"Faithful fellow!" cried Captain Delano. "Don Benito, I envy you such a friend; slave I cannot call him."

As master and man stood before him, the black upholding the white, Captain Delano could not but bethink him of the beauty of that relationship which could present such a spectacle of fidelity on the one hand and confidence on the other. The scene was heightened by the contrast in dress, denoting their relative positions. The Spaniard wore a loose Chili jacket of dark velvet; white small clothes and stockings, with silver buckles at the knee and instep; a high-crowned sombrero, of fine grass; a slender sword, silver mounted, hung from a knot in his sash; the last being an almost invariable adjunct, more for utility than ornament, of a South American gentle-man's dress to this hour. Excepting when his occasional nervous contortions brought about disarray, there was a certain precision in his attire, curiously at variance with the unsightly disorder around; especially in the belittered Ghetto, forward of the main-mast, wholly occupied by the blacks.

The servant wore nothing but wide trousers, apparently, from their coarseness and patches, made out of some old topsail; they were clean, and confined at the waist by a bit of unstranded rope, which, with his composed, deprecatory air at times, made him look something like a begging friar of St. Francis.

However unsuitable for the time and place, at least in the blunt-thinking American's eyes, and however strangely surviving in the midst of all his afflictions, the toilette of Don Benito might not, in fashion at least, have gone beyond the style of the day among South Americans of his class. Though on the present voyage sailing from Buenos Ayres, he had avowed himself a native and resident of Chili, whose inhabitants had not so generally adopted the plain coat and once plebeian pantaloons; but, with a becoming modification, adhered to their provincial costume, picturesque as any in the world. Still, relatively to the pale history of the voyage, and his own pale face, there seemed something so incongruous in the Spaniard's apparel, as almost to suggest the image of an invalid courtier tottering about London streets in the time of the plague.

The portion of the narrative which, perhaps, most excited interest, as well as some surprise, considering the latitudes in question, was the long calms spoken of, and more particularly the ship's so long drifting about. Without communicating the opinion, of course, the American could not but impute at least part of the detentions both to clumsy seamanship and faulty navigation. Eyeing Don Benito's small, yellow hands, he easily inferred that the young captain had not got into command at the hawse-hole but the cabin-window, and if so, why wonder at incompetence, in youth, sickness, and aristocracy united? Such was his democratic conclusion.

But drowning criticism in compassion, after a fresh repetition of his sympathies, Captain Delano having heard out his story, not only engaged, as in the first place, to see Don Benito and his people supplied in their immediate bodily needs, but, also, now further promised to assist him in procuring a large permanent supply of water, as well as some sails and rigging; and, though it would involve no small embarrassment to himself, yet he would spare three of his best seamen for temporary deck officers; so that without delay the ship might proceed to Concepcion, there fully to refit for Lima, her destined port.

Such generosity was not without its effect, even upon the invalid. His face lighted up; eager and hectic, he met the honest glance of his visitor. With gratitude he seemed overcome.

"This excitement is bad for master," whispered the servant, taking his arm, and with soothing words gently drawing him aside.

When Don Benito returned, the American was pained to observe that his hopefulness, like the sudden kindling in his cheek, was but febrile and transient.

Ere long, with a joyless mien, looking up toward the poop, the host invited his guest to accompany him there, for the benefit of what little breath of wind might be stirring.

As during the telling of the story, Captain Delano had once or twice started at the occasional cymballing of the hatchet-polishers, wondering why such an interruption should be allowed, especially in that part of the ship, and in the ears of an invalid; and, moreover, as the hatchets had anything but an attractive look, and the handlers of them still less so, it was, therefore, to tell the truth, not without some lurking reluctance, or even shrinking, it may be, that Captain Delano, with apparent complaisance, acquiesced in his host's invitation. The more so, since with an untimely caprice of punctilio, rendered distressing by his cadaverous aspect, Don Benito, with Castilian bows, solemnly insisted upon his guest's preceding him up the ladder leading to the elevation; where, one on each side of the last step, sat four armorial supporters and sentries, two of the ominous file. Gingerly enough stepped good Captain Delano between them, and in the instant of leaving them behind, like one running the gantlet, he felt an apprehensive twitch in the calves of his legs.

But when, facing about, he saw the whole file, like so many organ-grinders, still stupidly intent on their work, unmindful of everything beside, he could not but smile at his late fidgeting panic.

Presently, while standing with Don Benito, looking forward upon the decks below, he was struck by one of those instances of insubordination previously alluded to. Three black boys, with two Spanish boys, were sitting together on the hatches, scraping a rude wooden platter, in which some scanty mess had recently been cooked. Suddenly, one of the black boys, enraged at a word dropped by one of his white companions, seized a knife, and though called to forbear by one of the oakum-pickers, struck the lad over the head, inflicting a gash from which blood flowed.

In amazement, Captain Delano inquired what this meant. To which the pale Benito dully muttered, that it was merely the sport of the lad.

"Pretty serious sport, truly," rejoined Captain Delano. "Had such a thing happened on board the *Bachelor's Delight,* instant punishment would have followed."

At these words the Spaniard turned upon the American one of his sudden, staring, half-lunatic looks; then, relapsing into his torpor, answered, "Doubtless, doubtless, Señor."

Is it, thought Captain Delano, that this helpless man is one of those paper captains I've known, who by policy wink at what by power they cannot put down? I know no sadder sight than a commander who has little of command but the name.

"I should think, Don Benito," he now said, glancing toward the oakum-picker who had sought to interfere with the boys, "that you would find it advantageous to keep all your blacks employed, especially the younger ones, no matter at what useless task, and no matter what happens to the ship. Why, even with my little band, I find such a course indispensable. I once kept a crew on my quarter-deck thrumming mats for my cabin, when, for three days, I had given up my ship—mats, men, and all—for a speedy loss, owing to the violence of a gale in which we could do nothing but helplessly drive before it."

"Doubtless, doubtless," muttered Don Benito.

"But," continued Captain Delano, again glancing upon the oakum-pickers and then at the hatchet-polishers, near by, "I see you keep some at least of your host employed."

"Yes," was again the vacant response.

"Those old men there, shaking their pows from their pulpits," continued Captain Delano, pointing to the oakum-pickers, "seem to act the part of old dominies to the rest, little heeded as their admonitions are at times. Is this voluntary on their part, Don Benito, or have you appointed them shepherds to your flock of black sheep?"

"What posts they fill, I appointed them," rejoined the Spaniard in an acrid tone, as if resenting some supposed satiric reflection.

"And these others, these Ashantee conjurors here," continued Captain Delano, rather uneasily eyeing the brandished steel of the hatchet-polishers, where in spots it had been brought to a shine, "this seems a curious business they are at, Don Benito?"

"In the gales we met," answered the Spaniard, "what of our general cargo was not thrown overboard was much damaged by the brine. Since coming into calm weather, I have had several cases of knives and hatchets daily brought up for overhauling and cleaning."

"A prudent idea, Don Benito. You are part owner of ship and cargo, I presume; but not of the slaves, perhaps?"

"I am owner of all you see," impatiently returned Don Benito, "except the main company of blacks, who belonged to my late friend, Alexandro Aranda."

As he mentioned this name, his air was heart-broken, his knees shook; his servant supported him.

Thinking he divined the cause of such unusual emotion, to confirm his surmise, Captain Delano, after a pause, said, "And may I ask, Don Benito, whether—since awhile ago you spoke of some cabin passengers—the friend, whose loss so afflicts you, at the outset of the voyage accompanied his blacks?"

"Yes."

"But died of the fever?"

"Died of the fever.—Oh, could I but—"

Again quivering, the Spaniard paused.

"Pardon me," said Captain Delano slowly, "but I think that, by a sympathetic experience, I conjecture, Don Benito, what it is that gives the keener edge to your grief. It was once my hard fortune to lose at sea a dear friend, my own brother, then supercargo. Assured of the welfare of his spirit, its departure I could have borne like a man; but that honest eye, that honest hand—both of which had so often met mine—and that warm heart; all, all—like scraps to the dogs—to throw all to the sharks! It was then I vowed never to have for fellow-voyager a man I loved, unless, unbeknown to him, I had provided every requisite, in case of a fatality, for embalming his mortal part for interment on shore. Were your friend's remains now on board this ship, Don Benito, not thus strangely would the mention of his name affect you."

"On board this ship?" echoed the Spaniard. Then, with horrified gestures, as directed against some spectre, he unconsciously fell into the ready arms of his attendant, who, with a silent appeal toward Captain Delano, seemed beseeching him not again to broach a theme so unspeakably distressing to his master.

This poor fellow now, thought the pained American, is the victim of that sad superstition which associates goblins with the deserted body of man, as ghosts with an abandoned house. How unlike are we made! What to me, in like case, would have been a solemn satisfaction, the bare suggestion, even, terrifies the Spaniard into this trance. Poor Alexandro Aranda! what would you say could you here see your friend—who, on former voyages, when you for months were left behind, has, I dare say, often longed, and longed, for one peep at you—now transported with terror at the least thought of having you anyway nigh him.

At this moment, with a dreary graveyard toll, betokening a flaw, the ship's forecastle bell, smote by one of the grizzled oakum-pickers, proclaimed ten o'clock through the leaden calm; when Captain Delano's attention was caught by the moving figure of a gigantic black, emerging from the general crowd below, and slowly advancing toward the elevated poop. An iron collar was about his neck, from which depended a chain, thrice wound round his body; the terminating links padlocked together at a broad band of iron, his girdle.

"How like a mute Atufal moves," murmured the servant.

The black mounted the steps of the poop, and, like a brave prisoner, brought up to receive sentence, stood in unquailing muteness before Don Benito, now recovered from his attack.

At the first glimpse of his approach, Don Benito had started, a resentful shadow swept over his face; and, as with the sudden memory of bootless rage, his white lips glued together.

This is some mulish mutineer, thought Captain Delano, surveying, not without a mixture of admiration, the colossal form of the negro.

"See, he waits your question, master," said the servant.

Thus reminded, Don Benito, nervously averting his glance, as if shunning, by anticipation, some rebellious response, in a disconcerted voice, thus spoke:

"Atufal, will you ask my pardon now?"

The black was silent.

"Again, master," murmured the servant, with bitter upbraiding eyeing his countryman; "Again, master; he will bend to master yet."

"Answer," said Don Benito, still averting his glance, "say but the one word *pardon,* and your chains shall be off."

Upon this, the black, slowly raising both arms, let them lifelessly fall, his links clanking, his head bowed; as much as to say, "No, I am content."

"Go," said Don Benito, with inkept and unknown emotion.

Deliberately as he had come, the black obeyed.

"Excuse me, Don Benito," said Captain Delano, "but this scene surprises me; what means it, pray?"

"It means that that negro alone, of all the band, has given me peculiar cause of offence. I have put him in chains; I—"

Here he paused; his hand to his head, as if there were a swimming there, or a sudden bewilderment of memory had come over him; but meeting his servant's kindly glance seemed reassured, and proceeded:

"I could not scourge such a form. But I told him he must ask my pardon. As yet he has not. At my command, every two hours he stands before me."

"And how long has this been?"

"Some sixty days."

"And obedient in all else? And respectful?"

"Yes."

"Upon my conscience, then," exclaimed Captain Delano, impulsively, "he has a royal spirit in him, this fellow."

"He may have some right to it," bitterly returned Don Benito; "he says he was king in his own land."

"Yes," said the servant, entering a word, "those slits in Atufal's ears once held wedges of gold; but poor Babo here, in his own land, was only a poor slave; a black man's slave was Babo, who now is the white's."

Somewhat annoyed by these conversational familiarities, Captain Delano turned curiously upon the attendant, then glanced inquiringly at his master;

but, as if long wonted to these little informalities, neither master nor man seemed to understand him.

"What, pray, was Atufal's offence, Don Benito?" asked Captain Delano; "if it was not something very serious, take a fool's advice, and, in view of his general docility, as well as in some natural respect for his spirit, remit his penalty."

"No, no, master never will do that," here murmured the servant to himself, "proud Atufal must first ask master's pardon. The slave there carries the padlock, but master here carries the key."

His attention thus directed, Captain Delano now noticed for the first time that, suspended by a slender silken cord, from Don Benito's neck hung a key. At once, from the servant's muttered syllables divining the key's purpose, he smiled and said: "So, Don Benito—padlock and key—significant symbols, truly."

Biting his lip, Don Benito faltered.

Though the remark of Captain Delano, a man of such native simplicity as to be incapable of satire or irony, had been dropped in playful allusion to the Spaniard's singularly evidenced lordship over the black; yet the hypochondriac seemed in some way to have taken it as a malicious reflection upon his confessed inability thus far to break down, at least, on a verbal summons, the entrenched will of the slave. Deploring this supposed misconception, yet despairing of correcting it, Captain Delano shifted the subject; but finding his companion more than ever withdrawn, as if still slowly digesting the lees of the presumed affront above-mentioned, by-and-by Captain Delano likewise became less talkative, oppressed, against his own will, by what seemed the secret vindictiveness of the morbidly sensitive Spaniard. But the good sailor himself, of a quite contrary disposition, refrained, on his part, alike from the appearance as from the feeling of resentment, and if silent, was only so from contagion.

Presently the Spaniard, assisted by his servant, somewhat discourteously crossed over from Captain Delano; a procedure which, sensibly enough, might have been allowed to pass for idle caprice of ill-humour, had not master and man, lingering round the corner of the elevated skylight, begun whispering together in low voices. This was unpleasing. And more: the moody air of the Spaniard, which at times had not been without a sort of valetudinarian stateliness, now seemed anything but dignified; while the menial familiarity of the servant lost its original charm of simple-hearted attachment.

In his embarrassment, the visitor turned his face to the other side of the ship. By so doing, his glance accidentally fell on a young Spanish sailor, a coil of rope in his hand, just stepped from the deck to the first round of the mizzen-rigging. Perhaps the man would not have been particularly noticed, were it not that, during his ascent to one of the yards, he, with a sort of covert intentness, kept his eye fixed on Captain Delano, from whom, presently, it passed, as if by a natural sequence, to the two whisperers.

His own attention thus redirected to that quarter, Captain Delano gave a slight start. From something in Don Benito's manner just then, it seemed as if the visitor had, at least partly, been the subject of the withdrawn consultation going on—a conjecture as little agreeable to the guest as it was little flattering to the host.

The singular alternations of courtesy and ill-breeding in the Spanish captain were unaccountable, except on one of two suppositions—innocent lunacy, or wicked imposture.

But the first idea, though it might naturally have occurred to an indifferent observer, and, in some respects, had not hitherto been wholly a stranger to Captain Delano's mind, yet, now that, in an incipient way, he began to regard the stranger's conduct something in the light of an intentional affront, of course the idea of lunacy was virtually vacated. But if not a lunatic, what then? Under the circumstances, would a gentleman, nay, any honest boor, act the part now acted by his host? The man was an impostor. Some low-born adventurer, masquerading as an oceanic grandee; yet so ignorant of the first requisites of mere gentlemanhood as to be betrayed into the present remarkable indecorum. That strange ceremoniousness, too, at other times evinced, seemed not uncharacteristic of one playing a part above his real level. Benito Cereno—Don Benito Cereno—a sounding name. One, too, at that period, not unknown, in the surname, to supercargoes and sea captains trading along the Spanish Main, as belonging to one of the most enterprising and extensive mercantile families in all those provinces; several members of it having titles; a sort of Castilian Rothschild, with a noble brother, or cousin, in every great trading town of South America. The alleged Don Benito was in early manhood, about twenty-nine or thirty. To assume a sort of roving cadetship in the maritime affairs of such a house, what more likely scheme for a young knave of talent and spirit? But the Spaniard was a pale invalid. Never mind. For even to the degree of simulating mortal disease, the craft of some tricksters had been known to attain. To think that, under the aspect of infantile weakness, the most savage energies might be couched—those velvets of the Spaniard but the velvet paw to his fangs.

From no train of thought did these fancies come; not from within, but from without; suddenly, too, and in one throng, like hoar frost; yet as soon to vanish as the mild sun of Captain Delano's good-nature regained its meridian.

Glancing over once again toward Don Benito—whose side-face, revealed above the skylight, was now turned toward him—Captain Delano was struck by the profile, whose clearness of cut was refined by the thinness incident to ill-health, as well as ennobled about the chin by the beard. Away with suspicion. He was a true off-shoot of a true hidalgo Cereno.

Relieved by these and other better thoughts, the visitor, lightly humming a tune, now began indifferently pacing the poop, so as not to betray to Don Benito that he had at all mistrusted incivility, much less duplicity; for such mistrust would yet be proved illusory, and by the event; though, for the present, the circumstance which had provoked that distrust remained unexplained. But when that little mystery should have been cleared up, Captain Delano thought he might extremely regret it, did he allow Don Benito to become aware that he had indulged in ungenerous surmises. In short, to the Spaniard's black-letter text, it was best, for a while, to leave open margin.

Presently, his pale face twitching and overcast, the Spaniard, still supported by his attendant, moved over toward his guest, when, with even more than his usual embarrassment, and a strange sort of intriguing intonation in his husky whisper, the following conversation began:

"Señor, may I ask how long you have lain at this isle?"

"Oh, but a day or two, Don Benito."

"And from what port are you last?"

"Canton."

"And there, Señor, you exchanged your seal-skins for teas and silks, I think you said?"

"Yes. Silks, mostly."

"And the balance you took in specie, perhaps?"

Captain Delano, fidgeting a little, answered—

"Yes; some silver; not a very great deal, though."

"Ah—well. May I ask how many men have you on board, Señor?"

Captain Delano slightly started, but answered:

"About five-and-twenty, all told."

"And at present, Señor, all on board, I suppose?"

"All on board, Don Benito," replied the captain now with satisfaction.

"And will be to-night, Señor?"

At this last question, following so many pertinacious ones, for the soul of him Captain Delano could not but look very earnestly at the questioner, who, instead of meeting the glance, with every token of craven discomposure dropped his eyes to the deck; presenting an unworthy contrast to his servant, who, just then, was kneeling at his feet adjusting a loose shoe-buckle; his disengaged face meantime, with humble curiosity, turned openly up into his master's downcast one.

The Spaniard, still with a guilty shuffle, repeated his question:

"And—and will be to-night, Señor?"

"Yes, for aught I know," returned Captain Delano,—"but nay," rallying himself into fearless truth, "some of them talked of going off on another fishing party about midnight."

"Your ships generally go—go more or less armed, I believe, Señor?"

"Oh, a six-pounder or two, in case of emergency," was the intrepidly indifferent reply, "with a small stock of muskets, sealing-spears, and cutlasses, you know."

As he thus responded, Captain Delano again glanced at Don Benito, but the latter's eyes were averted; while abruptly and awkwardly shifting the subject, he made some peevish allusion to the calm, and then, without apology, once more, with his attendant, withdrew to the opposite bulwarks, where the whispering was resumed.

At this moment, and ere Captain Delano could cast a cool thought upon what had just passed, the young Spanish sailor before mentioned was seen descending from the rigging. In act of stooping over to spring inboard to the deck, his voluminous, unconfined frock, or shirt, of coarse woollen, much spotted with tar, opened out far down the chest, revealing a soiled under-garment of what seemed the finest linen, edged, about the neck, with a narrow blue ribbon, sadly faded and worn. At this moment the young sailor's eye was again fixed on the whisperers, and Captain Delano thought he observed a lurking significance in it, as if silent signs of some freemason sort had that instant been interchanged.

This once more impelled his own glance in the direction of Don Benito, and, as before, he could not but infer that himself formed the subject of the conference. He paused. The sound of the hatchet-polishing fell on his ears. He cast another swift side-look at the two. They had the air of conspirators. In connection with the late questionings, and the incident of the young sailor, these things now begat such return of involuntary suspicion, that the singular guilelessness of the American could not endure it. Plucking up a gay and humorous expression, he crossed over to the two rapidly, saying: "Ha, Don Benito, your black here seems high in your trust; a sort of privy-counsellor, in fact."

Upon this, the servant looked up with a good-natured grin, but the master started as from a venomous bite. It was a moment or two before the Spaniard sufficiently recovered himself to reply; which he did, at last, with cold constraint: "Yes, Señor, I have trust in Babo."

Here Babo, changing his previous grin of mere animal humour into an intelligent smile, not ungratefully eyed his master.

Finding that the Spaniard now stood silent and reserved, as if involuntarily, or purposely, giving hint that his guest's proximity was inconvenient just then, Captain Delano, unwilling to appear uncivil even to incivility itself, made some trivial remark and moved off; again and again turning over in his mind the mysterious demeanour of Don Benito Cereno.

He had descended from the poop, and, wrapped in thought, was passing near a dark hatchway, leading down into the steerage, when, perceiving motion there, he looked to see what moved. The same instant there was a sparkle in the shadowy hatchway, and he saw one of the Spanish sailors, prowling there, hurriedly placing his hand in the bosom of his frock, as if hiding something. Before the man could have been certain who it was that was passing, he slunk below out of sight. But enough was seen of him to make it sure that he was the same young sailor before noticed in the rigging.

What was that which so sparkled? thought Captain Delano. It was no lamp—no match—no live coal. Could it have been a jewel? But how come sailors with jewels?—or with silk-trimmed undershirts either? Has he been robbing the trunks of the dead cabin passengers? But if so, he would hardly wear one of the stolen articles on board ship here. Ah, ah—if now that was, indeed, a secret sign I saw passing between this suspicious fellow and his captain awhile since; if I could only be certain that in my uneasiness my senses did not deceive me, then—

Here, passing from one suspicious thing to another, his mind revolved the point of the strange questions put to him concerning his ship.

By a curious coincidence, as each point was recalled, the black wizards of Ashantee would strike up with their hatchets, as in ominous comment on the white stranger's thoughts. Pressed by such enigmas and portents, it would have been almost against nature, had not, even into the least distrustful heart, some ugly misgivings obtruded.

Observing the ship now helplessly fallen into a current, with enchanted sails, drifting with increased rapidity seaward; and noting that, from a lately intercepted projection of the land, the sealer was hidden, the stout mariner began to quake at thoughts which he barely durst confess to himself. Above all, he began to feel a ghostly dread of Don Benito. And yet when he roused himself, dilated his chest, felt himself strong on his legs, and coolly considered it—what did all these phantoms amount to?

Had the Spaniard any sinister scheme, it must have reference not so much to him (Captain Delano) as to his ship (the *Bachelor's Delight*). Hence the present drifting away of one ship from the other, instead of favouring any such possible scheme, was, for the time at least, opposed to it. Clearly any suspicion, combining such contradictions, must need be delusive. Beside, was it not absurd to think of a vessel in distress—a vessel by sickness almost dismanned of her crew—a vessel whose inmates were parched for water— was it not a thousand times absurd that such a craft should, at present, be of a piratical character; or her commander, either for himself or those under him, cherish any desire but for speedy relief and refreshment? But then, might not general distress, and thirst in particular, be affected? And might not that same undiminished Spanish crew, alleged to have perished off to a remnant, be at that very moment lurking in the hold? On heartbroken pretence of entreating a cup of cold water, fiends in human form had got into lonely dwellings, nor retired until a dark deed had been done. And among the Malay pirates, it was no unusual thing to lure ships after them into their treacherous harbours, or entice boarders from a declared enemy at sea, by the spectacle of thinly manned or vacant decks, beneath which prowled a hundred spears with yellow arms ready to upthrust them through the mats. Not that Captain Delano had entirely credited such things. He had heard of them—and now, as stories, they recurred. The present destination of the ship was the anchorage. There she would be near his own vessel. Upon gaining that vicinity, might not the *San Dominick,* like a slumbering volcano, suddenly let loose energies now hid?

He recalled the Spaniard's manner while telling his story. There was a gloomy hesitancy and subterfuge about it. It was just the manner of one making up his tale for evil purposes, as he goes. But if that story was true, what was the truth? That the ship had unlawfully come into the Spaniard's possession? But in many of its details, especially in reference to the more calamitous parts, such as the fatalities among the seamen, the consequent prolonged beating about, the past sufferings from obstinate calms, and still continued suffering from thirst; in all these points, as well as others, Don Benito's story had corroborated not only the wailing ejaculations of the indiscriminate multitude, white and black, but likewise—what seemed impossible to be counterfeit—by the very expression and play of every human feature, which Captain Delano saw. If Don Benito's story was throughout an invention, then every soul on board, down to the youngest negress, was his carefully drilled recruit in the plot: an incredible inference. And yet, if there was ground for mistrusting the Spanish captain's veracity, that inference was a legitimate one.

In short, scarce an uneasiness entered the honest sailor's mind but, by a subsequent spontaneous act of good sense, it was ejected. At last he began to laugh at these forebodings; and laugh at the strange ship for in its aspect someway siding with them, as it were; and laugh, too, at the odd-looking blacks, particularly those old scissors-grinders, the Ashantees; and those bed-ridden old knitting-women, the oakum-pickers; and in a human way, he almost began to laugh at the dark Spaniard himself, the central hobgoblin of all.

For the rest, whatever in a serious way seemed enigmatical, was now good-naturedly explained away by the thought that, for the most part, the poor invalid scarcely knew what he was about; either sulking in black vapours, or putting random questions without sense or object. Evidently, for the present, the man was not fit to be entrusted with the ship. On some benevolent plea withdrawing the command from him, Captain Delano would yet have to send her to Concepcion in charge of his second mate, a worthy person and good navigator—a plan which would prove no wiser for the *San Dominick* than for Don Benito; for—relieved from all anxiety, keeping wholly to his cabin—the sick man, under the good nursing of his servant, would probably, by the end of the passage, be in a measure restored to health and with that he should also be restored to authority.

Such were the American's thoughts. They were tranquillizing. There was a difference between the idea of Don Benito's darkly preordaining Captain Delano's fate, and Captain Delano's lightly arranging Don Benito's. Nevertheless, it was not without something of relief that the good seaman presently perceived his whale-boat in the distance. Its absence had been prolonged by unexpected detention at the sealer's side, as well as its returning trip lengthened by the continual recession of the goal.

The advancing speck was observed by the blacks. Their shouts attracted the attention of Don Benito, who, with a return of courtesy, approaching Captain Delano, expressed satisfaction at the coming of some supplies, slight and temporary as they must necessarily prove.

Captain Delano responded; but while doing so, his attention was drawn to something passing on the deck below: among the crowd climbing the landward bulwarks, anxiously watching the coming boat, two blacks, to all appearances accidentally incommoded by one of the sailors, flew out against him with horrible curses, which the sailors someway resenting, the two blacks dashed him to the deck and jumped upon him, despite the earnest cries of the oakum-pickers.

"Don Benito," said Captain Delano quickly, "do you see what is going on there? Look!"

But, seized by his cough, the Spaniard staggered, with both hands to his face, on the point of falling. Captain Delano would have supported him, but the servant was more alert, who, with one hand sustaining his master, with the other applied the cordial. Don Benito, restored, the black withdrew his support, slipping aside a little, but dutifully remaining within call of a whisper. Such discretion was here evinced as quite wiped away, in the visitor's eyes, any blemish of impropriety which might have attached to the attendant, from the indecorous conferences before mentioned; showing, too, that if the servant were to blame, it might be more the master's fault than his own, since when left to himself he could conduct thus well.

His glance thus called away from the spectacle of disorder to the more pleasing one before him, Captain Delano could not avoid again congratulating Don Benito upon possessing such a servant, who, though perhaps a little too forward now and then, must upon the whole be invaluable to one in the invalid's situation.

"Tell me, Don Benito," he added, with a smile—"I should like to have your man here myself—what will you take for him? Would fifty doubloons be any object?"

"Master wouldn't part with Babo for a thousand doubloons," murmured the black, overhearing the offer, and taking it in earnest, and, with the strange vanity of a faithful slave appreciated by his master, scorning to hear so paltry a valuation put upon him by a stranger. But Don Benito, apparently hardly yet completely restored, and again interrupted by his cough, made but some broken reply.

Soon his physical distress became so great, affecting his mind, too, apparently, that, as if to screen the sad spectacle, the servant gently conducted his master below.

Left to himself, the American, to while away the time till his boat should arrive, would have pleasantly accosted some one of the few Spanish seamen he saw; but recalling something that Don Benito had said touching their ill conduct, he refrained, as a ship-master indisposed to countenance cowardice or unfaithfulness in seamen.

While, with these thoughts, standing with eye directed forward toward that handful of sailors—suddenly he thought that some of them returned the glance and with a sort of meaning. He rubbed his eyes, and looked again; but again seemed to see the same thing. Under a new form, but more obscure than any previous one, the old suspicions recurred, but, in the absence of Don Benito, with less of panic than before. Despite the bad account given of the sailors, Captain Delano resolved forthwith to accost one of them. Descending the poop, he made his way through the blacks, his movement drawing a queer cry from the oakum pickers, prompted by whom the negroes, twitching each other aside, divided before him; but, as if curious to see what was the object of this deliberate visit to their Ghetto, closing in behind, in tolerable order, followed the white stranger up. His progress thus proclaimed as by mounted kings-at-arms, and escorted as by a Caffre guard of honour, Captain Delano, assuming a good-humoured, offhand air, continued to advance; now and then saying a blithe word to the negroes, and his eye curiously surveying the white faces, here and there sparsely mixed in with the blacks, like stray white pawns venturously involved in the ranks of the chessmen opposed.

While thinking which of them to select for his purpose, he chanced to observe a sailor seated on the deck engaged in tarring the strap of a large block, with a circle of blacks squatted round him inquisitively eyeing the process.

The mean employment of the man was in contrast with something superior in his figure. His hand, black with continually thrusting it into the tar-pot held for him by a negro, seemed not naturally allied to his face, a face which would have been a very fine one but for its haggardness. Whether this haggardness had aught to do with criminality could not be determined; since, as intense heat and cold, though unlike, produce like sensations, so innocence and guilt, when, through casual association with mental pain, stamping any visible impress, use one seal—a hacked one.

Not again that this reflection occurred to Captain Delano at the time, charitable man as he was. Rather another idea. Because observing so singular a haggardness to be combined with a dark eye, averted as in trouble and shame, and then, however illogically, uniting in his mind his own private suspicions of the crew with the confessed ill-opinion on the part of their captain, he was insensibly operated upon by certain general notions, which, while disconnecting pain and abashment from virtue, as invariably link them with vice.

If, indeed, there be any wickedness on board this ship, thought Captain Delano, be sure that man there has fouled his hand in it, even as now he fouls it in the pitch. I don't like to accost him. I will speak to this other, this old Jack here on the windlass.

He advanced to an old Barcelona tar, in ragged red breeches and dirty night-cap, cheeks trenched and bronzed, whiskers dense as thorn hedges. Seated between two sleepy-looking Africans, this mariner, like his younger shipmate, was employed upon some rigging—splicing a cable—the sleepy-looking blacks performing the inferior function of holding the outer parts of the ropes for him.

Upon Captain Delano's approach, the man at once hung his head below its previous level; the one necessary for business. It appeared as if he desired to be thought absorbed, with more than common fidelity, in his task. Being addressed, he glanced up, but with what seemed a furtive, diffident air, which sat strangely enough on his weatherbeaten visage, much as if a grizzly bear, instead of growling and biting, should simper and cast sheep's eyes. He was asked several questions concerning the voyage—questions purposely referring to several particulars in Don Benito's narrative—not previously corroborated by those impulsive cries greeting the visitor on first coming on board. The questions were briefly answered, confirming all that remained to be confirmed of the story. The negroes about the windlass joined in with the old sailor, but, as they became talkative, he by degrees became mute, and at length quite glum, seemed morosely unwilling to answer more questions, and yet, all the while, this ursine air was somehow mixed with his sheepish one.

Despairing of getting into unembarrassed talk with such a centaur, Captain Delano, after glancing round for a more promising countenance, but seeing none, spoke pleasantly to the blacks to make way for him; and so, amid various grins and grimaces, returned to the poop, feeling a little strange at first, he could hardly tell why, but upon the whole with regained confidence in Benito Cereno.

How plainly, thought he, did that old whiskerando yonder betray a con-sciousness of ill-desert. No doubt, when he saw me coming, he dreaded lest I, apprised by his captain of the crew's general misbehaviour, came with sharp words for him, and so down with his head. And yet—and yet, now that I think of it, that very old fellow, if I err not, was one of those who seemed so earnestly eyeing me here awhile since. Ah, these currents spin one's head round almost as much as they do the ship. Ha, there now's a pleasant sort of sunny sight; quite sociable, too.

His attention had been drawn to a slumbering negress, partly disclosed through the lace-work of some rigging, lying, with youthful limbs carelessly disposed, under the lee of the bulwarks, like a doe in the shade of a woodland rock. Sprawling at her lapped breasts was her wide-awake fawn, stark naked, its black little body half lifted from the deck, crosswise with its dam's; its hands, like two paws, clambering upon her; its mouth and nose ineffectually rooting to get at the mark; and meantime giving a vexatious half-grunt, blending with the composed snore of the negress.

The uncommon vigour of the child at length roused the mother. She started up, at distance facing Captain Delano. But, as if not at all concerned at the attitude in which she had been caught, delightedly she caught the child up, with maternal transports, covering it with kisses.

There's naked nature, now; pure tenderness and love, thought Captain Delano, well pleased.

This incident prompted him to remark the other negresses more particularly than before. He was gratified with their manners; like most uncivilized women, they seemed at once tender of heart and tough of constitution; equally ready to die for their infants or fight for them. Unsophisticated as leopardesses; loving as doves. Ah! thought Captain Delano, these perhaps are some of the very women whom Mungo Park saw in Africa, and gave such a noble account of.

These natural sights somehow insensibly deepened his confidence and ease. At last he looked to see how his boat was getting on; but it was still pretty remote. He turned to see if Don Benito had returned; but he had not.

To change the scene, as well as to please himself with a leisurely observation of the coming boat, stepping over into the mizzen-chains he clambered his way into the starboard quarter-gallery; one of those abandoned Venetian-looking water-balconies previously mentioned; retreats cut off from the deck. As his foot pressed the half-damp, half-dry seamosses matting the place, and a chance phantom cat's-paw—an islet of breeze, unheralded, unfollowed —as this ghostly cat's-paw came fanning his cheek, as his glance fell upon the row of small, round dead-lights—all closed like coppered eyes of the coffined—and the state-cabin door, once connecting with the gallery, even as the deadlights had once looked out upon it, but now caulked fast like a sarcophagus lid; and to a purple-black, tarred-over panel, threshold, and post; and he bethought him of the time, when that state-cabin and this state-balcony had heard the voices of the Spanish king's officers, and the forms of the Lima viceroy's daughters had perhaps leaned where he stood—as these and other images flitted through his mind, as the cat's-paw through the calm, gradually he felt rising a dreamy inquietude, like that of one who alone on the prairie feels unrest from the repose of the noon.

He leaned against the carved balustrade, again looking off toward his boat; but found his eye falling upon the ribboned grass, trailing along the ship's water-line, straight as a border of green box; and parterres of sea-weed, broad ovals and crescents, floating nigh and far, with what seemed long formal alleys between, crossing the terraces of swells, and sweeping round as if leading to the grottos below. And overhanging all was the balustrade by his arm, which, partly stained with pitch and partly embossed with moss, seemed the charred ruin of some summer-house in a grand garden long running to waste.

Trying to break one charm, he was but becharmed anew. Though upon the wide sea, he seemed in some far inland country; prisoner in some deserted château, left to stare at empty grounds, and peer out at vague roads, where never wagon or wayfarer passed.

But these enchantments were a little disenchanted as his eye fell on the corroded main-chains. Of an ancient style, massy and rusty in link, shackle and bolt, they seemed even more fit for the ship's present business than the one for which probably she had been built.

Presently he thought something moved nigh the chains. He rubbed his eyes, and looked hard. Groves of rigging were about the chains; and there, peering from behind a great stay, like an Indian from behind a hemlock, a Spanish sailor, a marlingspike in his hand, was seen, who made what seemed an imperfect gesture toward the balcony—but immediately, as if alarmed by some advancing step along the deck within, vanished into the recesses of the hempen forest, like a poacher.

What meant this? Something the man had sought to communicate unbeknown to any one, even to his captain. Did the secret involve aught unfavorable to his captain? Were those previous misgivings of Captain Delano's about to be verified? Or, in his haunted mood at the moment, had some random, unintentional motion of the man, while busy with the stay, as if repairing it, been mistaken for a significant beckoning?

Not unbewildered, again he gazed off for his boat. But it was temporarily hidden by a rocky spur of the isle. As with some eagerness he bent forward, watching for the first shooting view of its beak, the balustrade gave way before him like charcoal. Had he not clutched an outreaching rope he would have fallen into the sea. The crash, though feeble, and the fall, though hollow, of the rotten fragments, must have been overheard. He glanced up. With sober curiosity peering down upon him was one of the old oakum-pickers, slipped from his perch to an outside boom; while below the old negro—and, invisible to him, reconnoitring from a port-hole like a fox from the mouth of its den—crouched the Spanish sailor again. From something suddenly suggested by the man's air, the mad idea now darted into

Captain Delano's mind; that Don Benito's plea of indisposition, in withdrawing below, was but a pretence: that he was engaged there maturing some
plot, of which the sailor, by some means gaining an inkling, had a mind to
warn the stranger against; incited, it may be, by gratitude for a kind word
on first boarding the ship. Was it from foreseeing some possible interference
like this, that Don Benito had, beforehand, given such a bad character of
his sailors, while praising the negroes; though, indeed, the former seemed
as docile as the latter the contrary? The whites, too, by nature, were the
shrewder race. A man with some evil design, would not he be likely to speak
well of that stupidity which was blind to his depravity, and malign that
intelligence from which it might not be hidden? Not unlikely, perhaps.
But if the whites had dark secrets concerning Don Benito, could then Don
Benito be any way in complicity with the blacks? But they were too stupid.
Besides, who ever heard of a white so far a renegade as to apostatize from
his very species almost, by leaguing in against it with negroes? These difficulties recalled former ones. Lost in their mazes, Captain Delano, who had
now regained the deck, was uneasily advancing along it, when he observed
a new face; an aged sailor seated cross-legged near the main hatchway. His
skin was shrunk up with wrinkles like a pelican's empty pouch; his hair
frosted; his countenance grave and composed. His hands were full of ropes,
which he was working into a large knot. Some blacks were about him
obligingly dipping the strands for him, here and there, as the exigencies of
the operation demanded.

Captain Delano crossed over to him, and stood in silence surveying the
knot; his mind, by a not uncongenial transition, passing from its own
entanglements to those of the hemp. For intricacy such a knot he had never
seen in an American ship, or indeed any other. The old man looked like an
Egyptian priest, making gordian knots for the temple of Ammon. The
knot seemed a combination of double-bow-line-knot, treble-crown-knot,
back-handed-well-knot, knot-in-and-out-knot, and jamming-knot.

At last, puzzled to comprehend the meaning of such a knot, Captain
Delano, addressed the knotter:—

"What are you knotting there, my man?"

"The knot," was the brief reply, without looking up.

"So it seems; but what is it for?"

"For some one else to undo," muttered back the old man, plying his
fingers harder than ever, the knot being now nearly completed.

While Captain Delano stood watching him, suddenly the old man threw
the knot toward him, and said in broken English,—the first heard in the
ship,—something to this effect—"Undo it, cut it, quick." It was said lowly,
but with such condensation of rapidity, that the long, slow words in Spanish,
which had preceded and followed, almost operated as covers to the brief
English between.

For a moment, knot in hand, and knot in head, Captain Delano stood mute; while, without further heeding him, the old man was now intent upon other ropes. Presently there was a slight stir behind Captain Delano. Turning, he saw the chained negro, Atufal, standing quietly there. The next moment the old sailor rose, muttering, and, followed by his subordinate negroes, removed to the forward part of the ship, where in the crowd he disappeared.

An elderly negro, in a clout like an infant's, and with a pepper and salt head, and a kind of attorney air, now approached Captain Delano. In tolerable Spanish, and with a good-natured, knowing wink, he informed him that the old knotter was simple-witted, but harmless; often playing his old tricks. The negro concluded by begging the knot, for of course the stranger would not care to be troubled with it. Unconsciously, it was handed to him. With a sort of congé, the negro received it, and turning his back ferreted into it like a detective Custom House officer after smuggled laces. Soon, with some African word, equivalent to pshaw, he tossed the knot overboard.

All this is very queer now, thought Captain Delano, with a qualmish sort of emotion; but as one feeling incipient seasickness, he strove, by ignoring the symptoms, to get rid of the malady. Once more he looked off for his boat. To his delight, it was now again in view, leaving the rocky spur astern.

The sensation here experienced, after at first relieving his uneasiness, with unforeseen efficiency, soon began to remove it. The less distant sight of that well-known boat—showing it, not as before, half blended with the haze, but with outline defined, so that its individuality, like a man's, was manifest; that boat, *Rover* by name, which, though now in strange seas, had often pressed the beach of Captain Delano's home, and, brought to its threshold for repairs, had familiarly lain there, as a Newfoundland dog; the sight of that household boat evoked a thousand trustful associations, which, contrasted with previous suspicions, filled him not only with lightsome confidence, but somehow with half-humorous self-reproaches at his former lack of it.

"What, I, Amasa Delano—Jack of the Beach, as they called me when a lad—I, Amasa; the same that, duck-satchel in hand, used to paddle along the waterside to the schoolhouse made from the old hulk;—I, little Jack of the Beach, that used to go berrying with cousin Nat and the rest; I to be murdered here at the ends of the earth, on board a haunted pirate-ship by a horrible Spaniard?—Too nonsensical to think of! Who would murder Amasa Delano? His conscience is clean. There is some one above. Fie, fie, Jack of the Beach! you are a child indeed; a child of the second childhood, old boy; you are beginning to dote and drule, I'm afraid."

Light of heart and foot, he stepped aft, and there was met by Don Benito's servant, who, with a pleasing expression, responsive to his own present feelings, informed him that his master had recovered from the effects of his coughing fit, and had just ordered him to go present his compliments to his good guest, Don Amasa, and say that he (Don Benito) would soon have the happiness to rejoin him.

There now, do you mark that? again thought Captain Delano, walking the poop. What a donkey I was. This kind gentleman who here sends me his kind compliments, he, but ten minutes ago, dark-lantern in hand, was dodging round some old grind-stone in the hold, sharpening a hatchet for me, I thought. Well, well; these long calms have a morbid effect on the mind. I've often heard, though I never believed it before. Ha! glancing toward the boat; there's *Rover;* a good dog; a white bone in her mouth. A pretty big bone though, seems to me.—What? Yes, she has fallen afoul of the bubbling tide-rip there. It sets her the other way, too, for the time. Patience.

It was now about noon, though, from the greyness of everything, it seemed to be getting toward dusk.

The calm was confirmed. In the far distance, away from the influence of land, the leaden ocean seemed laid out and leaded up, its course finished, soul gone, defunct. But the current from landward, where the ship was, increased; silently sweeping her further and further toward the tranced waters beyond.

Still, from his knowledge of those latitudes, cherishing hopes of a breeze, and a fair and fresh one, at any moment, Captain Delano, despite present prospects, buoyantly counted upon bringing the *San Dominick* safely to anchor ere night. The distance swept over was nothing; since, with a good wind, ten minutes' sailing would retrace more than sixty minutes' drifting. Meantime, one moment turning to mark "Rover" fighting the tide-rip, and the next to see Don Benito approaching, he continued walking the poop.

Gradually he felt a vexation arising from the delay of his boat; this soon merged into uneasiness; and at last, his eye falling continually, as from a stage-box into the pit, upon the strange crowd before and below him, and by-and-by recognizing there the face—now composed to indifference—of the Spanish sailor who had seemed to beckon from the main chains, something of his old trepidations returned.

Ah, thought he—gravely enough—this is like the ague: because it went off, it follows not that it won't come back.

Though ashamed of the relapse, he could not altogether subdue it; and so, exerting his good nature to the utmost, insensibly he came to a compromise.

Yes, this is a strange craft; a strange history, too, and strange folks on board. But—nothing more.

By way of keeping his mind out of mischief till the boat should arrive, he tried to occupy it with turning over and over, in a purely speculative sort of way, some lesser peculiarities of the captain and crew. Among others, four curious points recurred.

First, the affair of the Spanish lad assailed with a knife by the slave boy; an act winked at by Don Benito. Second, the tyranny in Don Benito's treatment of Atufal, the black; as if a child should lead a bull of the Nile by the ring in his nose. Third, the trampling of the sailor by the two negroes; a piece of insolence passed over without so much as a reprimand. Fourth, the cringing submission to their master of all the ship's underlings, mostly blacks; as if by the least inadvertence they feared to draw down his despotic displeasure.

Coupling these points, they seemed somewhat contradictory. But what then, thought Captain Delano, glancing toward his now nearing boat,— what then? Why, this Don Benito is a very capricious commander. But he is not the first of the sort I have seen; though it's true he rather exceeds any other. But as a nation—continued he in his reveries—these Spaniards are all an odd set; the very word Spaniard has a curious, conspirator, Guy-Fawkish twang to it. And yet, I dare say, Spaniards in the main are as good folks as any in Duxbury, Massachusetts. Ah, good! At last "Rover" has come.

As, with its welcome freight, the boat touched the side, the oakum-pickers, with venerable gestures, sought to restrain the blacks, who, at the sight of three gurried water-casks in its bottom, and a pile of wilted pumpkins in its bow, hung over the bulwarks in disorderly raptures.

Don Benito with his servant now appeared; his coming, perhaps, hastened by hearing the noise. Of him Captain Delano sought permission to serve out the water, so that all might share alike, and none injure themselves by unfair excess. But sensible, and, on Don Benito's account, kind as this offer was, it was received with what seemed impatience; as if aware that he lacked energy as a commander, Don Benito, with the true jealousy of weakness, resented as an affront any interference. So, at least, Captain Delano inferred.

In another moment the casks were being hoisted in, when some of the eager negroes accidentally jostled Captain Delano, where he stood by the gangway; so that, unmindful of Don Benito, yielding to the impulse of the moment, with good-natured authority he bade the blacks stand back; to enforce his words making use of a half-mirthful, half-menacing gesture. Instantly the blacks paused, just where they were, each negro and negress suspended in his or her posture, exactly as the word had found them—for a few seconds continuing so—while, as between the responsive posts of a telegraph, an unknown syllable ran from man to man among the perched oakum-pickers. While Captain Delano's attention was fixed by this scene, suddenly the hatchet-polishers half rose, and a rapid cry came from Don Benito.

Thinking that at the signal of the Spaniard he was about to be massacred, Captain Delano would have sprung for his boat, but paused, as the oakum-pickers, dropping down in to the crowd with earnest exclamations, forced every white and every negro back, at the same moment, with gestures friendly and familiar, almost jocose, bidding him, in substance, not be a fool. Simultaneously the hatchet-polishers resumed their seats, quietly as so many tailors, and at once, as if nothing had happened, the work of hoisting in the casks was resumed, whites and blacks singing at the tackle.

Captain Delano glanced toward Don Benito. As he saw his meagre form in the act of recovering itself from reclining in the servant's arms, into which the agitated invalid had fallen, he could not but marvel at the panic by which himself had been surprised on the darting supposition that such a commander, who upon a legitimate occasion, so trivial, too, as it now appeared, could lose all self-command, was, with energetic iniquity, going to bring about his murder.

The casks being on deck, Captain Delano was handed a number of jars and cups by one of the steward's aides, who, in the name of Don Benito, entreated him to do as he had proposed: dole out the water. He complied, with republican impartiality as to this republican element, which always seeks one level, serving the oldest white no better than the youngest black; excepting, indeed, poor Don Benito, whose condition, if not rank, demanded an extra allowance. To him, in the first place, Captain Delano presented a fair pitcher of the fluid; but, thirsting as he was for fresh water, Don Benito quaffed not a drop until after several grave bows and salutes: a reciprocation of courtesies which the sight-loving Africans hailed with clapping of hands.

Two of the less wilted pumpkins being reserved for the cabin table, the residue were minced up on the spot for the general regalement. But the soft bread, sugar, and bottled cider, Captain Delano would have given the Spaniards alone, and in chief Don Benito; but the latter objected; which disinterestedness, on his part, not a little pleased the American; and so mouthfuls all around were given alike to whites and blacks; excepting one bottle of cider, which Babo insisted upon setting aside for his master.

Here it may be observed that as, on the first visit of the boat, the American had not permitted his men to board the ship, neither did he now; being unwilling to add to the confusion of the decks.

Not uninfluenced by the peculiar good humour at present prevailing, and for the time oblivious of any but benevolent thoughts, Captain Delano, who from recent indications counted upon a breeze within an hour or two at furthest, despatched the boat back to the sealer with orders for all the hands that could be spared immediately to set about rafting casks to the watering-place and filling them. Likewise he bade word be carried to his chief officer, that if against present expectation the ship was not brought to anchor by sunset, he need be under no concern, for as there was to be a full moon that night, he (Captain Delano) would remain on board ready to play the pilot, should the wind come soon or late.

As the two captains stood together, observing the departing boat—the servant as it happened having just spied a spot on his master's velvet sleeve, and silently engaged rubbing it out—the American expressed his regrets that the *San Dominick* had no boats; none, at least, but the unseaworthy old hulk of the long-boat, which, warped as a camel's skeleton in the desert, and almost as bleached, lay potwise inverted amidships, one side a little tipped, furnishing a subterraneous sort of den for family groups of the blacks, mostly women and small children; who, squatting on old mats below, or perched above in the dark dome, on the elevated seats, were descried, some distance within, like a social circle of bats, sheltering in some friendly cave; at intervals, ebon flights of naked boys and girls, three or four years old, darting in and out of the den's mouth.

"Had you three or four boats now, Don Benito," said Captain Delano, "I think that, by tugging at the oars, your negroes here might help along matters some.—Did you sail from port without boats, Don Benito?"

"They were stove in the gales, Señor."

"That was bad. Many men, too, you lost then. Boats and men.—Those must have been hard gales, Don Benito."

"Past all speech," cringed the Spaniard.

"Tell me, Don Benito," continued his companion with increased interest, "tell me, were these gales immediately off the pitch of Cape Horn?"

"Cape Horn?—who spoke of Cape Horn?"

"Yourself did, when giving me an account of your voyage," answered Captain Delano with almost equal astonishment at this eating of his own words, even as he ever seemed eating his own heart, on the part of the Spaniard. "You yourself, Don Benito, spoke of Cape Horn," he emphatically repeated.

The Spaniard turned, in a sort of stooping posture, pausing an instant, as one about to make a plunging exchange of elements, as from air to water.

At this moment a messenger-boy, a white, hurried by, in the regular performance of his function carrying the last expired half-hour forward to the forecastle, from the cabin time-piece, to have it struck at the ship's large bell.

"Master," said the servant, discontinuing his work on the coat sleeve, and addressing the rapt Spaniard with a sort of timid apprehensiveness, as one charged with a duty, the discharge of which, it was foreseen, would prove irksome to the very person who had imposed it, and for whose benefit it was intended, "master told me never mind where he was, or how engaged, always to remind him, to a minute, when shaving-time comes. Miguel has gone to strike the half-hour afternoon. It is *now*, master. Will master go into the cuddy?"

"Ah—yes," answered the Spaniard, starting, somewhat as from dreams into realities; then turning upon Captain Delano, he said that ere long he would resume the conversation.

"Then if master means to talk more to Don Amasa," said the servant, "why not let Don Amasa sit by master in the cuddy, and master can talk, and Don Amasa can listen, while Babo here lathers and strops."

"Yes," said Captain Delano, not unpleased with this sociable plan, "yes, Don Benito, unless you had rather not, I will go with you."

"Be it so, Señor."

As the three passed aft, the American could not but think it another strange instance of his host's capriciousness, this being shaved with such uncommon punctuality in the middle of the day. But he deemed it more than likely that the servant's anxious fidelity had something to do with the matter; inasmuch as the timely interruption served to rally his master from the mood which had evidently been coming upon him.

The place called the cuddy was a light deck-cabin formed by the poop, a sort of attic to the large cabin below. Part of it had formerly been the quarters of the officers; but since their death all the partitionings had been thrown down, and the whole interior converted into one spacious and airy marine hall; for absence of fine furniture and picturesque disarray, of odd appurtenances, somewhat answering to the wide, cluttered hall of some eccentric bachelor-squire in the country, who hangs his shooting-jacket and tobacco-pouch on deer antlers, and keeps his fishing-rod, tongs, and walking-stick in the same corner.

The similitude was heightened, if not originally suggested, by glimpses of the surrounding sea; since, in one aspect, the country and the ocean seem cousins-german.

The floor of the cuddy was matted. Overhead, four or five old muskets were stuck into horizontal holes along the beams. On one side was a claw-footed old table lashed to the deck; a thumbed missal on it, and over it a small, meagre crucifix attached to the bulkhead. Under the table lay a dented cutlass or two, with a hacked harpoon, among some melancholy old rigging, like a heap of poor friar's girdles. There were also two long, sharp-ribbed settees of malacca cane, black with age, and uncomfortable to look at as inquisitors' racks, with a large, misshapen arm-chair, which, furnished with a rude barber's crutch at the back, working with a screw, seemed some grotesque Middle Ages engine of torment. A flag locker was in one corner, exposing various coloured bunting, some rolled up, others half unrolled, still others tumbled. Opposite was a cumbrous washstand, of black mahogany, all of one block, with a pedestal, like a font, and over it a railed shelf, containing combs, brushes, and other implements of the toilet. A torn hammock of stained grass swung near; the sheets tossed, and the pillow wrinkled up like a brow, as if whoever slept here slept but illy, with alternate visitations of sad thoughts and bad dreams.

The further extremity of the cuddy, overhanging the ship's stern, was pierced with three openings, windows or port holes, according as men or cannon might peer, socially or unsocially, out of them. At present neither men nor cannon were seen, though huge ring-bolts and other rusty iron fixtures of the wood-work hinted of twenty-four-pounders.

Glancing toward the hammock as he entered, Captain Delano said, "You sleep here, Don Benito?"

"Yes, Señor, since we got into mild weather."

"This seems a sort of dormitory, sitting-room, sail-loft, chapel, armoury, and private closet together, Don Benito," added Captain Delano, looking round.

"Yes, Señor; events have not been favourable to much order in my arrangements."

Here the servant, napkin on arm, made a motion as if waiting his master's good pleasure. Don Benito signified his readiness, when, seating him in the malacca arm-chair, and for the guest's convenience drawing opposite it one of the settees, the servant commenced operations by throwing back his master's collar and loosening his cravat.

There is something in the negro which, in a peculiar way, fits him for avocations about one's person. Most negroes are natural valets and hairdressers; taking to the comb and brush congenially as to the castanets, and flourishing them apparently with almost equal satisfaction. There is, too, a smooth tact about them in this employment, with a marvelous, noiseless, gliding briskness, not ungraceful in its way, singularly pleasing to behold, and still more so to be the manipulated subject of. And above all is the great gift of good humour. Not the mere grin or laugh is here meant. Those were unsuitable. But a certain easy cheerfulness, harmonious in every glance and gesture; as though God had set the whole negro to some pleasant tune.

When to all this is added the docility arising from the unaspiring contentment of a limited mind, and that susceptibility of blind attachment sometimes inhering in indisputable inferiors, one readily perceives why those hypochondriacs, Johnson and Byron—it may be something like the hypochondriac, Benito Cereno—took to their hearts, almost to the exclusion of the entire white race, their serving men, the negroes, Barber and Fletcher. But if there be that in the negro which exempts him from the inflicted sourness of the morbid or cynical mind, how, in his most prepossessing aspects, must he appear to a benevolent one? When at ease with respect to exterior things, Captain Delano's nature was not only benign, but familiarly and humourously so. At home, he had often taken rare satisfaction in sitting in his door, watching some free man of colour at his work or play. If on a voyage he chanced to have a black sailor, invariably he was on chatty, and half-gamesome terms with him. In fact, like most men of a good, blithe heart, Captain Delano took to negroes, not philanthropically, but genially, just as other men to Newfoundland dogs.

Hitherto the circumstances in which he found the *San Dominick* had repressed the tendency. But in the cuddy, relieved from his former uneasiness, and, for various reasons, more sociably inclined than at any previous period of the day, and seeing the coloured servant, napkin on arm, so debonair about his master, in a business so familiar as that of shaving, too, all his old weakness for negroes returned.

Among other things, he was amused with an odd instance of the African love of bright colours and fine shows, in the black's informally taking from the flag-locker a great piece of bunting of all hues, and lavishly tucking it under his master's chin for an apron.

The mode of shaving among the Spaniards is a little different from what it is with other nations. They have a basin, specially called a barber's basin, which on one side is scooped out, so as accurately to receive the chin, against which it is closely held in lathering; which is done, not with a brush, but with soap dipped in the water of the basin and rubbed on the face.

In the present instance salt-water was used for lack of better; and the parts lathered were only the upper lip, and low down under the throat, all the rest being cultivated beard.

These preliminaries being somewhat novel to Captain Delano he sat curiously eyeing them, so that no conversation took place, nor for the present did Don Benito appear disposed to renew any.

Setting down his basin, the negro searched among the razors, as for the sharpest, and having found it, gave it an additional edge by expertly stropping it on the firm, smooth, oily skin of his open palm; he then made a gesture as if to begin, but midway stood suspended for an instant, one hand elevating the razor, the other professionally dabbling among the bubbling suds on the Spaniard's lank neck. Not unaffected by the close sight of the gleaming steel, Don Benito nervously shuddered, his usual ghastliness was heightened by the lather, which lather, again, was intensified in its hue by the contrasting sootiness of the negro's body. Altogether the scene was somewhat peculiar, at least to Captain Delano, nor, as he saw the two thus postured, could he resist the vagary, that in the black he saw a headsman, and in the white, a man at the block. But this was one of those antic conceits, appearing and vanishing in a breath, from which, perhaps, the best regulated mind is not free.

Meantime the agitation of the Spaniard had a little loosened the bunting from around him, so that one broad fold swept curtain-like over the chair-arm to the floor, revealing, amid a profusion of armorial bars and ground-colours—black, blue and yellow—a closed castle in a blood-red field diagonal with a lion rampant in a white.

"The castle and the lion," exclaimed Captain Delano—"why, Don Benito, this is the flag of Spain you use here. It's well it's only I and not the King, that sees this," he added with a smile, "but"—turning toward the black,—

"it's all one, I suppose, so the colours be gay," which playful remark did not fail somewhat to tickle the negro.

"Now, master," he said, readjusting the flag, and pressing the head gently ·further back into the crotch of the chair; "now, master," and the steel glanced nigh the throat.

Again Don Benito faintly shuddered.

"You must not shake so, master.—See, Don Amasa, master always shakes when I shave him. And yet master knows I never yet have drawn blood, though it's true, if master will shake so, I may some of these times. Now, master," he continued. "And now, Don Amasa, please go on with your talk about the gale, and all that, master can hear, and between times master can answer."

"Ah yes, these gales," said Captain Delano; "but the more I think of your voyage, Don Benito, the more I wonder, not at the gales, terrible as they must have been, but at the disastrous interval following them. For here, by your account, have you been these two months and more getting from Cape Horn to St. Maria, a distance which I myself, with a good wind, have sailed in a few days. True, you had calms, and long ones, but to be becalmed for two months, that is, at least, unusual. Why, Don Benito, had almost any other gentleman told me such a story, I should have been half disposed to a little incredulity."

Here an involuntary expression came over the Spaniard, similar to that just before on the deck, and whether it was the start he gave, or a sudden gawky roll of the hull in the calm, or a momentary unsteadiness of the servant's hand; however it was, just then the razor drew blood, spots of which stained the creamy lather under the throat; immediately the black barber drew back his steel, and remaining in his professional attitude, back to Captain Delano, and face to Don Benito, held up the trickling razor, saying, with a sort of half humorous sorrow, "See, master,—you shook so—here's Babo's first blood."

No sword drawn before James the First of England, no assassination in that timid King's presence, could have produced a more terrified aspect than was now presented by Don Benito.

Poor fellow, thought Captain Delano, so nervous he can't even bear the sight of barber's blood; and this unstrung, sick man, is it credible that I should have imagined he meant to spill all my blood, who can't endure the sight of one little drop of his own? Surely, Amasa Delano, you have been beside yourself this day. Tell it not when you get home, sappy Amasa. Well, well, he looks like a murderer, doesn't he? More like as if himself were to be done for. Well, well, this day's experience shall be a good lesson.

Meantime, while these things were running through the honest seaman's mind, the servant had taken the napkin from his arm, and to Don Benito had said: "But answer Don Amasa, please, master, while I wipe this ugly stuff off the razor, and strop it again."

As he said the words, his face was turned half round, so as to be alike visible to the Spaniard and the American, and seemed by its expression to hint, that he was desirous, by getting his master to go on with the conversation, considerably to withdraw his attention from the recent annoying accident. As if glad to snatch the offered relief, Don Benito resumed, rehearsing to Captain Delano, that not only were the calms of unusual duration, but the ship had fallen in with obstinate currents and other things he added, some of which were but repetitions of former statements, to explain how it came to pass that the passage from Cape Horn to St. Maria had been so exceedingly long, now and then mingling with his words, incidental praises, less qualified than before, to the blacks for their general good conduct.

These particulars were not given consecutively, the servant now and then using his razor, and so, between the intervals of shaving, the story and panegyric went on with more than usual huskiness.

To Captain Delano's imagination, now again not wholly at rest, there was something so hollow in the Spaniard's manner, with apparently some reciprocal hollowness in the servant's dusky comment of silence, that the idea flashed across him, that possibly master and man, for some unknown purpose, were acting out, both in word and deed, nay, to the very tremor of Don Benito's limbs, some juggling play before him. Neither did the suspicion of collusion lack apparent support, from the fact of those whispered conferences before mentioned. But then, what could be the object of enacting this play of the barber before him? At last, regarding the notion as a whimsey, insensibly suggested, perhaps, by the theatrical aspect of Don Benito in his harlequin ensign, Captain Delano speedily banished it.

The shaving over, the servant bestirred himself with a small bottle of scented waters, pouring a few drops on the head, and then diligently rubbing; the vehemence of the exercise causing the muscles of his face to twitch rather strangely.

His next operation was with comb, scissors and brush; going round and round, smoothing a curl here, clipping an unruly whisker-hair there, giving a graceful sweep to the temple-lock, with other impromptu touches evincing the hand of a master; while, like any resigned gentleman in barber's hands, Don Benito bore all, much less uneasily, at least, than he had done the razoring; indeed, he sat so pale and rigid now, that the negro seemed a Nubian sculptor finishing off a white statue-head.

All being over at last, the standard of Spain removed, tumbled up, and tossed back into the flag-locker, the negro's warm breath blowing away any stray hair which might have lodged down his master's neck; collar and cravat readjusted; a speck of lint whisked off the velvet lapel; all this being done; backing off a little space, and pausing with an expression of subdued self-complacency, the servant for a moment surveyed his master, as, in toilet at least, the creature of his own tasteful hands.

Captain Delano playfully complimented him upon his achievement; at the same time congratulating Don Benito.

But neither sweet waters, nor shampooing, nor fidelity, nor sociality, delighted the Spaniard. Seeing him relapsing into forbidding gloom, and still remaining seated, Captain Delano, thinking that his presence was un-desired just then, withdrew, on pretense of seeing whether, as he had prophesied, any signs of a breeze were visible.

Walking forward to the mainmast, he stood awhile thinking over the scene, and not without some undefined misgivings, when he heard a noise near the cuddy, and turning, saw the negro, his hand to his cheek. Advanc-ing, Captain Delano perceived that the cheek was bleeding. He was about to ask the cause, when the negro's wailing soliloquy enlightened him.

"Ah, when will master get better from his sickness; only the sour heart that sour sickness breeds made him serve Babo so; cutting Babo with the razor, because, only by accident, Babo had given master one little scratch; and for the first time in so many a day, too. Ah, ah, ah," holding his hand to his face.

Is it possible, thought Captain Delano; was it to wreak in private his Spanish spite against this poor friend of his, that Don Benito, by his sullen manner, impelled me to withdraw? Ah, this slavery breeds ugly passions in man! Poor fellow!

He was about to speak in sympathy to the negro, but with a timid reluc-tance he now re-entered the cuddy.

Presently master and man came forth; Don Benito leaning on his servant as if nothing had happened.

But a sort of love-quarrel, after all, thought Captain Delano.

He accosted Don Benito, and they slowly walked together. They had gone but a few paces, when the steward—a tall, rajah-looking mulatto, orientally set off with a pagoda turban formed by three or four Madras handkerchiefs wound about his head, tier on tier—approaching with a salaam, announced lunch in the cabin.

On their way thither, the two captains were preceded by the mulatto, who, turning round as he advanced, with continual smiles and bows, ushered them in, a display of elegance which quite completed the insignificance of the small bare-headed Babo, who, as if not unconscious of inferiority, eyed askance the graceful steward. But in part, Captain Delano imputed his jealous watchfulness to that peculiar feeling which the full-blooded African entertains for the adulterated one. As for the steward, his manner, if not bespeaking much dignity of self-respect, yet evidenced his extreme desire to please; which is doubly meritorious, as at once Christian and Chesterfieldian.

Captain Delano observed with interest that while the complexion of the mulatto was hybrid, his physiognomy was European; classically so.

"Don Benito," whispered he, "I am glad to see this usher-of-the-golden-rod of yours; the sight refutes an ugly remark once made to me by a Barbados planter that when a mulatto has a regular European face, look out for him; he is a devil. But see, your steward here has features more regular than King George's of England; and yet there he nods, and bows, and smiles; a king, indeed—the king of kind hearts and polite fellows. What a pleasant voice he has, too?"

"He has, Señor."

"But, tell me, has he not, so far as you have known him, always proved a good, worthy fellow?" said Captain Delano, pausing, while with a final genuflexion the steward disappeared into the cabin; "come, for the reason just mentioned, I am curious to know."

"Francesco is a good man," rather sluggishly responded Don Benito, like a phlegmatic appreciator, who would neither find fault nor flatter.

"Ah, I thought so. For it were strange indeed, and not very creditable to us white-skins, if a little of our blood mixed with the African's, should, far from improving the latter's quality, have the sad effect of pouring vitriolic acid into black broth; improving the hue, perhaps, but not the wholesomeness."

"Doubtless, doubtless, Señor, but"—glancing at Babo—"not to speak of negroes, your planter's remark I have heard applied to the Spanish and Indian intermixtures in our provinces. But I know nothing about the matter," he listlessly added.

And here they entered the cabin.

The lunch was a frugal one. Some of Captain Delano's fresh fish and pumpkins, biscuit and salt beef, the reserved bottle of cider, and the *San Dominick's* last bottle of Canary.

As they entered, Francesco, with two or three coloured aids, was hovering over the table giving the last adjustments. Upon perceiving their master they withdrew, Francesco making a smiling congé, and the Spaniard, without condescending to notice it, fastidiously remarking to his companion that he relished not superfluous attendance.

Without companions, host and guest sat down, like a childless married couple, at opposite ends of the table, Don Benito waving Captain Delano to his place, and, weak as he was, insisting upon that gentleman being seated before himself.

The negro placed a rug under Don Benito's feet, and a cushion behind his back, and then stood behind, not his master's chair, but Captain Delano's. At first, this a little surprised the latter. But it was soon evident that, in taking his position, the black was still true to his master; since by facing him he could the more readily anticipate his slightest want.

"This is an uncommonly intelligent fellow of yours, Don Benito," whispered Captain Delano across the table.

"You say true, Señor."

During the repast, the guest again reverted to parts of Don Benito's story, begging further particulars here and there. He inquired how it was that the scurvy and fever should have committed such wholesale havoc upon the whites, while destroying less than half of the blacks. As if this question reproduced the whole scene of plague before the Spaniard's eyes, miserably reminding him of his solitude in a cabin where before he had had so many friends and officers round him, his hand shook, his face became hueless, broken words escaped; but directly the sane memory of the past seemed replaced by insane terrors of the present. With starting eyes he stared before him at vacancy. For nothing was to be seen but the hand of his servant pushing the Canary over toward him. At length a few sips served partially to restore him. He made random reference to the different constitutions of races, enabling one to offer more resistance to certain maladies than another. The thought was new to his companion.

Presently Captain Delano, intending to say something to his host concerning the pecuniary part of the business he had undertaken for him, especially—since he was strictly accountable to his owners—with reference to the new suit of sails, and other things of that sort; and naturally preferring to conduct such affairs in private, was desirous that the servant should withdraw; imagining that Don Benito for a few minutes could dispense with his attendance. He, however, waited awhile; thinking that, as the conversation proceeded, Don Benito, without being prompted, would perceive the propriety of the step.

But it was otherwise. At last catching his host's eye, Captain Delano, with a slight backward gesture of his thumb, whispered, "Don Benito, pardon me, but there is an interference with the full expression of what I have to say to you."

Upon this the Spaniard changed countenance; which was imputed to his resenting the hint, as in some way a reflection upon his servant. After a moment's pause, he assured his guest that the black's remaining with him could be of no disservice; because since losing his officers he had made Babo (whose original office, it now appeared, had been captain of the slaves) not only his constant attendant and companion, but in all things his confidant.

After this, nothing more could be said; though, indeed, Captain Delano could hardly avoid some little tinge of irritation upon being left ungratified in so inconsiderable a wish, by one, too, for whom he intended such solid services. But it is only his querulousness, thought he; and so filling his glass he proceeded to business.

The price of the sails and other matters was fixed upon. But while this was being done, the American observed that, though his original offer of assistance had been hailed with hectic animation, yet now when it was reduced to a business transaction, indifference and apathy were betrayed. Don Benito, in fact, appeared to submit to hearing the details more out of regard to common propriety, than from any impression that weighty benefit to himself and his voyage was involved.

Soon, this manner became still more reserved. The effort was vain to seek to draw him into social talk. Gnawed by his splenetic mood, he sat twitching his beard, while to little purpose the hand of his servant, mute as that on the wall, slowly pushed over the Canary.

Lunch being over, they sat down on the cushioned transom; the servant placing a pillow behind his master. The long continuance of the calm had now affected the atmosphere. Don Benito sighed heavily, as if for breath.

"Why not adjourn to the cuddy," said Captain Delano; "there is more air there." But the host sat silent and motionless.

Meantime his servant knelt before him, with a large fan of feathers. And Francesco, coming in on tiptoes, handed the negro a little cup of aromatic waters, with which at intervals he chafed his master's brow, smoothing the hair along the temples as a nurse does a child's. He spoke no word. He only rested his eye on his master's, as if, amid all Don Benito's distress, a little to refresh his spirit by the silent sight of fidelity.

Presently the ship's bell sounded two o'clock; and through the cabin-windows a slight rippling of the sea was discerned; and from the desired direction.

"There," exclaimed Captain Delano, "I told you so, Don Benito, look!"

He had risen to his feet, speaking in a very animated tone, with a view the more to rouse his companion. But though the crimson curtain of the stern-window near him that moment fluttered against his pale cheek, Don Benito seemed to have even less welcome for the breeze than the calm.

Poor fellow, thought Captain Delano, bitter experience has taught him that one ripple does not make a wind, any more than one swallow a summer. But he is mistaken for once. I will get his ship in for him, and prove it.

Briefly alluding to his weak condition, he urged his host to remain quietly where he was, since he (Captain Delano) would with pleasure take upon himself the responsibility of making the best use of the wind.

Upon gaining the deck, Captain Delano started at the unexpected figure of Atufal, monumentally fixed at the threshold, like one of those sculptured porters of black marble guarding the porches of Egyptian tombs.

But this time the start was, perhaps, purely physical. Atufal's presence, singularly attesting docility even in sullenness, was contrasted with that of the hatchet-polishers, who in patience evinced their industry; while both spectacles showed, that lax as Don Benito's general authority might be, still, whenever he chose to exert it, no man so savage or colossal but must, more or less, bow.

Snatching a trumpet which hung from the bulwarks, with a free step Captain Delano advanced to the forward edge of the poop, issuing his orders in his best Spanish. The few sailors and many negroes, all equally pleased, obediently set about heading the ship toward the harbour.

While giving some directions about setting a lower stu'n'-sail, suddenly Captain Delano heard a voice faithfully repeating his orders. Turning, he saw Babo, now for the time acting, under the pilot, his original part of captain of the slaves. This assistance proved valuable. Tattered sails and warped yards were soon brought into some trim. And no brace or halyard was pulled but to the blithe songs of the inspirited negroes.

Good fellows, thought Captain Delano, a little training would make fine sailors of them. Why, see, the very women pull and sing, too. These must be some of those Ashantee negresses that make such capital soldiers, I've heard. But who's at the helm? I must have a good hand there.

He went to see.

The *San Dominick* steered with a cumbrous tiller, with large horizontal pulleys attached. At each pulley-end stood a subordinate black, and between them, at the tiller-head, the responsible post, a Spanish seaman, whose countenance evinced his due share in the general hopefulness and confidence at the coming of the breeze.

He proved the same man who had behaved with so shamefaced an air on the windlass.

"Ah,—it is you, my man," exclaimed Captain Delano—"well, no more sheep's-eyes now;—look straightforward and keep the ship so. Good hand, I trust? And want to get into the harbour, don't you?"

"Sí, Señor," assented the man with an inward chuckle, grasping the tiller-head firmly. Upon this, unperceived by the American, the two blacks eyed the sailor askance.

Finding all right at the helm, the pilot went forward to the forecastle, to see how matters stood there.

The ship now had way enough to breast the current. With the approach of evening, the breeze would be sure to freshen.

Having done all that was needed for the present, Captain Delano, giving his last orders to the sailors, turned aft to report affairs to Don Benito in the cabin; perhaps additionally incited to rejoin him by the hope of snatching a moment's private chat while his servant was engaged upon deck.

From opposite sides, there were, beneath the poop, two approaches to the cabin; one further forward than the other, and consequently communicating with a longer passage. Marking the servant still above, Captain Delano, taking the nighest entrance—the one last named, and at whose porch Atufal still stood—hurried on his way, till, arrived at the cabin threshold, he paused an instant, a little to recover from his eagerness. Then, with the words of his intended business upon his lips, he entered. As he advanced toward the

Spaniard, on the transom, he heard another footstep, keeping time with his. From the opposite door, a salver in hand, the servant was likewise advancing.

"Confound the faithful fellow," thought Captain Delano; "what a vexatious coincidence."

Possibly, the vexation might have been something different, were it not for the buoyant confidence inspired by the breeze. But even as it was, he felt a slight twinge, from a sudden involuntary association in his mind of Babo with Atufal.

"Don Benito," said he, "I give you joy; the breeze will hold, and will increase. By the way, your tall man and time-piece, Atufal, stands without. By your order, of course?"

Don Benito recoiled, as if at some bland satirical touch, delivered with such adroit garnish of apparent good-breeding as to present no handle for retort.

He is like one flayed alive, thought Captain Delano; where may one touch him without causing a shrink?

The servant moved before his master, adjusting a cushion; recalled to civility, the Spaniard stiffly replied: "You are right. The slave appears where you saw him, according to my command; which is, that if at the given hour I am below, he must take his stand and abide my coming."

"Ah now, pardon me, but that is treating the poor fellow like an ex-king denied. Ah, Don Benito," smiling, "for all the license you permit in some things, I fear lest, at bottom, you are a bitter hard master."

Again Don Benito shrank; and this time, as the good sailor thought, from a genuine twinge of his conscience.

Conversation now became constrained. In vain Captain Delano called attention to the now perceptible motion of the keel gently cleaving the sea; with lack-lustre eye, Don Benito returned words few and reserved.

By-and-by, the wind having steadily risen, and still blowing right into the harbour, bore the *San Dominick* swiftly on. Rounding a point of land, the sealer at distance came into open view.

Meantime Captain Delano had again repaired to the deck, remaining there some time. Having at last altered the ship's course, so as to give the reef a wide berth, he returned for a few moments below.

I will cheer up my poor friend, this time, thought he.

"Better and better, Don Benito," he cried as he blithely reentered; "there will soon be an end to your cares, at least for awhile. For when, after a long, sad voyage, you know, the anchor drops into the haven, all its vast weight seems lifted from the captain's heart. We are getting on famously, Don Benito. My ship is in sight. Look through this sidelight here; there she is; all a-taunt-o! The *Bachelor's Delight,* my good friend. Ah, how this wind braces one up. Come, you must take a cup of coffee with me this evening.

My old steward will give you as fine a cup as ever any sultan tasted. What say you, Don Benito, will you?"

At first, the Spaniard glanced feverishly up, casting a longing look toward the sealer, while with mute concern his servant gazed into his face. Suddenly the old ague of coldness returned, and dropping back to his cushions he was silent.

"You do not answer. Come, all day you have been my host; would you have hospitality all on one side?"

"I cannot go," was the response.

"What? it will not fatigue you. The ships will lie together as near as they can, without swinging foul. It will be little more than stepping from deck to deck; which is but as from room to room. Come, come, you must not refuse me."

"I cannot go," decisively and repulsively repeated Don Benito.

Renouncing all but the last appearance of courtesy, with a sort of cadaverous sullenness, and biting his thin nails to the quick, he glanced, almost glared, at his guest; as if impatient that a stranger's presence should interfere with the full indulgence of his morbid hour. Meantime the sound of the parted waters came more and more gurglingly and merrily in at the windows; as reproaching him for his dark spleen; as telling him that, sulk as he might, and go mad with it, nature cared not a jot; since, whose fault was it, pray?

But the foul mood was now at its depth, as the fair wind at its height.

There was something in the man so far beyond any mere unsociality or sourness previously evinced, that even the forbearing good-nature of his guest could no longer endure it. Wholly at a loss to account for such demeanour, and deeming sickness with eccentricity, however extreme, no adequate excuse, well satisfied, too, that nothing in his own conduct could justify it, Captain Delano's pride began to be roused. Himself became reserved. But all seemed one to the Spaniard. Quitting him, therefore, Captain Delano once more went to the deck.

The ship was now within less than two miles of the sealer. The whaleboat was seen darting over the interval.

To be brief, the two vessels, thanks to the pilot's skill, ere long in neighborly style lay anchored together.

Before returning to his own vessel, Captain Delano had intended communicating to Don Benito the practical details of the proposed services to be rendered. But, as it was, unwilling anew to subject himself to rebuffs, he resolved, now that he had seen the *San Dominick* safely moored, immediately to quit her, without further allusion to hospitality or business. Indefinitely postponing his ulterior plans, he would regulate his future actions according to future circumstances. His boat was ready to receive him; but his host still tarried below. Well, thought Captain Delano, if he has little breeding, the more need to show mine. He descended to the cabin to bid a ceremonious, and, it may be, tacitly rebukeful adieu. But to his great satisfaction, Don Benito, as if he began to feel the weight of that treatment with which his slighted guest had, not indecorously, retaliated upon him, now supported by his servant, rose to his feet, and grasping Captain Delano's hand, stood tremulous; too much agitated to speak. But the good augury hence drawn was suddenly dashed, by his resuming all his previous reserve, with augmented gloom, as, with half-averted eyes, he silently reseated himself on his cushions. With a corresponding return to his own chilled feelings, Captain Delano bowed and withdrew.

He was hardly midway in the narrow corridor, dim as a tunnel, leading from the cabin to the stairs, when a sound, as of the tolling for execution in some jail-yard, fell on his ears. It was the echo of the ship's flawed bell, striking the hour, drearily reverberated in this subterranean vault. Instantly, by a fatality not to be withstood, his mind, responsive to the portent, swarmed with superstitious suspicions. He paused. In images far swifter than these sentences, the minutest details of all his former distrusts swept through him.

Hitherto, credulous good-nature had been too ready to furnish excuses for reasonable fears. Why was the Spaniard, so superfluously punctilious at times, now heedless of common propriety in not accompanying to the side his departing guest? Did indisposition forbid? Indisposition had not forbidden more irksome exertion that day. His last equivocal demeanour recurred. He had risen to his feet, grasped his guest's hand, motioned toward his hat; then, in an instant, all was eclipsed in sinister muteness and gloom. Did this imply one brief, repentant relenting at the final moment, from some iniquitous plot, followed by remorseless return to it? His last glance seemed to express a calamitous, yet acquiescent farewell to Captain Delano for ever. Why decline the invitation to visit the sealer that evening? Or was the Spaniard less hardened than the Jew, who refrained not from supping at the board of Him whom the same night he meant to betray? What imported all those day-long enigmas and contradictions, except they were intended to mystify, preliminary to some stealthy blow? Atufal, the pretended rebel, but punctual shadow, that moment lurked by the threshold without. He seemed a sentry, and more. Who, by his own confession, had stationed him there? Was the negro now lying in wait?

The Spaniard behind—his creature before: to rush from darkness to light was the involuntary choice.

The next moment, with clenched jaw and hand, he passed Atufal, and stood unarmed in the light. As he saw his trim ship lying peacefully at her anchor, and almost within ordinary call; as he saw his household boat, with familiar faces in it, patiently rising and falling on the short waves by the *San Dominick's* side; and then, glancing about the decks where he stood, saw the oakum-pickers still gravely plying their fingers; and heard the low, buzzing whistle and industrious hum of the hatchet-polishers, still bestirring themselves over their endless occupation; and more than all, as he saw the benign aspect of Nature, taking her innocent repose in the evening; the screened sun in the quiet camp of the west shining out like the mild light from Abraham's tent; as his charmed eye and ear took in all these, with the chained figure of the black, the clenched jaw and hand relaxed. Once again he smiled at the phantoms which had mocked him, and felt something like a tinge of remorse, that, by indulging them even for a moment, he should, by implication, have betrayed an almost atheist doubt of the everwatchful Providence above.

There was a few minutes' delay, while, in obedience to his orders, the boat was being hooked along to the gangway. During this interval, a sort of saddened satisfaction stole over Captain Delano, at thinking of the kindly offices he had that day discharged for a stranger. Ah, thought he, after good actions one's conscience is never ungrateful, however much so the benefited party may be.

Presently, his foot, in the first act of descent into the boat, pressed the first round of the side-ladder, his face presented inward upon the deck. In the same moment, he heard his name courteously sounded; and, to his pleased surprise, saw Don Benito advancing—an unwonted energy in his air, as if, at the last moment, intent upon making amends for his recent discourtesy. With instinctive good feeling, Captain Delano, revoking his foot, turned and reciprocally advanced. As he did so, the Spaniard's nervous eagerness increased, but his vital energy failed; so that, the better to support him, the servant, placing his master's hand on his naked shoulder, and gently holding it there, formed himself into a sort of crutch.

When the two captains met, the Spaniard again fervently took the hand of the American, at the same time casting an earnest glance into his eyes, but, as before, too much overcome to speak.

I have done him wrong, self-reproachfully thought Captain Delano; his apparent coldness has deceived me; in no instance has he meant to offend.

Meantime, as if fearful that the continuance of the scene might too much unstring his master, the servant seemed anxious to terminate it. And so, still presenting himself as a crutch, and walking between the two captains, he advanced with them toward the gangway; while still, as if full of kindly contrition, Don Benito would not let go the hand of Captain Delano, but retained it in his, across the black's body.

Soon they were standing by the side, looking over into the boat, whose crew turned up their curious eyes. Waiting a moment for the Spaniard to relinquish his hold, the now embarrassed Captain Delano lifted his foot, to overstep the threshold of the open gangway; but still, Don Benito would not let go his hand. And yet, with an agitated tone, he said, "I can go no further; here I must bid you adieu. Adieu, my dear, dear Don Amasa. Go—go!" suddenly tearing his hand loose, "go, and God guard you better than me, my best friend."

Not unaffected, Captain Delano would now have lingered; but catching the meekly admonitory eye of the servant, with a hasty farewell he descended into his boat, followed by the continual adieus of Don Benito, standing rooted in the gangway.

Seating himself in the stern, Captain Delano, making a last salute, ordered the boat shoved off. The crew had their oars on end. The bowsman pushed the boat a sufficient distance for the oars to be lengthwise dropped. The instant that was done, Don Benito sprang over the bulwarks, falling at the feet of Captain Delano; at the same time, calling towards his ship, but in tones so frenzied, that none in the boat could understand him. But, as if not equally obtuse, three Spanish sailors, from three different and distant parts of the ship, splashed into the sea, swimming after their captain, as if intent upon his rescue.

The dismayed officer of the boat eagerly asked what this meant. To which, Captain Delano, turning a disdainful smile upon the unaccountable Benito Cereno, answered that, for his part, he neither knew nor cared; but it seemed as if the Spaniard had taken it into his head to produce the impression among his people that the boat wanted to kidnap him. "Or else—give way for your lives," he wildly added, starting at a clattering hubbub in the ship, above which rang the tocsin of the hatchet-polishers; and seizing Don Benito by the throat he added, "this plotting pirate means murder!" Here, in apparent verification of the words, the servant, a dagger in his hand, was seen on the rail overhead, poised, in the act of leaping, as if with desperate fidelity to befriend his master to the last; while, seemingly to aid the black, the three Spanish sailors were trying to clamber into the hampered bow. Meantime, the whole host of negroes, as if inflamed at the sight of their jeopardized captain, impended in one sooty avalanche over the bulwarks.

All this, with what preceded, and what followed, occurred with such involutions of rapidity, that past, present, and future seemed one.

Seeing the negro coming, Captain Delano had flung the Spaniard aside, almost in the very act of clutching him, and, by the unconscious recoil, shifting his place, with arms thrown up, so promptly grappled the servant in his descent, that with dagger presented at Captain Delano's heart, the black seemed of purpose to have leaped there as to his mark. But the weapon was wrenched away, and the assailant dashed down into the bottom of the boat, which now, with disentangled oars, began to speed through the sea.

At this juncture, the left hand of Captain Delano, on one side, again clutched the half-reclined Don Benito, heedless that he was in a speechless faint, while his right foot, on the other side, ground the prostrate negro;

and his right arm pressed for added speed on the after oar, his eye bent forward, encouraging his men to their utmost.

But here, the officer of the boat, who had at last succeeded in beating off the towing Spanish sailors, and was now, with face turned aft, assisting the bowsman at his oar, suddenly called to Captain Delano, to see what the black was about; while a Portuguese oarsman shouted to him to give heed to what the Spaniard was saying.

Glancing down at his feet, Captain Delano saw the freed hand of the servant aiming with a second dagger—a small one, before concealed in his wool—with this he was snakishly writhing up from the boat's bottom, at the heart of his master, his countenance lividly vindictive, expressing the centered purpose of his soul; while the Spaniard, half-choked, was vainly shrinking away, with husky words, incoherent to all but the Portuguese.

That moment, across the long benighted mind of Captain Delano, a flash of revelation swept, illuminating in unanticipated clearness Benito Cereno's whole mysterious demeanour, with every enigmatic event of the day, as well as the entire past voyage of the *San Dominick*. He smote Babo's hand down, but his own heart smote him harder. With infinite pity he withdrew his hold from Don Benito. Not Captain Delano, but Don Benito, the black, in leaping into the boat, had intended to stab.

Both the black's hands were held, as, glancing up toward the *San Dominick*, Captain Delano, now with the scales dropped from his eyes, saw the negroes, not in misrule, not in tumult, not as if frantically concerned for Don Benito, but with mask torn away, flourishing hatchets and knives, in ferocious piratical revolt. Like delirious black dervishes, the six Ashantees danced on the poop. Prevented by their foes from springing into the water, the Spanish boys were hurrying up to the topmost spars, while such of the few Spanish sailors, not already in the sea, less alert, were descried, helplessly mixed in, on deck, with the blacks.

Meantime Captain Delano hailed his own vessel, ordering the ports up, and the guns run out. But by this time the cable of the *San Dominick* had been cut; and the fag-end, in lashing out, whipped away the canvas shroud about the beak, suddenly revealing, as the bleached hull swung round toward the open ocean, death for the figurehead, in a human skeleton; chalky comment on the chalked words below, *"Follow your leader."*

At the sight, Don Benito, covering his face, wailed out: "'Tis he, Aranda! my murdered, unburied friend!"

Upon reaching the sealer, calling for ropes, Captain Delano bound the negro, who made no resistance, and had him hoisted to the deck. He would then have assisted the now almost helpless Don Benito up the side; but Don Benito, wan as he was, refused to move, or be moved, until the negro should have been first put below out of view. When, presently assured that it was done, he no more shrank from the ascent.

The boat was immediately despatched back to pick up the three swimming sailors. Meantime, the guns were in readiness, though, owing to the *San Dominick* having glided somewhat astern of the sealer, only the aftermost one could be brought to bear. With this, they fired six times; thinking to cripple the fugitive ship by bringing down her spars. But only a few inconsiderable ropes were shot away. Soon the ship was beyond the guns' range, steering broad out of the bay; the blacks thickly clustering round the bowsprit, one moment with taunting cries toward the whites, the next with upthrown gestures hailing the now dusky expanse of ocean—cawing crows escaped from the hand of the fowler.

The first impulse was to slip the cables and give chase. But, upon second thought, to pursue with whale-boat and yawl seemed more promising.

Upon inquiring of Don Benito what firearms they had on board the *San Dominick*, Captain Delano was answered that they had none that could be used; because, in the earlier stages of the mutiny, a cabin-passenger, since dead, had secretly put out of order the locks of what few muskets there were. But with all his remaining strength, Don Benito entreated the American not to give chase, either with ship or boat; for the negroes had already proved themselves such desperadoes, that, in case of a present assault, nothing but a total massacre of the whites could be looked for. But, regarding this warning as coming from one whose spirit had been crushed by misery, the American did not give up his design.

The boats were got ready and armed. Captain Delano ordered twenty-five men into them. He was going himself when Don Benito grasped his arm.

"What! have you saved my life, Señor, and are you now going to throw away your own?"

The officers also, for reasons connected with their interests and those of the voyage, and a duty owing to the owners, strongly objected against their commander's going. Weighing their remonstrances a moment, Captain Delano felt bound to remain; appointing his chief mate—an athletic and resolute man, who had been a privateer's man, and, as his enemies whispered, a pirate—to head the party. The more to encourage the sailors, they were told, that the Spanish captain considered his ship as good as lost; that she and her cargo, including some gold and silver, were worth upwards of ten thousand doubloons. Take her, and no small part should be theirs. The sailors replied with a shout.

The fugitives had now almost gained an offing. It was nearly night; but the moon was rising. After hard, prolonged pulling, the boats came up on the ship's quarters, at a suitable distance laying upon their oars to discharge their muskets. Having no bullets to return, the negroes sent their yells. But, upon the second volley, Indian-like, they hurtled their hatchets. One took off a sailor's fingers. Another struck the whale-boat's bow, cutting off the rope there, and remaining stuck in the gunwale, like a woodman's axe. Snatching it, quivering from its lodgment, the mate hurled it back. The returned gauntlet now stuck in the ship's broken quarter-gallery, and so remained.

The negroes giving too hot a reception, the whites kept a more respectful distance. Hovering now just out of reach of the hurtling hatchets, they, with a view to the close encounter which must soon come, sought to decoy the blacks into entirely disarming themselves of their most murderous weapons in a hand-to-hand fight, by foolishly flinging them, as missiles, short of the mark, into the sea. But ere long perceiving the stratagem, the negroes desisted, though not before many of them had to replace their lost hatchets with handspikes; an exchange which, as counted upon, proved in the end favourable to the assailants.

Meantime, with a strong wind, the ship still clove the water; the boats alternately falling behind, and pulling up, to discharge fresh volleys.

The fire was mostly directed toward the stern, since there, chiefly, the negroes, at present, were clustering. But to kill or maim the negroes was not the object. To take them, with the ship, was the object. To do it, the ship must be boarded; which could not be done by boats while she was sailing so fast.

A thought now struck the mate. Observing the Spanish boys still aloft, high as they could get, he called to them to descend to the yards, and cut adrift the sails. It was done. About this time, owing to causes hereafter to be shown, two Spaniards, in the dress of sailors and conspicuously showing themselves, were killed; not by volleys, but by deliberate marksman's shots; while, as it afterwards appeared, during one of the general discharges, Atufal, the black, and the Spaniard at the helm likewise were killed. What now, with the loss of the sails, and loss of leaders, the ship became unmanageable to the negroes.

With creaking masts she came heavily round to the wind; the prow slowly swinging into view of the boats, its skeleton gleaming in the horizontal moonlight, and casting a gigantic ribbed shadow upon the water. One extended arm of the ghost seemed beckoning the whites to avenge it.

"Follow your leader!" cried the mate; and, one on each bow, the boats boarded. Scaling-spears and cutlasses crossed hatchets and handspikes. Huddled upon the long-boat amidships, the negresses raised a wailing chant, whose chorus was the clash of the steel.

For a time, the attack wavered; the negroes wedging themselves to beat it back; the half-repelled sailors, as yet unable to gain a footing, fighting as troopers in the saddle, one leg sideways flung over the bulwarks, and one without, plying their cutlasses like carters' whips. But in vain. They were almost overborne, when, rallying themselves into a squad as one man, with a huzza, they sprang inboard; where, entangled, they involuntarily separated again. For a few breaths' space there was a vague, muffled, inner sound as of submerged sword-fish rushing hither and thither through shoals of black-fish. Soon, in a re-united band, and joined by the Spanish seamen, the whites came to the surface, irresistibly driving the negroes toward the stern. But a barricade of casks and sacks, from side to side, had been thrown up by the mainmast. Here the negroes faced about, and though scorning peace or truce, yet fain would have had a respite. But, without pause, overleaping the barrier, the unflagging sailors again closed. Exhausted, the blacks now fought in despair. Their red tongues lolled, wolf-like, from their black mouths. But the pale sailors' teeth were set; not a word was spoken; and, in five minutes more, the ship was won.

Nearly a score of the negroes were killed. Exclusive of those by the balls, many were mangled; their wounds—mostly inflicted by the long-edged scaling-spears—resembling those shaven ones of the English at Preston Pans, made by the poled scythes of the Highlanders. On the other side, none were killed, though several were wounded; some severely, including the mate. The surviving negroes were temporarily secured, and the ship, towed back into the harbour at midnight, once more lay anchored.

Omitting the incidents and arrangements ensuing, suffice it that, after two days spent in refitting, the two ships sailed in company for Concepcion in Chili, and thence for Lima in Peru; where, before the vice-regal courts, the whole affair, from the beginning, underwent investigation.

Though, midway on the passage, the ill-fated Spaniard, relaxed from constraint, showed some signs of regaining health with free-will; yet, agreeably to his own foreboding, shortly before arriving at Lima, he relapsed, finally becoming so reduced as to be carried ashore in arms. Hearing of his story and plight, one of the many religious institutions of the City of Kings opened an hospitable refuge to him, where both physician and priest were his nurses, and a member of the order volunteered to be his one special guardian and consoler, by night and by day.

The following extracts, translated from one of the official Spanish documents, will, it is hoped, shed light on the preceding narrative, as well as, in the first place, reveal the true port of departure and true history of the *San Dominick's* voyage, down to the time of her touching at the island of Santa Maria.

But, ere the extracts come, it may be well to preface them with a remark.

The document selected, from among many others, for partial translation, contains the deposition of Benito Cereno; the first taken in the case. Some disclosures therein were, at the time, held dubious for both learned and natural reasons. The tribunal inclined to the opinion that the deponent, not undisturbed in his mind by recent events, raved of some things which could never have happened. But subsequent depositions of the surviving sailors, bearing out the revelations of their captain in several of the strangest particulars, gave credence to the rest. So that the tribunal, in its final decision, rested its capital sentences upon statements which, had they lacked confirmation, it would have deemed it but duty to reject.

I, Don José de Abos and Padilla, His Majesty's Notary for the Royal Revenue, and Register of this Province, and Notary Public of the Holy Crusade of this Bishopric, etc.

Do certify and declare, as much as is requisite in law, that, in the criminal cause commenced the twenty-fourth of the month of September, in the year seventeen hundred and ninety-nine, against the Senegal negroes of the ship *San Dominick,* the following declaration before me was made.

Declaration of the first witness, Don Benito Cereno.

The same day, and month, and year, His Honour Doctor Juan Martinez de Dozas, Councillor of the Royal Audience of this Kingdom, and learned in the law of this Intendancy, ordered the captain of the ship *San Dominick,* Don Benito Cereno, to appear; which he did in his litter, attended by the monk Infelez; of whom he received, before Don José de Abos and Padilla, Notary Public of the Holy Crusade, the oath, which he took by God, our Lord, and a sign of the Cross; under which he promised to tell the truth of whatever he should know and should be asked;—and being interrogated agreeably to the tenor of the act commencing the process, he said, that on the twentieth of May last, he set sail with his ship from the port of Valparaiso, bound to that of Callao; loaded with the produce of the country and one hundred and sixty blacks, of both sexes, mostly belonging to Don Alexandro Aranda, gentleman, of the city of Mendoza; that the crew of the ship consisted of thirty-six men, beside the persons who went as passengers; that the negroes were in part as follows:

[*Here, in the original, follows a list of some fifty names, descriptions, and ages, compiled from certain recovered documents of Aranda's, and also from recollections of the deponent, from which portions only are extracted.*]

—One, from about eighteen to nineteen years, named José, and this was the man that waited upon his master, Don Alexandro, and who speaks well the Spanish, having served him four or five years; . . . a mulatto, named Francesco, the cabin steward, of a good person and voice, having sung in the Valparaiso churches, native of the province of Buenos Ayres, aged about thirty-five years. . . . A smart negro, named Dago, who had been for many years a grave-digger among the Spaniards, aged forty-six years. . . . Four old negroes, born in Africa, from sixty to seventy, but sound, caulkers by trade, whose names are as follows:—the first was named Muri, and he was killed (as was also his son named Diamelo); the second, Nacta; the third, Yola, likewise killed; the fourth, Ghofan; and six full-

grown negroes, aged from thirty to forty-five, all raw, and born among
the Ashantees—Martiniqui, Yan, Lecbe, Hapenda, Yambaio, Akim; four
of whom were killed; . . . a powerful negro named Atufal, who, being
supposed to have been a chief in Africa, his owners set great store by
him. . . . And a small negro of Senegal, but some years among the Spaniards, aged about thirty, which negro's name was Babo; . . . that he
does not remember the names of the others, but that still expecting the
residue of Don Alexandro's papers will be found, will then take due account of them all, and remit to the court; . . . and thirty-nine women and
children of all ages.

[*After the catalogue, the deposition goes on as follows:*]

. . . That all the negroes slept upon deck, as is customary in this navigation, and none wore fetters, because the owner, his friend Aranda, told
him that they were all tractable; . . . that on the seventh day after leaving
port, at three o'clock in the morning, all the Spaniards being asleep except
the two officers on the watch, who were the boatswain, Juan Robles, and
the carpenter, Juan Bautista Gayete, and the helmsman and his boy, the
negroes revolted suddenly, wounded dangerously the boatswain and the
carpenter, and successively killed eighteen men of those who were sleeping upon deck, some with handspikes and hatchets, and others by throwing them alive overboard, after tying them; that of the Spaniards upon
deck, they left about seven, as he thinks, alive and tied, to manœuvre the
ship and three or four more who hid themselves, remained also alive.
Although in the act of revolt the negroes made themselves masters of the
hatchway, six or seven wounded went through it to the cockpit, without
any hindrance on their part; that in the act of revolt, the mate and another
person, whose name he does not recollect, attempted to come up through
the hatchway, but having been wounded at the onset, they were obliged
to return to the cabin; that the deponent resolved at break of day to come
up the companionway, where the negro Babo was, being the ringleader,
and Atufal, who assisted him, and having spoken to them, exhorted them
to cease committing such atrocities, asking them, at the same time, what
they wanted and intended to do, offering, himself, to obey their com-
mands; that, notwithstanding this, they threw, in his presence, three men,
alive and tied, overboard; that they told the deponent to come up, and
that they would not kill him; which having done, the negro Babo asked
him whether there were in those seas any negro countries where they
might be carried, and he answered them, no; that the negro Babo afterwards told him to carry them to Senegal, or to the neighbouring islands
of St. Nicholas; and he answered, that this was impossible, on account of
the great distance, the necessity involved of rounding Cape Horn, the bad
condition of the vessel, the want of provisions, sails, and water; but that

the negro Babo replied to him he must carry them in any way; that they would do and conform themselves to everything the deponent should require as to eating and drinking; that after a long conference, being absolutely compelled to please them, for they threatened him to kill all the whites if they were not, at all events, carried to Senegal, he told them that what was most wanting for the voyage was water; that they would go near the coast to take it, and hence they would proceed on their course; that the negro Babo agreed to it; and the deponent steered toward the intermediate ports, hoping to meet some Spanish or foreign vessel that would save them; that within ten or eleven days they saw the land, and continued their course by it in the vicinity of Nasca; that the deponent observed that the negroes were now restless and mutinous, because he did not effect the taking in of water, the negro Babo having required, with threats, that it should be done, without fail, the following day; he told him he saw plainly that the coast was steep, and the rivers designated in the maps were not to be found, with other reasons suitable to the circumstances; that the best way would be to go to the island of Santa Maria, where they might water and victual easily, it being a desert island, as the foreigners did; that the deponent did not go to Pisco, that was near, nor make any other port of the coast, because the negro Babo had intimated to him several times, that he would kill all the whites the very moment he should perceive any city, town, or settlement of any kind on the shores to which they should be carried: that having determined to go to the island of Santa Maria, as the deponent had planned, for the purpose of trying whether, in the passage or in the island itself, they could find any vessel that should favour them, or whether he could escape from it in a boat to the neighbouring coast of Arruco; to adopt the necessary means he immediately changed his course, steering for the island; that the negroes Babo and Atufal held daily conferences, in which they discussed what was necessary for their design of returning to Senegal, whether they were to kill all the Spaniards, and particularly the deponent; that eight days after parting from the coast of Nasca, the deponent being on the watch a little after day-break, and soon after the negroes had their meeting, the negro Babo came to the place where the deponent was, and told him that he had determined to kill his master, Don Alexandro Aranda, both because he and his companions could not otherwise be sure of their liberty, and that, to keep the seamen in subjection, he wanted to prepare a warning of what road they should be made to take did they or any of them oppose him; and that, by means of the death of Don Alexandro, that warning would best be given; but, that what this last meant, the deponent did not at the time comprehend, nor could not, further than that the death of Don Alexandro was intended; and moreover, the negro Babo proposed to the deponent to call the mate Raneds, who was sleeping in the cabin, before the thing was done, for fear, as the deponent understood it, that the mate, who was a good navigator, should be killed with Don Alexandro and the rest; that the deponent, who was the friend, from youth of Don Alexandro, prayed and conjured, but all was useless; for the negro Babo answered him that the thing could not be prevented, and that all the Spaniards risked their death if they should attempt to frustrate his will in this matter, or any other; that, in this conflict, the deponent called the mate, Raneds, who was forced to go apart, and immediately the negro Babo commanded the Ashantee Martinqui and the Ashantee Lecbe to go and commit the murder; that those two went down with hatchets to the berth of Don Alexandro; that, yet half alive and mangled, they dragged him on deck; that they were going to throw him overboard in that state, but the negro Babo stopped them, bidding the murder be completed on the deck before him, which was done, when, by his orders, the body was carried below, forward; that nothing more was seen of it by the deponent for three days; . . . that Don Alonzo Sidonia, an old man, long resident at Valparaiso, and lately appointed to a civil office in Peru, whither he had taken passage, was at the time sleeping in the berth opposite Don Alexandro's; that, awakening at his cries, surprised by them, and at the sight of the negroes with their bloody hatchets in their hands, he threw himself into the sea through a window which was near him, and was drowned, without it being in the power of the deponent to assist to take him up; . . . that, a short time after killing Aranda, they brought upon deck his german-cousin, of middle-age, Don Francisco Masa, of Mendoza, and the young Don Joaquin, Marques de Aramboalaza, then lately from Spain, with his Spanish servant Ponce, and the three young clerks of Aranda, José Mozairi, Lorenzo Bargas, and Hermenegildo Gandix, all of Cadiz; that Don Joaquin and Hermenegildo Gandix, the negro Babo for purposes hereafter to appear, preserved alive; but Don Francisco Masa, José Mozairi, and Lorenzo Bargas, with Ponce, the servant, beside the boatswain, Juan Robles, the boatswain's mates, Manuel Viscaya and Roderigo Hurta, and four of the sailors, the negro Babo ordered to be thrown alive into the sea, although they made no resistance, nor begged for anything else but mercy; that the boatswain, Juan Robles, who knew how to swim, kept the longest above water, making acts of contrition, and, in the last words he uttered, charged this deponent to cause mass to be said for his soul to our Lady of Succour: . . . that, during the three days which followed, the deponent, uncertain what fate had befallen the remains of Don Alexandro, frequently asked the negro Babo where they were, and, if still on board, whether they were to be preserved for interment ashore, entreating him so to order it; that the negro Babo answered nothing till the fourth day, when at sunrise, the deponent coming on deck, the negro Babo showed him a skeleton, which had been substituted for the ship's proper figure-head, the image of Christopher Colon, the discoverer of the New World; that the negro Babo asked him whose skeleton that was, and whether, from its whiteness, he should not think it a white's; that, upon his covering his face, the negro Babo, coming close, said words to this effect: "Keep faith with the blacks from here to Senegal, or you shall in spirit, as now in body, follow your leader," pointing to the prow; . . . that the same morning the negro Babo took by succession each Spaniard forward, and asked him whose skeleton that was, and whether, from its whiteness, he should not think it a white's; that each Spaniard covered his face; that then to each the negro Babo repeated the words in the first place said to the deponent; . . . that they (the Spaniards), being then assembled aft, the negro Babo harangued them, saying that he had now done all; that the deponent (as navigator for the negroes) might pursue his course, warning him and all of them that they should, soul and body, go the way of Don Alexandro if he saw them (the Spaniards) speak or plot anything against them (the negroes) —a threat which was repeated every day; that, before the events last mentioned, they had tied the cook to throw him overboard, for it is not known what thing they heard him speak, but finally the negro Babo spared his life, at the request of the deponent; that a few days after, the deponent, endeavouring not to omit any means to preserve the lives of the remaining whites, spoke to the negroes peace and tranquillity, and agreed to draw up a paper, signed by the deponent and the sailors who could write, as also by the negro Babo, for himself and all the blacks, in which the deponent obliged himself to carry them to Senegal, and they not to kill any more, and he formally to make over to them the ship, with the cargo, with which they were for that time satisfied and quieted. . . . But the next day, the more surely to guard against the sailors' escape, the negro Babo commanded all the boats to be destroyed but the long-boat, which was unseaworthy, and another, a cutter in good condition, which, knowing it would yet be wanted for lowering the water casks, he had it lowered down into the hold.

[*Various particulars of the prolonged and perplexed navigation ensuing here follow, with incidents of a calamitous calm, from which portion one passage is extracted, to wit:*]

—That on the fifth day of the calm, all on board suffering much from the heat, and want of water, and five having died in fits, and mad, the negroes became irritable, and for a chance gesture, which they deemed suspicious—though it was harmless—made by the mate, Raneds, to the deponent, in the act of handing a quadrant, they killed him; but that for this they afterwards were sorry, the mate being the only remaining navigator on board, except the deponent.

—That omitting other events, which daily happened, and which can only serve uselessly to recall past misfortunes and conflicts, after seventy-three days' navigation, reckoned from the time they sailed from Nasca, during which they navigated under a scanty allowance of water, and were afflicted with the calms before mentioned, they at last arrived at the island of Santa Maria, on the seventeenth of the month of August, at about six o'clock in the afternoon, at which hour they cast anchor very near the American ship, *Bachelor's Delight,* which lay in the same bay, commanded by the generous Captain Amasa Delano; but at six o'clock in the morning, they had already descried the port, and the negroes became uneasy, as soon as at distance they saw the ship, not having expected to see one there; that the negro Babo pacified them, assuring them that no fear need be had; that straightway he ordered the figure on the bow to be covered with canvas, as for repairs, and had the decks a little set in order; that for a time the negro Babo and the negro Atufal conferred; that the negro Atufal was for sailing away, but the negro Babo would not, and, by himself, cast about what to do; that at last he came to the deponent, proposing to him to say and do all that the deponent declares to have said and done to the American captain; . . . that the negro Babo warned him that if he varied in the least, or uttered any word, or gave any look that should give the least intimation of the past events or present state, he would instantly kill him, with all his companions, showing a dagger, which he carried hid, saying something which, as he understood it, meant that that dagger would be alert as his eye; that the negro Babo then announced the plan to all his companions, which pleased them; that he then, the better to disguise the truth, devised many expedients, in some of them uniting deceit and defence; that of this sort was the device of the six Ashantees before named, who were his bravos; that them he stationed on the break of the poop, as if to clean certain hatchets (in cases, which were part of the cargo), but in reality to use them, and distribute them at need, and at a given word he told them that, among other devices, was the device of presenting Atufal, his righthand man, as chained, though in a moment the chains could be dropped; that in every particular he informed the deponent what part he was expected to enact in every device, and what story he was to tell on every occasion, always threatening him with instant death if he varied in the least: that, conscious that many of the negroes would be turbulent, the negro Babo appointed the four aged negroes, who were caulkers, to keep what domestic order they could on the decks; that again and again he harangued the Spaniards and his companions, informing them of his intent, and of his devices, and of the invented story that this deponent was to tell, charging them lest any of them varied from that story; that these arrangements were made and matured during the interval of two or three hours, between their first sighting the ship and the arrival on board of Captain Amasa Delano; that this happened at about half-past seven in the morning, Captain Amasa Delano coming in his boat, and all gladly receiving him; that the deponent, as well as he could force himself, acting then the part of principal owner, and a free captain of the ship, told Captain Amasa Delano, when called upon, that he came from Buenos Ayres, bound to Lima, with three hundred negroes; that off Cape Horn, and in a subsequent fever, many negroes had died; that also, by similar casualties, all the sea officers and the greatest part of the crew had died.

[*And so the deposition goes on, circumstantially recounting the fictitious story dictated to the deponent by Babo, and through the deponent imposed upon Captain Delano; and also recounting the friendly offers of Captain Delano, with other things, but all of which is here omitted. After the fictitious, strange story, etc., the deposition proceeds:*]

—That the generous Captain Amasa Delano remained on board all the day, till he left the ship anchored at six o'clock in the evening, deponent speaking to him always of his pretended misfortunes, under the fore-mentioned principles, without having had it in his power to tell a single word, or give him the least hint, that he might know the truth and state of things; because the negro Babo, performing the office of an officious servant with all the appearance of submission of the humble slave, did not leave the deponent one moment; that this was in order to observe the deponent's actions and words, for the negro Babo understands well the Spanish; and besides, there were thereabout some others who were constantly on the watch, and likewise understood the Spanish; . . . that upon one occasion, while deponent was standing on the deck conversing with Amasa Delano, by a secret sign the negro Babo drew him (the deponent) aside, the act appearing as if originating with the deponent; that then, he being drawn aside, the negro Babo proposed to him to gain from Amasa Delano full particulars about his ship, and crew, and arms; that the deponent asked "For what?" that the negro Babo answered he might conceive; that, grieved at the prospect of what might overtake the generous Captain Amasa Delano, the deponent at first refused to ask the desired questions, and used every argument to induce the negro Babo to give up this new design; that the negro Babo showed the point of his dagger; that, after the information had been obtained, the negro Babo again drew him aside, telling him that that very night he (the deponent) would be captain of two ships instead of one, for that, great part of the American's ship's crews going to be absent fishing, the six Ashantees, without any one else, would easily take it; that at this time he said other things to the same purpose; that no entreaties availed; that before Amasa Delano's coming on board, no hint had been given touching the capture of the American ship: that to prevent this project the deponent was powerless; . . . —that in some things his memory is confused, he cannot distinctly recall every event; . . . —that as soon as they had cast anchor at six of the clock in the evening, as has before been stated, the American captain took leave to return to his vessel; that upon a sudden impulse, which the deponent believes to have come from God and his angels, he, after the farewell had been said, followed the generous Captain Amasa Delano as far as the gunwale, where he stayed, under the pretence of taking leave, until Amasa Delano should have been seated in his boat; that on shoving off, the deponent sprang from the gunwale, into the boat, and fell into it, he knows not how, God guarding him; that—

[*Here, in the original, follows the account of what further happened at the escape, and how the "San Dominick" was retaken, and of the passage to the coast, including in the recital many expressions of "eternal gratitude" to the "generous Captain Amasa Delano." The deposition then proceeds with recapitulatory remarks, and a partial renumeration of the negroes, making record of their individual part in the past events, with a view to furnishing, according to command of the court, the data whereon to found the criminal sentences to be pronounced. From this portion is the following:*]

—That he believes that all the negroes, though not in the first place knowing to the design of revolt, when it was accomplished, approved it. . . . That the negro, José, eighteen years old, and in the personal service of Don Alexandro, was the one who communicated the information to the negro Babo, about the state of things in the cabin, before the revolt; that this is known, because, in the preceding midnight, he used to come from his berth, which was under his master's, in the cabin, to the deck where the ringleader and his associates were, and had secret conversations with the negro Babo, in which he was several times seen by the mate; that, one night, the mate drove him away twice; . . . that this same negro José, was the one who, without being commanded to do so by the negro Babo, as Lecbe and Martinqui were, stabbed his master, Don Alexandro, after he had been dragged half-lifeless to the deck; . . . that the mulatto steward, Francesco, was of the first band of revolters, that he was, in all things, the creature and tool of the negro Babo; that, to make his court, he, just before a repast in the cabin, proposed, to the negro Babo, poisoning a dish for the generous Captain Amasa Delano; this is known and believed, because the negroes have said it; but that the negro Babo, having another design, forbade Francesco; . . . that the Ashantee Lecbe was one of the worst of them; for that, on the day the ship was retaken, he assisted in the defence of her, with a hatchet in each hand, with one of which he wounded, in the breast, the chief mate of Amasa Delano, in the first act of boarding; this all knew; that, in sight of the deponent, Lecbe struck, with a hatchet, Don Francisco Masa when, by the negro Babo's orders, he was carrying him to throw him overboard, alive; beside participating in the murder, before mentioned, of Don Alexandro Aranda, and others of the cabin-passengers; that, owing to the fury with which the Ashantees fought in the engagement with the boats, but this Lecbe and Yan survived; that Yan was bad as Lecbe; that Yan was the man who, by Babo's command, willingly prepared the skeleton of Don Alexandro, in a way the negroes afterwards told the deponent, but which he, so long as reason is left him, can never divulge; that Yan and Lecbe were the two who, in a calm by night, riveted the skeleton to the bow; this also the negroes told him; that the negro Babo was he who traced the inscription below it; that the negro Babo was the plotter from first to last; he ordered every murder, and was the helm and keel of the revolt; that Atufal was his lieutenant in all; but Atufal, with his own hand, committed no murder; nor did the negro Babo; . . . that Atufal was shot, being killed in the fight with the boats, ere boarding; . . . that the negresses, of age, were knowing to the revolt, and testified themselves satisfied at the death of their master, Don Alexandro; that, had the negroes not restrained them, they would have tortured to death, instead of simply killing, the Spaniards slain by command of the negro Babo; that the negresses used their utmost influence to have the deponent made away with; that, in the various acts of murder, they sang songs and danced—not gaily, but solemnly; and before the engagement with the boats, as well as during the action, they sang melancholy songs to the negroes, and that this melancholy tone was more inflaming than a different one would have been, and was so intended; that all this is believed, because the negroes have said it. —That of the thirty-six men of the crew—exclusive of the passengers (all of whom are now dead), which the deponent had knowledge of—six only remained alive, with four cabin-boys and ship-boys, not included with the crew; . . . —that the negroes broke an arm of one of the cabin-boys and gave him strokes with hatchets.

[*Then follow various random disclosures referring to various periods of time. The following are extracted:*]

—That during the presence of Captain Amasa Delano on board, some attempts were made by the sailors, and one by Hermenegildo Gandix, to convey hints to him of the true state of affairs; but that these attempts were ineffectual, owing to fear of incurring death, and furthermore owing to the devices which offered contradictions to the true state of affairs; as well as owing to the generosity and piety of Amasa Delano, incapable of sounding such wickedness; . . . that Luys Galgo, a sailor about sixty years of age, and formerly of the king's navy, was one of those who sought to

convey tokens to Captain Amasa Delano; but his intent, though undis-
covered, being suspected, he was, on a pretence, made to retire out of
sight, and at last into the hold, and there was made away with. This the
negroes have since said; . . . that one of the ship-boys feeling, from Captain Amasa Delano's presence, some hopes of release, and not having enough
prudence, dropped some chance-word respecting his expectations, which
being overheard and understood by a slave-boy with whom he was eating
at the time, the latter struck him on the head with a knife, inflicting a
bad wound, but of which the boy is now healing; that likewise, not long
before the ship was brought to anchor, one of the seamen, steering at the
time, endangered himself by letting the blacks remark a certain unconscious hopeful expression in his countenance, arising from some cause
similiar to the above; but this sailor, by his heedful after conduct, escaped;
. . . that these statements are made to show the court that from the beginning to the end of the revolt, it was impossible for the deponent and his
men to act otherwise than they did; . . . —that the third clerk, Hermenegildo Gandix, who before had been forced to live among the seamen, wearing a seaman's habit, and in all respects appearing to be one for the time;
he, Gandix, was killed by a musket-ball fired through a mistake from the
American boats before boarding; having in his fright ran up the mizzen-
rigging, calling to the boats—"don't board," lest upon their boarding the
negroes should kill him; that this inducing the Americans to believe he
some way favoured the cause of the negroes, they fired two balls at him,
so that he fell wounded from the rigging, and was drowned in the sea;
. . . —that the young Don Joaquin, Marques de Arambaolaza, like Hermenegildo Gandix, the third clerk, was degraded to the office and appearance of a common seaman; that upon one occasion, when Don Joaquin
shrank, the negro Babo commanded the Ashantee Lecbe to take tar and
heat it, and pour it upon Don Joaquin's hands; . . . —that Don Joaquin
was killed owing to another mistake of the Americans, but one impossible to be avoided, as upon the approach of the boats, Don Joaquin, with
a hatchet tied edge out and upright to his hand, was made by the negroes
to appear on the bulwarks; whereupon, seen with arms in his hands and
in a questionable attitude, he was shot for a renegade seaman; . . . —that
on the person of Don Joaquin was found secreted a jewel, which, by
papers that were discovered, proved to have been meant for the shrine
of our Lady of Mercy in Lima; a votive offering, beforehand prepared and
guarded, to attest his gratitude, when he should have landed in Peru, his
last destination, for the safe conclusion of his entire voyage from Spain;
. . . —that the jewel, with the other effects of the late Don Joaquin, is
in the custody of the brethren of the Hospital de Sacerdotes, awaiting the
decision of the honourable court; . . . —that, owing to the condition of
the deponent, as well as the haste in which the boats departed for the

attack, the Americans were not forewarned that there were, among the
apparent crew, a passenger and one of the clerks disguised by the negro
Babo; . . . —that, beside the negroes killed in the action, some were killed
after the capture and reanchoring at night, when shackled to the ring-
bolts on deck; that these deaths were committed by the sailors, ere they
could be prevented. That so soon as informed of it, Captain Amasa Delano
used all his authority, and, in particular with his own hand, struck down
Martinez Gola, who, having found a razor in the pocket of an old jacket
of his, which one of the shackled negroes had on, was aiming it at the
negro's throat; that the noble Captain Amasa Delano also wrenched from
the hand of Bartholomew Barlo, a dagger secreted at the time of the massacre of the whites, with which he was in the act of stabbing a shackled
negro, who, the same day, with another negro, had thrown him down
and jumped upon him; . . . —that, for all the events, befalling through so
long a time, during which the ship was in the hands of the negro Babo,
he cannot here give account; but that, what he has said is the most sub-
stantial of what occurs to him at present, and is the truth under the oath
which he has taken; which declaration he affirmed and ratified, after
hearing it read to him.

He said that he is twenty-nine years of age, and broken in body and
mind; that when finally dismissed by the court, he shall not return home
to Chili, but betake himself to the monastery on Mount Agonia without;
and signed with his honour, and crossed himself, and, for the time, departed as he came, in his litter, with the monk Infelez, to the Hospital de
Sacerdotes.

BENITO CERENO.

DOCTOR ROZAS.

If the deposition of Benito Cereno has served as the key to fit into the
lock of the complications which preceded it, then, as a vault whose door
has been flung back, the *San Dominick's* hull lies open to-day.

Hitherto the nature of this narrative, besides rendering the intricacies
in the beginning unavoidable, has more or less required that many things,
instead of being set down in the order of occurrence, should be retrospec-
tively, or irregularly given; this last is the case with the following passages,
which will conclude the account:

During the long, mild voyage to Lima, there was, as before hinted, a
period during which Don Benito, a little recovered his health, or, at least
in some degree, his tranquillity. Ere the decided relapse which came, the
two captains had many cordial conversations—their fraternal unreserve
in singular contrast with former withdrawments.

Again and again, it was repeated, how hard it had been to enact the
part forced on the Spaniard by Babo.

"Ah, my dear Don Amasa," Don Benito once said, "at those very times when you thought me so morose and ungrateful—nay when, as you now admit, you half thought me plotting your murder—at those very times my heart was frozen; I could not look at you, thinking of what, both on board this ship and your own, hung, from other hands, over my kind benefactor. And as God lives, Don Amasa, I know not whether desire for my own safety alone could have nerved me to that leap into your boat, had it not been for the thought that, did you, unenlightened, return to your ship, you, my best friend, with all who might be with you, stolen upon, that night, in your hammocks, would never in this world have wakened again. Do but think how you walked this deck, how you sat in this cabin, every inch of ground mined into honey-combs under you. Had I dropped the least hint, made the least advance toward an understanding between us, death, explosive death—yours as mine—would have ended the scene."

"True, true," cried Captain Delano, starting, "you saved my life, Don Benito, more than I yours; saved it, too, against my knowledge and will."

"Nay, my friend," rejoined the Spaniard, courteous even to the point of religion, "God charmed your life, but you saved mine. To think of some things you did—those smilings and chattings, rash pointings and gesturings. For less than these, they slew my mate, Raneds; but you had the Prince of Heaven's safe conduct through all ambuscades."

"Yes, all is owing to Providence, I know; but the temper of my mind that morning was more than commonly pleasant, while the sight of so much suffering—more apparent than real—added to my good nature, compassion, and charity, happily interweaving the three. Had it been otherwise, doubtless, as you hint, some of my interferences with the blacks might have ended unhappily enough. Besides that, those feelings I spoke of enabled me to get the better of momentary distrust, at times when acuteness might have cost me my life, without saving another's. Only at the end did my suspicions get the better of me, and you know how wide of the mark they then proved."

"Wide, indeed," said Don Benito, sadly; "you were with me all day; stood with me, sat with me, talked with me, looked at me, ate with me, drank with me; and yet, your last act was to clutch for a villain, not only an innocent man, but the most pitiable of all men. To such degree may malign machinations and deceptions impose. So far may even the best men err, in judging the conduct of one with the recesses of whose condition he is not acquainted. But you were forced to it; and you were in time undeceived. Would that, in both respects, it was so ever, and with all men."

"I think I understand you; you generalize, Don Benito; and mournfully enough. But the past is passed; why moralize upon it? Forget it. See, yon bright sun has forgotten it all, and the blue sea, and the blue sky; these have turned over new leaves."

"Because they have no memory," he dejectedly replied; "because they are not human."

"But these mild trades that now fan your cheek, Don Benito, do they not come with a human-like healing to you? Warm friends, steadfast friends are the trades."

"With their steadfastness they but waft me to my tomb, Señor," was the foreboding response.

"You are saved, Don Benito," cried Captain Delano, more and more astonished and pained; "you are saved; what has cast such a shadow upon you?"

"The negro."

There was silence, while the moody man sat, slowly and unconsciously gathering his mantle about him, as if it were a pall.

There was no more conversation that day.

But if the Spaniard's melancholy sometimes ended in muteness upon topics like the above, there were others upon which he never spoke at all; on which, indeed, all his old reserves were piled. Pass over the worst and, only to elucidate, let an item or two of these be cited. The dress so precise and costly, worn by him on the day whose events have been narrated, had not willingly been put on. And that silver-mounted sword, apparent symbol of despotic command, was not, indeed, a sword, but the ghost of one. The scabbard, artificially stiffened, was empty.

As for the black—whose brain, not body, had schemed and led the revolt, with the plot—his slight frame, inadequate to that which it held, had at once yielded to the superior muscular strength of his captor, in the boat. Seeing all was over, he uttered no sound, and could not be forced to. His aspect seemed to say: since I cannot do deeds, I will not speak words. Put in irons in the hold, with the rest, he was carried to Lima. During the passage Don Benito did not visit him. Nor then, nor at any time after, would he look at him. Before the tribunal he refused. When pressed by the judges he fainted. On the testimony of the sailors alone rested the legal identity of Babo. And yet the Spaniard would, upon occasion, verbally refer to the negro, as has been shown; but look on him he would not, or could not.

Some months after, dragged to the gibbet at the tail of a mule, the black met his voiceless end. The body was burned to ashes; but for many days, the head, that hive of subtlety, fixed on a pole in the Plaza, met, unabashed, the gaze of the whites; and across the Plaza looked toward St. Bartholomew's church, in whose vaults slept then, as now, the recovered bones of Aranda; and across the Rimac bridge looked toward the monastery, on Mount Agonia without; where, three months after being dismissed by the court, Benito Cereno, borne on the bier, did, indeed, follow his leader.

JOSEPH CONRAD

The Secret Sharer 🐚

I

On my right hand there were lines of fishing-stakes resembling a
mysterious system of half-submerged bamboo fences, incomprehensible in its division of the domain of tropical fishes, and crazy
of aspect as if abandoned forever by some nomad tribe of fishermen now
gone to the other end of the ocean; for there was no sign of human habita-
tion as far as the eye could reach. To the left a group of barren islets, suggesting ruins of stone walls, towers, and blockhouses, had its foundations
set in a blue sea that itself looked solid, so still and stable did it lie below
my feet; even the track of light from the westering sun shone smoothly,
without that animated glitter which tells of an imperceptible ripple. And
when I turned my head to take a parting glance at the tug which had just
left us anchored outside the bar, I saw the straight line of the flat shore joined
to the stable sea, edge to edge, with a perfect and unmarked closeness, in
one leveled floor half brown, half blue under the enormous dome of the sky.
Corresponding in their insignificance to the islets of the sea, two small
clumps of trees, one on each side of the only fault in the impeccable joint,
marked the mouth of the river Meinam we had just left on the first preparatory stage of our homeward journey; and, far back on the inland level, a
larger and loftier mass, the grove surrounding the great Paknam pagoda,
was the only thing on which the eye could rest from the vain task of exploring the monotonous sweep of the horizon. Here and there gleams as of a
few scattered pieces of silver marked the windings of the great river; and
on the nearest of them, just within the bar, the tug steaming right into the
land became lost to my sight, hull and funnel and masts, as though the
impassive earth had swallowed her up without an effort, without a tremor.
My eye followed the light cloud of her smoke, now here, now there, above
the plain, according to the devious curves of the stream, but always fainter
and farther away, till I lost it at last behind the miter-shaped hill of the
great pagoda. And then I was left alone with my ship, anchored at the head
of the Gulf of Siam.

She floated at the starting-point of a long journey, very still in an immense
stillness, the shadows of her spars flung far to the eastward by the setting
sun. At that moment I was alone on her decks. There was not a sound in

her—and around us nothing moved, nothing lived, not a canoe on the water, not a bird in the air, not a cloud in the sky. In this breathless pause at the threshold of a long passage we seemed to be measuring our fitness for a long and arduous enterprise, the appointed task of both our existences to be carried out, far from all human eyes, with only sky and sea for spectators and for judges.

There must have been some glare in the air to interfere with one's sight, because it was only just before the sun left us that my roaming eyes made out beyond the highest ridge of the principal islet of the group something which did away with the solemnity of perfect solitude. The tide of darkness flowed on swiftly; and with tropical suddenness a swarm of stars came out above the shadowy earth, while I lingered yet, my hand resting lightly on my ship's rail as if on the shoulder of a trusted friend. But, with all that multitude of celestial bodies staring down at one, the comfort of quiet communion with her was gone for good. And there were also disturbing sounds by this time—voices, footsteps forward; the steward flitted along the main-deck, a busily ministering spirit; a hand-bell tinkled urgently under the poop-deck. . . .

I found my two officers waiting for me near the supper table, in the lighted cuddy. We sat down at once, and as I helped the chief mate, I said: "Are you aware that there is a ship anchored inside the islands? I saw her mastheads above the ridge as the sun went down."

He raised sharply his simple face, overcharged by a terrible growth of whisker, and emitted his usual ejaculations: "Bless my soul, sir! You don't say so!"

My second mate was a round-cheeked, silent young man, grave beyond his years, I thought; but as our eyes happened to meet I detected a slight quiver on his lips. I looked down at once. It was not my part to encourage sneering on board my ship. It must be said, too, that I knew very little of my officers. In consequence of certain events of no particular significance, except to myself, I had been appointed to the command only a fortnight before. Neither did I know much of the hands forward. All these people had been together for eighteen months or so, and my position was that of the only stranger on board. I mention this because it has some bearing on what is to follow. But what I felt most was my being a stranger to the ship; and if all the truth must be told, I was somewhat of a stranger to myself. The youngest man on board (barring the second mate), and untried as yet by a position of the fullest responsibility, I was willing to take the adequacy of the others for granted. They had simply to be equal to their tasks; but I wondered how far I should turn out faithful to that ideal conception of one's own personality every man sets up for himself secretly.

Meantime the chief mate, with an almost visible effect of collaboration

on the part of his round eyes and frightful whiskers, was trying to evolve a
theory of the anchored ship. His dominant trait was to take all things into
earnest consideration. He was of a painstaking turn of mind. As he used to
say, he "liked to account to himself" for practically everything that came in
his way, down to a miserable scorpion he had found in his cabin a week
before. The why and the wherefore of that scorpion—how it got on board
and came to select his room rather than the pantry (which was a dark place
and more what a scorpion would be partial to), and how on earth it managed to drown itself in the inkwell of his writing-desk—had exercised him
infinitely. The ship within the islands was much more easily accounted for;
and just as we were about to rise from table he made his pronouncement.
She was, he doubted not, a ship from home lately arrived. Probably she
drew too much water to cross the bar except at the top of spring tides. Therefore she went into that natural harbor to wait for a few days in preference
to remaining in an open roadstead.

"That's so," confirmed the second mate, suddenly, in his slightly hoarse
voice. "She draws over twenty feet. She's the Liverpool ship *Sephora* with
a cargo of coal. Hundred and twenty-three days from Cardiff."

We looked at him in surprise.

"The tugboat skipper told me when he came on board for your letters,
sir," explained the young man. "He expects to take her up the river the day
after tomorrow."

After thus overwhelming us with the extent of his information he slipped
out of the cabin. The mate observed regretfully that he "could not account
for that young fellow's whims." What prevented him telling us all about it
at once, he wanted to know.

I detained him as he was making a move. For the last two days the crew
had had plenty of hard work, and the night before they had very little
sleep. I felt painfully that I—a stranger—was doing something unusual when
I directed him to let all hands turn in without setting an anchor-watch. I
proposed to keep on deck myself till one o'clock or thereabouts. I would get
the second mate to relieve me at that hour.

"He will turn out the cook and the steward at four," I concluded, "and
then give you a call. Of course at the slightest sign of any sort of wind we'll
have the hands up and make a start at once."

He concealed his astonishment. "Very well, sir." Outside the cuddy he put
his head in the second mate's door to inform him of my unheard-of caprice
to take a five hours' anchor-watch on myself. I heard the other raise his
voice incredulously—"What? The Captain himself?" Then a few more
murmurs, a door closed, then another. A few moments later I went on deck.

My strangeness, which had made me sleepless, had prompted that uncon-
ventional arrangement, as if I had expected in those solitary hours of the
night to get on terms with the ship of which I knew nothing, manned by

men of whom I knew very little more. Fast alongside a wharf, littered like any ship in port with a tangle of unrelated things, invaded by unrelated shore people, I had hardly seen her yet properly. Now, as she lay cleared for sea, the stretch of her main-deck seemed to me very fine under the stars. Very fine, very roomy for her size, and very inviting. I descended the poop and paced the waist, my mind picturing to myself the coming passage through the Malay Archipelago, down the Indian Ocean, and up the Atlantic. All its phases were familiar enough to me, every characteristic, all the alternatives which were likely to face me on the high seas—everything! . . . except the novel responsibility of command. But I took heart from the reasonable thought that the ship was like other ships, the men like other men, and that the sea was not likely to keep any special surprises expressly for my discomfiture.

Arrived at that comforting conclusion, I bethought myself of a cigar and went below to get it. All was still down there. Everybody at the after end of the ship was sleeping profoundly. I came out again on the quarter-deck, agreeably at ease in my sleeping-suit on that warm breathless night, barefooted, a glowing cigar in my teeth, and, going forward, I was met by the profound silence of the fore end of the ship. Only as I passed the door of the forecastle I heard a deep, quiet, trustful sigh of some sleeper inside. And suddenly I rejoiced in the great security of the sea as compared with the unrest of the land, in my choice of that untempted life presenting no disquieting problems, invested with an elementary moral beauty by the absolute straightforwardness of its appeal and by the singleness of its purpose.

The riding-light in the fore-rigging burned with a clear, untroubled, as if symbolic, flame, confident and bright in the mysterious shades of the night. Passing on my way aft along the other side of the ship, I observed that the rope side-ladder, put over, no doubt, for the master of the tug when he came to fetch away our letters, had not been hauled in as it should have been. I became annoyed at this, for exactitude in small matters is the very soul of discipline. Then I reflected that I had myself peremptorily dismissed my officers from duty, and by my own act had prevented the anchor-watch being formally set and things properly attended to. I asked myself whether it was wise ever to interfere with the established routine of duties even from the kindest of motives. My action might have made me appear eccentric. Goodness only knew how that absurdly whiskered mate would "account" for my conduct, and what the whole ship thought of that informality of their new captain. I was vexed with myself.

Not from compunction certainly, but, as it were mechanically, I proceeded to get the ladder in myself. Now a side-ladder of that sort is a light affair and comes in easily, yet my vigorous tug, which should have brought it flying on board, merely recoiled upon my body in a totally unexpected jerk. What the devil! . . . I was so astounded by the immovableness of that ladder that I remained stock-still, trying to account for it to myself like that imbecile mate of mine. In the end, of course, I put my head over the rail.

The side of the ship made an opaque belt of shadow on the darkling glassy shimmer of the sea. But I saw at once something elongated and pale floating very close to the ladder. Before I could form a guess a faint flash of phosphorescent light, which seemed to issue suddenly from the naked body of a man, flickered in the sleeping water with the elusive, silent play of summer lightning in a night sky. With a gasp I saw revealed to my stare a pair of feet, the long legs, a broad livid back immersed right up to the neck in a greenish cadaverous glow. One hand, awash, clutched the bottom rung of the ladder. He was complete but for the head. A headless corpse! The cigar dropped out of my gaping mouth with a tiny plop and a short hiss quite audible in the absolute stillness of all things under heaven. At that I suppose he raised up his face, a dimly pale oval in the shadow of the ship's side. But even then I could only barely make out down there the shape of his black-haired head. However, it was enough for the horrid, frost-bound sensation which had gripped me about the chest to pass off. The moment of vain exclamations was past, too. I only climbed on the spare spar and leaned over the rail as far as I could, to bring my eyes nearer to that mystery floating alongside.

As he hung by the ladder, like a resting swimmer, the sea-lightning played about his limbs at every stir; and he appeared in it ghastly, silvery, fish-like. He remained as mute as a fish, too. He made no motion to get out of the water, either. It was inconceivable that he should not attempt to come on board, and strangely troubling to suspect that perhaps he did not want to. And my first words were prompted by just that troubled incertitude.

"What's the matter?" I asked in my ordinary tone, speaking down to the face upturned exactly under mine.

"Cramp," it answered, no louder. Then slightly anxious, "I say, no need to call anyone."

"I was not going to," I said.

"Are you alone on deck?"

"Yes."

I had somehow the impression that he was on the point of letting go the ladder to swim away beyond my ken—mysterious as he came. But, for the moment, this being appearing as if he had risen from the bottom of the sea (it was certainly the nearest land to the ship) wanted only to know the time. I told him. And he, down there, tentatively:

"I suppose your captain's turned in?"

"I am sure he isn't," I said.

He seemed to struggle with himself, for I heard something like the low, bitter murmur of doubt. "What's the good?" His next words came out with a hesitating effort.

"Look here, my man. Could you call him out quietly?"

I thought the time had come to declare myself.

"*I* am the captain."

I heard a "By Jove!" whispered at the level of the water. The phosphorescence flashed in the swirl of the water all about his limbs, his other hand seized the ladder.

"My name's Leggatt."

The voice was calm and resolute. A good voice. The self-possession of that man had somehow induced a corresponding state in myself. It was very quietly that I remarked:

"You must be a good swimmer."

"Yes. I've been in the water practically since nine o'clock. The question for me now is whether I am to let go this ladder and go on swimming till I sink from exhaustion, or—to come on board here."

I felt this was no mere formula of desperate speech, but a real alternative in the view of a strong soul. I should have gathered from this that he was young; indeed, it is only the young who are ever confronted by such clear issues. But at the time it was pure intuition on my part. A mysterious communication was established already between us two—in the face of that silent, darkened tropical sea. I was young, too; young enough to make no comment. The man in the water began suddenly to climb up the ladder, and I hastened away from the rail to fetch some clothes.

Before entering the cabin I stood still, listening in the lobby at the foot of the stairs. A faint snore came through the closed door of the chief mate's room. The second mate's door was on the hook, but the darkness in there was absolutely soundless. He, too, was young and could sleep like a stone. Remained the steward, but he was not likely to wake up before he was called. I got a sleeping-suit out of my room and, coming back on deck, saw the naked man from the sea sitting on the main-hatch, glimmering white in the darkness, his elbows on his knees and his head in his hands. In a moment he had concealed his damp body in a sleeping-suit of the same gray-stripe pattern as the one I was wearing and followed me like my double on the poop. Together we moved right aft, barefooted, silent.

"What is it?" I asked in a deadened voice, taking the lighted lamp out of the binnacle, and raising it to his face.

"An ugly business."

He had rather regular features; a good mouth; light eyes under somewhat heavy, dark eyebrows; a smooth, square forehead; no growth on his cheeks; a small, brown mustache, and a well-shaped, round chin. His expression was concentrated, meditative, under the inspecting light of the lamp I held up to his face; such as a man thinking hard in solitude might wear. My sleeping-suit was just right for his size. A well-knit young fellow of twenty-five at most. He caught his lower lip with the edge of white, even teeth.

"Yes," I said, replacing the lamp in the binnacle. The warm, heavy tropical night closed upon his head again.

"There's a ship over there," he murmured.

"Yes, I know. The *Sephora*. Did you know of us?"

"Hadn't the slightest idea. I am the mate of her—" He paused and corrected himself. "I should say I *was*."

"Aha! Something wrong?"

"Yes. Very wrong indeed. I've killed a man."

"What do you mean? Just now?"

"No, on the passage. Weeks ago. Thirty-nine south. When I say a man—"

"Fit of temper," I suggested, confidently.

The shadowy, dark head, like mine, seemed to nod imperceptibly above the ghostly gray of my sleeping-suit. It was, in the night, as though I had been faced by my own reflection in the depths of a somber and immense mirror.

"A pretty thing to have to own up to for a Conway boy," murmured my double, distinctly.

"You're a Conway boy?"

"I am," he said, as if startled. Then, slowly . . . "Perhaps you too—"

It was so; but being a couple of years older I had left before he joined. After a quick interchange of dates a silence fell; and I thought suddenly of my absurd mate with his terrific whiskers and the "Bless my soul—you don't say so" type of intellect. My double gave me an inkling of his thoughts by saying: "My father's a parson in Norfolk. Do you see me before a judge and jury on that charge? For myself I can't see the necessity. There are fellows that an angel from heaven—And I am not that. He was one of those creatures that are just simmering all the time with a silly sort of wickedness. Miserable devils that have no business to live at all. He wouldn't do his duty and wouldn't let anybody else do theirs. But what's the good of talking! You know well enough the sort of ill-conditioned snarling cur—"

He appealed to me as if our experiences had been as identical as our clothes. And I knew well enough the pestiferous danger of such a character where there are no means of legal repression. And I knew well enough also that my double there was no homicidal ruffian. I did not think of asking him for details, and he told me the story roughly in brusque, disconnected sentences. I needed no more. I saw it all going on as though I were myself inside that other sleeping-suit.

"It happened while we were setting a reefed foresail, at dusk. Reefed foresail! You understand the sort of weather. The only sail we had left to keep the ship running; so you may guess what it had been like for days. Anxious sort of job, that. He gave me some of his cursed insolence at the sheet. I tell you I was overdone with this terrific weather that seemed to have no end to it. Terrific, I tell you—and a deep ship. I believe the fellow himself was half crazed with funk. It was no time for gentlemanly reproof, so I turned round and felled him like an ox. He up and at me. We closed just as an awful sea made for the ship. All hands saw it coming and took to the rigging, but I had him by the throat, and went on shaking him like a rat, the men above us yelling, 'Look out! look out!' Then a crash as if the sky had fallen on my head. They say that for over ten minutes hardly anything was to be seen of the ship—just the three masts and a bit of the forecastle head and of the poop all awash driving along in a smother of foam. It was a miracle that they found us, jammed together behind the fore-bits. It's clear that I meant business, because I was holding him by the throat still when they picked us up. He was black in the face. It was too much for them. It seems they rushed us aft together, gripped as we were, screaming 'Murder!' like a lot of lunatics, and broke into the cuddy. And the ship running for her life, touch and go all the time, any minute her last in a sea fit to turn your hair gray only a-looking at it. I understand that the skipper, too, started raving like the rest of them. The man had been deprived of sleep for more than a week, and to have this sprung on him at the height of a furious gale nearly drove him out of his mind. I wonder they didn't fling me overboard after getting the carcass of their precious ship-mate out of my fingers. They had rather a job to separate us, I've been told. A sufficiently fierce story to make an old judge and a respectable jury sit up a bit. The first thing I heard when I came to myself was the maddening howling of that endless gale, and on that the voice of the old man. He was hanging on to my bunk, staring into my face out of his sou'wester.

" 'Mr. Leggatt, you have killed a man. You can act no longer as chief mate of this ship.' "

His care to subdue his voice made it sound monotonous. He rested a hand on the end of the skylight to steady himself with, and all that time did not stir a limb, so far as I could see. "Nice little tale for a quiet tea-party," he concluded in the same tone.

One of my hands, too, rested on the end of the skylight; neither did I stir a limb, so far as I knew. We stood less than a foot from each other. It occurred to me that if old "Bless my soul—you don't say so" were to put his head up the companion and catch sight of us, he would think he was seeing double, or imagine himself come upon a scene of weird witchcraft; the strange captain having a quiet confabulation by the wheel with his own gray ghost. I became very much concerned to prevent anything of the sort. I heard the other's soothing undertone.

"My father's a parson in Norfolk," it said. Evidently he had forgotten he had told me this important fact before. Truly a nice little tale.

"You had better slip down into my stateroom now," I said, moving off stealthily. My double followed my movements; our bare feet made no sound;

I let him in, closed the door with care, and, after giving a call to the second mate, returned on deck for my relief.

"Not much sign of any wind yet," I remarked when he approached.

"No, sir. Not much," he assented, sleepily, in his hoarse voice, with just enough deference, no more, and barely suppressing a yawn.

"Well, that's all you have to look out for. You have got your orders."

"Yes, sir."

I paced a turn or two on the poop and saw him take up his position face forward with his elbows in the ratlines of the mizzen-rigging before I went below. The mate's faint snoring was still going on peacefully. The cuddy lamp was burning over the table on which stood a vase with flowers, a polite attention from the ship's provision merchant—the last flowers we should see for the next three months at the very least. Two bunches of bananas hung from the beam symmetrically, one on each side of the rudder-casing. Everything was as before in the ship—except that two of her captain's sleeping-suits were simultaneously in use, one motionless in the cuddy, the other keeping very still in the captain's stateroom.

It must be explained here that my cabin had the form of the capital letter L, the door being within the angle and opening into the short part of the letter. A couch was to the left, the bed-place to the right; my writing-desk and the chronometers' table faced the door. But anyone opening it, unless he stepped right inside, had no view of what I call the long (or vertical) part of the letter. It contained some lockers surmounted by a bookcase; and a few clothes, a thick jacket or two, caps, oilskin coat, and such like, hung on hooks. There was at the bottom of that part a door opening into my bathroom, which could be entered also directly from the saloon. But that way was never used.

The mysterious arrival had discovered the advantage of this particular shape. Entering my room, lighted strongly by a big bulkhead lamp swung on gimbals above my writing-desk, I did not see him anywhere till he stepped out quietly from behind the coats hung in the recessed part.

"I heard somebody moving about, and went in there at once," he whispered.

I, too, spoke under my breath.

"Nobody is likely to come in here without knocking and getting permission."

He nodded. His face was thin and the sunburn faded, as though he had been ill. And no wonder. He had been, I heard presently, kept under arrest in his cabin for nearly seven weeks. But there was nothing sickly in his eyes or in his expression. He was not a bit like me, really; yet, as we stood leaning over my bed-place, whispering side by side, with our dark heads together and our backs to the door, anybody bold enough to open it stealthily would have been treated to the uncanny sight of a double captain busy talking in whispers with his other self.

"But all this doesn't tell me how you came to hang on to our side-ladder," I inquired, in the hardly audible murmurs we used, after he had told me something more of the proceedings on board the *Sephora* once the bad weather was over.

"When we sighted Java Head I had had time to think all those matters out several times over. I had six weeks of doing nothing else, and with only an hour or so every evening for a tramp on the quarter-deck."

He whispered, his arms folded on the side of my bed-place, staring through the open port. And I could imagine perfectly the manner of this thinking out—a stubborn if not a steadfast operation; something of which I should have been perfectly incapable.

"I reckoned it would be dark before we closed with the land," he continued, so low that I had to strain my hearing, near as we were to each other, shoulder touching shoulder almost. "So I asked to speak to the old man. He always seemed very sick when he came to see me—as if he could not look me in the face. You know, that foresail saved the ship. She was too deep to have run long under bare poles. And it was I that managed to set it for him. Anyway, he came. When I had him in my cabin—he stood by the door looking at me as if I had the halter round my neck already—I asked him right away to leave my cabin door unlocked at night while the ship was going through Sunda Straits. There would be the Java coast within two or three miles, off Angier Point. I wanted nothing more. I've had a prize for swimming my second year in the Conway."

"I can believe it," I breathed out.

"God only knows why they locked me in every night. To see some of their faces you'd have thought they were afraid I'd go about at night strangling people. Am I a murdering brute? Do I look it? By Jove! if I had been he wouldn't have trusted himself like that into my room. You'll say I might have chucked him aside and bolted out, there and then—it was dark already. Well, no. And for the same reason I wouldn't think of trying to smash the door. There would have been a rush to stop me at the noise, and I did not mean to get into a confounded scrimmage. Somebody else might have got killed—for I would not have broken out only to get chucked back, and I did not want any more of that work. He refused, looking more sick than ever. He was afraid of the men, and also of that old second mate of his who had been sailing with him for years—a gray-headed old humbug; and his steward, too, had been with him devil knows how long—seventeen years or more—a dogmatic sort of loafer who hated me like poison, just because I was the chief mate. No chief mate ever made more than one voyage in the *Sephora*, you know. Those two old chaps ran the ship. Devil only knows what the skipper wasn't afraid of (all his nerve went to pieces altogether in that hellish spell of bad weather we had)—of what the law would do to him —of his wife, perhaps. Oh, yes! she's on board. Though I don't think she would have meddled. She would have been only too glad to have me out of the ship in any way. The 'brand of Cain' business, don't you see. That's all right. I was ready enough to go off wandering on the face of the earth—and that was price enough to pay for an Abel of that sort. Anyhow, he wouldn't listen to me. 'This thing must take its course. I represent the law here.' He was shaking like a leaf. 'So you won't?' 'No!' 'Then I hope you will be able to sleep on that,' I said, and turned my back on him. 'I wonder that *you* can,' cries he, and locks the door.

"Well, after that, I couldn't. Not very well. That was three weeks ago. We have had a slow passage through the Java Sea; drifted about Carimata for ten days. When we anchored here they thought, I suppose, it was all right. The nearest land (and that's five miles) is the ship's destination; the consul would soon set about catching me; and there would have been no object in bolting to these islets there. I don't suppose there's a drop of water on them. I don't know how it was, but tonight that steward, after bringing me my supper, went out to let me eat it, and left the door unlocked. And I ate it—all there was, too. After I had finished I strolled out on the quarter-deck. I don't know that I meant to do anything. A breath of fresh air was all I wanted, I believe. Then a sudden temptation came over me. I kicked off my slippers and was in the water before I had made up my mind fairly. Somebody heard the splash and they raised an awful hullabaloo. 'He's gone! Lower the boats! He's committed suicide! No, he's swimming.' Certainly I was swimming. It's not so easy for a swimmer like me to commit suicide by drowning. I landed on the nearest islet before the boat left the ship's side. I heard them pulling about in the dark, hailing, and so on, but after a bit they gave up. Everything quieted down and the anchorage became as still as death. I sat down on a stone and began to think. I felt certain they would start searching for me at daylight. There was no place to hide on those stony things—and if there had been, what would have been the good? But now I was clear of that ship, I was not going back. So after a while I took off all my clothes, tied them up in a bundle with a stone inside, and dropped them in the deep water on the outer side of that islet. That was suicide enough for me. Let them think what they liked, but I didn't mean to drown myself. I meant to swim till I sank —but that's not the same thing. I struck out for another of these little islands, and it was from that one that I first saw your riding-light. Something to swim for. I went on easily, and on the way I came upon a flat rock a foot or two above water. In the daytime, I dare say, you might make it out with a glass from your poop. I scrambled up on it and rested myself for a bit. Then I made another start. That last spell must have been over a mile."

His whisper was getting fainter and fainter, and all the time he stared straight out through the port-hole, in which there was not even a star to be seen. I had not interrupted him. There was something that made comment impossible in his narrative, or perhaps in himself; a sort of feeling, a quality, which I can't find a name for. And when he ceased, all I found was a futile whisper: "So you swam for our light?"

"Yes—straight for it. It was something to swim for. I couldn't see any stars low down because the coast was in the way, and I couldn't see the land, either. The water was like glass. One might have been swimming in a confounded thousand-feet deep cistern with no place for scrambling out anywhere; but what I didn't like was the notion of swimming round and round like a crazed bullock before I gave out; and as I didn't mean to go back . . . No. Do you see me being hauled back, stark naked, off one of these little islands by the scruff of the neck and fighting like a wild beast? Somebody would have got killed for certain, and I did not want any of that. So I went on. Then your ladder—"

"Why didn't you hail the ship?" I asked, a little louder.

He touched my shoulder lightly. Lazy footsteps came right over our heads and stopped. The second mate had crossed from the other side of the poop and might have been hanging over the rail, for all we knew.

"He couldn't hear us talking—could he?" My double breathed into my very ear, anxiously.

His anxiety was an answer, a sufficient answer, to the question I had put to him. An answer containing all the difficulty of that situation. I closed the port-hole quietly, to make sure. A louder word might have been overheard.

"Who's that?" he whispered then.

"My second mate. But I don't know much more of the fellow than you do."

And I told him a little about myself. I had been appointed to take charge while I least expected anything of the sort, not quite a fortnight ago. I didn't know either the ship or the people. Hadn't had the time in port to look about me or size anybody up. And as to the crew, all they knew was that I was appointed to take the ship home. For the rest, I was almost as much of a stranger on board as himself, I said. And at the moment I felt it most acutely. I felt that it would take very little to make me a suspect person in the eyes of the ship's company.

He had turned about meantime; and we, the two strangers in the ship, faced each other in identical attitudes.

"Your ladder—" he murmured, after a silence. "Who'd have thought of finding a ladder hanging over at night in a ship anchored out here! I felt just then a very unpleasant faintness. After the life I've been leading for nine weeks, anybody would have got out of condition. I wasn't capable of swimming round as far as your rudder-chains. And, lo and behold! there was a ladder to get hold of. After I gripped it I said to myself, 'What's the good?' When I saw a man's head looking over I thought I would swim away presently and leave him shouting—in whatever language it was. I didn't mind being looked at. I—I liked it. And then you speaking to me so quietly—as if you had expected me—made me hold on a little longer. It had been a confounded lonely time—I don't mean while swimming. I was glad to talk a little to somebody that didn't belong to the *Sephora*. As to asking for the captain, that was a mere impulse. It could have been no use, with all the ship knowing about me and the other people pretty certain to be round here in the morning. I don't know—I wanted to be seen, to talk with somebody, before I went on. I don't know what I would have said. . . . 'Fine night, isn't it?' or something of the sort."

"Do you think they will be round here presently?" I asked with some incredulity.

"Quite likely," he said, faintly.

He looked extremely haggard all of a sudden. His head rolled on his shoulders.

"H'm. We shall see then. Meantime get into that bed," I whispered. "Want help? There."

It was a rather high bed-place with a set of drawers underneath. This amazing swimmer really needed the lift I gave him by seizing his leg. He tumbled in, rolled over on his back, and flung one arm across his eyes. And then, with his face nearly hidden, he must have looked exactly as I used to look in that bed. I gazed upon my other self for a while before drawing across carefully the two green serge curtains which ran on a brass rod. I thought for a moment of pinning them together for greater safety, but I sat down on the couch, and once there I felt unwilling to rise and hunt for a pin. I would do it in a moment. I was extremely tired, in a peculiarly intimate way, by the strain of stealthiness, by the effort of whispering and the general secrecy of this excitement. It was three o'clock by now and I had been on my feet since nine, but I was not sleepy; I could not have gone to sleep. I sat there, fagged out, looking at the curtains, trying to clear my mind of the confused sensation of being in two places at once, and greatly bothered by an exasperating knocking in my head. It was a relief to discover suddenly that it was not in my head at all, but on the outside of the door. Before I could collect myself the words "Come in" were out of my mouth, and the steward entered with a tray, bringing in my morning coffee. I had slept, after all, and I was so frightened that I shouted, "This way! I am here, steward," as though he had been miles away. He put down the tray on the table next the couch and only then said, very quietly, "I can see you are here, sir." I felt him give me a keen look, but I dared not meet his eyes just then. He must have wondered why I had drawn the curtains of my bed before going to sleep on the couch. He went out, hooking the door open as usual.

I heard the crew washing decks above me. I knew I would have been told at once if there had been any wind. Calm, I thought, and I was doubly vexed. Indeed, I felt dual more than ever. The steward reappeared suddenly in the doorway. I jumped up from the couch so quickly that he gave a start.

"What do you want here?"

"Close your port, sir—they are washing decks."

"It is closed," I said, reddening.

"Very well, sir." But he did not move from the doorway and returned my stare in an extraordinary, equivocal manner for a time. Then his eyes wavered, all his expression changed, and in a voice unusually gentle, almost coaxingly:

"May I come in to take the empty cup away, sir?"

"Of course!" I turned my back on him while he popped in and out. Then I unhooked and closed the door and even pushed the bolt. This sort of thing could not go on very long. The cabin was as hot as an oven, too. I took a peep at my double, and discovered that he had not moved, his arm was still over his eyes; but his chest heaved; his hair was wet; his chin glistened with perspiration. I reached over him and opened the port.

"I must show myself on deck," I reflected.

Of course, theoretically, I could do what I liked, with no one to say nay to me within the whole circle of the horizon; but to lock my cabin door and take the key away I did not dare. Directly I put my head out of the companion I saw the group of my two officers, the second mate barefooted, the chief mate in long india-rubber boots, near the break of the poop, and the steward half-way down the poop-ladder talking to them eagerly. He happened to catch sight of me and dived, the second ran down on the main-deck shouting some order or other, and the chief mate came to meet me, touching his cap.

There was a sort of curiosity in his eyes that I did not like. I don't know whether the steward had told them that I was "queer" only, or downright drunk, but I know the man meant to have a good look at me. I watched him coming with a smile which, as he got into point-blank range, took effect and froze his very whiskers. I did not give him time to open his lips.

"Square the yards by lifts and braces before the hands go to breakfast."

It was the first particular order I had given on board that ship; and I stayed on deck to see it executed, too. I had felt the need of asserting myself without loss of time. That sneering young cub got taken down a peg or two on that occasion, and I also seized the opportunity of having a good look at the face of every foremast man as they filed past me to go to the after braces. At breakfast time, eating nothing myself, I presided with such frigid dignity that the two mates were only too glad to escape from the cabin as soon as decency permitted; and all the time the dual working of my mind distracted me almost to the point of insanity. I was constantly watching myself, my secret self, as dependent on my actions as my own personality, sleeping in that bed, behind that door which faced me as I sat at the head of the table.

It was very much like being mad, only it was worse because one was aware of it.

I had to shake him for a solid minute, but when at last he opened his eyes it was in the full possession of his senses, with an inquiring look.

"All's well so far," I whispered. "Now you must vanish into the bath-room."

He did so, noiseless as a ghost, and then I rang for the steward, and facing him boldly, directed him to tidy up my stateroom while I was having my bath—"and be quick about it." As my tone admitted of no excuses, he said, "Yes, sir," and ran off to fetch his dust-pan and brushes. I took a bath and did most of my dressing, splashing, and whistling softly for the steward's edification, while the secret sharer of my life stood drawn up bold upright in that little space, his face looking very sunken in daylight, his eyelids lowered under the stern, dark line of his eyebrows drawn together by a slight frown.

When I left him there to go back to my room the steward was finishing dusting. I sent for the mate and engaged him in some insignificant conversation. It was, as it were, trifling with the terrific character of his whiskers; but my object was to give him an opportunity for a good look at my cabin. And then I could at last shut, with a clear conscience, the door of my stateroom and get my double back into the recessed part. There was nothing else for it. He had to sit still on a small folding stool, half smothered by the heavy coats hanging there. We listened to the steward going into the bath-room out of the saloon, filling the water-bottles there, scrubbing the bath, setting things to rights, whisk, bang, clatter—out again into the saloon—turn the key—click. Such was my scheme for keeping my second self invisible. Nothing better could be contrived under the circumstances. And there we sat; I at my writing-desk ready to appear busy with some papers, he behind me out of sight of the door. It would not have been prudent to talk in daytime; and I could not have stood the excitement of that queer sense of whispering to myself. Now and then, glancing over my shoulder, I saw him far back there, sitting rigidly on the low stool, his bare feet close together, his arms folded, his head hanging on his breast—and perfectly still. Anybody would have taken him for me.

I was fascinated by it myself. Every moment I had to glance over my shoulder. I was looking at him when a voice outside the door said:

"Beg pardon, sir."

"Well!" . . . I kept my eyes on him, and so when the voice outside the door announced, "There's a ship's boat coming our way, sir," I saw him give a start—the first movement he had made for hours. But he did not raise his bowed head.

"All right. Get the ladder over."

I hesitated. Should I whisper something to him? But what? His immobility seemed to have been never disturbed. What could I tell him he did not know already? ... Finally I went on deck.

II

The skipper of the *Sephora* had a thin red whisker all round his face, and the sort of complexion that goes with hair of that color; also the particular, rather smeary shade of blue in the eyes. He was not exactly a showy figure; his shoulders were high, his stature but middling—one leg slightly more bandy than the other. He shook hands, looking vaguely around. A spiritless tenacity was his main characteristic, I judged. I behaved with a politeness which seemed to disconcert him. Perhaps he was shy. He mumbled to me as if he were ashamed of what he was saying; gave his name (it was something like Archbold—but at this distance of years I hardly am sure), his ship's name, and a few other particulars of that sort, in the manner of a criminal making a reluctant and doleful confession. He had had terrible weather on the passage out—terrible—terrible—wife aboard, too.

By this time we were seated in the cabin and the steward brought in a tray with a bottle and glasses. "Thanks! No." Never took liquor. Would have some water, though. He drank two tumblerfuls. Terrible thirsty work. Ever since daylight had been exploring the islands round his ship.

"What was that for—fun?" I asked, with an appearance of polite interest.

"No!" He sighed. "Painful duty."

As he persisted in his mumbling and I wanted my double to hear every word, I hit upon the notion of informing him that I regretted to say I was hard of hearing.

"Such a young man, too!" he nodded, keeping his smeary blue, unintelligent eyes fastened upon me. "What was the cause of it—some disease?" he inquired, without the least sympathy and as if he thought that, if so, I'd got no more than I deserved.

"Yes; disease," I admitted in a cheerful tone which seemed to shock him. But my point was gained, because he had to raise his voice to give me his tale. It is not worth while to record that version. It was just over two months since all this had happened, and he had thought so much about it that he seemed completely muddled as to its bearings, but still immensely impressed.

"What would you think of such a thing happening on board your own ship? I've had the *Sephora* for these fifteen years. I am a well-known shipmaster."

He was densely distressed—and perhaps I should have sympathized with him if I had been able to detach my mental vision from the unsuspected sharer of my cabin as though he were my second self. There he was on the other side of the bulkhead, four or five feet from us, no more, as we sat in the saloon. I looked politely at Captain Archbold (if that was his name), but it was the other I saw, in a gray sleeping-suit, seated on a low stool, his bare feet close together, his arms folded, and every word said between us falling into the ears of his dark head bowed on his chest.

"I have been at sea now, man and boy, for seven-and-thirty years, and I've never heard of such a thing happening in an English ship. And that it should be my ship. Wife on board, too."

I was hardly listening to him.

"Don't you think," I said, "that the heavy sea which, you told me, came aboard just then might have killed the man? I have seen the sheer weight of a sea kill a man very neatly, by simply breaking his neck."

"Good God!" he uttered, impressively fixing his smeary blue eyes on me. "The sea! No man killed by the sea ever looked like that." He seemed positively scandalized at my suggestion. And as I gazed at him, certainly not prepared for anything original on his part, he advanced his head close to mine and thrust his tongue out at me so suddenly that I couldn't help starting back.

After scoring over my calmness in this graphic way he nodded wisely. If I had seen the sight, he assured me, I would never forget it as long as I lived. The weather was too bad to give the corpse a proper sea burial. So next day at dawn they took it up on the poop, covering its face with a bit of bunting; he read a short prayer, and then, just as it was, in its oilskins and long boots, they launched it amongst those mountainous seas that seemed ready every moment to swallow up the ship herself and the terrified lives on board of her.

"That reefed foresail saved you," I threw in.

"Under God—it did," he exclaimed fervently. "It was by a special mercy, I firmly believe, that it stood some of those hurricane squalls."

"It was the setting of that sail which—" I began.

"God's own hand in it," he interrupted me. "Nothing less could have done it. I don't mind telling you that I hardly dared give the order. It seemed impossible that we could touch anything without losing it, and then our last hope would have been gone."

The terror of that gale was on him yet. I let him go on for a bit, then said, casually—as if returning to a minor subject:

"You were very anxious to give up your mate to the shore people, I believe?"

He was. To the law. His obscure tenacity on that point had in it something incomprehensible and a little awful; something, as it were, mystical, quite apart from his anxiety that he should not be suspected of "countenancing any doings of that sort." Seven-and-thirty virtuous years at sea, of which over twenty of immaculate command, and the last fifteen in the *Sephora*, seemed to have laid him under some pitiless obligation.

"And you know," he went on, groping shamefacedly amongst his feelings, "I did not engage that young fellow. His people had some interest with my owners. I was in a way forced to take him on. He looked very smart, very gentlemanly, and all that. But do you know—I never liked him, somehow. I am a plain man. You see, he wasn't exactly the sort for the chief mate of a ship like the *Sephora*."

I had become so connected in thoughts and impressions with the secret sharer of my cabin that I felt as if I, personally, were being given to understand that I, too, was not the sort that would have done for the chief mate of a ship like the *Sephora*. I had no doubt of it in my mind.

"Not at all the style of man. You understand," he insisted, superfluously, looking hard at me.

I smiled urbanely. He seemed at a loss for a while.

"I suppose I must report a suicide."

"Beg pardon?"

"Sui-cide! That's what I'll have to write to my owners directly I get in."

"Unless you manage to recover him before tomorrow," I assented, dispassionately. . . . "I mean, alive."

He mumbled something which I really did not catch, and I turned my ear to him in a puzzled manner. He fairly bawled:

"The land—I say, the mainland is at least seven miles off my anchorage."

"About that."

My lack of excitement, of curiosity, of surprise, of any sort of pronounced interest, began to arouse his distrust. But except for the felicitous pretense of deafness I had not tried to pretend anything. I had felt utterly incapable of playing the part of ignorance properly, and therefore was afraid to try. It is also certain that he had brought some ready-made suspicions with him, and that he viewed my politeness as a strange and unnatural phenomenon. And yet how else could I have received him? Not heartily! That was impossible for psychological reasons, which I need not state here. My only object was to keep off his inquiries. Surlily? Yes, but surliness might have provoked a point-blank question. From its novelty to him and from its nature, punctilious courtesy was the manner best calculated to restrain the man. But there was the danger of his breaking through my defense bluntly. I could not, I think, have met him by a direct lie, also for psychological (not moral) reasons. If he had only known how afraid I was of his putting my feeling of identity with the other to the test! But, strangely enough—(I thought of it only afterwards)—I believe that he was not a little disconcerted by the reverse side of that weird situation, by something in me that reminded him of the man he was seeking—suggested a mysterious similitude to the young fellow he had distrusted and disliked from the first.

However that might have been, the silence was not very prolonged. He took another oblique step.

"I reckon I had no more than a two-mile pull to your ship. Not a bit more."

"And quite enough, too, in this awful heat," I said.

Another pause full of mistrust followed. Necessity, they say, is mother of invention, but fear, too, is not barren of ingenious suggestions. And I was afraid he would ask me point-blank for news of my other self.

"Nice little saloon, isn't it?" I remarked, as if noticing for the first time the way his eyes roamed from one closed door to the other. "And very well fitted out, too. Here, for instance," I continued, reaching over the back of my seat negligently and flinging the door open, "is my bath-room."

He made an eager movement, but hardly gave it a glance. I got up, shut the door of the bath-room, and invited him to have a look round, as if I were very proud of my accommodation. He had to rise and be shown round, but he went through the business without any raptures whatever.

"And now we'll have a look at my stateroom," I declared, in a voice as loud as I dared to make it, crossing the cabin to the starboard side with purposely heavy steps.

He followed me in and gazed around. My intelligent double had vanished. I played my part.

"Very convenient—isn't it?"

"Very nice. Very comf . . ." He didn't finish and went out brusquely as if to escape from some unrighteous wiles of mine. But it was not to be. I had been too frightened not to feel vengeful; I felt I had him on the run, and I meant to keep him on the run. My polite insistence must have had something menacing in it, because he gave in suddenly. And I did not let him off a single item; mate's room, pantry, storerooms, the very sail-locker which was also under the poop—he had to look into them all. When at last I showed him out on the quarter-deck he drew a long, spiritless sigh, and mumbled dismally that he must really be going back to his ship now. I desired my mate, who had joined us, to see to the captain's boat.

The man of whiskers gave a blast on the whistle which he used to wear hanging round his neck, and yelled, "Sephora's away!" My double down there in my cabin must have heard, and certainly could not feel more relieved than I. Four fellows came running out from somewhere forward and went over the side, while my own men, appearing on deck too, lined the rail. I escorted my visitor to the gangway ceremoniously, and nearly overdid it. He was a tenacious beast. On the very ladder he lingered, and in that unique, guiltily conscientious manner of sticking to the point:

"I say . . . you . . . you don't think that—"

I covered his voice loudly:

"Certainly not. . . . I am delighted. Good-by."

I had an idea of what he meant to say, and just saved myself by the privilege of defective hearing. He was too shaken generally to insist, but my mate, close witness of that parting, looked mystified and his face took on a thoughtful cast. As I did not want to appear as if I wished to avoid all communication with my officers, he had the opportunity to address me.

"Seems a very nice man. His boat's crew told our chaps a very extraordinary story, if what I am told by the steward is true. I suppose you had it from the captain, sir?"

"Yes. I had a story from the captain."

"A very horrible affair—isn't it, sir?"

"It is."

"Beats all these tales we hear about murders in Yankee ships."

"I don't think it beats them. I don't think it resembles them in the least."

"Bless my soul—you don't say so! But of course I've no acquaintance whatever with American ships, not I, so I couldn't go against your knowledge. It's horrible enough for me. . . . But the queerest part is that those fellows seemed to have some idea the man was hidden aboard here. They had really. Did you ever hear of such a thing?"

"Preposterous—isn't it?"

We were walking to and fro athwart the quarter-deck. No one of the crew forward could be seen (the day was Sunday), and the mate pursued:

"There was some little dispute about it. Our chaps took offense. 'As if we would harbor a thing like that,' they said. 'Wouldn't you like to look for him in our coal-hole?' Quite a tiff. But they made it up in the end. I suppose he did drown himself. Don't you, sir?"

"I don't suppose anything."

"You have no doubt in the matter, sir?"

"None whatever."

I left him suddenly. I felt I was producing a bad impression, but with my double down there it was most trying to be on deck. And it was almost as trying to be below. Altogether a nerve-trying situation. But on the whole I felt less torn in two when I was with him. There was no one in the whole ship whom I dared take into my confidence. Since the hands had got to know his story, it would have been impossible to pass him off for anyone else, and an accidental discovery was to be dreaded now more than ever. . . .

The steward being engaged in laying the table for dinner, we could talk only with our eyes when I first went down. Later in the afternoon we had a cautious try at whispering. The Sunday quietness of the ship was against us; the stillness of air and water around her was against us; the elements, the men were against us—everything was against us in our secret partnership; time itself—for this could not go on forever. The very trust in Providence was, I suppose, denied to his guilt. Shall I confess that this thought cast me down very much? And as to the chapter of accidents which counts for so much in the book of success, I could only hope that it was closed. For what favorable accident could be expected?

"Did you hear everything?" were my first words as soon as we took up our position side by side, leaning over my bed-place.

He had. And the proof of it was his earnest whisper, "The man told you he hardly dared to give the order."

I understood the reference to be to that saving foresail.

"Yes. He was afraid of it being lost in the setting."

"I assure you he never gave the order. He may think he did, but he never gave it. He stood there with me on the break of the poop after the maintopsail blew away, and whimpered about our last hope—positively whimpered about it and nothing else—and the night coming on! To hear one's skipper go on like that in such weather was enough to drive any fellow out of his mind. It worked me up into a sort of desperation. I just took it into my own hands and went away from him, boiling, and— But what's the use telling you? *You* know! . . . Do you think that if I had not been pretty fierce with them I should have got the men to do anything? Not it! The bo's'n perhaps? Perhaps! It wasn't a heavy sea—it was a sea gone mad! I suppose the end of the world will be something like that; and a man may have the heart to see it coming once and be done with it—but to have to face it day after day—I don't blame anybody. I was precious little better than the rest. Only—I was an officer of that old coal-wagon, anyhow—"

"I quite understand," I conveyed that sincere assurance into his ear. He was out of breath with whispering; I could hear him pant slightly. It was all very simple. The same strung-up force which had given twenty-four men a chance, at least, for their lives, had, in a sort of recoil, crushed an unworthy mutinous existence.

But I had no leisure to weigh the merits of the matter—footsteps in the saloon, a heavy knock. "There's enough wind to get under way with, sir." Here was the call of a new claim upon my thoughts and even upon my feelings.

"Turn the hands up," I cried through the door. "I'll be on deck directly."

I was going out to make the acquaintance of my ship. Before I left the cabin our eyes met—the eyes of the only two strangers on board. I pointed to the recessed part where the little campstool awaited him and laid my finger on my lips. He made a gesture—somewhat vague—a little mysterious, accompanied by a faint smile, as if of regret.

This is not the place to enlarge upon the sensations of a man who feels for the first time a ship move under his feet to his own independent word. In my case they were not unalloyed. I was not wholly alone with my command; for there was that stranger in my cabin. Or rather, I was not completely and wholly with her. Part of me was absent. That mental feeling of being in two places at once affected me physically as if the mood of secrecy had penetrated my very soul. Before an hour had elapsed since the ship had begun to move, having occasion to ask the mate (he stood by my side) to take a compass bearing of the Pagoda, I caught myself reaching up to his ear in whispers. I say I caught myself, but enough had escaped to startle the man. I can't describe it otherwise than by saying that he shied. A grave, preoccupied manner, as though he were in possession of some perplexing intelligence, did not leave him henceforth. A little later I moved away from the rail to look at the compass with such a stealthy gait that the helmsman noticed it—and I could not help noticing the unusual round-ness of his eyes. These are trifling instances, though it's to no commander's advantage to be suspected of ludicrous eccentricities. But I was also more seriously affected. There are to a seaman certain words, gestures, that should in given conditions come as naturally, as instinctively as the winking of a menaced eye. A certain order should spring on to his lips without thinking; a certain sign should get itself made, so to speak, without reflection. But all unconscious alertness had abandoned me. I had to make an effort of will to recall myself back (from the cabin) to the conditions of the moment. I felt that I was appearing an irresolute commander to those people who were watching me more or less critically.

And, besides, there were the scares. On the second day out, for instance, coming off the deck in the afternoon (I had straw slippers on my bare feet) I stopped at the open pantry and spoke to the steward. He was doing something there with his back to me. At the sound of my voice he nearly jumped out of his skin, as the saying is, and incidentally broke a cup.

"What on earth's the matter with you?" I asked, astonished.

He was extremely confused. "Beg your pardon, sir. I made sure you were in your cabin."

"You see I wasn't."

"No, sir. I could have sworn I heard you moving in there not a moment ago. It's most extraordinary . . . very sorry, sir."

I passed on with an inward shudder. I was so identified with my secret double that I did not even mention the fact in those scanty, fearful whispers we exchanged. I suppose he had made some slight noise of some kind or other. It would have been miraculous if he hadn't at one time or another. And yet, haggard as he appeared, he looked always perfectly self-controlled, more than calm—almost invulnerable. On my suggestion he remained almost entirely in the bath-room, which, upon the whole, was the safest place. There could be really no shadow of an excuse for anyone ever wanting to go in there, once the steward had done with it. It was a very tiny place. Sometimes he reclined on the floor, his legs bent, his head sus-tained on one elbow. At others I would find him on the camp-stool, sitting in his gray sleeping-suit and with his cropped dark hair like a patient, unmoved convict. At night I would smuggle him into my bed-place, and we would whisper together, with the regular footfalls of the officer of the watch passing and repassing over our heads. It was an infinitely miserable time. It was lucky that some tins of fine preserves were stowed in a locker in my stateroom; hard bread I could always get hold of; and so he lived on stewed chicken, paté de foie gras, asparagus, cooked oysters, sardines— on all sorts of abominable sham delicacies out of tins. My early morning coffee he always drank; and it was all I dared do for him in that respect.

Every day there was the horrible maneuvering to go through so that my room and then the bath-room should be done in the usual way. I came to hate the sight of the steward, to abhor the voice of that harmless man. I felt that it was he who would bring on the disaster of discovery. It hung like a sword over our heads.

The fourth day out, I think (we were then working down the east side of the Gulf of Siam, tack for tack, in light winds and smooth water)— the fourth day, I say, of this miserable juggling with the unavoidable, as we sat at our evening meal, that man, whose slightest movement I dreaded, after putting down the dishes ran up on deck busily. This could not be dangerous. Presently he came down again; and then it appeared that he had remembered a coat of mine which I had thrown over a rail to dry after having been wetted in a shower which had passed over the ship in the afternoon. Sitting stolidly at the head of the table I became terrified at the sight of the garment on his arm. Of course he made for my door. There was no time to lose.

"Steward," I thundered. My nerves were so shaken that I could not govern my voice and conceal my agitation. This was the sort of thing that made my terrifically whiskered mate tap his forehead with his forefinger. I had detected him using that gesture while talking on deck with a confidential air to the carpenter. It was too far to hear a word, but I had no doubt that this pantomime could only refer to the strange new captain.

"Yes, sir," the pale-faced steward turned resignedly to me. It was this maddening course of being shouted at, checked without rhyme or reason, arbitrarily chased out of my cabin, suddenly called into it, sent flying out of his pantry on incomprehensible errands, that accounted for the growing wretchedness of his expression.

"Where are you going with that coat?"

"To your room, sir."

"Is there another shower coming?"

"I'm sure I don't know, sir. Shall I go up again and see, sir?"

"No! never mind."

My object was attained, as of course my other self in there would have heard everything that passed. During this interlude my two officers never raised their eyes off their respective plates; but the lip of that confounded cub, the second mate, quivered visibly.

I expected the steward to hook my coat on and come out at once. He was very slow about it; but I dominated my nervousness sufficiently not to shout after him. Suddenly I became aware (it could be heard plainly enough) that the fellow for some reason or other was opening the door of the bath-room. It was the end. The place was literally not big enough to swing a cat in. My voice died in my throat and I went stony all over. I expected to hear a yell of surprise and terror, and made a movement, but had not the strength to get on my legs. Everything remained still. Had my second self taken the poor wretch by the throat? I don't know what I could have done next moment if I had not seen the steward come out of my room, close the door, and then stand quietly by the sideboard.

"Saved," I thought. "But, no! Lost! Gone! He was gone!"

I laid my knife and fork down and leaned back in my chair. My head swam. After a while, when sufficiently recovered to speak in a steady voice, I instructed my mate to put the ship round at eight o'clock himself.

"I won't come on deck," I went on. "I think I'll turn in, and unless the wind shifts I don't want to be disturbed before midnight. I feel a bit seedy."

"You did look middling bad a little while ago," the chief mate remarked without showing any great concern.

They both went out, and I stared at the steward clearing the table. There was nothing to be read on that wretched man's face. But why did he avoid my eyes, I asked myself. Then I thought I should like to hear the sound of his voice.

"Steward!"

"Sir!" Startled as usual.

"Where did you hang up that coat?"

"In the bath-room, sir." The usual anxious tone. "It's not quite dry yet, sir."

For some time longer I sat in the cuddy. Had my double vanished as he had come? But of his coming there was an explanation, whereas his disappearance would be inexplicable. . . . I went slowly into my dark room, shut the door, lighted the lamp, and for a time dared not turn round. When at last I did, I saw him standing bolt-upright in the narrow recessed part. It would not be true to say I had a shock, but an irresistible doubt of his bodily existence flitted through my mind. Can it be, I asked myself, that he is not visible to other eyes than mine? It was like being haunted. Motionless, with a grave face, he raised his hands slightly at me in a gesture which meant clearly, "Heavens! what a narrow escape!" Narrow indeed. I think I had come creeping quietly as near insanity as any man who has not actually gone over the border. That gesture restrained me, so to speak.

The mate with the terrific whiskers was now putting the ship on the other tack. In the moment of profound silence which follows upon the hands going to their stations I heard on the poop his raised voice: "Hard alee!" and the distance shout of the order repeated on the maindeck. The sails, in that light breeze, made but a faint fluttering noise. It ceased. The ship was coming round slowly; I held my breath in the renewed stillness of expectation; one wouldn't have thought that there was a single living soul on her decks. A sudden brisk shout, "Mainsail haul!" broke the spell, and in the noisy cries and rush overhead of the men running away with the main-brace we two, down in my cabin, came together in our usual position by the bed-place.

He did not wait for my question. "I heard him fumbling here and just managed to squat myself down in the bath," he whispered to me. "The fellow only opened the door and put his arm in to hang the coat up. All the same—"

"I never thought of that," I whispered back, even more appalled than before at the closeness of the shave, and marveling at that something unyielding in his character which was carrying him through so finely. There was no agitation in his whisper. Whoever was being driven distracted, it was not he. He was sane. And the proof of his sanity was continued when he took up the whispering again.

"It would never do for me to come to life again."

It was something that a ghost might have said. But what he was alluding to was his old captain's reluctant admission of the theory of suicide. It would obviously serve his turn—if I had understood at all the view which seemed to govern the unalterable purpose of his action.

"You must maroon me as soon as ever you can get amongst these islands off the Cambodge shore," he went on.

"Maroon you! We are not living in a boy's adventure tale," I protested. His scornful whispering took me up.

"We aren't indeed! There's nothing of a boy's tale in this. But there's nothing else for it. I want no more. You don't suppose I am afraid of what can be done to me? Prison or gallows or whatever they may please. But you don't see me coming back to explain such things to an old fellow in a wig and twelve respectable tradesmen, do you? What can they know whether I am guilty or not—or of *what* I am guilty, either? That's my affair. What does the Bible say? 'Driven off the face of the earth.' Very well. I am off the face of the earth now. As I came at night so I shall go."

"Impossible!" I murmured. "You can't."

"Can't? . . . Not naked like a soul on the Day of Judgment. I shall freeze on to this sleeping-suit. The Last Day is not yet—and . . . you have understood thoroughly. Didn't you?"

I felt suddenly ashamed of myself. I may say truly that I understood—

and my hesitation in letting that man swim away from my ship's side had been a mere sham sentiment, a sort of cowardice.

"It can't be done now till next night," I breathed out. "The ship is on the off-shore tack and the wind may fail us."

"As long as I know that you understand," he whispered. "But of course you do. It's a great satisfaction to have got somebody to understand. You seem to have been there on purpose." And in the same whisper, as if we two whenever we talked had to say things to each other which were not fit for the world to hear, he added, "It's very wonderful."

We remained side by side talking in our secret way—but sometimes silent or just exchanging a whispered word or two at long intervals. And as usual he stared through the port. A breath of wind came now and again into our faces. The ship might have been moored in dock, so gently and on an even keel she slipped through the water, that did not murmur even at our passage, shadowy and silent like a phantom sea.

At midnight I went on deck, and to my mate's great surprise put the ship round on the other tack. His terrible whiskers flitted round me in silent criticism. I certainly should not have done it if it had been only a question of getting out of that sleepy gulf as quickly as possible. I believe he told the second mate, who relieved him, that it was a great want of judgment. The other only yawned. That intolerable cub shuffled about so sleepily and lolled against the rails in such a slack, improper fashion that I came down on him sharply.

"Aren't you properly awake yet?"

"Yes, sir! I am awake."

"Well, then, be good enough to hold yourself as if you were. And keep a look-out. If there's any current we'll be closing with some islands before daylight."

The east side of the gulf is fringed with islands, some solitary, others in groups. On the blue background of the high coast they seem to float on silvery patches of calm water, arid and gray, or dark green and rounded like clumps of evergreen bushes, with the larger ones, a mile or two long, showing the outlines of ridges, ribs of gray rock under the dank mantle of matted leafage. Unknown to trade, to travel, almost to geography, the manner of life they harbor is an unsolved secret. There must be villages— settlements of fishermen at least—on the largest of them, and some communication with the world is probably kept up by native craft. But all that forenoon, as we headed for them, fanned along by the faintest of breezes, I saw no sign of man or canoe in the field of the telescope I kept on pointing at the scattered group.

At noon I gave no orders for a change of course, and the mate's whiskers became much concerned and seemed to be offering themselves unduly to my notice. At last I said:

"I am going to stand right in. Quite in—as far as I can take her."

The stare of extreme surprise imparted an air of ferocity also to his eyes, and he looked truly terrific for a moment.

"We're not doing well in the middle of the gulf," I continued, casually. "I am going to look for the land breezes tonight."

"Bless my soul! Do you mean, sir, in the dark amongst the lot of all them islands and reefs and shoals?"

"Well—if there are any regular land breezes at all on this coast one must get close inshore to find them, mustn't one?"

"Bless my soul!" he exclaimed again under his breath. All that afternoon he wore a dreamy, contemplative appearance which in him was a mark of perplexity. After dinner I went into my stateroom as if I meant to take some rest. There we two bent our dark heads over a half-unrolled chart lying on my bed.

"There," I said. "It's got to be Koh-ring. I've been looking at it ever since sunrise. It has got two hills and a low point. It must be inhabited. And on the coast opposite there is what looks like the mouth of a biggish river— with some town, no doubt, not far up. It's the best chance for you that I can see."

"Anything. Koh-ring let it be."

He looked thoughtfully at the chart as if surveying chances and distances from a lofty height—and following with his eyes his own figure wandering on the blank land of Cochin-China, and then passing off that piece of paper clean out of sight into uncharted regions. And it was as if the ship had two captains to plan her course for her. I had been so worried and restless running up and down that I had not had the patience to dress that day. I had remained in my sleeping-suit, with straw slippers and a soft floppy hat. The closeness of the heat in the gulf had been most oppressive, and the crew were used to see me wandering in that airy attire.

"She will clear the south point as she heads now," I whispered into his ear. "Goodness only knows when, though, but certainly after dark. I'll edge her in to half a mile, as far as I may be able to judge in the dark—"

"Be careful," he murmured, warningly—and I realized suddenly that all my future, the only future for which I was fit, would perhaps go irretrievably to pieces in any mishap to my first command.

I could not stop a moment longer in the room. I motioned him to get out of sight and made my way to the poop. That unplayful cub had the watch. I walked up and down for a while thinking things out, then beckoned him over.

"Send a couple of hands to open the two quarter-deck ports," I said, mildly.

He actually had the impudence, or else so forgot himself in his wonder at such an incomprehensible order, as to repeat:

"Open the quarter-deck ports! What for, sir?"

"The only reason you need concern yourself about is because I tell you to do so. Have them opened wide and fastened properly."

He reddened and went off, but I believe made some jeering remark to the carpenter as to the sensible practice of ventilating a ship's quarter-deck. I know he popped into the mate's cabin to impart the fact to him because the whiskers came on deck, as it were by chance, and stole glances at me from below—for signs of lunacy or drunkenness, I suppose.

A little before supper, feeling more restless than ever, I rejoined, for a moment, my second self. And to find him sitting so quietly was surprising, like something against nature, inhuman.

I developed my plan in a hurried whisper.

"I shall stand in as close as I dare and then put her round. I will presently find means to smuggle you out of here into the sail-locker, which communicates with the lobby. But there is an opening, a sort of square for hauling the sails out, which gives straight on the quarter-deck and which is never closed in fine weather, so as to give air to the sails. When the ship's way is deadened in stays and all the hands are aft at the main-braces you will have a clear road to slip out and get overboard through the open quarter-deck port. I've had them both fastened up. Use a rope's end to lower yourself into the water so as to avoid a splash—you know. It could be heard and cause some beastly complication."

He kept silent for a while, then whispered, "I understand."

"I won't be there to see you go," I began with an effort. "The rest . . . I only hope I have understood, too."

"You have. From first to last"—and for the first time there seemed to be a faltering, something strained in his whisper. He caught hold of my arm, but the ringing of the supper bell made me start. He didn't, though; he only released his grip.

After supper I didn't come below again till well past eight o'clock. The faint, steady breeze was loaded with dew; and the wet, darkened sails held all there was of propelling power in it. The night, clear and starry, sparkled darkly, and the opaque, lightless patches shifting slowly against the low stars were the drifting islets. On the port bow there was a big one more distant and shadowily imposing by the great space of sky it eclipsed.

On opening the door I had a back view of my very own self looking at a chart. He had come out of the recess and was standing near the table.

"Quite dark enough," I whispered.

He stepped back and leaned against my bed with a level, quiet glance. I sat on the couch. We had nothing to say to each other. Over our heads the officer of the watch moved here and there. Then I heard him move quickly. I knew what that meant. He was making for the companion; and presently his voice was outside my door.

"We are drawing in pretty fast, sir. Land looks rather close."

"Very well," I answered. "I am coming on deck directly."

I waited till he was gone out of the cuddy, then rose. My double moved too. The time had come to exchange our last whispers, for neither of us was ever to hear each other's natural voice.

"Look here!" I opened a drawer and took out three sovereigns. "Take this anyhow. I've got six and I'd give you the lot, only I must keep a little money to buy some fruit and vegetables for the crew from native boats as we go through Sunda Straits."

He shook his head.

"Take it," I urged him, whispering desperately. "No one can tell what—"

He smiled and slapped meaningly the only pocket of the sleeping-jacket. It was not safe, certainly. But I produced a large old silk handkerchief of mine, and tying the three pieces of gold in a corner, pressed it on him. He was touched, I suppose, because he took it at last and tied it quickly round his waist under the jacket, on his bare skin.

Our eyes met; several seconds elapsed, till, our glances still mingled, I extended my hand and turned the lamp out. Then I passed through the cuddy, leaving the door of my room wide open. . . . "Steward!"

He was still lingering in the pantry in the greatness of his zeal, giving a rub-up to a plated cruet stand the last thing before going to bed. Being careful not to wake up the mate, whose room was opposite, I spoke in an undertone.

He looked round anxiously. "Sir!"

"Can you get me a little hot water from the galley?"

"I am afraid, sir, the galley fire's been out for some time now."

"Go and see."

He flew up the stairs.

"Now," I whispered, loudly, into the saloon—too loudly, perhaps, but I was afraid I couldn't make a sound. He was by my side in an instant—the double captain slipped past the stairs—through a tiny dark passage . . . a sliding door. We were in the sail-locker, scrambling on our knees over the sails. A sudden thought struck me. I saw myself wandering barefooted, bareheaded, the sun beating on my dark poll. I snatched off my floppy hat and tried hurriedly in the dark to ram it on my other self. He dodged and fended off silently. I wonder what he thought had come to me before he understood and suddenly desisted. Our hands met gropingly, lingered united in a steady, motionless clasp for a second. . . . No word was breathed by either of us when they separated.

I was standing quietly by the pantry door when the steward returned.

"Sorry, sir. Kettle barely warm. Shall I light the spirit-lamp?"

"Never mind."

I came out on deck slowly. It was now a matter of conscience to shave the land as close as possible—for now he must go overboard whenever the ship was put in stays. Must! There could be no going back for him. After a moment I walked over to leeward and my heart flew into my mouth at the nearness of the land on the bow. Under any other circumstances I would not have held on a minute longer. The second mate had followed me anxiously.

I looked on till I felt I could command my voice.

"She will weather," I said then in a quiet tone.

"Are you going to try that, sir?" he stammered out incredulously.

I took no notice of him and raised my tone just enough to be heard by the helmsman.

"Keep her good full."

"Good full, sir."

The wind fanned my cheek, the sails slept, the world was silent. The strain of watching the dark loom of the land grow bigger and denser was too much for me. I had shut my eyes—because the ship must go closer. She must! The stillness was intolerable. Were we standing still?

When I opened my eyes the second view started my heart with a thump. The black southern hill of Koh-ring seemed to hang right over the ship like a towering fragment of the everlasting night. On that enormous mass of blackness there was not a gleam to be seen, not a sound to be heard. It was gliding irresistibly towards us and yet seemed already within reach of the land. I saw the vague figures of the watch grouped in the waist, gazing in awed silence.

. "Are you going on, sir?" inquired an unsteady voice at my elbow.

I ignored it. I had to go on.

"Keep her full. Don't check her way. That won't do now," I said, warningly.

"I can't see the sails very well," the helmsman answered me, in strange, quavering tones.

Was she close enough? Already she was, I won't say in the shadow of the land, but in the very blackness of it, already swallowed up as it were, gone too close to be recalled, gone from me altogether

"Give the mate a call," I said to the young man who stood at my elbow as still as death. "And turn all hands up."

My tone had a borrowed loudness reverberated from the height of the land. Several voices cried out together: "We are all on deck, sir."

Then stillness again, with the great shadow gliding closer, towering higher, without a light, without a sound. Such a hush had fallen on the ship that she might have been a bark of the dead floating in slowly under the very gate of Erebus.

"My God! Where are we?"

It was the mate moaning at my elbow. He was thunderstruck, and as it were deprived of the moral support of his whiskers. He clapped his hands and absolutely cried out, "Lost!"

"Be quiet," I said, sternly.

He lowered his tone, but I saw the shadowy gesture of his despair. "What are we doing here?"

"Looking for the land wind."

He made as if to tear his hair, and addressed me recklessly.

"She will never get out. You have done it, sir. I knew it'd end in something like this. She will never weather, and you are too close now to stay. She'll drift ashore before she's round. O my God!"

I caught his arm as he was raising it to batter his poor devoted head, and shook it violently.

"She's ashore already," he wailed, trying to tear himself away.

"Is she? ... Keep good full there!"

"Good full, sir," cried the helmsman in a frightened, thin, child-like voice.

I hadn't let go the mate's arm and went on shaking it. "Ready about, do you hear? You go forward"—shake—"and stop there"—shake—"and hold your noise"—shake—"and see these head-sheets properly overhauled"—shake, shake—shake.

And all the time I dared not look towards the land lest my heart should fail me. I released my grip at last and he ran forward as if fleeing for dear life.

I wondered what my double there in the sail-locker thought of this commotion. He was able to hear everything—and perhaps he was able to understand why, on my conscience, it had to be thus close—no less. My first order "Hard alee!" re-echoed ominously under the towering shadow of Koh-ring as if I had shouted in a mountain gorge. And then I watched the land intently. In that smooth water and light wind it was impossible to feel the ship coming-to. No! I could not feel her. And my second self was making now ready to slip out and lower himself overboard. Perhaps he was gone already ... ?

The great black mass brooding over our very mastheads began to pivot away from the ship's side silently. And now I forgot the secret stranger ready to depart, and remembered only that I was a total stranger to the ship. I did not know her. Would she do it? How was she to be handled?

I swung the mainyard and waited helplessly. She was perhaps stopped, and her very fate hung in balance, with the black mass of Koh-ring like the gate of the everlasting night towering over her taffrail. What would she do now? Had she way on her yet? I stepped to the side swiftly, and on the shadowy water I could see nothing except a faint phosphorescent flash revealing the glassy smoothness of the sleeping surface. It was impossible to tell—and I had not learned yet the feel of my ship. Was she moving? What I needed was something easily seen, a piece of paper, which I could throw

overboard and watch. I had nothing on me. To run down for it I didn't
dare. There was no time. All at once my strained, yearning stare distinguished a white object floating within a yard of the ship's side. White on the
black water. A phosphorescent flash passed under it. What was that thing?
. . . I recognized my own floppy hat. It must have fallen off his head . . .
and he didn't bother. Now I had what I wanted—the saving mark for my
eyes. But I hardly thought of my other self, now gone from the ship, to
be hidden forever from all friendly faces, to be a fugitive and a vagabond
on the earth, with no brand of the curse on his sane forehead to stay a
slaying hand . . . too proud to explain.

And I watched the hat—the expression of my sudden pity for his mere
flesh. It had been meant to save his homeless head from the dangers of the
sun. And now—behold—it was saving the ship, by serving me for a mark
to help out the ignorance of my strangness. Ha! It was drifting forward,
warning me just in time that the ship had gathered sternway.

"Shift the helm," I said in a low voice to the seaman standing still like a
statue.

The man's eyes glistened wildly in the binnacle light as he jumped round
to the other side and spun round the wheel.

I walked to the break of the poop. On the overshadowed deck all hands
stood by the forebraces waiting for my order. The stars ahead seemed to be
gliding from right to left. And all was so still in the world that I heard the
quiet remark, "She's round," passed in a tone of intense relief between two
seamen.

"Let go and haul."

The foreyards ran round with a great noise, amidst cheery cries. And now
the frightful whiskers made themselves heard giving various orders. Already the ship was drawing ahead. And I was alone with her. Nothing!
no one in the world should stand now between us, throwing a shadow on
the way of silent knowledge and mute affection, the perfect communion
of a seaman with his first command.

Walking to the taffrail, I was in time to make out, on the very edge of
a darkness thrown by a towering black mass like the very gateway of Erebus
—yes, I was in time to catch an evanescent glimpse of my white hat left
behind to mark the spot where the secret sharer of my cabin and of my
thoughts, as though he were my second self, had lowered himself into the
water to take his punishment: a free man, a proud swimmer striking out
for a new destiny.

Biographical Notes on the Authors

Biographical Notes on the Authors ❦

SHERWOOD ANDERSON was born in Camden, Ohio, in 1876. After achieving success in business, he turned abruptly to a writing career. He won the *Dial* award in 1921. His novels include *Windy McPherson's Son* (1916), *Marching Men* (1917), *Poor White* (1920), and *Dark Laughter* (1925). His best-known short-story collections are *Winesburg, Ohio* (1919), *The Triumph of the Egg* (1921), and *Death in the Woods and Other Stories* (1933). Most of his time after 1925 was spent in Marion, West Virginia, where he owned two local newspapers. He died in 1941.

KAY BOYLE was born in 1903 in St. Paul, Minnesota. Many of her early years were spent in Europe, and she settled there permanently in 1922. The recent war years were spent in the United States, where her husband, an Austrian by birth, was a member of the U. S. ski troops. In 1935 she won the O. Henry Memorial Award with her short story "The White Horses of Vienna." She has published five volumes of short stories, a pamphlet of verse, and a children's book in addition to such novels as *Plagued by the Nightingale* (1931) and *Death of a Man* (1936). She returned to Europe in 1946.

IVAN BUNIN was born October 22, 1870, in Voronezh, Russia. He traveled widely in the years preceding World War I, and became a permanent exile from Russia in 1918. He won the Nobel Prize for literature in 1933. His best-known novels are *The Village* (1910), *Dry Valley* (1912), and *The Well of Days* (1930). His first work to appear in English was "The Gentleman from San Francisco" in 1922.

WALTER VAN TILBURG CLARK was born in Maine in 1909, but he has spent most of his life in Nevada, where his father was president of the state university. His two novels, *The Ox-Bow Incident* (1940) and *The City of Trembling Leaves* (1945), reflect a feeling for both the history and the background of the West. His short stories, uncollected as yet, have been widely anthologized.

JOSEPH CONRAD (Téodor Jósef Konrad Korzeniowski) was born December 3, 1857, in the Ukraine, Russian Poland, of Polish parents. As a young man he shipped as a sailor; he worked on ships for twenty years, under the British merchant service, and finally became a master mariner commanding his own ship. The story of his first command at sea constitutes *The Shadow Line* (1917). His autobiographies are *The Mirror of the Sea* (1906) and *A Personal Record* (1912). His first novel was *Almayer's Folly*, which appeared in 1895. His early reputation as the greatest writer of sea stories in the English language was based upon such works as *The Nigger of the "Narcissus"* (1897), *Typhoon* (1902), and *Youth* (1902). His two greatest short works are "Heart of Darkness" (1902) and "The Secret Sharer," which first appeared in *'Twixt Land and Sea* (1912). His best novels are *Lord Jim* (1900), *Nostromo* (1904), *The Secret Agent* (1907), *Under Western Eyes* (1911), *Chance* (1914), and *Victory* (1915). He died in 1924 at his home near Canterbury.

STEPHEN CRANE was born in Newark, New Jersey, in 1871. An admirer of Tolstoi and Flaubert, Crane has been called the first important American author writing in the realistic tradition. Trained as a journalist, he believed that fiction should truly represent the life he knew. His first novel, *Maggie* (1893), was privately printed and did not become well known until after the success of his *The Red Badge of Courage* (1895), said to be the forerunner of all modern war novels. Crane spent the last years of his life in England, where he had settled as the result of rumors in the United States concerning his life and habits. He died in Germany in 1900.

EDWARD DONAHOE, born in 1900, is a native of Oklahoma, but he has spent much of his life abroad. He has published one novel and several short stories. He lives at present in Ponca City, Oklahoma.

WILLIAM FAULKNER, born in Mississippi in 1897, comes from a long line of Southern governors, statesmen, and other public figures. His first publication was a poem in the *Double-Dealer* (1922). His first novel, *Soldiers' Pay*, appeared in 1926, but Faulkner first became widely known after the publication of *Sanctuary* (1931). Probably his best two works, *The Sound and the Fury* (1929) and *As I Lay Dying* (1930), attracted little attention until after the popular success of *Sanctuary*. He has published five volumes of short stories: *Idyll in the Desert* (1931), *These Thirteen Stories* (1931), *Miss Zilphia Gant* (1932), *Doctor Martino and Other Stories* (1934), *Go Down Moses* (1942), and *Intruder in the Dust* (1948). He still lives in Oxford, Mississippi, where his family settled soon after he was born.

CAROLINE GORDON (Mrs. Allen Tate), born in 1895, is a native of Kentucky. She is the author of seven novels, among which are *Alec Maury, Sportsman,* and *The Women on the Porch.* "Her Quaint Honour" is from Miss Gordon's collection of short stories *The Forest of the South,* published in 1946.

NATHANIEL HAWTHORNE, born in Salem, Massachusetts, in 1804, is best known as the author of *The Scarlet Letter,* an American classic. Underrated during most of his life, and especially by his distinguished New England contemporaries, he has since taken his place as the first truly important writer of fiction in America. His chief works are *Twice-Told Tales* (1837), *Mosses from an Old Manse* (1846), *The Scarlet Letter* (1850), *The House of the Seven Gables* (1851), and *The Marble Faun* (1860). He died at Plymouth, New Hampshire, May 19, 1864.

ERNEST HEMINGWAY was born in Oak Park, Illinois, in 1899. During World War I he served in an ambulance unit on the Italian front, becoming later a Paris correspondent for the Hearst newspapers. He has published some verse, but is best known for his novels and his short stories. *In Our Time,* a collection of stories, appeared in 1925, followed by two novels, *Torrents of Spring* and *The Sun Also Rises,* in 1926. *A Farewell to Arms,* probably his most highly regarded novel, was published in 1929; his most recent, *For Whom the Bell Tolls,* in 1940. His short-story collections include *Men without Women* (1927), *Winner Take Nothing* (1933), and his collected stories in 1938. The last-named volume included "The Short Happy Life of Francis Macomber" and "The Snows of Kilimanjaro," two of his best stories, which had not appeared in the earlier collections.

HENRY JAMES, considered by many the outstanding American author of fiction, was born in New York in 1843. He traveled widely, even in his youth, and finally settled in England, where he became a British subject in 1915 in protest over America's early failure to enter the war against Germany. His change of allegiance has caused some historians to classify him as a British author, but the question of his nationality need not concern us, except to point out that the present tendency is to point to the evidence in his works of strong emotional ties which bound him to his native country. His literary career portrays a continuing and complete dedication to his art. He produced more than a hundred short stories and twenty novels, among which the best known are *The American* (1877), *The Europeans* (1878), *Daisy Miller* (1879), *The Portrait of a Lady* (1881), *The Spoils of Poynton* (1897), *The Wings of the Dove* (1902), and *The Ambassadors* (1903). The New York edition (26 vols.) of his *Novels and Tales* was published between 1907 and 1917, the uniform edition during 1915 and 1916. He died in England in 1916.

JAMES JOYCE, perhaps the most significant novelist of the twentieth century, was born in Dublin in 1882. Most of his life he lived away from Ireland, though his native country furnished him subject matter for all of his novels and short stories. *Dubliners,* a collection of short stories, was published in 1914 and shows only slight indication of the experiments in language which Joyce conducted in the later novels: *A Portrait of the Artist as a Young Man* (1916), *Ulysses* (1920), and *Finnegan's Wake* (1939). Joyce died in 1941.

FRANZ KAFKA was born in 1883 in Prague "Old Town" in Bohemia. His major works, including three novels, were published posthumously. Many of his short stories have not yet been translated into English. Readers have recognized in his works (*The Trial, The Castle, Amerika,* and such short stories as "A Hunger-Artist," "The Penal Colony," and "Metamorphosis") a true reflection of the disorder of our age. Kafka died in 1924.

D. H. LAWRENCE was born in Nottinghamshire, England, in 1885. He lived in England until after the publication of his first novel, *The White Peacock* (1911), then spent many years abroad in Germany, Italy, Sicily, Australia, Switzerland, France, and America. He is best known for such novels as *Sons and Lovers* (1913), *The Rainbow* (1915), *Women in Love* (1920), and *Lady Chatterley's Lover* (1928). His short stories appeared in such collections as *The Prussian Officer* (1914), *England, My England* (1922), *The Ladybird,* known in America as *The Captain's Doll* (1923), and *The Man Who Died* (1929). Lawrence died in 1930.

THOMAS MANN, born in Lübeck, Germany, in 1875, is thought by many critics to be the outstanding author of fiction produced by Germany in the twentieth century. Certainly his influence was great at the time he became an exile from his country during the rise of the Hitler regime. He had produced two important novels, *Buddenbrooks* (1901) and *The Magic Mountain* (1924), as well as a great number of short stories and short novels. An American edition of his short fiction, *Stories of Three Decades,* appeared in 1936. He is now a naturalized American citizen and lives in southern California.

KATHERINE MANSFIELD was born Katherine Beauchamp in Wellington, New Zealand, in 1888. She attended Queen's College, London, between 1902 and 1906, settling permanently in London in 1909. In 1913 she married the English critic, John Middleton Murry. During her brief career (she died in 1923), she published more than seventy short stories, leaving a great many more unfinished at her death. Some of her best-known collections are *Bliss* (1920), *The Garden Party* (1922), and *The Dove's Nest* (1923).

GUY DE MAUPASSANT has long been considered the French master of the short story. He was born in 1850. He became a protégé of Flaubert and imitated his methods. Considered a "naturalist," his stories deal, for the most part, with ordinary, if not always simple, people. Best known are "The Diamond Necklace," "The Piece of String," and "Little Soldier," in addition to the story included in this volume. He died in 1893.

HERMAN MELVILLE is sometimes called the American Conrad. The comparison is apt, but Melville's reputation as a major novelist would be secure without it. He was born in New York in 1819. After a brief experience as clerk, farm laborer, and schoolmaster, he sailed in 1841 on the whaler *Acushnet*. His experiences at sea and in the Marquesas Islands furnished him with subject matter for most of his literary works. After his return from sea in 1844, he established himself as an author with the publication of such works as *Typee* (1846), *Omoo* (1847), *Mardi* (1849), *Redburn*

(1849), and *White Jacket* (1850). His great work, *Moby Dick,* appeared in 1851, followed by *Pierre* (1852), *The Piazza Tales* (1856), and *The Confidence Man* (1857). He published two volumes of verse. Disappointed at the reception of his most ambitious works, Melville wrote little during his later years. He died in New York in 1891.

LUIGI PIRANDELLO was born in Girgenti, Sicily, in 1867, the son of a mineowner. He was educated at Rome and at the University of Bonn, Germany. He began writing fiction about 1900, publishing many volumes of short stories and novels during the next twenty-five years. His best-known novel is *The Late Mattia Pascal* (1904). Turning to playwriting, Pirandello wrote approximately fifty dramas after 1910, the best known in America being *Six Characters in Search of an Author* (1921).

KATHERINE ANNE PORTER, a descendant of Daniel Boone, was born in Texas in 1894. She has traveled widely in Europe and Central America, and many of her stories are set in Germany and in Mexico. She has received Guggenheim awards, and in 1937 was given a special prize of $2500 by the Book-of-the-Month Club for her distinguished service to American letters. She has published three collections of short stories, beginning with *Flowering Judas* (1930), and including *Pale Horse, Pale Rider* (1939) and *The Leaning Tower* (1944). She lives at present in California and is at work upon a long novel titled *No Safe Harbour.*

JEAN-PAUL SARTRE, born in 1905, is a professor of philosophy in Paris, the founder and chief exponent of the philosophical system known as "Existentialism." During the war he was taken prisoner by the Germans, but he escaped and participated actively in the resistance movement. His dramatic works have had great success all over Europe since the end of the war. Two of his novels—*L'Age de Raison* (The Age of Reason) and *Le Sursis* (The Reprieve)—have recently been translated and published in America. "The Wall" is from a collection of stories titled *Le Mur.*

WALLACE STEGNER became known when his first novel, *Remembering Laughter,* won the Little, Brown and Company novelette award of $2500 in 1937. Mr. Stegner was born in 1909 in Iowa, educated in Montana and Utah. His short stories have been widely anthologized, several having been printed in *Best Short Stories* and the O. Henry Memorial Award volume. His best-known novel is *The Big Rock Candy Mountain.* At present he is in charge of creative writing at Stanford University.

ANTON TCHEKHOV is the acknowledged master of a great many present-day short-story writers, including the late Katherine Mansfield. He was born in 1860, the son of a freed serf in South Russia. Trained as a physician at the University of Moscow, he did not practice except once briefly during an epidemic. In addition to his short stories, he is also well known as a playwright, having written such important dramas as *The Cherry Orchard* and *Uncle Vanya.* He died in 1904.

LEO N. TOLSTOI was born in 1827 and is generally recognized as one of the greatest novelists of all time. *War and Peace* (1864) and *Anna Karenina* (1875) are regarded as his outstanding achievements, but he is also the author of a great many significant short stories, among which the better known are "The Kreuzer Sonata" and "The Death of Ivan Ilyitch." In his later years, Tolstoi, a member of the Russian nobility, turned to religious and to didactic writing, and he attempted in various ways to improve the conditions of the Russian lower class. He died in 1910.

LIONEL TRILLING (born in 1905) is a member of the English faculty of Columbia University. He is the author of books on Matthew Arnold, E. M. Forster, and Mark Twain. His only novel, *The Middle of the Journey,* appeared in 1947. "The Other Margaret" appeared originally in *Partisan Review* and was the center of critical discussion for several months following its publication.

EUDORA WELTY was born in 1909 in Jackson, Mississippi, where her father was head of a Southern insurance company. She attended the University of Wisconsin and the Columbia School of Business. Her first collection of short stories, *A Curtain of Green* (1941), brought her work to the attention of critics. Since then she has published three additional volumes: *The Robber Bridegroom,* a short novel (1942), *The Wide Net,* a collection of stories (1943), and *Delta Wedding,* a short novel (1946). She has won prizes in the O. Henry Memorial Award several times. She is presently living in Jackson, Mississippi.

STEFAN ZWEIG was born in Vienna in 1881. He died by his own hand in Petropolis, a suburb of Rio de Janeiro, Brazil, in August, 1941, while an exile from his Hitler-occupied homeland. Best known in America for his biographies, Zweig nevertheless had built an imposing reputation in Europe as playwright, novelist, and short-story writer, as well as biographer. Fiction available in English translations includes *Passion and Pain* (1924), *The Invisible Collection* (1926), *Conflicts* (1927), *Amok* (1931), *Letter from an Unknown Woman* (1932), *Kaleidoscope* (1934), *The Buried Candelabrum* (1937), and *Beware of Pity* (1939).

END